FINANCE AND ACCOUNTING

FINANCE AND ACCOUNTING

Third Edition

R.S. Giles

Assisted by J. W. Capel

MACMILLAN

First edition 1987
Reprinted once
Second edition 1991
Reprinted twice
Third edition 1994

Published by
THE MACMILLAN PRESS LTD
Houndmills, Basingstoke, Hampshire RG21 2XS
and London
Companies and representatives
throughout the world

ISBN 0–333–61585–9

A catalogue record for this book is available
from the British Library.

10 9 8 7 6 5 4 3
03 02 01 00 99 98

Printed in Hong Kong

Contents

Preface   ix
Acknowledgements   x
Introduction   xi

PART I   FINANCIAL RESOURCES AND BUSINESS PLANNING

1   Financial Resources   3
2   Business Planning   22
3   The Role of the Accountant   41
4   Introducing the Balance Sheet   46

PART II THE DEVELOPMENT, PURPOSE AND FUNCTION OF ACCOUNTING

5   The Ledger System   67
6   An Alternative Method of Recording   90
7   The Sales Day Book   105
8   The Purchases Day Book   121
9   The Returns Day Books   136
10 The Cash Book   149
11 The Bank Reconciliation Statement   168
12 The Petty Cash Book   185
13 Computer-based Accounts   199

PART III   THE CONSTRUCTION OF FINANCIAL STATEMENTS

14 Final Accounts: Calculating Profits   219
15 Final Accounts: Adjustments   234

16 Capital Transactions   256
17 Partnership Accounts   287
18 Company Accounts   309
19 Cash Flow Statements   332
20 Accounts of Clubs and Societies   347

PART IV   THE PROVISION OF FINANCIAL INFORMATION

21 Accounting Ratios and Preparing Reports   365
22 Vat and Vat Returns   396
23 SSAPs and FRSs   407

PART V   SOURCES OF PERSONAL FINANCE

24 Personal Income   425
25 Saving and Borrowing   443
26 Personal Cash Budgeting   452

PART VI   PLANNING AND DECISION MAKING: ACCOUNTING FOR COSTS

27 Manufacturing Accounts   461
28 Costing Principles and Classification of Costs   482
29 Accounting for Materials   494
30 Accounting for Labour   517
31 Accounting for Overheads; Cost Centres   525
32 Job, Batch and Contract Costing   538
33 Process and Standard Costing   552
34 Marginal Costing   569
35 Budgeting and Planning   597
36 Capital Investment Appraisal   616

PART VII   FURTHER ACCOUNTING ISSUES

37 Control Accounts   629
38 The Trial Balance, Journal and Suspense Accounts   642
39 Incomplete Records   661
40 The Extended Trial Balance   682
41 Examination Success   698

An Assignment Programme
1   *Preparation of Balance Sheets and Calculation of
    Current Ratios*   701
2   *Planning Your Own Business*   703
3   *An Investigation into Different Forms of Business
    Organisation in Your Area*   706
4   *Manufacturing Accounts and Costing*   708
5   *Allied Components Plc: Diversification*   711
6   *Incomplete Records and the Extended Trial Balance*   714
Glossary of Terms   717
Abbreviated Answers to Text Questions   720
Index   751

Preface

The third edition of *Finance and Accounting* has been fully up-dated and can be used with confidence on a wide range of courses. It is intended to be student-friendly, interesting to read and designed to stimulate learning by the use of clear examples and lots of wide-ranging questions. It is going to be of benefit to you in your examinations.

The courses for which the text will be suitable include:

GNVQ Accounting
BTEC National
Association of Accounting Technicians (AAT)
Chartered Association of Certified Accountants (ACCA)
Chartered Institute of Management Accountants (ACMA)
Chartered Institute of Purchasing and Supply (CIPS)
Institute of Chartered Accountants (ACA)
Institute of Commercial Management (ICM)
General Certificate of Secondary Education
General Certificate of Education Advanced Level

It will also be of value to those students who have embarked on a first-year tertiary course in business studies and related subjects.

Throughout the text masculine pronouns have been used for the sake of simplicity: no offence is meant!

The more work and effort you put into all your studies, the greater the chance of success. Be determined, have a positive attitude and all the very best in your future courses and exams.

RICHARD S. GILES
Bournemouth & Poole College

Acknowledgements

My colleague and I would like to take this opportunity to thank the members of staff of the Business Studies and Computing Department at Bournemouth & Poole College for all their kind assistance and guidance in the development of this work over the years.

In addition, many thanks to the Examining Boards who have kindly allowed us to use their questions, particularly AAT. Others include ICM, CIPS, the Associated Examining Board (AEB), Royal Society of Arts, Chartered Institute of Management Accountants and Chartered Association of Certified Accountants and the Chartered Institute of Bankers. I would also like to thank Microsoft Ltd for the use of the computer-based accounts and Michael Upton for allowing us to use his very thorough business plan when he began as a sole trader.

Introduction

Each chapter of *Finance and Accounting* has been designed to engage you in the process of learning and to accelerate the acquiring of the skills you will need to gain the right level of competence in this subject.

Each chapter introduces you to the topic, emphasises key points, illustrates these with clear examples and then provides numerous activities to test learning and understanding.

Finance and Accounting has been divided into eight major parts. The first three of them develop financial accounting and concentrate on how a business is resourced and planned, how it records its financial transactions and how the financial statements are prepared as a result of these transactions. The preparation of the statements will be for different types of business organisations such as sole traders, partnerships and companies.

Part IV includes accounting ratios and preparing reports, and also takes a look at some management accounting. The inclusion of Statements of Standard Accounting Practice (SSAPs) is important because it gives us the profession's guide-lines on what should be a standard approach to preparing financial statements. There is also a significant chapter on VAT.

Part V emphasises personal rather than business finance. There is a comprehensive chapter on the payroll system and sections on investing, borrowing and personal budgeting.

Part VI provides very comprehensive chapters on cost and management accounting which indicate how important accounting is to management decision making. Many courses now include these as part of their syllabus and that is why an extensive examination of them has been made.

Part VII includes further accounting issues which are required to complement your studies on a number of courses. Part VIII contains a programme of assignments which should be useful to both students and teachers. Answers are also provided to give students guidance and to make sure they are on the right track.

PART I

FINANCIAL RESOURCES AND BUSINESS PLANNING

CHAPTER 1

Financial Resources

Finance

The word 'finance' can conjure up a number of thoughts and meanings both as a noun and as a verb. Accounts, business, economics and commerce, financial affairs, investments, funding and capital are just some of the words which may be associated with finance. Essentially, it is about money: the management of money, the control of it, the raising and spending of it and, the making of it.

From the business's point of view, the word finance is important because it wants to know:

(a) where it gets its money from (that is, the sources of finance);
(b) what happens to its money (that is, how is it used) and whether or not the business is making more money (profits).

In a similar way, the Government also needs to know about finance because, in the preparation of its Budget, it must be able to forecast accurately what it is to spend in the next fiscal period and match this up against how it is to raise the finance to do so.

In the following pages, the raising of finance in both the private and public sectors of business will be developed in more detail.

Accounting

This word is a derivative of the word 'account' and gives us the commercial definition of what it is: accounting books, to compute, charge, balance accounts, to maintain records of finances, etc. Every business organisation needs to maintain accurate accounting records to help it manage and control its finances efficiently.

Records must be kept by all businesses so that they can be run properly. Without these day-to-day records, it would be difficult to know if the business was making a profit or a loss or, indeed, whether it was worth keeping the business going. (If it were making losses, then it might as well pack up and cease trading.)

The book-keeping side of a business is to ensure that financial records such as sales, purchases and expenses are maintained accurately so that it then becomes possible to know what prices to charge for goods or services. From these figures, it's just a short step to work out how profitable the business is.

Records are also vital in business because they are needed for taxation and VAT purposes. The Inland Revenue will need to know what profits a business has made in order to assess the liability for tax and HM Customs & Excise say that if you are registered for VAT, you are obliged to keep a record of VAT accounts.

The bank will be interested in a business's records because it will have a bank account or could have a bank overdraft. If the business exceeds its overdraft limit, the bank can quickly stop it from writing more cheques which will then embarrass any further trading it wants to conduct.

Accounting is an onward step from book-keeping in that it is used for preparing financial statements and reports from the business's day-to-day records. Financial statements, such as the profit and loss account and the balance sheet, help both owners and managers in business to understand what has gone on, and whether the business is a success or failure, whether it requires further financing because it is short of cash or needs longer-term funds to ensure its survival; will the business be able to survive another week, in fact!

It is therefore a function of accounting to provide those interested parties such as owners, managers, banks, tax and VAT offices with the appropriate financial information which will indicate important aspects such as profits or losses, VAT, and the financial stability of a business both in the short and long term.

Types of accounting

In this text, there are different aspects of accounting which need to be briefly explained.

Financial accounting

This concerns the recording of financial information on a historical basis and is the book-keeping side of the business: that is, the maintenance of records. It also includes the preparation of financial statements such as the profit and loss account and the balance sheet.

The better the quality of accounting records, the better control the business has. It must record every financial transaction. How it performs this will depend upon the size and nature of the business. The larger and more complex a business, the more it will need in terms of extensive and computerised accounting systems in order to give it the information and control it wants. On the other hand, a small business, like the local shop, which conducts most of its transactions by cash, may only require a Cash Book and any supporting invoices when it buys goods and services.

Cost accounting

This is largely required to support management in decision making, and concerns how much things cost to produce. How much will it cost, for example, to make a television set in terms of materials, labour and overheads? Will it cost the same to produce 100 sets a week as it would 1,000 a week? How many sets would need to be produced for a business to cover its costs (break-even)? It's not going to do a business any good if it sells its televisions for £150 each only to discover they actually cost £175 to make! This is vital information for management, particularly in the manufacture of products.

Management accounting

All information, in the form of financial reports, can assist management to arrive at better, more informed decisions. Financial and cost accounting will be used in management accounting to provide the business with essential information so that it can target its aims and objectives more effectively. If the aim of a business is to expand and achieve a growth rate which can expect a good return of profit, what must it do to get it? The objectives set out how this may be done, and management accountants will be expected to provide the reports to do it. Planning, control and the forecasting of results will be an important role of management accounting.

Types of business organisations in the private sector

In the private sector of business, as distinct from the public sector (State-owned enterprises), there are three basic types of organisations which are primarily profit-motivated:

(a) sole trader;
(b) partnership;
(c) limited company.

The essential difference between these lies in the size of the business. This is directly related to the initial investment in the business – that is, the provision of capital, the most important ingredient in determining the size of a business enterprise.

The sole trader is a one-man business unit. Capital is raised by the resources of one person, including any borrowing from banks, building societies or other financial institutions.

Partnerships may have as many as twenty partners and subsequently have greater potential to raise more capital if each partner contributes a share. The more partners, the more capital is available for use in the business.

Limited companies are basically of two types. They are either public limited or private limited companies. Although there is no restriction on the number of shareholders who can contribute capital in either type of company, the private private company may only sell its shares privately (that is, without resort to advertising) and therefore the number of shareholders is likely to be limited, shares being sold within the boundaries of family, friends and business acquaintances.

A public limited company has no such restriction and can raise its capital by issuing a prospectus (an invitation to the public to buy its shares). A merchant bank or issuing house can act on behalf of the company and make the necessary arrangements for the sale. In this way, very large amounts of capital can be raised and public companies can take credit for being responsible for stimulating growth in capital investment during the last 100 years. For a public company, at least £50,000 of share capital must be registered with the company, of which at least 25% must be issued and paid for before it can start operating.

Shareholders are part-owners of their companies. The reward for owning shares may come from the payment of dividends from company profits, or from the increase in value of the shares (capital gain). Dividends are paid on the nominal value of shares (their face value) and not their market value. Dividends are usually determined as so much in the £; for example, 12p/£ would gain £12 per 100 shares.

Limited companies have 'limited liability,' and sole traders and partnerships are disadvantaged by not having this. This means that in the event of a company's collapse, shareholders are protected against the debts of the company up to the value of their paid-up capital, but nothing more. Sole traders or partnerships are unlimited, which means they are personally liable for all debts. This could involve the selling of personal possessions in order to settle business debts.

Sources of finance

To commence in business takes money. How much money depends upon the nature and size of the business. To start up a large industrial manufacturing business, for example, would require millions of pounds and this would most likely be financed by shareholders of a public limited company. On the other hand, a florist's shop on the High Street may only need a few thousand pounds financed by a sole trader.

Most financing is either of a short- or long-term nature. For day-to-day business operations, there is a need for sufficient cash flow (available money in the bank) to pay for the basic things such as purchases of stock, wages and working expenses. Often, to support cash flow, a business needs to have an overdraft facility with the bank. On a longer-term basis, financing may be required to buy fixed assets such as land, plant and machinery, equipment or motor vehicles; for these items of what is called capital expenditure there may be a need to call on a specific long-term loan from the bank, or other forms of financing such as leasing, or the hiring of fixed assets.

Whether on a short- or long-term basis, every type of business organisation needs to be adequately financed. One of the major causes of business failure is lack of solvency, which means not having sufficient liquidity (cash) to be able to pay debts when these fall due. A business is said to become 'insolvent' when it cannot pay its creditors. This could quickly turn to bankruptcy and the owners will probably lose their capital and their business, while employees will lose their jobs and suppliers will lose what is due to them. In fact, it's a sad story and everyone loses out. A business must maintain control of its finances and be able to plan its resources carefully and also try to forecast ahead of time what it will need.

It is not surprising, therefore, that when a new business starts up and goes to the bank to ask for money, the bank wants to know as much as it can about how the business is to be financed. It would also like to see some kind of planning (that is, a business plan) concerning what is involved in the set-up of the new venture.

The major sources of finance are:

(a) the owner's capital;
(b) loan capital;
(c) debenture issues;
(d) profits;
(e) leasing/hiring of fixed assets;
(f) factor finance;
(g) creditors;
(h) Government funds;
(i) other sources.

The owner's capital

When a business enterprise begins, the owner(s) put resources into the business, representing the capital. The capital may be in the form of money, equipment, tools, premises or indeed any other resource. The total value of these resources will be expressed in monetary terms and will establish the initial capital (or net worth) of the owner(s) at the commencement of business. Capital may stay the same or may increase or decrease depending on how successful the business is and what the owner decides to do.

Limited companies have shareholders who have subscribed share capital and are therefore part-owners of a business. The more shares they own, the more of the business they own. A shareholder of a public limited company whose shares are listed on the Stock Exchange may sell his shares if he wishes. Shares listed are 'marketable' securities and may be bought or sold by shareholders or by new investors to the market. Private limited companies are not listed on the Stock Exchange and are therefore not marketable securities. Transfer of share is restricted to those members who can sell their shares privately.

A company must register with the Registrar of Companies at Companies House, London, and state the amount of capital it wants to raise. This is known as the *authorised capital*. The shares issued and purchased by shareholders are known as *issued and paid-up capital*, which may be less than the authorised capital. A company may wish to issue further shares at a later date when it may require more capital for future investment and growth.

Classes of shares

There are basically two distinct classes of shares:

Ordinary shares. These are the most common type of shares and are often referred to as *equities*. The rate of dividend depends on how much profit the company has made, and how much the directors decide to pay out as dividends and how much they want to retain in the company (in what is known as *reserves*). Ordinary shareholders are paid last, after preference shareholders, the rate of dividend depending on how much the directors recommend. Large companies may pay an 'interim' dividend half-way through the financial year and a final dividend at the end of the financial year.

Preference shares. These entitle shareholders to a fixed rate of dividend (for example, 8% preference shares). These shares may be more suitable to the investor who wants a regular and fixed dividend and a more reliable investment than that offered by ordinary shares.

There are also different classes of preference shares. Some may be 'cumulative': that is, if there are any arrears of dividends owing from previous years, these can be paid when improved profits allow. Participating preference shares are those that may be paid a bonus or higher rate of dividend on top of the fixed rate, particularly when ordinary shareholders receive a higher rate than their own. Note that dividends are always paid on the nominal value of shares and not their market value.

A rights issue' is a situation where a company wants to expand its share capital and where the existing shareholders are invited to buy the new issue first, being offered shares in proportion to their existing shareholding at a favourable price: for example, the offer may be two shares for every five held. If the existing shareholders do not take up the offer, then the shares may be sold via prospectus on the open market. Shareholders are part-owners of a company and represent ownership capital and not loan capital.

Borrowing: loan capital

Loans may come from a variety of different sources but the most significant source is the bank. The commercial (or High Street) banks are generally recognised as the 'Big Five' – Barclays, National Westminster, Lloyds, Midland, and the TSB.

A loan may be short-term (for example, within one year) like a bank overdraft, or a medium-term to long-term loan (for example, two to twenty years), used for specific capital purposes.

Loans on short-term credit are usually required to finance the day-to-day running of the business – for example, to purchase materials, to pay wages, to pay for overhead costs. It is unlikely that a long-term loan would be negotiated to finance short-term expenditure. An overdraft arrangement with the bank usually allows a person or business to reach a certain fixed limit in the current account – for example, £5,000 'in the red'. If the limit is exceeded, the bank may take steps to reduce the overdraft facility or even cancel it. Interest is charged on a daily basis and is usually a percentage above what is termed the bank's *base rate*.

A business bank loan is for a specific period of time with arrangements to repay by regular instalments over the period of the loan. For medium-term to long-term loans, the loan capital may be required for specific projects: for example,

- to purchase machinery or equipment
- to mortgage buildings or land
- to develop new products
- to finance an export campaign

There is also a Government-sponsored scheme which was started in 1981. Termed the *Loan Guarantee Scheme* it operates via the clearing banks and is designed to assist small firms to obtain finance for new projects and ventures, especially in the areas of technology and manufacturing. The maximum that can be lent under this scheme is £75,000, the Government reimbursing the bank 70% of the sum lent if the company subsequently fails. The Government has promised more help for small businesses and the maximum which can be borrowed is likely to increase.

Debenture issues

Debentures represent loan capital. Debentures may be issued by companies for the purpose of raising finance over a specific period of time (for example, 5, 10, 15 years). Interest payment to creditors (debenture holders) is a fixed percentage of the nominal value of the stock and is payable even if profits are not made. They are usually secured on the assets of the company in that if the company goes into liquidation, the debenture holders can be paid from the proceeds of the asset sales. These are often known as *mortgage debentures*.

The nominal value of a 'block' of debenture stock is £100 and it is this figure which is paid back to the stock holder when the debenture matures. However, it is possible to sell one's stock on the Stock Exchange before the maturity date – that is, they are marketable just like shares. But, unlike shares, the value of debentures is not dependent on the current and expected profits of the company. Their value is primarily determined by the rate of interest paid on the stock in relation to current rates of interest elsewhere, say, in a bank; generally, if interest rates are 'high' in relation to the rate paid on the stock, then the market value will be below £100. When interest rates fall, therefore, the value of the stock can rise to £100 or sometimes even more if interest rates are very low.

Profits

The profits of a business are one of the most important sources of business finance. For sole traders and partners, most of the profits may be withdrawn from the business through the financial year as part of their income.

Companies need to pay corporation tax to the Inland Revenue and dividends to shareholders. Any profit which is left can be ploughed back into the business to finance its expansion or to provide for specific projects or replacement of assets like machinery, equipment and plant. Companies who retain their profits usually transfer them to what is known as *reserves*.

Leasing/hiring of fixed assets

A fixed asset is part of a business's capital expenditure and includes assets such as premises, equipment, plant and machinery, motor vehicles, etc. A business does not need to purchase its fixed assets outright but can either lease them or buy them on hire purchase.

There are two basic forms of lease: a finance lease, or an operating lease. A finance lease gives virtually the full advantages of acquiring an asset but without the legal ownership of them. Depreciation and interest charges can be written off against profits. An operating lease, however, is merely a form of rental and the fixed asset is hired for a fixed charge paid, say, quarterly which is also written off against profits. The firm which leases the assets is known as the lessor, and may be a bank or finance house or the actual manufacturer or supplier of the asset. The firm acquiring the use of the asset is known as the lessee. Leasing contracts can also have the advantage of servicing arrangements so that the maintenance and regular servicing of assets is the responsibility of the lessor. Both leasing and hire-purchase finance can help the cash flow of a business, giving it more funds at its disposal to finance other operations.

Hire purchase can be an expensive form of credit and, although it can ease the acquisition of buying a fixed asset outright, it only becomes the legal property of the business when the last payment is made. The interest and depreciation charges of acquiring an asset under a hire-purchase agreement may be written off against profits.

Factor finance

This has become a very popular way by which firms can ensure an adequate cash flow and thus short-term finance coming into the business to meet current expenditure. It involves a firm employing a debt factoring company. The firm employing the company passes all its invoices (trade debts) on to the factoring company which pays a major percentage of their value immediately and the rest when the debt is paid. In this way the firm has immediate funds (liquidity) because its funds (or a major part of them) are not tied up in debtors. The factoring company charges interest on the sum advanced until the debt is cleared; administration charges are payable too. A considerable number of factor financing arrangements are 'without recourse' – that is, the factoring company bears any losses occurring as a result of bad debts. Both large and small firms will employ factoring companies on a fairly continuous basis; the kind of financing provided can be a 'lifeline' to small firms who are experiencing cash-flow problems because of slow debtors.

Creditors

Suppliers of goods and services to business enterprises provide firms with an important source of short-term finance. If credit facilities are granted to a business for the purpose of buying goods or services allowing, say, two months to pay, the two months' credit is a short-term loan without interest charged.

Government funds

Investors in industry was originally set up in 1945 as two separate bodies – the Industrial and Commercial Finance Corporation, and the Finance Corporation for Industry. In 1975 the two companies were merged and renamed Finance for Industry, and in 1983 that name was changed to Investors in Industry.

The whole purpose of this body is to sponsor small, medium-sized and large companies who are seeking 'venture capital' for projects which are not likely to yield a profitable return for many years to come. Backed by the English and Scottish clearing banks and the Bank of England, Investors in Industry has sufficient capital backing to take the longer-term view – lending money for periods of up to fifteen years. It thus plays an essential role in helping the development of British industry, especially in the highly competitive world of computer technology.

The Enterprise Allowance Scheme can pay £40 per week for up

to a year to those people who wish to set up their own businesses. Applicants must be at least 18 and under 65 and must have £1,000 available to invest. This could be their own capital, or a grant, or a loan. Local job centres or training agencies and enterprise allowance offices can provide full details of the scheme.

There are funds available from local councils at both county and district levels which can offer a variety of help and financial support in the form of grants. These range from start-up grants and grants towards an exhibition. The Loan Guarantee Scheme is for small businesses wishing to obtain loans where the local Business Enterprise Scheme may be prepared to guarantee the loan through any of the major banks.

Other sources

There are various other sources available for assisting businesses; for instance, the Prince's Youth Business Trust provides finance for young people (normally 18–26) in the form of grants and low-interest loans. Disabled people up to the age of 30 can also seek assistance. The grants are for business start-up schemes and the loans can be used for further financing of the business.

The Shell Enterprise Loan Fund offers loans (usually up to £5,000) to favour young people wishing to start up in business at low rates of interest. The British Coal Enterprise Scheme is a similar venture which assists new businesses starting up in coal-mining areas and which offers up to £5,000 per job created or 25% of the cost of the project.

Other assistance can come from unlikely sources such as the Crafts Council, which offers loans and grants to those wishing to set up a workshop or requiring further training. The Arts Council can offer grants and loans to acquire equipment for those businesses concerned with performing or visual arts. Even the English Tourist Board can get in on the act by the offer of grants and loans if the business is tourist-related!

The Rural Development Commission offers financial assistance, training and business advice to small firms with less than 20 skilled employees. Grants can be up to 25% of costs whilst loans are usually below £75,000.

In conclusion, there is a wide variety of finance available to a business organisation. The larger the organisation, the more it may require to finance itself. The major source of external finance is borrowed capital, usually obtained from a bank. For small businesses wishing to start up new ventures, there are a number of helpful schemes available, which are often open to young people, whereby grants and loans are on offer to those with energy, ideas and a determination to succeed.

Public finance

Public finance refers to Government (or State) finances. It involves the raising of money through taxation and borrowing for the purpose of spending money on public goods and services such as health, social security, education, the environment and defence. Public finance is either in the hands of central government or local authorities. Increasingly, however, it is central government which exercises greater control of the public purse and which has taken over much of the spending power of councils to prevent them from over-spending. The Government has the power to cap any local authority if it overspends its budget limits. For example, if a district has a budget of, say, £80 million and wants to spend £90 million, the Government will cut its financial support in the form of grants or other measures, and force the district to cut back to within the budget level imposed.

The local authorities provide many community services and include a complex mixture of spending between county, district and parish council services. The county councils provide the majority of services including the heavy costs of local education, police, transport and highways. The district councils provide services for their own areas, including council houses, environmental health, recreation and leisure amenities and the maintenance of parks, libraries, roads and other features unique to their district. Parish councils spend relatively little in proportion to the finances they receive and spend money on projects such as a new sports pavilion or a Girl Guides' hall.

Local authority finance

Local government finance has been largely reformed. The domestic rating system was replaced by the Community Charge (Poll Tax), introduced in April 1990 in England and Wales, and a year earlier in Scotland. Its introduction was most unpopular and caused a great deal of controversy and public unrest. It may also have played a part in removing from office the then Prime Minister, Mrs Thatcher, because she was instrumental in its passage through the Commons.

According to the calculations made by the Department of the Environment, no one should have been asked to pay more than about £150 extra in total community charges than previously was paid in rates. This figure was greatly exceeded by almost every council and it worked out that the average charge per adult head would be in the region of nearly £400, far in excess of the estimated figures. This meant that many people suffered, particularly those in over-crowded homes and poor tenants in rented housing, cramped bedsits in the cities and also students, pensioners and the disabled.

The Council Tax

The Poll Tax had an extremely short political life and indeed, from 1 April 1993, the Government's Council Tax took over and replaced it. The Council Tax is a local charge imposed by the local councils to raise finance for the services they provide, although central government still provides at least half the finance in grants and other support.

The Council Tax works almost in the same way as the old rate system in that the charge is made on the basis of the value of each residence/ dwelling. Each dwelling is placed on the Council's valuation list at the time, broken down into 8 separate bands.

Band A   up to a value of £40,000
     B   over £40,000 to £52,000
     C   over £52,000 to £68,000
     D   over £68,000 to £88,000
     E   over £88,000 to £120,000
     F   over £120,000 to £160,000
     G   over £160,000 to £320,000
     H   over £320,000

Therefore the more expensive the dwelling, the higher the dwelling is coded and the more is paid in Council Tax by the occupants. The full chargeable value assumes that there are two adults living in the home. If only one person resides, the tax is reduced by 25%. If the dwelling is not the principal home, the tax is reduced by 50%. Not all persons are subject to Council Tax charges: full-time students, student nurses and those on youth training schemes, for example, are exempt.

Raising Government finance

The majority of central government finance comes from taxation in one form or another, including National Insurance contributions (NICs). Any short-fall in raising Government finance is made up by borrowing money. The Treasury is the Government department responsible for the control of public finance. The Bank of England acts in the capacity of financial adviser to the Treasury as well as functioning as the Government's bank, keeping the records of its receipts and expenditure in what is called the 'Exchequer Account'. The finance raised is used to pay for the vast programme of public spending as mentioned above.

The aim of the Government is to control public expenditure and borrowing as a proportion of national output, so that if expenditure is held more or less level in real terms (allowing for inflation), any growth in the economy will lead to the required reduction of Government expenditure as a percentage of national income.

Public sector borrowing

The Government's medium-term financial strategy (MTFS) is to reduce public borrowing as a percentage of national output from about 2% in 1985–86 to approximately 1% between 1989 and 1993.

However, the steep rise of unemployment which occurred in the UK in the late 1980s and the early 1990s (approximately 3 million out of work), affected the financial strategy and increased public expenditure on social security payments, sharply upturning the need for public sector borrowing. The estimate for the borrowing requirement to the period ending April 1994 was in excess of £40 billion.

The Government's response was to increase indirect taxes including VAT, and an unpopular measure was to charge fuel and power with 8% VAT in its first year of introduction in 1994 and then at the standard rate from 1995 onwards. Other measures were to cut public spending and to try to create an economic atmosphere of recovery, allowing more employment and thereby reducing the burden to the public purse.

Borrowing is necessary when public expenditure is more than public receipts. If the Government did not resort to borrowing, the increases in taxation levels needed to pay for expenditure would be relatively high and largely unacceptable to the public.

The Treasury is responsible for borrowing (generally known as the PSBR – Public Sector Borrowing Requirement), and via the Bank of England uses the Stock Exchange to sell Government Stock (or Gilts). The Government raises about 70% of its borrowing in this way, most of the stock being taken up by insurance companies and pension funds because there is little risk of the Government defaulting. The other 30% of borrowing comes in the form of National Savings via the Post Office, selling National Savings Certificates, Income Bonds, Premium Savings Bonds, Deposit Bonds and the accounts of the National Savings Bank. Both Government Stock and National Savings are at fixed interest rates, the difference being that the former is marketable on the Stock Exchange and the latter is not.

The Government's reform of the nationalised industries during the 1980s meant that a massive privatisation programme transferred many of the public sector industries into the private sector.

Proceeds from the sale of public sector businesses boosted the finances of the Treasury to a sum approaching £20 billion which not only helped to reduce the PSBR, but positively to replace it with PSDR (Public Sector Debt Repayment). These repayments commenced in the latter part of the 1980s and the Chancellor's forecast for the early years of the 1990s was about £6–£8 billion per annum. This had not only reduced the national debt, but significantly had helped to reduce the massive interest payments made each year on the total debt.

When the Government requires short-term funds to meet its current expenditure, as it often does, it arranges to sell Treasury Bills via the Bank of England, Each Treasury Bill has a nominal or part value, say £10,000, and each has a maturity period of 91 days.

However, unlike virtually all other kinds of fund-raising by the Government, Treasury Bills do not carry a rate of interest. In reality, no one is going to lend the Government money 'for free', so every week the Bank of England actions off the bills – invites tenders – to the highest bidders. The bidders include foreign banks, financial institutions and discount house, but not the UK clearing banks. The higher the bids or tenders (that is, the nearer to the Bill's part value), the greater the chance an institution has of receiving some Bills). In practice, the financial institutions are adept at putting in tenders such that the difference between what they pay for the bills and the money they get back after 91 days – the par value – reflects the current cost of borrowing. For example, a £50,000 Treasury Bill might be sold for £48,500. The annualised cost to the Government is

$$£50,000 - £48,500 \ = £1,500$$

$$\frac{£\ 1,500}{£48,500} \times \frac{100}{1} \times \frac{365}{91} = 12.4\%$$

The 12.4% is likely to reflect the current costs of borrowing from banks and financial markets.

The Budget

The Budget relates to the proposals planned by Government for changes in taxation and is also an annual review of the Government's economic policies for the year.

The Budget proposals are laid down in the Budget statement prepared by the Chancellor of the Exchequer, usually in March each year, and presented to the House of Commons. How will the Government finance its expenditure programme? What changes in taxation are to be made and how is it to be spent?

As far as public expenditure is concerned, at least half of it will finance health, social security, education and defence.

The Budget is not only a means of financing public expenditure. It is also a very important statement that reviews the Government's economic proposals for the year and is a means of implementing its policies. It has been the policy of successive Governments to make the control of inflation its primary objective through the use of both monetary and fiscal measures. Other significant objectives include invigorating the economy to make it more productive and competitive, and developing an economy which relates strongly to market forces so as to provide opportunities for growth and employment.

Finance for nationalised industries

After the Second World War the newly elected Labour Government set about its vast nationalisation programme to ensure that the nation had what they considered essential needs and services under public control. Acts of Parliament took over private sector industries such as coal (1946), railways and electricity (1947) and gas (1948). The shareholders of these former companies were paid off in cash or Government securities at fixed interest rates, or a combination of both.

Government ministers were made responsible for appointing the chairman and members of each board running the nationalised industries. Today they have the responsibility of agreeing with the management of each board the general planning and direction of how the industries should be run – for example, the general standard of services to be provided, the pricing policy and so forth. However, the day-to-day running of the industries is left to the individual management of each of the boards.

Over the years, governments have issued guide-lines to the nationalised industries to ensure, as far as possible, that they are run in the same way as commercial enterprises in the private sector, and hence make profits or break even. Some nationalised industries like the Post Office make very good returns on capital while others, including coal, steel and railways, tend to struggle from year to year and often make losses which need to be supported by funds from the Exchequer (in other words, the taxpayers).

The rate of return on capital before taxation was 5% per annum, although financial targets were individualised for each industry depending to a great extent on what services they needed to provide the public. The Government also sets external financing limits when it comes to the industries borrowing capital, to ensure they stay within specific targets and do not over-reach their spending powers.

Financing for nationalised industries basically comes from the following sources.

(a) Revenue from sales of goods and or services.
(b) Profits which are used to pay back interest and loans, and/or retained in the industry to improve services.
(c) Government grants and subsidies. Grants tend to be used for specific purposes such as capital projects (for example, building programmes) or to reduce the price of certain services (for example, Post Office charges).
(d) Loans from Government. This comprises the bulk of the board's borrowing requirements, using the National Loans Fund.
(e) Temporary borrowing needs from the finance markets, including loans and overdrafts.
(f) Loans from foreign sources (such as banks), but subject to Treasury approval.

Nationalised industries are monopolies subject to public scrutiny. The House of Commons Select Committee on Nationalised Industries is responsible for examining the reports and accounts of the industries and for making recommendations to Government. Findings from the annual reports and accounts can then be subject to debate in the House.

The interests of the industry's consumers are also protected by Consumers' Councils (such as the Post Office Users' National Council) which deal with a wide range of complaints and suggestions from consumers.

The privatisation of the public sector

The Conservative Government, which came to power in May 1979, set about its major policy of reforming the nationalised industries throughout the 1980s. The Conservative Party saw this as one of its essential methods of economic recovery. At the same time, it saw an opportunity to pursue its policy of wider share ownership by the general public and the employees of the nationalised industries.

The 1980s saw a massive privatisation programme where the public was offered the sale of shares for the ownership of the following industries:

British Aerospace	Enterprise Oil
British Airways	Britoil
British Gas	Associated British Ports
British Telecom	British Shipbuilders
Cable & Wireless	Rolls-Royce
The National Freight Consortium	British Airports Authority
The Rover Group	The Regional Water Authorities
Jaguar	The Electricity Boards

In all, almost 750,000 jobs have been transferred from the public to the private sector, thereby altering the 'balance' between public and private ownership. The process has not been without its critics. The former Conservative Prime Minister, the late Harold Macmillan (first Earl Stockton), criticised the Government for selling the 'family silver', and upsetting the balance of Britain's mixed economy between the private and public sectors of business.

Other privatisations in the pipeline include British Coal, the British Steel Corporation and perhaps British Rail.

Proceeds from these sales have brought about £20 billion into the Treasury and have helped to increase the budget surplus in the late 1980s and early 1990s. The surplus funds from the domestic budgets in turn helped to repay our national debt. The PSBR was reduced and replaced by the PSDR. Billions of pounds were repaid, reducing not only the national debt but, significantly, reducing the high cost of borrowing through interest rates.

Questions

1. How does the function of book-keeping differ from the function of accounting?
2. Why does the provision of capital influence the size of a business?
3. What do you consider the main sources of finance are for (a) a sole trader and (b) a plc?

4. What is the essential difference between the private sector of business and the public sector?
5. How does a local authority finance its expenditure programme?
6. How does central government raise its finance? What is meant by PSBR and PSDR?
7. Name the main sources of central government revenue and expenditure.
8. What are the economic objectives of the Budget? With regard to taxation, what is the difference between direct and indirect tax?
9. How do nationalised industries finance their expenditure? What kind of control can central government exert?
10. Clearly differentiate between ordinary and preference shares.
11. Why should a company want to lease its fixed assets?
12. Why did the Government privatise so many of the nationalised industries?

CHAPTER 2

Business Planning

Business planning

If anyone wanted to start up in business and went to their local bank to ask for advice and loan facilities, the bank's business adviser would, without doubt, recommend that a business plan be drawn up.

The business plan would provide essential information not only to the owner of the business, but also to any other party which may wish to support it. We have already discussed, in some detail, the various sources of finance available to small business ventures. Grants and loans are available but they are not given freely without the supporting evidence that a new business idea needs. A business plan provides the criteria whereupon the offer of a grant or loan may be given.

All the major banks have financial advisers for the small business sector. Barclays, for example, has provided what is called a 'Business Opportunity Profile' which give ideas for business plans in a wide variety of areas, from a florist's shop to a fitness centre. Each venture gives an outline of the market conditions, the type of customers, the competition to be expected, the advertising required, the start-up costs, qualifications and training needed and the legal aspects involved. The profiles are very useful in giving some guidance as to what is expected when a new business idea is ready to begin.

The banks also provide ample booklets, leaflets and forms giving a wide variety of information to the new business, not only from the bank's point of view of whether or not to offer finance, but from the business's view of how to start up, where to go, details of tax and VAT regulations, legal aspects, cashflow projections and so forth. It is neither in the bank's nor the client's interest that the new venture should fail, and therefore banks are keen to provide as much material as they can to help get a new business started.

Districts in the United Kingdom also have their own Business Enterprise Schemes which provide training, advice and financial assistance for people wishing to start their own businesses. For example, the Dorset Enterprise Agency provides a full package of assistance to potential new businesses. Many of the staff have started businesses of their own and so are able to give first-hand knowledge of their experiences.

The business plan

Does the business look a viable proposition? That's going to be a key element in the decision as to whether financial support is going to be offered. It is therefore important to prepare as professional a plan as possible and, if you are to present it to the bank or any other organisation, you need to know its contents thoroughly and look determined and committed. It's no good only being half-hearted and not being able to answer any questions posed by those who may be in a position to offer financial assistance. It's no use looking vacant or hoping for the best: money is a serious subject, particularly if you are asking someone for it!

A business plan may be organised as follows.

(a) *The Business.* Introduce and describe what it is, giving details of the product/service to be marketed.

(b) *The Market.* Give an outline of any research that has been completed, the type of customers and the level of competition.

(c) *The Marketing Plan.* Give details of the pricing policy, how the product/service is going to be advertised and distributed, and the areas to be marketed.

(d) *Management.* Outline the strengths and weakness of the business. Show how the business is to be organised. Give curriculum vitae details of personnel. State what equipment and other fixed assets are needed to run the business.

(e) *Finances.* State the sources of finance required.
Prepare the cash-flow forecast up to 12 months.
Try to give a break-even point of the business (the level of sales needed to cover costs).

(f) *Legal Requirements.* Any regulations which may affect the business should be stated, such as the Business Names Act, Sale of Goods Act or Trade Descriptions Act, etc.

(g) *The Presentation of the Plan.* This needs to be convincing and determined. The plan must look viable, be reasonably concise and provide good, factual evidence that it will be a success.

A business plan in action

Michael Upton recently began his own business which turned out to be successful. He is a trained engineer and had worked for large organisations in the electrical servicing departments. Once he had made up his mind to start his own business, he went to his local Business Enterprise Centre to find out what was involved. He also visited a number of banks to assess which of them might offer the best services at the most competitive rates.

Introduction

The business was to be called 'Aftercare' and was to provide a service to customers in the local community, in their homes, repairing electrical appliances (namely washing machines, refrigerators, freezers and cookers).

The list of appliances which could be serviced/repaired was quite extensive and included the popular brand names of Hoover, Creda, Indesit, Hotpoint, Zanussi, etc.

Michael thought that although there were a number of electrical engineers listed in the Yellow Pages, there were very few of them in his own area and he was sure there was a significant gap in the market available. In other words, there were potential customers to be gained.

The location of his premises was to be his own home, where a spare room was simply converted into an office.

The start-up of this business had an owner with the right technical background and he had both the experience and determination to succeed. The type of business organisation was to be sole trader, at least in the initial stages. The initial finance required was therefore the responsibility of the one owner.

If the business was to commence as a partnership, a business contract between the partners (in writing) should have been prepared, called the 'Deeds of Partnership'. More information on partnerships can be found in Chapter 17.

When the name Aftercare had been chosen, a check had to be made to make sure that it complied with the rules under the Business Names Act 1985 and that it was an approved title. The Act regulates the use of certain words and expressions and there are laws that protect the rights which persons may already have in relation to names and words used.

The market

It was found that in the local area, the main stream of customers would be in the domestic market rather than the commercial one of shops and other businesses. Consumer data stated that approximately 95% of homes have a washing machine and a refrigerator, while 80% have a freezer, and 67% have electric cookers. Michael decided, therefore, to press ahead and concentrate on the domestic market, believing this would have greater potential in finding an adequate number of customers.

As far as competition was concerned, there were no fewer than 15 engineers already advertising their services and working in an extensive area covering two major towns of Bournemouth and Poole and many other smaller districts.

These competitors were all located and it was decided that there was still room available for a further engineer in close proximity to Michael's residence. It was difficult to tie down how much per hour the engineers actually charged for their services but about £20 per hour seemed to be an average figure. To summarise, a market investigation must cover:

(a) who the customers are;
(b) what the customers are looking for;
(c) what the market is (whether it's restricted to the local area, or wider afield);
(d) whether you have got what the customers want;
(e) the level of competition;
(f) the prices already being charged;
(g) the best way to contact any potential customers and gain a share of the market.

The marketing plan

The aim of the owner was to establish himself in business and have self-sufficiency. He would need a turnover which he and his family could comfortably live on without resort to working for any other employer.

A marketing plan needs to determine everything possible about the market: that is, research into its likely customers, the prices to charge, the products to be sold, the advertising and the promotion needed to sell (the right goods sold at the right price, in the right place at the right time). Part of this plan concerns the marketing mix. The marketing mix refers to the 4 Ps of marketing, that is, product, price, place and promotion.

Product

The product, of course, was an engineering service called After-care with the object of repairing/servicing electrical goods such as washing machines and refrigerators.

Whatever is being sold, whether it is a product or service, a business must specify in precise terms what it has to offer. The message to the customer must include any individual or special features that the product may have and which should be communicated clearly to potential customers. This may be an attractive price, a high-quality product, an immediate 24-hour service or delivery, a built-in guarantee or something novel in the product itself. Whatever it is, you need to draw the customer's unwavering attention to it.

Price

The price must be set at the right level. There is always a danger of setting it too low. Once this is done, it may be difficult to raise it to the correct level. There is the feeling that you want to undercut the competition too much. A price should be set bearing in mind what customers expect to pay. If it is too low, they may feel suspicious that the service will be the same, too low a standard.

Michael decided to undercut the competition marginally by setting his charges at an estimated 20% lower than that of his rivals. He also produced a price list of typical repairs and servicing costs to give him a ready guide-line of how much to quote his customers. The prices in Tables 2.1 and 2.2 represent some typical charges for both repair and servicing.

The wholesale cost of parts can vary enormously from a trade profit of 20% to figures upwards of 50%. The cost of repairs can provide income from two sources: the profit margin on the part or component used and the hourly rate charged for the job.

It is quite difficult actually to decide what hourly rate to charge your customers. Obviously, you must make it worthwhile and be able to support yourself and your family. At the same time, you need to keep in step with your competitors. What a business needs to cover is: (a) the sum for drawings (what is, what you need to draw out in cash or through the bank each week for yourself); and (b) all overhead costs such as rent, rates, light, heat, telephone, etc. In Michael's case, he considered his drawings to be about £225 per week and his overheads for the year were estimated to cost £6,000. Based on working at least 45 weeks a year, 30 hours per week, his charge per hour should be:

TABLE 2.1   Example of washing machine repair

Item	Amount	Total
Water valve cost	£13.00	
Labour charge	£15.00	£28.00
Actual valve cost	£ 6.80	
Travel cost	£ 2.50	£ 9.30
Profit on typical repair:		£18.70

TABLE 2.2   Servicing charge of washing machine

Item	Amount
Labour charge	£16.00
Travel cost	£ 2.50
Profit on typical service	£13.50

$$\text{Hourly rate charge} = \frac{£6,000 + (£225 \times 52)}{45 \times 30} = \frac{£17,700}{1,350}$$

$$= £13.11 \text{ per hour}$$

If the service on a washing machine took just over an hour (including some travel), then £16 per hour seems to be a reasonable rate for the job at the time it was calculated. For further information concerning costs and price, see Part VI of the text.

Place

Concerns itself with the market. Customers have to be targeted and careful thought given to how to enter the market. In Michael's case, the place refers to people's homes. The area of the market was restricted to about a radius of 30 miles from the business location. No particular type of home was targeted because almost all homes have both a washing machine and refrigerator.

In other organisations, getting the product or service to the right place at the right time is of vital importance. Place may be every conceivable vantage point in getting the product to the customer. This could include direct customer access to their residence; wholesale or retail outlets; selling agents and other distributors; mail order business; or vending machines.

Place must also consider distribution. If you are selling goods as a wholesaler, distributor or manufacturer, you need to consider the best method of transport: how to get the goods to the customer by the most appropriate means. This could be by rail, road, air or sea. If it is by road, you may have your own vehicles or need to hire a haulage firm to carry your goods.

Promotion

How best to attract the customers and let them know what you have to offer? This concerns projecting a certain image to the customer. How are customers going to be attracted to your product/service? you may have an excellent service to offer but this must be backed up with the right promotional package. How and what to say to your customers will be important in getting the right message across.

Getting Aftercare on the road started with the distribution of a special offer leaflet, circulated by hand. About 2,000 of these were distributed in the local area, of which a 2% response was the result. This enabled the business to start rolling slowly. It is always likely that a new business moves very slowly in the initial stages until a customer clientele has been built up.

There was also free press advertising in the small circulation magazines which helped to get the right message to customers. In the larger circulation papers, like the *Poole and Dorset Advertiser* and the *Evening Echo*, a weekly or monthly charge had to be paid. It was these papers that kept customers informed that an electrical repair service was available.

AFTERCARE

washing machines
fridge-freezers
electric cookers

No call out charge

MIKE UPTON

0202 687331

The local shop windows can be used as well, and the Michael did try some post-card sized adverts at the post office and other shops for a number of weeks to help become established.

A small sticker was also printed to stick on the customer's appliances once they had been repaired.

The Yellow Pages was contacted and, once the business was heading towards success, an entry was booked for the next edition.

When choosing advertising media one must bear in mind the image the business is trying to convey to its customers. For small businesses like Michael's, the local press is ideal because it is relatively cheap and gets the message to the local customers almost like a directory. Obviously, for larger organisations a much wider range of advertising and publicity is required, such as the national press, magazines, trade journals, radio and television.

Management

If any business is to run smoothly and effectively, it must be well organised. Even a sole trader who makes all his own decisions in the business should think carefully of all the things he must do. He must be able to plan ahead and know the kind of activities to be achieved if he is to be successful. In a partnership or limited company where there is more than one person to share the decision making, it is wise to decide who is going to be responsible for what right at the outset. For example, if a florist's shop was in trade as a two-person partnership, one person could be responsible for all purchasing of stock, the other for all the administration and financial details.

Management policy

Part of management policy should be to specify activities to certain individuals and make them responsible for them. In large organisations, these activities would be broken down into various departments, headed by individual managers. An organisation chart would specify who those managers were and the subordinates under them.

Any business plan needs to identify the key staff in the organisation and their roles and responsibilities. The personal details of these individuals can be outlined in the form of a curriculum vitae which would include their age, marital status, education and training, qualifications and relevant work experience.

In Michael's case, he was qualified as an electrical engineer, having gained his City & Guilds in electrical installation. Later on in his career, he also studied management and became an associate of the Institute of Supervisory Management. On top of this, he had a long period of varied experiences in electrical servicing and

TABLE 2.3   **Michael's business assets**

Item	£	Total
Hand tools	250	
Electric drill	60	
Ladders/steps	100	
Como digital meter	30	
Van stocks	500	940
Casio calculator	35	
Erika portable typewriter	120	
Audio line 860 telephone (answering machine)	55	
BT tone Master Pager	20	230

management of staff. This made him particularly suitable to run his own business in his own specialised field.

To commence his operations as a sole trader, he deposited a sum of £2,000 to start up the business and required another £1,000 from the NatWest Bank. He also had a motor van which was needed to visit customers. His plan in the first year was to produce a turnover of at least £20,000 which should have generated sufficient profit/income to survive.

Suppliers

To purchase all the parts he required for his business, Michael made a list of the major suppliers of electrical components in the area. He contacted them and discussed in detail the type of goods he could buy, delivery times, trade discounts and other important facets of information. He decided, initially, to keep to two major suppliers and see how reliable and effective they are.

Equipment

Michael made a list of equipment he wanted and, in some cases, had already acquired. The assets (excluding vehicle) were as shown in Table 2.3.

Location of premises

Finding suitable premises can be a real pain. The location must be both appropriate and suitable, and preferably close to the market area with good transport links both for the marketing of the product and for staff.

In Michael's case this was not a problem because he used part of his own residence as his office and was able to apportion rent, rates and the use of power as part of his business expenses. His location was central and perfectly suitable for reaching his customers.

Administration

Michael intended using a Simplex D Cash Book system to keep records of his accounts. This is a straightforward book-keeping system which records, on a daily basis, all income including any banking details, and all expenses paid in cash and those incurred by invoice, particularly for purchases of parts.

Management of time

This is an important aspect for all of us. You can always tell who the better students are at college because it is they who organise their time so well. They don't idle their time away for weeks on end and then rush about insanely trying to finish an assignment in the tea-break before it is due in! Goals must be set in a given period of time and the activities required to achieve them parcelled out appropriately.

Priorities should also be given greater importance as regards time. If a list of calls come in from customers, it may be that some are far more urgent. The location of them will also play a part as to when the work could be completed. Even when times are hectic, making a list of jobs to be done, putting priorities first, leads to better organisation and efficiency of the business. Planning activities in periods when work is slack can help in targeting what needs to be done to improve the general functioning of the business.

Strengths and weaknesses

It is said that an organisation is only as strong as its weakest link. If there is a weak link in the overall business plan, something must be done to correct it. It may be that the business is under-capitalised and needs far more funding if it is to be a success. It could be that not all avenues to attract customers have been explored, therefore a so-called gap in the market becomes no more than a narrow slit! In a partnership, one of its members may not be suitable for the responsibilities that he has taken on. In a company, a weak department cannot be tolerated because any weak link can be a fatal factor and cause the disintegration of a business.

In Michael's case, the strengths were his qualifications and experience and a determination to succeed. The weaknesses were very marginal in that he restricted himself to domestic repairs and servicing and therefore neglected the commercial sector. The results, however, have shown that after two years' trading, the business is soundly successful.

Finances

This is what this text is really about. As you read and study the subject further, you will find that all businesses need to have good financial control. One of the most frequent causes of business failure is the lack of it.

Why is it important to have a basic understanding of a business's finances? Because without it, a business will not have the information it needs to be able to run properly. For example, it won't have much idea about the amount of money expected to flow into and out of the business and this could easily lead to a lack of liquidity (that is, insufficient funds to pay off creditors).

Nearly half of all businesses fail within three years of commencement of trading and, although a number of reasons can be found why they fail, it is this lack of financial knowledge that is a key factor in business bankruptcies.

Every business should plan ahead and have some sort of aim and objectives.

Aim:	What does it want to achieve?
Objective:	How does it go about getting what it wants?

The aim of all businesses is to make sufficient income to survive. Therefore, a business must plan to make profits. Revenue is the income of the business, either in cash or invoiced sales (credit sales). Against this are matched all the business expenses. The difference between them is profit. How this profit, is achieved depends upon how many customers it can attract and keeping costs as low as possible.

The business plan should therefore include figures which:

(a) forecast the cash flow for 12 months ahead;
(b) indicate the forecast of profit or loss for the same period;
(c) if possible, produce a forecast balance sheet at the end of the period which will indicate its financial position.

What were Michael's financial forecasts? Did things go according to plan? Figure 2.1 and Tables 2–4–5 show his cash flow, profit and loss account and balance sheet for the period 12 months ahead of his business starting.

Evaluation of results

The cash-flow forecast for the 12 months commencing 1 April indicated that Aftercare would have little problem with finding sufficient cash to meet all payments when they fell due. There was no month where an overdraft facility looked likely to be needed. Indeed, the bank account was estimated to rise from £1,065 at the start of the business to £4,621 at the period end.

The key to this very sound position was, of course, the income estimated to come from customers. This was based on the number of jobs, costed at approximately £18 each visit. The forecast was a modest start of 48 jobs in the first month, rising steadily to 96 jobs by the half year and 120 jobs in the final month. The total number of jobs was estimated to be 1,064.

The actual results after the first year surpassed those estimated. The number of jobs was closer to 1,200 and turnover (sales) cleared £24,000. This had the effect of increasing the profit expected in the first year and the business was certainly successful.

Both the gross and net profit returns were about 15% higher than forecast. The second year's trading figures looked just as promising, and the balance sheet indicated a very sound financial position. There was adequate working capital and sufficient inflow of cash resources every month to warrant excess sums to be transferred to a higher earnings account, providing further income from interest payments received.

From the cash-flow forecast, it was seen that a bank loan of £1,000 may not have been necessary, and therefore no business loan from the bank was ever negotiated. The bank also offered their services free for the first year's trading, so no charges were recorded in the profit and loss account.

There were no figures indicated for VAT because Michael was exempt, being below the Chancellor's threshold for registration. If Aftercare's turnover had been above the threshold, VAT registration would have been necessary. VAT would have had to be charged to customers and a VAT account opened. The balance owing to Customs & Excise would be the difference between what Michael collected in VAT and what he would pay for in VAT (VAT outputs on sales less VAT inputs on purchases and other costs).

The figures in the trading and profit and loss account would

Figure 2.1 Cash FLow Forecast for AFTERCARE
31 March 19- period ended

MONTH	April	May	June	July	August	Sept.	October	Nov.	Dec.	Jan	Feb	March	Total
Sales													
Sales by volume [Jobs]	48	56	64	72	80	88	96	104	108	112	116	120	1,064
Sales by value £	664	1,008	1,152	1,296	1,440	1,584	1,728	1,872	1,944	2,016	2,088	2,160	19,152
Receipts													
Sales - cash													
Sales - debtors													
Capital introduced	2,000												2,000
Grants & loans	1,000												1,000
Enterprise Allow.	80	160	160	240	160	160	80						1,040
Total	3,944	1,168	1,312	1,536	1,600	1,744	1,808	1,872	1,944	2,016	2,088	2,160	23,192
Payments													
Raw Materials	490	100	110	120	130	140	150	160	170	180	190	200	2,140
Employee wages & NI													
Rent, rates & HLP				35				35				290	360
Advertising etc	147	147	147	150	150	350	150	150	150	150	150	150	1,991
Insurance	55			120								120	295
Transport & packaging	150	120	120	120	120	120	120	120	150	150	350	150	1,790
Telephone	43	23	405	23	23	23	23	23	23	23	23	23	678
Stationery, postage, etc	200	10	10	10	10	10	10	10	10	10	35	20	345
Professional fees													
HP & lease payments													
Capital items	80	400			300								780
Loan repayments						300						300	600
Loan interest													
Bank charges													
Other NIC [personal]	21	21	21	21	21	21	21	21	21	21	21	21	252
Other Sundries	30	30	30	30	30	30	30	30	30	30	50	50	400
Principals drawings/wages	420	420	600	600	600	900	900	900	900	900	900	900	8,940
VAT													
VAT to C & E													
Total	1,636	1,271	1,443	1,229	1,384	1,894	1,404	1,449	1,454	1,464	1,719	2,224	18,571
Balances													
Cash increase (decrease)	2,308	[103]	[131]	307	216	[150]	404	423	490	552	369	[64]	–
Opening balance		2,308	2,205	2,074	2,381	2,597	2,447	2,851	3,274	3,764	4,316	4,685	–
Closing balance	2,308	2,205	2,074	2,381	2,597	2,447	2,851	3,274	3,764	4,316	4,685	4,621	4,621

TABLE 2.4   Forecast trading and profit and loss account
for Aftercare
(period ending 31 March 19—)

	£	£
Sales		19,152
Less cost of sales:		
Purchases	2,140	
– stock unused	(310)	1,830
GROSS PROFIT (90%)		17,322
Less overhead expenses:		
Rates	230	
Light, heat	130	
Telephone	678	
Transport costs	1,790	
Stationery	345	
Advertising	1,991	
Bank interest	100	
Insurances	295	
NIC (self)	252	
Sundries	400	
Depreciation		
Vehicle	800	
Equipment	320	
Accountant's fees due	300	7,631
		9,691
Add other revenue		
Enterprise allowance		1,040
NET PROFIT	(55%)	10,731

Notes:(a) The gross profit margin = 90% (17,322/19,152).
 (b) The net profit margin = 55% (10,731/19,152).
 (c) Depreciation: loss of value of vehicle and equipment.
 (d) Enterprise allowance received for 6 months only; without this income, net
  profit margin falls to 51%.
For further information concerning trading and profit and loss accounts, refer to part III
of the text.)

exclude any VAT charges if a business was registered for VAT.
The balance sheet would indicate either the balance owing or due
from Customs & Excise, depending on whether the sales outputs
were greater than inputs, or vice versa. Further information on
VAT is to be found in Part IV.

TABLE 2.5   Forecast balance sheet for Aftercare
(period ending as on 31 March 19—)

	£		£
Fixed assets:			
Equipment	1,280		
– Depreciation	(320)		960
Motor Vehicle	3,000		
– Depreciation	(800)		2,200
			3,160
Current assets:			
Stock	310		
Debtors	0		
Bank	4,621	4,931	
less			
current liabilities:			
Creditors	0		
Accountant's fees	300	300	
Working Capital			4,631
			7,791
less			
long-term liabilities:			
bank loan (1,000 – 500)			500
			7,291
Financed by:			
Capital (M. Upton)	5,500		
+ Profit	10,731		
	16,231		
– Drawings	8,940		7,291

Notes: (a) The balance sheet indicates Aftercare's financial position as forecast on 31 March.
     (b) Michael's initial capital at start was £2,000 in the bank and a vehicle worth £3,000 and equipment worth £500 = £5,500.
     (c) Working capital represents the value of current assets less current liabilities (debts).
     (d) The value of the business is £7,291 which represents the worth of the owner, £7,291.
For further information concerning the balance sheet, see Chapter 4.)

Legal requirements

When a new business is to commence, it is advisable that the owner(s) seek the services of a solicitor to lend guidance as regards setting the business up. He may be required if premises are to be purchased, leased or rented. He would do the conveyancing and see if there are any difficulties regarding a mortgage or contract.

Franchising

If a franchise was purchased, there would be a legal obligation between the seller and the buyer. A franchise is a monopoly right to trade in a particular activity, such as McDonald's or Kentucky Fried Chicken. Many petrol stations and public houses also operate on a franchise system, giving the suppliers major channels of distribution for their goods. It gives the franchise seller the right to dictate the terms of the trading functions of the business but, at the same time, it does provide an opportunity for anyone to become their own boss. A solicitor would be needed to check and clarify to the buyer of the franchise all the relevant details of the purchase and to ensure these were understood before any contract was signed and the business went ahead.

Business formation

If a partnership was to be formed, a solicitor's advice would be sought to ensure that the contract between the partners, the Deeds of Partnership, was acceptable to all members and that the interests of each member were protected, particularly from the point of view of how profits or losses were to be shared, and the rights and obligations of each member. If a limited company was to be the form of organisation, the solicitor would prepare the initial documents, such as the Memorandum and Articles of Association, and send them to Companies House.

Once the organisation was under way, his services may be required in other directions such as clarifying any consumer laws or investigating other contracts with suppliers or customers, etc. The significant consumer law acts are shown below.

The Sale of Goods Act 1979

This requires that goods correspond with their description and are fit for the purpose (that is, the goods are of merchantable quality and fit the purpose they were intended for). If a new pair of shoes is purchased and the sole falls off after a short period of time, the buyer has every chance of redress against the seller.

The Supply of Goods and Services Act 1982

This covers the same ground as above and also refers to goods which are supplied under contract for service or on lease or hire (that is, that the goods or service are of merchantable quality and are fit for the purpose).

The Trades Descriptions Act 1968

This states that any description of the goods or services offered must be true and fair. Any false representations gives the buyer the right to sue the seller or producer of the product. If a holiday was advertised stating it was sufficient to accommodate six persons and this was later to be discovered to mean that six bodies were expected to share a single room, then again there is every right of redress against the seller or agent offering the product or service.

The Consumer Protection Act 1987

This Act protects the consumer against goods which fail to meet standard safety regulations, particularly in electrical goods, in certain use of materials and in toys.

The Fair Trading Act 1973

The Act covers any trade practices which may be considered economically detrimental to the interests of consumers. For example, to state that a firm does not operate a refund policy is against the Sale of Goods Act and therefore a criminal offence. Companies which are seen to have an unfair monopoly of goods and control prices are subject to investigation by the Office of Fair Trading.

The Consumer Credit Act 1974

This applies to organisations offering credit, hire purchase, credit agreements, credit cards, etc., and obliges the seller of credit trading to clarify to the consumer aspects such as interest charges and 'cooling-off' periods, and so on.

The Interference of Goods Act 1977

This Act covers any civil wrong (tort) as opposed to any criminal wrong. A civil court would deal with torts such as negligence, breach of statutory duty and defamation. If a business is accused of any of these breaches of civil justice, it may have to pay out damages to whoever the injured party was.

Health and Safety Acts

There are also a number of important Acts which concern health and safety and, overall, these are in place to oblige all employers, as far as is reasonably possible, to ensure that their employees' safety, health and general welfare are protected.

The Health and Safety at Work act 1974, The Offices, Shops and Railway Premises Act 1963, and the Factories Act 1961 all require that certain basic standards are met as regards the general safety and welfare of their employees.

Insurance

New businesses are also obliged to have at least the minimum insurance cover to protect themselves, their employees and their customers. The business, including premises, stocks, motor vehicles, etc., should all be covered by insurance policies. Employers' Liability Insurance Act 1969 is compulsory if a business has employees, in the event that they have an accident whilst at work. Public liability insurance also protects members of the public if damage or injury is caused by the business (for example, if you walked into a shop and slipped on a newly polished floor and were injured as a result.

The presentation of the business plan

The business plan should be a complete and concise description of a business and its plans for the period ahead. At least the first year's trading should be forecast and, if possible, even further ahead. The plan, as guided in the above headings, should clearly explain what the business hopes to achieve, what its market is likely to be, the product it wishes to sell and how it is to be promoted. The financial information should be reasonably accurate and be the result of factual evidence wherever practicable. Estimations of income, particularly in the early months of business, should be conservatively calculated; a lender would be pessimistic if, on the cash flow, the initial sales figures looked like an established business.

The plan must be the selling-point of the business and look professional. Ideally, it should always be typed up, concise and factual, and generally look attractive.

In its presentation to a bank or other financial institution, or an Enterprise Scheme, be sure to know your facts well relating to the plan and be ready to answer any questions put to you, particularly about the quality of your product, the marketing of it and the financial forecast you have made.

You may also need to give details of any securities you could offer the lenders (that is, any assets you might own as financial backing to the business). This could be your house, car, or any other form of security which a bank or other lender may want before granting a loan.

Questions

1. If you wanted to start a business, where could you go to find information?
2. Why is it strongly advisable to prepare a business plan?
3. What do you think are the critical aspects of a business plan?
4. Define the 4 Ps of a marketing mix.
5. What factors determine the price of a product/service?
6. For a small business, how would you promote the product?
7. Why is it important to establish some form of management policy even in the smallest of businesses?
8. Why is financial information essential in the forming of a business plan?
9. What purpose does a cash budget serve?
10. Financial statements concern the trading and profit and loss account and the balance sheet. What is the essential difference between them?
11. If a business was registered for VAT, how would the figures in the trading and profit and loss account differ from that of a business which is exempt from VAT?
12. What is meant by a franchise?
13. Why is it important for a trader to have some knowledge of consumer law? Give an example to clarify.
14. What are the key points to consider in the presentation of a sound business plan?

CHAPTER 3

The Role of the Accountant

The accountant's work is often varied and interesting, as well as far reaching. Many people think they have a boring job to do, recording figures all day long and checking the work of others.

Accountants do this of course as part of their work but, more importantly, they are managers of finance whether they work in private practice or in an organisation where accounting is one of a number of departments like sales, marketing, production and personnel. Not only are they concerned with recording financial information, they are also interested in planning and forecasting results. They are financial consultants helping other managers to decide the way ahead, playing a critical part in evaluating business problems and being part of a team which plans, controls and takes decisions in an organisation.

Accountants, when qualified, may take on different roles. There are four main accounting qualifications:

The Institute of Chartered Accountants (letters ACA);

The Chartered Association of Certified Accountants (letters ACCA);

The Chartered Institute of Public Finance and Accountancy (letters CIPFA);

The Chartered Institute of Management Accountants (letters ACMA).

An ACA may work in a private practice; providing auditing and financial accounting services, such as preparing annual accounts for clients, and advising on taxation matters. In fact, the large professional firms of accountants engage in a whole range of financial consultancy work. Many ACAs work as senior accountants in industry and commerce. An ACCA may similarly work in a private practice and is qualified to audit and provide the same services as an ACA. Probably, a higher proportion of ACCA qualified accountants work in industry and commerce than do so in private practice.

A CIPFA accountant will mainly work for local authorities, where a specialist knowledge of public sector financial accounting is required. An ACMA is not qualified to audit; consequently most ACMAs work in industry and commerce as management accountants, concerned with assisting management to assess business performance and cost-effectiveness. However, some ACMAs are employed in private practice as management consultants. Much of the management accountant's work is involved with assessing future performance.

The purpose of auditing accounts

An audit is an examination of the accounts to check that everything is as it should be. Accounts are subject to annual audits by professional accountants like ACAs or ACCAs. The purpose is to ensure that records and statements are accurate and purport to be what they say. The role of the auditor is to examine a fair sample of the accounting books, documents, vouchers and statements of an organisation in order to verify that they are accurate, truthful and fair. A typical Auditors' Report concerning the accounts of a public limited company would appear in the Annual Report and Accounts as:

> We have audited the financial statements on pages 28 to 39 of the Annual Report & Accounts in accordance with Auditing Standards.
>
> In our opinion, these financial statements give a true and fair view of the state of affairs of the Company and of that of the Group as at 31 December, 19.. and of the profit and cash flow statement of the Group, for the year then ended and have been prepared in accordance with the Companies Act, 1985.
>
> PRICE WATERHOUSE
> Chartered Accountants
> and Registered Auditor

In the case of limited companies, the audit is a legal obligation Auditors act as 'watchdogs' over the shareholders' interests. There is no provision laid down for small businesses (such as sole traders and partnerships) to have their accounts audited although, if an owner wanted verification of the accounts, an auditor could be appointed to act on their behalf.

Every auditor is not only entitled to examine the books of a company, but may also ask for further papers or documents, or call in the directors of the company to add to, or clarify, any information he requires. If, in his opinion, there is insufficient data to make a valid examination, this would be stated in his report. If the auditor is unsatisfied with any aspect of the accounts or with any explanations or returns made by the directors of the company, these would be stated in the Auditors' Report.

The 1985 Companies Act states that every limited company must appoint an auditor (or auditors) to examine the books and accounts and to report on their correctness or otherwise, to the shareholders of the company (see Chapter 18, Company Accounts, and the 1985 and 1989 Companies Acts).

The accounts office

The role of the accountant either in private practice or working in an organisation may be listed as:

(a) the collection and recording of financial data;
(b) the organisation of financial data into books of account;
(c) the control of cash resources;
(d) the preparation of financial statements, such as profit and loss account and balance sheet;
(e) the assessment of financial performance through the analysis and evaluation of accounting reports;
(f) the examination of accounts in the role of auditor;
(g) the preparation of budgets to forecast estimation of expenditure against income for planning, control and evaluation of trading performance;
(h) the preparation of costing estimates, including marginal costing and break-even;
(i) the preparation of cash flow to ensure that sufficient cash is available to meet day-to-day expenditure;
(j) the arrangements and negotiations necessary for raising capital including loans or overdraft facilities;
(k) the role of financial adviser or consultant.

The recording of financial information is the key function of an accounts office. Customers' and suppliers' records must be accurately recorded by the sales and bought ledger clerks, information for these records coming from business documents like the invoice and credit note as well as from the receipts and payments of cash.

The cashier is responsible for all matters involving the receipt

Figure 3.1   Jobs and responsibilities in a typical accounts office

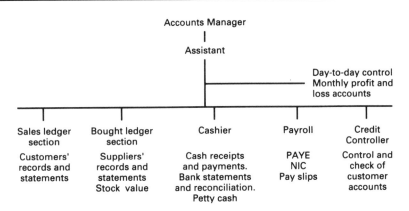

and payment of money and the checking of statements with the business's bank account records. There may be a junior clerk delegated to take care of petty cash payments (see Figure 3.1).

Wages must also be calculated for each of the firm's employees, including payments for overtime or bonus schemes. Appropriate deductions need to be made for taxation, National Insurance and other stoppages from pay.

Stock must be recorded either on stock record cards or using a stock program on the computer, showing both the quantity and type of stock in balance as well as its value.

The accountant and his assistant will have overall control of the staff and be responsible for preparing monthly statements of profit and loss as well as the final accounting reports at the end of the financial period. They may also be involved in the preparation of budget accounts which are used to forecast and control income and expenditure figures for all departments of the business.

The computer is playing an important role in the recording of financial information. Computer programs are available for sales and bought ledgers, stock control, payroll and the preparation of final accounts. The accounts clerk will tend to type in data on a computer keyboard rather than traditionally writing the information in the accounting books.

Finance is one of the most important aspects of an organisation because the whole operation is dependent on its expertise. The preparation of accounts helps to explain what is happening in the business: whether it is successful or not, whether it has sufficient cash to pay its way, whether it should make this decision or that.

It should also be noted that accountants do look ahead and help management make better informed decisions which concern the organisation, at the same time ensuring that finances are under sound control.

Questions

1. People often think that an accountant's job is boring. Can you offer an alternative adjective(s)?
2. One of the accountant's functions is to act as an auditor. Find out what this service is.
3. What would be the difference in working for an accountant in private practice or working in an organisation which has its own accounting department?
4. In an accounts office, what may be considered a key function?
5. What advantages are evident in the use of computerised accounts?

CHAPTER 4

Introducing the Balance Sheet

The balance sheet is a statement which lists the assets, the liabilities and the capital of a business organisation.

Assets represent a business's resources. They may be financed by a combination of the owner's capital and any capital borrowed, referred to in accounting as 'liabilities'. One of the major functions of a business is to make profits and this is achieved by financing resources which will make money and, in turn, produce more resources.

The following tables show the assets and the liabilities of G. Harrison, who is the owner of a small retail shop. He has recently started in business and is learning by experience. He left his job in a bank because he felt more than a little adventurous and wanted to make a success of being in business for himself.

TABLE 4.1   G. Harrison's assets: the resources owned by a business

	£	£
Premises	12,000	
Fixtures and fittings	2,000	
Equipment	3,000	
Stock	—	
Debtors (customers who owe money)	—	
Bank account	3,000	
Total assets:		20,000

TABLE 4.2   Liabilities: the finance owed by a business

	£	£
Creditors (money owed to suppliers)	—	
Mortgage on premises	8,000	
Bank loan	2,000	
Total liabilities:		10,000

What is G. Harrison worth? Simply the *difference* between assets and liabilities.

Total assets:	£20,000
Less total liabilities:	£10,000
Harrison's 'net worth' = (his capital)	£10,000

The balance sheet is simply a list of assets, liabilities and capital of a business at any given time. These are constantly changing in response to the business's trading activity.

The balance sheet of G. Harrison on 1 January is shown in Table 4.3.

TABLE 4.3   G. Harrison's balance sheet

	£	£
Fixed assets (at cost)		
Premises	12,000	
Fixtures and Fittings	2,000	
Equipment	3,000	17,000
Current assets		
Stock	—	
Debtors	—	
Bank	3,000	
		3,000
Total assets		20,000
Less		
Current liabilities		
Creditors	—	

TABLE 4.3 *continued*

	£	£
Long-term liabilities		
Mortgage on premises	8,000	
Bank loan	2,000	
	10,000	
Total liabilities		10,000
		10,000
Financed by		
Capital: G. Harrison		10,000

These figures are represented by the accounting equation:

Capital	=	Assets	–	Liabilities
£10,000	=	£20,000	–	£10,000

Alternatively, the equation may be represented as

Assets	=	Capital	+	Liabilities
£20,000	=	£10,000	+	£10,000

The first equation (C = A - L) tends to emphasise the net worth of the owner. The alternative equation (A = C + L) tends to emphasise the business as financed by a combination of the owner's capital + borrowed capital.

The accounting equation

Capital   =   Assets

The capital provided by the owner equals the resources owned by the business.

Capital   +   Liabilities   =   Assets

That is, the combination of the owner's capital plus what is borrowed equals the financing of the assets.
    From the owner's point of view:

Capital   =   Assets   –   Liabilities

Categories of assets and liabilities

The two main categories of *assets* are:

Fixed   that is, those more or less used permanently in the business: premises, equipment, fixtures and fittings, motor vehicles.

Current that is, those assets used for trading purposes and constantly circulating from cash, bank, stock and debtors. Current assets have a higher liquidity than fixed assets because they can be converted into cash more quickly.

Other types:

Intangible assets
that is, those assets not included above which tend to be 'invisible'. For example, *goodwill* – a business willing to pay to purchase another business may have to include a sum for the reputation or good name of that business.

Investments
that is, when a business buys property, stocks or shares in other business enterprises.

There are two main categories of *liabilities*:

Long-term (deferred)
for example, bank loans, mortgages.
The debt to be repaid runs longer than the business's financial year (that is, creditors after 12 months).

Current for example, creditors, banks overdraft, bills still outstanding, and short-term debts which will be repaid within the business's financial year (that is, creditors within 12 months).

Exercise

Table 4.4 represents the assets and liabilities of H. Brown, a retail proprietor, as on 1 January:

TABLE 4.4 H. Brown's assets and liabilities

	£
Assets	
Land and buildings	15,000
Bank a/c	2,500
Stock at cost	3,000
Equipment	1,800
Motor van	750
Debtors	150
Cash	100
Fixtures	1,750
Liabilities	
Mortgage on land and buildings	10,000
Bank loan (4 years)	2,000
Creditors	1,850
Bills outstanding	120

Required:

(a) Place the above in their appropriate categories.
(b) Calculate the net worth (or capital) of H. Brown.
(c) Prepare a balance sheet as at 1 January.
(d) Show the accounting equation from the point of view of the proprietor, including the figures.
(e) Show the alternative equation including the figures.
(f) The assets are the resources of the business. Which parties are financing the resources of the business?
(g) Make a list of the financial institutions where a businessman can borrow money to finance his enterprise.

Check your answers below.

(a)

Assets		Liabilities	
Fixed	Current	Long-term	Current
Land and buildings	Stock	Mortgage	Creditors
Equipment	Debtors	Bank loan	Bills outstanding
Fixtures	Bank		
Motor van	Cash		

(b) Net worth: the owner's capital

$$C = \text{Assets} - \text{Liabilities}$$
$$£11,080 \quad £25,050 \quad £13,970$$

(c) Balance Sheet of H. Brown as on 1 January

	£	£
Fixed assets		
Land and Buildings	15,000	
Fixtures	1,750	
Equipment	1,800	
Motor Van	750	19,300
Current assets		
Stock	3,000	
Bank	150	
Debtors	2,500	
Cash	100	5,750
Total assets		25,050
Less		
Current liabilities		
Creditors	1,850	
Bills outstanding	120	
	1,970	
Long-term liabilities		
Mortgage on Land and Buildings	10,000	
Bank Loan	2,000	
	12,000	
Total liabilities		13,970
Net assets		11,080
Financed by		
Capital: H. Brown		11,080

(d) Capital = Assets − Liabilities
    £11,080   £25,050   £13,970

(e) Assets = Capital + Liabilities
    £25,050   £11,080   £13,970

(f) Parties financing the resources:
     H. Brown   £11,080
     Total
     Liabilities   13,970   £25,050

(g) Some of the financial institutions where a businessman could borrow capital to help finance his enterprise:

● The banks (for example, loans and overdrafts).
● The building societies (for example, mortgages on premises).
● The insurance companies (for example, mortgages and loans on policies).
● The finance companies (for example, loans and hire-purchase finance).

The following is an incomplete balance sheet of Arthur Smith. Complete the exercise yourself.

Balance Sheet of Arthur Smith as on 1 June

Fixed Assets	£
Premises	19,500
Fixtures and Fittings	1,750
Motor Vehicle	800
tools, Equipment	500
Current	
Stock	1,650
Debtors	1,020
Bank	—
Cash	150
Current Liabilities	
Creditors	1,245
Bank Overdraft	875
Bills due	80
Long-term	
Mortgage on Premises	10,000
Hire-Purchase Finance	1,200
Financed by	?
Capital: Arthur Smith	———

Changes in the balance sheet

When G. Harrison started his business, he had £10,000 of his own money which he put into his business bank account. The accounting equation is

Capital   =   Assets
£10,000   =   £10,000 (Bank a/c)

He then used his capital to finance the business resources:

(a) He bought the shop for £12,000 by depositing £4,000 cash and getting a mortgage from the local building society for the balance of £8,000.
(b) He paid a £2,000 cheque for fixtures and fittings.
(c) He paid a further £3,000 cheque for equipment.
(d) He needed to borrow £2,000 from the bank on a two-year loan to ensure he had sufficient resources for future expenditure.

Table 4.5 Shows his financial position after these transactions, and Table 4.6 shows his balance sheet.

Check the accounting equation:

A   =   C   +   L
or   C   =   A   −   L

TABLE 4.5   G. Harrison's financial position

Bank account	£	£
Balance		10,000
less payments:		
Premises	4,000	
Fixtures	2,000	
Equipment	3,000	9,000
		1,000
Add loan		2,000
New balance		3,000

TABLE 4.6   G. Harrison's balance sheet

	£	£
Fixed assets		
Premises	12,000	
Fixtures and fittings	2,000	
Equipment	3,000	17,000
Current assets		
Bank	3,000	3,000
		20,000
Less		
long-term liabilities		
Mortgage	8,000	
Bank loan	2,000	10,000
		10,000
Financed by		
Capital: G. Harrison		10,000

The balance sheet of Mr Harrison has changed because of the financial transactions. His balance sheet still balanced, however, because for each transaction there were *two* aspects to record: for example, when he bought the equipment for £3,000:

> He *received* the equipment (Asset +) Equipment a/c £3,000
> He *gave* the cheque   (Asset −) Bank a/c   −£3,000

This is the basic convention in accounting: there is a *dual-aspect* for each transaction.

In the next part of the text, the dual-aspect of recording will be shown by using the ledger.

Alternative presentation of the balance sheet

The balance sheet has been presented in a vertical format relating to the accounting equation:

> Assets   −   Liabilities   =   Capital

This method has the distinct advantage of having figures listed in columnar form which makes it easier for comparison purposes. The vertical method of presentation is the most commonly used.

TABLE 4.7 G. Harrison's balance sheet

	£	£		£	£
Fixed assets			*Liabilities*		
Premises	12,000		Long-term		
Fixtures and fittings	2,000		Mortgage	8,000	
Equipment	3,000	17,000	Bank loan	2,000	10,000
Current assets			*Capital*		
Bank		3,000	G. Harrison		10,000
		20,000			20,000

The alternative format (shown in Table 4.7) is a horizontal lay-out listing assets on the left and capital and liabilities on the right. This method relates to the alternative accounting equation:

Assets = Liabilities + Capital

Both formats are acceptable in accounting practice. One of the conventions of accounting is consistency. Once a particular method of doing things is decided, then that method is applied consistently. The text will follow the vertical format because of the advantage of showing comparison figures if required.

G. Harrison's balance sheet as at 31 December

After a year's trading Harrison's financial position is shown through his balance sheet (see Table 4.8). Note that he has made a profit of £5,500. (The calculation of profit is shown in the part concerning trading and profits and loss account.) He has also drawn money from his business for his own living expenses. This is the proprietor's 'drawings' which is deducted from his capital.

In this presentation. Harrison's *working capital* is also shown by simply deducting current liabilities from current assets. Working capital is an important concept because it indicates the business's ability to pay off its current debts. The business must have sufficient liquidity to trade comfortably without wondering if there is money available to pay off creditors. Harrison is in a sound position on 31 December because there is twice the value of current assets over current liabilities.

TABLE. 4.8   Balance sheet of G. Harrison as at 31 December

	£	£	£
Fixed assets (at cost)			
Premises	10,000		
Fixtures and fittings	3,000		
Equipment	5,000		18,000
Current assets			
Stock	8,000		
Debtors	1,500		
Bank	2,400		
Cash	100	12,000	
Less			
Current liabilities			
Creditors	5,500		
Bill outstanding	500	6,000	
Working capital			*6,000*
			24,000
Less			
long-term liabilities			
Mortgage on premises	7,750		
Bank loan	4,250		12,000
Net assets			12,000
Financed by			
Capital (1 January)	10,000		
+ Profit	5,500	15,500	
– Drawings		3,500	12,000

Note: This presentation of the balance sheet is a little more sophisticated than the earlier examples and will be used as the standard format in the remainder of the text.

Example

Table 4.9 shows the balance sheet changes of a trader, H. Jones. He commenced business on 1 January when he inherited a small retailing business from his uncle. Table 4.10 shows the balance sheet after January's transactions.

TABLE 4.9 H. Jones's balance sheet changes

Transaction	A (£)	L (£)	C (£)	Result (£)
1. Started business: inherited premises £20,000 and also put £5,000 into bank	25,000		25,000	Capital: 25,000 Assets: 25,000
2. Bought £3,500 of stock on credit from XYZ	3,500	3,500		A: 28,500 L: 3,500
3. Bought £1,500 of stock by cheque	+ 1,500 − 1,500			No change
4. Bought a motor vehicle £2,500: cheque £500 (deposit); balance from Jack's Garage on credit	+ 2,500 − 500	2,000		A: 30,500 L: 5,500
5. Put another £500 cash into bank from own resources	+ 500		500	A: 31,000 L: 5,500 C: 25,500
6. Bought equipment £2,000 by cheque	+ 2,000 − 2,000			No change
7. Paid £1,000 to Jack's Garage on account	− 1,000	− 1,000		A: 30,000 L: 4,500

Notes: A = Assets; L = Liabilities; C = Capital.

TABLE 4.10 Balance sheet at end of January

	£	£	£
Fixed assets			
Premises	20,000		
Equipment	2,500		
Motor vehicle	2,000		24,500
Current assets			
Stock	5,000		
Bank	500	5,500	

TABLE 4.10 *continued*

	£	£	£
Current liabilities			
Creditors		3,500	
Working capital			2,000
			26,500
Deferred liabilities			
Garage (2 years)			1,000
			25,500
Financed by			
Capital: H. Jones			25,500

Accounting Equation:	C	=	A	−	L
	£25,500	=	£30,000	−	£4,500

Questions

1. Show these assets and liabilities of J. Smith, hardware merchant, in the form of a balance sheet.

Shop	8,000		
Equipment	1,500	Bank Mortgage	7,000
Motor van	900	Creditors*	115
Bank	120	Loan from	
		Insurance Company	500
Cash	35		
		Capital:	
Stocks	1,175	J. Smith	4,335
Debtors*	220		

*Debtors represent people who owe Mr Smith money; creditors represent people to whom Mr Smith owes money.

(a) Illustrate Mr Smith's figures by means of the accounting equation.
(b) Which party holds the most claim on the business's assets?
(c) If Mr Smith paid off his creditors by cheque, how would this affect his balance sheet?

(d) Could he buy £125 worth of stock without money in the bank? How could the transaction be financed?

(e) Prepare a new balance sheet incorporating the changes in (c) and (d) above.

2. John Jones started up in business during the first week of April with a motor vehicle worth £800 and deposited £3,000 in the bank as his investment in the business.
The accounting equation would therefore be:

Capital	=	Assets	−	Liabilities
£3,800	=	£3,800	−	0

During the month of April, John Jones's initial transactions were involved in using the capital to commence business operations:

	£
Bought stock, paying by cheque	1,500
Bought equipment on credit from Jackson & Co. Ltd	2,000
Paid £300 cheque for tools and other equipment	300
Paid a cheque for a trailer to be used on the motor vehicle	240
Borrowed from the bank a loan extended over two years	
Paid Jackson & Co. Ltd 10% of the sum owing	1,000

Required:

(a) Show the dual effect of each of John Jones's transactions during April. The first one is done for you:

Stock a/c increases £1,500 (asset +)
Bank a/c decreases £1,500 (asset −)

(b) Prepare a statement to show how much John has in his bank account after the above transactions have been completed.

(c) Prepare a balance sheet for John Jones as at 30 April listing his resources and the financing of them.

(d) Calculate John's working capital on 30 April. Do you consider it sufficient? Give a brief explanation.

3. The following accounts represent the financial interests of M. Crooks on 1 June. He runs a small business associated with the building trade.

	£
Premises	33,500
Machinery and equipment	12,500
Tools	1,500
Motor vehicle	4,200
Furniture in the office	1,500
Stocks (at cost)	15,000
Debtors	1,275
Cash	100
Bank overdraft	1,750
Creditors for supplies	13,450
Bills outstanding	750
Interest payments due	125
Mortgage on premises	22,500
Hire-purchase loan on motor vehicle (2 years)	1,000
Bank loan (5 years)	10,000
Capital a/c: M. Crooks	20,000

Required:

(a) Group the above accounts in their appropriate categories – for example, current asset, fixed asset, etc.
(b) Prepare the balance sheet of M. Crooks as at 1 June.
(c) Show the accounting equation which would emphasise the ownership of M. Crooks.
(d) The liabilities of the owner look rather excessive. Has he sufficient funds to meet his current debts?
(e) Crooks must find at least £2,000 by the end of the month to pay off bills and creditors outstanding. Suggest how he could pay them!

4. Complete the following table. Enter the figures in the appropriate columns.

		Assets		Liabilities		Capital
		Current	Fixed	Current	Fixed	
		£	£	£	£	£
Proprietor's capital:	£					
Robert David	13,985					
Plant, Equipment	4,000					
Premises	12,000					
Debtors	3,725					
Creditors	4,630					
Loan from P. Jackson	3,500					
Building society loan	8,000					
Drawings for proprietor's personal use*	2,000					
Stocks	6,500					
Bank	1,850					
Cash	40					

*Drawings are a *deduction* from proprietor's capital. Anything taken from the business for *personal* use reduces the owner's capital.

Required:

(a) Prepare a balance sheet on 1 June for the proprietor, Robert David. Show working capital as part of the presentation.
(The loans from P. Jackson and the building society are both longer than 12 months and therefore are to be treated as long term.)
(b) Why is adequate working capital important?

5. Redraft the balance sheet below of Harry Smith as at 30 June in vertical form: it is a poor presentation which needs adjustment.

Capital		£	Assets	£
H. Smith		12,000	Premises	25,500
Liabilities			Motor vehicles	4,500
Loan from Frank		24,000	Drawings of Harry	1,000
Overdraft		1,505	Office equipment	3,000
Creditors	4,500		Cash	100
−Debtors	3,490	1,010	Stocks	3,780
Gas bill due		55	Fixtures and fittings	1,050
HP on vehicles				
outstanding ($\frac{1}{2}$ year)		360		
		38,930		38,930

Also required:

(a) A brief comment regarding the extent of liabilities in relation to Harry's own capital. (The loan from Frank is over a period of 5 years.)

(b) An opinion as to whether Harry's cash resources are adequate.

(c) A comment on Harry's capital tied up in fixed assets relative to capital tied up in his trading assets (current assets).

(d) Show the accounting equation illustrating $C = A − L$.

6. The following represents the financial figures of R. James as at year ended 30 June.

Assets	£	Capital a/c	£
Land and Buildings	25,000	R. James 1 January	20,000
Furniture and fittings	5,500		
Equipment	7,000	*Liabilities*	
Motor van	6,500	Mortgage	15,500
Bank	2,500	Bank loan (5 years)	10,500
Cash	50	Interest owing	750
Debtors	1,450	Creditors	4,500
Stock	8,000	Bills outstanding	1,000
Profit from trading	8,250		
Proprietor's personal			
expenses	4,500		

Required:

(a) Prepare a balance sheet for R. James as at 30 June.
   Show his working capital as part of the presentation.
(b) Comment on the owner's working capital.
(c) On a capital outlay of £20,000 on 1 January, would you
   say that the profit was reasonable?
      What would you receive in income if the money was
   invested in the bank or building society at current rates?
(d) What other motives are there for going into business
   besides making profit?

7. *Balance Sheet of J. Robertson as on 31 December*

Assets	£	Capital	£	£
Plant and machinery	7,875	J. Robertson (1/1)?		
Motor vans	8,350	Net loss	3,850	
Tools and equipment	1,875	Drawings	2,910	17,740
Stocks	51,450			
Debtors	2,421	*Liabilities*		
Cash	904	Loan a/c (8 years)		11,460
		HP finance (3 years)		9,293
		Creditors		20,170
		Bank overdraft		14,212
	72,875			72,875

Required:

(a) Calculate J. Robertson's capital on 1 January.
(b) Prepare the balance sheet of J. Robertson in the vertical method showing the amount of working capital.
(c) What kind of trading year do you consider Robertson
   has had? Make a brief comment.

8. The information below relates to the summarised balance
   sheets of R. D. Andrews:

	Year 1 £	Year 2 £	Year 3 £
Stock	800	1,040	2,920
Debtors	740	700	620
Bank/Cash	440	300	—
Premises	16,000	16,000	16,000
Other fixed assets	1,300	1,300	1,460
	19,280	19,340	21,000
Capital	18,000	18,220	19,180
Bank O/D	—	—	1,020
Creditors	1,280	1,120	800
	19,280	19,340	21,000

Required:

(a) Calculate the working capital of R. D. Andrews at the end of each year.
(b) Calculate the working capital ratio (the working capital ratio is current assets divided by current liabilities, so in year one it is 1,980 ÷ 1,280, or 1.5:1) correct to 1 decimal place.
(c) In which of the three years do you consider R. D. Andrews is best able to meet his current debts? Explain why.

PART II

THE DEVELOPMENT, PURPOSE AND FUNCTION OF ACCOUNTING

The Ledger System

By keeping records of accounts it is possible to know more accurately and efficiently the state of affairs of a business. It is essential to know the exact balances of accounts because when the time comes to, say, pay a creditor or collect money from a debtor, accurate figures must be available to ensure the right amount is paid at the right time.

In a small business of a sole trader or partnership, the keeping of formalised accounts may be absent. Financial record-keeping may be restricted to the basic and simple: for example, a book for receipts and payments of money (Cash Book); the processing of documents like the invoice and credit note relating to sales and purchases and the filing of all bills relating to the business.

In larger business enterprises, the paper work expands as the business expands and becomes more complex. The financial accounts of the enterprise must be prepared in a more formalised way. Accurate records must be kept in order to provide the business with day-to-day information. Relevant information can then be extracted from the records and passed on to those persons who need to use it. Suppliers' accounts can then be paid at the right time and customers can be chased up if their accounts are overdue.

One of the most important functions of accounting is to summarise financial information periodically in order to prepare profit and loss reports and balance sheets for owners and management and other interested parties, such as the Inland Revenue. From these records, the performance of the business can be evaluated, giving those interested parties vital information on which to base their decisions.

In this section, the *ledger is the key to the recording process*. It is based on the principle of *double-entry* which simply means that each transaction has a dual aspect and each aspect must be recorded in an account in the ledger.

The recording of accounts in the ledger system enables the business to be better organised and controlled.

Large businesses have several ledgers for the purpose of organising their accounts more efficiently. Sales ledgers are used to record debtors only, purchase (bought) ledgers for creditors only, the cash book for cash transactions, and a general ledger for other groups of accounts. In this way, accounting serves the needs of the organisation, providing of framework for the collection and recording of financial data.

The ledger is a system in accounting to record all financial transactions. It is a book or collection of accounts and provides the fundamental basis of keeping accounting records. It is designed to record the principle of 'double-entry' – that is, every financial transaction has two aspects and each aspect is recorded in an account; for example:

Paid a cheque of £500 for equipment

Equipment account is one aspect because the value of equipment will increase by £500. The bank account is the other because the cheque paid will reduce the amount in the bank. How is this recorded?

The double entry

Equipment a/c	Debit	£500
Bank a/c	Credit	£500

Figure 5.1 gives an example of the traditional ledger headings where the page is divided into two to show debits on the left side and credits on the right.

Key points in recording ledger transactions

Double-entry recording is a method in which *two* entries are recorded for every transaction.

Every transaction has two aspects to it: (a) the receiving of goods or services is one aspect, and (b) the payment for these by cash or credit is the other. *Each of these aspects is recorded in an account.* One account will record the value received on the *debit* side (Dr.), and the value given on the *credit* side (Cr.).

FIGURE 5.1 Traditional double-entry ledger layout

Debit   Credit

Date	Particulars	Amount £	Date	Particulars	Amount £

The name of
the account

(a) The ledger has two sides.
(b) The left side is the debit side.
(c) The right side is the credit side.
(d) The name of an account is placed in the centre of the ledger page.
(e) The particulars column is used to record the details of a transaction.

A basic rule in accounting is

All *asset* accounts received are debited and
All *capital* and *liability* accounts received are credited.

Therefore, if an asset is increased, it is a debit entry and if it is decreased, it is a credit entry. For example, furniture £200, is purchased for cash:

    Furniture a/c   Debit   £200
    Cash a/c   Credit   £200

Two entries are recorded for each transaction and in this case, the asset furniture is increased (Dr.) and cash decreased (Cr.).

Conversely, when either a capital or liability account is increased, it represents a credit entry and when decreased, a debit entry. For example, if a motor van was purchased on credit terms for £3,000 from Henley Ford Ltd:

    Motor van a/c   Debit   £3,000
    Henley Ford Ltd. a/c   Credit   £3,000

The asset, motor van, is increased (Dr.), and the liability, Henley Ford Ltd, is also increased (Cr.).

Example: The Ledger of G. Harrison

	Account Dr.	Account Cr.
1/1 G. Harrison started business with £10,000 in the bank. Which account is Dr. and which account is Cr.	Bank (A+)	Capital (C+)
5/1 Harrison paid a £3,000 cheque for equipment and £4,000 cheque as a deposit on premises.	Equipment (A+) Premises (A+)	Bank (A–) Bank (A–)
Obtained a mortgage (£8,000 over 10 years) on the premises.	Premises (A+)	Mortgage (L+)
7/1 Obtained a bank loan £2,000 from NatWest over 3 years.	Bank (A+)	Bank Loan (L+)
10/1 Paid £2,000 cheque for fixtures.	Fixtures (A+)	Bank (A–)

A = Asset
L = Liability

The ledger entries of G. Harrison are as shown in Figure 5.2.

Balancing the accounts in the ledger

The balance of each account is the *difference* between the two sides of an account. The balance of Harrison's bank account is £3,000 because the debit side is greater than the credit side by this amount.

Procedure (shown in Figure 5.3)

(a) Enter 'Balance c/d' (carried down) on the lesser value of the two sides.
(b) This has the effect of making both sides equal. The total amounts of both sides must appear on the same line.

FIGURE 5.2 G. Harrison's ledger entries

Debit   Credit

Date	Particulars	Amount £	Date	Particulars	Amount £
		Bank a/c			
Jan. 1	Capital	10,000	Jan. 5	Equipment	3,000
7	Bank loan	2,000	5	Premises	4,000
			10	Fixtures	2,000
		Capital a/c			
			Jan. 1	Bank	10,000
		Equipment a/c			
Jan. 5	Bank	3,000			
		Premises a/c			
Jan. 5	Bank	4,000			
	B.S. Mortgage	8,000			
		Building Society Mortgage a/c			
			Jan. 5	Premises	8,000
		Bank Loan a/c			
			Jan. 7	Bank	2,000
		Fixtures a/c			
Jan. 10	Bank	2,000			

Notes: (a) Where an asset increases, the entry is debited. where it decreases (bank a/c) the entries are credited.
(b) Where capital or liability accounts increase, the entries are credited.
(c) What is the balance of each account? That is, the difference in values between the debit and credit entries (bank a/c £3,000).

(c) Once the totals have been entered, the word 'Balance b/d' (brought down) is entered under the totals, on the opposite side of 'Balance c/d'. This shows the value standing in an account at a particular time.

(d) Accounts in the ledger may be balanced as frequently as the volume of transactions allow. The greater the volume of transactions, the greater the need to keep accounts up to date and therefore balanced.

FIGURE 5.3 G. Harrison's bank account

Debit (Dr.)   Credit (Cr.)

		£			£
		Bank a/c			
Jan. 1	Capital	10,000	Jan. 5	Equipment	3,000
7	Bank loan	2,000	5	Premises	4,000
			10	Fixtures	2,000
			12	Balance c/d	3,000
		12,000			12,000
Jan.13	Balance b/d	3,000			

The balancing of G. Harrison's bank account

Where entries occur on one side of an account only, these need only be added-or if there is only a single entry, this may be left until further transactions occur.

Premises a/c

Jan. 5	Bank	4,000
	B.S. Mortgage	8,000
		12,000

Equipment a/c

Jan. 5	Bank	3,000

Questions

---

1. Which of the following accounts have debit balances? Which have credit balances? Tick the appropriate column.

Account	Debit	Credit
Fixtures and fittings		
Debtors		
Creditors		
Bank		
Motor vehicles		
Stock		
Mortgage		
Premises		
Bank overdraft		
Cash		
Capital		
Equipment		

2. Balance the following accounts on 31 January; bring down the balances the next day.

R. Green a/c (creditor)

		£			£
Jan. 10	Bank	500	Jan. 22	Balance	1,180
30	Bank	1,830	20	Goods	1,000
			27	Goods	150

Bank a/c

Jan. 1	Balance	3,500	Jan. 3	ABC Ltd	850
3	R. Smith	500	4	Southern Gas	275
			8	Rent	85
			10	R. Green	500
			12	Wessex Water	125
			30	R. Green	1,830
			31	Goods	200

Goods a/c (Purchases)

Jan. 1	Balance	250
20	R. Green	1,000
27	R. Green	150
31	Bank	200

3. The following transactions are to be recorded in the ledger of R. David during the month of June:

June
1   Commenced business with a motor van valued at £600 and a bank account of £1,500.
2   Bought stock on credit from XYZ Co. £1,800.
4   Bought tools and equipment, paying by cheque £300.
8   Paid XYZ Co. £500 on account.
11 Arranged a loan from Barclay's Bank for £2,500 which was entered in the business bank account.
14 Won £500 on the races and put it into the business!
15 Sold the motor van for £600 on credit to J. Briggs.
21 Briggs sent a cheque £250 on account.

Balance each account at the end of the month and bring down the balance on 1 July.

4. Record the following transactions of J. Bird for the month of January in his ledger:

January
1   The owner invested £60,000 in the business by depositing the money into his bank account.
5   A cheque of £26,000 was paid for premises.
11 A motor van was purchased on credit from Jackson, a local car salesman, valued at cost £5,000.
15 Office equipment was paid by cheque £1,750.
23 Paid £1,250 by cheque to a local builder for fixtures and fittings.
25 Arranged a loan from the local bank for £4,000.

Balance each account at the end of the month and bring down the balance.

5. Jack Jones put £5,000 into the bank on 1 January for the purpose of setting up business. Ledger entries would be:

Bank a/c   £5,000 debit
Capital a/c   £5,000 credit

The following are details of his transactions during the month of January:

January
5   Bought a new typewriter for the office, £250 cheque.
6   Bought stock from ABC Co. on credit terms £3,000.
7   Bought a second-hand motor van £800. This was financed by a cheque of £250 as a deposit and the rest is on credit from Jake Smith (Car Dealers)
10 Paid £500 cheque to ABC Co. on account.
12 The proprietor decides to put another £2,000 in the business from his own savings.
15 Purchased fixtures and fittings for the office which was paid by cheque, £750.
20 Paid the garage the balance owing on the motor vehicle.
21 More stock was purchased for his business: some of the stock was paid by cheque £254 and there was also £1,125 stock on credit from the supplier, ABC Co.
25 Paid a cheque to ABC Co. on the balance outstanding. On the same day, the owner ordered another £2,400 of stock on credit terms.

Required:

(a) Enter each transaction in the ledger of Jack Jones for the month of January.
(b) Balance the accounts on 31 January, and bring down the balances.

Introducing revenue and expenses in the ledger

There are *five* distinct groups of accounts:

(a) assets;
(b) capital;
(c) liabilities;
(d) revenue;
(e) expenses.

The first three of these groups have already been recorded in the ledger (asset balances shown as debits and capital and liability balances shown as credits).

What are revenue and expense accounts?

Revenue   Refers to the income earned by a business by sell-
             ing its goods or services. Sales is the main form
             of revenue earned by a business enterprise. Manu-
             facturers make goods to sell. Wholesalers and re-
             tailers form part of the distribution chain to sell
             the goods to consumers. Professional and trades
             people sell their services – for example, solici-
             tor's fees, estate agent's commission, an electrician's
             services.

             Income may also come from other sources – for
             example, rent received, bank interest, dividends
             and discount received are some of these sources.
             Banks earn the major part of their revenue from
             the interest they charge their borrowers, while
             insurance companies earn their income from selling
             premiums to their clients. Income may also be
             invested to earn more income.

Expenses   Refers to goods and services paid for by a busi-
             ness. Expenses (or costs) basically fall into three
             categories: the cost of labour (wages and salaries),
             the cost of goods or materials (purchases), and the
             general running expenses of the business (such as
             light and heat, rates and insurances, advertising,
             distribution expenses, administration expenses, sta-
             tionery, printing, and a good number of other over-
             head costs).

The recording of revenue and expenses

Which side of the ledger to record expenses?

Expenses are debited in the same way as asset accounts: when an
expense is increased, it is a debit entry. When an expense is decreased, it is credited.

Which side of the ledger to recrod revenue?

When revenue accounts are increased, they are credited in the same
way as for capital and liability accounts.
  A decrease in revenue will therefore be a debit entry (see Figure 5.4).
  The ledger account entries of G. Harrison are as shown in Figure
5.5.

FIGURE 5.4 The ledger of G. Harrison

	Account Dr.	Account Cr.
15/1 Paid wages by cheque, £125.	Wages (E+)	Bank (A-)
18/1 Purchased goods by cheque, £500.	Purchases (E+)	Bank (A-)
27/1 Paid gas bill, cheque, £75	Light and heat (E+)	Bank (A-)
30/1 and electricity, cheque, £40		
21/1 Purchased goods from J. Jones £250, a supplier, on credit.	Purchases (E+)	J. Jones (L+)
10/1 Cash sales paid into bank £750.	Bank (A+)	Sales (R+)
14/1 Sold goods on credit to J. Hunt, a customer, £285.	J. Hunt (A+)	Sales (R+)

A = Asset   E = Expenses
L = Liabilities   R = Revenue

The recording of stock and returns

The value of unsold stock is an asset to the organisation. At stock-taking time, which takes place at the end of a financial period, the stock is valued (usually at cost price) and recorded in the stock account.

When the purchasing and selling of stock takes place within the financial period, it is recorded in the purchases and sales accounts respectively and not in the stock account. In the purchases account it is recorded at its cost price, while in the sales account it is recorded at its selling price.

The main documentation for the sale or purchase of goods/services on a credit basis is the invoice. It is a bill of sale which states the total cost of the transaction: that is, its quantity, unit price, value, trade discount, VAT, etc. If goods are returned to a supplier, the credit note is the documentary evidence for the returns or allowances. If a customer returns goods the entry is:

Debit   returns inward account;
Credit   debtor's account.

If goods are returned to a supplier, the entry is:

Debit   creditor's account;
Credit   returns outward account.

FIGURE 5.5   G. Harrison's Ledger account entries

Dr.   Cr.

Bank a/c

8/1	Balance	3,000	15/1	Wages	125
10/1	Sales	750	18/1	Purchases	500
			27/1	Light and heat	75
			30/1	Light and heat	40
			31/1	Balance c/d	3,010
		3,750			3,750
1/2	Balance b/d	3,010			

Wages a/c

15/1	Bank	125

Light and heat a/c

27/1	Bank (gas)	75
30/1	Bank (elect.)	40
		115

Purchases a/c

18/1	Bank	500
21/1	Jones	250
		750

Sales a/c

			10/1	Bank	750
			14/1	Hunt	285
					1,035

Jones, J. a/c (creditor)

			21/1	Purchases	250

Hunt, J. a/c (debtor)

14/1	Sales	285

Example

			£
Jan. 1		Value of unsold stock	1,500
	5	Purchased stock from Brown	1,000
	10	Cash purchases by cheque	400
	12	Sold stock to Jackson	250
	17	Purchased stock from Brown	1,750
	18	Sold stock to Jackson	485
	27	Cash sales paid to Bank	1,250
	28	Returned 10% of goods to Brown purchased on 5/1 (damaged).	
	31	Jackson returned £50 goods to us, we sold on 12/1 (surplus).	

A record of these stock transactions in the ledger is shown in Figure 5.6.

FIGURE 5.6 Recording Stock in the ledger

Dr.   Cr.

Stock a/c

5/1	Balance	1,500			

Purchases a/c

5/1	Brown	1,000			
10/1	Bank	400			
17/1	Brown	1,750			
		3,150			

Sales a/c

			12/1	Jackson	250
			18/1	Jackson	485
			27/1	Bank	1,250
					1,985

Bank a/c

27/1	Sales	1,250	10/1	Purchases	400

FIGURE 5.6 *(continued)*

Brown a/c

28/1	Returns outward	100	5/1	Purchases	1,000
31/1	Balance c/d	2,650	17/1	Purchases	1,750
		2,750			2,750
			1/2	Balance b/d	2,650

Jackson a/c

12/1	Sales	250	31/1	Returns inward	50
18/1	Sales	485		Balance c/d	685
		735			735
1/2	Balance b/d	685			

Returns inward a/c

| 31/1 | Jackson | 50 |

Returns outward a/c

| | | | 28/1 | Brown | 100 |

Note: always assume transactions of personal accounts of debtors and creditors to be on a *credit* basis unless otherwise stated.

Review of the five groups

Assets	Things of value *owned* by the business enterprise; for instance, land, building, equipment, bank, cash, debtors, etc.
Liabilities	Things of value *owing* by the business enterprise; for instance, creditors, overdrafts at the bank, loans, mortgages, etc.
Capital	The difference between the two above is what is owned less what is owed:

C = Assets – Liabilities

This is the basic accounting equation
and may alternatively be written:

Assets = Capital + Liabilities

Thus C = A – L

or A = C + L

Revenue	The value of goods and services sold; for instance, sales, commission received.
Expenses	The value of goods and services paid; for example, purchases, wages, rent, salaries, heating, etc.

Review of recording procedure

A basic scheme is shown in Table 5.1 below.

TABLE 5.1   Recording procedure: a basic scheme

Accounting group	Type of balance (Dr. or Cr.)		Increase in the a/c	Decrease in the a/c
Assets	Debit		Debit	Credit
Capital		Credit	Credit	Debit
Liabilities		Credit	Credit	Debit
Revenue		Credit	Credit	Debit
Expenses	Debit		Debit	Credit

The trial balance

The trial balance may be defined as: 'A summary of all the account balances in the ledger to prove the arithmetical accuracy of double-entry recording.' In other words, there should be a debit entry as well as a credit entry for every transaction. This is the double-entry principle.

At frequent intervals, ledger account balances are listed in the trial balance to prove that the recording process is arithmetically correct.

For instance, Mr G. Harrison prepares a trial balance at the end of each month. At 31 January, his trial balance is as shown below in Table 5.2. The totals agree and therefore the arithmetical accuracy of double-entry recording has proved to be correct. If the principle of double-entry is not recorded, the trial balance will fail to balance.

TABLE 5.2   Trial balance of G. Harrison at 31 January

	Dr. £	Cr. £
Bank	3,010	
Premises	12,000	
Fixtures and fittings	2,000	
Equipment	3,000	
Mortgage		8,000
Bank loan		2,000
Capital G. Harrison		10,000
Wages	125	
Light and Heat	115	
Purchases	750	
Sales		1,035
Creditors		250
Debtors	285	
	21,285	21,285

Example

Prepare from the following information, a trial balance for P. Jackson, as on 1 January (the solution is given in Table 5.3).

	£		£
Bank overdraft	300	Sales	48,575
Cash	200	Purchases	35,450
Motor van	2,420	General expenses	2,485
Debtors	515	Motor expenses	850
Creditors	1,225	Rent received	840
Capital	10,500		
Bank loan	3,400		
Premises	25,300		
Mortgage	8,950		
Equipment	6,570		

**TABLE 5.3 Trial balance of P. Jackson
as on 1 January 19—**

| | Dr.
£ | Cr.
£ |
|---|---|---|
| Bank overdraft | | 300 |
| Cash | 200 | |
| Motor van | 2,420 | |
| Debtors | 515 | |
| Creditors | | 1,225 |
| Capital: P. Jackson | | 10,500 |
| Bank loan | | 3,400 |
| Premises | 25,300 | |
| Sales | | 48,575 |
| Purchases | 35,450 | |
| General expenses | 2,485 | |
| Motor expenses | 850 | |
| Rent received | | 840 |
| Mortgage | | 8,950 |
| Equipment | 6,570 | |
| | 73,790 | 73,790 |

Questions

1. The balances of R. James extracted from his ledger on 31
January were as follows:

Account	£
Capital: R. James	12,125
Premises	11,900
Fixtures and fittings	800
Stock	320
Debtors	1,020
Creditors	890
Sales	6,950
Purchases	4,050
General expenses	1,875

Required:

(a) Prepare a trial balance for R. James as on 31 January.
(b) Categorise each account into one of the five accounting groups.
(c) Which of the above accounts would be listed in the balance sheet?

2. The balances of D. Andrew were taken from the ledger on 30 June:

Account	£
Bank	3,305
Stock	750
Equipment	4,000
Motor van	1,750
Sales	2,095
Purchases	1,115
Wages	880
Rent	565
General overheads	480
Debtors	955
Creditors	1,560
Bank loan	1,250
Bills outstanding	55
Capital: D. Andrew	8,840

Required:

Prepare the trial balance on 30 June.

3. The following balances were taken from the books of P. McCartney (Music Publisher) on 1 June.

		£
Bank	Dr. Balance	1,240
Stock	Dr. Balance	2,150
Motor vehicle	Dr. Balance	1,175
J. Jones	Dr. Balance	248
N. Diamond	Cr. Balance	152
B. Manilow	Cr. Balance	502
Capital: P. McCartney		4,159

Enter the six accounts in Mr McCartney's ledger. The transactions below relate to the month of June. Make appropriate entries in McCartney's ledger.
(*Assume transactions to be on a credit basis unless other wise stated.*)

		£
June 2	Bought stock from N. Diamond	258
4	J. Jones paid on account	100
5	Bought stock from B. Manilow	374
10	The proprietor paid N. Diamond the balance owing 1 June	
15	Sold vehicle receiving the full book value to Harry Belafonte on credit	
18	Paid by cheque 10% deposit on a new vehicle costing (The balance is on credit from Jake's Garage)	2,750
20	Paid a cheque to B. Manilow $33\frac{1}{3}$ % of his outstanding balance	
28	Paid N. Diamond on account	158
30	Paid cheque for new stereo equipment to be used on premises	399

Required:

(a) Balance each of the above accounts on 30 June. Ensure that after entering 'balance c/d' that totals are on the same line.

(b) Bring down the balances on 1 July to begin the new month's transactions.

(c) Extract a trial balance as at 30 June.

4. The following represents the ledger entries of Jack Jones, music publisher:

Balances of Debtors, 1 April
Smith   £250
Lillee   £115
Thomson   £25

Balances of Creditors, 1 April
May   £85
Cowdrey   £172

Capital a/c: J. Jones 1 April: £18
Bank a/c: £115[overdraft]

Transactions occurring during April

April 2 Sold goods to Lillee £287 and to Smith £415
       5 Bought goods from Cowdrey £150
      10 Sold goods to Thomson £37
      15 Settled May's account of 1 April
      17 Smith settled his account of 1 April
      21 Paid £75 to Cowdrey on account
      22 Sold goods to Thomson £156
      25 Thomson paid £62 on account
      26 Bought goods from May £195
      29 Paid Cowdrey a further £95 on account
      30 Received £201 cheque from Lillee.

Required:

(a) Enter all the above information in Jack's ledger.
(b) Extract a trial balance for the month ending 30 April.

5. The following represents the financial position of Harry Smith, shop proprietor, on 1 June.

Assets	£	Liabilities	£	Capital
Premises	15,000	Long-term		?
Stock	2,150	Bank loan	10,000	
Equipment	1,500			
Bank	463			
		Creditors:		
Debtors:		Brown	1,247	
White	1,150	Jackson	353	
Jones	1,037			

Required:

(a) Draw up a balance sheet as on 1 June to illustrate Harry's financial position.
(b) Using traditional two-sided ledger paper, enter the above account balances as on 1 June.

The transactions below relate to Harry's business during June. Enter them in the ledger.

			£
June	2	Bought stock from Jackson	1,500
	3	Bought stock by cheque	275
	4	Jones paid £750 cheque on account	
	5	Harry paid Jackson on account	600
	8	Bought stock from Brown	550
	10	Purchased a motor vehicle valued	2,400
		Paid 10% Deposit by cheque	
		The balance outstanding from Jake's Garage Co.	
	13	Paid a cheque to Brown	500
		and to Jackson on a/c	300
	16	Harry needed to inject a further £1,500 into the business from his own resources	
	18	Sold £1,000 of his old equipment to Gordon on credit	
	20	Bought new equipment on credit from ABC Co. Ltd	1,750

21	Gordon sent a cheque to cover 50% of his debt
25	Paid Jake's garage a cheque which would leave a balance of £1,500 owing
27	Agreed to pay £25 extra for installing new equipment to ABC Co. Ltd (Asset to be dr.)
30	Paid ABC Co. Ltd £775 on account
30	Received a cheque from White 337

(c) Extract a trial balance for Harry Smith as on 30 June

6. Mrs J. Boddy decided to commence business by opening a small retail shop in the High Street on 1 May. Her finances on that day were: cash, £2,500, and a motor van valued at £1,500. Hire purchase still outstanding on the vehicle was £1,000.

During her first month's trading, the following transactions took place:

May
1	Deposited £2,000 into the business bank account, retaining £500 in cash.
2	Rented shop premises paying £250 cheque in advance.
4	Cash purchases of goods for resale £300.
5	Purchased £550 goods from Arthur Daley on credit.
7	Paid £40 cash on stationery items.
10	Cash sales £120.
12	Sold goods on credit for Jack Smith £180.
14	Purchased £750 goods on credit from Donna Steele.
16	Paid motor expenses £30 cheque.
17	Cash sales £235 into bank.
18	Returned goods to Arthur £150 as stock damage.
19	Paid £100 cheque on the hire purchase of van.
20	Bought equipment on credit from Land Supplies Ltd £1,800, paying 25% deposit by cheque, the balance on credit.
24	Cash sales £130 into bank.
26	Paid general expenses by cash £80.
27	Received 50% of the sum due from Jack Smith, by cheque.
28	Sold goods on credit to David Wheelbarrow £330.

30 David Wheelbarrow returned 10% of goods to us as beng unsuitable.
31 Cash sales £225 into bank.
31 Paid Donna Steele £500 on account.
31 Paid Land Supplies Ltd on account £270 by cheque.

Required:

(a) Enter all the above information in the ledger of Mrs J. Boddy for the month of May.
(b) Extract a trial balance as on 31 May.

CHAPTER 6

An Alternative Method of Recording

This method of recording ledger accounts is more updated. Computerised systems use this format rather than the traditional method of dividing ledger pages in half with Dr. entries on the left and Cr. entries on the right.

The ledger is designed to look more like the page of a bank statement. Dr. and Cr. columns appear side-by-side with the balance column at the end (see Table 6.1).

TABLE 6.1 An example of a ledger format

Date		Particulars	Dr.	Cr.	Balance
Jan.	1	Balance			200 dr.
	4	Sales	150		350
	15	Sales	100		450
	28	Bank		300	150
Feb.	1	Balance			150 dr.

(a) After each transaction the balance is updated and has the distinct advantage of balances instantly being known.

(b) In the traditional method of ledger recording, balances may have been brought down at frequent intervals but not with the instant result of having a balance after each entry.

(c) Is the ledger account above a debtor or a creditor? What information tells you it is a debtor/creditor?

(d) Were the sales made for cash or on a credit basis?

Figure 6.1 shows four ledger accounts entered in the traditional method. Table 6.2 shows a bank account in the running balance

FIGURE 6.1 Traditional ledger account entries
Bank a/c

Jan. 1	Capital	8,000	Jan. 3	Premises	4,000
			7	Stock	750
			12	Equip.	380
			19	Stock	80
			27	Tools	180
			31	Balance c/d	2,610
		8,000			8,000
Feb. 1	Balance b/d	2,610*			

Premises a/c

Jan. 1	Bank	4,000

Stock a/c

Jan. 7	Bank	750
19	Bank	80
		830

Equipment and tools a/c

Jan. 12	Bank	380
27	Bank	180
		560

style which can be checked with the bank account above. The bank balance of £2,610 ends up the same, of course; only the method of recording is different.

Now enter premises, stock and equipment and tools accounts in the running balance format.

Example: ledger and trial balance

The ledger uses the running balance method of recording transactions.

TABLE 6.2   The running balance method

			Debit	Credit	Balance
Jan.	1	Capital	8,000		8,000 Dr.
	3	Premises		4,000	4,000
	7	Stocks		750	3,250
	12	Equipment		380	2,870
	19	Stock		80	2,790
	27	Tools		180	2,610*

Note: The bank a/c finishes the month with the identical balance irrespective of the method of ledger recording.

J. Jones, the proprietor of a small business enterprise, had £5,000 in his bank account and also a motor vehicle (value £585) on 1 May.
Transactions during May:

May 2   Paid rent for premises £25 per week paying by cheque, 4 weeks in advance.
  3   Paid for shop fixtures by cheque £475.
  5   Bought on credit terms goods for resale from:
              J. Randle   £150
              T. Smith   £225

  7   Cash sales £125 into bank.
  8   Shop assistant's wages £55 paid by cheque.
  9   Cash sales £85 into bank.
  12   Paid by cheque:
              J. Randle   £100 on account
              T. Smith   £75 on account

  15   Shop assistant's wages £55 paid by cheque.
  16   Cash sales £98 into bank.
  20   Bought on credit terms from J. Randle £300 goods.
  24   Sold goods on credit to Corfe Mullen Social Club £120.
  27   Shop assistant's wages £82 by cheque.
  30   Received from Corfe Mullen Social Club £50 on account.
  31   Cash sales £84 into bank.

Required:

(a) The ledger of J. Jones using the running balance method of recording for the month ending 31 May (this is done for you in Figure 6.2).
(b) Enter the figures for the trial balance as on 31 May (see Figure 6.3). The trial balance will fail to balance because of an error in the ledger. Find the error and adjust the balance in the ledger.

Divisions of the ledger

The ledger is the book of accounts; or rather, the ledgers are the books of account. When a business enterprise expands its trading operations, invariably the paper work increases too. There is a greater volume of accounts to handle. It may be that the business has a great number of debtors and creditors and wants to keep these in separate ledgers.

To improve the organisation of accounting, the ledger may be divided into four main sections:

Personal ledgers:
1. *The sales ledger* to record all transactions of customers who are sold goods or services on a credit basis. The ledger for debtors only.
2. *The bought ledger* (or purchase ledger) to record all transactions of suppliers for the supply of goods or services on a credit basis. The ledger for creditors only.

The personal ledgers are for *personal* accounts – that is, individual debtors and creditors.

3. *The nominal ledger* (or general ledger) to record all impersonal accounts, that is:
   (a) all the nominal accounts which are the revenue and expense accounts of the business, such as rent, wages, sales, purchases, etc.;
   (b) all the *real* accounts which are the tangible assets of the business (those which can be seen), such as premises, equipment, stock, bank, etc.;
   (c) the capital account of the owner or owners.

4. *The cash ledger (or Cash Book)* to record all cash and cheque receipts and payments. It may also include the recording of

FIGURE 6.2 Ledger of J. Jones

Date	Particulars	Dr.	Cr.	Balance	
Capital a/c					
1/5	Bank		5,000	5,000	(Cr.)
	Motor vehicle		585	5,585	
Bank a/c					
1/5	Capital	5,000		5,000	(Dr.)
2	Rent		100	4,900	
3	Fixtures		475	4,425	
7	Sales	125		4,550	
8	Wages		55	4,495	
9	Sales	85		4,580	
12	Randle, J.		100	4,480	
	Smith, T.		75	4,405	
15	Wages		55	4,350	
16	Sales	98		4,448	
27	Wages		82	4,366	
30	Corfe Mullen Social Club	50		4,416	
31	Sales	84		4,500	
Motor Vehicle a/c					
1/5	Capital	585		585	(Dr.)
Fixtures a/c					
3/5	Bank	475		475	(Dr.)
Corfe Mullen Social Club a/c (Debtor)					
24/5	Sales	120		120	(Dr.)
30	Bank		50	70	
Rent a/c					
2/5	Bank	100		100	(Dr.)
Purchases a/c					
5/5	Randle, J.	150		150	(Dr.)
	Smith, T.	225		375	
20/5	Randle, J.	300		675	

Date	Particulars	Dr.	Cr.	Balance	
Sales a/c					
7/5	Bank		125	125	(Cr.)
9	Bank		85	210	
16	Bank		98	308	
24	Corfe Mullen		120	428	
31	Bank		84	512	
Wages a/c				*Expenses*	
8/5	Bank	55		55	(Dr.)
15	Bank	55		110	
27	Bank	82		192	
J. Randle a/c					
5/5	Purchases		150	150	(Cr.)
12	Bank	100		50	
20	Purchases		300	450	
T. Smith a/c					
5/5	Purchases		225	225	(Cr.)
12/5	Bank	75		150	

**FIGURE 6.3 Trial balance of J. Jones
as at month ending 31 May**

	Dr.	Cr.
	£	£
Capital – J. Jones		
Bank		
Motor vehicle		
Fixtures		
Rent		
Purchases		
Wages		
Sales		
J. Randle		
T. Smith		
Corfe Mullen Social Club		

cash discounts – that is, a discount from a sum owing, given for prompt payment.

The three categories of accounts from the above information are:

Personal accounts – names of individual debtors and creditors

Nominal accounts – impersonal accounts of the revenue and expenses of a business

Real accounts – asset accounts of a business – that is, the value of the business's resources such as premises, stock, bank/cash

Table 6.3 shows a list of accounts taken from the ledgers of G. Harrison. A tick is made in the appropriate column for each account.

Questions

1. The following information relates to the ledger accounts of David Robert as on 31 December.

	£
Premises	15,000
Furniture and fittings	2,750
Equipment, tools	2,375
Motor van	1,340
Bank (Dr.)	320
Purchases	14,050
Sales	16,950
R. Smith (Dr.)	800
J. Hunt (Dr.)	220
S. Jones (Cr.)	1,890
N. Fox (Cr.)	2,000
Wages	3,000
General expenses	985
Bank loan: Southern Bank	5,000
Capital: D. Robert	15,000

Required:

(a) Extract a trial balance as on 31 December.
(b) If more than a single ledger was used, list the accounts

TABLE 6.3 Accounts taken from G. Harrison's ledgers

Account	Cash book	Sales ledger	Bought ledger	Nominal ledger
Debenhams PLC (supplier)			✓	
T. Smith (customer)		✓		
Stock				✓
Bank	✓			
Sales				✓
Purchases				✓
Plant and machinery				✓
Cash	✓			
Marks & Spencer (supplier)			✓	
Cash discount	✓			
Wages				✓
Light and heat				✓
Commission				✓
Premises				✓
Admin. expenses				✓

Nominal accounts:	Sales, Purchase, Cash Discount, Wages, Light and Heat, Commission, Admin. Expenses.
Personal accounts:	Debenhams, Smith, Marks & Spencer.
Real accounts:	Stock, Bank, Plant and Machinery, Cash and Premises.

which would be entered in each ledger.
(c) Which of the above accounts would not be entered in the balance sheet?

2. Roger Lee has the following accounts in his ledger on 1 May.

	£	
Jackson, P	336	Dr.
Newman, J.	450	Cr.
Sales	1,755	Cr.
Purchases	1,565	Dr.
Bank	525	Dr.
Capital: R. Lee	221	Cr.

The transactions below took place during the month of May.
Enter them in the ledger using the running balance method
of recording.

May	3	Paid a cheque to Newman on account	275
	5	Sold goods to Jackson	122
	8	Jackson paid on account	168
	10	Cash sales	375
	12	Bought goods from Newman	227
	15	Sold goods to Jackson	210
	16	Cash sales	280
	21	Bought goods, paying by cheque	187
	23	Bought further goods from Newman	156
	25	Paid Newman a cheque on account	125
	28	Received a cheque from Jackson which	
		would leave £250 outstanding in his account	
	30	Cash sales	156
		Cash purchases paid by cheque	450
		New account opened. Sold goods to	
		R. Fanshawe	300

Required:

(a) Enter the opening accounts in the ledger or R. Lee on
    1 May.
(b) Enter the above transactions in Lee's ledger for the month
    of May and also extract a trial balance as at 31 May.
    Assume transactions of personal accounts are on credit
    unless otherwise stated.

3. Freddy Smith had the following ledger balances on 1 January.

	£	
Premises (cost)	20,000	(dr.)
Motor van	1,875	(dr.)
Stock	1,900	(dr.)
Bank	850	(dr.)
Debtors:		
Rollin	420	(dr.)
Vines	268	(dr.)
Mortgage on premises	16,750	(cr.)
Creditors:		
Boston	1,950	(cr.)
Turner	350	(cr.)

The transactions for the month of January were as follows:

£

January		
1	General expenses paid by cheque	35
2	Cash sales	125
4	Goods from Boston	2,000
5	Sold to Rollin goods	500
7	Cash sales	225
9	Insurance by cheque	84
11	Purchases by cheque, goods	100
14	Rollin settles account balance of 1 January, by cheque	
15	Cash sales	585
16	Paid cheque to Boston on account	1,000
18	Bought from Turner, goods	750
22	Paid general expenses, cheque	80
24	Sold goods to Vines	450
26	Cash sales	378
27	Vines paid cheque to clear balance owing on 1 January	
30	Cash sales	225
31	Paid Turner £500 on account	

Required:

(a) Extract a trial balance as on 1 January for Freddy Smith, including your calculation of his capital account. Enter the balances in his ledger.

(b) Enter the above transaction in the ledger of Freddy Smith using the running balance method. Assume all cash received entered in Smith's bank account.

(c) Extract a trial balance for Freddy Smith as at 31 January.

4. On January 1, Jack Briggs's financial position was as follows:

	£	
Premises	17,000	(dr.)
Fixtures	1,500	(dr.)
Stocks	1,200	(dr.)
Bank (overdraft)	675	(cr.)
Cash	150	(dr.)
Debtors		
J. Collins	1,100	(dr.)
D. Smith	925	(dr.)
Creditors		
R. Jones	1,200	(cr.)

Required:

(a) Find the capital account of J. Briggs and enter the figure in his ledger.

(b) Enter all other accounts in the ledger listed above.

Transactions during January

Jan.	3	Sold goods to Collins £2,850
	5	Cash sales £1,300 into bank
	8	Purchased goods from Jones £1,605
	12	Paid salaries by cheque £300
	13	Owner withdrew £20 cash for personal use (drawings a/c)
	14	Paid £260 cheque for general repairs
	16	Cash sales £455. Banked £400
	19	Sold goods to Smith £720
	26	Paid salaries by cheque £300
	27	Cash purchases £90

29 Received cheques from:
Collins and Smith in settlement of their accounts of Jan. 1
30 Paid Jones by cheque £1,750 on a/c
31 Paid purchases of goods by cheque £175
31 Sold £500 of fixtures cash

Required:

(a) Enter all the above transactions in the ledger of Jack Briggs.
(b) Extract a trial balance as at 31 January.

5. On 1 July the following balances were extracted from the books of George Harrison, record shop owner.

	£	
Capital George Harrison	1,860	(cr.)
As represented by:		
Cash/bank	1,812	(dr.)
Lloyd, C.	440	(dr.)
Jones, D.	168	(dr.)
Bloggs, H.	560	(cr.)

(a) You are required to enter the above information in George's ledger.
(b) Enter the transactions below in the ledger for the month of July. Use the running balance method of recording.

Transactions during July

July 1 Cash sales £140
2 General expenses cheque £30
3 Harrison drew a cheque for personal use £40
6 Sold to Lloyd £250 goods on credit and to Jones £156 goods on credit
7 Purchased from Bloggs £400 goods on credit
8 Cash sales £160
9 Paid for purchases of goods by cheque £215
10 Purchased a motor vehicle £350 cash
15 Paid by cheque:

Salaries	£85
General expenses	£27
Insurance	£54

21 Cash sales £85
22 Sold further goods to Jones on credit   £44
24 Cash Sales £80
26 Paid by cheque Bloggs a/c – settled 1 July balance
27 Received cheques from:
   Lloyd having settled the 1 July balance
   Jones £100 on account
28 Paid Bloggs another £150 on account
29 bought goods on credit from T. Jones £580 (new a/c)
30 Paid salaries by cheque £80

(c) Extract a trial balance as at month ending 31 July.

6. Mr Les Dawson commenced business on 1 January with capital of £30,000. He put £28,000 into a business bank account and kept the remainder in a cash account as cash in hand.
   During the first two weeks in January the following business transactions occurred:

Jan. 1 Credit purchases: Green & Co. £4,000 Black & Co. £2,500
    2 Purchased fixtures and fittings £6,200, paying by cheque
    5 Paid by cheque £56, advertising in the local paper
    6 Paid rent six months in advance £6,000 by cheque
    7 Cash sales £400. Credit sales: Redhill & Co. £3,500
    8 Wages paid by cheque £86
    9 Paid insurance premium for 12 months £400, by cheque
   12 Credit purchases: Green & Co. £3,000
   13 Paid postage and stationery by cash £38
   14 Withdrew cash £500 for personal use
   15 Paid Green & Co. 50% of his outstanding balance
   15 Wages paid by cash £84
   16 Cash sales £880. Credit sales: Redhill & Co. £4,600 Shaw Ltd £2,100
   17 Redhill & Co. send a cheque £5,000 on account
   18 Paid Black & Co. in full, by cheque

Required:

(a) Open appropriate ledger accounts for the business, recording the above transactions. Extract a trial balance
as at 18 January.
(b) Why is it necessary to have more than a single ledger
system for different types of business organisations?

7. Jack Jones started in his own business on 1 March having
the following:

£1,000   in cash which he deposited in his new business bank account
£1,800   motor van which he will use in the business
£ 550   equipment
£1,150   is on hire purchase from XYB Garages Ltd over
two years.

Your task is to assist Jack set up a ledger to record the
day to day transactions as they occur.
Calculate Jack's capital as on 1 March and enter the above
information in the accounts required in the ledger.
The following transactions occurred during March:

March
3   Purchased goods on credit from D. Guest £350 and J.
Good £245
4   Bought some office furniture, paying by cheque £150
5   Sold goods on credit to M. Bright £180
8   Cash sales £125, into bank
10 Bought further goods from J. Good £300
11 Sold goods on credit to M. Bright £85
12 Bought goods from Cash & Carry Warehouse, £220
by cheque
14 Sold goods to C. Taylor, on credit £300
19 Paid general overheads by cheque £115
20 20% of the goods bought on the 10th were returned
to J. Good as unsatisfactory (debit J. Good, Credit Returns Outward)
22 Sold goods on credit to M. Bright, £125
26 Cash sales into bank £190
27 M. Bright returned £40 goods to us which he had purchased on the 22nd (debit Returns Inward, Credit
M. Bright)

29   Paid general overheads by cheque £135
29   C. Taylor sent a cheque £150 on account
30   Drew a cheque for £200 for personal use
30   Bought goods by cheque £480
30   Cash sales into bank £400
31   Purchased further equipment for £1,200, paying a deposit of 20% by cheque. The balance outstanding is on credit from Rawlings Ltd over three years
31   Paid off the account outstanding to D. Guest and paid J. Good £250 on account.
31   Received a cheque £225 from M. Bright on account.

Required:

(a) Enter all the above information in the ledger of J. Jones.
(b) Prepare a trial balance as on 31 March.

CHAPTER 7

The Sales Day Book

Accounts are compiled from business documents like the invoice and credit note as well as from actual receipts and payments of money. These may first be recorded in the day books, or books of prime entry. They are subsidiary books in the accounting system which help to 'feed' information in a collective way to the ledgers.

The function of the day books is to list and summarise all goods and services bought and sold on credit. When these are bought or sold on credit, the invoice acts as the bill of sale and is the evidence of the transaction. When goods are returned to a supplier, the credit note is the documentary evidence of the return.

The day books (or journals) may be listed as:

1. *The Sales Day Book*
   Records all sales on credit to customers by listing the key figures of the invoices sent to customers.
2. *The Purchases Day Book*
   Records all purchases from suppliers on credit by listing all the key figures from the invoices received from suppliers.
3. *The Returns Day Book*
   There are two of these to record:
   (a) Returns Inward Day Book
       Records all returns from customers (sales return). Credit notes sent to customers are listed with the key figures.
   (b) Returns Outward Day Book
       Records all returns back to suppliers (purchases return). Credit notes received from suppliers are listed with the key figures.
4. *The Cash Book*
   This is the cash ledger and records all receipts and payments of cash or cheques. The Cash Book 'doubles up' as both sub-

sidiary book and ledger. The Petty Cash Book which records small payments of cash falls into the same category.

5. *The Journal*
   This is also a subsidiary book, but it is not dealt with in this chapter. It is a book to record transactions that are outside the scope of the above books. See Chapters 16 and 36.

The accounting system

So far it has been stated that the recording of transactions is the basis of preparing accounts in a business organisation. Financial transactions are basically by payment of cash or on credit terms, which are then fed through the system via the day books and Cash Book to the ledger system. The trial balance is a check of the ledger system (see Figure 7.1). From these records it then becomes possible to prepare accounting statements, particularly at the end of a financial period, to show whether the business has made a profit or loss. The statement showing profit or lost is called the trading

Figure 7.1 The Accounting system

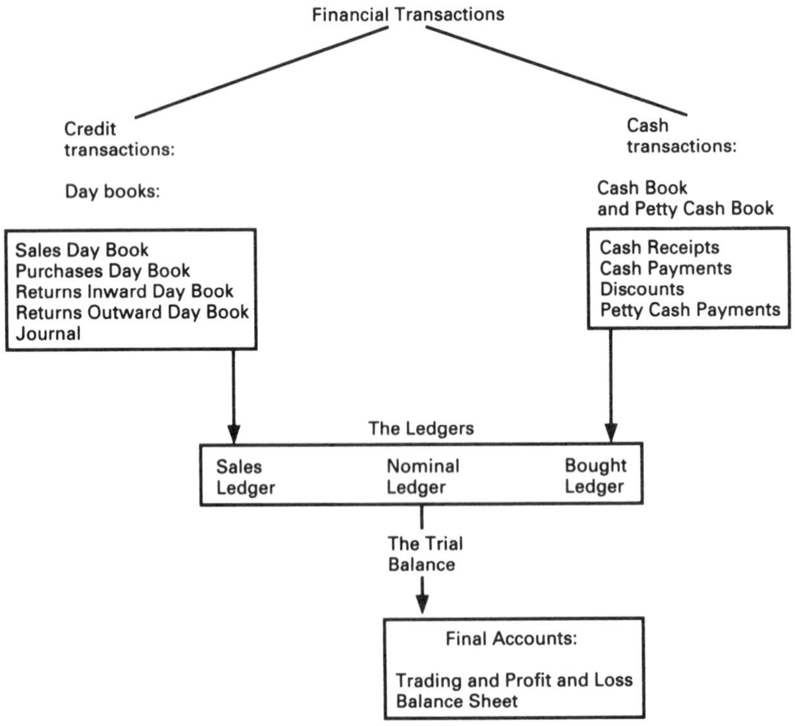

and profit and loss account. The balance sheet may also be prepared at the same time to show the firm's financial position at that time. These statements are referred to as the 'final accounts' of the business.

Sales documentation

In any business, to sell goods is the life-blood of its existence because a business which cannot sell simply cannot survive. A business must be able continuously to sell its goods or services which customers want to buy.

Selling and finding new customers is a very demanding job and a successful salesman is an important asset to the business. The reward to the salesman is normally a basic salary plus commission based on the volume of sales achieved.

It is important for a business to research its market thoroughly if it wishes to maximise its sales and therefore its profits. This may require the function of marketing which attempts to identify what the customer wants and then makes sure that the business is in a position to satisfy consumer demand as effectively as possible.

Finding out what the market wants may require market research into the business's past records, into government statistics, trade journals and directories, newspapers and any other information which might point the business in the right direction.

A business needs to advertise its goods in order to attract customer attention. Small businesses may be able to afford some minor advertisements in the local newspapers to attract customers. Larger companies may require a wide range of facilities from the advertising media including newspapers, television, radio, magazines, etc., in order to attract a much wider audience which may be international as well as national. Businesses may also advertise their price lists or send catalogues to its potential customers as a way of stimulating sales. Without sales, there is no income or profit and, without these, there is no business.

The invoice

The invoice usually comes in sets of, say, five or six copies, because each copy has a specific function in helping to administer the sale and despatch of goods.

An example of copies required:
1 Top copy: the customer's bill of sale, showing details of prices and terms of sale.

2 Sales copy:	the sales office copy for filing (also used to make a record of sales, etc.).
3 Delivery note:	usually accompanies the delivery of goods and signed by the customer as evidence of receiving order.
4 Advice note:	the customer may be advised when the goods are to be despatched.
5 Accounts copy:	required as evidence of transaction and for recording in sales day book and ledgers.
6 Stores copy:	recording the despatch and entering details on a stock record card.

The sales day book

The sales ledger clerk usually records the sale on credit to the customer from the copy of the invoice sent from the Sales Department. The invoice copy is checked for accuracy before entry.

Details from the invoice to record in the sales day book are:

(a) Date of sale.
(b) Name of customer.
(c) Invoice No.
(d) The sales total net (that is, gross sales *less* trade discount).
(e) VAT if applicable.
(f) The total net sales + VAT (if applicable).

The sales day book may be totalled when convenient. This may be daily or weekly or monthly, depending on the volume of sales on credit. The greater the volume of invoices to enter, the more frequently it must be totalled and details posted to the ledgers.

Posting from the Day Book to the Ledgers

The sales ledger

> *Debit*   each debtor account with the net sales value + VAT where applicable (asset +).

The nominal ledger

> *Credit*   the total value of net sales to Sales a/c
> the total value of VAT   to VAT a/c   (revenue +)

Below are illustrate a simplified sales day Book without VAT, and a sales day book with VAT.

A simplified sales day book (without VAT)

TABLE 7.1   Sales Day Book

Date	Customer's a/c	Invoice No.	Amount
1 May	J. Smith	1285	300 Dr.
5 May	R. Jones	1286	255 Dr.
7 May	F. Brown	1287	100 Dr.
15 May	J. Smith	1288	125 Dr.
26 May	F. Brown	1289	120 Dr.
		Sales (Cr.)	900

TABLE 7.2   Ledger posting

Date	Particulars	Dr.	Cr.	Balance
J. Smith a/c				
1 May	Sales	300		300 dr.
15 May	Sales	125		425
R. Jones a/c				
5 May	Sales	255		255 dr.
F. Brown a/c				
7 May	Sales	100		100 dr.
26 May	Sales	120		220
Sales a/c				
31 May	Debtors		900	900 cr.

Note: The double-entry
(a) Each individual customer (debtor) is debited (Asset +).
(b) The total sales for the monthare credited (Revenue +).

The sales invoice

An invoice sent from Mr G. Harrison to one of his customers, R. Thomson, is shown in Figure 7.2.

FIGURE 7.2 A sales invoice

	INVOICE

INVOICE

G Harrison
214 The High Street
Poole
Dorset

To: R Thomson
   14 West Way
   Broadstone
   Poole

VAT Reg: 424 28422 56
Invoice No: INV/ 1136

Date: 4th June 19–5   Your Order Ref: 30 May 19–5   Terms: 10% Trade
                           Despatch Date: 4 June 19–5   Carriage Paid

Code Number	Qty	Description	Unit Price	Total Price	Less Trade	Net
1042Z	10	SLAZENGER MK5 tennis rackets	20	200	20	180

	= = = =
TOTAL NET:	£180
E&OE VAT	£31.5

Delivery Address: as above

TOTAL VALUE: £211.5

   Payment within 28 days of invoice date

Notes: Trade discount refers to a deduction to the customer allowing him to buy the goods at a reduced price. It is normally given to people who are traders.
Cash discount is offered to customers to encourage them to pay their accounts promptly. Mr. Harrison offers trade discount but not cash.
VAT has been changed at 17.5%.

Example

Sales day book with VAT (and also using the control a/c)
On 1 June the balances in the ledgers of Mr G. Harrison were as shown in Table 7.3.

   During June, sales invoices (all at 17.5% VAT) were sent to customers as shown in Table 7.4.

TABLE 7.3 G. Harrison's ledger balances

Sales Ledger:	£		Nominal Ledger	£
Thomson	45	Dr.	Sales a/c	8,500 Cr.
Simpson	110	Dr.	VAT a/c	350 Cr.
Jackson	180	Dr.	Sales Ledger	
	335		Control a/c*	335 Dr.

TABLE 7.4 Sales invoices sent

	Invoice no.	Date	Net sales £	VAT £
Thomson	1136	4/6	180	
Simpson	1137	10/6	200	
Thomson	1138	11/6	100	
Jackson	1139	15/6	360	
Simpson	1140	20/6	160	

Cheques received from customers at the end of June were:

Thomson	£300
Simpson	£450
Jackson	£500 (£1,250)

Required:

(a) Prepare the Sales Day Book for June, calculating the VAT.
(b) Enter the opening balances on 1 June in the ledgers of G. Harrison.
(c) Post from the day book to the appropriate ledgers.
(d) Enter the cheques received in the appropriate accounts, including the control account.
(e) Prepare a schedule of debtors to cross-check with the sales ledger control account.
See Figure 7.3 and Tables 7.5–7 for the answers.

* *Sales ledger Control a/c: [S/L Control a/c]*
This is a total account representing the total individual accounts in the Sales Ledger (£335). It may be used for both sales and purchases ledgers and is a measure of control; that is, a check can be made to ensure that total balances in the sales ledger (or purchases ledger) = the control account balance. *The sales ledger control a/c is also referred to as the debtor's control a/c.*

FIGURE 7.3 Sales Day Book: Harrison

Folio No. 25*

Date	Customer's a/c	Invoice No.	Sales a/c £	VAT a/c £	Total debtors £
4/6	Thomson	1136	180	31.5	211.50 Dr.
10/6	Simpson	1137	200	35	235 Dr.
11/6	Thomson	1138	100	17.5	117.50 Dr.
15/6	Jackson	1139	360	63.	423 Dr.
20/6	Simpson	1140	160	28	188 Dr.
			1,000	175	1,175
			(Cr.)	(Cr.)	(Dr.)

TABLE 7.5 Sales Ledger: Harrison

Date	Particulars	Folio	Dr. £	Cr. £	Balance £
Thomson a/c					
1/6	Balance				45 Dr.
4/6	Sales	*S 25	180		
	VAT		31.5		256.5
11/6	Sales	S 25	100		
	VAT		17.5		374
30/6	Bank			300	74
1/7	Balance				74 Dr.
Simpson a/c					
1/6	Balance				110 Dr.
10/6	Sales	S 25	200		
	VAT		35		345
20/6	Sales	S 25	160		
	VAT		28		533
30/6	Bank			450	83
1/7	Balance				83 Dr.
Jackson a/c					
1/6	Balance				180 Dr.
15/6	Sales	S 25	360		
	VAT		63		603
30/6	Bank			500	103
1/7	Balance				103

* Folio cross-reference to the page number of the day book.

TABLE 7.6 General Ledger: Harrison

Date	Particulars	Folio	Dr.	Cr.	Balance
Sales a/c			£	£	£
1/6	Balance				8,500 Cr.
30/6	Debtors	S 25		1,000	9,500
1/7	Balance				9,500 Cr.
VAT a/c					
1/6	Balance				350 Cr.
30/6	Debtors	S 25		175	525
1/7	Balance				525 Cr.
*S/L Control a/c**					
1/6	Balance				335 Dr.
30/6	Sales	S 25	1,000		
	VAT		175		1,485
30/6	Bank			1,250	260
1/7	Balance				*260 Dr.

Notes: (a) The key figures from the invoice are entered in the day book – invoice number, sales, VAT and total cost.
(b) Debtors' accounts are debited with their individual totals in the Sales Ledger.
(c) Total for Sales and VAT accounts are credited in the General Ledger.
(d) Total debtors in the sales day book will be debited to the S/L Control account. The Control account is simply a means of cross-checking the total individual balances in the Sales Ledger.
*Sales Ledger Control a/c.

TABLE 7.7 Schedule of Debtors (June)

Name	£
Thomson	74 Dr.
Simpson	83
Jackson	103
	*260

The sales day book can be adapted to give businesses more information. Extra columns may be added to provide sales data for different types of product. This type of day book is often referred to as 'columnar' because of the extra columns used.

Large wholesalers and retailers need to know how various categories of goods are moving. It is inadequate for them merely to have a total of all their sales. Stores such as Comet, Rumbelows and Curry's want to know, for example, how their 'white' goods (washing machines, dishwashers, refrigerators) are selling in contrast with their 'brown' goods (televisions, stereos, videos) because, they need to know how much profit each of their major categories is earning. This type of information helps management in making decisions. It also helps to keep better control of sales, and therefore purchases and stock levels. If some goods are slow-moving, these can be more readily identified and action taken to remedy the situation.

Example

Table 7.8 provides some information for you.

(a) Check the figures down and across for accuracy.
(b) Sales ledger posting:
    The total debtors column is used to post individual customer's figures to the debit side of their sales ledger account in the normal way.
(c) Nominal ledger posting:
    The total of each sales category is posted to the credit side of that account (3 sales accounts). VAT is also posted to the credit side of the VAT account. The total of debtors (£3,478) is posted to the debit side of the control account (see Table 7.9).

TABLE 7.8   Sales data

Date	Customer a/c	Invoice number	Golf a/c	Cricket a/c	Tennis a/c	VAT a/c	Total debtors
7/1	Faldo	3364	400		120	91	611
8/1	Boycott	3365	100	180		49	329
9/1	Woosnam	3366	580	60	140	136.5	916.5
10/1	Bates	3367		130	110	42	282
10/1	Gooch	3368	60	440		87.5	587.5
11/1	Castle	3369	100	126	74	52.5	352.5
12/1	Lyle	3370	240		100	59.5	399.5
			1,480	936	544	518	3,478

TABLE 7.9 General ledger

	Dr.	Cr.	Balance
Golf Sales a/c			
12/1 Debtors		1,480	1,480 Cr.
Cricket Sales a/c			
12/1 Debtors		936	936 Cr.
Tennis Sales a/c			
12/1 Debtors		544	544 Cr.
VAT a/c			
12/1 Debtors		518	518 Cr.
S/L Control a/c			
12/1 Sales and VAT	3,478		3,478 Dr.

Questions

1. The credit sales of Royston Carlton were listed for the week ending 8 June. You need to calculate the VAT (15%) for each of them:

	Customer's Account	Invoice No.	No. 27 Amount £
4/6	Thomson	1136	180
5/6	Jackson	1137	200
6/6	Brown	1138	380
7/6	Warren	1139	300
7/6	Thomson	1140	420
8/6	Wilson	1141	60
8/6	Jones	1142	150

Required:

(a) Prepare the sales day book for the week ending 8 June.
(b) What ledger are the individual debtors posted to? On which side of their account?
(c) What ledger are the totals of the day book posted to? On which side of the relevant account is each of the totals posted?
(d) What purpose has the sales ledger control account? Why is it not part of the double-entry?

2. Debtor's balances on 1 June in G. Harrison's sales ledger were:

		£	
Arthur	100	Dr.
Brian	120	Dr.
Colin	150	Dr.

During the month of June, Harrison sold on credit:

		Invoice	£
5/6	Arthur	421	250
8/6	Brian	422	160
15/6	Arthur	423	200
20/6	Colin	424	280

On 28 June, Harrison received cheques from Arthur, Brian and Colin settling their accounts on 1 June.

Required:

(a) The sales day book for the month of June.
(b) Sales ledger accounts of Arthur, Brian and Colin for June.
(c) The sales account as it would appear in the nominal ledger (opening balance £1,240 Cr.).

3. Prepare the *same* information as above in the books of G. Harrison with the following exceptions:

(a) 15% VAT is charged on the sale of goods.
(b) A Sales Ledger Control account is opened in the nomi-

nal ledger with a balance of £370 Dr. on 1 June (that is, the three debtors).

(c) The nominal ledger has the following balances on 1 June:

Sales a/c	£1,240	Cr.
VAT a/c	£ 125	Dr.
Sales ledger Control a/c	£ 370	Dr.

(d) Prepare a schedule of debtors to check with the control account balance as on 30 June.

4. The balances on 1 May in the sales ledger of Brian Boddy were:

	£	
Bremner W.	575	(dr.)
Lorimer P.	255	(dr.)
Jones M.	250	(dr.)
Gray E.	100	(dr.)
	1,180	
Sales Ledger Control a/c	1,180	

The sales invoices issued for the month of May were as follows:

	Customer	Invoice No.	Amount	VAT [15%]
1 May	Bremner	2742	200	
6 May	Gray	2743	280	
14 May	Bremner	2744	450	
18 May	Jones	2745	180	
21 May	Lorimer	2746	800	
22 May	Giles (New a/c)	2747	100	
24 May	Bremner	2748	300	
28 May	Jones	2749	150	

Required:

(a) Prepare the sales day book for the month of May.
(b) Prepare the individual debtor's accounts in the sales ledger.

(c) Prepare the debtors control account for the month of May.

5. The following represents the sales day book of Graham Whitehall for the month of June:

Customer	Total	Bats	Balls	Pads
	£	£	£	£
Brearley, M.		172	12.50	35.00
Botham, I.		60	4.25	20.50
Boycott, G.		250	43.75	55.80
Bailey, T.		78	12.50	70.00
Benaud, R.		195	38.75	61.50

(a) Complete the totals for the sales day book for the month of June (no VAT).
(b) Enter the opening balances in XYZ's sales ledger for each of the following (1 June):

Brearley	£200.96
Botham	£ 15.00
Boycott	£ 66.30
Bailey	£ 27.88
Benaud	£ 40.25

(c) Post the additional transactions for June to the personal accounts of the above.
(d) Make the necessary postings to the general ledger using a *separate* sales a/c for each of the above items. The debtors control balance 1 June 21 was £350.39 (dr.).
(e) Check the individual debtors' total with the debtors control as at 30 June.

6. The following information represents the sales day book of Dawson's Ltd, a seller of furniture in three grades, basic, standard and deluxe models. All sales are charged with the standard rate of VAT at 17.5%.

Customer	Basic model	Standard model	Deluxe model	Total sales	VAT a/c	Total debtors
Jackson	200	420	160			
Thompson	125	500	365			
Illingworth	0	0	660			
Rocastle	280	400	820			
James	320	640	1,040			

Required:

(a) Complete the totals of the sales day book for the week ended 7 April (across and down).
(b) The following balances are to be entered in the sales ledger on 1 April:

£

Jackson	740.50 Debit
Thompson	356.76 Debit
Illingworth	125.50 Debit
Rocastle	1,040.50 Debit
James	1,360.00 Debit

(c) Post the transactions from the sales day book for the week ended 7 April to the sales ledger. Cheques received included £1,000 from Jackson and £2,000 from James.
(d) Post the sales figures and VAT to the nominal ledger using separate sales accounts for each grade of furniture (assume balances are nil on 1 April). The S/L control account on 1 April was £3,623.25 Dr. Cross-check the control account with the sales ledger.

7. The accounts in the sales ledger of Jones Enterprises Ltd on 1 January were:

Davies, J.	£800.00 Dr
Smith, P.	£450.00 Dr
Forbes, B.	£100.00 Dr

During January, the following invoices were sent to these customers:

	Invoice number	Amount	Sales code
5/1 Davies	2334	200 + VAT	S161
12/1 Smith	2335	80 + VAT	S162
17/1 Davies	2336	120 + VAT	S162
21/1 Forbes	2337	400 + VAT	S163
28/1 Smith	2338	300 + VAT	S161
30/1 Forbes	2339	160 + VAT	S163
31/1 Davies	2334	340 + VAT	S161

On 31 January, cheques were received from Davies (£1,000), Forbes (£250) and Smith (£544). VAT is at 17.5%.

Required:

(a) Prepare the sales day book for January, using separate columns to record each type of sales.
(b) Prepare the sales ledger account for each customer.
(c) How would the sales and VAT accounts be posted to the general ledger?

CHAPTER 8

The Purchases Day Book

Purchase documentation

Only those invoices checked and authorised as correct can be passed for payment. Invoices need to be cross-checked against the purchase order and either the goods received note (GRN) or delivery note to ensure that the goods were physically checked into stock.

If an invoice agrees with the purchase order and the GRN, then the invoice is passed to the accounts office for recording and is authorised for payment.

Errors to check:

(a) the invoice may be arithmetically wrong;
(b) the invoice may fail to agree with the terms of the purchase order, such as an incorrect trade discount;
(c) the GRN may not agree with the invoice because there is a discrepancy between quantities received and quantities charged. (Some stock could also have been damaged.)

Action must be taken to solve any discrepancies which may have been found. It may be the firm's policy to return to the supplier any invoice which is incorrect. Alternatively, the buying office may telephone, fax or telex the supplier explaining the nature of the error and come to some mutual agreement: for example, it may be more convenient for the supplier to send the shortfall of goods later or, alternatively, a credit note may be issued to make up for any discrepancies in favour of the buyer.

If a computerised system is used to record incoming invoices in the ledgers, it is very important to ensure that any document which is entered in the program is checked and initialled as to its correctness. Once the information is entered, it is a permanent record and any error will require an adjusting entry to correct it.

Document check

1. The invoice is the bill of sale from the seller to the buyer.
2. The delivery note comes with the driver of the goods and is signed by the person receiving them only if the delivery is seen as satisfactory.
3. The GRN is a record of stock delivered and is normally prepared by the storeman who has received the delivery note and checked over the goods to see that they are satisfactory.
4. The credit note is used if there has been any over-charge on an invoice: for example, goods may have been returned as unsatisfactory or there may be a shortfall on quantity.
5. The statement is sent from the supplier of goods to the buyer, usually monthly, to indicate how much the buyer owes.

Procedure for invoice control

The responsibility for checking the correctness of the invoice normally lies with either the buying office or the accounts office. If it is the buying office, it should tie in with the copies of the purchase order raised for the goods in the first place. Copies of the delivery note or GRN can then be sent to the buying office to check the physical goods that came in.

The invoices are stamped with the control grid (see Figure 8.1) to ensure that a full check on each invoice is made. The control grid should have checks for goods received, price terms and calculations. Each check should be initialled by the person authorised to do so. Any major errors arising from these checks may require the supplier to be contacted and the discrepancies solved.

When an invoice is received

The invoice is stamped with a control grid such as that shown in Figure 8.1. When a full check is completed and is found to be satisfactory, the invoice can then be passed to the accounts office for entry into the purchases day book and be authorised for payment.

An example of the grid can be seen on the invoice from ROCCO Sports in Figure 8.2.

The flow chart (shown in Figure 8.3) illustrates the basic procedure for buying, commencing with an initial authorisation for the goods and ending with the statement from the supplier.

FIGURE 8.1   control grid

CONTROL GRID	INITIALS
date invoice received	
internal reference no.	
order price check	
extensions check	
goods received check	

FIGURE 8.2 ROCCO Sports invoice

INVOICE
B/ 184285

ROCCO SPORTS
15 – 47 Cheviot Lane
Wakefield
Yorkshire
Telephone 0602 5571

VAT Reg 584 5691 48

Area 16	Customer Order details 0/15672 2.MAY.	Fwd	Date 25.5.88	Account No. H1452	Invoice No. 184285	Page 1/1
Invoice Address G HARRISON 214 HIGH STREET POOLE DORSET		Consignee				

Code Z451 F	Qty 10	Description SWINGBALL SET	Price 8.41	Goods value 84.10	VAT rates 17.5	VAT 14.13

CONTROL GRID INITIALS
Date invoice in   Rg
Reference no.   Wt
Price check   RP
GRN check   SB

	Goods value	VAT
Total Goods	84.10	
Total VAT	14.13	← 14.13
INVOICE TOTAL	98.23	

Terms: cash discount 4% within 7 days or 2% payment by 20th of following month.

FIGURE 8.3 Basic buying procedure

AUTHORISATION   ⟶   The buyingoffice must be authorised to order goods to an agreed budget or re-order level.

INQUIRY   ⟶   To investigate sources of supply from quotations estimates, price lists, etc.

PURCHASE ORDER ⟶   To place an official order for the goods to the supplier.

INVOICE   ⟶   The bill of sale for the goods stating what is owed by the buyer.

STATEMENT   ⟶   A summary of the buyer's account over a specific period (for example, a month) and sent to the buyer.

The purchase invoice

Figure 8.2 is an invoice from ROCCO Sports supplier of sports goods. The details are:

Name of supplier	ROCCO Sports Co.
Date of invoice	25 May
No. of invoice	184285
Quantity/description of goods	10 Swingball sets
Price	£8.41 each plus VAT 17.5%.
Terms	No trade discount offered. Cash discount: 4% within 7 days or 2% for payment by 20th of month following invoice date The 17.5% VAT calculated is £14.13. It is not based on the goods value of £84.10 because cash discount has been offered. This allows the VAT to be calculated on the lower figure of £80.74 (£84.10 − £3.36), that is, less 4% cash discount.

The purchases day book

The function of the purchases day book is to list, summarise and, where applicable, analyse all purchase invoices over a period of time. The total of purchases may be required daily, weekly or monthly depending on the number of credit purchases made from suppliers.

The purchase ledger clerk does not take action in recording until the supplier's invoice is fully checked and initialled.

Any returns sent back to a supplier must await the credit note which will be received by the Buying Department and checked for accuracy. It is then sent to Accounts to be debited to the supplier's account.

Monthly statements received from suppliers stating the sum owing to them are not paid by the Accounts Department until checked against the supplier's account in the purchase ledger.

Posting from the purchases day book to ledgers:

(a) *The purchase or bought ledger. Credit* each creditor account with the net purchase plus VAT if charged.
(b) *The nominal ledger. Debit* purchases account and *debit* VAT a/c if charged.

The following pages illustrate:

(a) a simplified purchases day book without VAT;
(b) a purchases day book with VAT.

Double-entry:
(1) Each supplier (creditor) is credited with the amount of the purchase (Liability +).
(2) The *total* purchases is debited (Expense +).

Example

Purchases day book with VAT and also using the control account

Table 8.3 represents the purchases day book of G. Harrison for the month of June: VAT is at 17.5%.

TABLE 8.1   A simplified purchases day book (without VAT)

Date	Supplier's a/c	Invoice no. received	amount £
4 May	R. Bates	415	155 Cr.
12 May	J. Snow	0276	276 Cr.
15 May	R. Bates	627	359 Cr.
20 May	J. Sorrell	A253	180 Cr.
28 May	J. Sorrell	A322	190 Cr.
		Purchases (Dr.)	1,160

TABLE 8.2   Ledger posting

Date	Particulars	Debit	Credit	Balance
R. Bates a/c				
4 May	Purchases		155	155 (cr.)
15 May	Purchases		359	514
J. Snow a/c				
12 May	Purchases		276	276 (cr.)
J. Sorrell a/c				
20 May	Purchases		180	180 (cr.)
28 May	Purchases		190	370
Purchases a/c				
31 May	Creditors	1,160		1,160 (dr.)

TABLE 8.3   G. Harrison's purchases day book

Date	Supplier	Invoice no.	Purchases £	VAT £	Total £
June 4	Decca	4,242	450	78.75	528.75
8	Decca	5,789	200	35.00	235.00
15	EMI	687	360	63.00	423.00
22	Jacksons	1,425	120	21.00	141.00
			1,130.00	197.75	1,327.75
			(Dr.)	(Dr.)	(Cr.)

1 June Balances from Ledgers:

			£
General Ledger:	Purchases a/c	(debit)	3,576.50
	VAT a/c	(credit)	421.25
	Purchase Ledger:		
	Control Account	(credit)	5,646.50

			£
Purchase Ledger:	Decca	(credit)	3,465.00
	EMI	(credit)	1,572.50
	Jacksons	(credit)	609.00

Required:

(a) Enter the above balances on 1 June in the ledger of G. Harrison.
(b) Post the month's details from the day book to the appropriate ledger accounts. The purchase ledger control account [P/L control] is also referred to as the creditors' control account.
(c) Enter the payment details: all cheques on 30 June.

£1,500 to Decca on a/c
£1,000 to EMI on a/c
£200 to Jacksons on a/c.

See Tables 8.4 and 8.5 for the answers.

Check the control account with the Purchase Ledger:

			Cr.
June 30	P/L Control a/c		4,274.25

		£
30	Purchase Ledger Schedule:	
	Decca	2,728.75
	EMI	995.50
	Jacksons	550.00
		4,274.25

TABLE 8.4 General ledger

Date	Particulars	Folio	Debit £	Credit £	Balance £
Purchases a/c					
June 1	Balance				3,567.50 (Dr)
30	Creditors	P 42	1,130		4,697.50
VAT a/c					
June 1	Balance				421.25 (Cr)
30	Creditors	P 42	197.75		223.50
P/L Control a/c					
June 1	Balance				5,646.50 (Cr)
30	Purchases	P 42		1,130.00	
	VAT			197.75	6,974.25
	Bank		2,700		4,274.25

TABLE 8.5 Purchase ledger

Date	Particulars	Folio	Debit £	Credit £	Balance £
Decca Records a/c					
June 1	Balance				3,465.00 (Cr)
4	Purchases	P 42		450.00	
	VAT			78.75	3,993.75
8	Purchases	P 42		200.00	
	VAT			35.00	4,228.75
30	Bank		1,500		2,728.75
EMI Records a/c					
June 1	Balance				1,572.50 (Cr)
15	Purchases	P 42		360.00	
	VAT			63.00	1,995.50
30	Bank		1,000		995.50
Jackson a/c					
June 1	Balance				609 (Cr)
22	Purchases	P 42		120.00	
	VAT			21.00	750.00
30	Bank		200		550.00

Balances agree:

When preparing the trial balance, the control accounts represent the totals of both debtors and creditors. They are useful because if control accounts cross-check with personal ledgers it is assumed that double-entry recording is correct. In the event that the trial balance failed to balance, personal accounts need not be checked to locate the error(s) if they already agree with the control accounts.

Notes: (a) The purchase ledger: each creditor account is credited with the purchase + VAT.
(b) The nominal ledger: totals for both purchases a/c and VAT a/c are debited.
(c) The total of the purchases day book is credited to the P/L Control a/c.
(d) The purchase ledger is commonly referred to as the bought ledger.

The analysed purchases day book

Example

Prepare the day book of ABC Shoes Ltd using analysis columns for men's, women's and children's shoes from the information given in Tables 8.6 and 8.7 (note VAT at 15%):

How would these entries be posted to the ledgers?

(a) Each supplier's account is credited with the total sum.
(b) The total sum of men's, women's and children's shoes is debited to the purchase account of each category:

Purchases a/c		
(Men's)	£855	Dr.
(Women's)	£345	Dr.
(Children's)	£285	Dr.
(c) VAT a/c	£222.75	Dr.
(d) Purchase Ledger Control a/c	£1,707.75	Cr.

TABLE 8.6 Goods supplied

Date	Supplier	Invoice no.	Description	Value £
3/2	Footwear Ltd	F223674	5 pairs men's casuals @ £24 pair + VAT	120
6/2	Freeman, Hardy & Willis	08476	10 pairs of kiddies sandals @ £9.50 + VAT	95
7/2	Country Casuals Ltd	14279K	5 pairs of ladies dress shoes @ £15 + VAT	75
14/2	Footwear Ltd	F223989	10 pairs of men's brogues @ £21 pair + VAT	210
16/2	Freeman, Hardy & Willis	08979	20 pairs of children's school casuals @ £9.50 + VAT	190
21/2	Footwear Ltd	F224028	25 pairs of country casuals for men @ £21 + VAT	525
28/6	Jones Leather Goods	26011	18 pairs ladies dress shoes @ £15 + VAT	270

TABLE 8.7 Purchases Day Book: ABC Company Shoes Ltd

Date	Supplier	Invoice no.	Men's shoes £	Women's shoes £	Children's shoes £	VAT £	Total creditor £
3/2	Footwear Ltd.	F2236	120			18	138
6/2	F.H.&W.	08476			95	14.25	109.25
7/1	Country Cas'l	14279		75		11.25	86.25
14/2	Footwear Ltd.	F2239	210			31.50	241.50
16/2	F.H.&W.	08979			190	28.50	218.50
21/2	Footwear Ltd.	F2240	525			78.75	603.75
28/2	Jones Leather	26011		270		40.50	310.50
			855	345	285	222.75	1,707.75

Questions

1. See Invoice no. 1185 from G. Harrison to R. Jones. Answer the following questions from the point of view of R. Jones receiving the invoice from Harrison.

   (a) In which book is the invoice entered?
   (b) Complete the totals across. (Trade discount is 25%.)
   (c) Calculate the VAT (17.5%). Note $2\frac{1}{2}$ % cash discount is offered.
   (d) Complete the totals of the invoice at the bottom.
   (e) How would you complete the postings to the ledgers?

INVOICE

G Harrison
214 The High Street
Pools
Dorset

To: R Jones
14 Ship Road
The Quay
Poole

VAT Reg: 424 28422 56
Invoice No: INV/1185

Date: 10 June   Your Order Ref: 275   Terms: 25% Trade
          Despatch Date : 10 June   Carriage Paid

Code Number	Qty	Description	Unit Price	Total Price	Less Trade	Net
1042	4	Tennis Rackets (Slazenger) (special edition)	32			
1070	10	Squash Rackets (Dunlop)	8.25			

===

TOTAL NET: £

E&OE   VAT @ 17.5%: £

Delivery Address: as above   TOTAL VALUE: £

Payment within 20 days of invoice date, Cash Discount $2\frac{1}{2}$ %

2. The following supplier's invoices were received by G. Harrison for the week ending 29 May.

	Supplier's account	Invoice no.	Amount £	No. 26 VAT £
25/5	ROCCO Sports Co.	184285	84.10	12.10
26/5	Arena	4556	152.	22.80
26/5	Sondico	X4443	350.	52.50
28/5	ROCCO Sports Co.	184789	126.	18.14
29/5	Arena	5287	80.	12.
29/5	Dunlop Sports Co.	199774	215.	32.25

Required:

(a) Prepare the purchases day book of G. Harrison for the week ending 29 May.
(b) What ledger would the individual suppliers be posted to? On which side of their respective accounts? Explain why it is on the side you have chosen.
(c) What ledger is used to post the totals of the purchases day book? On which side of the account do each of the three totals go?
(d) What is the purchases control account used for?
(e) Which of the above suppliers offers a cash discount?

3. Creditor's balances on 1 June in G. Harrison's bought ledger were:

Dick	£280 Cr.
Eric	£100 Cr.
Fred	£120 Cr.

During the month of June, Harrison bought on credit from his suppliers:

		Invoice	£
8/6	Dick	3478	400
12/6	Eric	51729	220
15/6	Eric	51915	160
23/6	Fred	283	100

One 29 June Harrison sent cheques to:

	£
Dick	180
Eric	100
Fred	60

Required:

(a) The purchases day book for June.
(b) Bought ledger accounts of Dick, Eric and Fred for June.
(c) The purchases a/c as it would appear in the nominal ledger (opening balance £1,100 Dr.) at the end of June.

4. Prepare the *same* information as above in the books of G. Harrison with the following exceptions:

(a) 15% VAT is charged on goods purchased.
(b) A bought ledger control account is opened in the nominal ledger with a balance of £500 Cr. on 1 June.
(c) The nominal ledger has the following balances on 1 June:

Purchases a/c	£1,100	Dr.
VAT a/c	£ 125	Dr.
Bought ledger control a/c	£ 500	Cr.

(d) Prepare a schedule of creditors to check with the control account balance on 30 June.

5. The following represents the transactions of Harry Smith – a retailer – during the month of July:

Invoice Nos

July	1	Bought goods from ABC: 200 units @ £5 units less 25% trade discount	27491
	2	Bought goods from XYZ: 150 units @ £2 units less 20% trade discount	X427
	7	Sold to R. Green 100 units @ £7 less 10% trade discount	142

9	Sold to R. Jones	
	100 units @ £5.50 less 10% trade discount	143
12	Bought goods from ABC:	
	500 units @ £4 unit less 25% trade discount	9278
14	Sold goods to F. Smith	
	100 units @ £3.50 trade discount nil	144
17	Bought goods from XYZ:	
	200 units @ £2 unit less 20% trade discount	X588
21	Sold to R. Green	
	150 units @ £7 less 10% trade discount	145
26	Bought from ABC:	
	500 units @ £4.50 less 25% trade discount	10429

Required:

(a) Enter the above in Harry Smith's purchases and sales day books (no VAT).
(b) Post to the ledgers:
   Personal ledger for individual debtors and creditors.
   General ledger for total sales and total purchases.

6. The personal accounts in Harry Smith's ledger were as follows:

1 May balances

	£	
R. Mellows	200	Cr.
Paterson Bros	150	Cr.
J. Hudson	95	Cr.
D. Moorcroft	24	Cr.

The following invoices were received from the above suppliers during May:

		Invoice No.	Net Purchase £	VAT (+17.5%) £
May				
3	Mellows	2784	200.00	
7	Hudson	149	150.00	
10	Paterson Bros	87632	400.00	
14	Hudson	251	180.00	
20	Mellows	3219	350.00	
21	Hudson	267	225.00	
26	Moorcroft	4929	100.00	

On 30 May Harry Smith paid off the *opening balances* of each creditor.

Required:

(a) The purchases day book for the month of May. You need to calculate the VAT at 17.5% on each purchase.
(b) The personal ledger accounts of Smith as they would appear on 31 May.

7. The following information concerns the analysed purchases day book of Harriet Prince for the first fortnight of January:

Date	Supplier a/c	Invoice number	Footwear a/c	Leisure a/c	Sports a/c	VAT a/c	Total a/c
7/1	Foulks Ltd	48735	850	70			
8/1	Johnsons	564/33		350			
9/1	Foulks Ltd	49822	436	164	80		
10/1	Hardcastle	3388	200		325		
10/1	Johnsons	648/33	236	164			
11/1	Dougas Ltd	4422		346			
12/1	Just Sport	1889	140		825		

Required:

(a) Complete the totals across including the calculation of VAT at the 17.5% standard rate.
(b) Total the figures down and cross-check for accuracy.
(c) Explain how the individual accounts are posted.
(d) Post the totals to the nominal ledger.

CHAPTER 9

The Returns Day Books

The returns day books

The two books to record returns are:

(a) the returns inward day book – to record sales returns from customers (debtors);
(b) the returns outward day book – to record purchases returns to suppliers (creditors).

Situations arise in business where goods may be returned to the seller for a variety of reasons. They may have been damaged in transit, the wrong type may have been sent, or the buyer may have changed his mind and sent them back. The invoice could have been added incorrectly and over-charged. There may be bottles, crates or barrels involved where a credit is given for the return of them.

The *credit note* is the documentary evidence for any return or allowance. It signifies that a reduction is to be made from the account where the credit note is sent.

The returns inward day book

The credit notes sent to customers to cover their returns are listed in sequence (numerically) and in date order. Posting to the ledgers will include:

(a) the sales ledger. *Credit* the debtor's account with the value of the return plus VAT if charged.
(b) The nominal ledger. *Debit* the returns inward account and *debit* the VAT if VAT is charged.
     Where a control account is used, *credit* the total value of

returns, plus VAT if charged, to the sales ledger control account (in line with crediting individual debtors).

The returns outward day book

Credit notes received from suppliers cover the return of purchases to them. The credit notes are listed in date order.

Posting to ledgers will include:

(a) The purchase ledger. *Debit* the creditor's account with the value of the return plus VAT if charged.
(b) The nominal ledger. *Credit* the returns outward account and *credit* VAT if charged.

   Where a control account is used, *debit* the total value of returns plus VAT if charged, to the purchase ledger control account (in line with debiting individual creditors).

Example 1

A credit note (shown in Figure 9.1) is sent to a customer of G. Harrison.

The credit note is the documentary evidence for returns and allowances. A credit note sent to a customer has the effect of reducing the customer's account. In this case Mr Smith's account will be credited by £28.20.

Example 2

The returns inward day book

The debtor's balances in G. Harrison's Sales Ledger on 1 June were:

J. Jones	£156	Dr.
T. Smith	£385	Dr.
T. Dooley	£224	Dr.

The returns inward day book for the month of June is shown in (note VAT at 17.5%).

FIGURE 9.1   Credit note from G. Harrison to a customer

	Credit note	

From	G Harrison 214 High Street Poole Dorset	Credit No.: B/ 427
To	T Smith 56–57 Ringwood Road Poole	

Credit in respect of		Date 7 May
☒ Retd Goods ☐ Error		Inv 253
☐ Discount ☐ O'chge		Order 67231
☐ Shortage ☐		Ref

Date	Details	£	p
June 15	200 Tennis Balls (poor quality)	32	00
	Less 25% Trade	8	00
		24	00
	Plus 17.5 VAT	4.	20

	Total Credit:	£ 28.	20

Example 3

The returns outward day book

Creditor's balances in G. Harrison's Purchase Ledger on 1 June were:

Dunlop Sports	£96.21	Cr.
Sondico	£124.62	Cr.
Arena Sports	£150.00	Cr.

Table 9.3 shows the returns outward day book for the month of June.

TABLE 9.1 Returns inward day book (June)

	Customer's a/c	C/N no.	Returns Inward a/c	VAT a/c	Total debtor's a/c
			£	£	£
June 15	T. Smith	427	24	4.20	28.20 Cr.
23	T. Dooley	428	60	10.50	70.50 Cr.
30	T. Jones	429	10	1.75	11.75 Cr.
			94	16.45	110.45
			(Dr.)	(Dr.)	(Cr.)

TABLE 9.2 G. Harrison's sales ledger

Date	Particulars	Folio	Dr.	Cr.	Balance	
J. Jones a/c						
June 1	Balance				156	
30	Returns In	RI 4		11.75	144.25	Dr.
T. Smith a/c						
June 1	Balance				385.	Dr.
15	Returns In	RI 4		28.20	356.80	
T. Dooley a/c						
June 1	Balance				224.	Dr.
23	Returns In	RI 4		70.50	153.50	

TABLE 9.3 Returns outward day book (June)

	Supplier's a/c	C/N no.	Returns Outward a/c	VAT a/c	Total creditor's a/c
			£	£	£
June 4	Dunlop Sports	142	16.82	2.94	19.76 Dr.
18	Sondico	234/C	10.86	1.90	12.76 Dr.
26	Arena	67	24.60	4.30	28.90 Dr.
			52.28	9.14	61.42
			(Cr.)	(Cr.)	(Dr.)

TABLE 9.4   G. Harrison's purchase ledger

Date	Particulars	Folio	Dr.	Cr.	Balance
Dunlop Sports a/c					
June 1	Balance				96.21 Cr.
4	Returns Out	RO 2	19.76		76.45
Sondico a/c					
June 1	Balance				124.62 Cr.
18	Returns Out	RO 2	12.76		111.86
Arena a/c					
June 1	Balance				150.00 Cr.
26	Returns Out	RO 2	28.90		121.10

TABLE 9.5   G. Harrison's nominal ledger

Date	Particulars	Folio	Dr.	Cr.	Balance
Returns Inward a/c					
June 1	Balance				—
30	Debtors	RI 4	94.		94. Dr.
VAT a/c					
June 1	Balance				—
30	Debtors	RI 4	16.45		16.45 Dr.
30	Creditors	RO2	9.14		7.31
Sales Ledger Control a/c					
June 1	Balance				765. Dr.
30	Returns In	RI 4		110.45	654.55
	+ VAT				
Returns Outward a/c					
June 1	Balance				—
30	Creditors	RO2		52.28	52.28 Cr.
Purchase Ledger Control a/c					
June 1	Balance				942.50 Cr.
30	Returns Out				
	+ VAT	RO2	61.42		881.08

The statement

Statements are normally sent to customers once a month to remind them of their outstanding balance. In Figure 9.2, T. Smith owes Harrison £163.80 at the end of June. This balance should cross-check with Smith's sales ledger account balance. A debit note was sent on 25 June because Invoice No. 1156 was incorrectly valued by £23, due to the omission of an item.

FIGURE 9.2   Statement from G. Harrison to a Customer

STATEMENT

G. Harrison
214 The High Street
POOLE
DORSET

T. Smith
56, 57 Ringwood Rd.
POOLE
Dorset

Telephone: 674221
VAT Reg:
  42428422

All accounts are
rendered on a
net basis and
are due for
settlement within
30 days

Account No. S 25

Date	Details	Debit £	Credit £	Balance £
1 June	Balance			385.00
15	C/n 427 Returns		28.20	356.80
21	Invoice 1156 Sales	160.		
	VAT	24.		540.80
24	Debit Note 46	20		
	VAT	3		563.80
28	Cash – thank you		400.00	163.80
30	Balance now due			163.80

Checking statements with ledger accounts

When statements are received from creditors they are checked with the purchases ledger account to see if balances agree. If they do and all details are correct, the statement is passed on to the Cashier for payment.

If statements do not agree with the ledger accounts, they must be checked and reconciled before they are passed on for payment. For example, G. Harrison received a statement from Dunlop Sports Ltd. The balance owing was £3.08. The date of the statement was 16 June.

On checking the ledger account, it was found that the Dunlop balance had been settled (see Table 9.6).

Dunlop Sports Ltd had not taken cash discount into account, whereas Harrison had deducted 4% for payment within 7 days. If the statement is believed to be in error it must be settled with the supplier in order to solve the problem. Either the discount is valid or it is not. Did Harrison pay on time or was it an error by the accounts section at Dunlops?

Dunlop confirm by telephone that the discount should have been deducted in Harrison's favour, so the reconciliation of account is shown below.

Balance as per statement:	£3.08
Less cash discount received	£3.08
Balance as per purchases ledger	0

TABLE 9.6   Purchases ledger entry

Dunlop	Sports a/c	Dr.	Cr.	Balance
June 1	Balance			96.21 Cr.
4	Returns out	19.76		76.45
6	Bank	73.37		
	Discount Recd	3.08		0

Questions

1. Debtor's balances on 1 June in the books of G. Harrison were:

Sales ledger:	£	
Arthur	100	Dr.
Brian	120	Dr.
Colin	150	Dr.

Nominal ledger: £

	£	
Returns inward a/c	257	Dr.
VAT a/c	125	Dr.
Sales ledger control a/c	370	Dr.

Harrison sent credit notes to customers who had returned goods during June (VAT at 15% in this question).

		£	Credit Note No.
12/6	Brian	60 + VAT	261
20/6	Arthur	20 + VAT	262
24/6	Colin	50 + VAT	263

Required:

(a) The returns inward day book for June.
(b) Sales ledger accounts of Arthur, Brian and Colin for June.
(c) Nominal ledger accounts for June.

2. Creditor's balances on 1 June in the books of G. Harrison were:

Bought ledger: £

	£	
Dick	280	Cr.
Eric	100	Cr.
Fred	120	Cr.

Nominal ledger: £

	£	
Returns outward a/c	352	Cr.
VAT a/c	125	Dr.
Bought ledger control	500	Cr.

Harrison received credit notes from suppliers for returns outward during June (VAT at 15% in this question).

		£	Credit Note No.
13/6	Dick	80 + VAT	42
20/6	Eric	48 + VAT	215
26/6	Fred	60 + VAT	88

Required:

(a) The returns outward day book for June.
(b) Bought ledger accounts of Dick, Eric and Fred for June.
(c) Nominal ledger accounts for June.

3. The books of G. Harrison:

Suppliers' Summary of Invoices 31 May

Date	Supplier	Invoice No.	Quantity	Unit Price
				£
May 7	Dunlop Sports	3427	100	5.95
			250	4.50
10	Sondico	84521	500	1.25
			100	3.25
			50	10.65
15	Dunlop Sports	3692	200	4.50
24	Metre Sports	895	100	6.75
			50	8.50
27	Sondico	85971	150	3.25
			50	10.65
31	Metre Sports	1052	125	6.50
			200	8.50
31	Dunlop Sports	4573	100	4.50
			50	6.00

Terms:

Dunlop and Sondico allow Taylor a 10% trade discount.
Metre Sports allow a 20% trade discount.

On 31 May, Harrison returned goods, Dunlop Sports [invoice 3692] 100 units @ £4.50 and Sondico [invoice 85971] 150 units @ £3.25 and received credit notes for them. [17.5% VAT charged.]

Required:

(a) The appropriate day books to record the above information.
(b) The individual accounts of Dunlop, Metre and Sondico as on 31 May.

4. The balances in the bought ledger of *Freddy Smith* (outfitter) as on 1 June were:

	£	
Trueman, F. S.	1,090	(cr.)
Statham, B.	250	"
Tyson, F.	975	"
Snow, J.	340	"
Illingworth, R.	420	"
P/L Control a/c	3,075	"

Invoices were received during June from the following:

	Invoice no.	Supplier	Amount	VAT
6/6	27481	Trueman, F.	£580	+17.5%
8/6	4278W	Snow, J.	520	+17.5%
15/6	992	Illingworth, R.	210	+17.5%
22/6	52833	Statham, B.	330	zero-rate
25/6	888	Tyson, F.	360	+17.5%
30/6	A998	Old, C.	580	+17.5%

Credit notes were received from:

Illingworth	No. C447	29/6	£ 6.30 + VAT	17.5%
Tyson	No. 42/82	30/6	£90.00 + VAT	17.5%

Required:

(a) The purchases day book of Smith, for the month of June.
(b) The individual suppliers accounts in the bought ledger.
(c) A separate returns outward day book.
(d) The purchase ledger control account for the month of June.

5. M. Crooks has the following accounts in his ledgers on 1 May [VAT at 15% in this question]:

Sales ledger:

J. Hunt	£600	Dr.
R. Speedie	£240	
J. Milton	£400	

Bought ledger:

R. Ball	£500	Cr.
J. Carlson	£400	Cr.
D. Smith	£150	Cr.

Invoices issued during May:

	£		
Hunt	130	+	VAT
Milton	200	+	VAT
Speedie	180	+	VAT

Invoices received during May:

	£		
Ball	250	+	VAT
Smith	120	+	VAT

Credit note received during May:

Carlson   £200   + VAT

Cheques received during May:

Hunt	£580	in settlement of account of 1 May
Milton	£390	in settlement of account of 1 May
Speedie	£200	on account

Cheques paid during May:
    Settled all creditors accounts due 1 May less $2\frac{1}{2}$% cash discount.

Required:

(a) Enter the opening personal accounts in the ledgers of M. Crooks.
(b) Post all the above transactions to these ledger accounts and balance off at the end of the month.

6. On 1 June personal accounts in J. Smith's ledger had the following balances:

	£	
R. Morton	175	Cr.
W. Pierce	184	Cr.
L. Appleby	150	Dr.
T. Shuttleworth	210	Dr.
M. Vincent	145	Dr.

The following transactions took place during the month of June:

			£
June 3	Sold goods on credit to T. Shuttleworth		150
4	Sold goods on credit to M. Vincent		210
8	Bought goods on credit from R. Morton		470
	Paid R. Morton by cheque		175
9	T. Shuttleworth settled his account to date by cheque		
11	Bought goods on credit from W. Pierce		197
12	Returned goods to R. Morton		10
	Sold goods on credit to L. Appleby		240
	Sold goods on credit to T. Shuttleworth		160
15	L. Appleby returned goods		10
	Returned goods to W. Pierce		15
19	Paid W. Pierce by cheque		184
25	L. Appleby paid by cheque		150
26	Sold goods on credit to M. Vincent		310
29	Bought goods on credit from W. Pierce		180
	Sold goods on credit to T. Shuttleworth		160
30	M. Vincent returned goods		14
	Paid W. Pierce by cheque		182

From the information given above write up the *personal accounts* in J. Smith's ledger. To obtain full marks the accounts should be of the three-column type, with columns headed Dr., Cr. and balance. The amount of the balance on each account should be calculated afresh after each entry in the account.

[Royal Society of Arts]

CHAPTER 10

The Cash Book

The Cash Book is used to record all cash and banking transactions. It is an extension of the ledger itself, concentrating only on cash or bank entries. Therefore, instead of having a separate bank and cash account in the nominal ledger as we had before, a Cash Book can be used to record these cash and bank entries, making it more convenient to keep them together.

Any money paid into the business bank account either in cheques or in cash, using the bank's paying-in-slip as documentary evidence, may be recorded in the bank column of the Cash Book. Entries which are merely in cash are recorded in the cash column: Figure 10.1 shows an example of a Cash Book.

FIGURE 10.1   Cash Book lay-out

Debit   Credit

Receipts			Payments		
	Cash £	Bank £		Cash £	Bank £

Recording: Debit – cash or bank in.
        Credit – cash or bank out.

Some businesses also use a Petty Cash Book to pay for insignificant items of expenditure such as office cleaning, refreshments, small items of stationery, postage, newspapers, etc. The form of Petty Cash Book can be seen in Chapter 12. For items of expenditure which may be in excess of, say, £10 or £20, the recording would have to be made in the Cash Book.

Some organisations may want to analyse their receipts and payments of cash. There may be several extra columns used for this purpose for VAT, debtors and different categories of sales on the receipts side. On the payments side, there could be columns used for VAT, creditors and various types of expenses.

A Cash Book may be in the form of two separate books: a Cash Receipts Book and a Cash Payments Book, particularly if there are a great number of transactions for both receipts and payments.

The three-column Cash Book has columns to record cash discounts. Discount allowed is on the left and discount received on the right (see Figure 10.2).

FIGURE 10.2   Three-column Cash Book

Debit   Credit

Receipts				Payments			
	Disc. Allwd £	Cash £	Bank £		Disc. Recd £	Cash £	Bank £
Jones	3		57	Fox	4		76

Cash discounts

These may take one of two forms:

(a) Discount Allowed: this is entered on the *left side* of the Cash Book and is given to debtors for prompt payment of their accounts and is treated as an expense to the business.
(b) Discount Received: this is entered on the *right side* of the Cash Book and is received from creditors for prompt payment of debts and is treated as revenue to the business.

In practice, Cash Books rarely look the same because they are adapted to suit the needs of the business. Some businesses may prefer multi-columns for receipts and payments because they may want to analyse various aspects of the business, such as different categories of sales, VAT, or different types of expenses.

The need to record cash transactions in the Cash Book

Cash and credit transactions

Transactions basically fall into two categories: those for cash and those on credit. Cash transactions refer to actual cash or cheques

FIGURE 10.3   Transaction recording flowchart

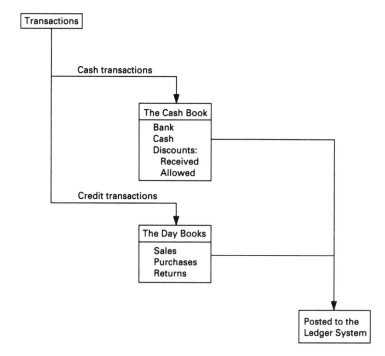

received or given. Credit transactions refer to sales or purchases where a period of time is given for payment.

The business must therefore record a transaction on credit at two stages:

(a) At the point of sale or purchase.
(b) At the point of payment received or given.

Example

Cash Book transactions for G. Harrison during the month of January:

January
    1 Balances in cash £25, bank £900.
    4 Paid stationery by cash £20.
    5 Cash sales £72.
  13 Paid rates £125 by cheque.
  15 Cash sales £15.

25   Paid cash to creditor James £115 on account.
26   Cash sales £80.
28   Paid Fox, another creditor, a cheque £76 in settlement of an £80 account (£4 discount received).
28   Received £57 cheque from Jones (debtor) in settlement of a £60 account (£3 discount allowed).
29   Received from Smith (debtor) cheque for £152 in settlement of £160 owing (£8 discount allowed).

Balancing G. Harrison's Cash Book [see Figure 10.4]

(a) The cash balance c/d 31/1:

Total cash in (Dr. column)	£192
less Total cash out (Cr. column)	£135
	£ 57

(b) Bank Balance: c/d 31/1:

Total bank in (Dr. column)	£1,109
less Total bank out (Cr. column)	£ 201
	£ 908

Ledger posting from Cash Book

To complete the double-entry, entries on the debit side of the Cash Book are posted to the credit side of the respective ledger account.

Entries on the credit side of the Cash Book are posted to the debit side of the respective ledger account.

When posting cash discounts to the nominal ledger, the totals posted remain on the *same* side.

Discount Allowed	£11 Dr.
Discount Received	£ 4 Cr.

FIGURE 10.4   Cash Bank and Discount in the Cash Book of G. Harrison

Dr.   Page No. 42   Cr.

Date	Particular	Disc. All.	Cash	Bank		Particulars	Disc. Rec.	Cash	Bank
1 Jan	Balance		25	900	4 Jan	Stationery		20	
5 Jan	Sales		72		13 Jan	Rates			125
15 Jan	Sales		15		25 Jan	James		115	
26 Jan	Sales		80		28 Jan	Fox	4		76
28 Jan	Jones	3		57					
29 Jan	Smith	8		152	31 Jan	Balance c/d		57	908
		11	192	1,109			4	192	1,109
1 Feb	Balance b/d		57	908					

Notes:

(a) DEBIT   *Increases* in cash and bank   + A

      CREDIT   *Decreases* in cash and bank   – A

(b) The double entry is completed when entries in the Cash Book are posted to their corresponding accounts in the ledger.

For example, cash sales: Dr. cash column as above (Asset +)
                                Cr. Sales a/c in the ledger (Revenue +)

For example, paid rates: Cr. bank column above (Asset–)
                                Cr. Rates a/c in ledger (Expense +)

TABLE 10.1   General ledger: Harrison

Date	Particulars	Folio	Dr. £	Cr. £	Balance £
Sales a/c					
1/1	Balance				0
5/1	Cash	C 42		72	72 Cr.
15/1	Cash	C 42		15	87
26/1	Cash	C 42		80	167
Stationery a/c					
1/1	Balance				0
4/1	Cash	C 42	20		20 Dr.
Rates a/c					
1/1	Balance				0
13/1	Bank	C 42	125		125 Dr.
Discount Allowed a/c					
1/1	Balance				0
31/1	Sundries	C 42	11		11 Dr.
Discount Received a/c					
1/1	Balance				0
31/1	Sundries	C 42		4	4 Cr.

Note: The folio C 42 refers to the Cash Book page number and is used as a cross-reference to the source of information.

TABLE 10.2   Sales ledger: Harrison

Date	Particulars	Folio	Dr. £	Cr. £	Balance £
J. Jones a/c					
1/1	Balance				60 Dr.
28/1	Bank	C 42		57	
	Discount Allowed	C 42		3	0
R. Smith a/c					
1/1	Balance				160 Dr.
29/1	Bank	C 42		152	
	Discount Allowed	C 42		8	0

TABLE 10.3   Purchase ledger: Harrison

Date	Particulars	Folio	Dr. £	Cr. £	Balance £
N. Fox a/c					
1/1	Balance				80 Cr.
28/1	Bank	C 42	76		
	Discount Received	C 42	4		0
R. James a/c					
1/1	Balance				115 Cr.
25/1	Cash	C 42	115		0

Note: The double-entry includes the discounts, for example:
   J. Jones a/c 28/1   Bank £57 & Discount Alld. £3 Credit
   N. Fox a/c 28/1   Bank £76 & Discount Red. £4 Debit

A revised Cash Book

Entries made in the Cash Book must have their sources of information in the same way as the day books and their sets of invoices and credit notes.

For example, if actual cash is received, this could be entered on something like a 'cash receipts abstract' form. The balances of the day's till rolls could be entered on this type of document.

Cheques received could also be listed on the receipts abstract. Most sizeable payments are normally made by writing out a cheque and there is always the cheque stub or a list of cheque counterfoils as the evidence of payment made.

If an organisation (for example, one of our retail outlets) makes numerous transactions by cash/cheques, the Cash Book may be modified in order to accommodate the posting procedure to the ledger system – basically to improve posting efficiency and information.

TABLE 10.4   G. Harrison: receipts abstract

	Customer's a/c	Discount allowed £	Cheques £	Cash sales till roll £	Day's bank totals £
1 May				76.48	
				38.30	114.78
2				38.45	
				83.72	122.17
3				42.40	
				33.29	75.49
4	Jackson, P.	5.79	109.93	79.43	
				28.32	217.68
5	Thomson, J.	3.27	60.90	32.08	
				42.30	135.28
	Week's summary	£ 9.06	170.83	494.57	665.40

TABLE 10.5   G. Harrison: cash payments abstract

Date	Particulars	Cheque no.	Amount £	Suppliers (creditors) £	Disc. rec'd £	Wages £	Other expenses £
1 May	Wages	272348	186.48			186.48	
2	Light/Heat	349	44.54				44.54
2	Dunlop Co.	350	482.16	482.16	24.10		
3	Goldboro's	351	322.40	322.40	18.02		
4	Petty Cash	352	48.00				48.00
5	Slazenger Co.	353	82.00	82.00	–		
	Week's summary		£1,165.58	886.56	42.12	186.48	92.54

Note: (a) Columns could be extended to facilitate further analysis of figures, such as a break-down of expenses.
(b) The abstracts summarise the week's cash/bank transactions.
(c) The abstracts facilitate transfer of entries to the Cash book.

FIGURE 10.5 The use of a modified Cash Book showing extra columns for debtors. Cash sales, creditors, wages and miscellaneous expenses.

CASH BOOK

Date	Particulars	Disc. All.	Debtors	Cash sales	Bank	Date	Particulars	Disc. Rec'd	Creditors	Wages	Misc. expenses	Bank
1 May	Balance b/d				124.16	1 May	Wages			186.48		186.48
1	Sales			114.78	114.78	2	Light and Heat				44.54	44.54
2	Sales			122.17	122.17	2	Dunlop Co.	24.10	482.16			482.16
3	Sales			75.49	75.49	3	Goldboro's	18.02	322.40			322.40
4	Jackson, P	5.79	109.93	107.75	217.68	4	Petty Cash				48.00	48.00
5	Thomson, J	3.27	60.90	74.38	135.28	5	Slazenger	—	82.00			82.00
6	Balance c/d				376.02							
		9.06	170.83	494.57	1,165.58			42.12	886.56	186.48	92.54	1,165.58

£ Balance b/d (overdraft) 376.02

Note: The advantages of using extra columns include:
(a) totals are available to show *where* the money is received and *where* it is paid out;
(b) they facilitate ledger posting in total; for example, sales £494.57 is posted to the Cr. side of sales a/c in the nominal ledger.

TABLE 10.6 Sales ledger (debtors)

Date	Particulars	Folio	Dr. £	Cr. £	Balance £
Jackson, P. a/c					
1 May	Balance				364.86 Dr.
4	Bank			109.93	
	+ Disc. All.	CB 17		5.79	249.14 Dr.
Thomson, J. a/c					
1 May	Balance				64.17 Dr.
5	Bank			60.90	
	+ Disc. All.	CB 17		3.27	Nil

TABLE 10.7 Purchase ledger (creditors)

Date	Particulars	Folio	Dr. £	Cr. £	Balance £
Dunlop and Co.					
1 May	Balance				846.82 Cr.
2	Bank		482.16		
	+ Disc. Rec'd	CB 17	24.10		340.56 Cr.
Goldboro's					
1 May	Balance				340.42 Cr.
3	Bank		322.40		
	+ Disc. Rec'd	CB 17	18.02		Nil
Slazenger					
1 May	Balance				482.00 Cr.
5	Bank	CB 17	82.00		400.00 Cr.

Using the Cash Book to analyse sales and VAT

ABC Co. wants to analyse its sports sales in three distinct categories:

Sports equipment	code A
Clothing	code B
Shoes	code C

All goods will be coded and the cash registers will be set up to make such analysis including appropriate VAT calculations.

The cash receipts and the week's sales figures entered in the Cash Book were as shown in Tables 10.9 and 10.10.

TABLE 10.8   General ledger

Date	Particulars	Folio	Dr. £	Cr. £	Balance £
Sales a/c					
1 May	Balance				8,424.10 Cr.
6	Cash	CB 17		494.57	9,418.67
Wages a/c					
1 May	Balance				511.22 Dr.
6	Bank	CB 17	186.48		697.70
Misc. Expenses a/c					
1 May	Balance				54.20 Dr.
6	Bank	CB 17	92.54		146.74
*Discount a/c**					
1 May	Balance				26.50 Dr.
6	Sundries	CB 17	9.06	42.12	6.56 Cr.
S/L Control a/c [debtors]					
1 May	Balance				1,215.90 Dr.
6	Bank			170.83	1,045.07
	Disc. All.	CB 17		9.06	1,036.01
P/L Control a/c [creditors]					
1 May	Balance				2,927.75 Cr.
6	Bank		886.48		2,041.27
	Disc. Rec'd	CB 17	42.12		1,999.15

* Using the same account for both discount allowed and received.
Discount allowed is regarded as an expense   (Dr.).
Discount received is regarded as revenue   (Cr.).

TABLE 10.9   Cash receipts

	Disc. All. £	Debtors £	SALES A £	B £	C £	Total £	VAT £	Bank £
8 May Sales			60		24	84	12.60	96.60
9 May Sales			42	12	22	76	11.40	87.40
10 May Smith	2.50	97.50	75	20	25	120	18.00	235.50
11 May Sales			47	25	22	94	14.10	108.10
12 May Sales			85	40	35	160	24.00	184.00
	2.50	97.50	309	97	128	534	80.10	711.60

TABLE 10.10 Posting to nominal ledger [Credit side of the sales account]

		A	B	C	Total	
					£	
12/5	Bank	309	97	128	534	Cr.
	VAT a/c					
					£	
12/5	Bank				80.10	Cr.
	S/L Control a/c					
					£	
12/5	Bank				97.50	Cr.
	Disc. All.				2.50	Cr.

Questions

1. Balance the cash book as at 31/5:

Cash Book – George Harrison

Dr.

Date	Particulars	Disc. All.	Cash	Bank
1 May	Balances		41	300
7 May	Sales			162
16 May	Rogers	2		80
24 May	Lee			9
	Sales			60
30 May	Bank (contra)*		80	
31 May	Sales		79	40
	ICI PLC	15		285
1 June	Balance b/d			

Cr.

Date	Particulars	Disc. Rec'd	Cash	Bank
1 May	Johnstone and Smith	1		28
14 May	Crookes			50
15 May	Capel Stores		7	
29 May	Gibbs			10
30 May	Cash (contra)*			80
31 May	Wages		110	
	Southern Gas		33	
	Bank Charges			38
	Balance c/d			

* Contra entry: Cash withdrawn from the bank: or Cash deposited to bank:
Bank Cr.   Bank Dr.
Cash Dr.   Cash Cr.

2. The following balances were brought down from the Cash Book of Harry Palmer on 1 July:

Cash   £747   Dr.   Bank   £1,022 Dr.

The transactions which took place during July were as follows:

			£
July	1	Paid rent by cheque	44
		General expenses by cheque	32
	3	Cash sales	156
	4	Paid a cheque of £95 to H. Smith, having been allowed £5 discount	
	6	Paid shop assistant's wages, cash	60
	10	Cash sales	188
	12	Paid for general expenses, cash	14
	15	Paid an advertising bill, cheque	35
	17	Cash sales	204
	18	Transferred to bank [contra entry] (Dr. bank, Cr. cash columns)	500
	20	Paid cheque to J. Jones £185, having been allowed a £15 discount	
	22	Received £98 cheque from A. Knott in settlement of £100 Received £296 from P. May in settlement of £300.	
	24	Cash sales £156 directly paid to bank	
	26	Paid shop assistant's wages, cash	60
	28	Received a cheque from C. Daley on a/c	140
	30	Paid rent by cheque	44
	31	Paid a cheque to J. Johnson of £180 in settlement of £200 owing.	

Required:

(a) Prepare the Cash Book of Harry Palmer for the month of July, bringing down the balances the next day.
(b) If Harry operated two personal ledgers and a nominal ledger, indicate how posting from the Cash Book to these would be done, using four of the above as examples.

3. On 1 July ABC Co. has the following balances in its Cash Book:

Cash in hand   £484
Bank   £276

During the month the transactions were as follows:

		£			£
Cheques Received:				Discount Allowed:	
2/7	Jackson and Son	186			14
3/7	Chappell Ltd	250			18.75
12/7	Clogg and Co.	100			—
28/7	Hughes, K.	358			17.90
Cheques Issued:				Discount Received:	
2/7	Mitre Sports	500			12.50
4/7	Arena	160			8.00
22/7	Dunlop	80.50			—
28/7	Slazenger Sport	172.50			7.50

Cash Received:
Week

ending	6/7	Shop takings	258.75	Paid £200 into Bank
	13/7	Shop takings	196.80	Paid £150 into Bank
	20/7	Shop takings	220.00	Paid £175 into Bank
	27/7	Shop takings	187.75	Paid £150 into Bank

Cash Paid Out:

6, 13, 20, 27 July, Assistant salaries	£56.75 (each date)
22/7	Advertising	£42.24
23/7	Delivery expenses	£14.75
25/7	Petty expenses	£ 8.50
29/7	Delivery expenses	£10.50

Required:

(a) Enter the above transactions in *date order* for the month of July. Balance as on 31 July and bring down the new balances.
(b) Ledger accounts for nominal accounts only. Assume balances are nil on 1 July.

4. The following personal accounts were in P. Land's ledger on 1 January:

	£
Smith, J.	220 Dr.
Jones, S.	84 Dr.
Bloggs, H.	280 Cr.

The following transactions took place during January:

			£
Jan.	1	Balances b/d Cash	25
		Bank	381 Dr.
	2	Cash sales	140
	3	General expenses – cash	15
		– cheque	27
	5	Personal drawings cheque	40
	8	Cash sales	185
	15	Salaries – cheque	85
	16	Insurance premium – cheque	54
	21	General expenses – cash	27
	24	Cash sales	80
	26	Smith pays a cheque to settle a/c less 5% discount	
	28	Jones pays a cheque to settle a/c less 5% discount	
	29	Cash sales paid directly into bank	285
	31	Paid salaries – cheque	85
		General expenses – cheque	54
	31	Paid Bloggs sum owing and was allowed $2\frac{1}{2}$ % discount	

Required:

(a) Prepare the Cash Book of P. Land for the month of January and balance on 31 January.
(b) Write up the personal accounts of P. Land using the running balance method, as they would appear in January.
(c) Write up the nominal accounts in P. Land's ledger as they would appear in January.

5. On 1 January D. Dawson had the following balances in his books:

	£
Cash	142 (Dr.)
Bank (overdrawn)	150 (Cr.)
R. Smith	200 (Dr.)
J. Green	160 (Dr.)
D. Land	200 (Cr.)
A. Land	80 (Cr.)
J. Jones	300 (Cr.)

During the month of January, his cash/bank transactions were as follows:

Cheques paid

January	3	To D. Land £195 in settlement of his a/c
	9	To A. Land £76 in settlement of his a/c
	17	To Jones, £150 on account
	22	Withdrew from bank for personal use £100

Cheques received

January	16	From R. Smith £195 in settlement of a/c
	23	From J. Green £152 in settlement of a/c

Cash Received

January	5	Cash sales for the week £125, £100 in bank
	12	Cash sales for the week £200, £100 in bank
	19	Cash sales for the week £150, £125 in bank
	26	Cash sales for the week £135, £100 in bank

Cash Paid

January	5	Shop assistant's wages £45 per week for the month (to 26 January)
	22	To Southern Gas, cash £55
	27	General expenses £27
	29	Petty expenses £3

Required:

(a) Prepare the Cash Book for D. Dawson for the month of January, balancing on 31 January.

(b) Show the personal accounts of D. Dawson in his ledger as they would appear on 31 January.

6. Jack Jones used a modified cash book in his music shop. All payments were made by cheque and shop takings were banked daily. On the receipts side of his Cash Book he used columns for the following:

| Discount allowed | Debtors | Record sales | Other sales | Bank |

On the payments side:

| Discount received | Creditors | Assistant's wages | Other expenses/ drawings | Bank |

Jack's bank balance on 1 May was £850.55 (dr.). During May the transactions were summarised as follows:

(a) *Cheques Issued*

2 May	To J. Brown £95 in settlement of £100 debt.
2	To wages for assistant £56 per week to 30 May.
4	To F. Smith £1,150 on account.
8	To A. Jackson £190 in settlement of £200 debt.
12	Delivery expenses £27.
15	Jack withdrew for personal use £150.
22	To Wimborne DC for rates £196.
24	To British Telecom for telephone £77.
26	Delivery expenses £42.
28	Jack withdrew for personal use £125.
30	Petty cash expenses £85.

(b) *Cheques/Cash received*

		£
May 5	shop takings* for week ending amounted to	227.75
12	shop takings* for week ending amounted to	187.00
19	shop takings* for week ending amounted to	245.60
26	shop takings* for week ending amounted to	310.25
31	shop takings* for week ending amounted to	156.20
	(All banked the same day.)	

May 7 From G. Chappell £142.50, discount allowed £7.50
  10   From D. Walters £50 on account
  18   From R. Benaud £285, discount allowed £15
  25   From D. Lillee £25 on account

*Shop takings: take 'record sales' to be 20% of week's takings.

Required:

Draw up the Cash Book of J. Jones for the month of May, balancing at the end of the month.

7. A wine shop owned by R. Lees kept an analysis Cash Book using columns for wine, beer and lager, spirits, other sales, total sales, VAT and bank.
   The daily takings are banked each day at the local branch. The cash register calculates the VAT separately when a sale goes through the till.
   The takings over four days were as follows:

June		Wine £	Beer & lager £	Spirits £	Other sales £	Total sales £	Bank £
2	Takings	200	250	80	30		
	VAT	30	37.5	12	4.5		
3	Takings	150	200	50	20		
	VAT	22.5	30	7.5	3		
4	Takings	180	240	60	24		
	VAT	27	36	9	3.60		
5	Takings	300	340	100	60		
	VAT	45	51	15	9		

Required:

(a) Prepare a suitable Cash Book using the above columns to analyse the different sale categories.
(b) Post the sales and VAT to the ledger.
(c) Why is it sometimes useful to make analysis columns?

8. On 1 October the Cash Book of Hawksworth Ltd showed a cash balance of £142 and an overdraft at the bank of £177. The business has been registered for VAT and during the first week of October the following transactions took place:

October 1 Settlement made by cheque between Hawksworth Ltd and HM Customs & Excise relating to the last VAT return. This showed £2,890 as being the total VAT paid on purchases and £3,425 as the total VAT collected on sales.

October 1 Withdrew £250 cash from the bank for use within the business.

October 2 Paid telephone bill for £207, inclusive of VAT, by cheque.

October 3 During September credit sales had been made to P. Donavon for £200 plus VAT and to G. Stevens for £600 plus VAT.
(The two customers have now paid by cheque.)

October 3 Sold goods for £736 inclusive of VAT, the customer paying by cheque.

October 4 Received a cheque for £90 from S. Turnbull.

October 4 Paid a cheque for £297 to M. Palmer in repayment of a debt.

October 4 A cheque drawn by N. Collins for £110 and originally paid into the bank in September has now been dishonoured and returned by the bank 'Refer to Drawer'.

October 5 Sold goods to M. Peters for £380 plus VAT. M. Peters paid in cash.

October 5 £450 cash was paid into the bank.
The rate of VAT is 15%. (To find VAT when inclusive, multiply by 3/23.)

Required:

(a) Write up Hawksworth Ltd's Cash Book for the week and then balance off at the end of the week. The Cash Book should have separate columns for VAT, cash and bank. Folio numbers are not required.
(b) Show how the totals of the VAT columns would appear in the VAT account.
(c) Show how the payment made on 2 October would appear in the telephones account.

[Association of Accounting Technicians]

CHAPTER 11

The Bank Reconciliation Statement

The Cash Book's bank balance needs to be confirmed with the bank statement at frequent intervals to check that its receipts and payments are in line with the banks recording of these.

Bank reconciliation is a method of bringing together the bank balance as shown on the bank statement with the balance as shown in the Cash Book.

These balances may not agree at any specific time because: (a) items in the Cash Book may not yet have reached the bank in time for these to be entered in the bank statement, or (b) items in the bank's statement may not be in the Cash Book. Some examples follow.

Items in the Cash Book not yet recorded in the statement:

- (a) cheque payments entered on the credit side of the Cash Book but not yet presented for payment at the bank – these are 'unpresented cheques';
- (b) cheques, cash entered on the debit side of the Cash Book, but not yet deposited at the bank – these are 'undeposited cheques, cash'.

Items in the bank statement not yet recorded in the Cash Book:

- (a) payments and charges made by the bank and charged against the business:

Standing orders
Direct debits
Interest and bank charges
Cheques r/d (returned to drawer, insufficient funds)

These items will be entered on the *credit* side of the Cash Book.

(b) receipts by the bank on the business's behalf and not yet recorded in the Cash Book:

Cheques from customers paid through the Bank Giro
Interest received on deposits at the bank
Dividends received from investments

These items will be entered on the *debit* side of the Cash Book.

Procedure for reconciliation

Checking must be made in some systematic order. Have the appropriate Cash Book pages ready to be compared with the latest batch of bank statements.

1. Tick those items which appear on *both* sets of records – for example, the receipts side of the Cash Book with the receipts side of the statement. Check the payments side of both records.

   If entries appear on both sets of records, no action is required.

   Also check the opening and closing balances for any differences.

2. If there are unticked items on the bank statement, such as bank charges, standing orders or interest received, these need to be first entered in the Cash Book.

   The Cash Book balance will then have been adjusted. Once the Cash Book has been adjusted the final stage is set for the reconciliation – that is, preparation of a simple bank reconciliation statement. This is composed of those items left unticked in the Cash Book.

3. The Bank Reconciliation Statement
   (a) Balance as per bank statement (end balance).
   (b) *Add* any *undeposited* cheques.
   (c) *Deduct* any *unpresented* cheques.
   (d) This should equal the balance as per Cash Book (adjusted).

An example is given below, illustrated in Figures 11.1 and 11.2.

Example: Bank Reconciliation

Procedure so far:

After checking entries on both sets of records, the Cash Book was brought up to date by entering the bank charges and the standing order for insurance on the credit side. The adjusted bank balance in the Cash Book is now £876.

The final stage is to prepare the reconciliation statement commencing with the final balance on the statement of £800, to be reconciled with the Cash Book balance of £876 (see Table 11.1).

Difference in opening balances

In most cases, when a cross-check is made between the Cash Book entries and those of the bank statement, the opening balances do not agree. This is because transactions are recorded at different times at the bank, as already discussed. Most of the questions which follow will have the opening balances agreeing, but this is only for convenience. In practice, we require the previous bank reconciliation to tick off items like unpresented cheques which do become presented at the bank and are recorded in the following bank statement.

FIGURE 11.1 Cash, bank and discounts in the Cash Book of G. Harrison

Dr.   Page No. 42   Cr.

Date	Particulars	Disc. All.	Cash	Bank	Date	Particulars	Disc. Rec'd	Cash	Bank
1 Jan.	Balance		25	900✓	4 Jan.	Stationery		20	125✓
5 Jan.	Sales		72		13 Jan.	Rates		115	
15 Jan.	Sales		15		25 Jan.	James			(76)
26 Jan.	Sales		80		28 Jan.	Fox	4		
27 Jan.	Jones	3		57✓	31 Jan.	Balance c/d		57	908
29 Jan.	Smith	8		(152)					
		11	192	1,109			4	192	1,109
1 Feb.	Balance b/d		57	908		Bank charges			7
						Insurance			25
						Balance c/d			876
			57	908				57	908
1 Feb.	Balance b/d		57	876					

FIGURE 11.2   G. Harrison's bank statement

BARCLAYS BANK PLC

Account: G. Harrison			*STATEMENT OF ACCOUNT* Account No. 44494410 31 January	

Details	Payments	Receipts	Date	Balance
	£	£		£
Balance forward			1 Jan.	900√ Cr.
100111 (rates)	125√		18 Jan.	775
Cornhill Insurance STO	(25)		20 Jan.	750
Credits (Jones)		57√	27 Jan.	807
Charges	0		30 Jan.	800

TABLE 11.1   Bank reconciliation as on 31 January

	£	£
Balance per Bank Statement		800
Add		
Deposits not yet credited:		
Smith	152	152
		952
less		
Cheques not presented:		
Fox	76	76
Balance as per Cash Book		876

Example

The Cash Book of Rod Pearce had the following entry:

    Mar. 1   Balance b/d   142.80 Cr. (overdrawn)

The bank statement is shown in Table 11.2.

TABLE 11.2 Bank statement: Rod Pearce

		Dr.	Cr.	Balance
Mar. 1	Balance			350.80 Dr. (Overdrawn)✓
2	credit		440 ✓	
3	05634	133.20 ✓		
7	05637	98.80 ✓		
10	05651	200.		
12	credit		500	

Have you calculated this? Only the entries on 2, 3 and 7 March affect the opening balance and these should cancel out. The opening balances differ by £208 (£350.80–£142.80) This is matched against the entries listed on the statement.

Questions

1. From the information given below, prepare the bank reconciliation of John Lloyd for the month of January. Adjust the Cash Book with the appropriate entries first.

Cash Book – John Lloyd (Bank columns)

			£					£
Jan.	1	Balance	93	Jan.	1	Jack Jones	52
	4	Sales	88		8	Office Expenses	24
	7	Tom Jones	87		9	Harry Smith	141
	16	A. Knott	228		10	Gas, Electricity	34
	18	J. Snow	74		12	Freddy Smith	108
	21	Sales	255		17	Rates	46
	28	A. Clarke	54		21	Salaries	84
	31	R. Wilson	36		30	George Fame	116
						Balance c/d	?
			915				915

Bank Statement – John Lloyd – for month of January

			Debit £	Credit £	Balance £
Jan.	1	Balance			93 Cr.
	4	Sundries		88	181
	8	Sundries		87	268
	11	452	52		
		453	24		192
	12	SO	55		137
	14	DD	18		119
	16	Sundries		228	347
	17	455	34		313
.	18	456	108		205
	19	Sundries		74	279
	21	Sundries		255	534
	22	457	46		488
	24	458	84		404
.	29	Dividend		16	420

Notes: SO = Standing Order
DD = Direct Debit

2. The following represents the Cash Book and bank statement figures of J. Jones (sportsman/businessman) for the month of June:

Cash Book (bank columns only)

		£			£
1/6	Balance b/d	469	6/6	Jones, F.	130
14/6	Doyle, C.	393	9/6	Singleton, S.	63
17/6	Cronin, A.	200	20/6	Jackson, J.	292
28/6	Smith, W.	205	27/6	Hemmings, R.	78
				Balance c/d	?

Bank of education   Statement of J. Jones – for the month of June

		Dr. £	Cr. £	Balance £
1/6	Balance			469 Cr.
5/6	Credit		393	862 Cr.
12/6	123971	130		732 Cr.
19/6	123972	63		669 Cr.
20/6	Credit		200	869 Cr.
26/6	Credit			
	Smith, R.		100	969 Cr.
28/6	SO			
	Leicester BSC	86		883 Cr.
29/6	Charges	19		864 Cr.

Required:

(a) Bring down the balance of J. Jones's Cash Book and check both sets of records and action any unticked items.
(b) Adjust the Cash Book.
(c) Prepare the bank reconciliation statement as at 30 June.

3. The Cash Book of P. Bentley in the 1st and 2nd weeks of May appeared as follows:

			£				£
May 1	Balance		2,300	May 2	Harrison		168
3	Smith	125		4	Rent, Rates		154
	Jones	217	342	8	Wages		218
6	Sales	115		10	Jackson		517
	Jones	13	128	12	Robson		26
					Balance c/d		?
10	Fox	259					
	Sales	175	434				
12	Knott	189					
	Sales	215	404				

Bank statement to 12 May was as follows:

		Dr.	Cr.	Balance	
May 1	Balance			2,300	Cr.
1	Counter Credit		342	2,642	
5	449	168		2,474	
6	Credit transfer R. White		435	2,909	
6	Counter Credit		128	3,037	
7	450	218		2,819	
9	SO (AB Soc.)	125		2,694	
10	Counter Credit		434	3,128	
12	Direct Debit (SEB)	44		3,084	

Required:

(a) Adjust the Cash Book with the appropriate entries. Balance on 12 May.
(b) Prepare the reconciliation statement on 12 May.

4. The following information refers to the accounts of G. Fame:

Bank Statement received on 6 August

LLOYDS BANK PLC

Account: G. Fame   *STATEMENT OF ACCOUNT*
                                   Account No. 44244214
                                   5 August ....

Date	Details	Payments £	Receipts £	Balance £
Aug. 1	Balance			471.19 Dr.
2	CC		80.	391.19
3	DV B.D.H. PLC		4.28	386.91
4	CC		97.	289.91
5	465725	48.		337.91
5	DD Wimborne DC	41.49		379.40

Abbreviations:

CC Cash or cheques deposited
DV Dividends

Required:

(a) Check the details of the above statement with the Cash Book of G. Fame on p. 178. Tick the items which are the same on both sets of records. Bring the Cash Book up to date and balance on 6 August.
(b) Prepare the bank reconciliation statement on 6 August.

Cash Book – George Fame:

Dr.

Date	Particulars	Disc. All.	Cash	Bank
1 Aug.	Balance		41.00	
	Sales		88.00	
2 Aug.	Robertson Co.	3.00		97.00
	Cash (contra)			80.00
4 Aug.	Jackson and Son			24.00
5 Aug.	Balance c/d			
		3.00	129.00	
6 Aug.	%			

Cr.

Date	Particulars	Disc. Rec'd	Cash	Bank
1 Aug.	Balance			471.19
2 Aug.	Bank (contra)	2.00	80.00	48.00
3 Aug.	Jones			48.00
	General expenses		6.24	
5 Aug.	Boston Bros			22.10
5 Aug.	Balance c/d			
		2.00	129.00	
6 Aug.	Balance b/d (overdrawn)			

5. The Cash Book of J. Jones is as follows:

Dr.		Bank £			Bank £	Cr.
1/5	Balance b/d	850.55	2/5		95	
5/5		227.75			56	
7/5		142.50	4/5		1,150	
10/5		50	8/5		190	
12/5		187	9/5		56	
18/5		285	12/5		27	
19/5		245.60	15/5		150	
25/5		25	16/5		56	
26/5		310.25	22/5		196	
31/5		156.20	23/5		56	
					77	
			26/5		42	
			28/5		125	
			30/5		85	
					56	
					25	
			31/5	Balance c/d	37.85	
		2,479.85			2,479.85	

Required:

Check the Cash Book entries with Jones's bank statement below and bring it up to date. Prepare the reconciliation statement   dated 31 May.

Details	Payments £	Receipts £	Balance £
Balance forward			850.55 Cr.
2741	56	227.75	795.55
CC		142.50	
CC			1,164.80
2742	95		
2743	1,150	50.	80.20 Dr.
CC			30.20 Dr.
2746	56		86.20 Dr.
CC		187.	100.80 Cr.
2744	150		
2745	27	285.	76.20 Dr.
CC		245.60	
CC		200.	
Bank Giro			654.40 Cr.
(R. Smith)		25.	
CC			679.40
2747	56	310.25	623.40
CC			933.65
2748	56		
Charges	31.50		
Lillee R/D	25		
2749	196		625.15 Cr.

6. The following information refers to a summary of R. David's Cash Book as at the month ended 31 May.

Receipts		£	Payments	£
May 1	Balance b/d	2,706	General expenses	7,225
	Cash sales	11,142	Creditors	6,955
	Debtors	3,100	Wages	2,580
	Commission	2,152	Office equipment	1,000

The bank statement dated 31 May received by R. David had an overdrawn balance of £893 (Dr.).

When checking with the Cash Book records the following facts were revealed:

- A payment of £420 to a supplier had been entered as a receipt.
- Bank commission of £19 and administrative charges and interest payment of £23 had not yet been entered in the Cash Book records.
- A cheque of £215 from a customer of R. David had been dishonoured by the bank and marked 'R/D'.
- A credit transfer of £426 from an R. David customer had been directly paid through the bank.
- Cheques of £375, £410, £72 and £95 had not yet been presented to the bank for payment.
- The opening Cash Book balance of £2,706 was b/d in error and should have read £2,607.
- A request to transfer £850 from deposit to current account, and entered in the Cash Book, had been misinterpreted by the bank and the transfer had been made the opposite way round. Cash Book to be corrected.
- Cash sales of £11,142 were under-cast in error and should have read £11,642.
- The final paying-in-book deposit of £1,215 had not yet been credited by the bank.

Required:

(a) Reconstruct the Cash Book incorporating the information above and bring down the balance on 31 May.
(b) Prepare the bank reconciliation statement for the month ended 31 May.
(c) Why is there a need to reconcile banking transactions?

7. The following information relates to the cash ledger of A. D. Robert for the month of 19 June.

	£		£
1/6 Balance b/f	2,870	General expenses	2,420
Debtors	8,755	Creditors	10,455
Cash sales	6,420	Salaries	2,815
Other receipts	895	Rental charges	400

The bank statement received by the business on 30 June showed a balance of £1,935 (credit).

When the proprietor checked his records with those of the statement, the following facts were revealed:

- The bank's commission and other charges amounted to a total of £79.
- A customer's cheque, which had been sent to Robert, had been marked 'R/D' and dishonoured by the bank. The cheque was for £1,353.
- A receipt of £300 from a customer of Robert had been wrongly entered as a payment in his cash ledger.
- The opening cash ledger balance of £2,870 was brought forward in error and should have been £2,780.
- Several cheques signed by Robert and presented for payment, had not yet been cleared by the bank. The cheques were for £315, £455, £170 and £595.
- Wages of £200 had been under-cast in error and had not been recorded in the cash ledger.
- A credit transfer of £420 from a Robert customer had been directly paid into the bank.
- Other entries in the statement included £122 paid to Robert as a dividend from ACY Ltd, and a direct debit relating to an insurance premium for £70.
- The final paying-in-book deposit of £1,800 had not yet been credited by the bank.

Required:

(a) Reconstruct the cash ledger for the month of June, bringing down the balance on 30 June.
(b) Prepare the bank reconciliation statement for the month ending 30 June.

8. Kirsty McDonald has recently received the following bank statement:

National Bank plc				
Kirsty McDonald Statement of Account				
Date	Details	Debits £	Credits £	Balance £
Oct 30	Balance			841
Oct 31	606218	23		818
Nov 5	Sundry Credit		46	864
Nov 7	606219	161		703
Nov 9	Direct Debit	18		685
Nov 12	606222	93		592
Nov 15	Sundry Credit		207	799
Nov 19	606223	246		553
Nov 19	Bank Giro Credit		146	699
Nov 20	Bank Giro Credit		246	945
Nov 21	606221	43		902
Nov 21	Sundry Credit		63	965
Nov 22	Bank Giro Credit		79	1,044
Nov 23	Loan Interest	391		653
Nov 26	606220	87		566
Nov 26	Deposit A/C Interest		84	650
Nov 27	606226	74		576
Nov 28	Sundry Credit		88	664
Nov 30	606225	185		479

Her Cash Book showed the following details:

		£				Cheque No.	£
Nov 1	Balance b/d	818	Nov 2	Rent	219	161
Nov 5	B. Mason	46	Nov 5	H. Gibson	220	87
Nov 8	K. Dean	146	Nov 7	G. Wise	221	43
Nov 14	G. Hunt	207	Nov 8	T. Allen	222	93
Nov 16	C. Charlton	79	Nov 12	Gas	223	246
Nov 19	D. Banks	63	Nov 15	F. Causer	224	692
Nov 26	P. Perry	88	Nov 19	M. Lewis	225	185
Nov 28	A. Palmer	29	Nov 23	G. Bridges	226	74
Nov 30	J. Dixon	17	Nov 29	L. Wilson	227	27
Nov 30	Balance c/d	206	Nov 29	P. Brown	228	91
		1,699				1,699

Required:

(a) Bring the Cash Book balance of £206 up to date as at 30 November.
(b) Draw up a bank reconciliation statement as at 30 November.

[Association of Accounting Technicians]

CHAPTER 12

The Petty Cash Book

The main points which concern the Petty Cash Book are:

(a) It is a subsidiary book of the Cash Book and is primarily used to record small payments of cash as an alternative to the credit side of the Cash Book. In this way, numerous small cash payments need not interfere with the main channels of cash entries.

(b) It uses a voucher system as evidence that cash payments have been made. These must be countersigned by an authorised person before money can be released.

(c) It is based on using a 'float' such as £100 per month from which these petty cash payments ar made. When this sum is used up, it is reimbursed from further cash received through the Cash Book.

(d) Analysis columns can be used in the Petty Cash Book to identify the different areas of payments.

The advantages of having a Petty Cash Book include:

(a) The handling of work can be subdivided between a number of employees. The cashier who is responsible for the Cash Book may delegate petty cash control to a junior accounts clerk.

(b) It frees the Cash Book from too many small and less significant figures.

(c) The style of the Petty Cash Book allows for the analysis columns to be totaled, which facilitates easier ledger posting.

The Petty Cash Book is also known as the 'imprest system' because it uses a float or 'imprest'. A sum of money, transacted through the Cash Book, is used to make payments for minor expenses such as travel, office cleaning, office refreshments, stationery and so forth.

When the float or imprest is used up after a set of period of time, it is reimbursed by further payment via the Cash Book. Reimbursements may be made weekly, monthly or whenever appropriate to the business.

Petty cash vouchers must be signed by any person who receives a cash payment and also by a person authorised to make the payments, such as the cashier or office manager. Vouchers are numbered and receipts are filed with vouchers because they will be required for audit purposes.

Control of petty cash

Each payment from the Petty Cash Book should be supported by a cash voucher. The voucher shows why the petty cash is required and who has authorised the payment. The petty cashier should always support the giving of petty cash by the signature of the person taking the cash. An example of a petty cash voucher is given in Figure 12.1.

The vouchers are numbered consecutively from the beginning of the month. They should be authorised by the person responsible for allowing petty cash to be paid. The person signing the petty cash is the person entitled to receive the money.

It is advisable that receipts for money spent on items of petty

FIGURE 12.1   A petty cash voucher

PETTY CASH VOUCHER	No.: 1 Date: 2 June	
Description	Amount	

Office refreshments:
      Coffee
      Buns
	1	12
		38

	1	50
Signature: *fom fm* Authorisation: *F.P. Slm*		

cash should be produced. On some items, VAT may be reclaimable if receipts are attached as evidence of spending.

Random checks can be made on the petty cashier. At any particular time, the total sum of the number of vouchers used in the month – that is, their total value – added to the balance of petty cash should equal the petty cash float (or imprest). For example

Petty cash balance	£ 4.25
Vouchers used	£45.75
= Float	£50.00

Double-entry with cash book

When any sum for petty cash is to be withdrawn from the Cash Book and entered in the Petty Cash Book, the double-entry is

Debit the Petty Cash Book
Credit the Cash Book

In the following example the petty cash float is £125 per month. During May, £87.25 was used for petty cash expenses leaving a balance brought down on 1 June of £37.75. A reimbursement of £87.25 is required to give the Petty Cash Book its float of £125:

Dr. Petty Cash Book	£87.25
Cr. Cash Book	£87.25

The calculation of VAT

VAT is an indirect source of taxation charged by the Government on most of our goods and services. Some goods are not yet subject to VAT, such as most of our food, books, children's clothing and postage.

The standard rate of tax is currently 17.5% and goods and services which are at the standard rate must be charged at this percentage rate. The responsibility for collecting this money lies with HM Customs & Excise. The tax charged on sales is called an 'output tax' and tax charged on purchases or expenses is called an 'input tax'.

Where some items are purchased by petty cash, which include VAT, the amount of VAT included is recorded as a separate sum in the petty cash records because it can be recovered as 'input tax' and must be recorded in the VAT account. For further information concerning VAT, see Chapter 23.

Examples:

Envelopes and typing paper   £5.17
inclusive of 17.5% VAT

Cleaning materials   £9.40
inclusive of 17.5% VAT

If a payment is given which is inclusive of VAT, it is still necessary to calculate the VAT charged (the fraction 7/47 equals the VAT charged):

$$\frac{7 \times 9.40}{47} = 1.40 \quad \text{(cleaning £8.00, VAT £1.40)}$$

$$\frac{7 \times 5.17}{47} = 0.77 \quad \text{(stationery £4.40, VAT £0.77)}$$

However, if VAT was charged at the 15% rate and it was inclusive in the value, the fraction to use is 3/23:

Stationery inclusive of 15% VAT £8.05

$$\frac{3 \times 8.05}{23} = 1.05 \quad \text{(stationery £7.00, VAT £1.05)}$$

Example

R. Taylor uses a Petty Cash Book in his business. He uses small sums of cash frequently for items such as office refreshments, packing materials, travel expenses, postage and telegrams, sundry expenses and VAT.

Petty Cash float: £125 month
Balance brought forward from 31 May: £37.75

The entries for the month of June were as shown in Table 12.1.

TABLE 12.1 Petty cash record, June

June		Amount £	VAT £	Voucher No.
1	Petty Cash reimbursement	87.25		
2	Office refreshments	1.50		1
5	Taxi fares	5.00		2
6	Packing materials	15.44	2.32	3
7	Petrol	5.45	0.82	4
12	Postage	8.50		5
14	Replacement glass	17.17	2.57	6
16	Telegrams	4.20		7
18	Office refreshments	2.12		8
21	Packing materials	14.43	2.17	9
22	Petrol	3.03	0.45	10
24	Miscellaneous expenses	16.21		11
28	Refreshments and taxi fares	15.50		12

Required:

(a) Enter the above details in the appropriate columns of R. Taylor's Petty Cash Book for the month of June (see Figure 12.2).
(b) Balance the Petty Cash Book on 30 June and bring down the balance on 1 July (see Figure 12.2).
(c) R. Taylor decided to increase the float to £150 per month. Show the appropriate reimbursement on 1 July (see Table 12.2).

Questions:

---

1. On page 193 is an incomplete Petty Cash Book of Jack Smith for the month of June. Complete the analysis columns across the page. (VAT is deducted from the total, where applicable.)

   Balance the Petty Cash Book on 30 June and include the appropriate reimbursement from the Cash Book after the balance has been brought down on 1 July.

Figure 12.2 Petty Cash Book: R. Taylor

Dr.   Cr.   No. 42

Dr £		Date	Details	No.	Total £	Office refresh. £	Packing material £	Travel expenses £	Post and telegrams £	Sundries £	VAT £
37	75	1/6	Balance b/d								
87	25	1	Cash Book (reimbursement)								
125											
		2	Office refreshments	1	1 50	1 50					
		5	Taxi fare	2	5 00			5 00			
		6	Packing materials	3	17 76		15 44				2 32
		7	Petrol and oil	4	6 27			5 45			0 82
		12	Postage	5	8 50				8 50		
		14	Replacement glass	6	19 74					17 17	2 57
		16	Telegrams	7	4 20				4 20		
		18	Office refreshments	8	2 12	2 12					
		21	Packing materials	9	16 60		14 43				2 17
		22	Petrol and oil	10	3 48			3 03			0 45
		24	Misc. costs	11	16 21			14 40	1 26	0 55	
		24	Office refresh., taxi	12	15 50	5 50		10 00			
					116 88	9 12	29 87	37 88	13 96	17 72	8 33
		30	Balance c/d		8 12						
125					125 00						
8	12	1/7	Balance b/d		8 12						
141	88	1	Cash Book (reimbursement)								
150											

TABLE 12.2 Nominal Ledger: G. Harrison

	Folio	Debit £	Credit £	Balance £
Office Refreshments a/c				
June 1 Balance				20.15 Dr.
30 Petty Cash	PC 42	9.12		29.27
Packing Materials a/c				
June 1 Balance				50.10 Dr.
30 Petty Cash	PC 42	29.87		79.87
Travel Expenses a/c				
June 1 Balance				40.06 Dr.
30 Petty Cash	PC 42	37.88		77.94
Postage and Telegrams a/c				
June 1 Balance				15.24 Dr.
30 Petty Cash	PC 42	13.96		29.20
Sundry Expenses a/c				
June 1 Balance				12.20 Dr.
30 Petty Cash	PC 42	17.72		29.92
VAT a/c				
June 1 Balance				12.15 Dr.
30 Petty Cash	PC 42	8.33		20.48

Note: each of the analysis columns identifying the petty cash expenses is posted from the credit side of the Petty Cash Book to the debit side of its respective ledger account.

2. Prepare a Petty Cash Book from the following information for the month of May and balance it at 31 May.

   Your analysis columns should be for:

   (a) cleaning;
   (b) stationery;
   (c) postage;
   (d) sundry expenses.

   The agreed amount of the imprest is £100.

Transactions during the month of May:

		£
1	Balance of cash on hand	14.50
3	Cash received from Cashier to make up total of imprest	
3	Postage	2.85
4	Envelopes	1.40
5	Cleaner's wages	5.65
6	Bus fares	2.50
7	Gummed paper	1.30
10	Postage stamps	2.60
11	Cleaner's wages	5.65
12	Rail fares	4.82
13	Cleaning materials	1.85
14	Typing paper	12.26
18	Cleaner's wages	6.65
19	Paper clips, etc.	1.60
20	Postage	1.80
24	Typing paper	14.75
25	Cleaner's wages	5.65
28	Bus fares	2.28
31	Cleaning materials	2.14
31	Parcel post	1.10
31	Received cash from cashier to make up total of imprest.	

Ledger entries:

Post the totals of the analysis columns to the nominal ledger and commence each petty cash expense with a 'nil' balance on 1 May.

This refers to Q1 on p. 189
Petty Cash Book of J. Smith:

£	Date	Details	Voucher No.	Total £	VAT £	Postages £	Stationery £	Travel £	Cleaning £	Sundries £
200	1/6	Balance b/d								
	4	Stamps	1	14 34						
	6	Bus fares	2	3 24						
	7	Taxi	3	8 50						
	10	Typing paper	4	20 70	2 70					
	12	Petrol	5	9 20	1 20					
	15	Envelopes, etc.	6	18 86	2 46					
	16	Window clean	7	11 50	1 50					
	20	Washing liquid etc.	8	1 80	0 24					
	22	Taxi	9	22 00						
	23	Stamps, telegrams	10	15 50						
	23	Crockery	11	9 48	1 23					
	24	Car repairs	12	31 05	4 05					
	26	Tea, coffee, etc.	13	4 83	0 63					
	28	Typing paper	14	2 60	0 34					
	30	Petrol, oil	15	14 29	1 85					
	30	Window clean	16	11 50	1 50					

3. Prepare a Petty Cash Book from the balance brought down in question 2. The imprest is £100. You will need to add *two* further columns: packing materials and VAT. Transactions for the month of June were as follows:

			£
June	1	Typing paper, pencils	10.50
	2	Taxi fares	5.75
	3	Postages, telegrams	6.55
	5	Cleaner's wages	5.65
	7	Bus fares	2.25
	10	Miscellaneous stationery	15.15
	12	Packing materials	8.00
		VAT	1.20
	16	Cleaner's wages	8.21
	17	Taxi fares	11.50
	18	Received a further £50 imprest to increase float to £150	
	19	Packing materials	16.00
		VAT	2.40
	20	Typing paper	12.00
	21	Parcel post	4.50
	23	Postage	6.75
	25	Cleaner's wages	8.21
	26	Packing materials	8.00
		VAT	1.20
	28	Pens, pencils etc.	2.25

July 1 Received cash from cashier to make up imprest

Required:

(a) Balance the Petty Cash Book on 30 June. Bring down the balance and show the reimbursement entry on 1 July.

(b) Ledger entries:
Post the totals of the analysis columns to the same accounts in the nominal ledger. Add the two further accounts.

4. ABC Co. uses its bank for all significant receipts and payments of cash. All cash payments under £10 come out of the petty cash. The imprest is £100 and is reimbursed every month by a cheque payment from the Cash Book.

The headings used by ABC Co. are as follows: cleaning, travelling expenses, stationery, Post Office, refreshments, general and VAT. The balance of the petty cash on 30 June was £15.65. The firm uses the voucher system and all vouchers begin from No. 1 on the first of the month.

The transactions for July were as follows:

			£
July	2	Reimbursement from Cash Book	
	2	Cleaning materials	1.50
		VAT	0.22
	3	Stamps and parcel post	8.68
	6	Window cleaning	6.00
		VAT	0.90
	8	Pens, pencils, typing paper	10.00
		VAT	1.50
	11	Newspapers	0.85
	12	Tea, coffee, and sugar	3.76
	15	Envelopes, ribbons	2.40
		VAT	0.36
	19	Telegrams	4.60
	20	Taxi fares	3.85
	23	Charity donations	1.50
	27	Bus fares	4.50
	28	Window cleaning	6.00
		VAT	0.90
	29	Floor polish and dusters	2.80
		VAT	0.42

Required:

(a) Draw up a Petty Cash Book using the appropriate columns. Bring the imprest balance up to date on 2 July.
(b) Enter the above transactions and balance the book on 31 July. Bring down the balance and make the appropriate reimbursement on 1 August.
(c) Post the analysis totals to the nominal ledger on 31 July, commencing with a 'nil' balance for each of the petty cash expenses on 1 July.

5. The following details refer to J. Smith's petty cash. He keeps the amount of imprest at £50 per month. The balance on hand, 1 January, is £8.42 and the necessary reimbursement is made. VAT is at 15%.

				£	
Jan. 7	Voucher No.	1	Petrol and oil	8.05	(VAT inc.)
10		2	Stationery	4.50	(VAT inc.)
14		3	Cleaning materials	2.20	(VAT inc.)
25		4	Refreshment supplies	4.85	
26		5	Postage stamps	3.00	
27		6	Envelopes and typing paper	7.60	(VAT inc.)
29		7	Cleaning materials	2.80	(VAT inc.)
30		8	Petrol and oil	7.20	(VAT inc.)

Required:

Draw up a Petty Cash Book and balance on 31 January.

6. Gilly Graham runs her petty cash on the imprest system, having a float of £200 per month. She uses analysis columns for VAT, postage, travel, cleaning, refreshments, stationery and sundries. At the end of August, she had £28.75 to carry forward to the new month. During the first three weeks of September, the following transactions occurred:

September
1   Enter the balance brought down from August in the Petty Cash Book.
2   Cashier reimburses Gilly to bring up to required float.
3   Purchased stamps £12.50.
5   Rail fares to Bristol, £13.60.
6   Typing paper, biros, etc., £14.10 (inc. VAT 17.5%).
8   New kettle and cups £18.80   (inc. VAT 17.5%).
11 Window cleaner £10.50.
12 Postal orders £8.75.
15 Taxi expenses £7.80.
16 Repairs to typewriter £12.80 + VAT 17.5%.
18 Window cleaner, £10.50.
20 Donation for Poppy Appeal £2.00.
20 Milk money £6.25.
21 Tea, coffee, etc., £4.80.
    For the remainder of September, there are eight further vouchers to record.

Required:

(a) Enter the above petty cash transactions in the Petty Cash Book of Gilly Graham. Record the remaining eight petty cash vouchers (see p. 000).
(b) Balance the Petty Cash Book on 30 September, bringing down the balance the next day.
(c) Post the individual analysis columns to the ledger.

Petty Cash Voucher	Folio 13		
	Date 22/9		
For what required	Amount	£	P
Stationery items		1	80
VALUE ADDED TAX:		0	32
		2	12
Signature _____			
Passed by _____			

Petty Cash Voucher	Folio 17		
	Date 27/9		
For what required	Amount	£	P
Twin Jones		11	40
VALUE ADDED TAX:		—	—
		11	40
Signature _____			
Passed by _____			

Petty Cash Voucher	Folio 14		
	Date 24/9		
For what required	Amount	£	P
Coffee, tea, etc		4	24
VALUE ADDED TAX:		—	—
		4	24
Signature _____			
Passed by _____			

Petty Cash Voucher	Folio 18		
	Date 28/9		
For what required	Amount	£	P
Magazines, newspapers		3	40
VALUE ADDED TAX:		—	—
		3	40
Signature _____			
Passed by _____			

Petty Cash Voucher	Folio 15		
	Date 25/9		
For what required	Amount	£	P
Milk		8	20
VALUE ADDED TAX:		—	—
		8	20
Signature _____			
Passed by _____			

Petty Cash Voucher	Folio 19		
	Date 28/9		
For what required	Amount	£	P
Stamps, envelopes		6	86
Card		1	50
VALUE ADDED TAX:		—	—
		8	36
Signature _____			
Passed by _____			

| Petty Cash Voucher | Folio | 16 |
| | Date | 27/9 |

For what required	Amount	
	£	P
Window cleaning	10	50
VALUE ADDED TAX:	—	—
	10	50

Signature _____

Passed by _____

| Petty Cash Voucher | Folio | 20 |
| | Date | 30/9 |

For what required	Amount	
	£	P
Stationery	4	24
VALUE ADDED TAX:		74
	4	98

Signature _____

Passed by _____

CHAPTER 13

Computer-based Accounts

The ledger programs have been operated on the Pegasus Accounting System. This system includes a wide range of accounting programs such as invoicing, stock control, payroll and job costing.

This section will concentrate on the two personal ledgers, that is, the sales and purchase ledger programs, for the purpose of drawing students' attention to the reality of recording accounts by using a micro-computer, a system they are more likely to use in the business world.

The same principles of accounting apply whether data is entered via the use of a computer keyboard or manually in an accounting book. However, once data is entered into a computer, the facilities offered by the computer's memory for listing and analysing data are far easier and superior. At the press of a button on the computer's keyboard, instant analysis is possible of anything which has been previously entered, with the additional bonus of a printout if required.

The Pegasus Accounting Package is user-friendly in that it takes little time for students to become acquainted with what is called the 'Menu System'. This is a system which offers a menu of functions on screen, for the user to choose. One of the most frequent functions to be operated is 'Ledger Processing' which deals with the entry of day-to-day transactions.

Computer programs

Computers in business have helped to modernise and speed up the whole system of financial reporting. In particular, repetitive, routine transactions can be recorded, classified, up-dated and recalled in an instant.

Accurate recording of financial information is regarded as one of the most important and fundamental functions in accounting and keeping a track of the business's accounts provides management with vital day-to-day information:

- Is sufficient cash coming in?
- Which products sell the best?
- Is adequate stock available?
- Which customers pay regularly?
- Which customers are slow payers?
- How much is owed to creditors?
- How much has been spent on overheads?

These are the type of questions which need constant answers. Accounting provides management with vital information needed to make sound decisions. A good software program can help management by providing a means to record quickly and display instantly as much detailed information as required.

Software refers to the program disks which are designed for the computer to carry out precise instructions. A program disk contains the instructions which the computer carries out and some hold a number of different programs (or files) on the same disk: for example, files for sales, bought and nominal ledgers on a single disk.

The program is loaded into the computer's memory and data can then be stored on the disk. Data may be filed on the same program disk although much of the 'memory capacity' of the computer may be taken up by the program and therefore the amount of data which can be input might then be restricted. A separate data disk is often required on micro-computers.

Loading data

Data comes from the day-to-day financial transactions which occur in a business. The disk is fed into the computer and is then ready to receive the facts and figures from the source of documents like an invoice. Data is typed in from the computer's keyboard and the information is fed into the computer's memory system and relayed to the appropriate accounts.

The computer can be used to operate any account in a business. The computer's printer enables all kinds of information to be run off and can provide a whole range of important printouts such as customer statements, employee pay slips, bank payment notices, stock records and receipt slips, as well as the financial statements.

A computer program can provide a flow of information which helps a business make better, informed decisions. The key areas of a business must be carefully monitored for better control:

Sales	Which products are moving?
Customers	Which customers are paying?
Suppliers	Which suppliers need paying?
Stock	What level of stocks are carried?
Cash	Is there adequate cash?

The right software can provide the right supply of information to a business at the time it is needed.

A computer network

The computer 'hardware' relates to the computer itself. In Figure 13.1 the basic parts of a system are illustrated.

1. The screen, which visually displays the program details and the information required from the program.
2. The keyboard, which is like that of a typewriter but with a greater number of keys to provide further functions.
3. The disk drive, where the disks are loaded into the computer.
4. The printer, which prints out the information, including business documents and financial statements.
5. The program disks. These are the compact floppy disk type which are fed into the disk drive and give the computer its precise instructions.

The sales ledger program

An accounting program may either be part of a network system or mainframe where it may be conveniently called upon the screen when required by simply pressing the appropriate command key, or it may be necessary to load a program disk which has the program instructions written on it to run a particular function, such as the sales or purchase ledgers.

A data disk will be used to record the program and the information stored on it.

Once a disk is loaded on to the computer, the operator will choose which file or menu is required. There may be several files on an accounting package and the computer may require an identifying letter or number: for example, '1' may be the code for the sales ledger program, '2' for the purchase ledger.

Programs in business usually operate on what is called a 'menu' system, that is, it gives the operator a number of choices or functions on which to use. The user will choose a particular function and press the relevant key in order to get started. For example, in

FIGURE 13.1   Basic elements of a computer system

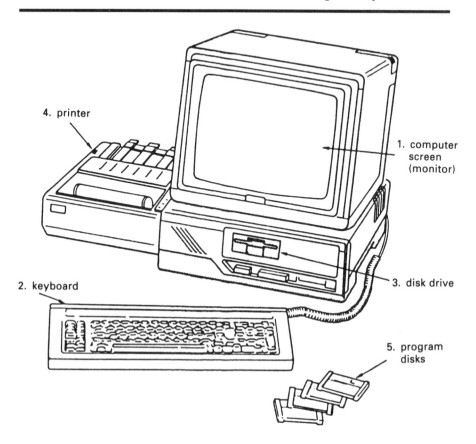

the programs shown in this section, the Jenkins Jeans Company Ltd displays the main menu as shown in Figure 13.2.

The first function we need is the Sales Ledger, therefore the number 1 would be pressed on the keyboard. The sub-menu of the sales ledger would then be displayed as shown in Figure 13.3.

The most frequently used function would be number 1, 'Ledger Transactions', which would give a list of further options to operate such as entering invoices, credit notes and receipts.

The function 'Period End' may be used to end a financial period and sales turnover may be zeroed to commence a new period. The customers' balances are not zeroed, of course, the balance being brought forward.

The 'Analysis of Sales' function may be particularly useful to those types of business which want to know which stocks are moving and which may be slow. Someone may want an analysis of sales

FIGURE 13.2 Screen message

MAIN MENU

1. Sales Ledger
2. Purchases Ledger
3. Nominal Ledger
4. Stock Control
5. Payroll
6. Invoicing
7. Costing
8. Terminate

Select and Press Number Required

FIGURE 13.3 Screen message

MENU: SALES LEDGER

1. Ledger Transactions
2. Period End
3. Analysis of Sales
4. Reports

Select and Press Number Required

geographically, or by department, or by sales executive. Sales may easily be coded for this purpose.

The fourth function, 'Reports', may be used to indicate batches of sales over periods of time or any other statistical information provided by a particular program.

The general features of reasonable sales ledger program would include:

- A facility to store a large number of accounts.
- Details of each debtor's records.
- Individual customer turnover to date.
- Automatic processing to the nominal ledger, thereby completing the double-entry.
- Sales journal.
- VAT analysis.
- Credit control limits for customers.
- Aged debtors analysis.
- Receipts analysis and details of discounts.
- Customer statements.

Most of the above items would be available for printout and this gives computer-based accounting a further edge. Not only can this information be stored on a tiny-sized disk, it can be retrieved instantly when needed and a copy taken on the printer whenever the information is required. Unbeatable over a manual system any time! In large organisations the use of computerised information is essential for management and helps them in their daily decision-making.

If the user selected function 1 of the Sales Ledger Menu, Ledger Transactions, a further menu would appear, giving a further list of options, as shown in Figure 13.4.

FIGURE 13.4   Screen message

MENU: LEDGER TRANSACTIONS

```
 1. Accounts Up-Date
 2. Ledger Postings
 3. Invoice & Credit Note Listing
 4. Receipts & Adjustments
 5. Customer Accounts
 6. Customer Statements
 7. Aged Debtors List
 8. List of Accounts
 9. Outstanding Debtors Total
10. Terminate
```

Select and Press Number Required

The Ledger Transactions function would be used on a daily basis to enter details relating to customers. What each of the options provide is summarised below:

1. *Accounts Up-Date*:
   The screen would show information such as that shown in Figure 13.5.

The cursor is awaiting an instruction from the user; in this case it is flashing over the Account Number and is waiting for the operator to enter the relevant number. If the account is new, the computer will state 'New Account' and await further input. If the account is an existing one, all other relevant information will be displayed on screen (as above).

FIGURE 13.5 Screen information

*ACCOUNT NUMBER	NAME & ADDRESS
A001	Chappell Bros. 570 Alton Rd Lower Parkstone Poole Dorset BH3 12YU

COMMENT	CREDIT LIMIT	CODE
Tele. 730256	2,500	S

* Cursor flashing

2. *Ledger Postings*:

The cursor on the screen would prompt which account was required and then the details of the customer would be automatically displayed, as shown in Figure 13.6. Here the opening balance of a customer, Chappell Bros. has been entered. Under 'TYPE', the letter 'A' signifies the appropriate code to enter an opening balance. The letter 'I' could signify invoice, the letter 'C' credit note, and so forth. Once details of any transaction are entered, the sales ledger file is automatically up-dated and may be viewed when required.

Note: Printouts of functions 3, 4, 5, 7 and 8 are shown on pages 211–14 and relate to the illustrated example of Jenkins Jeans Co. Ltd.

FIGURE 13.6 Customer details

ACCOUNT NUMBER	DATE	TYPE	REFERENCE	VALUE	VAT/ DISC	PERIOD
A001	1/1/90	A	Open/Bal	1025		1

Chappel Bros

3. *Invoice & Credit Note Listing*:
   This function lists the invoice and credit notes for any given period, for example, a day, or a week, a month, or longer. In the printout, the month's invoices and credit notes are listed. This detail woulld be the same as given in the sales day book.

4. *Receipts & Adjustments*:
   This function allows the operator to list the receipts and adjustments for the period required as in the same case as the invoice and credit note listing.

5. *Customer Accounts*:
   This function is used to display, either on screen or printout, the details of each customer's account. All transactions to the debtor are shown, including:

   (a) date of entries;
   (b) invoice and credit note numbers;
   (c) cheque numbers;
   (d) discounts given;
   (e) the age of the debt in months.

   This function is used frequently to check records of individual customers and will be an important check on credit control.
   How much does the customer owe?
   When did he last pay his account?
   Does he pay in reasonable time?
   These are important questions which need answers in order to keep adequate control of customer accounts. The speed of debt collection is vital to a business's cash flow and working capital.

6. *Customer Statements*:
   If a customer statement needs to be printed and sent, this function will give details of the account as found in option number 5, above.

7. *Aged Debtors List*:
   This function may be viewed on screen or as a printout, as shown in the example. The balance of each customer is indicated and 'aged' according to how old the debt is.
   In the printout, all the debts are listed as 'current', the total debt being £4,209.50. This figure should equal the Sales

Ledger Control account as in the nominal ledger. The credit limit and telephone numbers of each customer are also printed for convenience.

8. *List of Accounts*:
This function gives a list of the customer accounts required. In the printout, the 5 accounts of Jenkins Jeans are listed, also indicating the turnover to date, credit limit and telephone number of each customer. Code 'S' can refer to the geographical area the customer comes from.

9. *Outstanding Debtors Total*:
This function will display on the computer screen the outstanding debt owed by the total of the business's customers.
It should equal the total sum in option 7 (the Aged Debtors List) and is used as a quick check on how much debtors owe.
The screen should display:

Total Debtors = £4,209.50

10. *Terminate*:
This function is used to return the operator back to the main Sales Ledger menu.

Illustrated example of a software program

The following information refers to the Sales and Purchase Ledgers of Jenkins Jeans Co. Ltd. The accounts have been fed into the microcomputer using the Pegasus Accounting Package.

On 1 January the balances of customers and suppliers were as shown in Figures 13.7 and 13.8.

Required:

(a) Set up the ledgers of the company using sales and purchase programs. Make up appropriate addresses for each customer and supplier and any further information which might prove useful (telephone numbers).

Credit Sales and Credit Purchases

The credit sales for January were as shown in Figure 13.9.

FIGURE 13.7 Sales Ledger

Customer	Account number	Balance on 1/1
		£
Chappell Bros.	A001	1,025
Lawrie & Sons	A002	200
Redpath & Edwards	A003	600
Walker Ltd.	A004	285
Walters & Co. Ltd.	A005	465

All balances are debit.

FIGURE 13.8 Purchase Ledger

Supplier	Account number	Balance on 1/1
		£
Illingworth & Edwards	B001	1,975
Milburn & Harries	B002	300
Snow Material Supplies	B003	1,215
Underwood Mills Ltd.	B004	2,150

All balances are credit.

(b) Calculate VAT at 15% and total the columns. Post the transactions to the ledgers.

The credit purchases of stock for January were as shown in Figure 13.10.

(c) Check the accuracy of the invoices before totalling the columns. Underwood Mills Ltd. and Illingworth & Edwards give 20% trade and 5% cash discounts. Milburn & Harris and Snow Supplies give 15% trade and 5% cash discounts. Post to the ledgers.

Receipts & Payments for January

Figure 13.11 is an extract from Jenkins Jeans Cash Book.

(d) Post the above receipts and payments to the relevant accounts in the sales and purchase ledgers. Ensure that the totals of

FIGURE 13.9   Credit sales, January

Date	Customer a/c	Invoice no.	Net sales	VAT total
Jan.5	Chappell Bros	4219	500	
8	Lawrie & Sons	4220	240	
12	Chappell Bros	4221	200	
17	Walker Ltd	4222	350	
18	Redpath & Edwards	4223	450	
24	Lawrie & Sons	4224	180	
25	Chappell Bros	4225	290	
27	Redpath & Edwards	4226	650	
30	Walters Ltd	4227	300	
31	Chappell Bros	cn 42	(30)	
			3,130	

FIGURE 13.10   Credit purchases of stock, January

Date	Supplier a/c	Inv. no. rec'd	Gross purchases	Net	VAT	Total
			£	£	£	£
Jan5	Underwood Mills Ltd	3046	1,000	800	114	
7	Illingworth & Edwards	29851	1,200	960	136.8	
10	Milburn & Harris Ltd	4367	500	425	60.56	
15	Underwood Mills Ltd	4768	380	304	43.32	
20	Illingworth & Edwards	34420	530	424	60.42	
25	Snow Material Supplies	2321	240	204	29.07	
			3,850	3,117		

FIGURE 13.11   Jenkins Jeans: Cash Book extract

Receipts

Date	Customer	Amount	Discount
		£	£
Jan.5	Redpath & Edwards	290	10
10	Walker Ltd.	200	
15	Redpath & Edwards	290	10
17	Chappell Bros.	480	20
20	Lawrie & Son	200	
29	Walter Ltd.	465	

Payments

Date	Supplier	Amount	Discount
		£	£
Jan.5	Illingworth & Edwards	1,000	50
8	Snow Material Supplies	500	12.5
13	Underwood Mills Ltd.	1,500	
16	Milburn & Harries	292.5	7.5

debtors and creditors cross-check with the control accounts in the nominal ledger.

The sales ledger program

Printouts from ledger transactions

Figures 13.12–16 show the following:

Option 3:	Invoice & Credit Notes
Option 4:	Receipts & Adjustments
Option 5:	Customer Accounts
Option 7:	Aged Debtors List
Option 8:	List of Accounts

FIGURE 13.12   Option 3: Invoice & Credit Notes

Jenkins Jeans Co. Ltd.

01.01.90   SL Invoices & Credit Notes (To Date) Page 1

Ac	Date	Type	Ref	Value	Goods	VAT	
A001	05.01.90	Invce	4219	575.00	500.00	75.00	Chappell Bros.
A002	08.01.90	Invce	4220	276.00	240.00	36.00	Lawrie & Sons
A001	12.01.90	Invce	4221	230.00	200.00	30.00	Chappell Bros.
A004	17.01.90	Invce	4222	402.50	350.00	52.50	Walker Ltd
A003	18.01.90	Invce	4223	517.50	450.00	67.50	Redpath & Edwards
A002	24.01.90	Invce	4224	207.00	180.00	27.00	Lawrie & Sons
A001	25.01.90	Invce	4225	333.50	290.00	43.50	Chappell Bros.
A003	27.01.90	Invce	4226	747.50	650.00	97.50	Redpath & Edwards
A005	30.01.90	Invce	4227	345.00	300.00	45.00	Walters Co. Ltd
A001	31.01.90	Cnote	cn 42	-34.50	-30.00	-4.50	Chappell Bros.

Total Invoices				3634.00	3160.00	474.00	
Total Cr. Notes				-34.50	-30.00	-4.50	
Total				3599.50	3130.00	469.50	

FIGURE 13.13   Option 4: Receipts & Adjustments

Jenkins Jeans Co. Ltd.

01.01.90   SL Receipts & Adjusts (To Date) Page 1

Ac	Date	Type	Reference	Value	Period	
A001	01.01.90	Adjust	open bal	1025.00	1	Chappell Bros.
A002	01.01.90	Adjust	open bal	200.00	1	Lawrie & Sons
A003	01.01.90	Adjust	open bal	600.00	1	Redpath & Edwards
A004	01.01.90	Adjust	open bal	285.00	1	Walker Ltd
A005	01.01.90	Adjust	open bal	465.00	1	Walters Co. Ltd
A003	08.01.90	Recpt	chq 9809	-290.00	1	Redpath & Edwards
A003	08.01.90	Discnt	chq 9809	-10.00	1	Redpath & Edwards
A004	10.01.90	Recpt	chq 8908	-200.00	1	Walker Ltd
A003	15.01.90	Recpt	chq 6577	-290.00	1	Redpath & Edwards
A003	15.01.90	Discnt	chq 6577	-10.00	1	Redpath & Edwards
A001	17.01.90	Recpt	chq 6754	-480.00	1	Chappell Bros.
A001	17.01.90	Discnt	chq 6754	-20.00	1	Chappell Bros.
A002	20.01.90	Recpt	chq 5645	-200.00	1	Lawrie & Sons
A005	29.01.90	Recpt	chq 5656	-465000	1	Walters Co. Ltd

Total Discounts	-40.00	
Total Receipts	-1925.00	
Total Refunds	.00	
Total Adj - Contras	.00	
Total Adj - Bad Debts	.00	
Total Adj - Write Offs	.00	
Total Adj - Misposts	.00	
Total Adj - Discounts	.00	
Total Adj - Interest	.00	
Total Adj - Sundry	2575.00	
Total	610.00	

FIGURE 13.14   Option 5: Customer Accounts

Chappell Bros.   Account A001   01 Jan 1990
570 Alton Road
Lower Parkstone
Poole   TOver   960 Jan   Cr. Lim 2500
DORSET   Interest Rate 0.00%
BH3 12YU

Date	Type	Reference	Status	Debit	Credit Balance
01.01.90	Adjust	open bal	Jan	1025.00	
05.01.90	Invoice	4219		575.00	
12.01.90	Invoice	4221		230.00	
25.01.90	Invoice	4225		333.50	
31.01.90	Cr. Note	cn 42			34.50
17.01.90	Receipt	chq 6754	Jan.		480.00
17.01.90	Discnt	chq 6754	Jan		20.00

3 Months	+ 2 Months	1 Month	Currrent		Total
.00	.00	.00	1629.00		1629.00

Lawrie & Sons   Account A002   01 Jan 1990
1 Selfrige Close
Southbourne
Bournemouth
DORSET   TOver 420 Jan Cr.Lim 1020
BH4 6LU   Interest Rate 0.00%

Date	Type	Reference	Status	Debit	Credit Balance
01.01.90	Adjust	open bal	Jan	200.00	
08.01.90	Invoice	4220		276.00	
24.01.90	Invoice	4224		207.00	
20.01.90	Receipt	chq 5645	Jan		200.00

3 Months	+ 2 Months	1 Month	Current		Total
.00	.00	.00	483.00		483.00

Redpath & Edwards   Account A003   01 Jan 1990
120 Hintonwood Avenue
Highcliffe
Christchurch
DORSET   TOver 1100 Jan Cr.Lim 2000
BH4 57W   Interest Rate 0.00%

Date	Type	Reference	Status	Debit	Credit Balance
01.01.90	Adjust	open bal	Jan	600.00	
18.01.90	Invoice	4223		517.50	
27.01.90	Invoice	4226		747.50	
08.01.90	Receipt	chq 9809	Jan		290.00
08.01.90	Discnt	chq 9809	Jan		10.00
15.01.90	Receipt	chq 6577	Jan		290.00
15.01.90	Discnt	chq 6577	Jan		10.00

3 Months	+ 2 Months	1 Month	Current		Total
.00	.00	.00	1265.00		1265.00

Walker Ltd   Account A004   01 Jan 1990
Footloose Industrial
  Estate
Footloose Way
Highcliffe
DORSET
BH7 89Y

                          TOver 350 Jan Cr.Lim 1500
                          Interest Rate 0.00%

Date	Type	Reference	Status	Debit	Credit Balance
01.01.90	Adjust	open bal	Jan	285.00	
17.01.90	Invoice	4222		402.50	
10.01.90	Receipt	chq 8908	Jan		200.00

3 Months +	2 Months	1 Month	Current		Total
.00	.00	.00	487.50		487.50

Walters Co. Ltd   Account A005   01 Jan 1990
134 Jeremy Way
Charlie Industrial Estate
Christchurch
DORSET   TOver   300 Jan   Cr.Lim 1000
BH7 560   Interest Rate 0.00%

Date	Type	Reference	Status	Debit	Credit Balance
01.01.90	Adjust	open bal	Jan	465.00	
30.01.90	Invoice	4227		345.00	
29.01.90	Receipt	chq 5656	Jan		465.00

3 Months +	2 Months	1 Month	Current		Total
.00	.00	.00	345.00		345.00

FIGURE 13.15   Option 7: Aged Debtors List

Jenkins Jeans Co. Ltd.

01.01.90   Aged Debtors List   Page 1

Ac	3 Mths +	2 Mths	1 Mth	Current	Total	Cr. Limit	
A001	.00	.00	.00	1629.00	1629.00	2500	Chappell Bros. 000 Tel 730256
A002	.00	.00	.00	483.00	483.00	1020	Lawrie & Sons 000 Tel 465712
A003	.00	.00	.00	1265.00	1265.00	2000	Redpath & Edwards 000 Tel 272713
A004	.00	.00	.00	487.50	487.50	1500	Walker Ltd 000 Tel 536765
A005	.00	.00	.00	345.00	345.00	1000	Walters Co. Ltd 000 Tel 478095
Total	.00	.00	.00	4209.50	4209.50		

FIGURE 13.16   Option 8: List of Accounts

A001	Chappell Bros. 570 Alton Road Lower Parkstone Poole DORSET BH3 12YU	000 Tel 730256 Code S Type B Cr Limit 2500 TOver 960Jan
A002	Lawrie & Sons 1 Selfrige Close Southbourne Bournemouth DORSET BH4 6LU	000 Tel 465712 Code S Type B Cr Limit 1020 TOver 420Jan
A003	Redpath & Edwards 120 Hintonwood Avenue Highcliffe Christchurch DORSET BH4 57W	000 Tel 272713 Code S Type B Cr Limit 2000 TOver 1100Jan
A004	Walker Ltd Footloose Industrial Estate Footloose Way Highcliffe DORSET BH7 89Y	000 Tel 536765 Code S Type B Cr Limit 1500 TOver 350 Jan
A005	Walters & Co Ltd 134 Jeremy Way Charlie Industrial Estate Christchurch DORSET BH7 560	000 Tel 478095 Code S Type B Cr Limit 1000 TOver 300 Jan

The purchase ledger program

This program operates in an almost identical way to the Sales Ledger Program and is used to record the individual suppliers of a business, giving details of purchases, returns, payments, and any other information which relates to creditors.

The control of purchasing is a key management function. All purchases must be bought and paid for at the right time, at the right quantity and quality and at the right price. Management needs to have up-to-date information about all its suppliers. How long will they wait before payment? What discounts do they offer? Who is the person(s) to contact in the event of queries?

The amount of money a business spends on its stock can be a major expenditure and therefore affects its cash flow and working capital. Has the business sufficient cash resources to pay its creditors on time? A good computer program can provide up-to-the minute information management needs, including:

- A facility to store a large number of accounts
- Details of supplier's records
- Supplier turnover
- Printouts of the purchase journal
- VAT analysis
- Automatic processing to the nominal ledger
- Analysis of purchases, payments, discounts
- Aged creditors analysis
- A link up to stock control

The options available on the Purchase Ledger Program are virtually the same as those of the Sales Program and the sub-menu, 'Ledger Transactions' is the one most frequently in use on a daily basis to record all transactions which concern suppliers. The menus and printouts of supplier details are very similar to those of the sales program.

FIGURE 13.17 Nominal Ledger

		Debit	Credit	Balance
Sales Ledger Control Account				
1190	Balance			2,575 Dr.
31190	Sales	3,130		
	VAT	469.5		6,174.5
31190	Bank		1,925	
	Dis. Alld.		40	4,209.5

Note: Check the Aged Debtors List, Option 7 in the Sales Ledger with the above account. Make sure the balances cross-check.

Remember the following points:

(a) Computer-based accounts give immediate access to any section of information needed. The menu system of a program represents the various options (functions) which an operator may use.
(b) The sales and purchase ledger programs may have many features, including the ageing of debtors and creditors, which

helps a business to monitor and control its information more easily and assists management to make better decisions.

(c) The sales and purchase ledger programs may be integrated with the nominal ledger. When information is entered in the personal ledgers, the double-entry may automatically be transferred to the appropriate nominal accounts.

Questions

1. What advantages do you think a computer program has to offer over a manual system of recording a relatively large number of personal accounts?
2. When data is typed into the computer, the appropriate menu is used. Use a specific example to explain what this means.
3. In a sales or purchase ledger program, which functions tend to be used most frequently?
4. In the printouts of the sales ledger program, what functions does option 3 relate to when compared with a manual system of accounts?
   In option 5, check how the accounts of customers compare with recording accounts in a manual system.
5. If it is possible for you to obtain and use a computer, why not try an exercise yourself by using a question from the sales or purchases day books chapters?
6. Refer to Figures 13.10 and 13.11 and see if you can complete the purchase ledger and purchase ledger control accounts. The control account should equal £5838.67 credit.

PART III

THE CONSTRUCTION OF FINANCIAL STATEMENTS

CHAPTER 14

Final Accounts: Calculating Profits

Accounting reports or statements attempt to explain what has happened in an organisation's financial year. Reports are required for a number of reasons. An organisation wants to know how successful or otherwise it has been; whether it has earned profits or incurred losses. It wants to know how its money has been used, where it has come from and where it has gone. It wants to know the value of its resources and how these resources have been financed.

The Inland Revenue needs to have accounting reports in order to assess an organisation's tax liability. Creditors require reports to inform them about the reliability and financial stability of their clients. Potential investors also require accounting reports to help them investigate whether or not it is worth risking their capital.

Making a profit is one of the most significant objectives of an organisation in the private sector as distinct from the public sector. Not that the State is averse to making profits.

Profit is basically the difference between revenue and expenses. If revenue is more than expenses, then a profit is made. The profit and loss account is the report which states an organisation's position of profit or loss.

The balance sheet identifies the value of an organisation's resources and the financing of them. Any profit which is retained by an organisation is reflected as an increase in its resources and also as an equivalent increase in its net worth (or capital). In this way the five groups of accounts are linked together. The difference between revenue and expenses equals profit or loss which is related to an equivalent increase or decrease in net assets.

These two financial statements, the trading and profit and loss account as one and the balance sheet as the other, are collectively known as the 'final accounts'.

219

G. Harrison's accounting year runs from 1 January to 31 December. This represents his accounting period. To calculate whether or not he has made a profit in this period, he will need to match his revenue accounts with his expenses accounts.

This matching process must be done precisely and this means that all revenue earned within the period and all expenses paid or incurred within the period must be accounted for.

This may include expenses which have been used up in this period but are still unpaid (accrued expenses), or expenses paid which relate to the subsequent period (pre-paid expenses). Adjustments such as these will have to be made to the accounts in order to get a 'true and fair view' of them and of the profit or loss for the period under review. Other adjustments to the accounts include depreciation of fixed assets and provisions against debtors going bad. These will be dealt with in subsequent parts of this section.

Basically, profit = revenue *less* expenses. There are two types of profit:

1. *Gross Profit*

   Gross profit is the difference between sales *less* cost of sales; in other words selling price *less* cost price. For example:

(a) Sales	£11,000
Purchases	£ 5,000
Gross profit	£ 6,000

   However, the *stock* value both at the beginning and end of an accounting period affects the value of purchases.

   (b) If stock value on 1 January was £1,000 and the unsold stock value on 31 December was £1,500:

Cost of sales	=		Stock (1/1)	£1,000
		+	Purchases	5,000
				6,000
		−	Stock (31/12)	1,500
				4,500

Gross profit	=	Sales - Cost of sales
£6,500		£11,000 - £4,500

   (c) Returns: if there were returns inward of £250 (sales returns) and returns outward of £350 (purchases returns),

TABLE 14.1   Calculation of gross profit

	£	£
Sales	11,000	
– Returns in	250	10,750
Less Cost of Sales		
Stock (1/1)	1,000	
+ Purchases	5,000	
	6,000	
– Returns out	350	
	5,650	
– Stock (31/12)	1,500	4,150
Gross profit		6,600

these would be deducted from sales and purchases value respectively (see Table 14.1).

The *trading account* is the account where gross profit is calculated.

2. *Net profit*
The net profit is the difference between the gross profit and all other expenses, plus any other revenue earned (other than sales):

Net Profit = Gross Profit – Other Expenses + any other revenue
see the example in Table 14.2.
The *profit and loss account* is the account where the net profit is calculated.
Table 14.3 shows G. Harrison's trial balance.

Required:

(a) Prepare the trading and profit and loss account of G. Harrison for the year ended 31 December.
(b) A balance sheet as at that date, 31 December.

The answers are given in Tables 14.4 and 14.5.

TABLE 14.2   Calculation of net profit

	£	£
Gross profit		6,600
less other expenses:		
Salaries	850	
Light and heat	300	
Printing and stationery	100	
Telephone	155	
Delivery expenses	125	
Advertising	300	
Packing materials	340	
Discount allowed	65	
Rates and water	285	
Motor expenses	500	
Interest paid	140	3,160
		3,440
add other revenue:		
Discount received	125	
Commission	85	210
Net Profit		3,650

Transfer of nominal ledger accounts to trading and profit and loss

All revenue and expense balances are transferred to the trading and profit and loss account at the end of an accounting period.

Once profit and loss has been calculated, revenue and expense accounts will start the new accounting period with new zero balances.

The stock account will also be transferred to trading and the unsold stock value at the end of the year will be entered in the stock account as the new stock value.

See Table 14.6 for examples.

TABLE 14.3 G. Harrison's trial balance as on 31 December

Account	£	£
Capital: G. Harrison		10,000
Drawings	2,600	
Premises	12,000	
Fixtures and Fittings	2,000	
Equipment	3,000	
Motor Van	1,250	
Building Society Mortgage		8,000
Bank Loan		1,000
Stock (1 January)	1,000	
Bank/cash	400	
Debtors	850	
Creditors		950
Sales		11,000
Returns Inward	250	
Purchases	5,000	
Returns Outward		350
Salaries	850	
Light and Heat	300	
Printing and Stationery	100	
Telephone	155	
Delivery Expenses	125	
Advertising	300	
Packing Materials	340	
Discount Allowed	65	
Rates and Water	285	
Motor Expenses	500	
Interest Paid	140	
Discount Received		125
Commission Received		85
	31,510	31,510

Note: Value of unsold stock
at cost 31 December   £1,500

TABLE 14.4   Trading and profit and loss account for the year ended 31 December

	£	£
Sales	11,000	
– Returns inward	250	10,750
Less cost of sales		
Stock (1/1)	1,000	
+ Purchases	5,000	
	6,000	
– Returns outward	350	
	5,650	
– Stock (31/12)	1,500	4,150
Gross profit		6,600
Less other expenses		
Salaries	850	
Printing and stationery	100	
Telephone	155	
Delivery expenses	125	
Advertising	300	
Packing materials	340	
Discount allowed	65	
Rates and water	285	
Motor expenses	500	
Interest paid	140	
Light and heat	300	3,160
		3,440
Add other revenue		
Discount received	125	
Commission	85	210
Net Profit		
(transferred to Capital account)		3,650

Notes: The value of unsold stock on 31 December is entered in the balance sheet as a current asset.

The Net Profit is added to the Capital a/c in the balance sheet, increasing the owner's net worth in the business. The owner's drawings will be deducted from his net worth.

TABLE 14.5   Balance sheet as at 31 December

	£	£	£
Fixed Assets (at cost)			
Premises	12,000		
Fixtures and Fittings	2,000		
Equipment	3,000		
Motor Van	1,250		18,250
Current Assets			
Stock (at cost) 31.12	1,500		
Debtors	850		
Bank/cash	400	2,750	
Less Current Liabilities			
Creditors	950	950	
Working Capital			1,800
*Capital Employed			20,050
Less Long-term Liabilities			
Mortgage (Building Society)	8,000		
Bank Loan	1,000		9,000
Net assets			11,050
Financed by:			
Capital: G. Harrison (1/1)	10,000		
+ Net Profit	3,650	13,650	
− Drawings		2,600	11,050

* Capital Employed:	=	Fixed Assets	+	Working Capital
£20,050	=	£18,250	+	£1,800

TABLE 14.6 Nominal ledger of G. Harrison after trading and profit and loss account

		Dr. £	Cr. £	Balance £
Sales a/c				
31 Dec.	Balance			11,000 Cr.
	Trading	11,000		0
Purchases a/c				
31 Dec.	Balance			5,000 Dr.
Trading			5,000	0
Returns Inward a/c				
31 Dec.	Balance	250		250 Dr.
	Trading		250	0
Returns Outward				
31 Dec.	Balance			350 Cr.
	Trading	350		0
Stock a/c				
1 Jan.	Balance			1,000 Dr.
31 Dec.	Trading		1,000	Nil
31 Dec.	Trading	1,500		1,500 Dr.
*1 Jan.	Balance			1,500 Dr.

* New accounting period. Note that the stock (end) £1,500 becomes stock (beg.) in the new period.

TABLE 14.6   Nominal ledger of G. Harrison (continued)

		Dr. £	Cr. £	Balance £
Salaries a/c				
31 Dec.	Balance			850 Dr.
	Profit and Loss		850	0
Printing and Stationery a/c				
31 Dec.	Balance			100 Dr.
	Profit and Loss		100	0
Telephone a/c				
31 Dec.	Balance			155 Dr.
	Profit and Loss		155	0
Delivery Expenses a/c				
31 Dec.	Balance			125 Dr.
	Profit and Loss		125	0
Advertising a/c				
31 Dec.	Balance			300 Dr.
	Profit and Loss		300	0
Packing Materials a/c				
31 Dec.	Balance			340 Dr.
	Profit and Loss		340	0

Note: The remaining revenue and expense accounts will also be transferred to Profit and Loss. All other accounts (that is, assets, liabilities and capital) are not affected in the same way and their balances are carried forward to the new accounting period.

Questions

1. The following represents the trial balance of J. Wright on 30 June:

Account	Dr. £	Cr. £
Capital: J. Wright		25,000
Premises	19,000	
Bank	1,250	
Equipment	4,075	
Motor vehicle	2,250	
Drawings: J. Wright	1,750	
Stock (1/7) beg.	1,250	
Debtors	1,000	
Creditors		2,100
Sales		50,000
Returns inward	200	
Returns outward		550
Purchases	44,500	
General expenses	650	
Salaries	1,125	
Administration expenses	450	
Rates and insurance	300	
Interest received		150
	77,800	77,800

Note: At the year ended 30 June, the value of unsold stock was £3,750.

Required:

(a) A trading and profit and loss account for the year ended 30 June.
(b) A balance sheet as at that date. Show working capital.

2. The following represents the trial balance of Jack Armstrong as at 31 December.

	Dr. £	Cr. £
Premises	27,000	
Motor van	2,000	
Fixtures and fittings	5,300	
Bank	4,250	
Cash	250	
Stock (1 Jan. 1988)	8,000	
Debtors	3,100	
Mortgage on premises		20,000
Interest owing		1,000
Creditors		9,000
Capital: J. Armstrong		7,000
Sales		71,000
Discount		300
Returns outward		1,000
Rates and water	500	
Motor and travel expenses	2,500	
Purchases	34,000	
Returns inward	2,250	
Light and heat	600	
Advertising	590	
Wages	16,500	
Insurance	360	
General expenses	2,100	
	109,300	109,300

Note: The ledger accounts are more or less listed in asset, liability, capital, revenue and expense order, making it a little easier to prepare the final accounts.

Required:

(a) Prepare the trading and profit and loss account of J. Armstrong for the period ended 31 December. The value of stock on 31 December was £4,200.
(b) Prepare the balance sheet as at 31 December, and clearly show working capital.

3. The following information relates to Freddy Smith, small retailer, as at year ended 31 December:

	Dr. £	Cr. £
Capital		2,000
Shop premises	1,950	
Fixtures	750	
Stock 1 Jan.	320	
Debtors	1,020	
Creditors		1,245
Sales		6,950
Purchases	4,050	
Returns inward	100	
Outward		150
Rent	250	
Wages and salaries	600	
General expenses	75	
Light and heat	355	
Bank	875	
	10,345	10,345

Note: Closing stock at 31 December was £650.

Required:

(a) Enter all the above accounts in the ledger of Freddy Smith as they would appear on 31 December. Transfer all revenue and expense accounts to the trading and profit and loss account. Adjust for stock end.
(b) Prepare the trading and profit and loss accounts for the year ending 31 December and a balance sheet as at that date.

4. The following balances were taken from the books of Freddy White as at 30 September:

Trial Balance as on 30 September

	Dr. £	Cr. £
Capital: F. White		12,730
Drawings: F. White	1,200	
Purchases	8,400	
Sales		12,900
Stock (beg.)	1,358	
Debtors	1,889	
Creditors		2,184
Commission		1,033
Water, rates, insurance	664	
Wages	3,173	
General expenses	125	
Equipment	1,500	
Motor van	410	
Cash	528	
Overdraft at bank		2,400
Premises	12,500	
Returns inward	153	
Returns outward		653
	31,900	31,900

Note: Stock value on 30 September was £2,415.

Required:

(a) Prepare the trading and profit and loss account of F. White for the year ended 30 September and a balance sheet as at that date.
(b) Why are some accounts transferred to the trading and profit and loss account and not others? Explain, giving examples.

5. James Robert has a small business enterprise. The following accounts were extracted from his ledgers at the financial year end 30 April:

Trial Balance as on 30 April

	Dr. £	Cr. £
Capital: J. Robert		18,000
Drawings	2,800	
Bank overdraft		725
Premises	15,700	
Motor van	1,000	
Equipment	1,400	
Debtors	2,900	
Creditors		3,850
Stock (beg.)	3,500	
Purchases	28,400	
Sales		42,650
Rent received		750
Wages	8,500	
Rates and insurance	270	
Light and heat	195	
Administrative expenses	325	
Selling and distribution costs	500	
VAT	275	
Returns inward	400	
Returns outward		190
	66,165	66,165

Note: Stock unsold on 30 April was valued £5,280.
        VAT is not an expense. Customs & Excise owe the money to J. Robert.

Required:

(a) The trading and profit and loss account for the year ended 30 April.
(b) A balance sheet as at this date.

6. The trial balance of G. Chappell on 31 March is shown below.

	Dr. £	Cr. £
Bank loan (2 Years)		402.77
Cash	48	
Bank	1,532.8	
Stock (beg.)	700	
Fixtures & fittings	200	
Motor van	1,025	
Sales ledger control	941.5	
Purchase ledger control		1,580.23
VAT	145.41	
Capital		4,050
Drawings	600	
Sales		1,867
Purchases	1,562.12	
Discount	42.15	
Overheads	546.25	
Wages	154	
Motor expenses	303.77	
Petty cash expenses	99	
	7,900	7,900

Note: Stock on 31 March still unsold, £1,300.

Required:

(a) The trading and profit and loss account for the year ended 31 March.
(b) A balance sheet as at that date, showing working capital.

CHAPTER 15

Final Accounts: Adjustments

It has been previously mentioned that Mr. G. Harrison's accounting period runs from 1 January to 31 December. Other organisations may not have the same financial year. Some businesses run from 1 April to 31 March, others from 1 June, and so forth. The important thing is that, once an accounting period is recognised and accepted, that period of time is consistently applied as to when the final accounts are prepared. In G. Harrison's case the final accounts are prepared at the end of the financial year, 31 December.

The accruals concept in accounting recognises that any transaction, part or whole, which relates to a specific accounting period must be brought to account. In this way, a true and fair assessment of the accounting year is more likely to be made.

It may be necessary to make adjustments to the accounts at the end of an accounting period in order to achieve a true and fair position of the financial affairs of the business. The three major adjustment in this section are accrued expenses, pre-payments and provisions for bad debts.

Accrued expenses

These are expenses which have been incurred during the financial period but not yet paid for. G. Harrison's financial period end is on 31 December and a wide range of bills such as telephone, light & heat, advertising, garage expenses, wages, etc. could be still be outstanding on this date. These MUST be charged to the profit & loss account for the year in which they were used up. Even if a bill has not yet been received, an estimate of the charge should still be included in the accounts for the period. This may mean calculating the number of units consumed and could be achieved

TABLE 15.1   Effect on final accounts

	£	£
Profit and loss a/c:		
Light and Heat	300	
+ accrued expense	54	354
Salaries	850	
+ accrued expense	34	884
Balance sheet:		
Current Liabilities		
Accrued Expenses	88	

Notes: (a) An accrued expense increases the expenses during the accounting period and therefore reduces the profit for the year.

(b) Because the expense is still owing for the period, it is treated as a current liability, until the payment is paid.

by looking at the bill for the same corresponding period in the previous year. Any accrued expense must be added to the expense account which it applies to and entered in the profit & loss account for the period. The amount owing is also included as a current liability in the balance sheet.

For example, in G. Harrison's trial balance as on 31 December, he paid for a number of expenses. Suppose a gas bill was outstanding for £54 and there was £34 owing to salaries, and both these related to the current year's expenses. What effect have they on the final accounts? See Table 15.1.

Prepayments

Some type of expenses, rather than being paid in arrear (such as accruals), are in effect, more likely to be paid in advance of the period under review. Members subscriptions, rent, rates, insurance and unused stationery are the type of expenses which are prepaid. Any payment made in advance of the accounting period, must be deducted from the expense it applies to and entered in the profit & loss account. The amount prepaid is also included as a current asset in the balance sheet.

For example, in Harrison's trial balance as on 31 December he paid rates and water expenses of £285. If £160 was paid for rates for the year ended 31 March, 3 months (1/4) has been paid in advance because it is related to the next financial period. £40 is therefore pre-paid. See Table 15.3. (Table 15.4 shows the prepayments as entered in the nominal ledger.)

TABLE 15.2 Accrued expenses in the nominal ledger

	Dr. £	Cr. £	Balance £
Light and Heat a/c			
31 Dec. Balance			300 Dr.
Accrued Expense	54		354
Profit and Loss		354	0
1 Jan. Accrued Expense		54	54 Cr.
7 Jan. Bank	54		0

Notes: (a) The accrued expense is brought down as a credit in the new financial period because £54 is still owing.
(b) When the bill was paid on 7 Jan. it cleared the bill. Any subsequent payments for gas or electricity will then be related to the new financial year.

TABLE 15.3 Effect of pre-payments

	£	£
Profit and loss a/c:		
Rates and water	285	
– Pre-paid expense	40	245
Balance sheet:		
Current assets		
Pre-paid expenses	40	

Note: A pre-payment decreases the current year's expenses, having the effect of increasing current profit.
Because some value of the expense is still to be used in the next accounting period, the pre-paid expense is regarded as a current asset in the balance sheet as on 31 December.

Other prepayments of G. Harrison

On 31 December, Harrison still had £20 stationery unused and £60 of packing materials. Because the unused stock of these can be used in the next accounting period, they are both treated as pre-paid expenses.

The total pre-paid expenses on 31 December were £120.

The trading and profit and loss account of Harrison for the period ended 31 December would now appear as shown in Table 15.5.

TABLE 15.4   Pre-paid expenses as shown in the nominal ledger

	Dr. £	Cr. £	Balance £
Rates and water a/c			
31 Dec. Balance			285 Dr.
Pre-paid expenses		40	245
Profit and loss		245	0
1 Jan. Pre-paid expenses 40			40 Dr.

Notes: (a) The pre-paid expense is brought down as a debit entry in the new financial period 1 Jan.
 (b) This indicates that £40 of rates already paid belongs to the new accounting period.

TABLE 15.5   G. Harrison's trading and profit and loss account

	£	£	£
Gross profit			6,600
Less other expenses			
Salaries	850		
+ Accrued expense	34	884	
Light and heat	300		
+ Accrued expense	54	354	
Rates and water	285		
– Pre-paid expense	40	245	
Printing and stationery	100		
– Pre-paid expense	20	80	
Packing materials	340		
– Pre-paid expense	60	280	
Other expenses		1,285	3,128
			3,472
Add other revenue			210
Net profit			3,682

How the adjustments affect profit

Before the accrued and pre-paid expenses were taken into account, Harrison's net profit was £3,650 for the year ended 31 December.

With adjustments taken into account, the profit has increased by £32 to £3,682. This is the result of:

Expenses + (accrued)	£88
Expenses − (pre-paid)	£120
Extra profit	£32

Provisions for bad and doubtful debts

Businesses tend to be conservative by nature in that if any asset is likely to be reduced in value, the accounting convention is to provide for the loss in advance. On 31 December, Harrison has £850 owing to him from debtors. Looking through his sales ledger, he may decide that one or more accounts look 'a little doubtful' and therefore make a 10% provision against his debtors.

What is the effect of a 10% provision for bad or doubtful debts in the final accounts (see Table 15.6) and how would this be shown in the nominal ledger (see Table 15.7). The double-entry is:

| Profit and Loss a/c | Debit |
| Provision for Bad and Doubtful Debts a/c | Credit |

Writing off a bad debt

In June of the new accounting period, Harrison had to write off one of his customers, J. Hunt, as a bad debt, £75. The double entry is:

| Bad Debts | a/c | Debit |
| J. Hunt | a/c | Credit |

Harrison's sales ledger:	Dr.	Cr.	Balance
J. Hunt a/c			
30/6 Balance			75 Dr.
Bad Debts		75	0

Harrison's nominal ledger:	Dr.	Cr.	Balance
Bad Debts a/c			
30/6 J Hunt	75		75 Dr.

TABLE 15.6   Effect of 10% provision on final accounts

	£	£
Profit and Loss a/c Provision for bad and doubtful debts	85	
Balance Sheet: Debtors	850	
less Provision for bad and doubtful debts	85	765

Notes: (a) The opening of a provision account for bad debts allows a sum to be set aside from profits, and is treated as an expense.
(b) The debtors in the balance sheet are shown as net, the provision reducing their value to a sum the debtors are expected to pay £765.

TABLE 15.7   Provision for bad and doubtful debts in the nominal ledger

		Dr. £	Cr. £	Balance £
Provision for bad and *doubtful debts a/c*				
31 Dec.	Profit and Loss		85	85 Cr.
1 Jan.	Balance			85 Cr.

Note: In the new accounting period, 1 January, the Provision account has £85 in credit.

At the end of the financial period, 31 December, Harrison had debtors totalling £1,550. He also wrote off another customer for £60, the total sum of £135 written off to bad debts account. It was decided to maintain the 10% provision against bad and doubtful debts. The appropriate entries for these in the accounts are shown in Table 15.8.

The profit and loss account and balance sheet at the year end would look as shown below.

Profit and Loss a/c 31/12

Bad Debts	135	
Provision for Bad Debts	70	

Balance Sheet 31/12

Debtors	1,550	
Provision for Bad Debts	155	1,395

TABLE 15.8   Harrison's nominal ledger

	Dr.	Cr.	Balance
Bad Debts a/c			
31/12 Balance			135 Dr.
Profit and loss		135	0
Provision for bad and			
doubtful debts a/c			
1/1 Balance		85	85 Cr.
31/12 Profit and Loss		70	155

Note: 10% of Debtors £1550 = £155. Only £70 needs to be charged to Profit and Loss because £85 is already in the account. In this way, the provision account is adjusted each year to equal the percentage required against debtors. If the adjustment is increased, it is credited in the provision as above. If it is reduced, it is debited in the provision account.

The need to check customers

When businesses trade with each other, it is accepted practice that the buying and selling of goods is on a credit basis. The invoice will be the bill of sale and used as the contract between the buyer and the seller.

When the statement is sent to the customer, the supplier will expect payment, or at least part payment, on the account within a reasonable period of time. Payment is likely to be by cheque or through the banking system, such as direct debit or credit transfer. Sometimes it is inevitable that some customers will fail to pay their accounts. If trade becomes slack and the demand for goods and services falls a recession can linger on as it did in the early 1990s. Some customers were unable to pay because they faced financial difficulties or even went bankrupt, as thousands did to their cost.

Credit control

It is important for a business to try to restrict the total of outstanding debts due from their customers. A system of internal control is needed to ensure that all customers pay their accounts on time, and particularly when the economy starts to take a downturn and liquidity becomes a problem for many businesses.

It would be foolhardy to allow just any customer to buy any amount of goods they wanted without first fully checking how reliable they were. If a customer shows that he can regularly pay

TABLE 15.9   Aged list of debtors

		£
60%	are current (1 month)	11,100
20%	are 2 months old	3,700
15%	are 3 months old	2,775
5%	are over 3 months old	925
	Total customers' debts	18,500

his outstanding debts, then trust is built up between the buyer and seller.

Where some customers take their time about paying and their debts are outstanding over a long period of time (say, beyond a period of three months), then firm action needs to be taken to recover the debts.

It is essential in business to have an 'aged debtors list': that is, a list which clearly establishes how old the debts of customers are. For example, a firm has debtors who owe a total of £18,500. The 'aged' list of debtors might be as shown in Table 15.9. It would seem that those debts which are 3 months old or more ought to be investigated to see what measures could be taken to expedite payment.

From this schedule of aged debtors, a business can make an estimate of the percentage debt which might be doubtful. The percentage provision for doubtful debts could be made upon a basis such as:

Current (up to a month)	1.5%
One–two months	2.0%
Two–three months	2.5%
Over three months	5.0%

Therefore: £11,100 × 1.5% = £166.50
£ 3,700 × 2.0% = £ 74.00
£ 2,775 × 2.5% = £ 69.38
£ 925 × 5.0% = £ 46.25   £356.13

A provision of £356 on a total debt of £18,5 = 1.92%, or approximately 2.0% overall. This could then be the figure in the final accounts for the provision for bad and doubtful debts.

A business may employ a credit controller with the responsibility of chasing up the older debts. A thorough and continuous system is required to ensure that customers do not exceed their credit limits and that they pay their bills on time.

A credit rating is a device which seeks to inform the controller how good or bad a customer is when paying his bills. For example, a 5-star rating might indicate an absolute top mark rating for those customers showing great reliability. At the other end of the scale, a 1-star rating would indicate that the customer needs close attention and that the value of sales would have to be closely monitored to make sure payment is made.

A credit limit is made on customers which indicates the limit of their purchases. In this way, payment must be made before further sales are made to the customer.

Credit ratings of customers can change, depending on whether they become more or less reliable. The credit rating also gives guidance as to the value of sales allowed to a customer. The higher the rating, it follows that the higher the sales value a customer is given.

The credit controller can make up the ratings according to past experiences with customers. With new customers, assistance can be gained from organisations like Dun & Bradstreet which make evaluations of company performance and estimate their ability to pay debts. A new customer would normally be expected to give references from other suppliers or from their bank.

If a computer program is used to record sales on credit (see chapter 13), the sales ledger program would have a function which would give the aged debtors list automatically. The list would print out precisely the age of each debtor and could also be asked to type out standard letters to late customers who need reminders to pay their accounts on time (see Table 15.10).

If we were to apply the same principle and calculate a percentage for overall bad debts from Table 15.10:

$$
\begin{aligned}
£\ 638 \times 1.5\% &= £\ 9.57 \\
£\ 888 \times 2.0\% &= £17.76 \\
£\ 633 \times 2.5\% &= £15.83 \\
£1{,}516 \times 5.0\% &= £75.80 \quad £18.96/3{,}675
\end{aligned}
$$

This works out at an average of approximately 3.24% provision for bad and doubtful debts.

Customers who fail to honour their debts must be placed on the stop list, which simply means that all further sales to them are withheld until payment is received from the client.

Credit control is of utmost importance. It's no good having lots of customers who buy but cannot pay. A customer is an asset to a

TABLE 15.10   Example of an aged debtors schedule

Debtors: A–D
Month: March

Customer	Current	1–2 months owing	2–3 months owing	3 months + owing	Totals
R. Anders			155	180	335
D. Andrews	148	210			358
J. Arkwright		160	50		210
P. Bailey				456	456
W. Barstow		351	428		779
F. Barton	370	125			495
R. Briggs				880	880
D. Dartman	120	42			162
	638	888	633	1,516	3,675

business because he owes money to it. But if he fails to pay, the asset is converted to an expense because the customer becomes a bad debt. Expenses reduce profits and no business can afford too many of these otherwise it may not be in business itself for much longer.

The recovery of bad debts

In the event of a customer paying back a debt which had previously been written off, either in part-payment or in full, the debt must first be reinstated in the customer's sales ledger account. It is important to do this because the record will then show that the customer did, in effect, honour the debt at some future point in time. Once the cheque has been received and banked, the posting to the ledger account clears the debt. The procedure for this type of transaction is therefore as follows:

1. Reinstate the debt
   Debit: the customer's account (and S/L Control a/c) with amount recovered;
   Credit: the bad debts accounts (or a bad debts recovered a/c)

2. Banking the amount received
   Debit: bank account
   Credit: customer's account (and S/L Control a/c).

Example

In June 19–4 Harry Smith, a customer, had been written off as a bad debt, owing £380 to George Harrison. In April, 19–5, a cheque for the full amount had been received from Smith's solicitor in settlement of the account. In Harrison's ledgers this appeared as shown in Tables 15.11 and 15.12.

The sales ledger control and the bank account would appear as shown below.

Sales ledger control a/c

30/4 H. Smith	380		380 Dr.
30/4 Bank (H.Smith)		380	0

Bank a/c

30/4 H.Smith	380	380 Dr.

Note: remember that the control account must reflect in total what affects the individual accounts in the sales ledger. Both the debts recovered and received in Smith's personal account must also be recorded in the control account, otherwise the schedule of debtors would not reconcile with the control account.

The provision for debtors discounts

If it is the policy of a business to allow customers to have cash discounts on their sales, it may be seen as prudent to make an appropriate provision for it in the same way as providing for bad and doubtful debts. The amount of provision for discount is therefore:

Debit: profit and loss account (an expense)
Credit: provision for discounts allowed account (negative asset)

The provision for discounts must always be calculated on the net value of debtors: that is, after deducting the provision for bad debts. The balance sheet will then indicate the gross debtors figure, less both provisions for discounts and bad debts.

The provision for discounts allowed to customers may then be adjusted each year in relation to the amount of discounts allowed and the provision for bad debts.

TABLE 15.11 Harrison's sales ledger

		Dr.	Cr.	Balance
Harry Smith a/c				
19-4				
30/6	Balance			380 Dr.
	Bad debts		380	0
19-5				
30/4	Bad debts	380		380 Dr.
	Bank		380	0

TABLE 15.12 Nominal ledger

		Dr.	Cr.	Balance
Bad Debts a/c				
19-5				
30/4	Harry Smith		380	380 Cr.

Example

George Harrison has £800 credit as the opening balance (1 January 19–4) in the provision for bad debts account. He decides to provide a 2.5% provision for discounts at the year end. The following figures relate to the two years ended 31 December 19–5:

19–4 Debtors £16,800   Bad debts written off £785
19–5 Debtors £18,000   Bad debts written off £700.

Provision for bad debts 5%
Provision for discounts 2.5%.

The relevant accounts for both years are as shown in Table 15.13.

TABLE 15.13 Harrison's accounts

	Dr.	Cr.	Balance
Provision for Bad Debts a/c			
19-4			
1/1 Profit & Loss a/c			800 Cr.
31/12 Bad debts	785		15
Profit & Loss a/c		825	840
19-5			
31/12 bad debts	700		140
Profit & Loss a/c		760	900
Provision for Discounts Allowed a/c			
19-4			
31/12 Profit & Loss a/c		399	399 Cr.
19-5			
31/12 Profit & Loss a/c		29	428
Profit and Loss Account year ended 31 December			
19-4 Provision for bad debts		825	
Provision for discounts		399	
19-5 Provision for bad debts		760	
Provision for discounts		29	
Balance Sheet as on 31 December			
19-4 Debtors			16,800
− Prov. for bad debts		840	
Prov. for discounts		399	1,239
			15,561
19-5 Debtors			18,000
− Prov. for bad debts		900	
Prov. for discounts		428	1,328
			16,682

Note:
To *increase* the provision for bad debts or discounts:
  Dr. profit and loss account (with the increase)
  Cr. provision for bad debts or discounts
To *reduce* the provision for either bad debts or discounts:
  Dr. provision for bad debts or discounts
  Cr. profit and loss account.

Questions

1. The following accounts were taken from the books of Harry Wright for the financial year ended 31 December

	Dr. £	Cr. £
Capital: H. Wright		16,000
Drawings	4,200	
Stock 1 Jan.	12,890	
Purchases	22,430	
Sales		32,300
Premises	12,000	
Equipment	760	
Motor van	2,250	
Debtors	23,220	
Creditors		33,600
Returns inward	250	
Returns outward		540
Rates and water	850	
Wages	4,480	
Advertising	250	
Office expenses	280	
Discount received		350
General expenses	820	
Bank overdraft		1,890
	84,680	84,680

Note: At 31 December.
   (a) The value of stock £10,500.
   (b) Wages owing £42.
   (c) Rats pre-paid £30.
   (d) At invoice for office stationery still unpaid £55.

Required:

   Prepare the trading and profit and loss account of H. Wright for the year ended 31 December, and a balance sheet as at that date. (Show working capital.)

2. The following informations represent the accounts of James Hunt on 31 December:

Account	£
Capital: J. Hunt	8,000
Drawings	2,500
Cash	100
Bank	400
Equipment	400
Motor vehicle	1,500
Stock (1/1)	4,800
Debtors	2,500
Creditors	3,130
Sales	12,200
Purchases	7,000
Returns outward	250
Rent	160
Discount received	20
Stationery	90
Wages	3,000
General expenses	1,000
Rates	150

Adjustments: 31 December

- Stock unsold £4,300.
- Rates pre-paid £38.
- A provision for bad debts is to be made to equal 5% of debtors.
- Wages outstanding £120.
- Stationery unused £40.

Required:

(a) A trading and profit and loss account for the year ended 31 December.
(b) A balance sheet as at that date.

3. You work for a firm of accountants and have to prepare the final accounts for a client, S. Waugh. The following trial balance was extracted on February 19–5.

	Dr. £	Cr. £
Capital		60,000
Loan from A. Boarder		
(repayable 2001)		25,000
Premises	39,000	
Drawings	15,000	
Stock at 1/3/19–4	26,500	
Motor vans (at cost)	35,000	
Carriage outwards*	4,000	
Fixtures (at cost)	15,000	
Purchases and sales	173,200	319,200
Debtors & creditors	21,400	14,200
Returns inwards and		
outwards	1,200	800
Discounts allowed and		
received	4,000	2,100
Motor expenses	9,200	
Rent and rates	12,400	
Postage and telephone	3,100	
Wages and salaries	49,800	
Insurance	6,100	
Interest paid	2,000	
Advertising	4,200	
Bank/Cash	200	
	421,300	421,300

* Profit and Loss expenses.

Notes at 29/2/19–5:

- Stock at cost £31,000.
- A provision for bad debts is to be created to equal 4% of debtors.
- Rent is prepaid (£850).
- There is £140 still outstanding on interest payments.
- Advertising paid in advance is £146.

Required:

(a) Prepare the trading and profit and loss account for the year ended 28 February 19–5.
(b) Prepare the balance sheet as at 28 February 19–5.

[Institute of Commercial Management]

4. You work as an accounts clerk for a company which is preparing its first year's accounts. You are in the process of writing up various expense accounts and transferring amounts into the profit and loss account and balance sheet, for the year ending 31 December 19–5.

Rent of £600 is payable quarterly in arrears and the following payments have been made:

1 April £600; 5 July £600; 20 October £600.

Insurances: After a few months of trading the company realised that it had not insured against a number of possible risks. Details of policies taken out were as follows:

1 January   Annual premium of £700 paid in respect of occupiers' and employers' liability.

1 April   Annual premium of £600 paid on building insurance.

1 July   Stock insured and an annual premium of £800 paid.

Required:

(a) Write up the rent account for year ended 31 December 19–5 clearly showing the amount transferred to the profit and loss account.
(b) Write up the insurance account for year ended 31 December 19–5 clearly showing the amount transferred to the profit and loss account.
(c) What amount in respect of rent and insurance would you include as accruals/pre-payments in the balance sheet?

5. Jones started a new business on 1/12/19–4 and made the following transactions regarding insurance for the business:-

1/12/19–4	Took out cover for occupiers liability	Annual premium paid £1,000
1/2/19–5	Took out cover on buildings	Annual premium paid £1,200
1/5/19–5	Took out cover on stock	Annual premium paid £800.

Required:

Write up the insurance account in the ledger, clearly showing the amount to be transferred to the profit and loss account for the year ending 30/11/19–5.

6. The following trial balance was extracted from the accounts of A. Farney on 30 November 19–5

	Dr. £	Cr. £
Bad debts written off in year	400	
Cash in hand	250	
Cash at Bank	6,250	
Purchases/sales	23,500	80,000
Motor vehicles	12,500	
Rent and rates	1,250	
Light and heat	600	
Carriage outwards*	350	
Opening stock	18,750	
Commissions received		1,350
Capital		75,740
Drawings	8,500	
Returns	1,650	2,000
Office salaries	25,000	
Debtors creditors	23,600	5,650
Provisions for bad debts		1,860
Fixture and fittings	8,000	
Land and buildings	46,000	
Bank Loan (repayable 1999)		10,000
	176,600	176,6000

* Profit and Loss expense

Notes at 30 November 19–5:
● Closing stock £19,500.
● £800 owing on office salaries.
● Rates had been paid £150 in advance.
● £100 is owed for heating.
● Provision for bad debts is to be increased to 10% of the debtors.
● Interest on loan of £1,000 is still outstanding.
● It was decided to create a provision for discounts for customers at a rate of 1.25% p.a.

Required:

(a) Prepare the trading and profit and loss account for the year ended 30 November 19–5.
(b) Prepare the Balance sheet as at 30 November 19–5.

[Institute of Commercial Management]

7. During the financial period ending 31 December, Charcoal Ltd wrote off bad debts totalled £6,420. The company rather surprisingly, also received £850 from a customer previously written off as a bad a few years ago.

On 31 December, its debtors were 'aged' as follows:

No. of days outstanding	Debtors £	
Over 90 days	4,210	
90 days	7,560	
60 days	20,800	
30 days	56,440	89,010

The company had an opening provision for bad and doubtful debts of £6,400.

When the customers of over 90 days' debt were investigated, it was decided to write off £800 as bad.

The company's policy concerning the provision for bad debts is to use a percentage sliding scale off (round up to nearest £:

Over 90 days	75%
90 days	50%
60 days	10%
30 days	0%

Required:

On 31 December:

(a) The bad debts account.
(b) The provision for bad debts account.
   (Bad debts to be transferred to this account.)
(c) The figure to be transferred to the profit and loss account and the debtors' presentation in the balance sheet.
(d) Explain briefly the double-entry procedure when a bad debt is recovered.

[Association of Accounting Technicians]

8. Bradshaw Limited produced the following aged debtor analysis as at the end of the financial year:

	Balance	Current	One month	Two months	Three months and over
	£	£	£	£	£
Debtors at 31/12/19–4	120,000	50,000	30,000	30,000	10,000
Debtors at 31/19–5	180,000	90,000	60,000	25,000	5,000

In both years the provision for bad debts account is made up by providing for bad debts at:

20%	on debtors over 3 months
10%	on debtors aged 2 months
2%	on debtors aged 1 month
0.5%	on current debtors

Required:

(a) (i) Calculate the provision for bad debts as at 31/12/19–4.
(ii) Calculate the provision for bad debts as at 31/12/19–5.
(b) Prepare the provision for bad debts account over the two years note provision at at 1/1/19–4 was £4,900 CR).
(c) Briefly state with reasons if you think Bradshaw's credit control has improved over the two years.
(d) If a provision for discount allowed was created to equal 2% of net debtors, show how the debtors would be shown in the balance sheet as on 31/12/19–5.

[Institute of Commercial Management]

9. The trial balance as at 31 May 19–5 Tip Top Dealers Limited included the following:

	Dr. £	Cr. £
Purchases ledger control account	654.00	7,348.00
Sales ledger control account	12,360.00	716.00
Provision for doubtful debts		410.00
Bad debts recovered (received from K. L. Blaney)		970.00

Additional information:

- K. L. Blaney's bad debts was written off in the accounts for the year ended 31 May 19–4.
- It had now been decided to write off the following debts due to the company, as irrecoverable.

  L. Pink   £210.00
  G. Slack   £50.00

- The provision for doubtful debts account is not used for actual bad debts written off or for bad debts recovered.
- The company's continuing policy is to maintain a provision for doubtful debts at 2% of outstanding debtors at each accounting year end.
- Control accounts may have both debit and credit balances where some customers and suppliers have overpaid their accounts.

Required:

(a) Prepare the provision for doubtful debts account for the year ended 31 May 19–5 in the books of Tip Top Dealers Limited.
(b) Prepare the entry for debtors and creditors which will be included in the balance sheet as at 31 May 19–5 of Tip Top Dealers Limited.

[Association of Accounting Technicians]

10. The financial period for ABC Co. Ltd runs from 1 June to 31 May and it maintains separate accounts for rent & rates in the nominal ledger. Rent is payable quarterly in advance and was £4,800 pa, year ended 31 December 19–2 and £6,000 pa year ended 31 December 19–3.
    The following payments have been made by cheque:

19–2	£	
5 January	1,200	Quarter to 31/3
4 April	1,200	Quarter to 30/6
3 July	1,200	Quarter to 30/9
5 October	1,200	Quarter to 31/12
19–3		
4 January	1,500	Quarter to 31/3
6 April	1,500	Quarter to 31/6

Rates are assessed by the local council annually, year ending 31 March, and are payable in one lump sum by the 30 September of that year. The assessment for rates was £4,080 for the period ended 31 March 19–3 and £4,560 for the period ended 31 March 19–4.

The company paid the rates for the year to April 19–2 to 31 March 19–3 on 15 September 19–2 and intends to pay the following year's rates on 15 September 19–3.

Required:

Prepare the rent account and rates account for the period ended, 31 May 19–3. Show the appropriate figures to be recorded in the profit and loss account and the balance sheet for the same period.

[Association of Accounting Technicians]

CHAPTER 16

Capital Transactions

A business spends money on two types of expenditure. One concerns the purchase of fixed assets such as vehicles and equipment, and the other concerns money spent on running the business with expenses such as purchases of stock, wages and salaries, light and heat, stationery, etc.

Capital expenditure

Capital expenditure, therefore, is money which is spent on fixed assets or money spent on improving their value. For example, if a second-hand vehicle was purchased for £3,500, and later required a new engine costing £1,000 which was seen as better than the one before, then the value of the vehicle under fixed assets should be £4,500. This is capital expenditure rather than revenue expenditure.

Revenue expenditure

On the other hand, all aspects of expenditure in running the vehicle for business purposes, including petrol, repairs and maintenance, car tax and insurance, depreciation of the vehicle, replacement tyres, etc., would be treated as revenue expenditure: that is, it would be seen as part of the day-to-day running of the business.

Capital expenditure on fixed assets must also include any cost which is involved in bringing their value in to the business. If premises were purchased, the value capitalised would include solicitor's and estate agent's fees, land registry fees and any other cost involved with the purchase. If new plant and machinery were to be installed in a factory, the capital cost would include the carriage of it to the premises and all costs in the installation.

In the financial statements all capital expenditure is listed in the balance sheet under fixed assets, whereas all revenue expenditure appears as expenses in the trading and profit and loss account. Any unsold stock is also entered under current assets.

It is extremely important, therefore, to make the distinction between these two expenditure types, otherwise serious errors will arise when the financial statements are prepared. For example, if machinery was purchased for £5,000 and it was wrongly treated as purchases under revenue expenditure, this would have the effect of under-stating the value of fixed assets and over-stating the value of chargeable expenses. Result: profits are under-stated and fixed assets are under-stated. The Inland Revenue would also be displeased and would demand an adjustment to the accounts because it would reduce the tax payable on profits.

An article recently published in the *Daily Mail*, 'The roof falls in and upsets the taxman', is a case in point. The problem concerned the repairing of a roof and whether or not it was repairs or improvement to the roof, the subtle difference being that it can cost companies many more thousands of pounds in the payment of tax.

According to the Inland Revenue, repairs to fixed assets are allowable against tax whereas improvements to them are not. A company called Cableduct fell foul of the tax office when they had part of their factory roof replaced. In this case, the old roof was made of asbestos and corrugated iron and its replacement was a profile metal sheeting. The tax office said that this was an improvement in roof covering because the roof had a different covering from that of the original. In other words, it should have been treated as a capital item, not revenue expenditure.

This would have been a big blow to Cableduct because the roof cost £55,000. It was very old and although they had temporary repairs, the lot had to come down and be replaced. Thus the problem was the tax office regarding something to be replaced in its entirety as improvement and therefore a capital cost.

At the time, the company was struggling hard to break even and the tax office's decision was an additional burden it could have done without. The accountants of the company argued that a roof was only part of a building and that profile metal sheeting was not available when the original roof was built.

Fortunately for Cableduct, their accountants won the case, saving the company £13,750 in tax.

The purchase of fixed assets is made on the assumption that they will benefit the business over a number of accounting periods, whereas when money is spent on day-to-day expenses their value

TABLE 16.1   Capital and revenue expenditure

Transaction	Revenue expenditure Profit and loss account £	Capital expenditure Balance sheet £
1 New computer £2,500		2,500
2 Installation of computer £1,000		1,000
3 Gas and electricity £450	450	
4 Modernisation of premises £8,000		8,000
5 Office buildings painted (every 5 years) £6,000	6,000	
6 Wages and salaries £17,500	17,500	
7 New vehicle for manager £9,500		9,500
8 Stock for resale £3,200	3,200	
9 Motor expenses £800	800	
10 Modernisation of offices £20,000	5,000	15,000

is consumed within the accounting period. There are some exceptions to this, such as painting or repairs and maintenance of buildings which could last far longer than the financial period. However, as a general rule, this is treated as revenue expenditure.

Check Table 16.1 to see how capital and revenue expenditure are treated. In the final transaction, the office modernisation could have had some element of repairs in the cost (say, £5,000), and therefore this sum would have been apportioned to revenue expenditure rather than the whole amount capitalised.

The distinction between capital and revenue income

When fixed assets are sold, the sale value of them is referred to as capital income. The profit or loss from the disposal of them will depend on how much they are sold for and this will be recorded in the profit and loss account as:

> Other revenue:
> profit on sale of fixed asset

or,

> Expenses:
> loss on sale of fixed asset.

Revenue income refers to the normal trading activities of the business when it sells its goods or services, including further income from rent, interest, commission received, etc.

Provision for depreciation of fixed assets

Assets lose their value over periods of time. Car owners will understand that as their vehicles become older, they lose their value. This is the case with most fixed assets. As the assets age, they lose their value because of wear and tear, damage, obsolescence and any other reason which may diminish their value.

G. Harrison has £18,250 of fixed assets valued at cost:

Premises	£12,000
Fixtures	£ 2,000
Equipment	£ 3,000
Motor vehicle	£ 1,250

Premises are unlikely to depreciate; in fact the property may well appreciate in value rather than reduce in price. The other fixed assets will lose their value over time.

Purchasing an asset is really like buying an expense which will be divided over the accounting periods it is expected to last. The loss in value of an asset will be charged as an expense in each accounting period it is used. As the asset diminishes in value, the balance sheet will show the cost, the depreciation to date and the net value of the asset. For example:

Equipment £3,000. Harrison expects to replace it in 5 years and he expects to receive an estimated £400 on its disposal.

How much depreciation should be charged each year?

Cost: £3,000
– Residual
   value   £ 400   £2,600/5 years = £520 per annum

In each accounting period, Harrison will depreciate the equipment £520, charged as an expense in the profit and loss account.

This method of depreciation, where the *same* amount is depreciated each year, is known as the fixed instalment method (or straight line).

The balance sheet will show the equipment's net value each year over its estimated 'life' of 5 years (see Table 16.2).

Formula for fixed instalment method

$$\frac{\text{Cost of fixed asset} - \text{Residual value}}{\text{Life of asset}}$$

TABLE 16.2   Depreciation of equipment

	Cost £	Depreciation £	Net value [net book value] £
Year 1	3,000	520	2,480
2	3,000	1,040	1,960
3	3,000	1,560	1,440
4	3,000	2,080	920
5	3,000	2,600	400 (residual value)

TABLE 16.3   Profit and loss account, year ended 31 December

	£	£
Depreciation:		
Equipment	520	
Fixtures	500	
Motor vehicle	250	1,270

Harrison decides to depreciate his fixtures by 25% on cost:

Fixtures £2,000 @ 25% = £500 depreciation

He revalues his motor vehicle to £1,000 in line with its market value on 31 December:

Motor vehicle   £1,250
Market value   £1,000   =   £250 depreciation

What effect have these in the final accounts of Harrison on 31 December? See Table 16.3.

A total of £1,270 is charged as expenses and written off against profits for the year. The balance sheet at the year end is shown in Table 16.4.

Depreciation on cost or net value

Harrison depreciated his fixtures 25% on a cost of £500. If he chose, Harrison could apply a fixed rate percentage based on the net value of the asset each year. This would mean that the depreciation charge each year would be reduced over the life of the asset. Using this method, the asset would lose more of its value in the earlier years and less in the later years.

TABLE 16.4   Balance sheet as at 31 December

	Cost £	Depreciation £	Net £
Fixed Assets			
Premises	12,000	—	12,000
Fixtures	2,000	500	1,500
Equipment	3,000	520	2,480
Motor vehicle	1,250	250	1,000
	18,250	1,270	16,980

The reducing balance method of depreciation

If Harrison used this method on his fixtures, what rate percentage would he apply for depreciation if:

Cost	£2,000
Estimated residual value	£400
Estimated 'life'	4 years

Formula:

$$\text{Rate } \% = 1 - \sqrt[n]{\frac{\text{Residual value}}{\text{Cost of asset}}} \quad (n = \text{no. of years})$$

$$1 - \sqrt[4]{\frac{400}{2,000}} = 33\% \text{ depreciation per year on the net value of the asset}$$

If the reduced balance method was applied, an estimated 33% depreciation would be deducted each year, as shown in Table 16.5.

$$\begin{aligned}
\textit{Check:} \quad \frac{\text{Residual value}}{\text{of asset}} &= \frac{\text{Cost of}}{\text{asset}} (1 - \text{Rate } \%)^n \\
&= \text{£2,000} (1 - 33\%)^{4 \text{ years}} \\
&= \text{£2,000} (0.67)^4 \\
&= \text{£403}
\end{aligned}$$

TABLE 16.5   Effect of reduced balance method

Year	Reduced value	Depreciation @ 33%	Net value
	£	£	£
1	2,000	660	1,340
2	1,340	442	898
3	898	296	602
4	602	199	403 (residual value)

Nominal ledger recording of depreciation

The double-entry for depreciation is:

Dr.   Profit and Loss a/c with the expense
Cr.   Provision for depreciation of asset a/c

In the above example, the fixtures and fittings account would be depreciated each year by 33% on reduced balance. This would mean that £660 would be debited to profit and loss in Year 1 and £199 debited in Year 4 (see Table 16.6).

The balance sheet in Year 4 would then read as shown in Table 16.7.

At this point, Harrison estimated he would replace the fixtures at a residual value of about £400. Whether he gets £400 depends on what the market will give.

Disposal of an asset account

When an asset is disposed of it can be transferred to a 'disposal of asset' account. Any depreciation to date associated with the asset is also transferred to the disposal account. If the asset is sold under its net value (or book value), a loss on the sale is charged against the year's profit and loss account. If the asset is sold for more than its net value, the gain is transferred to profit and loss. If Harrison disposed of the fixtures after Year 4 for £350, he would have made a loss on the net value of £53. (See the nominal ledger entries in Table 16.8.)

By selling the fixtures for £350, Harrison has lost £53 on the book value of the asset. This is charged as an expense loss in the profit and loss account (see Table 16.9).

If the fixtures had been sold for *more* than the book value of

TABLE 16.6   Recording depreciation

	Dr. £	Cr. £	Balance £
Fixtures and Fittings a/c			
Year 1			
1 Jan. Bank			2,000 Dr.
Provision for Depreciation of Fixtures and Fittings a/c			
Year 1			
31 Dec. Profit and Loss		660	660 Cr.
Year 2			
31 Dec. Profit and Loss		442	1,102 Cr.
Year 3			
31 Dec. Profit and Loss		296	1,398 Cr.
Year 4			
31 Dec. Profit and Loss		199	1,597 Cr.

TABLE 16.7   Balance sheet in Year 4

	Cost £	Depreciation £	Net £
Fixed Assets			
Fixtures and fittings	2,000	1,597	403

£403, for example, if Harrison received £450, he would have made a gain of £47 on the book value. This would have been entered as a gain in the profit and loss account and included under 'any other Revenue'.

The use of the journal

The journal is used as a prime record for those transactions which are normally outside the scope of other subsidiary books such as the day books and Cash Book. Part VII deals with the journal in more detail but we need to mention it here because it is used for the sale and purchase of fixed assets on credit.

The journal has two columns to record the double entry of the transaction: for example, a business purchased a new motor vehicle (M20 DXY) for £8,000 in total from Henley Ford Motors Ltd

TABLE 16.8   Nominal ledger entries

		Dr. £	Cr. £	Balance £
Fixtures and Fittings a/c				
Year 4				
31 Dec.	Balance			2,000 Dr.
	Disposal a/c		2,000	—
Provision for Depreciation				
Fixtures and Fittings a/c				
Year 4				
31 Dec.	Balance			1,597 Cr.
	Disposal a/c	1,597		—
Disposal of Asset a/c				
Year 4				
31 Dec.	Fixtures and			
	fittings	2,000		2,000 Dr.
	Provision for			
	depreciation		1,597	403
	Bank		350	53
	Profit and loss		53	—

TABLE 16.9   Profit and loss a/c G. Harrison, (Year 4) ended 31 December

	£
Depreciation	
Fixtures	199
Loss on sale of asset	53

using its old vehicle (A29 GLA) in part-exchange, value £2,000 (see Table 16.10).

The journal is also used to record adjustments such as providing for depreciation and bad debts, accruals, pre-payments, etc., and the correction of errors. It is seen as a useful diary where an original entry can be made to facilitate the posting of transactions to the relevant accounts in the ledgers.

TABLE 16.10   Journal

Date	Details	Folio	Debit	Credit
July				
3	Motor Vehicle	N35	8,000	
	Disposal of fixed asset	N55		2,000
	Henley Ford Ltd	P45		6,000
	Being purchase of vehicle M20 DXY			
	on credit using A29 GLA in part-exchange			

Notes: (a) The debit entry is always recorded first.
(b) The credit entry is slightly indented,
(c) A short narrative is used to describe the transaction.
(d) The folio may be used to record the ledger account number.

Example

A business depreciates its equipment at the rate of 20 per cent per annum, based on the straight-line method, applied on a month by month basis. The residual value is nil. Its financial period commences 1 January.

The following information relates to the purchase, depreciation and disposal of the equipment over a period of three years:

1991   purchased equipment code A300 costing £4,800 on 1 January.
purchased equipment code A310 costing £3,600 on 1 October.

1992   purchased equipment code A320 costing £2,400 on 1 July.

1994   on 1 October, traded in the equipment bought on 1 January 1991 for £1,500 and purchased new equipment coded A330 for £8,000 from Jackson & Turner Ltd on credit, on the same date.

It was decided that the remaining economic life of the equipment code A320 purchased in July 1992 should be reduced and written off in total by 30 June 1995.

Required:

(a) Prepare the equipment account, provision for depreciation of equipment account and disposal of equipment account over the four years, ending 31 December 1994.
(b) Show the appropriate journal entries which are required for 1994.
(c) Prepare an extract of the profit and loss account for each of the four years for the period ending 31 December.
(d) Prepare an extract of the balance sheets as at the end of each of the four years as on 31 December.

The answers are shown in Tables 16.11–16.

TABLE 16.11   Equipment account

		Debit £	Credit £	Balance £
1991				
1/1	Bank A300	4,800		4,800 Dr.
1/10	Bank A310	3,600		8,400
1992				
1/7	Bank A320	2,400		10,800
1994				
1/10	Disposal A300		4,800	6,000
1/10	Disposal A300	1,500		
	J & T Ltd. A330	6,500		14,000

Statement of Standard Accounting Practice 12 (SSAP 12): Accounting for depreciation

SSAPs represent the profession's accounting standards. These statements are prepared for the purpose of standardising the preparation of business accounts. Part IV deals with the various statements in more detail. SSAP 12, Accounting for Depreciation, is the accounting profession's guide-line for how to deal with depreciation.
    In this statement the SSAP states:

Depreciation is defined as the loss in value of fixed assets over periods of time, that is, the measure of the wearing out, consumption or other reduction in the useful life of a fixed asset through use, time, obsoles-

TABLE 16.12   Provision for depreciation of equipment account

			Debit £	Credit £	Balance £
1991					
31/12	Profit and Loss	A300		960	
		A310		180	1,140 Cr.
1992					
31/12	Profit and Loss	A300		960	
		A310		720	
		A320		240	3,060
1993					
31/12	Profit and Loss	A300		960	
		A310		720	
		A320		480	5,220
1994					
1/10	Disposal*	A300	3,600		1,620
31/12	Profit and Loss	A300		720	
		A310		720	
		A320		1,120	
		A330		400	4,580

* Calculation: £960 p.a. X   3   =   £2,880
                      + £960   X   (3/4) =   £ 720   3,600

Calculation: £1,680 depreciation left for 1.5 years, therefore 1 year:
   2/3 X 1,680 = 1,120

TABLE 16.13   Disposal of fixed asset account

		Debit £	Credit £	Balance £
1994				
1/10	Equipment A300	4,800		4,800 Dr.
	Provision for depreciation		3,600	1,200
	Trade-in J & T		1,500	300 Cr.
31/12	Profit and loss	300		0

cence or market changes. Depreciation should be allocated so as to charge a fair proportion of the cost of the fixed asset to each accounting period expected to benefit from its use.

The standard is to provide depreciation of all fixed assets having a finite life. However, there are some exceptions, such as in-

TABLE 16.14   Journal

Date	Details	Folio	Debit £	Credit £
1994				
1/10	Equipment A330		8,000	
	Disposal A300			1,500
	J & T Ltd.			6,500
	Being purchase of new equipment using A300 as part-exchange			
1/10	Disposal A300		4,800	
	Equipment A300			4,800
	Provision for depreciation		3,600	
	Disposal			3,600
	Being disposal of old equipment, A300			
31/12	Disposal		300	
	Profit and loss			300
	Being profit on disposal of A300			
31/12	Profit and Loss: depreciation of equipment		2,960	
	Provision for depreciation of equipment			2,960
	Being depreciation of equipment for the year.			

TABLE 16.15   Extract of profit and loss account for year ended 31 December

Year	Expenses	£
1991	Depreciation of Eqpt	1,140
1992	"	1,920
1993	"	2,160
1994	"	2,960
	Other Revenue:	
1994	Profit on disposal of fixed asset	300

TABLE 16.16 **Extract of balance sheet as at year ended 31 December**

Fixed assets		Cost £	Depreciation £	Net book value £
1991	Equipment	8,400	1,140	7,260
1992	Equipment	10,800	3,060	7,740
1993	Equipment	10,800	5,220	5,580
1994	Equipment	14,000	4,580	9,420

vestments, goodwill and freehold land. Buildings should be depreciated even though their market value may have increased. It is still prudent to depreciate them because they do deteriorate with time and need repairs and maintenance. The straight-line method is seen as the most common depreciation type, although it may not be the most appropriate for all types of assets. The standard indicates that a change of method (or base) is only acceptable if this is thought to give a better or fairer allocation of cost in the final accounts.

The standard recognises that goodwill (the value of a business in terms of its custom and reputation) should be written off as soon as is practicable, particularly if this is the cost arising from the purchase of a business.

The term 'amortisation' means the same as depreciation in that something is written off over its useful life. This can apply to the leasing of fixed assets whereby a bank or a finance house provides finance under a lease contract which will enable a business to acquire the use of a fixed asset over a fixed contractual period of time, usually over the greater part of its useful life. The business can then treat this acquisition as a fixed asset and amortise its writing-off in the profit and loss account and balance sheet in the normal way. However, the title of the fixed asset remains that of the lessor (providing the finance) not the lessee (acquiring the asset).

This should not be confused with that of an operating lease, where a fixed asset can be rented out at various times to different uses and where the rental charge for this use is treated as an expense in the profit and loss account. It is not recorded as a fixed asset in the balance sheet. SSAP 21, accounting for leases and hire-purchase contracts, is the profession's standard and guide-line which deals with this topic and is further discussed in Chapter 21.

The use of a fixed assets register

The purchase of capital transactions can cost a business large sums of money. It may have a fleet of motor vehicles or extensive factory equipment, plant and machinery, office equipment, etc. The journal, as we have already pointed out, can be used as a book of prime entry to record the buying of these fixed assets. Yet is this sufficient to record and control what happens to them? There could be a whole list of valuable fixed assets housed in various departments or factory floors, and occasionally some of these would be scrapped or sold off and replaced by new ones. What is required, therefore, is a fixed asset register which lists all these assets of a business, together with other important facts about each of them, such as:

(a) the date of purchase;
(b) description of the asset;
(c) internal control number or other number for identification;
(d) the location of the asset;
(e) the cost of the asset;
(f) the method of depreciation used;
(g) the estimated scrap/sale value;
(h) the estimated useful life of the asset;
(i) its disposal date and authorisation of disposal;
(j) the proceeds, if any, on disposal.

The fixed asset register is not part of the double entry system; it is simply used for the purpose of internal control. The register can be used to make physical checks for the location of fixed assets and the person (the supervisor or manager) who is in charge of them. The register should also be reconciled with the fixed asset accounts in the nominal ledger to ensure that all aspects match. In other words, if an asset is sold off, this should be properly authorised, the asset released, the register completed and the necessary entries made in the journal and ledger accounts.

If any discrepancies do arise as a result of checks between the ledger accounts and the register, these must be investigated to find out why there are differences. It could be that there is a delay in sending the appropriate authorisation form when an asset has been disposed of. It could, of course, be far more serious in that theft could have occurred. Whatever the cause of any discrepancy, a solution should be found and the appropriate action taken. It may also arise that some assets may require an adjustment in their expected life due to excessive wear and tear. Again, the proper authority to change any estimations to the life of an asset must have the correct authorisation, and the information should be communicated to the accounts department who will need to make the right adjustments in the journal and ledger.

The type of register for fixed assets will vary from one business to another. Some may have an individual page devoted to each type of fixed asset. Others may have columns across the page for various headings and list the assets in an organised way (for example, by department, or by the type of asset it is).

Tables 16.17 and 16.18 are examples of fixed asset registers. The first is a detailed register which has a full sheet of information given to each fixed asset. Table 16.18 lists the fixed assets as on a specific date.

TABLE 16.17   Fixed asset register Stringer & Mitchell Ltd

Title of Asset:	IBM Word Processor, 1286
Date of Purchase:	12 June 1994
Internal Control No.	377342/9
Location:	Personnel Office
Cost	£2,800 + VAT
Supplier	Lansdowne Computer Services Ltd
Nominal Ledger Account No.	N210
Method of Depreciation:	20% per annum Straight-Line
Estimated Residual Value:	200.00
Estimated Life:	5 years
Cumulative Depreciation:	560.00
Depreciation Account:	N220
Proceeds from Sale:	
Date of Disposal:	
Disposal Authorisation Number:	
Comments:	

When the IBM computer is finally disposed of, the rest of the register can be completed, including the authorisation number of the disposal form (the form requiring the authority to properly dispose of a fixed asset). By keeping such a detailed register, there is far greater control in the purchase, depreciation, movements and final disposal of a company's fixed assets.

In Table 16.18, a list of fixed assets is recorded giving details of individual items, although not in the same depth as in the first.

This is an example of a single page of a fixed asset register which, in the practice of this particular business, carries on for several pages, identifying not less than 72 individual fixed assets at a total

TABLE 16.18   Register of Fixed Assets as on 31 December 19–5

Compaq 386N	
Code No. 025	
Cost as at 1/1/19–5 :	2,600
Depreciation (straight-line)	
at 20% p.a. :	520
Net Book Value	2,080
Location: General Office	
Expected residual value: 10% cost	
Electronic Typewriter 4572	
Code No. 030	
Cost as at 30/3/19–5 :	360
Depreciation (straight-line)	
at 20% p.a. :	54
Net book value	306
Location: Technical Office	
Expected residual value: scrap 0	
Amstrad Computer 1428	
Code No. 028	
Cost as at 30/6/19–4 :	780
Depreciation (straight-line)	
at 20% p.a. :	234
Net book value:	546
Location: General Office	
Expected residual value: scrap 0	
Motor Vehicle: Peugeot GLA 242X	
Cost as at 30/04/19–4 :	10,800
Depreciation (reducing-balance)	
at 25% p.a. :	3,881
Net book value:	6,919
Location: Sales Director (RCP)	
Expected residual value £2000	

cost value of £286,540. It is not surprising, therefore, that a fixed asset register is required. There is a great amount of investment capital tied up in the purchase of them and a tight control of the details concerning each fixed asset is required.

A summary of major adjustments used in final accounts

Table 16.19 provides a summary of these.

TABLE 16.19   A summary

Type of adjustment	Effect on final accounts	
	Trading and profit and loss	Balance sheet
1. Accrued expense	Increase expense	Current liability
2. Pre-payment	Reduce expense	Current asset
3. Accrued revenue	Increase revenue	Current asset
4. Provision for bad debts (increase)	Increase expense	Reduce debtors
5. Personal stock drawings	Reduce cost of sales	Reduce capital
6. Provision for depreciation	Increase expense	Reduced fixed asset
7. Provision for Discounts	Increase expense	Reduce debtors (after provision)

Example

A trial balance was extracted from the accounts of R. Horden on 31 October 19–5, as shown in Table 16.20.

TABLE 16.20 R. Horden's trial balance

	Dr. £	Cr. £
Cash at bank/in hand	6,500	
Purchases/sales	26,000	75,100
Motor vehicles	12,500	
Provision for depreciation (motor vehicles)		5,000
Rent and rates	1,400	
Light and heat	700	
Carriage inwards*	500	
Carriage outwards	400	
Opening stock	18,300	
Commissions received		1,500
Drawings	9,000	
Returns	1,800	1,400
Office salaries	26,000	
Debtors/creditors	24,000	6,000
Provision for bad debts		2,000
Fixtures and fittings	8,000	
Provision for depreciations (fixtures and fittings)		2,400
Land and buildings	50,000	
Bank loan (repayable 1998)		10,000
Interest on loan (10% p.a.)	1,000	
Capital		82,700
	186,100	186,100

* Carriage inwards – a trading a/c expense.
Notes: 31 October 19–5
      (a) Closing stock £21,000.
      (b) Revenue accrued: £420 still to be received on commission.
      (c) Rates had been paid £200 in advance.
      (d) £120 is owed for electricity (heating and lighting).
      (e) Provision for bad debts is to be increased to 10% of the debtors.
      (f) Provision for depreciation of 10% p.a. on cost is to be made on fixtures and fittings.
      (g) Provision for depreciation of 20% p.a. on book value of motor vehicles.
      (h) During the financial year, R. Horden took goods for own use from the business which cost £800.

Required:

Prepare the trading & profit & loss account of R. Horden for the year ended 31 October 19–5 and a balance sheet as at that date. (The answers are shown in Tables 16.21 and 16.22.)

TABLE 16.21   R. Horden, trading and profit and loss account for year ending 31 October 19–5

	£	£	£
Sales			75,100
Less returns inwards			1,800
			73,300
Less Cost of Sales:			
Opening stock		18,300	
Purchases	26,000		
add carriage inwards	500		
less returns outwards	1,400		
less goods for own use	800	24,300	
		42,600	
Closing Stock		21,000	21,600
	Gross Profit		51,700
Rent and rates paid	1,400		
Rent and rates in advance	200	1,200	
Light and heat paid	700		
Light and heat owing	120	820	
Carriage outwards		400	
Office salaries paid		26,000	
Interest on loan		1,000	
Increase in provisions for bad debts		400	
Provision for depreciation – fix. & fitt.		800	
Provision for depreciation – vehicles		1,500	32,120
			19,580
Add other revenue – Commissions received	1,500		
Add other revenue – Accrued	420		1,920
	Net Profit		21,500

TABLE 16.22 R. Horden balance sheet as at 31 October 19–5

	£	£	£
	(Cost)	(Cumulative depn)	(Net book value)
Fixed Assets			
Land and buildings	50,000	—	50,000
Fixtures and fittings	8,000	3,200	4,800
Motor vehicles	12,500	6,500	6,000
	70,500	9,700	60,800
Current Assets			
Stock	21,000		
Debtors 24,000			
Less provision for bad debts 2,400	21,600		
Pre-payments	200		
Bank/cash	6,500		
Revenue accrued	420	49,720	
Current Liabilities			
Trade creditors			
Accruals	6,000		
	120	6,120	
Net current assets			43,600
Capital employed			104,400
Long Term Liabilities			
Bank loan			10,000
			94,400
Financed by:			
Capital	82,700		
Add net profit	21,500	104,200	
Less drawings (9,000 + 800)		9,800	94,400

Questions

1. Classify the following items as to whether they are capital or revenue expenditure:

   (a) The purchase of a new IBM computer for the office.
   (b) Cost of software for the use of the new computer.
   (c) Cost of computer paper.

(d) A refit of the stockroom with new shelving.

(e) The payment of gas and electricity bills.

(f) The purchase of stock for resale.

(g) Discounts allowed on the sale of stock.

(h) The acquisition of a new motor vehicle for the supervisor's use.

(i) The road tax and insurance of the vehicle.

(j) The repairs and maintenance of the motor vehicle.

(k) The cost of new floppy disks for the use of the computer.

(l) The complete decoration of the offices to last a number of years.

2. In the setting-up of a new business for Jack Ramsgate, classify the following between capital and revenue expenditure:

(a) The purchase price of premises.

(b) The estate and solicitor's fees.

(c) The cost of a computer system.

(d) The cost of delivery charges and installation fees of the new computer.

(e) The cost of training of personnel on the computer system.

(f) Running repairs to the computer.

(g) Oil and petrol for the motor vehicle.

(h) An extension built on the premises.

(i) The extension is painted on completion.

(j) The extension is repainted six months later.

(k) Improved roofing of the premises is installed two years later.

(l) The cost of an advertising campaign which is expected to benefit a number of accounting periods.

3. (a) Why is it important to make the distinction between capital and revenue costs as those stated in the two previous questions?

(b) If the cost of a computer, £2,800, was recorded in the purchases account and the cost of the vehicle insurances (£480) was recorded in the motor vehicles account, what effect, if any, would it have on the final accounts?

4. (a) Jim Barlow is the owner of a taxi business and his financial year runs from 1 July to 30 June. On 1 July

19–5 he had two vehicles, one a Ford purchased on 10 January 19–3 for £10,000 and the other, a Toyota, purchased on 12 August 19–3 for £8,000.

During November 19–5, Jim Barlow decided to replace the Ford and trade it in for a new Mercedes costing £15,500. Jim took delivery of the new car on 4 November 19–5. The garage accepted the Ford together with a cheque for £9,500 in payment.

Vehicles are depreciated at 10% per annum on the reducing balance method (alternatively known as diminishing balance), with a full year's depreciation charged in the year of purchase and no depreciation charged in the year a vehicle is disposed of.

Required:

(i) Calculate the value of the Ford and Toyota vehicles as on 1 July 19–5.

(ii) Write up the journal entries and draw up the appropriate ledger accounts for motor vehicles, provision for the depreciation of motor vehicles and the disposal of motor vehicles accounts for the year ended 30 June 19–6. Show clearly any transfers to the profit and loss account and the balance sheet.

(iii) If depreciation was applied on a month by month basis (in the final year only), how would it affect the ledger accounts on the trade-in and purchase of the new Mercedes in November 19–5? How would the final account be affected?

(b) When a fixed asset is purchased, a business will use depreciation as a means to set aside cash each year so that it eventually has the funds to purchase a replacement when it becomes necessary.

Required:

Comment briefly on this statement.

(Association of Accounting Technicians)

5. Prepare a trial balance from the following ledger account of Tom Dooley as at year ending 31 December.

Prepare trading, profit and loss accounts and balance sheet taking into consideration the adjustments at the foot of the accounts.

a/c	£	Dr. £	Cr. £
Capital	9,048		
Debtors	1,780		
Creditors	4,369		
Cash	125		
Bank	7,235		
Plant and machinery	2,800		
Motor vehicles	2,200		
Prov. for depreciation (plant and machinery)	560		
Prov. for depreciation (motor vehicles)	330		
Prov. for bad debts	60		
Rent received	1,160		
Wages and salaries	3,850		
Rent	830		
Rates, insurances	785		
Light and heat	325		
Carriage out	84		
Returns inwards	27		
Returns outwards	140		
Stock (1 Jan.)	2,362		
Purchases	5,990		
Sales	12,726		

Notes: (31 December)
1. Stock-taking figure £2,950.
2. Bad debts provision increased to £90.
3. Provide for depreciation on plant and machinery 10% of cost.
4. Provide for depreciation on motor vehicles 20% on book valuation.

6. The following accounts relate to Arthur Jones, a local businessman, as at year ended 31 December.

Prepare trading, profit and loss accounts and balance sheet from the information below:

Trial Balance as on 31 December

	Dr. £	Cr. £
Capital – A. S. Jones		71,000
Premises	57,500	
Equipment	23,000	
Provision for depreciation of equipment		6,000
Motor van	8,000	
Provision for depreciation of motor van		2,000
Stock (Jan. 1)	8,300	
Purchases and sales	30,800	66,600
Returns inward	700	
Returns outward		900
Wages	16,500	
Carriage inwards*	500	
Carriage outwards	400	
Commission received		500
Bank interest	350	
Lighting and heating	1,650	
Postage and stationery	600	
Insurance	1,200	
Telephone	500	
Rent receivable		750
Debtors, creditors	7,000	11,750
Bank	1,950	
Discount	100	
Bad debts	450	
	159,500	159,500

* Trading account.

Adjustments to be taken into account 31 December:

(a) Unsold stock valued at cost £9,500.
(b) Wages due to be paid £550.
(c) Jones, the proprietor, takes goods for own use valued at cost £800.
(d) Pre-paid stationery – unused stock valued £95.
(e) Rent receivable still outstanding £180.

(f) Depreciation: Motor van revalued to £4,500.
　　　　　　　　Equipment depreciated 20% on net value.
(g) Provision for bad and doubtful debts to equal 10% of
　　debtors.

7. The trial balance of ABC Co. as on 31 December was as
　follows:

Account	Dr. £	Cr. £
Premises (cost)	24,000	
Fixtures and fittings (cost)	4,000	
Motor vehicle (cost)	5,000	
Bank	3,305	
Stock	5,750	
Debtors	20,500	
Creditors		24,220
Loan (3 years) 10% p.a.		15,500
Capital: ABC Co.		18,000
Sales		21,274
Commission received		485
Discount		557
Salaries	2,864	
Light and heat	122	
Petty cash expenses	44	
General expenses	268	
Purchases	14,090	
Returns outward		484
Returns inward	577	
	78,520	78,520

The following information is to be taken into account as
on 31 December:

● The value of unsold stock £6,259.
● Gas bill still outstanding £42.
● Under general expenses, stationery unused was £70.
● The owner took stock for his own use £2,100.
● Depreciation:Furniture and fittings 10% on cost.
　　　　　　　　Motor vehicle revalued to £3,750.
● Provision for bad debts 5% of debtors.
● 6 months interest on loan unpaid.

Required:

(a) Prepare the trading and profit and loss account of ABC Co. for the year ended 31 December.
(b) A balance sheet as at that date, showing working capital and capital employed.
(c) Calculate the working capital ratio (current assets/current liabilities). Is it adequate?

8. The following trial balance was extracted from the accounts of Jack Jones, 31 December.
   Prepare trading and profit and loss accounts for the year and a balance sheet as at that date.

A/c	Dr. £	Cr. £
Premises	14,600	
Motor vehicles	1,250	
Provision for depn		500
Cash	125	
Bank	1,625	
Fixtures, fittings	800	
Provision for depn		240
Debtors	2,360	
Provision for bad debts		186
Bank loan		12,100
Creditors		565
Sales		7,260
Purchases	2,350	
Rent, rates	125	
Light and heat	60	
Carriage in*	50	
Carriage out	35	
Stock (1 Jan.)	1,825	
Commission		135
Returns	165	160
Wages (warehouse)*	1,520	
Office salaries	980	
Capital		7,574
Drawings	850	
	28,720	28,720

* Trading account.

Notes: 1. Stock (end) £1,950.   5. Depreciation of fixtures and
2. Warehouse wages due £20.   fittings by 10% of cost.
3. Pre-paid rates £15.   6. Motor vehicles revalued £500

4. Invoice of £5 electricity unpaid.

(net).
7. Provision for bad debts adjusted to equal 10% of debtors.

9. (a) Identify the factors which can cause fixed assets to depreciate.
   (b) Using these factors which depreciate fixed assets, which of them do you consider significant in the following:

   ● A new high-tech machine capable of increased productivity
   ● The purchase of a motor vehicle
   ● The mining of minerals
   ● The purchase of land
   ● A new long-term lease of a fleet of vehicles

   (c) What do you think are two important points which can be taken from SSAP 12 as regards the applying of depreciation to various fixed assets?
   (d) Outline the need for a business to maintain a fixed asset register.
   (e) What purpose does the use of the journal serve as regards capital transactions?

10. The following information relates to the fixed assets of Rockbourne Company Limited on 1 January 1987:

	Cost £	Depreciation to 31/12/86 £
Premises	1,200,000	—
Plant and machinery	950,000	413,500
	2,150,000	413,500

The company depreciates plant and machinery at the rate of 10% p.a., straight-line basis (a full year's depreciation being provided in the year of purchase, but none in the year of sale).

During the year ending 31 December 1987 the following took place:

● The Directors decided to revalue the premises to £1,500,000.
● Plant and machinery purchased in 1983 for £200,000 was sold in October 1987 for £130,000.
● New plant was purchased in July 1987 for £150,000.

Required:

Provide relevant ledger accounts including an asset disposal account as they would appear on 31 December 1987.

11. The following trial balance was extracted from the accounts of Harry Gallagher on 31 December:
    You are to prepare the trading and profit and loss account for the period and a balance sheet as at that date.

Trial Balance
H. Gallagher as on 31 December

	Dr. £	Cr. £
Sales		37,615
Purchases	26,470	
Returns	1,205	1,315
Stock (1/1)	2,355	
Carriage inwards	442	
Carriage outwards	580	
Drawings	2,560	
Maintenance and rates	998	
Insurance, telephone	334	
Light, heat	546	
Postage, stationery	350	
Bad debts	175	
Motor expenses	560	
Wages	6,285	
Provision for bad debts		300
Provision for discounts		65
Cash	500	
Bank overdraft		3,005
Equipment (cost)	21,600	
Prov. for depreciation of equipment (1/1)		2,160
Motor van (cost)	2,500	
Prov. for depreciation of van (1/1)		500
Debtors, creditors	12,420	12,560
Bank loan [Long term]		3,500
Capital: Gallagher		18,860
	79,880	79,880

Additional information was available on 31 December:

(a) Unsold stock was valued £3,895.
(b) Accrued expenses: wages £185, electricity bill £90.
(c) Pre-payments: stock of unused stationery £110, insurance £80.
(d) The bad debts provision is to be adjusted to equal 5% of debtors.
    The provision for discounts is to be adjusted to equal 1.5% of debtors.
(e) Depreciation: the van at 20% on the reducing balance method. Equipment at 10% of cost.
(f) Gallagher took £800 stock for personal use.

[BTEC National]

12. You are employed in the accounts department of Stringer & Mitchell Ltd, a small family-run wholesaling firm of fruit and vegetables. Your immediate boss, James Hardwick, the accountant, has made you responsible for maintaining the general ledger and records relating to the fixed asset register. Amongst the fixed assets, the company has various items of equipment and also has three delivery vans. You have been asked to maintain the records of the motor vehicles register and also make some necessary adjustments for the final accounts for the period ending 31 March 1993.

The fixed asset register for motor vehicles is:

Account number	Description of vehicle	Registration/ engine no.	Purchase date	Cost	Accum. depn.	Net book value
A229/1	Vauxhall	H29/GLB E2283694/88	1/10/89	8,500		
A229/2	Ford trans.	J928/BFC E3948255/89	1/04/90	12,000		
A229/3	Ford trans.	K342/CDF E4927622/91	1/04/92	16,000		

The register continues across:

Disposal date	Auth. no.	Proceeds of sale/scrap	Estimated residual value	Expected life (yrs)	
			2,500	5	A229/1
			2,000	8	A229/2
			4,000	8	A229/3

The company's policy on its motor vehicles is to provide depreciation at the end of each financial year using the straight-line method, applied on a monthly basis.

During the financial period ending 31 March 1993, the following transactions had occurred:

● On 30 June 1992, the Vauxhall van (H29 GLB) was traded in for a newer model Vauxhall (K897 JWX, Engine No. E5772436/92); the trade-in value was £5,000. The new vehicle price was £15,000 and the balance due was on credit from Harbour View Finance Corp. Ltd. The expected residual value of the new van is £4,000 after an estimated running life of 5 years.

● It was also decided on 31 March 1993 to reduce the remaining economic life of the Ford transit (J928 BFC) by half, from 6 to 3 years.

(a) Show all appropriate journal entries required which affect the above transactions. Use narratives.

(b) Record in the general ledger all the accounts relating to motor vehicles, including the provision for depreciation and a disposal of fixed asset account, as they would appear on 31 March 1993. Note that all vehicle acquisitions are recorded in a single motor vehicle account, number A229.

(c) Produce an extract for the final accounts which will show the correct figures to be transferred to the profit and loss account and the balance sheet as on 31 March 1993.

(d) You are to complete the fixed asset register for motor vehicles (draw up your own from the data provided), as it would appear on 31 March 1993. For the disposal of the Vauxhall van (H29 GLB) you are to devise and raise an asset disposal authorisation form.

Chapter 17

Partnership Accounts

A partnership is defined as two or more persons in business with a view to making a profit. There is little legal constraint and most partnerships can be formed without complex documentation or procedure. As far as the law is concerned, the 1890 Partnership Act and 1907 Partnership Act apply – the former to all partners and the latter to limited partners. A limited partner is one who has limited liability and has no control in the partnership because he is not involved in any decision-making in the business. Only general partners have the right to control the partnership. However, general partners do not have the advantage of limited liability and are therefore liable to the debts of the enterprise, even up to the extent of their personal wealth.

It is advisable that a *written agreement* should exist between partners (rather than merely a verbal arrangement(so that, if disagreements arise between the partners, the written agreement can be referred to in a court of law. A 'Deeds of Partnership' is such an agreement, where a contract is signed by each partner and witnessed, preferably by a member of the legal profession, outlining the proposed agreements by the partners. Agreements between partners usually include the following important items:

(a) the amount of capital to be contributed by each partner;
(b) how profits and losses are to be shared (for example, equally, or by some specific ratio);
(c) whether salaries are to be paid;
(d) whether interest is to be paid on capital or charged on partners' drawings from the business;
(e) whether loans by partners to the business are to be paid interest and at what rate;
(f) the level of control to which each partner is entitled;
(g) the length of time the partnership is to exist;
(h) the procedure to be followed in the event of a new partner

being admitted or an existing partner leaving;
(i) the procedure to be followed in the event of the partnership being dissolved (wound up).

In the event of non-agreement between partners, where a Deeds of Partnership does not exist, the 1890 Partnership Act applies. Under Section 24, the Act states:

(a) profit or loss is to be borne *equally* between partners;
(b) no interest is to be paid on capital or charged on drawings;
(c) no partnership salaries are to be paid;
(d) loans by partners are to be paid interest at 5% per annum.

Partnership final accounts

The final accounts of a partnership are prepared identically to those of other business units as far as the calculation of profit and the preparation of a balance sheet are concerned.

The partnership does have, however, an 'appropriation account' to show how profits (or losses) are shared between partners. This account is prepared after profit/loss is calculated. An example is given in Table 17.1.

Peter and Jane agreed to share profits equally. Other items such as salaries, interest paid on capital and interest charged on drawings are accounted for, leaving a residue of £4,350 to be divided equally.

Partners' current accounts

A current account is a record of a partner's personal finances in the business. Items recorded in this account include additions such as partner's share of profits, interest paid on capital, salary paid and any other money deposited by the partner. Deductions from the current account are mainly drawings of cash or stock and the interest charged on drawings.

The appropriation account at the end of the accounting period acts as a source of entry to the current account (in effect, being part of the double-entry): an example of nominal ledger entries is given in Table 17.2.

The balance sheet

In the balance sheet, each of the partners' capital and current account balances are recorded under the section 'financed by'. See Table 17.3.

TABLE 17.1 Profit and loss appropriation account of Peter & Jane (year ended 31 December ...)

	£	£	£
Net Profit			7,500
deduct:			
Salary: Peter	1,500		
Jane	1,500	3,000	
Interest on Capital (5%):			
Peter	250		
Jane	250	500	3,500
			4,000
Add:			
Interest charged on Drawings:			
Peter	200		
Jane	150		350
			4,350
Share of Profits:			
Peter	2,175		
Jane	2,175		4,350

TABLE 17.2 Nominal ledger

	Dr. £	Cr. £	Balance £
Current Account: Peter			
Dec. 31 Balance			200 Cr.
Salary		1,500	1,700
Interest on Capital		250	1,950
Profit		2,175	4,125
Drawings	2,000		2,125
Interest charged	200		1,925
Current Account: Jane			
Dec. 31 Balance			500 Dr.
Salary		1,500	1,000 Cr.
Interest on Capital		250	1,250
Profit		2,175	3,425
Drawings	1,500		1,925
Interest charged	150		1,775

Note: A debit balance in the partner's current account above indicates that the partner has overdrawn on his account.

TABLE 17.3   Balance sheet (extract) of Peter & Jane as at 31 December . . .

	£	£	£
Net Assets			13,700
Financed by:			
Capital accounts:			
Peter	5,000		
Jane	5,000	10,000	
Current accounts:			
Peter	1,925		
Jane	1,775	3,700	13,700

Example

Jim, Julie and Jake are in partnership, sharing profit and losses in the ratio of 2:2:1 respectively. During the financial year ended 31 December the net profit was £16,810. The partners' drawings for the year were:

Jim	£3,150
Julie	£3,000
Jake	£1,800

and the interest charged:

Jim	£320
Julie	£300
Jake	£275

These charges were based on average drawings over the year. Interest is to be paid on partners' capital accounts at the rate of 5% per annum. Only Julie is entitled to a salary of £1,500 per annum because of her extra duties. The balances of the partners' other accounts were as shown in Table 17.4.

Required:

(a) Prepare the partners' profit and loss appropriation account and partners' current accounts for year ended 31 December.

TABLE 17.4 Balances in the partners' accounts

Partner	Capital accounts	Current accounts
Jim	£10,000	£700 Cr.
Julie	£10,000	£450 Dr.
Jake	£ 5,000	£350 Dr.

TABLE 17.5 Profit and loss appropriation account

	£	£	£
Net Profit:			16,810
Salary: Julie		1,500	
– Interest on capital:			
Jim	500		
Julie	500		
Jake	250	1,250	2,750
			14,060
+ Interest changed on drawings:			
Jim	320		
Julie	300		
Jake	275		895
			14,955
Share of capital:			
Jim		5,982	
Julie		5,982	
Jake		2,991	14,955

Notes: After contingencies of salary, interest paid and interest charged, the residue was £14,955. This was divided in the ratio agreed by the partners of 2:2:1 respectively.

(b) Prepare an extract of the 'financed by' section of the partners' balance sheet as at 31 December.
(c) What is the difference between a general partner and a limited partner?

Answers:

(a) The profit and loss appropriation account of Jim, Julie & Jake for year ended 31 December is shown in Table 17.5 and their current accounts in Table 17.6.
(b) An extract from the partners' balance sheet is shown in Table 17.7.

TABLE 17.6   Partners' current accounts as shown in the nominal ledger

	Dr. £	Cr. £	Balance £
Current a/c Jim			
Dec. 31 Balance			700 Cr.
Interest on Capital		500	1,200
Profit		5,982	7,182
Drawings	3,150		4,032
Interest charged	320		3,712
Current a/c Julie			
Dec. 31 Balance			450 Dr.
Interest on Capital		500	50 Cr.
Salary		1,500	1,550
Profit		5,982	7,532
Drawings	3,000		4,532
Interest charged	300		4,232
Current a/c Jake			
Dec. 31 Balance			350 Dr.
Interest on Capital		250	100 Dr.
Profit		2,991	2,891 Cr.
Drawings	1,800		1,091
Interest charged	275		816

TABLE 17.7 Balance sheet of Jim, Julie & Jake as at 31 December . . .

	£	£	£
Net Assets			33,760
Financed by:			
Capital: Jim	10,000		
Julie	10,000		
Jake	5,000	25,000	
Current a/c's:			
Jim	3,712		
Julie	4,232		
Jake	816	8,760	33,760

(c) A general partner has a right to share in the decisions which affect the partnership and therefore shares in the control of the business. He is not protected by limited liability and therein he is liable for the debts of the business, even up to his own personal wealth.

A limited partner is one who has registered as a limited partner with the Registrar and is protected with limited liability. This means that, in the event of bankruptcy and debt, he is only liable to the extent of his capital contributed to the business and not his personal wealth. However, he must never be part of partnership decisions and holds no control or active part in the business. Retired partners sometimes wish to remain a part of the partnership, at the same time relinquishing control, and hence apply to become limited partners.

Goodwill

The term 'goodwill' may arise in a business because it may have earned itself a good name or reputation built up over a period of time through its business activities. The value of goodwill can be calculated on certain factors like average sales over a period of time, or profits earned over a number of accounting periods.

When a business is sold, the net value of the assets is assessed and a value may then be paid towards goodwill. If, for example, a business has an average turnover (sales) of £30,000 per annum based on the last three years' sales, the vendor (the seller) may want something in the region of 10 to 20% goodwill. The buyer and seller may agree on anything between £3,000 and £6,000 depending on how much the buyer wants to buy and how much he can afford.

If a new partner is admitted to the partnership, he may well have to pay the existing partners a sum for goodwill. Example two partners A and B decided to admit partner C to help expand the business and also to inject new capital. The three of them mutually agree to the proposal that C is to pay £2,000 as goodwill and that this should be credited to the partners' A and B capital accounts:

Double-entry: Dr. Bank a/c £2,000
                 Cr. Partner A   £1,000
                      Partner B   £1,000

Partner C is to introduce £3,000 of capital into the business which will also be debited to the bank account:

Double-entry: Dr. Bank a/c £3,000
                         Cr. Partner C   £3,000

Alternatively, if partner C had insufficient money to pay the £2,000 goodwill, a goodwill account may have been debited and partners A and B still credited with the £1,000 to their capital:

Double-entry: Dr. Goodwill a/c   £2,000
                         (Asset)
                         Cr. Partner A   £1,000
                              Partner B   £1,000

The writing-off of goodwill

It has been standard practice to write off the value of goodwill arising from the purchase or the commencement of a new business partnership. SSAP 22 (see Chapter 23) recognises that it is difficult to separate goodwill from the business as a whole, and it is largely a subjective valuation agreed by the partners. It has not been the practice to recognise goodwill in published accounts; therefore, if a value has been placed on a business, or partners come together with an agreed sum for goodwill, it ought to be written off as soon as practicable on the basis of the agreed partnership profit-sharing ratio. If this is not stated, it will be assumed that it is written off equally.

If goodwill is to be written off either immediately or over a period of time, the partners' capital accounts will be debited and the goodwill account credited.

Example

Tom, Dick and Harry were separate traders for a number of years and now have decided to form a partnership bringing their assets and liabilities into the new business. Their capital accounts at the time, 1 January, were:

Tom	£18,000	
Dick	£12,000	
Harry	£6,000	£36,000

It has been recognised by Tom, Dick and Harry that a sum for goodwill should be included in the accounts:

Tom	£ 6,000	
Dick	£ 8,000	
Harry	£10,000	£24,000

If the goodwill was to remain in the current year's accounts, then the partners would have these sums credited to their capital accounts and the goodwill account would be debited with the total (that is, £24,000) as an intangible fixed asset.

However, if the partners did not want a goodwill account to be maintained in the partnership books, then it would be written off in relation to their agreed profit sharing ratio at the time the goodwill was introduced. If the partners, Tom, Dick and Harry, were to share profit and losses in the ratio of 3:2:1 respectively, then the position would be as shown in Table 17.8.

TABLE 17.8 Writing-off a goodwill account

	Capital introduced £	Goodwill introduced £	Goodwill written off £	New balances £
Tom	18,000	6,000	(12,000)	12,000
Dick	12,000	8,000	(8,000)	12,000
Harry	6,000	10,000	(4,000)	12,000

What has occurred here is that Harry, who has benefited the most by introducing a greater value of goodwill (he may have brought in more trading customers) and because of the profit-sharing ratio, only loses 1/6 of total goodwill to be written off £24,000/6). On the other hand, Tom has most capital to lose because he takes half the profit share and therefore must apportion half the value of goodwill against his capital account. By coincidence, their capital accounts are now equal!

Questions

1. Alan and Brenda are in partnership and agree to share profits and losses equally. During the year to 31 December, the net profit of the firm was £14,680.

The partners' drawings for the year were:

£
Alan   4,950
Brenda 4,565

Interest charged on drawings is at 10% per annum based on average drawings for the year:

Average balance of   Alan   £2,500
                       Brenda   £2,100

Interest is paid on capital of 5% per annum
The balances on the partners' accounts were:

	Capital a/c (1/1) £	*Current a/c* (1/12) £
Alan	12,000	600 Cr.
Brenda	12,000	50 Dr.

Partners' salaries:

Alan   3,500
Brenda   2,500

Required:

(a) Prepare the partnership profit and loss appropriation account and the partners' current accounts for the year ended 31 December.
(b) An extract of the partners' balance sheet as at 31 December.
(c) Alan and Brenda decide to admit a new partner, Charlie. Goodwill is agreed at a value of £6,000. This account is to be debited on 1 January, the new financial period. Alan and Brenda are to be credited equally with the value of goodwill.

   Charlie will inject £10,000 of his own capital which will be debited to the business's bank account. If profits and losses are then to be shared on a capital input ratio, what will be the profit-sharing ratio? How would the balance sheet be affected on 1 January?

2. Smith and Jones are in partnership, sharing profits and losses in a ratio to their capital accounts. The trial balance as on 31 December was as follows:

		Dr. £	Cr. £
Premises		23,500	
Furniture and fittings		2,750	
Motor van		2,000	
Provision for bad debts			115
Carriage in		142	
Returns		288	343
Purchases		11,665	
Sales			21,429
Discounts		199	146
Stock (1/1)		3,865	
Debtors, creditors		2,355	3,569
Salaries		5,055	
Rates and insurance		645	
Light and heat		162	
Bank		522	
Capital:	Smith		18,000
	Jones		12,000
Current accounts:	Smith	625	
	Jones	540	
Drawing accounts:	Smith	2,303	
	Jones	1,500	
Rent received			2,514
		58,116	58,116

Notes: at 31 December,

- The value of unsold stock £4,200.
- Gas bill due for payment £65.
- Rates paid in advance £30.
- Provision for bad debts to be increased to £250.
- Depreciation: Furniture and fittings by 20%
                 Motor van revalued £1,800.
- Jones is awarded a salary of £1,000 for extra responsibilities.
- Interest charged on Drawings: Smith £209, Jones £160.

Required:

(a) Prepare the trading, profit and loss and appropriation accounts for the year ended 31 December and balance sheet as at that date.
(b) Show the current accounts as they would appear in the ledger.

3. Lee and Crooks are partners sharing profits and losses equally. At the end of the financial year, the trial balance extracted from the books was:

at 31 December		£	£
Premises		15,000	
Equipment (cost)		3,600	
Provision for depreciation of equipment a/c			360
Motor vehicle		3,500	
Stock (1/1)		3,742	
Debtors		5,188	
Creditors			3,165
Bank			850
Cash		255	
Provision for bad debts			70
Rates and insurance		450	
General overheads		600	
Wages		6,342	
Carriage in		450	
Carriage out		156	
Discount			440
Bank charges		235	
Advertising		350	
Printing, stationery		285	
Sales			24,565
Returns inward		350	
Purchases		13,080	
Returns outward			2,052
VAT			340
Current accounts:	Lee		300
	Crooks	155	
Drawings:	Lee	3,700	
	Crooks	2,704	

Capital accounts:	Lee		14,000
	Crooks		14,000
		60,142	60,142

Notes: at 31 December,
(a) The value of unsold stock (at cost) £5,150.
(b) Crooks took goods for his own use £420.
(c) Provision for Bad Debts increased to £500.
(d) Depreciation: Equipment 10% on Cost. Motor vehicle 20%.
(e) Partners' charge on drawings: Lee   £300
                                   Crooks   £249
(f) Partners' salaries: Lee   £1,500
                                   Crooks   £1,000.

Required:

Prepare the trading, profit and loss and appropriation accounts for the year ended 31 December, and a balance sheet as at that date.
4. May and Cowdrey are in partnership in a small business. They share profits (losses) three-quarters and one-quarter respectively. The trial balance of the business is indicated below. Prepare the trading and profit and loss account(s) for the year ending 31 December, and the balance sheet at that date after making all necessary adjustments.

Trial Balance at 31 December

	Dr.	Cr.
Capital Accounts – 1 January		
MAY		10,000.00
COWDREY		4,000.00
Drawings		
MAY	1,750.00	
COWDREY	1,250.00	
Current Accounts – 1 January		
MAY		500.00
COWDREY		300.00
Debtors and creditors	4,520.00	5,420.25
Warehouse wages*	3,200.00	

Trial Balance at 31 December

	Dr.	Cr.
Office salaries	1,500.00	
Stock 1 January	6,334.00	
Purchases and sales	10,472.00	22,232.75
Returns in and out	361.00	547.25
Bank	2,641.00	
Cash	142.25	
Light and heat	470.00	
Warehouse $\frac{4}{5}$, Office $\frac{1}{5}$*		
Rates	248.00	
Warehouse $\frac{3}{4}$, Office $\frac{1}{4}$*		
Freehold premises	6,500.00	
Fixtures and fittings	1,440.00	
Vehicles	1,600.00	
Stationery	156.75	
Sundry expenses	64.00	
Postage and telephone	136.00	
Insurance	60.50	
Discounts	248.00	426.75
Provision for bad debts		125.00
Bad debts	72.00	
Vehicle expenses	386.50	
	£43,552.00	£43,552.00

*Any warehousing costs to be attributed to the trading a/c.
Make provision for the following items:

(a) Stock at 31 December – £4,400.00.
(b) Depreciation: fixtures and fittings by 15%, and vehicles by 10%.
(c) Rates pre-paid amount to £64.00.
(d) Unexpired insurance amounts to £10.00.
(e) Provision for bad debts at 31 December is to be 5% of debtors' total.
(f) 5% interest is allowed on partners' capital and a salary of £1,046.00 is awarded to Cowdrey.

5. Jones, Smith and Brown are partners in a wholesaling enterprise. They have a warehouse and a small section of offices. Expenses attributed to the warehouse are to be listed

under 'Distribution Costs' in the profit and loss account. All other expenses in the profit and loss account are to be listed under 'Administration Expenses'. The accounts extracted for the trial balance at the year ended 31 December were:

Trial Balance of Jones, Smith and Brown as on 31 December

	£	£
Premises (at cost)	35,000	
Fixtures (at cost)	18,500	
Motor Vans (at cost)	12,750	
Bank		2,460
Cash	100	
Equipment (at cost)	11,000	
Stock (1 Jan.)	77,450	
Debtors	18,142	
Creditors		64,800
Purchases/sales	86,257	142,000
Returns	4,150	4,400
Provision for bad debts		180
Rates ($\frac{3}{4}$ Warehouse)	840	
Wages ($\frac{1}{4}$ Warehouse)	16,424	
General expenses ($\frac{1}{4}$ Warehouse	1,764	
Insurance	283	
Loan (5 years)		27,000
Capital accounts, balances 1 Jan.		
Jones		25,000
Smith		20,000
Brown		5,000
Current accounts, balances 1 Jan.		
Jones		1,242
Smith		1,615
Brown	37	
Drawings for the year:		
Jones	6,000	
Smith	4,000	
Brown	1,000	
	293,697	293,697

The following additional information is to be taken into account: as at 31 December:

- Unsold stock valued at cost £82,427.
- Rates unpaid £120.
- Invoice due on stationery £125 (Administration expense).
- Depreciation: Motor vans revalued to £11.250 (distribution cost)

    Equipment and fixtures 10% on cost
    (Administration expense).
- Insurance pre-paid £37.
- Smith was awarded a salary of £2,750.
  Drawings by partners to be charged 5% interest.
  Interest on capital to be paid 6%.
  Profits are shared according to their capital ratio on 1 January.

Required:

(a) Prepare the partners' trading, profit and loss account and appropriation account for the year ended 31 December.
(b) Prepare the partners' current accounts as they would appear in the ledger.
(c) Prepare the partners' balance sheet as at 31 December.

6. The following information refers to the accounts of Smith, Jones and Rogers who are in partnership and, according to their Deeds, share profits and losses in the ratio of 2:2:1 respectively.

   During the financial period ended 31 May 19–5, the net profit of the business was £7,300 and the partners' drawings for the year were:

Smith	£2,000
Jones	£1,900
Rogers	£1,500

   Interest on partners' drawings has been calculated as follows:

Smith	£65
Jones	£55
Rogers	£45

   As far as the partners' capital accounts are concerned, the agreement states that 6% will be allowed as interest payment.

The partners had agreed that Smith should withdraw £1,000 from his capital account on 1 December 19–4 and that Rogers should contribute the same amount on that date. Jones is awarded a salary of £900 for extra responsibilities. The opening balances on the partners' accounts on 1 June, 19–4 were:

	Capital a/c £	Current a/c £
Smith	9,000	600 Cr.
Jones	8,000	400 Dr.
Rogers	7,000	300 Dr.

Other balances on 31 May 19–5 were as follows:

	£
Fixed assets (net)	30,700
Stocks	12,750
Debtors	4,655
Cash	500
Bank (Cr.)	2,995
Creditors	14,560
Accruals	300
Bank loan (5 years)	4,950

Required:

(a) Prepare the partnership profit and loss appropriation account and the partners' current accounts for the year ended 31 May 19–5.
(b) Prepare the partners' balance sheet as at 31 May 19–5 and show net current assets as part of its construction.
(c) Make a brief comment on the partners' financial position as at 31 May 19–5.

[Associated Examining Board]

7. French and Saunders run a business consultancy and have the following account balances in their books on 31 March 19–5:

	£
Capital accounts:	
French	20,000
Saunders	25,000
Current accounts: [1/4/19–4]	
French	4,200 Cr.
Saunders	2,060 Dr.
Drawings for the year:	
French	12,000
Saunders	15,000
Premises	60,000
Vehicles	6,000
Depreciation of vehicles	5,000
Bank	3,800
Debtors	3,210
Creditors	6,970
Bank loan 11% [long term]	20,000
Net trading profit for year	19,800
Interest accrued on loan	
6 months	

Notes:

● The partners have agreed on equal sharing of profit/ losses.
● The partners have agreed 8% interest on capital accounts.
● Interest charges on drawings amount to: French £200, Saunders £600.

Required:

(a) The profit and loss appropriation account of French & Saunders for the year ended 31 March 19–5 and the current accounts of each partner.
(b) The balance sheet of the partnership as on 31 March 19–5.
(c) A brief memorandum, addressed to the partners, commenting on the partnership liquidity and suggesting how it could be improved.
(d) French has used her own premises for the business partnership and £500 has been agreed for running costs.

No entries have been made. What effect would this have on the preparation of the above accounts?

[BTEC National]

8. You work as Accountant for Wooldridge & James, a partnership, and have to prepare their final accounts for the year ended 31/5/19–5.

	Dr £	Cr. £
Capital a/c balances:		
Wooldridge		50,000
James		30,000
Current a/c balances: [1/6/19–4]		
Wooldridge		1,000
James		2,000
Drawings on 30/11/19–4		
Wooldridge	5,000	
James	8,000	
Drawings on 31/6/19–5		
Wooldridge	8,000	
James	10,000	
Fixed assets (Net)	114,000	
Current assets	80,650	
Deferred liabilities		29,000
Current liabilities		75,000
Profit for the year		38,650
	225,650	225,650

The Partnership agreement between Wooldridge and James stipulates:

● Profits and losses to be shared 60% Wooldridge and 40% James.
● Salaries to be received Wooldridge £9,000, James £12,000.
● Interest to be paid on capital and current account balances as on 1/6/19–4 at 10% per annum.
● Drawings also to be subject to interest at a rate of 10% per annum calculated on their half-yearly balances.

Required:

(a) Prepare the partnership profit and loss appropriation account for the year ending 31/5/19–5.
    Prepare the partners' current accounts after completion of the profit and loss and appropriation account.
(b) Prepare the partnership's balance sheet in its abbreviated form as on 31/5/19–5.
(c) Write a memorandum to the partners explaining the situation under Section 24 of the Partnership Act 1890 if no Partnership Agreement existed.
(d) Prepare a statement, to be sent with the above memorandum, showing how the profits would be divided if Section 24 of the Partnership Act 1890 applied.

[BTEC National]

9. Bell, Ring and Gong, who traded separately for several years, decided to form a partnership on 1 April 199–4 and transferred all the assets and liabilities of their individual businesses to the partnership at that date.

Whilst the assets and liabilities brought into the partnership have been recorded in the partnership books of account at agreed valuations, it has now been discovered that recognition has not been given in the partnership books for the goodwill as at 1 April 199–4 of the businesses transferred to the partnership:

Bell	£ 8,000
Ring	£12,000
Gong	£16,000

At the same time, it must be noted that the partners do not want a goodwill account to be maintained in the partnership books.

The partnership agreement provides for partners to be credited with interest on their capital account balances at the rate of 10% per annum, Ring and Gong to be credited with partners' salaries of £10,000 and £13,000 per annum respectively, and the balance of profits and losses to be shared between Bell, Ring and Gong in the ratio 5:3:2 respectively.

The following trial balance as at 31 March 199–5 has been extracted from the partnership accounts:

	£	£
Freehold land and buildings: at valuation	50,000	
provision for depreciation		1,250
Plant and machinery: at valuation	21,000	
provision for depreciation		2,100
Motor vehicles: at valuation	12,000	
provision for depreciation		3,000
Stock	9,000	
Debtors	4,000	
Balance at bank	600	
Creditors		5,250
Capital accounts: Bell		40,000
Ring		20,000
Gong		14,000
Drawings: Bell	13,000	
Ring	11,000	
Gong	9,000	
Net profit for the year ended 31 March 199–5		44,000
	£129,600	£129,600

Additional information:
- It is agreed that a current account be opened for each partner.
- On 1 October 199–4, by agreement between the partners, Ring acquired from the partnership a motor vehicle at a valuation of £2,000 – this vehicle was valued at £2,400 [cost] at 1 April 199–4. Entries have not yet been made in the partnership books for this transfer which is to be debited to the partner's drawings account.
- There have been no additions to any fixed assets since the commencement of the partnership.
- The partners have decided that depreciation is to be provided on the straight-line basis as follows:

	% per annum
Freehold land and buildings	$2\frac{1}{2}$
Plant and machinery	10
Motor vehicles	25

Required:

(a) Prepare the partnership's profit and loss appropriation account for the year ended 31 March 199–5.
(b) Prepare the partnership's balance sheet as at 31 March 199–5.

[Association of Accounting Technicians]

CHAPTER 18

Company Accounts

Company accounts are regulated by the consolidated 1985 Companies Act and the supplementary 1989 Companies Act.

The formation of a limited company needs only a minimum of two founder members who are willing to subscribe share capital. There is no maximum limit.

Basically, there are two distinct types of limited company:

(a) the private Limited Company;
(b) the Public Limited Company (PLC).

A PLC must bear these letters after its name on all correspondence to distinguish it from a private company (for example, Barclays Bank PLC). The word 'limited' means that shareholders' liabilities are limited to the nominal capital of their shares, in the same way a limited partner is limited to the amount of capital he has subscribed.

The private company can only sell its shares privately. It cannot issue a prospectus inviting the public to buy its shares. This privilege is only permitted to the PLC. A private company, therefore, is restricted in the amount of share capital it can raise because it cannot, by statute, advertise to sell its shares. It is likely to sell its shares to family and friends interested in financing a business venture.

Unlike the private company, the PLC has the potential to raise large sums of capital by offering its shares for public sale. A merchant bank or issuing house can arrange for the issue of shares and, indeed, could buy the shares outright, then offer them to the public for sale via the prospectus.

Most private companies are small business ventures with a limited number of members, and rarely employ more than twenty people. On the other hand, PLCs like the commercial banks, large retail chains and manufacturing enterprises are big business concerns which have thousands of members and employees.

PLC shares may be listed on the Stock Exchange once they have been vetted and accepted by the Stock Exchange Council. Private company shares cannot be listed.

The procedure to form a limited company is a little more involved than forming other business units. The sole trader has virtually no legal constraint and partnerships are advised to prepare Deeds of Partnership before starting up in business. A limited company must prepare two important documents which are sent to the Registrar at Companies House for companies to obtain approval before it can proceed. These documents are the Memorandum and Articles of Association.

The Memorandum gives the 'external' view of the company to the public, including details of its name, address, registered office, share capital and, most important, its objectives (that is, what it proposes to do).

The Articles give the 'internal' view of the company which relates to the rules and regulations governing the internal organisation of the company, such as voting rights, conduct at meetings, power of directors and so forth.

Once approval is given by the Registrar, a limited company is issued a Certificate of Incorporation which gives it the status of being a *separate legal entity* from the owners of the business (the shareholders). The company has then the right of its own identity and can proceed under its own name, acting under its own name in the course of its business.

A Board of Directors is elected by the shareholders to take control of the company on their behalf. The directors control, the shareholders own.

A private company, on receipt of its Certificate of Incorporation, can commence trading. A PLC must issue its prospectus to sell its shares before it can begin. The directors of the company must state, in the prospectus, the minimum amount of share capital it requires in order to start business and that the share issue has been underwritten (guaranteed) to ensure that the minimum capital is raised. Once this minimum capital is raised, the Registrar can issue the PLC its Certificate of Trading – its right to commence business operations.

The preparation of company accounts

The 1985 Companies Act gives guidance as to the preparation of final accounts relating to companies.

The trading and profit and loss account. The Act illustrates a choice of four formats of presentation. The first, Format 1, will be used because it is in the same style already used in the text. Expenses may be sub-divided into categories like distribution costs and administration expenses. The net profit is shown before and after taxation.

The appropriation account. This shows the division of profits before tax. Basically, profits are distributed by:

(a) provision for taxation;
(b) dividends to shareholders on the basis of the number of shares issued and paid up on the value of nominal capital;
(c) transfer of profit to the company reserves (profits retained in the company helping it to expand and grow).

There are two classes of share capital which may be issued to shareholders, ordinary shares and preference shares. The first type is the most common and represents the 'true' shares, taking the greater risks. The rate of dividend depends on how much profit is made and how much is to be distributed. These are also referred to as 'equity' shares and are given voting rights – one share, one vote. These votes may be used at annual general meetings but rarely are they exercised in PLCs because very few shareholders actually attend.

Preference shares are paid at a *fixed* rate of dividend and are entitled to be paid first before ordinary shares. The shares do not hold voting rights and are suitable for the less adventurous type of shareholder who wants a more reliable and consistent rate of dividend.

Debentures represent borrowed capital and not share capital. They are paid at a fixed rate of interest over the specified period of the loan. The interest paid is an expense entered in the profit and loss account, not the appropriation account.

The 1985 Companies Act

Under Part VII of the 1985 Companies Act, and particularly sections 221 and 222, the main points state:

1. Every limited company must keep accounting records, with reasonable accuracy, to disclose the financial position of the company.
2. Financial records must be kept daily including receipts and payments of money, the assets and liabilities of the company, including stocktaking at the year end. These records must be

kept for a period of 3 years for a private company and 6 years for a public company.

3. The final accounts of the company must be kept in accordance with the formats laid down in Schedule 4 of the Act. This must include:

- A profit and loss account
- A balance sheet, as at the same period
- An auditors' report
- A directors' report

Public companies must have at least two directors and a private company, one. Every company must have a secretary. The directors of a company must make a report as part of the annual accounts and must present a fair view of the business's development in its financial year. The directors must indicate the dividend they wish to recommend and also the amount they propose to withhold as reserves.

Annual reports must be filed with the Registrar, Companies House. For companies registered in England and Wales, there are addresses in London and Cardiff. For companies registered in Scotland, there is an address in Edinburgh.

A company must show its accounts to its members for each accounting period at its annual general meeting. It must ensure that a copy of its accounts is sent to the Registrar within a period of 10 months following the end of the financial period for a private company and 7 months for a public company.

The 1989 Companies Act

The new Companies Act, 1989, is a supplementary Act and does not replace the 1985 Companies Act which, in effect, consolidated all previous Acts from 1948 to 1981.

The 1989 Act amends and adds to the existing legislation of the 1985 Act. It is expected that the accounting provisions relating to Part I are likely to be effective in respect to accounting periods beginning on or after 1 January, 1990.

The necessity of the new Act comes about as a result of the United Kingdom's obligation to implement the European Community's 7th Directive on consolidated accounts and its 8th Directive on the regulation of company auditors. At the same time, the Government had an opportunity to take stock of its company law and to bring in desired amendments such as the power to investigate and obtain information, to make provision for the safeguarding of certain financial markets and to amend the Financial Services Act, 1986 and the Company Securities Act, 1985 (Insider Dealing).

As far as company accounts go, the provisions of the Act under sections 221 and 222 (Part VII) emphasise the duty of all companies to keep accounting records.

Some of the 1989 Act's interesting sections are outlined below:

221
(1):   Every company shall keep accounting records, sufficient to show and explain the company's transactions with reasonable accuracy at any time and the financial position of the company, and to enable the directors to ensure that the balance sheet and profit and loss account complies with the requirements of the Companies Act.

A company's accounts shall be kept at its registered office or such other place where the directors think fit and shall at all times be open to inspection by the company's officers.

221
(2):   Accounting entries shall contain day-to-day records of all sums of money received and spent as well as a record of its assets and liabilities.

221
(3):   If a company deals with goods for resale, the accounts must contain statements of the value of stock held at end of the financial year and show sufficient details of buyers and sellers, except by way of ordinary retail trade.

226   It is the duty of the directors to have individual, as well as group, company accounts prepared for each financial period, a balance sheet as at the last day of that period and a profit and loss account for that period. Both these financial reports must give a 'true and fair' view of the state of affairs of the company for the financial period under review.

227   Where a company acts as a parent company and has subsidiary companies, the directors must prepare individual accounts for each company and also consolidated accounts for the group, as whole.

238   The persons entitled to receive copies of the annual accounts and director's and auditors' reports are:

(a) every member of the company;
(b) every holder of the company's debentures;
(c) every person entitled to receive notice of general meetings and not less than 21 days before the meeting is held.

242   Copies to the Registrar, Companies House.
Directors must send to the Registrar a copy of the company's

annual accounts and also a copy of the director's and auditor's reports.

Penalties for not complying within the stated specified time (within 7 months of the financial period end for a public company and 10 months for a private company will be fined according to the length of time the accounts are delayed.

For a public company, the fine will range between £500 and £5,000, and for a private company, the fine will range between £100 and £1,000.

Other sections of the 1989 Companies Act deal with aspects largely outside the scope of this text. These include matters relating to the following:

(a) investigations and power to obtain information;
(b) the eligibility for the appointment of company auditors;
(c) various amendments to company law;
(d) mergers and related matters;
(e) financial markets and insolvency;
(f) the Financial Services Act 1986 – amendments;
(g) the transfer of securities.

Table 18.1 is an example for internal use (that is, a full set of figures for management purposes).

The company balance sheet

The Act lays down a choice of two formats. The first will be used because it is shown in the vertical form as used in the text. The alternative is represented in the horizontal form, showing assets on the left and liabilities and capital on the right. A full version of the balance sheet is required both for internal and external use. An example is given in Table 18.2.

When accounts are for external use, the profit and loss account is abbreviated (see Hardcastle Ltd in Table 18.4), and are available for distribution to shareholders and other interested parties. A copy of the external reports must be sent to the Registrar, Companies House, as required by the 1985 Companies Act.

TABLE 18.1 Presentation of trading and profit and loss account and appropriation account, y/e 31/12 (accounts for internal use)

	£	£	£
Turnover (net sales)			100,000
Less			
Cost of Sales			
Stock (1/1)	4,000		
+ Purchases	66,000		
	70,000		
– Stock (31/12)	10,000		60,000
Gross Profit			40,000
Less			
Distribution Costs			
Salesmen's salaries	8,500		
Distribution expenses	1,500		
Advertising	2,500		
Motor expenses	1,500		
Depreciation of motors	500		
Depreciation of equipment	2,000	16,500	
Administration Expenses			
Office salaries	7,350		
General office expenses	1,400		
Discount	250		
Bad debts provision	350		
Rates and Insurance	500		
Miscellaneous costs	1,200		
Light and heat	150		
Depreciation of equipment (office)	1,300	12,500	29,000
			11,000
add			
Other Income			
Discount	450		
Bank interest	350		800
			11,800
Income from Shares			
Dividends from other companies			800
			12,600
Less			
Interest Payable			
Bank loan interest accrued			250

Table 18.1 *continued*

The appropriation account			
Net Profit (before tax)			12,350
Corporation tax			3,150
Net Profit (after tax)			9,200
+ Profit and loss balance (1/1)			400
			9,600
Provision for dividends:			
8% Preference shares	1,600		
Ordinary shares	3,000	4,600	
Transfer to reserve		4,000	8,600
Profit and loss balance (31/12)			1,000
(transferred to shareholders' funds)			

Notes: (a) The profit and loss balance is the residue of profit after appropriations to dividends and reserves. The balance at the end of one accounting period becomes the opening balance in the next.

(b) The 8% dividend to preference shares was based on the issued and paid-up nominal capital of £20,000. The ordinary share dividend was based on a 6% share-out on £50,000 of issued and paid up nominal capital.

(c) Net profit (before tax) is the start of the appropriation account and ends with the profit and loss balance (31/12) £1,000.

TABLE 18.2   Balance sheet as at year end 31/21

	£ Cost	£ Depn	£ Net
Fixed Assets			
Premises	50,000		50,000
Equipment	35,000	8,000	27,000
Motor vehicles	4,000	1,000	3,000
Investments	10,000		10,000
	99,000	9,000	90,000
Current Assets			
Stock	10,000		
Debtors	17,500		
Bank	3,500		
Pre-payments	1,000	32,000	

Less
Current Liabilities

Creditors	16,000	
Accruals	250	
Provision for dividends	4,600	
Provision for taxation	3,150	24,000

Working Capital		8,000
Capital Employed		98,000
Less		
Long-term Liabilities		
Bank loan (5 years)		6,000
Net assets		92,000

Financed by

Shareholders Funds:	*Authorised Capital*	*Issued and Paid-Up Capital*
Ordinary Shares @ £1	100,000	50,000
8% Preference Shares @ £1	20,000	20,000
		70,000
Share Premium Account		5,000
Reserves		16,000
Profit and loss balance		1,000
		92,000

Notes: (a) The share premium account is the amount received in excess of the nominal value of shares when issued. In the above case, they sold at £1.10 each (50,000 x 10p).

(b) Authorised capital is the amount stated in the Memorandum of Association and also in the Prospectus. A PLC must have a minimum of £50,000 registered in its Memorandum.

(c) Issued and paid-up capital is the amount issued and paid up by shareholders. A PLC must have at least £12,500 of shares issued and paid up.

(d) Reserves refer to the profits retained in the company. When reserves are built up over the years, they may be capitalized by converting them into bonus shares for existing shareholders. In the above accounts, £4,000 was transferred to reserves in the appropriation account, indicating that £12,000 was already in the reserve account, the sum now being £16,000.

Company accounts for external use

The accounts of limited companies for publication and copies to the Registrar are in abbreviated format as amended by Financial Reporting Standard No. 3, *Reporting Financial Performance*. This standard changes the format of the profit and loss account and basically highlights:

- results of continuing operations (normal company business);
- results of discontinued operations;
- exceptional items, for example, profit/loss on sale of business;
- extraordinary items, any unusual items outside ordinary activities;
- earnings per share before and after any exceptional items.

Attention is focused on the results between continuing and discontinuing operations so that operating profit may be disclosed to show the proportion of each of these categories.

Exceptional items including profits or losses on the sale of an operation or on the disposal of fixed assets, should be shown separately, after operating profit and before any interest charges.

The objective of FRS No. 3 is to focus attention on a range of important components relating to financial performance in the profit and loss statement. An example with this objective in mind is given below. For futher information on SSAPs and FRSs see Chapter 23.

Example: company accounts for external use

The figures are for the financial year end of Hardcastle Co. Ltd, 31 December are for external use and shown in Tables 18.3 and 18.4.

TABLE 18.3 Trading and profit and loss account, Hardcastle Co. Ltd, year ending 31/12

	£
Turnover	
Continuing Operations	327,000
Cost of sales	191,500
Gross profit	135,500
Net operating expenses	(83,500)
	52,000
Other income/ (expenses)	500
Operating profit:	
Continuing Operations	52,500
Profit from discontinued operations	2,500
Profit before exceptional items	55,000

Exceptional items:	
Loss on sale of business	(3,000)
Profit before interest and tax	52,000
Interest	(5,500)
Profit before tax	46,500
Tax	(14,500)
Profit after tax	32,000
Dividends	(2,500)
Reserves	(25,000)
Profit and Loss account	4,500
Earnings per share:	64p

TABLE 18.4 Balance sheet, Hardcastle Co. Ltd, as at 31/12

	£	£	£
Fixed Assets [net value]			135,100
Current Assets			
Stock	68,750		
Debtors	76,750		
Pre-payments	500	146,000	
Creditors Falling Due < 12 months			
Creditors	89,400		
Accruals	4,900		
Taxation provision	14,500		
Dividends proposed	2,500		
Bank/cash	10,800	122,100	
Net Current Assets			23,900
Total assets – current liabilities			159,000
Creditors Falling Due > 12 Months			
Loans			52,000
			107,000

TABLE 18.4 *continued*

	£	£	£
Capital and Reserves			
Issued and paid-up capital:			
Ordinary Shares @ £1		50,000	
Share Premium a/c		10,000	
Revenue reserves		42,500	
Profit and loss a/c		4,500	107,000

Questions

1. XYZ Co. Limited had an authorised capital of £200,000 divided into 100,000 ordinary shares of £1 each and 100,000 $7\frac{1}{2}$% preference shares of £1 each. The following balances remained in the accounts of the company after the trading and profit and loss accounts had been prepared for the year ended 31 December.

	Debit £	Credit £
Ordinary share capital: fully paid		80,000
$7\frac{1}{2}$% preference shares: fully paid		50,000
Machinery and plant at cost	95,000	
Provision for depreciation on machinery and plant		19,000
Premises at cost	68,000	
Profit and loss account balance (1 January)		5,000
Net profit (for year ended 31 Dec.)		15,500
Accruals		2,150
Bank		395
Stock	9,750	
Debtors and creditors	3,100	3,955
Pre-payments	150	
	176,000	176,000

- The directors have recommended an ordinary dividend of 10% and wish to provide for payment of the year's preference share dividend.
- A Revenue Reserve is to be created of £2,000.
- Taxation of £3,760 to be provided for.

Required:

(a) The profit and loss appropriation account for the year ended 31 December.
(b) Prepare the balance sheet at 31 December to show clearly the working capital.
(c) Make brief comments with reference to the company's working capital.

2. The following balances remain on the books of ABC Co. Ltd after the preparation of trading and profit and loss accounts for the year ended 31 December:

	£	£
60,000 ordinary shares of £1 each fully paid		60,000
Machinery and plant (at cost)	52,500	
Motor vehicles (at cost)	4,000	
Furniture and fittings (at cost)	5,750	
General reserve		30,000
Premises (at cost)	45,000	
Profit and loss		
balance brought forward (1/1)		5,460
Net profit for year		18,750
Accrued expenses		2,810
Provision for depreciation:		
Machinery and plant		10,500
Motor vehicles		1,500
Furniture and fittings		1,000
Provision for bad and doubtful debts		650
Sundry debtors	10,855	
Sundry creditors		4,900
Stocks	11,985	
Cash in hand	500	
Bank	4,980	
	135,570	135,570

You are required to prepare a profit and loss appropriation account for the year ended 31 December, and a balance sheet at that date. The following information is available:

(a) The directors decided to transfer £10,000 to reserve and to recommend a dividend of 15% on the ordinary shares.
(b) The authorised capital of ABC Co. Ltd is 100,000 ordinary shares of £1 each.
(c) The provision for taxation payable next year is £1,500.
(d) Briefly comment on the adequacy of the company's working capital.

3. Bournemouth Trading Company Limited has extracted the following trial balance from its books at the end of the accounting period, 31 December.

	£	£
Issued Share Capital:		
60,000 @ £1 shares fully paid		60,000
6% Debentures		5,000
Share premium account		6,000
Stock (1/1)	20,600	
Purchases	118,940	
Debtors	12,460	
Wages, salaries	10,768	
Directors' fees	2,500	
Debenture Interest	150	
Furniture and fittings (cost)	4,000	
General expenses	1,820	
Insurances	42	
Provision for bad debts		750
Creditors		4,860
Bank overdraft		940
Freehold premises (cost)	52,000	
Sales		149,500
Maintenance and power	5,840	
Provision for depreciation of furniture and fittings		1,500
Returns inward	650	
Cash	80	
Profit and loss balance (1/1)		1,300
	229,850	229,850

You are to take the following into account on 31 December:

(a) Unsold stock valued at £22,000.
(b) Provision of 15% is to be made for ordinary shares. The outstanding debenture interest is also to be accounted for.
(c) Under maintenance and power, there is £76 due to rates and £14 insurance relates to the next financial period.
(d) Furniture and fittings to be depreciated 15% on cost.
(e) The provision for bad debts is to be adjusted to 5% of the debtors.
(f) The figure of £600 is to be transferred to reserve.
(g) £500 is to be provided for taxation.

Required:

Prepare the company's trading and profit and loss account and appropriation account for the year ended 31 December and a balance sheet as at that date (show full set of figures as for internal use).

4. The accounts of Robertson and David Co. Ltd were extracted from the books on 30 June 19–5.

Trial Balance as on 30 June 19–5

	Dr. £	Cr. £
Issued and paid-up capital:		
160,000 ordinary shares @ £1		160,000
40,000 8% preference shares @ £2		80,000
Profit and loss a/c (1 July 19–4)		7,780
General reserve		25,000
7% Debentures		40,000
Premises (cost)	287,910	
Motor vehicles (cost)	32,000	
Plant, equipment (cost)	16,880	
Provision for depreciation of motor vehicles		4,800
Stock (1 July 19–4)	49,600	
Bank		11,752

| | Dr. | Cr. |
	£	£
Cash	1,558	
Purchases	535,600	
Sales		696,500
Returns	500	1,600
Wages	65,460	
Rates, water, insurance	3,600	
General expenses	22,536	
Preference dividend paid		
(31 December 19–4)	3,200	
Debtors, creditors	63,380	53,944
Bad debts	2,150	
Provision for bad debts		3,120
Discount allowed	122	
	1,084,496	1,084,496

Notes: Additional details, 30 June 19–5

(a) Stock value £39,400.
(b) Rates pre-paid £1,000; wages still outstanding £3,360.
(c) Invoice unpaid for general expenses £30.
(d) Depreciation: Motor vehicles 20% on book valuation
                     Plant and equipment 25% on cost.
(e) Adjust the provision for bad debts to equal 5% of debtors.
(f) The Directors of the company propose a dividend of 10% for
     ordinary shares. The paid dividend is to be entered in the appro-
     priation account.
     Preference shares to receive their final dividend.
(g) No interest has been paid on the debentures.
(h) A transfer of £4,000 is to be made to reserve.
(i) A provision of £19,200 is to be made for taxation.

Required:

Prepare the trading, profit and loss appropriation accounts
for the year ended 30 June 19–5, and a balance sheet as
at that date.

5. The following trial balance represent the accounts of G.
    Chappell & Sons Ltd as on 31 December:

	£	£
Authorised and paid-up capital		
125,000 @ £1 shares (Equity)		125,000
Share premium		2,500
Premises	110,000	
Furniture and fittings (cost)	4,200	
Profit and loss a/c (1/1)		1,170
Discounts	422	329
Salaries	7,537	
Rates and insurance	2,333	
Rent received		825
Purchases	90,450	
Returns	782	1,789
Sales		105,411
Stock (1/1)	9,142	
General overheads	2,197	
Provision for bad debts		108
Dividend paid (30/6)	1,000	
Provision for depreciation of furniture and fittings		200
Debtors	9,920	
Creditors		5,226
Bank	6,575	
General reserve		2,000
	244,558	244,558

You are to take the following into account on 31 December:

(a) Value of unsold stock £12,498.
(b) Rates paid in advance £70.
(c) Salaries accrued: £263.
(d) Overheads: a bill for gas £103 was still outstanding.
(e) Depreciation of furniture and fittings 25% on book value.
(f) Provision for bad debts to be adjusted to equal 5% of debtors.
(g) The Directors propose to provide for a final dividend of 2.5% and to transfer £2,000 to reserve.
(h) Taxation: a sum of £1,250 is to be provided for.

Required:

Prepare trading, profit and loss and appropriation accounts for the period ended 31 December, and a balance sheet as on that date.

6. Harrison's is a small private company producing electrical components. It is a relatively new business and the Board are anxious to do well and hope that the year's final accounts will look promising.

   The following information has been extracted from the books:

Trial Balance of Harrison Co. Ltd on 31 December

	£	£
Stock (1 Jan.)	5,760	
Purchases	82,500	
Premises (at cost)	60,500	
Plant and equipment (at cost)	60,000	
Provision for depreciation of plant		18,000
Office equipment (at cost)	15,000	
Provision for depreciation of office equipment		6,000
Bank		2,400
Debtors, creditors	48,750	45,100
Cash	440	
Summary of expenses*	66,550	
Sales		176,000
Finance loan 12½%(5 years)		40,000
General reserve		2,000
Authorised and paid-up capital:		
50,000 £1 ordinary shares		50,000
	339,500	339,500

*Divided into Distribution Costs 60%
          Administration Expenses 40%.

Additional information available on 31 December:

- The value of unsold stocks (at cost) £6,485.
- Administration expenses: Stationery of stock unused valued £1,250.
  Rates pre-paid £110.
  Office salaries outstanding £260.
- Distribution costs: Salesmen's salaries outstanding £484.
- A provision for bad debts is to be created to equal 10% of debtors (enter under Administration Expenses above).
- Depreciation: both plant and office equipment is depreciated by reduced balance method, 20% on net value (enter under Administration expenses above).
- The Directors have proposed a dividend of $7\frac{1}{2}$% on ordinary shares.
  Taxation of £3,750 is to be provided.
- There was no profit and loss balance on 1 January.
- The interest on the loan has not yet been paid.

Required:

(a) Prepare the company's trading and profit and loss account, and appropriation account for the year ended 31 December.
(b) A balance sheet as at that date showing clearly working capital.
(c) Prepare a brief report for the directors of the company with regard to working capital.

[BTEC National]

7. You work as an assistant to the Accountant for Jason Limited which has a registered capital of £500,000, divided into 800,000 ordinary shares of 50p each and 200,000 8% preference shares of 50p each. The following balances remained in the accounts of the company after the trading and profit and loss accounts had been prepared for the year ended 30 November 19–5.

	Dr. £	Cr. £
General reserve		5,000
Ordinary share capital: fully paid		100,000
8% preference shares: fully paid		30,000
Premises at cost	140,000	
Light and heat owing		880
Profit and loss account balance		
(1 Dec. 19–4)		19,200
Bank		8,200
Debtors and creditors	5,800	1,120
Net profit (for year ended 30 Nov. 19–4)		40,600
Machinery and plant at cost	50,000	
Provision for depreciation on machinery		
and plant		30,000
Stock	38,340	
Insurance pre-paid	820	
Cash	40	
	235,000	235,000

Information as on 30 November 19–5:

The directors of Jason Ltd. have recommended:

- providing payment of the year's preference dividend
- providing for corporation tax of £8,400
- a maximum dividend which would maintain a working capital ratio of 1.5:1, the balance remaining from profits to be transferred to general reserve

Required:

(a) The profit and loss appropriation account for the year ended 30 November 19–5.
(b) The balance sheet as at 30 November 19–5.
(c) State the number of ordinary and preference shares which can still be issued by the company. Briefly explain the difference between these classes of shares.

[Institute of Commercial Management]

8. You work as Assistant to the Financial Accountant of Compton Ltd, manufacturers of cosmetics, and are working on the annual accounts.

The following balances remain in the ledger of Compton Ltd after the preparation of the profit and loss account for the year ended 31 March 19–5.

	£
Stocks and work in progress	98,000
Debtors	87,000
Provision for bad debts	4,000
£1 ordinary shares	400,000
[Authorised £600,000]	
16% preference shares of £1 each	100,000
[Authorised £200,000]	
Creditors	74,000
Balance at bank	4,000
Accruals	3,500
Pre-payment	2,500
General reserve account	14,000
Share premium account	20,000
Net profit for the year ended 31/3/19–5	108,000
Profit and loss account balance 1/4/19–4	22,000
Premises (at cost)	300,000
Plant and equipment (at cost)	310,000
Vehicles (at cost)	200,000

The Directors propose the following:

(a) To transfer £20,000 to reserves.
(b) To propose an ordinary dividend of 12% and to pay the preference dividend.
(c) To provide for corporation tax of £30,000.

Depreciation of fixed assets has been calculated as follows:

(a) Plant and equipment has a residual value of £30,000 and a 'life' estimated at 10 years. It is five years old and depreciation is based on the straight-line method.
(b) The vehicles are valued at current market value of £84,000.
(c) There is no depreciation on premises.

Required:

Draw up a profit and loss appropriation account for the year ended 31 March 19–5 and a balance sheet as at that date.

[BTEC National]

9. You are an assistant to the accountant at J. P. Davies plc, which has been in business for several years. The trial balance on 30 June 19–5 was as follows:

Trial Balance – J. P. Davies PLC as on 30 June 19–5

	Dr. £	Cr. £
£1 preference shares (15%)		100,000
(Authorised £200,000)		
£1 ordinary shares		200,000
(Authorised £500,000)		
Revenue reserves		45,000
Debenture stock (12.5%), 1999		100,000
Profit for year ending, 30/6/19–5		
(before debenture interest)		80,000
Profit and loss balance (1/7/19–4)		40,000
Stocks	200,000	
Premises	200,000	
Plant and machinery	180,000	
Vehicles	50,000	
Office equipment	90,000	
Provisions for depreciation:		
Premises		10,000
Plant and machinery		70,000
Vehicles		30,000
Office equipment		55,000
Debtors	220,000	
Creditors		190,000
Cash	500	
Provision for bad debts		11,000
Pre-payments	9,500	
Accruals		21,000
Bank overdraft		5,500
Interim preference dividend paid	7,500	
	957,500	957,500

Notes:

(a) A full year's debenture interest is still to be charged.
(b) Corporation tax is to be provided, £20,000.
(c) The final dividend on preference shares is to be provided for.
(d) To propose an ordinary dividend of 20%.
(e) To transfer £25,000 to Revenue Reserves.

Required:

Draw up the company's profit and loss appropriation account for the year ended 30 June 19–5 and a balance sheet as on that date.

[BTEC National]

CHAPTER 19

Cash Flow Statements

Historically, the balance sheet and the profit and loss account were always the most important financial statements of a business organisation. However, during the late 1960s and the early 1970s, it was considered necessary by the Accounting Standards Committee (ASC), representing the accounting profession, to try to highlight a business's cash flow position and they produced SSAP No. 10, The Statement for Sources and Application of Funds in 1975. (SSAPs are discussed in greater detail in Part IV of the text.) SSAP 10 attempted to indicate where the sources of funds came from and where the funds went.

In August 1990, the ASC was taken over by a new independent body responsible for setting standards, the Accounting Standards Board (ASB). In September 1991 they produced their first statement, Financial Reporting Standard No. 1 (FRS 1), The Cash Flow Statement, replacing SSAP No. 10, which is now obsolete.

The major purpose of this new FRS is basically the same as the old funds flow statement: that is, to emphasise a business's inflow and outflow of cash during the financial year. The cash flow statement may be described as the *Link* between:

    (a) two balance sheets in the financial period (that is, one at the beginning of the year and one at the end);
    (b) the profit and loss account for the year.

The cash flow statement is to be prepared under five separate sections which are:

1. *Net cash inflow/outflow from operating activities*
    (a) Net profit on normal trading activities (before taxation).
    (b) Non-cash flow expenses.
    (c) Adjustments in movements in working capital.

2. *Returns on investments and servicing of finance*
   (a) Interest received.
   (b) Interest paid.
   (c) Dividends paid.

3. *Taxation*

4. *Investing activities*
   (a) Purchases of tangible fixed assets/investments.
   (b) Sales of tangible fixed assets/investments.

5. *Financing activities*
   (a) Issuing shares/debentures.
   (b) Redemption of shares/debentures.
   (c) Repayment of loans.

From these headings, the statement should then balance off in relation to the increase or decrease in cash or the bank for the period. Interested parties, such as owners, managers, shareholders, etc., should be able to see the major inflows and outflows of funds through the financial year. Questions which could be raised include:

● Is enough cash being raised to finance the business's spending?
● Were profits sufficient to pay for tax, interest and dividends?
● How did the large overdraft occur in the bank?

Example

TABLE 19.1   Duran Ltd: balance sheets as at 31 December

	19–4		19–5	
	£	£	£	£
Fixed Assets				
Cost	60,000		100,000	
Less cumulative depreciation	20,000		34,000	
		40,000		66,000
Investments at cost		40,000		20,000
		80,000		86,000
Current Assets				
Stock	40,000		120,000	
Debtors	44,000		96,000	
Bank	2,000		6,000	
	86,000		222,000	
Current Liabilities				
Tax owing	12,000		28,000	
Dividend owing	8,000		10,000	
Creditors	14,000		20,000	
	34,000	52,000	58,000	164,000
		132,000		250,000
Long Term Loans		20,000		28,000
		112,000		222,000
Financed by:				
Ordinary shares		80,000		100,000
Share premium account		—		20,000
Profit/loss account balance		32,000		102,000
		112,000		222,000

Required:

Prepare a cash flow (FRS 1) Statement for the year ended 31 December, 19–5.
   (The answer is given in Table 19.3.)

TABLE 19.2 Duran Ltd: abbreviated profit and loss accounts for Year ended 31 December

	19–5 £
Sales	1,500,000
Cost of sales	(1,200,000)
Gross profit	300,000
Total expenses (inc. depn)	(196,500)
Operating profit for year	103,500
Add profit on sale of investments	8,000
Less interest payable	(3,500)
	108,000
Less tax provision	(28,000)
	80,000
Add retained profits	32,000
	112,000
Less proposed ordinary dividend	(10,000)
Retained profits c/f	102,000

Note: No fixed assets were disposed of during the year.

TABLE 19.3 Duran Ltd: cash flow statement for the year ended 31 December 19–5

	£	£
1. Net cash inflow/outflow from operating activities*		(8,500)
2. Returns on investments and servicing of finance		
Interest received	0	
Interest paid	(3,500)	
Dividends paid	(8,000)	
Net cash outflow from returns on investments and servicing		(11,500)
3. Taxation		(12,000)
4. Investing activities		
Purchases of tangible fixed assets	(40,000)	
Sale of tangible fixed assets	28,000	
Net cash outflow from investing activities		(12,000)
Net cash outflow before financing		(44,000)

TABLE 19.3 *continued*

	£	£
5. Financial activities		
Issue of shares	20,000	
Share premium account	20,000	
New loan	8,000	
Net cash inflow from financing		48,000
Net increase in cash and cash equivalents		4,000

* Calculation of no. 1:

	£	
Operating profit	103,500	
+ Depreciation charges	14,000	
Working capital:		
+ stock	(80,000)	
+ debtors	(52,000)	
+ creditors	6,000	8,500

Notes: (a) The net increase in cash, £4,000, corresponds with the balance sheet increase (£2,000 - £6,000) under the bank figures.
(b) The movements in working capital indicate that increased spending on current assets is an outflow of cash, reductions would be an inflow. Increase in creditors would increase the inflow of cash, a reduction in creditors would decrease it.
(c) Outflows of funds are in brackets, indicating deductions: payment for interest, tax, dividends and fixed assets.
(d) Inflows of funds for Duran come from the issuing of shares and an increase in the loan.

Other key facts

Dividends and taxation paid: because these are provided for in one period and actually paid in the next, it is the previous year's figures (in Duran Ltd 19–4) which will be entered in section number 2, Returns on investments and servicing of finance.

Fixed assets: when fixed assets are purchased and entered in section number 4, Investing activities, we need to know how much they cost; therefore the difference between the two periods is taken (£60,000 to £100,000), indicating £40,000 cost of new assets acquired.

If the assets were given at their net values (that is, after depreciation has been deducted), you must remember to add on any depreciation charges in order to arrive at the cost of purchase. The net asset value of the two periods (£40,000 to £66,000) indicates an increase of £26,000, add depreciation charges of £14,000 = £40,000 cost of fixed assets.

In the event that some fixed assets are disposed of during the financial period, any gain or loss in their disposal is not recorded as part of the inflow of cash section number 1. The actual sum received for the sale of the fixed assets are recorded under section number 4, Investing activities: £20,000 of the investments had been sold off (£40,000 down to £20,000) under fixed assets and the profit and loss account stated a profit of £8,000, therefore the assumption is that the actual sale of investments brought an inflow of cash of £28,000.

Reserves and profit and loss balances: these figures only represent internal transfers of funds and therefore play no part in the recording of figures in the cash flow statement.

Questions

1. The final accounts of ABC Co. Ltd for year ended 31 March were as follows:

Balance Sheet of ABC Co. Ltd as at 31 March:

	£19–4	£19–5
Assets		
Fixed (net)	140,000	195,000
Stocks	23,500	21,550
Debtors	14,725	18,450
Bank	4,150	2,925
Cash	500	500
	182,875	238,425
Liabilities		
Creditors	19,550	26,450
Provision for taxation	12,500	15,000
Provision for dividends (ordinary)	6,000	6,500
Debenture stock	35,000	50,000
	73,050	97,950
Net Assets:	109,825	140,475

	£19–4	£19–5
Shareholders' Funds:		
Issued and paid-up capital:		
Ordinary shares	75,000	75,000
Preference shares	15,000	25,000
Reserves	15,725	33,725
Profit and loss balance (31/3)	4,100	6,750
	109,825	140,475

Profit and Loss Account of ABC Co. Ltd
Year ended 31 March 19–5

Net trading profit		
(Depreciation charges £8,000)		44,150
Corporation tax		15,000
		29,150
+ Profit and loss balance (1/4 19–4)		4,100
		33,250
Preference dividends *paid*	2,000	
Provision for ordinary	6,500	
Reserves	18,000	26,500
Profit and loss balance (31/3 19–5)		6,750

Required:

A cash flow statement for the year ended 31 March 19–5.

2. The final accounts of K. Bishop Limited for the years ended 31 March 19–4 and 19–5 were as follows:

Summarised Balance Sheets at 31 March

	19–4 £	19–5 £
Assets:		
Fixed (Net)	420,000	585,000
Stocks	70,500	64,650
Debtors and pre-payments	44,175	55,350
Bank	12,450	8,775
Cash	1,500	1,500
	548,625	715,275

Liabilities:

Trade creditors and accruals	(58,650)	(79,350)
Provision for tax	(37,500)	(45,000)
Proposed final dividend	(18,000)	(19,500)
10% Debenture stock	(105,000)	(150,000)
	(219,150)	(293,850)
	329,475	421,425

Capital and Reserves:

£1 ordinary shares	225,000	225,000
£1 preference shares (8%)	45,000	75,000
Profit and loss account	59,475	121,425
	329,475	421,425

Note: There were no disposals of fixed assets during the year.

Summarised Profit and Loss Account for year ending 31 March 19–5

	£	£
Operating profit (after provision for depreciation of £24,000)		147,450
Interest payable		(15,000)
Profit for year before tax		132,450
Provision for tax		(45,000)
Profit for year after tax		87,450
Preference dividend paid	6,000	
Proposed ordinary dividend	19,500	(25,500)
		61,950

Required:

(a) Prepare a cash flow statement (as set out in FRS 1) for the year ending 31 March 19–5.
(b) Comment on the changes which have taken place during the year to 31 March 19–5.

[Chartered Institute of Purchasing & Supply]

3. The following information refers to the accounts of P. Jackson & Co. Ltd:

	31 Dec. 19–4 £	31 Dec. 19–5 £
Assets		
Premises (cost)	35,000	45,000
Machinery*	20,000	21,500
Stock	15,000	20,580
Debtors	8,450	12,375
Bank/cash	2,255	1,835
	80,705	101,290
Liabilities		
Creditors	10,150	12,755
Accruals	1,125	955
Taxation due	5,100	6,530
	16,375	20,240
Capital		
Issued @ £1 ordinary shares	50,000	60,000
Profit and Loss account	14,330	21,050
	64,330	81,050

*Machinery	Cost £	Depreciation £	Net £
Balance (31/12/19–4)	25,000	5,000	20,000
Additions 19–5	6,000		
	31,000		
Sale of old stock	(3,000)	(2,000)	
Depreciation 19–5		3,500	
Balance (31/12/19–5)	28,000	6,500	21,500

Profit and Loss Account, Year Ended 31 December, 19–5

Net trading profit	12,750
+ Gain on sale of machinery	500
	13,250
Corporation tax	6,530
Retained to profit and loss account	6,720

Note: Any gain or loss on the sale of a fixed asset *is not* included in section 1 as net profit although the actual sum received *is* included in section 4.

Required:

(a) A cash flow statement for the year ended 31 December 19–5.
(b) Comment on the change of working capital over the two periods.

4. Study the following balance sheets of Jones & Rogers PLC, and profit and loss account for the year ended 31 May 19–5.

Jones & Rogers PLC
Balance Sheets as at 31 May

	19–4 £	19–4 £	19–5 £	19–5 £
Ordinary shares	170,000		200,000	
Share premium a/c	17,000		20,000	
Profit and loss a/c	8,000	195,000	10,000	230,000
Fixed Assets (cost)	180,000		260,000	
Depreciation	40,000	140,000	60,000	200,000
Investment (cost)		10,000		5,000
Current Assets:				
Stock	50,000		60,000	
Debtors	30,000		47,000	
Bank	10,000	90,000	18,000	125,000
Current Liabilities:				
Creditors	17,000		18,000	
Provision for tax	16,000		18,000	
Provision for dividends	12,000	(45,000)	14,000	(50,000)
Deferred Liability:				
9% Debentures		—		(50,000)
		195,000		230,000

Jones & Rogers PLC Profit & Loss a/c Year ended 31 May 19–5

	£
Net trading profit	30,000
+ Profit on investment	4,000
	34,000
- Provision for taxation	18,000
	16,000
+ Profit and loss balance (1/6/19–4)	8,000
	24,000
- Provision for dividends	14,000
Profit and loss a/c (31/5/19–5)	10,000

Required:

(a) Calculate the working capital ratio over the two years and briefly comment on the business's liquidity.
(b) Prepare a cash flow statement for the year ended 31 May 19–5.

5. The following final accounts relate to Harry Fox Co. Ltd for the years ending 31 December 19–4, and 19–5. Study the figures carefully from the point of view of analysing the firm's performance between the two financial periods.

Profit and Loss account, Harry Fox Co. Ltd, Years ended 31 December 19–4 and 19–5

	19–4 £	19–5 £
Retail sales	128,640	196,480
Net profit (before tax)	12,850	21,590
Corporation tax (provision for year)	5,100	9,250
Net profit (after tax)	7,750	12,340
Dividends:		
Ordinary shares	6,500	9,000
Retained profits	1,250	3,340

Note: Depreciation charges for the year were £4,500.

Balance Sheet, Harry Fox Co. Ltd, as at year ended 31 December . . .

	19–4 £	19–5 £
Fixed Assets (net)	28,904	38,244
Current Assets		
Stock	7,288	10,338
Debtors	4,942	8,358
Bank	3,750	1,674
Cash	100	50
Current Liabilities		
Creditors	1,930	2,670
Accruals	550	1,000
Taxation	5,100	9,250
Dividends	6,500	9,000
Deferred		
Bank loan	5,000	2,500
Shareholders' Funds		
Authorised capital		
50,000 @ £1 ordinary shares	50,000	50,000
Issued and paid-up capital		
@ £1 ordinary shares	20,000	25,000
Reserves	5,904	9,244

Required:

(a) Prepare two separate balance sheets at the year ended 31 December 19–4 and 19–5 for Harry Fox Co. Ltd, showing clearly working capital and capital employed.
(b) Prepare a cash flow statement for the year ended 31 December 19–5.

6. You work in the accounts office of XYZ Ltd and the accountant has provided you with the following information at the end of the financial period, 31 March 19–5:

Balance Sheets of XYZ Ltd. at 31 March

	31 March 19-4 £	31 March 19-5 £		31 March 19-4 £	31 March 19-5 £
Freehold property at cost	25,000	25,000	Issued Share Capital	30,000	30,000
Equipment*			Profit and loss a/c	27,000	33,000
	18,000	22,200	Corporation tax		
Stock in trade	16,400	17,800	due:		
Debtors	13,600	14,000	1 January	6,000	—
Bank	2,000	1,000	1 January	—	4,000
			Creditors	12,000	13,000
	75,000	80,000		75,000	80,000

* Equipment movements during the year ended 31 March 19-5 were:

	Cost £	Depreciation £	Net £
Balance at 31 March 19-4	30,000	12,000	18,000
Additions during year	9,000		
Depreciation provided during year		3,800	
	39,000	15,800	
Disposals during year	4,000	3,000	
Balance at 31 March 19-5	35,000	12,800	22,200

The company's summarised profit calculation for the year ended 31 March 19-5, revealed:

	19-4 £	19-5 £
Sales	95,000	100,000
Gain on sale of equipment		2,500
Less		102,500
Cost of sales and other expenses	84,800	92,500
Net profit	10,200	10,000
Corporation tax on profits of the year	6,000	4,000
Retained profit of the year (after tax)	4,200	6,000

Required:

Prepare a cash flow statement for the year ended 31 March 19–5.

[Institute of Commercial Management]

7. You work for a small limited company and are assisting in the preparation of the annual accounts for year ending 30/5/19–5.

Aspen Limited Balance Sheet as at 30 May

	£	19–4 £	£	£	19–5 £	£
Fixed Assets						
at cost		173,000			243,400	
Less						
depreciation		57,800	115,200		78,100	165,300
Current Assets:						
Stock		74,400			72,080	
Debtors		97,920			100,020	
Bank		10,880			—	
		183,200			172,100	
Current Liabilities:						
Creditors	41,440			37,080		
Overdraft	—			2,320		
Provision						
for tax	17,120			12,400		
Proposed						
dividend	10,000	68,560	114,640	12,000	63,800	108,300
			£229,840			£273,600
Financed by:						
£1 ordinary						
shares			200,000			220,000
Reserves			29,840			53,600
			£229,840			£273,600

Aspen Limited, Profit and Loss Account for Year Ended 30/5/9–5

	£
Profit for the year	48,160
Provision for tax	12,400
	35,760
Undistributed profits from last year	29,840
	65,600
Proposed dividend	12,000
Undistributed profits carried to next year	53,600

Required:

(a) Prepare a cash flow statement of Aspen Limited for the year ended 30/5/19–5.
(b) Compute the current ratio for both years.

[Institute of Commercial Management]

CHAPTER 20

Accounts of Clubs and Societies

Most private sector businesses are profit motivated. Goods and services are produced and distributed for the purpose of making money. However, there are non-profit organisations which are not primarily set up to make profits. These are the clubs and societies which are organised for specific purposes – for example, social, sporting, political and other organisations.

In many regions up and down the country, there are local tennis, cricket, football and rugby clubs. There are also amateur dramatic and choral societies as well as political and other associations.

Finance is raised by the members of these social organisations in a number of ways. Members' subscriptions provide a major source of income, while donations from various bodies and fund-raising activities are ways of raising extra finance. The sources of finance are used to pay for the running and up-keep of the club or society.

Money which comes in and goes out of a social organisation should be properly accounted for in order to safeguard the members' interests. It is therefore necessary to keep some basic records of the accounts in order to know what funds are available at what time.

Most of the social organisations elect honorary members who take on specific responsibilities. The club chairman is usually the spokesman and figure-head of the organisation. The club secretary will have the responsibility of taking care of the essential paper work such as letters to members, agendas, minutes of meetings, reports of activities and so forth. The club treasurer will have the responsibility of looking after the accounts.

The Treasurer's accounting reports

Formal accounting methods tend to be uncommon because the treasurer may lack time or expertise or both when it comes to keeping the accounts of the club or society. However, he should be expected to keep a tight control of cash and be in a position to prepare for members the following financial reports at the end of the club or society's social year:

(a) a receipts and payments account;
(b) an income and expenditure account;
(c) a balance sheet showing the organisation's state of affairs.

The receipts and payments account

This statement is a summary of all cash receipts and payments of the organisation for the year and is, in effect, a simplified Cash Book. The purpose of it is to show members where the cash has come from and where it has gone and, significantly, how much is left in balance at the end of the year under review.

The income and expenditure account

This is a statement which is the equivalent of the business's trading and profit and loss account where expenses are matched against income. Adjustments such as accruals, pre-payments and depreciation are also accounted for because they affect the profit or loss for the year. A social organisation uses the words 'surplus' or 'deficit' to indicate its profit or loss. Some clubs and societies operate a bar or refreshment counter for the benefit of members. The treasurer can prepare a special bar or refreshment account to indicate whether or not such an activity has made a surplus or deficit.

The balance sheet

This statement may be prepared in the same way as any other organisation. The net resources of the club or society are financed by the 'accumulated funds' – that is, the capital or net worth of the social organisation. Accumulated funds represent assets less liabilities in the same way as capital. Any surplus from the income and expenditure account is added to the funds. Any deficit is deducted.

Example

Poole Tennis Club begins its social year on 1 April 19–5. Its accumulated funds at this date are £17,704, made up of:

Bank balance	£ 304
Equipment	£ 400
Club House	£15,000
Investment	£ 2,000
	£17,704

At the end of the social year, 31 March 19–5, the treasurer listed the receipts and payments for the year and prepared the club's receipts and payments account as shown in Table 20.1.

TABLE 20.1 Receipts and payments account for the period ended 31 March 19–5

Receipts	£	Payments	£
Bank balance (1 Apr. 19–4)	304	Sports equipment	108
Subscriptions	400	Tennis balls	30
Subscriptions in advance	55	Hire of courts	230
Refreshment sales	91	Light and heat	35
Dance tickets	25	General expenses	140
Tournament fees	72	Refreshment purchases	60
Donations	30	Club house improvement	350
		Bank balance (31 Mar. 19–5)	24
	977		977

Note: on 31 March 19–5 the following were to be taken into consideration before preparing the Club's income and expenditure account for the period ended:
(a) stock of refreshments £ 27
(b) subscriptions owing for current year £150
(c) electricity bill owing £ 35
(d) sports equipment to be depreciated by £ 58
(e) bill for refreshment purchases due £ 12

Preparing a refreshment or bar account

It may be useful to prepare a separate account to deal with these to show whether a surplus or deficit is made. A surplus or deficit may then be transferred to the income and expenditure account (see Tables 20.2–4).

TABLE 20.2   Refreshment account Poole Tennis Club

	£	£
Sales		91
Less cost of sales:		
Stock (1 Apr. 19–4)	—	
+ Purchases	60	
+ Purchases due	12	
	72	
– Stock (31 Mar. 19–5)	27	
		45
*Surplus**		46

* Transferred to the income side of the income and expenditure account.

TABLE 20.3   Poole Tennis Club: Income and expenditure account for the period ended 31 March 19–5

Expenditure		£	Income		£
Tennis balls		30	Subscriptions	400	
Hire of courts		230	+ owing	150	550
Light and heat	35		Refreshment surplus		46
+ owing	35	70	Dance tickets		25
General expenses		140	Tournament fees		72
Depreciation of			Donations		30
equipment		58			
Surplus		195			
(income greater than					
expenditure)					
		723			723

Note: The subscriptions owing £150 belong to the current period ending 31 March 1988 and are therefore added to income. The subscriptions in advance are not included because they belong to the next period ending 31 March 19–6. The last statement is the balance sheet showing the Club's resources and the financing of them via the accumulated funds.

TABLE 20.4   Poole Tennis Club balance sheet at 31 March 19–5

	£	£	£
Fixed Assets			
Club House	15,000		
+ improvements	350		15,350
Equipment	400		
+ new purchases	108	508	
– Depreciation		58	450
Investment			2,000
			17,800
Current Assets			
Stock of refreshment	27		
Bank	24		
Subscriptions due	150	201	
– Current Liabilities			
Subscription in advance	55		
Accrued expenses	47	102	99
			17,899
Financed by			
Accumulated funds	17,704		
+ Surplus	195		17,899

Questions

1. The following statement has been submitted to you by the
   Corfe Mullen Social Club whose year ends 31 March 19–5.

Receipts and Payments Account

	£		£
Bank balance		Insurance and rates	480
(1 Apr. 19–4)	2,000	Wages	5,650
Subscriptions	5,575	Light and heat	480
Surplus from Bingo	850	Bar purchases	6,500
Bar takings	10,225	General expenses	275
		New furniture	500
		Maintenance and	
		repairs to Club	1,275
		Bank balance	
		(31 Mar. 1988)	3,490
	18,650		18,650

Other information:

		£
1 April 19–4	Club premises valued	25,000
	Furniture and equipment	2,000
	Bar stock	1,600
	Bank balance (as above)	
31 March 19–5	Bar stock	850
	Subscriptions in arrears	480
	in advance	50
	Furniture and equipment valued	1,950
	Bar purchases still due	500
	Insurance pre-paid	35

Required:

(a) The Club's bar account for the period ended 31 March 19–5.
(b) The Club's income and expenditure account for the period ended 31 March 19–5.
(c) A balance sheet as at 31 March 19–5.

2. From the following receipts and payments account of the Parkstone Golf Club and the further particulars provided below prepare an income and expenditure account for the year ended 31 March 19–5 and a balance sheet as at that date.

Receipts and Payments Account for the year ended 31 March 19–5

Receipts	£	Payments	£
Balance from last year	1,600	Wages	4,800
Entrance fees	8,400	Payment for new Equipment	3,500
Subscriptions:		Printing and stationery	200
Current year	4,800	Postage	175
In advance	500	Lighting and heating	575
Profits and refreshments	1,160	Insurances	250
Equipment rented to		General expenses	1,850
members	750	Balance (bank)	5,860
	17,210		17,210
Balance b/d	5,860		

Additional information (31 March 19–5):

(a) £50 is owing for subscriptions for the year.
(b) £15 is owing by members for equipment rentals.
(c) Printing and stationery, value £28, is still unpaid.
(d) The Club House and equipment appear in the books on 1 April 19–4 at a value of £10,000.

3. The Sandal Rugby Club was started on 1 April 19–4 with a bank balance of £3,300 which was provided by its members. After its first season, the receipts and payments for the year ended 31 March, 19–5 was as follows:

	£
Pavilion and other buildings, land	8,150
Equipment	500
Gate money	3,500
Collections at matches	1,642
Donations from members and other	1,585
Refreshment expenses	756
Receipts from refreshments	1,100
Loan from local bank secured on land and buildings (@ 12% per annum)	5,000
Rates, water	185
Light, heat	75
Wages of groundsman (part-time)	800
Match expenses paid	115
Printing and other expenses	125

	£
Advertising	176
General expenses	80
Transport costs	1,050

Notes: 31 March 19–5.

● Rates pre-paid £45.
● The interest on loan has not yet been accounted for and was taken out on 1 July 19–4.
● Wages owing to groundsman £40.
● Stocks of catering amounted to £65.
● The equipment was to be depreciated by £100.

Required:

(a) Prepare the income and expenditure account for the year ended 31 March 19–5.
(b) A balance sheet as at that date.

4. The following is the trial balance of the Broadwent Rugby Club on 31 December.

	£	£
Accumulated Fund at 1 January		10,500
Club House	18,560	
Club-room equipment	755	
Sports equipment	150	
Sale of refreshments		3,765
Purchase of refreshments	2,400	
Interest accrued		50
Subscriptions received for current year		2,800
Subscriptions in advance		55
Receipts from Club-house games		200
Maintenance of games		
Equipment	500	
Postage	150	
Insurance	850	
Sundry expenses	275	
Printing and stationery	105	
Wages	1,450	

Bank		1,870
Loan from Building Society		5,955
	25,195	25,195

Required:

(a) An account to show the profit or loss on sale of re-freshments.
(b) The income and expenditure account for the year ended 31 December, and a balance sheet at that date.

Take into consideration the following:

● Sports equipment is to be depreciated at 10% per annum and club-room equipment at 20% per annum
● £75 subscriptions are due for the current year
● £95 is owing for the purchase of refreshments
● Stock of refreshments on hand at 31 December was £370

5. The following information relates to Broadstone Tennis Club at the beginning of their season 1 April 19–4:

	£
Club House	15,000
Equipment	800
Bank	500
Stock (refreshments)	250

A summary of receipts for the year.

Subscriptions	1,500
Subs in advance	150
Refreshments	1,855
Dances	550
Fees for tournaments	360
Donations from members	100
Members' loan (5% p.a.)	2,000
Sales of lottery	875

A summary of payments for the year.

Sports equipment	450
Tennis balls (expense)	50

	£
Lottery tickets, prizes	565
Light and heat	80
General expenses	240
Refreshment purchases	1,255
Club House re-building	1,850
Maintenance of grounds	200
Insurance, rates, water	375

At the end of the season, 31 March 19–5; the following information was available to the Club Treasurer:

- The sports equipment (including additions) was valued at £900
- Stock of refreshments valued at cost £165
- Subscriptions owing by members £80
- A gas bill was still to be paid £18
- Insurance was pre-paid £25
- Club House rebuilding is classified as a capital expense, not revenue expense
- Members' interest on loan had not been paid (from 1 April 19–4)

Required:

(a) Prepare a receipts and payments account for the year ended 31 March 19–5.
(b) Prepare the club's income and expenditure account for the year ended 31 March 19–5 and a balance sheet as at that date.

6. From the following details and the notes attached relating to the Wiltshire Tennis Club prepare the final accounts of the Club for the year ended December 31.

On 1 January, the club's assets were: freehold club-house, £1,000.00, equipment £70.00; club subscriptions in arrears £8.00; balance at bank £76.00. The club owed £40.00 to Caterer's Ltd for Christmas dance catering.

Summary of Receipts and Payments

Receipts	£	Payments	£
Subscriptions	164.00	Catering-Christmas dance	
Locker rents	10.00	(Caterer's Ltd)	40.00
Receipts from dances		This year's dances and	
and social	139.00	socials	95.00
Sales of used match		Band fees-dances	25.00
tennis balls	15.00	New lawn mower	55.00
Sale of old lawn mower	8.00	Repairs to tennis nets	19.00
		Match tennis balls	31.00
		Match expenses	17.00
		Repair and decoration	
		of Club House	65.00

Notes: (a) The book value on January 1 of the old lawn mower sold during the year was £15.
  (b) The club has 40 members and the subscription is £4.00 per annum. The subscriptions received included those in arrears for the previous year.
  (c) On 31 December £11.00 was owed to James Ltd for tennis balls supplied.
  (d) Equipment as at 31 December, is to be depreciated by 10%.
  (e) Tennis balls are regarded as revenue expenditure, not capital expenditure.

Why is it important to clearly distinguish between capital and revenue expenditure?

7. You have been asked to prepare some accounts for the local golf club. The treasurer of the Redbridge Golf Club, Chris Payne, has passed on to you all the necessary financial information consisting of a receipts and payments account for the year, the club's balance sheet for the previous year and some other relevant notes which were thought to be needed. This information now follows:

Redbridge Golf Club: Balance Sheet as at 30 June 19–5

	Cost £	Depreciation £	Net £
Fixed Assets:			
Club property	120,000	24,000	96,000
Fixtures and fittings	22,000	6,600	15,400
	142,000	30,600	111,400
Current Assets:			
Bar stock		1,420	
Subscriptions in arrears		2,140	
Bank		4,780	
		8,340	
Current Liabilities:			
Creditors for bar supplies	575		
Subscriptions in advance	1,165		
		1,740	
			6,600
			118,000
Financed By:			
Accumulated Fund:			
Balance as at 1 July 19–4			113,800
Surplus for the year			4,200
			118,000

Redbridge Golf Club: Receipts and Payments Account for the year ended 30 June 19–5

Receipts	£	Payments	£
Bank balance b/d	4,780	Bar purchases	7,248
Subscriptions	18,220	Bar steward's salary	4,926
Bar takings	12,435	General expenses	2,674
		Maintenance expenses	3,749
		Heating and lighting	788
		Bank Balance c/d	16,050
	35,435		35,435

Notes:

• The following balances were available at 30 June 19–5.

Bar stock	£1,540
Subscriptions in arrears	£1,875
Subscriptions in advance	£1,450
Creditors for bar supplies	£638

• The club's policy is to provide depreciation annually on fixed assets at the following rates:

Club property	2.5% of cost
Fixtures and fittings	10% of cost

Required:

(a) Showing clearly the profit or loss made on the bar, prepare the club's income and expenditure account for the year ended 30 June 19–5.

(b) Explain the difference between the receipts and payments account and the income and expenditure account of a club or association.

[Association of Accounting Technicians]

8. The following account has been prepared by the treasurer of the Phoenix Model Engineering Society:

Receipts and payments statement for the year ended 31 March 19–5

	£		£
1 April 19–4 Opening balance b/fwd	894	Purchase of building land	8,000
Subscriptions received	12,000	Purchase of machinery and tools	17,500
Sales of machinery and tools	21,000	Rent of temporary office and meeting room	600
Sale of wooden hut	1,100	Printing, stationery and postages	860
Sales of tickets for annual national exhibition	300	Deposit in building society investment account	7,500
		Secretary's honorarium	150
		Coach to annual national	

	£		£
		exhibition	110
		Admission charges to annual national exhibition	220
		31 March 19–5 closing balance c/fwd	354
	£35,294		£35,294

The following additional information has been obtained from the Society's records:

(a) In addition to the balances at bank shown in the above receipts and payments statement, the Society's assets and liabilities were:

As at	1 April 19–4	31 March 19–5
	£	£
Stocks of machinery and tools at cost	1,200	600
Subscriptions due to the Society	150	250
Wooden hut at valuation	1,300	—
Subscriptions pre-paid by members	300	To be determined
Outing to annual national exhibition	—	See note below

(b) The annual subscription for the year ended 31 March has been £50 per member since 1 April.
All subscriptions due at 1 April 19–4 have now been paid. The Society's membership was 238 during the year ended 31 March 19–5.

(c) All sales of machinery and tools are to members on a strictly cash basis.

(d) *Annual National Exhibition*, £40 for tickets was owing by a member to the Society on March 9–5 31 and at that date the Society owed £45 for the purchase of exhibition programmes distributed to members without charge.

(e) Since preparing the above receipts and payments statement, the treasurer has received a bank statement showing bank charges of £14 debited in the Society's bank account on 30 March 19–5; no adjustment was made for these charges in the above statement.

(f) Since the sale of the wooden hut on 1 July 19–4, the

Society has rented a temporary office and meeting room at an annual rent of £600 payable in advance.

Required:

Prepare an income and expenditure account for the year ended 31 March 19–5 and a balance sheet as at that date for the Society.

(Note: The income and expenditure account should show clearly the overall result of the trade in machinery and tools and the profit or loss of the visit to the annual national exhibition.)

[Association of Accounting Technicians]

PART IV

THE PROVISION OF FINANCIAL INFORMATION

CHAPTER 21

Accounting Ratios and Preparing Reports

Accounting ratios can assist both the owners and managers in business to improve their decision making. The performance of every business organisation is related to its aims and objectives. Whether the results look good or not will largely depend upon the objectives of the business. If a firm wanted a 20% return on its profits and the results showed only 10%, then the report on its performance will be disappointing. On the other hand, if the aim was to achieve 10% and 20% profit was reported, the result would be received far more cheerfully.

Accounting ratios help owners and managers in business to compare figures over periods of time and also to compare them with their competitors and with industries in the same field as themselves. From preparing these ratios, key questions about the business can be analysed, profitability, liquidity and efficiency being particularly significant. Is the business becoming more successful or less so? What factors might be identified to help management decide what to do for the best?

Groups of ratios

A business's accounts can be analysed into various groups, and text books are never consistent about this. The reason why they are not is because:

(a) there are so many different types of businesses producing a wide variety of different goods or services;
(b) accounting ratios are devised to be adapted to meet this wide variety of different business organisations.

However, the important thing is to be consistent from one financial period to the next, and at least businesses should try to use the same formula for calculation within their industry. The comparison of results will be greatly improved and more accurate as a result.

In the major areas of ratio categories, there are always two which are consistently in the list: that is, profitability and liquidity. Here are some of the groups to be considered:

Group A
Profitability
Liquidity
Long-term solvency
Effective use of resources

Group B
Performance ratios
Liquidity
Use of assets
Solvency (or gearing)

Group C
Profitability
Liquidity
Efficiency
Structure
Investment

There are other groupings, too, and these should not confuse your basic understanding of how to calculate the ratios and what they are meant to be used for. The High Street banks tend to use Group B where their performance ratios cover not only profitability, but also a group of efficiency ratios such as rate of stock turnover. In accounting, there are always different ways to say and mean the same thing.

It is by reducing the absolute figures taken from financial statements to accounting ratios that comparison from year to year and with different organisations becomes more easily analysed.

The following information will be used as an example for the calculation of accounting ratios. The company, Allied Components, Plc, is a small public company, recently quoted on the Stock Exchange. Ratios to test for profitability, liquidity, efficiency, structure and investment will be calculated, including a brief evaluation of the results (see Tables 21.1 and 21.2).

TABLE 21.1   Allied Components PLC profit and loss account, year ended 31 December

	£[000s]	£[000s]
Turnover		9,000
Cost of Sales		
Stock (1/1)	500	
Purchases	5,650	
Stock (31/12)	(150)	6,000
Gross Profit		3,000
Distribution costs	550	
Administration expenses	850	
Interest payable	400	1,800
Net Profit (before tax)		1,200
Provision for tax		300
Net Profit (after tax)		900
Profit and loss balance (1/1)		0
		900
Provision for Dividends:		
8% preference shares	160	
Ordinary shares	300	460
Retailed Profits (to Reserve)		440

TABLE 21.2   Allied Components PLC balance sheet, as at year ended 31 December

	£[000's]	£[000's]
Fixed Assets (net value)		20,000
Current Asssets:		
Stock (31/12)	150	
Debtors	1,080	
Bank cash	2,170	
Pre-payments	100	
	3,500	
Creditors falling within 12 months:		
Trade creditors	1,200	
Accruals	40	
Provision for tax	300	
Provision for dividends	460	
	2,000	

TABLE 21.2 *continued*

	£[000's]	£[000's]
Net Current Assets		1,500
Capital Employed		21,500
Creditors falling after 12 months:		
Debenture stock		6,500
		15,000
Capital and Reserves		
Ordinary Share Capital	3,000	
8% Preference Shares	2,000	
Reserves 9,560		
+ Retained Profits 440	10,000	15,000

Profitability ratios

These ratios are used to measure the trading performance of a business in terms of profit to sales or profit to capital. The ratios in themselves may have little meaning unless they are compared to past performances or with businesses in the same category (for example, supermarkets or electrical appliances). Allowing for factors such as inflation or other economic indicators which may influence demand, ratio analysis can be useful in detecting trends and the reasons behind them.

The ratios used are not the whole category available but they are amongst the most common:

(a) The Gross Profit % $= \dfrac{\text{Gross Profit} \times 100}{\text{Net Sales}}$

(b) The Net Profit % $= \dfrac{\text{Net Profit} \times 100}{\text{Net Sales}}$

(c) Return on Capital Employed $= \dfrac{\text{Net Profit} \times 100}{\text{Capital Employed}}$

(d) Return on Net Worth $= \dfrac{\text{Net Profit} \times 100}{\text{Net Worth (Owner's Equity)}}$

(e) Return on Total Assets $= \dfrac{\text{Net Profit} \times 100}{\text{Total Assets}}$

The net profit returns may be shown (for a company) as before or after tax, or both. When comparing ratios with other periods, it is important to be consistent. Compare like with like, otherwise distortions will occur and negate the usefulness of any comparison. The profitability ratios of Allied Components are:

(a) Gross Profit %
$$= \frac{£3,000 \times 100}{£9,000}$$
$$= 33.33\%$$

(b) Net Profit %
$$= \frac{£1,200 \times 100}{£9,000}$$
$$= 13.33\%$$

(c) Return on Capital Employed
$$= \frac{£1,200 \times 100}{£21,500}$$
$$= 5.58\%$$

(d) Return on Net Worth
$$= \frac{£1,200 \times 100}{£15,000}$$
$$= 8\%$$

(e) Return on Total Assets
$$= \frac{£1,200 \times 100}{£23,500}$$
$$= 5.1\%$$

Note: The net profit has been taken *before tax* in the above figures.

Are these profit returns reasonable? With no comparative figures to guide our analysis, it is difficult to make useful comment. However, if the 'norm' for Allied Components within its own industry was, for example, between 35% and 40% gross and between 14% and 18% net, then we could assume that the company's profitability was marginally lower than was expected.

Is the company satisfied receiving around £33 gross per £100 sales and £13 net per £100 sales (before tax)? Could it do any better? Is it buying its materials at optimum prices? Is its production as efficient as it could be if it manufactured its products?

Is its return on capital a reasonable figure? How does it measure up to interest rates? All Allied's profits to the balance sheet figures are between 5% and 8%. The return on capital employed, seen by the majority of organisations as *one of the most significant* returns on capital, is only a low 5.58%. If base interest rates were high, the return on capital is very mediocre. This measures profit to the business resources as a whole, and the directors of the company would need to seek improvement on a miserable 5%.

Is the sales department doing its job effectively? Could an improvement in marketing be the answer? Could some of the expenses be cut without affecting the quality of the product?

These are some of the questions management could be asking, to seek ways of improving profits.

Liquidity ratios (short-term solvency)

These ratios indicate the business's ability to have sufficient cash resources to meet current debts. The two most significant ratios are:

(a) working capital ratio (or current ratio);
(b) quick asset ratio (or acid test).

Calculation of ratios:

$$\text{Working Capital ratio} = \frac{\text{Current Assets}}{\text{Current Liabilities}}$$

$$= \frac{£3,500}{£2,000} = 1.75$$

$$\text{Quick Asset ratio} = \frac{\text{Current Assets (less Stock)}}{\text{Current Liabilities}}$$

$$= \frac{£3,500 - £150}{£2,000} = 1.68$$

Working capital needs to be adequate to enable the business to trade with reasonable 'comfort'. It should be enough to finance short-term debts (those which are due within the financial period). If creditors demand payment, the business should be in a sound enough financial position to meet the demands.

The working capital ratio should not fall below 1:1 because then there would be insufficient liquid resources to meet debts. A ratio falling below 1:1 means the business is potentially 'insolvent' – that is, it has insufficient liquidity to meet current debt.

Liquidity is as important as profit earning, if not more so. A business could be in an attractive profit-earning position and and yet still fail because it has disregarded its liquidity. Creditors can force a business to pay its debts by taking them to court. If the court ruled that the business must pay up within a specific time, it may well mean that it must be 'liquidated' to pay off its outstanding debts.

The quick asset ratio is an immediate test of liquidity because the value of stock is deducted from the total of current assets. Can a business, without relying on its stock, meet its immediate debts? However, the importance of this ratio is also related to the business's rate of stock turnover – the speed with which a business sells its stock. The faster stock is sold, the less important is the quick asset ratio. A supermarket like Sainsbury's, for example, has such a high rate of stock turnover that stock is almost like cash anyway. On the other hand, a manufacturing business making motor vehicles could have a much lower rate of turnover, therefore taking longer to produce and sell its goods and receive its cash.

Comparisons need to be made with previous years to check the business's liquidity trend. Expected ratios, depending on the type of business, should be:

Working Capital ratio   2.5:1 to 1.5:1
Quick Asset ratio   1.5:1 to 0.75:1

Ideally, the working capital and quick asset ratios should fall somewhere between these ratios, 2:1 and 1:1 respectively, although this depends on the size and nature of the business. As long as there is adequate liquidity to satisfy creditors, that is what is important.

Efficiency ratios

These ratios are used to try and identify the strengths and weaknesses of a business using a variety of different ratios, including the money incurred on relative expenses, stock turnover, debt collection, the investment of assets to turnover and productivity. This list is by no means exhaustive but it is emphasised that past figures and norms for similar industries are needed in order to give a better and more in-depth analysis.

Expense percentages

Each type of expense may be analysed in relation to sales for the purpose of evaluating in absolute or relative terms the significance of different types of expense and how they affect profit.

$$\text{Cost of Sales \%} = \frac{\text{Cost of Sales} \times 100}{\text{Sales}}$$

$$= \frac{£6,000 \times 100}{£9,000} = 66.66\%$$

$$\text{Distribution Expenses \%} = \frac{\text{Distribution Expenses} \times 100}{\text{Sales}}$$

$$= \frac{£550 \times 100}{£9,000} = 6.11\%$$

$$\text{Administration Expenses \%} = \frac{\text{Administration Expense} \times 100}{\text{Sales}}$$

$$= \frac{£850 \times 100}{£9,000} = 9.44\%$$

$$\begin{aligned}\text{Financial Expenses \%} \\ \text{[interest]}\end{aligned} = \frac{\text{Financial Expenses} \times 100}{\text{Sales}}$$

$$= \frac{£400 \times 100}{9,000} = \underline{4.44\%}$$

Total Expenses %	=	86.65%
Therefore Net Profit %	=	13.35%
		100%

These expenses may be related to pence in the £ to indicate an easy break-down of expenses to the number of pence profit in the £ (see Table 21.3).

TABLE 21.3   Relation of expenses to pence/£

	Pence/£
Cost of sales	67
Distribution expenses	6
Administration expenses	9
Financial expenses	4
	87 total;
	13 in the £ profit

Is 13p in the £ an adequate return? How does it compare with previous trading performances? How does it compare with similar organisations trading in similar goods or services?

If 13p is regarded as an insufficient return, investigation is needed in order to find out why the return is low. Is 67p/£ for cost of sales too high? Is the firm inefficient in buying or producing its goods? How do the other expenses compare with previous years? Is the selling price too low? These points need to be analysed and are important in assisting management and owners in making decisions.

The rate of stock turnover

This ratio refers to the number of times the stock is sold within an accounting period. It gives an indication of the business's selling efficiency.

$$\text{Calculation: Rate of Stock Turnover} = \frac{\text{Cost of Sales}}{\text{Average Stock}}$$

$$= \frac{£6,000}{£325} = 18.5 \text{ times per year}$$

This is a reasonably high rate of stock turnover where Stock is sold every 2.8 weeks $\left[\dfrac{52}{18.5}\right]$

The speed of stock turnover depends on the nature of goods sold. A large supermarket will have a high turnover rate because it sells goods required every day. For goods required less frequently, such as furniture, the stock rate will be less. Because turnover of stock measures the business's selling efficiency, the trend should be carefully checked and deviations from the normal patterns investigated.

If the rate of stock is sold every 2.8 weeks, it is seen as relatively fast compared with another organisation whose rate is, say, every 16 weeks and which sells goods like jewellery or furniture and not supermarket goods.

The stock turnover should be compared with the gross profit percentage (33.3%) to see the effect of selling prices on turnover figures. For example, if the rate of turnover increases, it may indicate a policy by the firm of reducing its selling prices in order to increase turnover and sales. If the gross profit percentage falls but actual gross profit increases, the policy will be seen as successful. On the other hand, if selling prices are forced down because of intense competition, the gross profit percentage may fall without either an increase in actual gross profit or stock turnover.

The actual calculation of stock turnover also needs a little caution. If stock taking is only carried out at the end of a financial year, the average stock is computed on the basis of adding stock beginning with stock end and dividing by 2:

Stock (1 Jan.)   £500
Stock (31 Dec.)   £150   £650/2 = £325

If stock levels at the end of the financial period are not an average indication of stock because of seasonal changes, the turnover ratio is likely to be a false representation of the business's true selling efficiency.

The collection of debt

This ratio is an indication of the period of credit taken by debtors; in other words, how long it takes them to pay their debts. The ratio has a significant bearing on both the efficiency of credit control and the accuracy of liquidity. If credit control is doing its job properly, the period of credit taken by debtors should be satisfactory. If debtors are paying their bills regularly, the liquidity ratio is more reliable.

$$\text{Average credit taken by debtors} = \frac{\text{Debtors} \times 365}{\text{Credit Sales}}$$

$$\text{(assume all sales in Allied's accounts are credit sales)} = \frac{£1,080 \times 365}{£9,000}$$
$$= \text{approximately 44 days to collect debts}$$

In general, a monthly invoice is usually paid within about 45 days.

Some manufacturing organisations which produce and sell highly expensive goods (like motor vehicles, machinery and equipment) may need to give distributors a far longer period of time in which to settle debts, such as 3 to 12 months. The method of payment may also be far more complex, involving time-payments calculated to suit both buyer and seller. The important thing to remember is that credit control should be constantly checking the reliability of individual debtors rather than merely observing an average collection period as a whole.

Creditors' payment period

This links with the collection of debt from customers. If debtors pay promptly, as in Allied's case, then there should be little problem in the payment of creditors if they are approximately in the same proportion. We will assume that all purchases of stock are on a credit basis.

$$\text{Average credit obtained from suppliers} = \frac{\text{Creditors} \times 365}{\text{Credit Purchases}}$$

$$= \frac{1{,}200 \times 365}{5{,}650}$$

$$= \text{approximately 77.5 days to pay debts.}$$

It is taking Allied Components about 2.5 months, on average, to pay creditors, and this contrasts with a more rapid response from customers who only take 1.5 months to pay. Obviously, this is a liquidity advantage to the company because it can use the extra funds provided by creditors as a significant source of capital for other projects. As long as the creditors accept this extended period of credit, then the position is sound. If, however, they always press for payment and discounts have been lost as a result, it may be time to review the situation and pay them more promptly.

Asset usage

There are a number of ratios that can be used to identify the amount of investment in assets which will generate turnover (sales). The term for these ratios varies, although asset usage or asset turnover are commonly applied.

$$\text{Sales: Capital Employed} = \frac{\text{Sales}}{\text{Capital Employed}}$$

$$= \frac{9{,}000}{21{,}500} = 0.42$$

$$\text{Sales: Trading Assets} = \frac{\text{Sales}}{\text{Current Assets}}$$

$$= \frac{9{,}000}{3{,}500} = 2.57$$

The commonly used sales: capital employed indicates the type of investment required in operational assets which are needed to produce the appropriate level of turnover. In this case, 0.42:1 may be considered very low because for every £1 invested in capital employed, only 42p is generated in sales. This is due to the very significant investment in fixed assets which may be required by this type of organisation. The sales: trading assets ratio is better and indicates that it takes £1 invested in current assets to generate £2.57 in sales. These figures must not be taken in isolation, of course, and comparisons must be made with past performances and with competitors in the same industry.

Productivity

Two ratios may be used to identify productivity in terms of the number employed. If we assume that Allied has a workforce of 200, two ratios may be calculated:

$$\text{Sales: Employees} = \frac{£9,000,000}{200}$$

$$= £45,000 \text{ turnover/employee}$$

$$\text{Profit (before tax): Employee} = \frac{£1,200,000}{200}$$

$$= £6,000 \text{ profit/employee}$$

Productivity has always been seen to be an important contributory factor to efficiency in business because the greater the productivity, the greater the profit and the more resources are available for distribution.

A business can afford to pay its workforce more if productivity increases, without it being inflationary. If productivity falls, the business is seen to be less efficient and employees produce less in terms of units to man-hours.

This could be caused by a number of factors, such as the inefficient use of manpower, plant and machinery, or technology may need up-dating. Are the figures for Allied adequate to satisfy the demand of management and shareholders?

Structure ratios (Long-term Solvency)

There are a number of ratios which may be used to identify the relationship between the members' capital and the extent of liabilities. In this sense, the structure only refers to how the business is financed: that is, internally by its owners, or, externally by the extent of its liabilities.

$$The\ Owner's\ Stake = \frac{Capital\ (Net\ Worth)}{Assets\ (Total\ Assets)}$$

$$= \frac{£15,000}{£23,000}$$

$$= 63.8\%$$

$$Interest\ Cover = \frac{Net\ Profit\ (before\ tax,\ interest)}{Interest\ Payable}$$

$$= \frac{1,600}{400} = 4:1$$

The owner's stake identifies how much the owners are worth in the business. In this case 63.8% is in the hands of the company's shareholders. This leaves 36.2% in the hands of its creditors.

The ratio of interest cover (net profit without the interest or tax payable) to the payment of interest signifies the number of times the interest can be paid from profits. Allied can cover the interest payments four times over from its profits. How sound this figure is will depend on the trend (that is, is the proportion better or worse than previous year's figures?).

Capital Gearing

Gearing refers to the relationship between ordinary shares and fixed interest payable shares plus fixed interest payable long-term liabilities, often in the shape of debentures. Gearing may be high or low, depending on the level of borrowed capital and preference capital.

The company which is high-geared has a high proportion of borrowed and preference capital relative to ordinary shares. If ordinary share capital predominates then the company is said to be low-geared.

Gearing plays an influential part in the payout of ordinary share dividends. If profits are good, the high-geared company can benefit its ordinary shareholders by paying higher dividends.

For example, if borrowing at fixed interest rates is $8\frac{1}{2}\%$ and return on investment is $14\frac{1}{2}\%$, the ordinary shareholders will obviously be delighted because they earn 6% above the fixed interest borrowed. Conversely, if returns are the opposite way around and fixed interest payments are greater than investment, the result may not only be disappointing but also financially precarious because fixed interest must be paid regardless of profits. If creditors hold the balance of financial power they can soon call in their loans and precipitate the collapse of the company.

$$\text{Capital Gearing} = \frac{\text{Debt}}{\text{Equity}}$$

$$= \frac{\text{Long-term Borrowing} + \text{Preference Share Capital}}{\text{Shareholders Funds (less Preference Shares)}}$$

Capital Gearing
of Allied Components: $= \dfrac{£8,500}{£13,000}$

$= 65\%$ (moderately low)

Example

Company A: Low-gearing – a high proportion of ordinary share capital

B: High-gearing – a low proportion of ordinary share capital

TABLE 21.4 The two companies' ratio and gearing

	Company A £	Company B £
Capital Employed:		
Issued £1 ordinary shares and paid up	100,000	25,000
11% Debenture Stock	25,000	100,000
	125,000	125,000
Ratio:	25%	400%
GEARING	LOW	HIGH

TABLE 21.5   Profit and Loss statement

	Company A £	Company B £
Trading Profit (before interest paid to Debentures)	20,000	20,000
11% Debenture Interest	2,750	11,000
Profit before Tax	17,250	9,000
Corporation tax (50%)	8,625	4,500
Profit after Tax	8,625	4,500
% Dividend available	8,625 x 100	4,500 x 100
to Equities:	100,000 1	25,000 1
	= 8.6%	= 17%

Note: Company a returns are not as high as Company B's. Company B rewards it shareholders more, even with the same level of profits. When times are goods, high returns will be expected; but when profits decline (or losses are made) interest must still be paid and a high-geared business may then be in a precarious financial position, vulnerable to its creditors. Debenture interest has also reduced the profit before tax of Company B and therefore their tax liability is less; a distinct advantage.

Investment ratios

The shares of public limited companies can be bought and sold on the Stock Exchange and these may be listed if the shares or debentures have obtained an official quotation from the Stock Exchange Council. It is these stocks and shares which are published in the daily national newspapers. Some public companies do not necessarily want official listing and may seek to be listed on the USM (the Unlisted Securities Market). This 'second division' of listing still permits the buying and selling of securities (stocks and shares) but is not under the same strict code of practice demanded of an official listing.

The shares of private limited companies do not appear on any listing of the Stock Exchange simply because securities of private companies must be dealt with privately and not publicly.

The major newspapers and particularly the *Financial Times*, list the securities each day, giving information about share prices, their change in value, dividends, yield, cover and price to earnings ratios and other significant information about the fluctuating fortunes of the stock market.

The *Financial Times Index* (FTI) is the barometer of the Exchange, and its rise or fall each day indicates how the market responds to the demand for stocks and shares. If the market believes there is confidence in the economy, demand for shares could pick up and the market is said to be 'bullish' and share prices are likely to rise. On the other hand, if confidence falls, demand can dry up and investors may rush out and sell, causing share prices to fall. This is a 'bear' market.

The investment ratios all concern ordinary shares (equities) rather than preference shares which are on a fixed rate of dividend. The following ratios of Allied Components are considered to be of significance:

(a) Earnings per Share (eps)

$$= \frac{\text{Net Profit (after tax)} - \text{Preference Dividend}}{\text{No. of Ordinary Shares}}$$

$$= \frac{\pounds 900 - \pounds 160}{3,000 \text{ shares}} = 25\text{p per share}$$

(b) Percentage Dividend

$$= \frac{\text{Sum to Ordinary Shares} \times 100}{\text{Issued \& Paid Up Capital}}$$

$$= \frac{\pounds 300 \times 100}{3,000} = 10\text{p per share} \atop (10\%)$$

(c) Yield Percentage

$$= \frac{\text{Dividend per share} \times 100}{\text{Market Value per Share*}}$$

$$= \frac{10\text{p} \times 100}{125} = 8\% \text{ yield}$$

* Market Value as listed on Exchange for Allied Components, £1.25 (125p per share).

(d) Cover

$$\frac{\text{Net Profit (after tax)} - \text{Preference Dividend}}{\text{Dividend on Ordinary Shares}}$$

$$= \frac{\pounds 900 - \pounds 160}{\pounds 300} = 2.5 \text{ times}$$

(e) Price/Earnings Ratio

$$= \frac{\text{Market Price per Share}}{\text{eps}}$$

$$= \frac{125\text{p}}{25\text{p}} = 5 \text{ times}$$

The eps is one of the most publicised ratios when companies report their half-yearly or yearly results. It indicates the earning potential of each ordinary share. Allied has an eps of 25p per share which may look very attractive to some shareholders, each share literally earning 25p in profit. This does not mean that the dividend is 25p per share, it simply indicates that each share has earned 25p.

The dividend per share is the dividend recommended by the board to its ordinary shareholders. Allied are recommending 10% or 10p per share. This links with the cover. Ordinary shares could have been paid 2.5 times what has been offered. The higher the cover, the greater the sum retained by the company, rather than paid as dividends. If the cover is low, it indicates that the board is offering the shareholders most of the available profit, less being retained by the company as reserves.

The price to earnings (P/E) ratio indicates the market value of a share in relation to the number of years' profits it represents. In other words, a P/E of 5 means that the current market price of £1.25 equals approximately 5 years of current profit earned. Generally speaking, the higher the P/E ratio, the better. It indicates what the market is prepared to pay for them.

The investment ratios concerning Allied PLC may then be analysed and compared with other stocks and shares on the Exchange.

eps	25p/share
Dividend to Ordinaries	10p/share or 10%
Yield/	8%
Cover	2.47 times
P/E ratio	5 times

The figures appear far from spectacular, but the market value of the shares is only 25p above the nominal value and it may be, given time, and with more profits retained for expansion purposes, that the market value of the shares could increase. The dividends to ordinary shareholders may remain relatively small. What does the investor want? Income from dividends or capital income derived from the increase in the market value of the shares?

A good investment or not? Retain or sell? It is difficult to say. The Stock Exchange is a reliable source as far as the reporting of figures is concerned, yet nothing is certain as to which shares will be successful.

The limitations of accounting ratios and parties interested in financial information

Accounting ratios need to be analysed and interpreted and not merely listed as a set of figures. They need to be compared with the previous year's performances and, where possible, with other similar organisations to investigate and evaluate what the figures indicate.

There have been a number of cases where accounting ratios have indicated a sound financial position but, on closer inspection of the accounts, evidence has revealed that the 'apparent soundness' of the figures is merely an empty shell and the organisation is far from sound.

For example, a liquidity ratio may indicate an 'ideal' situation of 2:1, yet this may be entirely because of a heavy stock position which is old or obsolete and, although measured at cost, in real terms is worth far less and would be difficult to off-load to the market.

It may be that a preponderance of debtors, who are at best unreliable, is responsible for achieving an unrealistic liquidity ratio which looks very sound on paper but in actual terms is precarious because a certain proportion of debtors should have been written down or written off. What of the 'ideal' 2:1 ratio when the business goes bankrupt or a company is liquidated a few months later?

Accounting ratios can never reveal the whole story about a business because they can never provide all the information needed to make a full evaluation. A business may look fine on paper, but what is it really like? Do the figures reveal anything about the ability of its management or the relationship between the management and the rest of its employees? Is the company dynamic, aggressive, attractive, traditional, bright or dull?

Not all organisations are the same because of the nature, size, structure, management policy and many other aspects which concern the running of a business. This will make it more difficult to compare financial performance between different organisations unless some of these aspects are addressed. The High Street banks do make performance comparisons between companies and bear in mind their size, turnover and nature of the industry being compared.

Not only owners and management are interested in the performance of their organisations. Bankers and creditors who may be asked to lend money to the business need to know if their investment is going to be sound. Accounting ratios may help them to decide whether or not to go ahead. They will also need to be cautious about the reliability of the accounts and the ratios calculated and may wish to make more inquiries to organisations like Dun & Bradstreet who specialise in assessing the 'credit rating' of different business organisations.

Employees may also be interested in the financial performance of their organisations from the point of view of productivity and profits. If the business is successful and productivity is improving, the trade unions have a solid platform when negotiating new pay awards and conditions.

Shareholders of companies and potential shareholders who may not be in a position to know the reliability of firms need investment advice from a bank or other financial institution. The *Financial Times* share section can also give current information concerning dividends and yields, etc., but professional help is still needed to guide shareholders through the maze of security (shares) dealings.

The Inland Revenue is also an interested party because it needs to assess the level of taxation to be charged against profits and against dividends paid to shareholders.

Example: Accounting Ratios and Evaluation

Table 21.6 and 21.7 represent the accounts of XYZ Co. for the year ended 31 December.

Required:

(a) Use appropriate accounting ratios to evaluate both Year 1 and 2 (see Table 21.8).
(b) Compare the performance of the firm over the two years.

TABLE 21.6 Trading and profit and loss account year ended 31 December

	Year 1 £	Year 2 £
Sales	50,000	60,000
Cost of sales	30,000	40,000
Gross Profit	20,000	20,000
Distribution costs and Selling expenses	5,000	7,000
Administration expenses	4,000	5,000
Net Profit	11,000	8,000

TABLE 21.7 Balance sheet as at 31 December

	£	£
Fixed assets	37,000	45,700
Current assets	20,900	24,000
	57,900	69,700
Current liabilities	9,900	18,500
Long-term liabilities	6,000	3,700
	42,000	47,500
Financed by:		
Capital: 40,000 (a £1 ord. shares	40,000	40,000
Reserves	2,000	7,500
	42,000	47,500
Note: Average stock	7,500	8,500

TABLE 21.8   Accounting ratios

	Year 1	Year 2
1. *Profitability*:		
Gross profit %	40%	33.33%
Net profit %	22%	13.33%
Return of capital employed	22.9%	15.6%
eps	27.5p	20.0p
2. *Liquidity*:		
Current ratio (working capital ratio)	2:1	1.3:1
Acid test	1.35:1	0.75:1
3. *Efficiency*:		
Stock turnover	4. times	4.7 times
Cost of Sales%	60.%	67.%
Distribution and Selling expenses	10.%	11.%
Administrative expenses	8.%	8.3%
4 *Ownership Structure*:		
Shareholder's stake	72.5%	68.1%
(Proprietorship ratio)		
Capital gearing	14.3%	7.8%

Evaluation of Performance

The Year 1 profit ratios are all superior to Year 2. The basic reason why this is the case lies in the cost of sales which increased from 60% to 67% in the year, thereby reducing the gross percentage by 7%. Why was this?

Sales had expanded by £10,000 in Year 2 and stock turnover had also increased marginally, but the actual gross profit remained the same at £20,000 in both years. Perhaps sales prices were marked too low (to generate greater sales) but sales did not respond sharply enough to gain more gross profit. It could also mean that insufficient savings were made when buying stocks.

The extra profit and loss expenses ensured that the net profit fell by £3,000, thereby reducing returns. The company has expanded (not only its sales but also in its fixed assets) but it has not yet generated greater profit returns.

Liquidity has also suffered with both current and acid test ratios declining markedly. From an 'ideal' 2:1, the current ratio has slipped to a more marginal 1:3. Creditors have doubled in the year due to expansion and this has weakened the company's ability to meet its short-term debts. Expanding the business has required greater credit, and the purchase of fixed assets (£8,700) has also added to the pressure.

However, the expansion scheme may show improved results in the following years depending on whether or not the company can increase its share of the market. It may take time for expansion schemes to develop towards full potential.

Although the shareholders' ownership in the business has declined marginally due to the extra burden of current liabilities capital gearing is halved to only 7.8% which is very low, indicating very sound long-term solvency.

Limitations

One must recognise the fact that figures alone cannot tell the full tale! What else is known about this company? Very little.

What does it produce/buy/sell? How do these figures compare with similar enterprises in terms of size and nature of business? What style of management exists? Is the workforce relatively stable? Are the figures realistic in terms of valuation (stock, premises, equipment, etc.)? Are provisions adequate?

In summary, we may say that the company has expanded its operations and in terms of accounting ratios, the results are virtually all inferior in Year 2. However, it may take some time for improvements to channel through and benefits to materialise. If they do, then financial performance will improve. It all rests with customers. They alone create the demand for goods or services and are the arbiters of fortune. Success or failure depends on them.

Questions

1. The following trading results refer to the accounts of P. Jackson & Co. during the last three years, year ending 31 December.

	Year 1 £	Year 2 £	Year 3 £
Trading and Profit and Loss			
Sales:			
Cash	5,000	6,000	8,000
Credit	25,000	30,000	37,000
Cost of sales	20,000	24,000	31,950
Distribution costs	3,000	3,200	4,100
Administration expenses	3,150	3,750	4,275
Stock:			
1 Jan.	1,950	2,050	2,950
31 Dec.	2,050	2,950	5,050
Balance Sheet (extract)			
Debtors	5,000	6,000	9,000
Capital Invested (1 Jan.)	26,500	30,000	31,750

Required:

(a) The trading and profit and loss account of P. Jackson & Co. for each of the 3 years ending 31 December.
(b) Accounting ratios to indicate:

Gross Profit %
Net Profit %
Expense %

Rate of stock turnover
Credit taken by debtors
Return on capital invested

(c) Brief comments using the accounting ratios to give some indication of the firm's performance over the 3 years. What limitations do the ratios impose?

2. Study the following information regarding companies A and B then answer the following questions below.

Profit and Loss Account	Company A £	Company B £
Turnover	9,000	24,000
Cost of goods	5,000	10,500
Other Expenses		
Selling	500	4,750
Administration	750	2,250
Financial	300	500
Balance Sheet		
Fixed assets	7,000	10,000
Current assets	4,275	6,750
Current liabilities	2,000	3,500

Required:

(a) Preparation of profit and loss accounts for the year ended 31 December and balance sheets as at that date.
(b) Profitability: Gross Profit %
             Net Profit %
             Return on Capital
(c) Working capital and working capital ratio.
(d) A brief comment on the results comparing the two firms.

3. Below are shown the summarised balance sheets of Harry Smith at the end of three consecutive years:

	Year 1 £	Year 2 £	Year 3 £
Creditors	6,480	9,740	12,565
Bank	—	—	1,500
Loan (long-term)	12,500	10,500	10,000
Capital	24,100	24,180	26,220
	43,080	44,420	50,285
Cash in hand	100	100	250
Bank	1,450	1,750	—
Debtors	8,455	7,940	9,165
Stock	4,575	6,230	10,120
Shop fittings	3,500	3,400	5,750
Premises	25,000	25,000	25,000
	43,080	44,420	50,285

From these balances you are required:

(a) to calculate the amount of the working capital at the end of each year;
(b) to calculate the ratio of current assets to current liabilities correct to one decimal place at the end of each year;
(c) to calculate the acid test correct to one decimal place at the end of each year;
(d) which year do you consider has been the 'safest' as far as Harry's ability to repay debts?

4. The following represents the accounts of XYZ Co. for the year ended 31 December

Trading and Profit and Loss a/c year ended 31 December

	Year 1 £	Year 2 £	Year 3 £
Sales	50,000	60,000	80,000
Cost of sales	30,000	40,000	48,000
Gross profit	20,000	20,000	32,000
Distribution costs and selling expenses	5,000	7,000	12,000
Administration expenses	4,000	5,000	6,000
Net profit	11,000	8,000	14,000

Balance Sheet as at 31 December

	Year 1	Year 2	Year 3
Fixed assets	37,000	45,700	55,000
Current assets	20,900	24,000	30,000
	57,900	69,700	85,000
Current liabilities	9,900	18,500	24,000
Long-term liabilities	6,000	3,700	5,500
Net assets	42,000	47,500	55,500
Financed by:			
Capital	31,000	42,000	47,500
Net profit	11,000	8,000	14,000
Drawings		(2,500)	(6,000)
	42,000	47,500	55,500

Required:

(a) Use appropriate accounting ratios to evaluate Year 1, Year 2 and Year 3.

(b) Compare the performance of the firm over the three years.

5. Rocco Bank Ltd and Ball Bearings Ltd are two independent companies in the type of business activity their names suggest.

As a young financial adviser, you are asked to assess the situation of both companies by studying the figures given below:

	Ball Bearings Ltd		Rocco Bank Ltd	
	£000s	£000s	£000s	£000s
Fixed assets (net)	39,000		4,000	
Intangibles	4,000		—	
Investments (long-term)	2,000	45,000	9,000	13,000
Stocks	27,000			
Debtors	25,000			
Advances			21,000	
Cash, liquid assets	—		59,000	
Investments	3,000	55,000	7,000	87,000
		100,000		100,000
Creditors	48,000			
Taxation	1,000		1,000	
Current and deposit accounts			91,000	
Bank	7,000	56,000		92,000
10% debenture stock		33,000		500
Shareholders' Funds				
Ordinary Shares @ £1	10,000		2,000	
Reserves	1,000	11,000	5,500	7,500
		100,000		100,000
Net Profit (before tax)		2,500		2,600
Proposed ordinary dividends		700		400

Required:

Choose accounting ratios which you consider will reveal the differences between the two companies. Discuss your calculations from the point of view of profitability and financial stability.

[Institute of Bankers]

6. ABC Co. Ltd is a small private company in the rag trade. Its first four years trading annually to 31 December were made up as follows:

Year	Sales	Purchases	Increase or decrease of material stocks during year	Selling and distribution costs	Rent	General administrative expenses
	£	£	£	£	£	£
1	36,000	39,000	+ 12,000	900	3,000	4,500
2	54,000	37,500	- 3,000	1,250	3,000	5,250
3	78,000	63,000	+ 4,500	2,500	3,000	6,000
4	120,000	108,000	+ 12,000	4,000	3,500	11,500

Required:

(a) Trading and profit and loss accounts in columnar form for each of the four years ending 31 December.
(b) Two accounting ratios for each of the four years.
(c) A brief discussion of the implication of these figures and the inferences drawn from them.

[Institute of Bankers]

7. The following figures relate to a retailing organisation which has expanded its business operations. Its premises were converted into a 'self-service' style during the 2nd year:

	Yr 1 £	Yr 2 £	Yr 3 £
Net sales	120,000	150,000	200,000
Gross profit %	30%	33$\frac{1}{3}$%	35%
Fixed expenses:	20,000	25,000	30,000
Variable expenses: (12% of sales)	?	?	?
Average stock held (cost):	8,000	8,500	10,000
Capital employed:	60,000	105,000	160,000

Required:

(a) Prepare the trading and profit and loss accounts for each trading year, preferably in columnar format.
(b) In tabular form, prepare the appropriate business profit

returns and also the rate of stock turnover for each of the above years.

(c) Briefly evaluate the business's progress over the three years in terms of its efficiency and profits.

8. Andrew Rob-David plc intends to expand its business activities and the Board of Directors are in agreement that an extra £500,000 will be required to meet their plans.
    The schemes which have been put forward are:

Scheme A
    To issue £500,000 10% preference shares @ £1 per share at par.
Scheme B
    To issue £500,000 ordinary shares @ £1 per share at par.
Scheme C
    To issue £500,000 10% redeemable debenture stock.

The company's current share capital consists of 3,000,000 @ £1 ordinary shares, issued and paid up.

Next year, it is estimated that a dividend of 12% will be declared by the board.

The accountant of the company has estimated that the profit for the budget year ended 31 December 199–5 will be £700,000, *before* the payment of interest or taxation.

This year's interest payments on the company's overdraft is £5,000 and it is estimated that the same payment will be made next year, 199–5.

Corporation tax on the company's profits is at a rate of 35%.

As the assistant to the accountant, you have been asked to prepare the following:

(a) An estimated profit and loss appropriation account for 31 December 199–5 for each of the three schemes, in tabular form. Commence your account with Net Profit *before* interest payments and taxation.
(b) Calculate, for each of the three schemes, the Eps and capital gearing and state which scheme, in your view, is likely to be the most appropriate.
(c) As an information leaflet is to be sent to existing shareholders, draft a suitable section to be included which will clearly differentiate between:

- equity shares
- preference shares
- redeemable debentures

[Institute of Bankers]

9. The summarised trading and profit and loss accounts for the three years ended 30 September and the balance sheets as at 30 September T. Carr Limited are as follows:

Trading and profit and loss accounts

Years ended 30 September	Yr 1		Yr 2		Yr 3	
	£'000	£'000	£'000	£'000	£'000	£'000
Sales		120		180		270
Less: Cost of sales		80		135		216
Gross profit		40		45		54
Less: Overhead expenses						
Variable	18		27		27	
Fixed	10	28	10	37	20	47
Net profit		12		8		7

Balance sheet

As at 30 September	£'000	£'000	£'000	£'000	£'000	£'000
Fixed assets		30		60		80
Current assets						
Stock	24		25		40	
Debtors	26		40		55	
Balance at bank	20		10		—	
	70		75		95	
Less: Current liabilities						
Creditors	20		35		45	
Bank overdraft	—		—		10	
	20	50	35	40	55	40
		80		100		120
Share capital:						
Ordinary shares of £1		50		62		75
Retained earnings		30		38		45
		80		100		120

The major objective of the company in each of the last two financial years has been to increase turnover by 50 % on the immediately preceding year.

Required:

(a) Prepare a table of four accounting ratios, each ratio showing a distinctly different aspect of changes in the company during the past three years.
(*Note*: The ratios may be expressed as percentages.)
(b) A brief, but reasoned, report addressed to James and Henry Carr concerning the advisability of the company continuing to concentrate on increasing turnover by 50% each year.

[Association of Accounting Technicians]

10. Jane Winters is currently considering which of two companies she should choose for the investment of a legacy from her late father's estate. The choice lies between purchasing all the share capital of A Limited and purchasing 40% of the share capital of B Limited. Whilst neither A Limited nor B Limited has paid any dividends in recent years, it is anticipated that the companies will resume dividends in the next year or two.

The summarised final accounts of the companies for their last completed financial year are as follows:

Trading and profit and loss accounts

| | A Limited | | | B Limited |
£	£		£	£
	160,000	Sales		240,000
		Cost of sales:		
10,000		Opening stock	70,000	
140,000		Purchases	160,000	
150,000			230,000	
30,000		Closing stock	50,000	
	120,000			180,000
	40,000	Gross profit		60,000
		Less:		
10,000		Establishment expenses	14,000	
12,000		Administrative expenses	18,000	
6,000		Sales and distribution expenses	9,500	
3,000		Financial expenses	500	
	31,000			42,000
	9,000	Net profit		18,000

Balance sheet

A Limited			B Limited	
£	£		£	£
	80,000	Fixed assets		180,000
		Current assets:		
30,000		Stock	50,000	
6,000		Debtors	20,000	
4,000		Balance at bank	10,000	
40,000			80,000	
		Creditors: Amounts falling due within one year		
10,000		Trade creditors	20,000	
	30,000			60,000
	110,000			240,000
		Creditors: Amounts falling due after more than one year		
	30,000	10% loan stock		5,000
	80,000			235,000
		Represented by:		
	60,000	Ordinary share capital		160,000
	20,000	Retained earnings		75,000
	80,000			235,000

Required:

(a) Prepare a schedule of appropriate accounting ratios or financial ratios utilising the information given on the two companies, A Limited and B limited, to permit a comparison to be made between these companies in each of the following areas: profitability; effective use of resources; short-term solvency; long-term solvency.
   Answers should include 8 ratios or other statistics, each one of which should be stated at 2 decimal places. Taxation is to be ignored.
(b) A report to Jane Winters drawing attention to the comparative strengths and weaknesses of each of the companies A limited and B Limited as revealed in the answer to (a) above and making reference to other significant matters which should be borne in mind by Jane Winters when making her investment decision.
   Note: Assume that the report is from a financial adviser.

[Association of Accounting Technicians]

CHAPTER 22

VAT and VAT Returns

As we have already mentioned, VAT is a charge on most of our goods and services in the United Kingdom and represents an indirect source of taxation for the Government. The cost of this tax, charged between traders in business, eventually falls to the consumer who is purchasing the product. Businesses, in effect, are the collectors of VAT along the chain of distribution, and consumers are the eventual payers.

Those businesses which are VAT registered (that is, they have received the Certificate of Registration from Customs & Excise, the Government Department responsible for the collection of VAT), are given a VAT registration number and the date of their tax period which, in most cases, lasts 3 months (a quarterly return). The VAT account is therefore normally settled on a quarterly basis.

Supplies of goods and services may be at the standard rate, zero rated or exempt. The current standard rate of VAT charged is 17.5% on most of our goods and services. The Chancellor of the Exchequer, responsible to the Government for deciding taxation rates, has over recent years imposed the standard rate on a wider area of products. Under much pressure to raise more revenue in order to cut the budget deficit, he imposed VAT from 1 April 1994 at 8% on all domestic fuel and power, which then increased to the standard rate a year later.

VAT calculations

When we purchase goods or services, we do not pay a separate sum for VAT; it is part of the price paid. Businesses charge VAT on goods sold (VAT outputs) and are themselves charged on goods purchased (VAT inputs).

The total VAT received in a tax period less the total VAT paid is completed on the traders' form VAT 100, the difference between the two being the balance due to the VAT office. In a simple example:

Sales in the quarter £4,230 (inclusive of VAT)
Purchases in the quarter £3,290 (inclusive of VAT)

How much VAT is due to the VAT office?

$$\text{VAT outputs (on sales)} \quad = \frac{4{,}230 \times 7}{47} = £630$$

$$\text{VAT inputs (on purchases)} = \frac{3{,}290 \times 7}{47} = £490$$

The difference between outputs and inputs (630 − 490) = the tax due: £140. This would be payable to the VAT office along with the tax return form VAT 100. If the inputs of VAT had been £630 against the outputs of VAT £490 because more goods and services were purchased in a tax period than sold, then the VAT office would owe the business £140 for that period.

Most tax periods are payable quarterly although some traders prefer to have monthly tax periods, particularly if they are likely to get refunds because they deal with zero-rated supplies. Other traders can have annual tax periods.

The cash accounting scheme allows traders the advantage of accounting for their VAT on the basis of receiving and paying cash, rather than on the normal invoice dates which are taken as the date of the tax point. In other words, the VAT return is prepared from the cash receipts (VAT outputs) less the cash payments (VAT inputs) in the given tax period. The turnover threshold of this scheme is currently for those traders whose taxable turnover, not including VAT, is less than £350,000 per annum.

The annual accounting scheme allows businesses to make a VAT return just once a year but again, there is a turnover threshold and it is intended for those traders having a turnover (excluding VAT) less than £300,00 per annum. Traders are directed to make payments on account to the VAT office through the year on the amount due to them.

Businesses which are not registered for VAT because they sell exempt supplies or are under the turnover threshold because they are a small business, do not need to account for VAT or keep records for VAT purposes.

Those businesses which are registered with the VAT office must retain records of their transactions for 6 years (unless Customs & Excise grant permission to destroy records at an earlier date).

Note that SSAP 5 (Accounting for VAT) is the standard dealing with this topic. For further details on this statement, see Chapter 23, SSAPs and FRSs.

Foreign trade

Goods and services imported to the UK are subject to the same rules and regulations when these same goods are available here at home. Since the Single European Market came into force on 1 January 1993, the idea of imports and exports between the member states of the EC has been abandoned. Instead of 'imports' the term is 'acquisition'. When a buyer from the UK acquires goods or services from a member state, he will account for VAT on the form VAT 100 in the normal way under VAT inputs.

If goods are imported from a non-EC country, the importer will have to account for them to Customs & Excise at the port of entry. Customs will provide a certificate as evidence that goods were imported and this can then be treated as a taxable input on the importer's next return on form VAT 100.

The export of goods from the UK is zero rated.

Input tax

For registered traders, input tax offsets the amount deductible to the VAT Office. Most of the business's capital and revenue expenditure is allowable for VAT inputs if they are wholly for business purposes. Not all expenditure items are allowable, however, and these concern:

(a) the acquisition of motor cars (unless it is for stock resale by a business buying and selling vehicles, or for taxi, car hire, driving school, or other purposes where the vehicle generates income);

(b) non-business expenses incurred by the organisation on items such as entertainment, meals, private use of facilities, etc., where the VAT office does not see these as business-related.

In such cases as these, the full charge for the expense (including VAT) can be made in the annual profit and loss account.

Bad debts

If bad debts occur when a trader is registered for VAT, bad debt relief may be claimed as a VAT input in the case where a customer's debt has been owing for a minimum period of 12 months and the debt has been written off as bad in the accounting books. If, at a later point, the customer repays the debt (bad debts recovered), the VAT office must be repaid with the input tax.

Assume that a business is registered with Customs & Excise. The end of the VAT quarter is 28 February and it will need to complete the VAT Form 100 and send it off with the sum payable (if any), not usually later than the 20th day of the following month.

In February, the quarter totals of sales and purchases figures were:

net sales (less returns in)	£60,000 (exc. VAT)
net purchases (less returns out)	£40,000 (exc. VAT)
sales (output tax)	£60,000 × 17.5% = £10,500
purchases (input tax)	£40,000 × 17.5% = £7,000

In addition to these figures, we have £800 of allowable expenses on which VAT of £140 was charged. This is an input tax in the same way as purchases.

The nominal ledger records and the VAT Form 100, completed on 28 February, would appear as shown in Table 22.1.

On 28 February, the VAT account shows a credit balance of £3,360, indicating that this sum is payable to the Customs & Excise VAT Central Unit not later than 20 March.

The VAT Form 100 is shown in Figure 22.1 indicating the sum payable to the VAT Office (£3,360).

TABLE 22.1   Nominal ledger

	Debit £	Credit £	Balance £
Sales account			
28/2 Balance			60,000 Cr.
Purchases account			
28/2 Balance			40,000 Dr.
Vat account			
28/2 Debtors		10,500	10,500 Cr.
28/2 Creditors	7,000		3,500
28/2 Expenses	140		3,360

H M Customs and Excise

Value Added Tax Return
For the period
1 November to 28 February

Due to reach the VAT Central Unit by
These dates must not be altered.

R. PEARCE SPORTS LTD.
77 Penhill Road
Parkstone
Poole

004766/03

For Official Use

Registration No	Period
76 48424	1

Before you fill in this form please read the notes on the other side. You must complete all boxes — writing "none" where necessary. If you need to show an exact amount of pounds, please write "00" in the pence column. Don't put a dash or leave the column blank. Please write clearly in ink.

You must ensure that the completed form and any VAT payable are received no later than the due date by the Controller, VAT Central Unit, H M Customs and Excise, 21 Victoria Avenue, SOUTHEND-ON-SEA X

SS99 1AL

An envelope is enclosed for your use

For Official Use				£	p

			£	p
VAT DUE in this period on OUTPUTS (sales, etc), certain postal imports and services received from abroad	1	10500		
Underdeclarations of VAT made on previous returns (but not those notified in writing by Customs and Excise)	2	none		
TOTAL VAT DUE (box 1 + box 2)	3	10500		
VAT DEDUCTIBLE in this period on INPUTS (purchases, etc)	4	7140		
Overdeclarations of VAT made on previous returns (but not those notified in writing by Customs and Excise)	5	none		
TOTAL VAT DEDUCTIBLE (box 4 + box 5)	6	7140		
NET VAT PAYABLE OR REPAYABLE (Difference between boxes 3 and 6)	7	3360		
Value of Outputs (excluding any VAT)	8	60000		00
Value of Inputs (excluding any VAT)	9	40800		00

WARNING

From 1.1.90 interest will be charged on underdeclared tax. There will also be a penalty for large errors. Accuracy will avoid these extra charges.

Please tick only ONE of these boxes:

box 3 greater than box 6 — payment by credit transfer [ ]   payment enclosed [✓]

box 6 greater than box 3 — repayment due [ ]

How to pay the VAt due

Cross all cheques and postal orders "A/C Payee only" and make them payable to "HM Customs and Excise". Make credit transfers through account 3078027 at National Girobank or 10-70-50 52055000 for Bank Giros and keep your payment slip. You can order pre-printed booklets of credit transfer slips from your local VAT office. In your own interest do not send notes, coins, or uncrossed postal orders through the post.

Please write your VAT registration number on the back of all cheques and credit transfer slips.

Please tick box(es) if the statement(s) apply:

box 5 includes bad debt relief [ ]   box 8 includes exempt outputs [ ]   box 8 includes exports [ ]

Retail schemes If you have used any of the schemes in the period covered by this return please tick the box(es) to show all the schemes used

A	B	C	D	E	F	G	H	J

Remember, you could be liable to a financial penalty if your return and all the VAT payable are not received by the due date.
DECLARATION by the signatory to be completed by or on behalf of the person named above.

I, ... JOHN CHAPPLE [accountant, R. PEARCE SPORTS] .... declare that the
(full name of signatory in BLOCK LETTERS)

information given above is true and complete.

Signed .... *J Chapple* .... Date .... 14 March .... 19 ......
*(Proprietor, partner, director, secretary, responsible officer, committee member of club or association, duly authorised person)   * Delete as necessary

FOR OFFICIAL USE

VAT 100

VAT at standard, zero rate and exempt

Remember that VAT is paid on most of our goods and services and is a charge on consumer expenditure. It is also collected on imports as well as domestic business transactions and is an indirect source of tax, payable to HM Customs & Excise Department.

A taxable element is an individual, firm or company which is, or is required to be, registered for VAT.

If traders are registered with Customs & Excise and buy and sell taxable supplies of goods or services, it means that they must account for VAT. When sales are made, VAT is charged at the standard rate and is the output tax. On purchases of goods or services supplied to the trader, the VAT is the input tax.

The VAT account records these outputs (sales) as credit entries, and inputs (purchases) as debit entries. If outputs in a given tax period are greater than inputs, then the difference in VAT is owed to the VAT office. Conversely, if inputs are greater than outputs, the VAT office will need to pay the trader the difference.

Zero-rated supplies

Most business transactions are at the *standard rate*, currently 17.5%, or the *zero rate*, which is nil. Zero-rated supplies include:

(a) most food (but not catering which includes meals in res-taurants, cafes, etc.);
(b) books and newspapers;
(c) young children's clothing and footwear;
(d) the export of goods;
(e) prescription charges;
(f) the construction (or long leasing) of new houses and some other buildings but not existing buildings;

Zero-rated supplies of goods or services cannot charge VAT on sales but a firm can recover its VAT charges on purchases or any other business expenses.

From the date on which a trader is first required to be regis-tered, all taxable supplies, either at the standard or zero rate, are liable for VAT.

Exempt supplies

Exempt supplies are transactions on which VAT is not charged. If a trader is exempt from VAT, he must not charge VAT on the supplies of goods or services to customers. At the same time, the trader is not allowed to reclaim any VAT he may have paid on purchases or other business expenses.

Those traders with a small turnover (below that set by the Chancellor's threshold), are exempt and need not keep VAT records. The taxable turnover is the value of all taxable supplies which are either at the standard rate or zero-rated, made in the UK. Note that the turnover does not include any supplies that are exempt. Exempt supplies also include:

(a) insurance;
(b) betting, gaming and lotteries (but not gaming machines, club subscriptions and admission to premises);
(c) certain education and training;
(d) the services of doctors, dentists, opticians;
(e) membership benefits provided by trade unions and professional bodies;
(f) entries to certain sports competitions;
(g) the letting, leasing and sales of most land and buildings (but not hotel and holiday accommodation or garages and parking spaces);
(h) the provision of credit services including the operation of bank accounts.

If a trader supplies mostly zero-rated goods, he or she may be exempt from VAT registration, particularly if the input tax would normally exceed the output tax. However, once exempted, the trader cannot recover VAT paid on purchases of goods or services.

On the other hand, a trader could still register for VAT even though his or her turnover may be under the required threshold. Before applying, however, a trader needs to think carefully whether registration would gain benefit, because once registered all outputs and inputs of VAT must be accurately accounted for, including the formality of sending VAT returns regularly to the VAT offices. The return is normally on a quarterly basis (on Form VAT 100). The period covered by the return is called the tax period and details of supplies made and received in that period will need to be entered on the form.

Tax invoices

All documents relating to VAT, including credit and debit notes, must be filed and retained in order to reclaim input tax. The invoice date is usually taken as the tax point when the supply is made. A business must comply strictly with the requirements as outlined by Customs & Excise as to the preparation of invoices, including:

(a) the business's name, address and VAT registration number;
(b) date of supply;
(c) customer's name and address;
(d) the description of the goods or services supplied;
(e) the total cost of the goods or services (excluding VAT charged);
(f) the rate of any trade or cash discounts offered;
(g) the total VAT payable;
(h) the total amount of the invoice.

A business's VAT details

To provide you with an example of inputs and outputs of VAT, the information in Table 22.2 relates to a business's activity for the quarter from January to March inclusive.

Assume that on 1 January the VAT account had a balance of £1,480 credit and this had been settled with the VAT office on the

TABLE 22.2   Business activity January–March

	£ (inc. VAT)	£ VAT
Sales (outputs)	61,428.0	9,148.85
Purchases (inputs)	47,700.0	7,104.26
Motor expenses	1,245.0	185.43
Telephone	380.0	56.60
Advertising	587.5	87.50
Accounts fees	493.5	73.50
General expenses	263.2	39.20
Total inputs	50,669.2	7,546.49
Outputs		9,148.45
Inputs		7,546.49
Total VAT payable:		1,601.96

Note: To calculate the VAT at 17.5% when it is inclusive, multiply by 7 and divide by 47.

TABLE 22.3   VAT accounts 31 March

VAT account	Debit £	Credit £	Balance £
1/1 Balance			1,480.00 Cr.
14/1 Bank	1,480.00		—
31/3 Outputs		9,148.45	9,148.45 Cr.
31/3 Inputs	7,546.49		1,601.96 Cr.

14th. The VAT account on 31 March would appear as shown in Table 22.3.

The balance owing to the VAT Office = £1,601.96.

Questions

---

1. Janet Jones provides you with the following information for her last quarter for VAT purposes:

   sales (taxable outputs) £393,390 (inclusive of VAT at standard rate);
   purchases (taxable inputs) £281,060 (inclusive of VAT at standard rate).

   During this period, Janet paid £9,875 in settlement of the previous quarter's return. (Open the VAT account with this as a credit.) Draft the VAT account to record these entries for the quarter.

2. The following data refers to the accounts of Susan Brambles Ltd for the VAT tax period April–June. Note that all the figures are *inclusive* of VAT.

	£
Sales	14,570
Purchases	11,327
Credits allowed to customers	940
Credits received from suppliers	799
Equipment purchases	987
New motor car for finance chief	8,850
Operating expenses allowable by VAT office	846

There was also an over-payment made to the VAT office of £62 in the previous period.
Note that credits refer to returns inward and outward.

Required:

(a) The VAT account for the period to 30 June.
(b) The sales and purchase figures to June (returns inclusive of these).
(c) The amounts which will be posted to equipment, vehicles and operating expenses accounts.

3. Answer the following questions in brief:

(a) Although VAT is normally collected on a quarterly basis, what other methods are allowed by the VAT office?
(b) At what date is the tax point normally identified?
(c) How would EC imports normally be dealt with if they were taxable items?
(d) When can bad debts relief be taken as a taxable input?
(e) Are all expenses by a business allowable for taxable input?
(f) How does a business, which is exempt from VAT, record VAT when it is charged against them?
(g) How does a business which is zero rated deal with VAT in its accounts?

4. Study form VAT 100 and see if you can enter the details derived from question 2 on to the form. Please note that in boxes 6 and 7 the value of all outputs and inputs (excluding VAT) is to include zero-rated and exempt supplies. For those items which are VAT exempt (car), where the VAT is blocked, the value of the VAT is added to the overall cost of items. Check your answers in the VAT return shown.

					£
Box 8 (Outputs) sales	12,400	–	800	=	11,600
Box 9 (Inputs)	purchases (–680)	8,960			
	equipment	840			
	allowable expenses	720			
	blocked motor VAT	1,318			11,838

Value Added Tax Return

For the period
to

Due to reach the VAT Central Unit by
These dates must not be altered.

H M Customs
and Excise

For Official Use

Registration No   Period

Before you fill in this form please read the notes on the other side. You must complete all boxes — writing "none" where necessary. If you need to show an exact amount of pounds, please write "00" in the pence column. Don't put a dash or leave the column blank. Please write clearly in ink.
You must ensure that the completed form and any VAT payable are received no later than the due date by the Controller, VAT Central Unit, H M Customs and Excise, 21 Victoria Avenue, SOUTHEND-ON-SEA X

An envelope is enclosed for your use

For Official Use	£	p

FOR OFFICIAL USE			£	p
VAT DUE in this period on OUTPUTS (sales, etc), certain postal imports and services received from abroad	1	2,030		
Underdeclarations of VAT made on previous returns (but not those notified in writing by Customs and Excise)	2	—		
TOTAL VAT DUE (box 1 + box 2)	3	2,030		
VAT DEDUCTIBLE in this period on INPUTS (purchases, etc)	4	1,841		
Overdeclarations of VAT made on previous returns (but not those notified in writing by Customs and Excise)	5	62		
TOTAL VAT DEDUCTIBLE (box 4 + box 5)	6	1,903		
NET VAT PAYABLE OR REPAYABLE (Difference between boxes 3 and 6)	7	127		

Please tick only ONE of these boxes:

box 3 greater than box 6   payment by credit transfer ☐   payment enclosed ☐

box 6 greater than box 3   repayment due ☐

		£	p
Value of Outputs (excluding any VAT)	8	11,600	00
Value of Inputs (excluding any VAT)	9	11,838	00

How to pay the VAt due
Cross all cheques and postal orders "A/C Payee only" and make them payable to "HM Customs and Excise". Make credit transfers through account 3078027 at National Girobank or 10-70-50   52055000 for Bank Giros and keep your payment slip. You can order pre-printed booklets of credit transfer slips from your local VAT office. In your own interest do not send notes, coins, or uncrossed postal orders through the post.
Please write your VAT registration number on the back of all cheques and credit transfer slips.

Please tick box(es) if the statement(s) apply:

box 5 includes bad debt relief ☐   box 8 includes exempt outputs ☐   box 8 includes exports ☐

Retail schemes   If you have used any of the schemes in the period covered by the return please tick the box(es) to show all the schemes used

A	B	C	D	E	F	G	H	J

Remember, you could be liable to a financial penalty if your return and all the VAT payable are not received by the due date.
DECLARATION by the signatory to be completed by or on behalf of the person named above.

I, ... declare that the
(full name of signatory in BLOCK LETTERS)

information given above is true and complete.

Signed .... Date .... 19 ....
*(Proprietor, partner, director, secretary, responsible officer, committee member of club or association, duly authorised person)   * *Delete as necessary*

FOR OFFICIAL USE

VAT 100

CHAPTER 23

SSAPs and FRSs

Statements of Standard Accounting Practice SSAPs and Financial Reporting Statements FRSs represent the profession's accounting standards. These statements are prepared for the purpose of standardising the preparation of the final accounts of a business, and all accounts of the profession are expected to conform to these standards.

The preparation and publication of the SSAPs had been the responsibility of the six major accounting bodies of the UK (the ASC), Accounting Standards Committee and provided both guidance and greater reliability to accountants in preparing the financial statements of a business. One of the principal statements is SSAP 2, Disclosure of Accounting Policies, issued in 1971, which has outlined the basic accounting concepts; these will be discussed in greater detail in the next few pages. Largely due to these published statements, there has been far greater conformity and therefore less variation in preparing final accounts, making them more objective and reliable, rather than subjective and open to controversy.

Up to 1988 there were some 24 statements which had been published by the profession, although a number of them have been withdrawn or revised. Some of the ones of interest, such as SSAPs 2 (accounting policies), 5 (VAT), 9 (stocks and work-in-progress), 12 (depreciation), 13 (research and development) and 21 (leases and hire purchase) will be briefly outlined.

In August 1990, the Accounting Standards Committee gave way to a new body, the Accounting Standards Board (ASB). The ASB is an independent body responsible for setting standards, taking over the functions of the ASC. It is giving the SSAPs a fresh overhaul, modifying and changing them to improve the accounting standards of the profession even further.

The Board's first standard was published in September 1991 and was given the new title of Financial Reporting Standard (FRS replacing the letters SSAP).

FRS 1, Cash Flow Statements, was published by the ASB and provides a standard for cash flow reporting. It supersedes SSAP 10, Statements of Sources and Application of Funds, which is now obsolete. (FRS 1 was discussed in greater detail in Chapter 19.)

Below we will briefly outline the SSAPs of interest.

SSAP 2, Disclosure of Accounting Policies

This statement is seen as one of the most fundamental because it relates to the four basic accounting concepts. The policies disclosed by a business concern the use of accounting bases or methods which were adopted when it prepared its financial reports. These methods concern the valuation of stock, or the method applied when depreciating fixed assets. A limited company is obliged in law to disclose which methods it adopts as notes to the final accounts.

The accounting concepts

All final accounts involve some element of judgement on the part of the accountant who has prepared them. Accountants could easily prepare different final accounts from the same data, and each would conform to fundamental principles. The accounting profession recognises four basic concepts which are assumed to be followed in preparing final accounts (unless otherwise stated). The four fundamental concepts are:

(a) going concern concept;
(b) accruals concept;
(c) consistency concept;
(d) prudence concept.

In addition to the above fundamental concepts there are a number of other accounting concepts which include:

(a) cost concept;
(b) materiality concept;
(c) realisation concept;
(d) money measurement concept;
(e) the dual-aspect concept.

Going concern concept

The value of an organisation's assets is based on the assumption that the firm will continue trading. Businesses tend to value their assets at cost less estimated depreciation. If for any reason (such as lack of working capital) there is a probability of closure because of bankruptcy or liquidation, then the balance sheet would have to reflect the situation – that is, assets would have to be valued at a realistic market valuation and other liabilities may arise, such as redundancy payments.

Accruals concept (or matching concept)

It is taken for granted that a set of final accounts includes *all* expenses incurred and *all* income earned, not merely the payment date: for example, if an organisation owed its employees £50,000 in wages at the end of the financial year it would have to include this figure as an accrued expense, otherwise the profits of the firm would appear over-stated. In this concept, the matching of revenue with expenses must include all items pertinent to the period, paid or unpaid.

Consistency concept

There are a number of bases of dealing with accounting data, such as the different methods of valuing stock or the different methods of depreciation. Organisations are expected to adopt consistent accounting policies in order to prevent profit distortions. Thus, if an organisation changed its method of depreciation from straight-line to market valuation, it must clearly state in the accounting reports the effect on the profit for the year.

Prudence concept (or the concept of conservatism)

Accountants are expected to take a pessimistic view when preparing the final accounts. Thus the accountant should provide in full for any expected loss (such as provisions for bad debts) but not take profit if there is any doubt regarding its realisation. Where, for instance, there may be two or more values relating to an asset, the lower value would tend to be chosen.

Cost concept

The common standard practice is for *all* items of either capital or revenue expenditure to be valued at cost. Therefore the purchase of assets, including stock, and the payment of expenses are at their cost price. Stock may be valued lower than cost if it has lost its value for reasons such as damage, obsolescence, etc.

Materiality concept

This is the view that small, insignificant items may be excluded from the normal accounting policy. The *size* of the business enterprise will dictate what is materially relevant. A large organisation may consider a valuation of a fixed asset under £500 insignificant. It will be treated as an expense item and written off in the year it was bought, irrespective of how long it will last. A smaller organisation may consider £500 as significant and depreciate the asset over a number of accounting periods.

Realisation concept

This concept is part of the matching process between income and expenditure. Only when a definite sale has been made can it be realised as income – for example, the date of issue of the sales invoice rather than the date of receipt of the order contract.

Money measurement concept

Essentially this concept recognises that a set of final accounts will only be the outcome of financial transactions. A profit and loss account or balance sheet cannot possibly measure the value to an organisation of intangibles like the morale or skill of its employees – even a football club cannot include the value (or fees paid) for its players in the balance sheet, although Tottenham Hotspur PLC once included players like Lineker and Gascoigne on its balance sheet.

The dual-aspect concept (the accounting equation)

The basic accounting equation recognises the fact that the assets represent the business. These assets are claimed by proprietor(s) and liabilities according to the value of their ownership:

```
Assets            =  capital + liabilities
(The business)    =  (proprietor's claim) + (external liabilities claim)
or A              =  C
or A              =  L
```

In a large organisation's final accounts, the statement of accounting policies followed (for example, regarding depreciation) will often take at least one full page to declare, as the application of accounting policies is of prime importance to all those concerned about the enterprise: 'Fixed assets are stated at cost less government grants or at valuation. No depreciation is provided on the book cost attributed to the site values of freehold property. Other fixed assets are depreciated over their estimated economic life by equal annual instalments.'

SSAP 5, Accounting for VAT

This standard aims to achieve uniformity in the treatment of VAT in published accounts. VAT is currently charged at the rate of 17.5% (standard rate) on a wide variety of goods and services. There are also goods which are zero-rated for VAT and exempt from VAT.

Businesses which are registered for VAT (those listed with HM Customs & Excise) are collectors of this indirect form of tax on behalf of the Government. Traders collect VAT on their sales (output tax), offset by what they pay on purchases and other expenses (input tax). The balance between these two figures in the VAT account will either indicate whether a sum is owing to the VAT office or whether the business is owed money from it. Chapter 22, VAT and VAT Returns, goes into more detail.

Standard rate supplies

Most of our goods and services are charged at the standard rate. This has been increased from 15% to the current 17.5%. Only those traders registered with Customs & Excise can charge VAT on their goods or services.

Zero-rated supplies

The zero rate is nil which means that traders do not charge VAT on their sales, but they can recover input VAT charges on their purchases and other expenses where VAT has been charged. Zero-rated supplies, for example, include most of our food (but not catering, which means food in restaurants, hotels, cafes, etc).

Exempt supplies

VAT is not charged on supplies which are exempt in the same way as zero-rated supplies. However, a trader cannot reclaim any VAT paid on purchases or other expenses where VAT has been charged. No VAT account is recorded in the books because there is no registration with HM Customs & Excise.

In the preparation of the final accounts, SSAP 5 states that those businesses registered with Customs & Excise should exclude VAT on all taxable inputs and taxable outputs. In other words, sales, purchases, taxable expenses and fixed assets are recorded net (excluding VAT). The VAT charges are recorded in a VAT account. At the end of the financial period, any VAT owing to Customs would be listed as a current liability (a credit balance), or a current asset (a debit balance) in the balance sheet.

With expenditure which is not VAT deductible, such as tax on motor vehicles or for expenses for which the VAT office will not allow recovery, the full amount will appear in the profit and loss account and balance sheet. The same will apply to those non-registered businesses which are exempt from VAT: all their expenditure will include VAT charges in the recording of their accounts as well as in their final accounts.

SSAP 9, Stocks and Work in Progress

This standard seeks to establish a broad band of generally accepted accounting techniques in the valuation of stock. There are a number of different ways that stocks can be valued, and this statement was written with a view to limiting the number of options open in valuation. Stocks may be comprised of finished goods, raw materials and partly finished goods; SSAP 9 states that: 'stock be valued at the lower of cost or net realisable value'. Net realisable value is referred to as the selling price of stock less any expenses involved in the selling process. In other words, stock should be valued as a general rule at the cost price, but if for any reason (such as a recession) the selling price is seen to fall lower than that of cost, then the net realisable value should be used. This is the conservatism or prudence in accounting, is it not? To be able to foresee possible losses, and not recognising profits until realised!

The statement, in defining cost, states that the purchase cost would include any import duties, carriage inwards, handling charges or other costs in the procurement of goods, less any trade discount which may be offered. The manufacturing cost should include the cost of direct labour and materials plus factory overheads as a result of what is considered 'normal' output levels. (Any idle or slack production affecting overheads should not be considered as part of the stock valuation.)

A system of costing stocks should be consistently adopted and, once a method or base in valuation has been used, the same system should be kept, otherwise distortion of profits will occur and the final accounts may not be accepted by the firm's auditors as being 'true and fair'. More details concerning the valuation of stocks and work-in-progress can be found in Part VI of the text.

SSAP 12, Accounting for Depreciation

Depreciation is defined as the loss of value in fixed assets over periods of time. The standard defines that 'depreciation is the measure of the wearing out of a fixed asset through use, time, or obsolescence and that charges of depreciation should be spread fairly over the fixed asset's life'. The depreciation charges for the period are written off to the profit and loss account as expenses and the cumulative depreciation to date is deducted from the cost value of fixed assets in the balance sheet. The concept of consistency must apply and, once a method of depreciation has been adopted, the same method should be used until the asset is finally disposed of. Again, if this were not the case, distortion of profits would occur and incorrect figures would be recorded in the profit and loss account and the balance sheet. If it were necessary to make revaluations in fixed assets which involved changing the method of depreciation, reasons as to why this should occur must accompany the final accounts.

This SSAP does not apply to all fixed assets and those excluded are those which concern investments (SSAP 19), goodwill (SSAP 22) and research and development (SSAP 13). For further information concerning SSAP 12, see Part III, chapter 16.

SSAP 13, Accounting for Research and Development

This standard concerns itself with the costs which are incurred by those companies spending money for research and development purposes. The key point is that of defining the type of expenditure incurred: that is, whether it is classed as capital or revenue expenditure.

Research falls into two basic categories: pure and applied. Pure research is classified as that research into new scientific or technological principles and is seen as original research. Applied research infers a more practical nature, building upon the work classed as original.

Pure research could investigate different principles involving the use of energy. A practical application could be the building of a revolutionary new car running on electricity, classified as applied research because there is a specific application or direction to an original research being put to practical use.

Research, whether pure or applied, is generally seen as revenue expenditure because it is of an on-going nature; it is part of the day-to-day costs of a business as it tries to stay ahead of its competitors in the manufacture of a wide range of products. Because one accounting period may not benefit substantially more than another from research, it is appropriate to see it as revenue expenditure, the costs being written off to the profit and loss account as they occur.

The standard defines development as the use of existing scientific or technical knowledge in order to produce improved products. Development could involve the manufacture of prototype models, testing them and modifying them for the purpose of earning future income. The development of a new type of car or a new medicine, therefore, could benefit a number of future accounting periods. If future revenues are to be affected, some developmental costs could be spread over a number of financial periods and could be capitalised in the same way as other fixed assets.

The 1985 Companies Act states that research costs should not be capitalised and should be written off as and when they occur. The Act states that development costs may be capitalised under fixed assets if, in the balance sheet, notes to the accounts explain the reasons why development is being capitalised and the period of time involved where the capitalisation is to be written off as future charges in the profit and loss account. A development project should be seen as technically feasible and have commercial potential over future accounting periods, otherwise there is little point in making it a capital project and treating it as any other fixed asset.

SSAP 21, Accounting for leases and hire-purchase contracts

This standard attempts to regularise the accounting treatment and disclosure of assets which are held under lease or hire-purchase agreement. The lease or hire purchase of fixed assets is an alternative method of financing assets rather than paying for them outright or by alternative credit terms.

When goods are sold on credit, the legal title to them immediately passes to the buyer, but if they are sold on a hire-purchase agreement, the title of the goods does not pass to the buyer until the last instalment has been paid. If fixed assets are acquired under a lease, there is no provision for the title to be passed to the lessee (the person who acquires the asset) under the terms of a lease contract.

If a fixed asset is acquired under a hire-purchase agreement it is treated as capital expenditure, even though the legal title of the goods is not passed to the buyer until the final instalment. The cost price of hire purchase is debited to the fixed asset account and the interest calculated in the period is charged to profit and loss account.

The amount owing to the creditor will be the cost price of the asset plus interest charges, less any repayments made. Depreciation of the fixed asset should be dealt with in the normal way, irrespective of how it is financed, and this will be based on the cost price of the asset (excluding interest charges).

Under the terms of a lease, the lessor (the party offering the lease) retains legal ownership of the asset and only hires it out to the lessee (the hirer), for an agreed length of time. SSAP 21 recognises two basic categories of lease: finance leases and operating leases.

A finance lease (similar to a hire-purchase agreement) offered by finance companies, banks and other organisations, provides either the finance of the asset or the asset itself, for the use by the lessee, normally on a fixed long-term contract. The lessee acquires the ownership of the asset without actually having the legal title to it. This is to be treated as acquiring a fixed asset by the lessee, therefore debiting the asset account and crediting the lessor (long-term liability) account. In other words, the transaction is capitalised and any interest payment is charged as an expense to profit and loss account.

Depreciation or amortisation (for leasing of premises) is calculated in the normal way and recorded both as an expense in the profit and loss account and as cumulative depreciation in the balance sheet. From the lessor's point of view, the financing of the lease will be seen as debiting the lessee (as a debtor) and crediting sales.

An operating lease is acquired more on a rental basis rather than a fixed long-term contract as in a finance lease. It is therefore viewed as a rental agreement and payment is charged against profits in the profit and loss account. This type of leasing therefore reflects revenue rather than capital expenditure. The lessor would normally be expected to take responsibility for repairs, maintenance, insurance or any other costs in ensuring the asset is operable.

The payment of rental by the lessee will normally be made up of interest charges on the finance provided by the lessor, and a repayment charge which covers the capital cost of the asset.

To summarise this standard, hire purchase and finance leasing are both capitalised and recorded as fixed assets, with appropriate charges for interest and depreciation in the profit and loss account. The balance owing to the supplier/lessor is recorded as a long-term liability. The operating lease is seen more as a rental charge and is treated as revenue expenditure in the profit and loss account.

SSAP 22, Goodwill

Goodwill is defined as an intangible fixed asset normally arising from the surplus or excess price of a business over the net asset value, due to the good name or reputation which a business has built up or the value of any concessions or patents which it may have as part of the business. The standard recognises that is difficult to separate goodwill as a whole from the other business assets, and its calculation is both subjective and liable to fluctuate in value over periods of time.

Therefore, after purchasing a business with a value for goodwill, one should normally eliminate the goodwill portion immediately upon the acquisition of a business. In the case of a partnership where goodwill is brought in by, the partners, it should be written off on the basis of the partners' profit-sharing ratio at the time the partners agree to it being written off.

In the case of a company, the purchase of goodwill may be written off immediately against identifiable reserves (or even some suitable but as yet unrealised reserves until realised reserves are obtained). Where in some cases there is 'negative goodwill' where the purchase price of the business is less than the net asset value, then reserves can be credited with the negative balance.

The standard, however, does allow the purchase of goodwill to be depreciated (or amortised) over its useful economic life. In this case, it is depreciated over time, the charge being made against the profit and loss appropriation account and then the cost, accumulated depreciation (amortisation) and net book value, is shown in the balance sheet.

The following statements have been prepared by the former ASC:

SSAP 1   Associate companies
SSAP 2   Disclosure of accounting policies

SSAP 3   EPS (earnings per share)
SSAP 4   Government grants
SSAP 5   VAT
SSAP 6   Extraordinary items
SSAP 7   Changes in the purchasing power of money
SSAP 8   Taxation
SSAP 9   Stocks and work in progress
SSAP 10   Funds statement (withdrawn; now FRS 1, Cash Flow)
SSAP 11   (Withdrawn)
SSAP 12   Depreciation
SSAP 13   Research and development
SSAP 14   Group accounts
SSAP 15   Deferred taxation
SSAP 16   Current cost accounting
SSAP 17   Post balance sheet events
SSAP 18   Contingencies
SSAP 19   Investment properties
SSAP 20   Foreign currency
SSAP 21   Leasing and hire-purchase contracts
SSAP 22   Goodwill
SSAP 23   Acquisitions and mergers
SSAP 24   Pension costs
SSAP 25   Segmental reporting

The ASB is now responsible for preparing new FRSs, and is currently in the process of up-dating, amending and changing the SSAPs as and when they feel it necessary. The major objective of the publishing of these statements is to have greater consistency in the preparing of financial reports and to oblige the accounting profession to conform to the published regulations and practice as laid down in them. At the time of publication, three FRSs, have so far been published by the ASB:

FRS 1 Cash flow statements (see Chapter 19)
FRS 2 Accounting for subsidiary undertakings
FRS 3 Reporting financial performance (see Chapter 18.)

The importance of finance on organisational decision making

In this section we have shown how important it is for an organisation to have adequate financial resources and to obtain an adequate return on those resources.

A 'young' business may find itself in a poor liquidity position since in an expanding situation the business will need to increase the amount invested in stock; it may have more debtors, and more fixed assets will be required. Therefore, if management does not consider the effect on working capital of taking on extra business then a position of insolvency may be the result. If acquiring more fixed assets, the drain on capital can be greatly reduced if the assets are leased rather than purchased outright. Each potential major order must be subject to the scrutiny of the accountant in order that the effect on cash flow can be assessed and extra finance obtained if necessary, such as by obtaining an overdraft or possibly by obtaining some payment in advance from customers (as long as this is done at the time of the contractual negotiations).

If an organisation does not carefully monitor its working capital position then, even though it has a profitable product/service, it may find itself in an insolvent position. In such a case it may end up being wound up through the court action of a creditor or become the subject of a takeover by a more stable organisation. Obviously, in the latter situation, the takeover organisation is in a very strong position and can drive a very hard bargain for itself – all through the financial laxity of the smaller organisation. Thus adequacy of finance is vital for survival. Financial control is exercised by the use of budgetary control, professional stock management, capital appraisal techniques and other cost and management controls, which are all dealt with in this book.

As far as profit is concerned, what is considered adequate for one type of organisation may not be adequate for another. The general rule, though, is that the higher the element of risk involved then the higher the rate of return would need to be. The major financial indicator for profit is that of return on capital employed. Most industrial and commercial organisations aim to achieve a return on investment in excess of 20% p.a. An objective of anything less would seem to be a waste of effort as capital can usually be safely invested with blue chip financial institutions at rates of interest of around 10% p.a. (for example, Government and Local Authority bonds). Thus an entrepreneur with capital invested in a business would want to achieve considerably above safe interest rates as a reward for the extra risks.

Throughout the text we stress the importance of profitability on business decision making but would acknowledge that, in arriving at key policy decisions, management should consider other aspects. Peter Drucker, author of many books on management, suggests there are eight key areas vital to the continued existence of any business organisation:

● Profitability
● Market standing

- Productivity
- Product leadership
- Personal development
- Employee attitudes
- Public responsibility
- Maintaining a balance between short- and long-term objectives

Earlier in the text we examined the public sector where, for the large part, commercial profit objectives cannot be applied. Central and Local Government place a lot of emphasis on providing services on a value for money (v.f.m.) basis – that is, constantly examining the methods employed in providing services with a view to providing the same level of service at a lower cost or a higher level of service at the same cost. In some instances, a public sector authority has carried out a v.f.m. analysis and concluded that privatisation of parts of the service is the best option – for example, private contractor employed for household refuse collection, outside caterers used in schools, hospitals, etc.

However, the objective of all organisations must clearly be to utilise the factors of production in the most efficient manner for the benefit of the owners, employees and customers. Therefore, ensuring both adequacy of finance and control of costs is of paramount importance in operating an organisation.

Questions

---

1. The following are extracts from the Chairman's financial report:

    'The Company adopts the accruals concept in the preparation of its accounts with the exception of items where in the opinion of the directors the inclusion would have no material effect on the profits of the organisation.'

    'The Company has a policy where it capitalises the cost of additions and major alterations to premises and records at cost.'

    'The Company adopts a 'straight-line' basis when providing for depreciation of machinery, equipment and furniture. Market value is adopted for the depreciation of the Company's motor vehicles. These policies will continue until the disposal of the assets.'

'Stock is to be valued at the "lower of cost and net realisable value", computed on the basis of selling price after deducting appropriate overheads.'

'Land and buildings will be recorded at the cost valuation.'

Required:

(a) Identify the fundamental concepts in the Chairman's report.
(b) Can you identify any other concepts?
    If certain assets are valued at cost rather than current value, how might this effect the accounting reports?

2. In the private sector of business, organisations are primarily motivated by making profits. What other considerations are thought to be relevant?

3. Explain and illustrate with examples, the four fundamental concepts of accounting:

(a) going concern;
(b) accruals;
(c) consistency;
(d) prudence.

4. *Accounting Policies for the year ended 31 December 1989*

The financial statements have been prepared under the historical cost convention.
    The principal accounting policies have remained unchanged from the previous year and are set out below.

Turnover

Turnover is the total amount receivable by the company in the ordinary course of business with outside customers for goods supplied as a principal and for services provided, excluding VAT, recorded on invoice.

Depreciation

Depreciation is calculated to write down the cost of all tangible fixed assets over their expected useful lives.

Depreciation is by equal annual instalments in the case of leasehold premises, fixtures and fittings, and plant and machinery and is calculated on the reducing balance method in the case of motor vehicles.

The periods generally applicable are:

Leasehold premises	Period of lease
Plant and equipment	5 years
Motor vehicles	5 years
Fixtures and fittings	5 years

Stock and work in progress

Stock and work in progress is stated at the lower cost and net realisable value.

In the case of raw materials and consumable stores, cost means purchase price less trade discounts, calculated on a first-in, first-out basis. In the case of work in progress and finished goods, cost consists of direct materials, direct labour and attributable production and other overheads. The amount of work in progress has been reduced by progress payments.

Net realisable value means estimated selling price (less trade discounts) less all further costs to completion and all costs to be incurred in marketing, selling and distribution.

Required:

(a) Identify the accounting concepts which may be apparent in the above accounting policies.
(b) Check terminology such as raw materials, work in progress, direct labour and net realisable value in later sections of the text.

PART V

SOURCES OF PERSONAL FINANCE

CHAPTER 24

Personal Income

Most people have to work for a living and the income they earn is a result of working five or more days a week. Wages are usually paid on a weekly basis and salaries are generally associated with office staff who are, more often than not, paid on a monthly basis by cheque or through the bank, building society or Post Office. Pay is also referred to as 'remuneration'. For the purpose of what counts as pay, the tax office gives the following examples:

(a) salaries, wages, overtime, bonuses, commission and perks;
(b) cash payments such as Christmas boxes;
(c) statutory Sick Pay or Statutory Maternity Pay;
(d) pay in respect of sickness or absence from work;
(e) holiday pay;
(f) tips received as an addition to normal pay;
(g) payment for travelling to and from work.

There are two major ways on which remuneration may be calculated:

● Time rates
● Payment by results.

Time rates

This is the most common way of being paid. This could be a flat rate where the same sum is paid each week or each month (for example, £120 per week), or it could be on an hourly rate basis where a higher rate of pay may be earned for overtime. A basic rate is paid for a certain number of hours and anything over this time would be at an agreed overtime rate.

For example, if the basic week was 37.5 hours and pay was £6.80

per hour and one and a quarter for overtime (over 37.5 hours), how much would you earn working 40 hours?

37.5 hours basic:	37.5 × 6.80/hr	=	255.00
2.5 hours overtime:	2.5 × 8.50/hr	=	21.25
Total gross pay:		=	276.25

Payment by results

This method of payment offers an incentive to workers to work harder and earn more income: more production, more pay. Piecework is a system particularly suitable where production is standard and repetitive. For example, £2.00 is paid for every 100 units produced, so if a worker produced 10,000 units in a week, he would earn £200:

$$\frac{10,000 \times 2.00}{100} = £200.00$$

There are also other incentives for workers. Sales assistants or representatives are often paid a commission on top of their usual basic salary. The more they sell, the better their pay. For example, a sales representative earns a flat basic salary of £150 per month and a commission is paid at 3% of gross sales. If his sales were £17,600 in one month, how much would he earn?

Commission: £17,600 x 3%	=	£528.00
basic pay	=	£150.00
total pay	=	£678.00

Gross and net pay

The gross pay of an employee refers to the total sum earned before any deductions from pay. There are what is called statutory and voluntary deductions.

Statutory deductions are legally required ones, such as income tax and NICs; both are collected using what is called the PAYE (Pay As You Earn) system. Voluntary deductions are those agreed to by the worker and may be for a pension fund, trade union, social club or professional subscriptions.

A pension fund or scheme is also referred to as superannuation. The Government has its own pension scheme, called SERPS (State Earnings-Related Pension Scheme). Those on this scheme pay NIC

TABLE 24.1   Example of calculating net pay

		£
Gross Pay (per week)		276.25
Deductions:		
income tax	40.60	
NIC	21.46	
pension fund	13.80	
trade union	2.50	78.36
Net pay		197.89

contributions from Table 1, 'not contracted out' contributions. Others may opt to 'contract out': that is, find an alternative private pension scheme of their own instead of paying SERPS contributions to the Government's scheme. The way to calculate net pay is shown in Table 24.1.

Processing pay

Wages are usually paid weekly to non-office staff, contrasting with salaried office employees who are paid monthly. Wages are associated with a wage packet and payment in cash, whereas a salary is more in keeping with payment by cheque or through a bank. It is, however, becoming far more frequent for all employees to be paid through the bank, building society or post office. This is seen as more efficient and better for security reasons. When employees are paid through the bank by credit transfer, it is known as BACS (Bankers Automatic Clearing System).

However, irrespective of how one is paid (whether in cash or through a bank), the documentation procedure is basically the same. The major documents involved are:

- Clock cards or time sheets
- Tax table A: free pay
- Tax table B: taxable pay
- National Insurance Tables 1 and 1A
- Tax deduction cards P11
- Employee's P45 and P46
- Pay slip advice
- Payroll

For all employees, the correct procedure for calculating the gross pay and making the correct deductions to arrive at net pay is of paramount importance, not only to the individual, but also to keep within the legal framework when making statutory deductions from pay. The tax office would want to see consistently accurate deductions for tax and NICs made by the accounts office of a business.

Clock cards

To record how long an employee is at work, the clock card may be used to time staff coming in and going out of their work place, including the lunch break. The cards will be used to provide for the payroll staff the data required to calculate the number of hours worked, including any overtime hours. They will then calculate the gross pay by multiplying the hours by the rate per hour.

The clock card is ideal for those staff on hourly rates of pay or those on what is called 'flexitime': that is, an employee works so many hours a week but is not entirely restricted to set times for clocking in and out of work.

Some firms use a time book rather than a card system, where staff would simply sign in and out, rather than clock in and out. What management do not ever want to seek is one member of staff clocking in for another because that person is late, or might not turn up at all! This is fraud and is often seen as a sackable offence.

The information in Figure 24.1 refers to the clock cards of Jackie Lomas and Roger Pebbles. Jackie works on factory floor 4 on a 40 hours per week basic time. Roger's work place is on floor 7. Any overtime from Monday to Friday is paid at the rate of time and a third. Saturday is at time and a half. Any additional overtime on Sundays is at double time. Each worker is allowed to be late up to just 3 minutes clocking in time. Time lost over 3 minutes means a deduction of a quarter of an hour's basic pay. Over 20 minutes late in any one hour results in an hour's pay lost.

Jackie is paid as a skilled worker at £6.42 per hour basic. Roger is unskilled on the assembly line and earns £4.50 per hour basic.

Study the two clock cards below and check them for accuracy. Jackie's card has been completed. Can you complete Roger's card? Check your answer after the Questions section at the end of this chapter.

Calculating statutory deductions

Income tax and NICs are both statutory deductions from pay. The amount to be deducted is decided by the Chancellor of the Ex-

FIGURE 24.1   Clock cards

| NAME | Jackie Lomas | | | WKS NO. 296 | |
| FACTORY | 4 | | | WK ENDING 9/4 | |
DAY	IN	OUT	IN	OUT	BASIC TIME	OVER TIME
MON	8.30	12.31	1.29	6.02	8	$\frac{1}{2}$
TUES	8.28	12.34	1.30	7.03	8	$1\frac{1}{2}$
WED	8.25	12.30	1.28	8.05	8	$2\frac{1}{2}$
THURS	8.32	12.32	1.27	6.01	8	$\frac{1}{2}$
FRI	8.20	12.32	1.28	5.32	8	
SAT	8.30	12.30				4
SUN						–

TOTAL NUMBER OF HOURS WORKED

BASIC TIME	40	OVER-* TIME	9	ADDL O/T	

RATE OF PAY £   PER HOUR

40 Hours @ £ 6.42 per hr   £ 256 – 80
9 Overtime Hours
5 M – F @ £ 8.56 per hr   £ 42 – 80
4 Sat @ £ 9.63 per hr   £ 38 – 52
___ Additional @ £ ___ per hour £

GROSS PAY £ 338 – 12

| NAME | Roger Pebbles | | | WKS NO. 429 | |
| FACTORY | 7 | | | WK ENDING 9/4 | |
DAY	IN	OUT	IN	OUT	BASIC TIME	OVER TIME
MON	8.32	12.32	1.30	6.04	8	$\frac{1}{4}$
TUES	8.26	12.34	1.31	6.06	8	$\frac{1}{4}$
WED	8.35	12.31	1.27	8.06	$7\frac{3}{4}$	$2\frac{1}{4}$
THURS	8.30	12.32	1.28	8.07	8	$2\frac{1}{4}$
FRI	8.28	12.34	1.27	5.31	8	
SAT	8.30	12.30				3
SUN						

TOTAL NUMBER OF HOURS WORKED

BASIC TIME		OVER-* TIME		ADDL. O/T	

RATE OF PAY £   PER HOUR

$39\frac{3}{4}$ Hours @ £ 4 –50 per hour   £ 177–88
9 Overtime Hours
___ M – F @ £ ___ per hr   £
___ Sat @ £ ___ per hr   £
___ Additional @ £ ___ per hour £

GROSS PAY £ _____

* (a) Mon–Fri overtime is paid at ordinary time plus one third.
  (b) Saturday overtime is paid at ordinary time plus one half.
  (c) Sunday overtime is paid at double ordinary time.

chequer and is presented to Parliament in his March budget speech each year.

Income tax in the UK is a progressive tax which means that the more you earn, the more you pay. There are three tax bands at present although the Chancellor may make any adjustments to these figures as and when he feels necessary:

the lower rate	20%	up to	£ 2,500
the basic rate	25%	£2,501 to	£23,700
the higher rate	40%	over	£23,700

If an employee earned, say, £33,500 per annum, he would most probably have to pay some of his earnings at the higher rate depending on how much his personal allowances were.

All employees are liable for income tax through the PAYE system. Your employer deducts income tax and NICs from your pay and this is sent in total to the Inland Revenue each month along with Form P30B.

Tax is not charged on your gross pay. Each person is entitled to tax allowances which are deducted from gross pay to arrive at what is called 'taxable pay'. Taxable allowances include:

- Single person's allowance
- Married couple's allowance
- Pension or superannuation allowances
- Mortgage interest relief allowance (if it is not already deducted by the lender on monthly payments)
- Subscriptions to professional bodies
- Some personal expenses at the place of work

The most significant allowances for most persons is the single and married couple's allowances. For example, if a married man has a tax allowances of £5,500 per annum, this is his 'tax-free' pay. He would only be liable to pay tax on any earnings above £5,500. If he did not earn this amount, he would not be liable for any tax.

Each person's tax code is prepared by the tax office on form P2(T). It lists the allowances you are entitled to and at the foot of the form it states:

Your code for the year to 5 April 199. is 344L

The code 344L represents a single person's allowance for that particular year. If a 5 is added to the three digits, it indicates the allowance of £3,445. The L indicates a single person, H a married person, P pensioner, etc. A married person may have a code of, say, 516H. This would indicate an allowance of £5,165.

Therefore, the greater the personal allowances you have, the less will be your taxable pay. For example, if a person had an income of £33,500 per annum and his allowances were £5,500, his taxable pay would be £28,000. How much tax would he be liable to pay?

				Tax(£)
Lower	rate	£2,500 × 20%	=	£500
Basic	rate	£21,200 × 25%	=	£5,300
Higher	rate	£4,300 × 40%	=	£1,720
		£28,000 to pay	=	£7,520

PAYE does not concern the self-employed. Their financial year-end accounts, indicating their income less allowable expenses, will be sent with their tax return to the Inland Revenue, who will determine how much tax they will pay, if any.

Tax tables

The Inland Revenue provide employers with two books of tax tables so that the correct deductions for tax can be calculated.

Table A gives the cumulative tax-free pay to date, shown opposite the tax code number. (Each employee has an individual tax code which determines his tax-free pay.) It is based on 52 weekly payments throughout the year. For those employees on monthly pay, the pay to date is shown at the back of Table A.

Table B gives the tax due to date and is used on conjunction with Table A. The total pay to date, less the cumulative tax-free pay to date equals the taxable pay to date. From this, the total tax due to date is given in the column opposite the taxable pay to date.

When the weekly or monthly taxable pay limits are exceeded, supplementary Tables C and D are used, where an additional higher tax rate of 40% will be charged on the higher earnings.

It sounds rather complicated, doesn't it, but an illustrated example may help you to understand it better. *Charlie Green* is an employee at Harrison's, and in Week 1 of the tax year commencing on 6 April, he earned £328.17. His tax code for the year is 435L. This represents £4,355 allowances. How much tax will Charlie pay?

Table A for Free Pay in Week 1 gives the code 435 = £83.83 tax-free pay.

Gross pay	£328.17
less free pay	£ 83.83
taxable pay	£244.34

For tax purposes, this is always rounded down to the pound, £244.

Now, using Table B for Taxable Pay at the basic rate on £244, we are given the figure £61. Using the lower relief table because tax is 20% on the first £2,500, in Week 1 the lower relief is £2.41

Therefore the tax due in Week 1 is £61 − £2.41 = £58.59.

National Insurance Contributions

This is, in effect, another form of tax to the employee but it does pay for benefits such as unemployment, sick pay, retirement pension, child benefits, maternity pay, industrial accident and benefits for the employee. Both the employee and the employer are charged NICs.

For persons who earn a low income and are below the threshold of earnings, for example, say under £60 per week, NICs are not paid by either the employee or the employer. Earnings higher than the threshold have usually been charged at 2% on the lower earnings up to the threshold and 9% on earnings above that figure. For example, Charlie would pay 2% on the first £60 and a further 9% on the balance of his gross pay, £268:

2% on £60.00	=	£ 1.20
9% on £268.00	=	£24.12
NIC due to pay	=	£25.32

However, there are NIC tables from which the amounts payable are extracted.

Table 1 are used for 'not contracted out' contributions that is, those persons who are still in SERPS. Tables 1 include the following tables.

(a) Table A (standard rate) is used for employees over 16 and under pension age and those employees who have their own personal pension from 1 July 1988.
(b) Table B (reduced rate) is used for married women and widows.
(c) Table C is used for employees over the pension age, including those previously contracted out and those employees who have made their own arrangements to pay NICs.
(d) Tables 1A are for those persons who have 'contracted out' of SERPS and have chosen their own personal pension plans.
(e) Table D is used for persons who have contracted out and pay the standard rate NICs.
(f) Table E is used for married women and widows who have contracted out and pay NICs at the reduced rate.

Both employee and employer are charged NICs and the tables will indicate the total of both employee's and employer's contributions and a separate figure for the employee's contributions, based on the earnings on which the contributions are payable (again in rounded pounds, not pence).

Figure 24.2 gives the Free Pay table, so you can check Charlie Green's free pay in Week 1.

FIGURE 24.2   Table A-Free Pay, week 1, Apr. 6 to Apr. 12

Code	Total free pay to date	Code	Total free pay to date	Code	Total free pay to date	Code	Total free pay to date	Code	Total free pay to date	Code	Total free pay to date	Code	Total free pay to date	Code	Total free pay to date
	£		£		£		£		£		£		£		£
0	NIL	61	11.91	121	23.45	181	34.99	241	46.52	301	58.06	361	69.60	421	81.14
1	0.37	62	12.10	122	23.64	182	35.18	242	46.72	302	58.25	362	69.79	422	81.33
2	0.56	63	12.29	123	23.83	183	35.37	243	46.91	303	58.45	363	69.99	423	81.52
3	0.75	64	12.49	124	24.02	184	35.56	244	47.10	304	58.64	364	70.18	424	81.72
4	0.95	65	12.68	125	24.22	185	35.75	245	47.29	305	58.83	365	70.37	425	81.91
5	1.14	66	12.87	126	24.41	186	35.95	246	47.49	306	59.02	366	70.56	426	82.10
6	1.33	67	13.06	127	24.60	187	36.14	247	47.68	307	59.22	367	70.75	427	82.29
7	1.52	68	13.25	128	24.79	188	36.33	248	47.87	308	59.41	368	70.95	428	82.49
8	1.72	69	13.45	129	24.99	189	36.52	249	48.06	309	59.60	369	71.14	429	82.68
9	1.91	70	13.64	130	25.18	190	36.72	250	48.25	310	59.79	370	71.33	430	82.87
10	2.10	71	13.83	131	25.37	191	36.91	251	48.45	311	59.99	371	71.52	431	83.06
11	2.29	72	14.02	132	25.56	192	37.10	252	48.64	312	60.18	372	71.72	432	83.25
12	2.49	73	14.22	133	25.75	193	37.29	253	48.83	313	60.37	373	71.91	433	83.45
13	2.68	74	14.41	134	25.95	194	37.49	254	49.02	314	60.56	374	72.10	434	83.64
14	2.87	75	14.60	135	26.14	195	37.68	255	49.22	315	60.75	375	72.29	435	83.83
15	3.06	76	14.79	136	26.33	196	37.87	256	49.41	316	60.95	376	72.49	436	84.02
16	3.25	77	14.99	137	26.52	197	38.06	257	49.60	317	61.14	377	72.68	437	84.22
17	3.45	78	15.18	138	26.72	198	38.25	258	49.79	318	61.33	378	72.87	438	84.41
18	3.64	79	15.37	139	26.91	199	38.45	259	49.99	319	61.52	379	73.06	439	84.60
19	3.83	80	15.56	140	27.10	200	38.64	260	50.18	320	61.72	380	73.25	440	84.79
20	4.02														

FIGURE 24.3 Table B (Tax at 25%)

Tax Due on Taxable Pay from £100 to £23,700

Total TAXABLE PAY to date	Total TAX DUE to date	Total TAXABLE PAY to date	Total TAX DUE to date	Total TAXABLE PAY to date	Total TAX DUE to date	Total TAXABLE PAY to date	Total TAX DUE to date
£	£	£	£	£	£	£	£
100	25.00	6100	1525.00	12100	3025.00	18100	4525.00
200	50.00	6200	1550.00	12200	3050.00	18200	4550.00
300	75.00	6300	1575.00	12300	3075.00	18300	4575.00
400	100.00	6400	1600.00	12400	3100.00	18400	4600.00
500	125.00	6500	1625.00	12500	3125.00	18500	4625.00
600	150.00	6600	1650.00	12600	3150.00	18600	4650.00
700	175.00	6700	1675.00	12700	3175.00	18700	4675.00
800	200.00	6800	1700.00	12800	3200.00	18800	4700.00
900	225.00	6900	1725.00	12900	3225.00	18900	4725.00
1000	250.00	7000	1750.00	13000	3250.00	19000	4750.00
1100	275.00	7100	1775.00	13100	3275.00	19100	4775.00
1200	300.00	7200	1800.00	13200	3300.00	19200	4800.00
1300	325.00	7300	1825.00	13300	3325.00	19300	4825.00
1400	350.00	7400	1850.00	13400	3350.00	19400	4850.00
1500	375.00	7500	1875.00	13500	3375.00	19500	4875.00
1600	400.00	7600	1900.00	13600	3400.00	19600	4900.00
1700	425.00	7700	1925.00	13700	3425.00	19700	4925.00
1800	450.00	7800	1950.00	13800	3450.00	19800	4950.00
1900	475.00	7900	1975.00	13900	3475.00	19900	4975.00
2000	500.00	8000	2000.00	14000	3500.00	20000	5000.00

Tax Due on Taxable Pay from £1 to £99

Total TAXABLE PAY to date	Total TAX DUE to date	Total TAXABLE PAY to date	Total TAX DUE to date
£	£	£	£
41	10.25	61	15.25
42	10.50	62	15.50
43	10.75	63	15.75
44	11.00	64	16.00
45	11.25	65	16.25
46	11.50	66	16.50
47	11.75	67	16.75
48	12.00	68	17.00
49	12.25	69	17.25
50	12.50	70	17.50
51	12.75	71	17.75
52	13.00	72	18.00
53	13.25	73	18.25
54	13.50	74	18.50
55	13.75	75	18.75
56	14.00	76	19.00
57	14.25	77	19.25
58	14.50	78	19.50
59	14.75	79	19.75
60	15.00	80	20.00

FIGURE 24.4 Weekly Table A, continued (6 April 1993 to 5 April 1994)

Earnings on which employee's contributions payable 1a	Total of employee's and employer's contributions payable 1b	Employee's contributions payable 1c	Employer's contributions*
£	£	£	£
256	45.84	19.16	26.68
257	46.03	19.25	26.78
258	46.22	19.34	26.88
259	46.42	19.43	26.99
260	46.61	19.52	27.09
261	46.81	19.61	27.20
262	47.00	19.70	27.30
263	47.19	19.79	27.40
264	47.39	19.88	27.51
265	47.58	19.97	27.61
266	47.78	20.06	27.72
267	47.97	20.15	27.82
268	48.16	20.24	27.92
269	48.36	20.33	28.03
270	48.55	20.42	28.13
271	48.75	20.51	28.24
272	48.94	20.60	28.34
273	49.13	20.69	28.44
274	49.33	20.78	28.55
275	49.52	20.87	28.65

Earnings on which employee's contributions payable 1a	Total of employee's and employer's contributions payable 1b	Employee's contributions payable 1c	Employer's contributions*
£	£	£	£
316	57.48	24.56	32.92
317	57.67	24.65	33.02
318	57.86	24.74	33.12
319	58.06	24.83	33.23
320	58.25	24.92	33.33
321	58.45	25.01	33.44
322	58.64	25.10	33.54
323	58.83	25.19	33.64
324	59.03	25.28	33.75
325	59.22	25.37	33.85
326	59.42	25.46	33.96
327	59.61	25.55	34.06
328	59.80	25.64	34.16
329	60.00	25.73	34.27
330	60.19	25.82	34.37
331	60.39	25.91	34.48
332	60.58	26.00	34.58
333	60.77	26.09	34.68
334	60.97	26.18	34.79
335	61.16	26.27	34.89

Pay slips

A pay slip or pay advice is the details of pay prepared for each employee. It informs them of how much gross pay they have earned, including overtime, bonus or other payments and the deductions from pay, statutory and voluntary, to arrive at net pay. Some pay slips also indicate the employee's total pay and deductions to date.

The examples below show the pay slips of Jackie Lomas and Roger Pebbles and, as this is their first week of pay in the new tax year, the total pay and deductions to date will be the same as for the first week's pay.

Check the figures for Jackie Lomas; note that her tax code is 344L, that of a single person. She is also not contracted out for NIC purposes and therefore Tables 1, Table A are used to extract the NIC figures.

Roger Pebbles has a partly prepared pay slip for you to complete. He is a married and has a tax code of 510H. The same NIC Tables 1 are used as for Jackie. Roger also pays out £10 a week towards a recognised voluntary pension fund, approved by the tax office. This entitles him to have this deducted from his gross pay, thereby reducing his tax liability:

$$£234.13 - £10 = £224.13$$

His personal allowance is then deducted to calculate tax:

$$£224.13 - £98.44 = £125.69 \text{ taxable pay at the basic rate (less}$$
$$\text{the lower rate on the first £2,500).}$$

The pay slips for you to check and complete are given in Figure 24.5.

Major payroll forms from the Inland Revenue

Deductions from pay need to be accurate both from the individual's and the tax office's point of view. The tax office produces an Employer's Guide to PAYE which includes a pack a cards as an illustration and guidance on income tax regulations. Card 11 is a quick reference to the type of forms in use. The major ones are:

P2(T)   Tax code number notification to the employee.
         Tax code number notification to the employer. P6 andP9 inform you and your employer of your tax code allowances, including any changes to these. The code number

FIGURE 24.5 Pay slips

PAY ADVICE Wk/endg._____9/4_____				PAY ADVICE Wk/endg._____9/1_____			
NAME_____J. LOMAS_____				NAME_____R. PEBBLES_____			
WORKS NO.__296_ DEPT.____F4____				WORKS NO._429____DEPT.__F7__			

	Earnings				Earnings		
	Basic Time				Basic Time		
	40 hrs @ 6.42	256	80		39 3/4 hrs @ 4.50	177	88
	Overtime				Overtime		
	5 8.56	42	80		6 6.00	36	00
	4 hrs @ 9.63	38	52		3 hrs @ 6.75	20	25
	Additional Overtime				Additional Overtime		
	____ hrs @_____				____ hrs @ _____		
	GROSS PAY	£338	12		GROSS PAY	£234	13

Deductions (J. LOMAS)

PAYE	65	34		
NI Contr.	26	50		
Other Deduct	1	50		
Pension				
	93	34		
TOTAL DEDUCTIONS			£ 93	34

Deductions (R. PEBBLES)

PAYE	—	—		
NI Contr.	—	—		
Other Deduct.				
Pension	10	00		
TOTAL DEDUCTIONS			£	

Additions (J. LOMAS)

Tax Refund	—	—		
Other Addns.	–	–		
TOTAL ADDITIONS			£	
NET PAY			£244	78

Additions (R. PEBBLES)

Tax Refund	—	—		
Other Addns				
TOTAL ADDITIONS			£	
NET PAY			£	

is used to calculate your tax-free pay to date.

P11   This is the tax deductions working sheet for each individual employee. It records weekly or monthly earnings, income tax, NIC, SSP (Statutory Sick Pay) and SMP (Statutory Maternity Pay).

P11D   Indicates all benefits and expenses paid to an employee.

P14   This is a year end summary of pay for each employee, showing total tax, NICs, etc. P60 is a certificate of the same information given to the employee, a copy of P14.

P15   Is used by an employee to claim tax allowances, particularly if on an emergency coding.

P30B   The pay slip to be completed by the employer showing totals deducted from employees for tax and NICs (less refunds, SSP and SMP) for the month, to be paid to the tax office within 14 days of the month end.

P30BC   Pay slip booklet containing pay slips.

P45   This is used when an employee either starts or leaves a job. Details of the tax code, total pay and tax due to date and tax paid to date are recorded.

P46   If a new employee is without a P45 (it might be the first job from school), an emergency tax code number 344L is used until a new tax code is provided by the tax office. A P15 (tax allowance claim) will be completed by the employee and sent to the tax office.

P47   This is an application to make a tax refund to a new employee if it exceeds £200.

P48   Is the tax office's authority to make the refund on P47.

P60   The certificate of an employee's pay and tax deductions for the year. It is either a separate form, or the third part of P14.

Tables A	The tax-free tables.
Tables B	The taxable pay tables.
NIC 268	A quick guide to NIC, SSP and SMP.
CF 391	National Insurance tables (not contracted out). Red Book 1.
CF 392	National Insurance tables (contracted out). Red Book 1a.
SSP 55	Statutory Sick Pay tables. Red Book 2.
SSP 55	Statutory Maternity Pay tables. Red Book 3.

Questions

1. Calculate the net pay of Harry Smith from the following:

No. of Hours	39
Basic Week:	36 hours @ £4.00 per hour
Overtime:	Paid @ $1\frac{1}{2}$ rate per hour

Deductions	
National Insurance:	@ 9% of gross pay.
Taxable income:	
Harry is allowed	£42.30 tax free pay
	Assume basic rate of tax
	at 30%

Other:	
Trade Union	0.85
Social fund	1.25
Pension	2.50 (tax free)

2. Calculate the gross pay for the following employees:

Jack	46 hours
Fred	43 hours
Harry	51 hours

The basic working week is 38 hours @ £2.80 hours. Over-time pay over 38 hours is at time and a quarter.

3 Calculate the gross pay of an employee who is paid a basic rate for attendance and piece-rate according to how much he produces:

Attendance money: £1.25 per hour

Production (piece-rates)

(a) from 500 to 1,000 units	2p per unit
(b) from 1,001 to 1,500 units	3p per unit
(c) over 1,500	2.5p per unit

How much will be earn on a 40 hour week if he produces 1,650 units?

4. Calculate the gross pay of S. Robbins from the following: A bonus system operates where the employee is paid a bonus a half-time saved.

	Time allowed	Time taken
Monday	12	8
Tuesday	10	8
Wednesday	11	8
Thursday	11	8
Friday	10	7

S. Robin's basic hourly rate is £3 per hour for a 39 hour week.

5. The following is a clock card for B. Balderstone who works a 38-hour basic week, and all additional hours are counted as overtime, at time and a half. His basic rate of pay is £2.40 per hour. As far as clocking in or out is concerned employees are allowed a 2-minute tolerance either way

(this means that arriving at 8.02 counts as 8.00 and leaving at 18.32 counts as 18.30).

From the above information calculate the gross pay, clearly showing the overtime amount. (You may use the blank sections on the clock card if you wish.)

NAME B BALDERSTONE					WKS No. 807	
DEPT ASSEMBLY					WK ENDING 9/8/86	
DAY	IN	OUT	IN	OUT	BASIC TIME	OVER TIME
MON	8.00	12.01	13.00	18.32		
TUE	7.59	12.02	13.00	17.31		
WED	8.01	12.00	13.01	18.33		
THU	7.59	12.00	13.00	18.02		
FRI	8.00	12.01	13.01	17.00		
SAT						
SUN						

NUMBER OF HOURS WORKED		
BASIC TIME	OVERTIME	TOTAL
RATE OF PAY £	PER HOUR	

____Hours @ £ _____ per hour   £

____Overtime

____Hours @ £ _____ per hour   £ _____

                    GROSS PAY £ _____

6. Calculate the gross pay of Harry Ford. Details taken from his clock cards are:

   Basic pay rate: 38-hour working week, £4.20 per hour
   Mon.–Fri. overtime rate: one and one-third.
   Saturday overtime rate: one and a half.
   Sunday overtime rate: double time.

		Week 1	Week 2
Mon.-Fri.	overtime:	6 hours	4.5 hours
Saturday	overtime:	3.5 hours	4.5 hours
Sunday	overtime:	0	3 hours

7. Calculate the net weekly pay of Imran from the following information:

Gross pay:		£226.80
Deduction:		
Superannuation	£14.00	(tax free)
National insurance	£16.34	
Union subs	£1.10	
Tax (to calculate)		

Imran has £110.00 per week tax-free allowances and deductions are at the basic rate of 25% and also at the lower rate of 20% on the first £3000 per annum (£57.69 per week).
8. Calculate the tax payable on the following:
    (a) a person who works only part-time and earns £74 a week((tax-free pay is £66.33 a week);
    (b) a person who earns £250 a week and has tax-free pay of £83.83 a week.

Note: Use the lower rate on the first £57.69 per week, then at the basic rate.

9. A person earns £36,800 a year; tax-free pay is £109.98 per week and he also pays 6% of his gross salary to a pension scheme (tax free).
    Use the lower rate at 20% on the first £3,000 p.a. the basic rate at 25% up to £23,700 and the higher rate at 40% on the remainder of his salary.
10. (a) A person earns £308 per week and is on Tables 1 `(A), not contracted out. NIC is 2% on the first £60 and 9% on the balance. Calculate the NIC payable.
    (b) A married woman earns £242 per week and is on Tables1 (B) not contracted out at the lower rate of 2% on the first £60 and 3.85% on the balance. Calculate the NIC payable.
11. What is meant by the term 'statutory deductions from pay'? Why is this different from voluntary deductions?
12. (a) When income tax is to be deducted, which tax forms are used?
    (b) When NIC is to be deducted, which forms are used?

13. NIC Tables 1 and Tables 1A are used for not contracted out and contracted out contributions. What is the difference between them?
14. Why do we pay NICs? Briefly explain the benefits available to us.

Note: Roger's gross pay was £234.13.

CHAPTER 25

Savings and Borrowing

What is saving?

Saving is refraining from spending all of your income and setting money aside for future use.

Reasons for saving?

People save for many reasons:

(a) as a protection against inflation;
(b) as a way of achieving capital growth;
(c) as a form of security, especially for retirement;
(d) as a way of achieving an asset, such as saving for a specific item like a motor bike;
(e) as a source of income.

In this part of the text we are mainly concerned with savings as a source of income.

The small saver can invest money in several different ways, the principal agencies concerned being:

- The national savings movement
- The building societies
- The commercial banks
- Investments in stocks and shares either directly or through unit trusts and investment trusts

Investing money

The national savings movement

The movement offers the following:

(a) ordinary savings account;
(b) investment account;
(c) savings certificates;
(d) index-linked savings certificates;
(e) Premium Bonds.

The ordinary savings account pays the first 'slice' of interest tax free. The investment account pays interest at a much higher rate but is taxable and one month's notice of withdrawal is required. One of the main advantages of the ordinary National Savings Bank (NSB) account is that of convenience – there is always an NSB somewhere near and they are open $5\frac{1}{2}$ days per week. However, with the increasing provision of electronic cash dispensers by banks and building societies, this is not the competitive factor it used to be. National Savings certificates offer a fixed return over a fixed period – the saver will lose interest if the certificate is cashed before the period expires. During, the mid-1970s, index-linked savings certificates were introduced to preserve the capital value of people's savings during periods of high inflation. Premium Bonds are not really a form of saving but in effect are a 'coward's form of gambling'.

The building societies

Building societies are now administered under the terms of the 1986 Building Society Act for the purpose of assisting the objective of home ownership. In order to attract funds, the societies offer a wide range of saving schemes:

(a) paid-up shares
(b) SAYE (Save As You Earn) schemes
(c) 'high interest' accounts

An important feature about building society interest is that it is paid to the investor net of tax. What this means is that if you pay tax at the standard rate you are not liable for further tax on the interest. Building society interest is not tax-free as the tax is paid direct to the Inland Revenue by the society. This is called composite rate tax and it cannot be reclaimed by non-tax payers.

Paid-up shares

Each £1 invested purchases a fully paid-up share on which interest is earned. Withdrawals can be paid on demand up to certain limits (say, £1,000) but for larger sums a short period of notice may be required. Unlike company shares, building society shares cannot be traded on the Stock Exchange.

SAYE schemes

For investors who are prepared to save on a regular basis, a higher rate of interest is paid. The investor agrees to save a fixed sum each month, often by having the agreed sum deducted from gross wages by his employer on behalf of the building society.

Higher interest accounts

Most societies have some form of 'higher interest' scheme, usually with a minimum investment (say, £500), which requires notice of withdrawal – often one month or 91 days. But, because of increased competition, the notice of withdrawal aspect is now often waived if there is a minimum limit to the account.

Like the NSB (Post Office), most building societies are open on Saturday mornings and some, such as the Halifax Building Society, now have electronic cashpoints for both depositing and withdrawing cash.

The commercial banks

In essence there are two main types of account that a private individual will tend to use:

(a) current account;
(b) deposit account.

Interest is paid on a deposit account but not on a current account. Seven days' notice is required for withdrawals from a deposit account but most banks waive this period of notice. With a current account, cash is repayable on demand and a cheque book is issued. Most banks currently make no bank charges as long as the current account remains in surplus.

Increasingly in the 1980s the clearing banks have introduced high interest accounts, which compete against the building societies. There are high interest current accounts and high interest deposit accounts – the latter usually requiring a minimum deposit of £1,000 and paying $2-2\frac{1}{2}\%$ above the normal deposit account rate; more interest is paid on larger sums deposited.

Investments in stocks and shares

Earlier, describing sources of business finance, we dealt with types of share. During the 1980s more private individuals have invested in shares with a view to receiving a regular income (dividends) and some capital appreciation. A popular way to invest in stocks and shares has been through unit trusts, many of which are run by banks. The trust uses people's savings and invests their money in a wide range of equities and gilts, so spreading the risk. Specialised unit trusts also exist. One of the major influences in the trend towards wider share ownership has been the privatisation of former public sector institutions – in financial terms, British Telecom and British Gas were the largest issues and were responsible for several million small investors.

Buying on credit

Most of the expenditure of a private individual, such as rent, rates, light, heat, petrol, entertainment costs, etc., is paid for out of current income. In accountancy terms this is called *revenue expenditure*.

But there are occasions when an individual wishes to purchase a major item, such as a television, motor car or freezer, and wishes to borrow in order to make the purchase. In accountancy terms this is called *capital expenditure* – that is, the item purchased will give several years of useful life.

The major sources of loan finance include:

(a) commercial banks – personal loan or overdraft;
(b) hire-purchase finance companies;
(c) credit card companies.

Commercial banks

The procedure for obtaining either a personal loan or an overdraft is a little different. If an overdraft is required, say, for 3 months, a simple letter of application to the bank manager will usually suffice. The Manager will arrange to mark the account with an overdraft limit – usually a few hundred pounds – for the pre-set period. With an overdraft, interest is only paid when one is overdrawn, on a daily basis, and is linked to the Bank's base rate.

A major company may be charged 1% over base rate, whereas a smaller company may be charged 3 or 4% over base and a personal borrower may pay 6 or 7% over base rate. The deciding factor is the degree of risk – that is, the safer the loan the lower the interest rate.

For a personal loan, most banks do not require to interview the applicant unless there is some problem. The customer will complete an application form giving full details of his income from all sources, and his outgoings (expenses). The customer has to state on his application form:

● How much he wishes to borrow
● For what purpose he wishes to borrow the money
● How he intends to repay it (his income source)
● How long he wants the loan for
● What contribution he is making from his own savings towards the cost of the item

This then introduces cash budgets; the preparation of such a cash budget would be essential in this instance. If the borrower is not a well-known customer the bank will make general status inquiries as to his job, salary, dependants and other financial commitments. Essentially, if the Manager or Loans Officer is satisfied that a customer is creditworthy, then a loan can be arranged – after all, this is why banks exist and how they make much of their profits. For a large loan the bank may require some form of collateral (security) such as property or life assurance policy.

One of the main advantages of bank finance is that the borrower has the freedom to purchase the actual goods wherever he prefers – which means that the best discount price can be obtained. Furthermore, the title to the goods moves to the buyer immediately, whereas in a hire-purchase situation this is not the case until the final payment is made.

Example

Amount of loan required	£600
Interest at 10% for 24 months	£120
	£720 ÷ 24 = £30

that is, 24 monthly instalments of £30

Note: The true rate of interest (APR) is approximately 19.85% p.a. (that is, nearly double the flat rate).

In addition, the bank may charge an arrangement fee in the above case; this may be in the region of £10.

Hire-purchase companies

Many retail stores offer hire-purchase facilities – sometimes through their own in-house company or by using an outside hire-purchase company. In most circumstances the rate of interest charged is much higher than that charged by the banks. The advantage to the customer is that obtaining hire purchase at the point of purchase is convenient; that is, you do not have to apply to or visit the bank, just complete the appropriate agreement form.

A major drawback of buying on hire purchase is that the buyer does not own the goods until the final instalment has been paid. The contract that exists is that the customer will hire the goods for the duration of the contract, paying rent for their use, and will complete the purchase at the end of the period. Until the final payment, the supplier has certain rights about regaining possession. Therefore, an individual would be well advised to look very seriously at the alternatives before purchasing on hire purchase.

Credit card companies

A credit card enables the holder to buy goods or services up to individual limits at shops, restaurants, garages, etc., which belong to the scheme, without paying at the time of purchase. The cardholder presents the card and the supplier completes a voucher in triplicate at the same time, imprinting the number of the card on the vouchers, which are then signed by the card holder.

The main types of credit card available are

● Barclaycard
● Access Card
● American Express ⎱ These are really charge cards, as the
● Diners Card   ⎰ balance *has* to be paid each month

Although these are mainly backed by different banks, cards are available to any suitable applicant, regardless of the bank to which he belongs. Note that retail companies such as Debenhams, Tesco, Comet and Marks & Spencer now operate their own in-house credit card schemes.

Advantages to the card-holder include:

(a) large sums of money do not have to be carried about;
(b) cash, up to a certain sum, can be withdrawn from any bank (interest is, charged immediately on such transactions);
(c) one cheque only is written each month to cover all transations;

(d) if used sensibly to time purchases carefully, a credit card can be economical (55/59 days credit can be obtained);

(e) Barclaycard also doubles as a cheque guarantee card for cheques drawn on Barclays Bank only.

Disadvantages to the card-holder include:

(a) there is always the temptation to spend more than one can afford;

(b) interest rates on accounts not paid in full are much higher than overdraft or personal loan rates – it is an expensive way to borrow!

Advantages to dealers include:

(a) higher sales result;

(b) payment is assured (as against cheques which may be returned after goods are taken)

Disadvantages to dealers include:

(a) vouchers have to be completed, distributed to card organisations and checked against payments from card organisations;

(b) a small charge is raised by the card organisations on every transaction, usually $1\frac{1}{2}$–2% of the cost of the sales.

Types of mortgage

There are two main types of mortgage:

- endowment mortgage and
- capital and interest mortgage (sometimes called repayment mortgage)

With an endowment mortgage the monthly payment falls into two parts. First there is the interest payment on the whole of the mortgage, paid to the lender over the full term. The second payment is to an insurance company for an endowment policy, with payments again being made throughout the term of the loan. Should the borrower die during the mortgage term, the endowment policy guarantees payment of the loan. At the end of the mortgage term, it will usually mature with a value sufficient to repay the full loan, often with a cash surplus as well, although this is not guaranteed.

With a capital and interest mortgage the monthly payment is made up of interest on the outstanding loan and capital repayment of the loan itself. In the early years the majority of the monthly payment is used to pay the interest, with only a small part being used as capital repayment. Then, as the outstanding loan is gradually repaid, the interest charges reduce so that eventually the major part of the monthly payment is used to repay capital.

Interest paid on mortgages

To encourage house ownership, the policy of successive governments has been to allow relief from interest paid on mortgages.

There is a 'ceiling' to the amount on mortgage on which relief of interest can be claimed (currently £30,000). To make administration easier the Inland Revenue introduced the MIRAS (Mortgage Interest Relief At Source) scheme. Under MIRAS most people with a mortgage obtain their tax relief through the lender, rather than have it added to their allowances. Their repayments to the lender are paid on a net basis – that is, tax relief already deducted. Some people with mortgages exceeding the relief of interest ceiling still get their tax relief via their tax coding numbers.

Questions

1. Go down your local High Street and visit banks and building societies to pick up various leaflets which inform you of their savings and investment accounts. List the type of accounts they have on offer such as deposit, higher interest rate, and Tessa accounts and the rates they pay.
2. Study the following investment offers which were featured in the *Daily Mail's* 'Money Mail':

Portman:	7% gross p.a. for 6 months, minimum investment £500.
Bristol & West:	7.15% gross p.a. Saver with no withdrawals p.a.
N & P:	6.00% gross p.a. minimum investment £500.

   (a) If interest is paid gross, what does it mean?
   (b) Convert the gross interest rates to net.
   (c) If you had £1,500 to invest for a period of 6 months,

how much interest would be earned on the three investment offers (net)?

3. What are the essential differences between an endowment and a capital repayment mortgage?
Explain MIRAS.

4. Hire purchase and credit cards are useful devices for acquiring goods and services but they do have their drawbacks. Explain.

Personal Cash Budgeting

'Annual income twenty pounds – annual expenditure nineteen pounds
nineteen and six, result happiness.
Annual income twenty pounds – annual expenditure twenty pounds
and six pence – result misery'
(Mr Micawber in *David Copperfield* by Charles Dickens)

It is just as important for an individual to consider cash flow as
it is for a business. For an individual or a business to be unable to
meet commitments is at the least embarrassing, will certainly cause
anxiety and can lead to bankruptcy.

It is recommended that an individual compiles a budget on a
regular basis. The mechanics of drawing up a budget are very simple;
the skill lies in forecasting income and expenditure. Certain expenditure is more or less known and can be regarded as fixed in
nature; for example, mortgage payments, rent, rates, insurance
premiums, car licence, hire-purchase commitments, etc. – in all these
cases we know when the amount is due and often how much.
Other expenditure, such as food and drink, entertainment, petrol
and oil, holidays, clothing, etc., is much more variable and much
more in the control of the individual.

Example: a Personal Cash Budget

Phillip, a single person, has the following regular income and
commitments.
Income
Net monthly salary £550.

Income from investments received at three-monthly intervals commencing in March of £40 (net of tax).

Known expenditure (fixed)
Rent £140 monthly; rates £20 monthly; car tax £100 due in February; gas bill due in March estimated at £80; electricity bill due in February estimated at £70; annual life assurance premium of £50 due in January; instalment on the car of £60 per month.

Unknown expenditure (variable)
Food and drink, say, £20 per week; entertainment, say, £25 per week: clothing £15 per week.

Other information
Assume Phillip has £100 on 1 January and wishes to prepare a cash budget to cover 3 months. Note that the expenditure in the 'unknown' category can be tailored to what can be afforded – the cash budget would indicate how much (if anything) can be saved for the future.

First of all it is probably best to make a schedule of payments as shown in Table 26.1.

Now we can show the cash budget (see Table 26.2).

TABLE 26.1 Schedule of payments

	Jan. (4 weeks in month) £	Feb. (4 weeks in month) £	March (5 weeks in month) £
Rent	140	140	140
Rates	20	20	20
Car tax	—	100	—
Gas	—	—	80
Electricity	—	70	—
Life assurance	50	—	—
Hire purchase	60	60	60
Food and drink	80	80	100
Entertainment	100	100	125
Clothing	60	60	75
	510	630	600*

*These totals can now be transferred to the expenditure line of the cash budget.

TABLE 26.2 Cash budget

	Jan. £	Feb. £	March £
Balance brought forward	100	140	60
Income	+ 550	550	590
	650	690	650
Expenditure	- 510	630	600
Balance carried forward	140	60	50

Thus Phillip can tell from the above projected cash flow that he must be very careful during this period as his cash in hand will reduce from £140 to £50. In addition he would have problems coping with an unexpected event, such as a car repair bill. Phillip should, therefore, be as prudent as possible with his spending on entertainment and clothing during this period.

By preparing a cash budget it will be known in advance if any surplus or deficit is likely to occur. This will mean that one can decide the most advantageous means of investing any surplus and can make proper plans to fund any deficit. A short-term deficit of a month or two might best be coped with on a credit card, but for longer periods bank finance may be the solution. The fact that one has prepared a cash-flow plan, showing when one expects to be back in surplus, will impress a bank manager, and assist in convincing him that one is a 'good risk'.

Questions

1. Margaret, a single person, has the following regular income and commitments:

   Income
   Net monthly salary of £500.

   'Known' expenditure (fixed)
   Housekeeping contribution to parents £20 per week; driving lesson £10 per week; hire purchase payment £25 per month; monthly rail ticket £35; life assurance payment due in July £60.

'Unknown' expenditure (variable)
Margaret plans to spend around £40 per week on enter-tainment, clothing, LPs, etc.

Other information
On 1 June Margaret has £80 in her current account and maintains a building society account.

Required:

(a) Draw up a personal cash flow budget for June to August inclusive, clearly showing the balance in her current account at each month end.
   (Assume 4 weeks in June and July and 5 in August.)
(b) Make recommendations as to what Margaret can do with any resulting surplus/deficit. You may assume no bank charges will occur as long as her current account is not overdrawn.

2. Cyril and Cecelia are a married couple with no children and have the following commitments:

Income
Cyril has a net monthly salary of £600 per month (payable on last day of month).
Cecelia has a net monthly salary of £450 per month (pay-able on the 10th day of each month).

'Known' expenditure (fixed)
Rent £200 per month; regular building society savings sub-scription of £150 per month; hire purchase payment of £30 per month; gas bill of £70 due in February; electricity bill of £80 due in January; credit card statement balance of £90 due on 12 January; car insurance of £90 due in March; petrol and oil £10 per week.

'Unknown' expenditure (variable)
Food and drink, say £30 per week; entertainment, say £30 per week; clothing £20 per week.

Other information
On 1 January their joint current account has £200 in it.

Required:

(a) Draw up a cash budget for the couple for January to March inclusive. (Assume 4 weeks in January and February and 5 weeks in March.)

(b) Assuming that Cyril and Cecelia like to keep about £200 in their joint current account, will they be able to save any more than they already do during the period? If so, how much in each month?

3. Jack, a single person, has just had to leave a well-paid job and take up a lower-paid job. His 'new' income and existing commitments are:

Income
Net monthly salary of £450.

'Known' expenditure
Rent £150 monthly (3 weeks' notice of termination is required, and the rent is payable in advance), rates £25 monthly; electricity bill £50 due in May; hire purchase payments of £40 monthly; gas bill £40 due in June.

'Unknown' expenditure
Jack has only been used to opening the odd pack of cornflakes and making tea and coffee, etc., at a cost of about £5 per week. He has been eating out a lot up until now, at a cost of about £60 per week. Jack has also been spending about £50 per week on clothes and entertainment.

Other information
On 1 April Jack starts his new job and has £250 in a current account and £600 in a building society account. His parents live nearby and have always maintained a room for his use.

Required:

(a) Assuming Jack maintains his existing style of living, draw up a personal cash flow budget for the period April to June inclusive. Start with an opening balance figure of £850 (£250 + £600). (Assume each month consists of 4 weeks.)

(b) Clearly Jack will be forced to alter his existing style of living; you are asked to make suggestions as to what he should do and to prepare a cash-flow budget taking account of your suggestions.

4. Robert Cambell, a single person, has worked as a clerk for a large insurance company for three years. Robert left school at 18 with two 'A' levels, and is currently part-way through the examinations of the Institute of Insurance. Roger has had one promotion since joining the company and can expect to gain further promotions in the future. Robert shares a flat with a colleague. Robert is also hoping to purchase a car, and his parents will pay any deposit.

Information

- Robert's current gross salary is £8,000 p.a., payable weekly
- The single person's personal tax allowance is £2,400
- Robert pays 5% of his salary as pension contribution
- Robert is not entitled to any other tax allowances
- Robert has to pay NICs at the rate of £12.30 per week
- Robert has no other deductions from his salary
- Income tax is 30% (standard rate)
- Robert's known weekly personal expenditure is:
    Rent £25 per week and food and drink £20 per week
    Bus fares £5 per week
- In addition to the above weekly expenditure Robert is aware of the following bills to pay:
    January – pay off credit card balance £80
    February – Life Assurance premium due £70
    March – snooker club subscription £20
- On 1 January, Robert has £40 in his current account
- Current interest charged on personal loans = 10% flat rate

Required:

(a) Compute Robert's net *weekly* salary.
(b) Using the above information, prepare a personal cash-flow budget for January to March inclusive. (Assume 4 weeks in January, 4 in February and 5 in March.)
(c) How much on average could Robert spend per month during the period January – March inclusive on entertainment and clothing?
(d) Robert has now seen a car he likes and needs to obtain a loan of £1,800.
    (i) Calculate the monthly repayments over 2 years.

(ii) Calculate the monthly repayments over 3 years.

(e) Robert has written to you, his uncle, and asked for your advice on how he should go about financing the purchase. You, therefore, have to write a letter to Robert giving him general advice on how to obtain finance, what sources are available, and specific advice regarding Robert's circumstances. You should also advise Robert on whether to borrow for 2 or 3 years.

Note: You may assume knowledge of all the preceding information.

PART VI

PLANNING AND DECISION MAKING: ACCOUNTING FOR COSTS

CHAPTER 27

Manufacturing Accounts

There is a wide range of different business organisations in our economic environment which require financial reports. The larger the organisation, the more important it is to provide it with essential information so that management can make objective and sound decisions.

A manufacturing organisation which makes its own products wants to know, among other things, how much it costs to produce its goods and how these costs are divided in terms of costs directly or indirectly related to production. From these figures it is possible to analyse cost types and their effect on production levels and price.

A business needs to know its total production costs for the purpose of setting its selling price. Given a certain production capacity (for example, 10,000 units) and a total cost (absorption cost) of say £100,000, the cost per unit is £10. From this, a selling price can be determined by adding a sum to the cost, a margin considered to be what the market will pay.

The purpose of preparing a manufacturing account is to calculate the cost of production – that is, the factory cost as distinct from other costs in the profit and loss account.

The cost of manufacturing a product can be divided into three parts:

(a) *Direct Costs*: These are directly involved with the making of the product, including the labour, the materials and any direct expense directly related to production.
  (i) Direct Labour. The factory wages related to the workers actively involved making the product; such as machinists or assembly workers.
  (ii) Direct Materials. The raw materials and components specifically used to make the product, such as the tube,

461

frame, stand and electrical/electronic parts of a television set.

(iii) Direct Expenses. There are few of these because most of them tend to be indirect and related to factory overheads. Direct expenses include direct power, the hiring or leasing of special equipment or plant for production, or the payment of royalties for patents or trade marks used in production.

The total of direct costs = the PRIME COST

(b) *Indirect Costs.* These refer to the factory overheads and include indirect labour, materials and expenses.

(i) Indirect Labour. This relates to the factory employees but excludes direct wages. Factory storemen, cleaners, progress chasers, production controllers, engineers and draftsmen are some examples.

(ii) Indirect Materials. These may relate to factory lubricants, fluids, stationery, safety clothing and any other materials used in the factory, but excluding direct materials.

(iii) Indirect Expenses. These relate to any factory overhead but exclude indirect labour and materials. Factory rates, insurance, light and heat, power (if not direct), rent, depreciation of factory equipment and any general factory expenses are examples.

(c) *Work-in-Progress.* This relates to the stock of partly finished goods both at the beginning and end of a financial period, such as televisions partly completed on the assembly line.

Presentation of manufacturing account

An example is given in Table 27.1.

TABLE 27.1 A manufacturing account

	£	£	£
Direct Costs			
Stock of raw materials (1 Jan.)	2,000		
+ Purchases of raw materials	25,000		
	27,000		
− Stock of raw materials (31 Dec.)	3,000	24,000	
Direct manufacturing wages	19,000		

+ Accrued wages		1,000	20,000	
Hire of special equipment			1,000	
Prime Cost				45,000
Indirect Costs				
Safety clothing			1,000	
Indirect factory wages			12,000	
Depreciation of plant		500		
Factory rates, insurance		2,500		
Factory maintenance		4,000		
Factory general expenses		1,000	8,000	
Factory Overheads				21,000
				66,000
Work-in-Progress				
+ Stock (Jan. 1)				1,500
				67,500
− Stock (Dec. 31)				2,500
Cost of Production				65,000
(Transferred to Trading a/c)				

Production (Factory) Cost ≥ Prime Cost + Factory Overheads
 + WIP (o/stock) - WIP (c/stock)

Note: Some factories may not have any work-in-progress because they may process their production, such as food or paint, and their stock maybe in the form of raw materials and finished goods.

The cost of production per unit

If 20,000 units were produced by the factory in the financial year:

(a) Production Cost per Unit $= \dfrac{£65,000}{20,000} \dfrac{\text{Cost of Production}}{\text{No. of Units}}$

 $= £3.25$ per Unit

(b) Prime Cost per Unit $= \dfrac{£45,000}{20,000} \dfrac{\text{Prime Cost of Production}}{\text{No. of Units}}$

 $= £2.25$ per Unit

(c) Factory Overheads per Unit $= \dfrac{£21,000}{20,000} \dfrac{\text{Factory OH Cost}}{\text{No. of Units}}$

 less adjustment for $= £1.05$ per Unit
 Work-in-Progress Stock $\dfrac{0.05}{£1.00}$ per Unit

The factory's production cost per unit is £3.25, made up of prime cost and factory overheads. It does not include the firm's profit and loss expenses per unit, such as distribution costs and administration expenses.

The production cost per unit is a guide to the factory to indicate whether the firm is cost-effective in the production of its goods.

Transfer of cost of production to the trading account

This is shown in Table 27.2.

TABLE 27.2   Transfer of production costs to trading account

	£	£	£
Sales			100,000
Less			
Cost of Sales			
Stock: finished goods (1 Jan.)	5,500		
+ Cost of production	65,000		
	70,500		
– Stock: Finished goods (31 Dec.)	3,500		67,000
Gross profit			33,000

Example

The following figures relate to the accounts of ABC Company Limited, television manufacturing business, for the year ended 31 December:

	£
Stocks of raw materials 1 January	3,186
Stocks of raw materials 31 December	4,479
Stocks of finished goods 1 January	4,264
Stocks of finished goods 31 December	9,651
Purchases of raw materials	23,766
Sales of finished goods net	79,695
Rent and rates	3,292
Manufacturing wages	23,463
Manufacturing power	765
Manufacturing heat and light	237
Manufacturing expenses and maintenance	819

Salaries and wages	13,870
Advertising	2,217
Office expenses	786
Depreciation of plant and machinery	745
Hiring of plant	504

One-half of the salaries and wages and three-quarters of the rent and rates are to be treated as a manufacturing charge.

Work-in-Progress (1 January)	£1,156
Work-in-Progress (31 December)	£1,066

Required:

Manufacturing, trading and profit and loss accounts for the year to show clearly:

(a) the cost of raw materials used;
(b) prime cost;
(c) cost of factory overheads;
(d) factory cost of goods completed;
(e) cost of goods sold;
(f) gross profit for the year;
(g) total of administrative and selling expenses;
(h) net profit for the year.

The manufacturing account of ABC Company Limited for the period ending 31 December is shown in Table 27.3.

Trading and profit and loss account of ABC Company Limited for the period ending 31 December is shown in Table 27.4.

TABLE 27.3 ABC's manufacturing account

		£	£	£
Direct Costs				
Stocks of raw materials (1/1)		3,186		
Purchases of raw materials		23,766		
		26,952		
Less stocks of raw materials (31/12)		4,479		
	(a)	22,473		
Direct wages		23,463		
Direct expenses		504		
	(b)			46,440
Indirect Costs				
Indirect wages and salaries			6,935	
Indirect expenses:				
Depreciation: plant		745		
Manufacturing heat and light		237		
Expenses and maintenance		819		
+ power		765		
+ rent and rates		2,469	5,035	
	(c)			11,970
				58,410
Add				
Work-in-Progress (1/1)				1,156
				59,566
less				
Work-in-Progress (31/12)				1,066
Cost of Production				
(transferred to Trading a/c)	(d)			58,500

TABLE 27.4 ABC's trading and profit and loss account

	£	£	
Sales		79,695	
– *Cost of Sales*			
Stocks of finished goods (1/1)	4,264		
+ Cost of Production	58,500		
	62,764		
– Stocks of finished goods (31/12)	9,651	53,113	(e)
Gross Profit		26,582	(f)
– *Other Expenses*			
Rent and rates	823		
Wages and salaries	6,935		
Advertising	2,217		
Office expenses	786	10,761	(g)
Net profit		15,821	(h)

Costs per unit

If 260 television sets had been produced by ABC Company Limited for the period to 31 December, then if we were to include *total costs* of running the firm (that is, production and profit and loss expenses)

Cost of production	£58,500
Profit and loss expenses	£10,761

£69,261

$$\text{Total cost per unit} \quad = \quad \frac{£69,261}{260} \quad = \quad £266.38$$

The cost of production would show the amount it costs to run the factory – as separate from running the office.

$$\text{Factory cost per unit} \quad = \quad \frac{£58,500}{260} \quad = \quad £225.00$$

This would be a check to see if the manufacturing side of the business was producing goods cost-effectively. Could the firm 'buy out' (that is, from other manufacturers) at less than £225 per unit?

Prime cost is a guide to show the *minimum* possible cost to produce a television in terms of direct labour and materials:

$$\text{Prime cost per unit} \quad \frac{£46{,}440}{260} = £178.60$$

The valuation of stock

The unsold stock of finished goods at the end of the financial year may be valued in a number of different ways (see Chapter 23, SSAP 9):

(a) at prime cost per unit;
(b) at production cost per unit;
(c) at total cost per unit;
(d) at lower of cost or net realisable value.

Whichever method is used, it must be applied consistently when preparing the final accounts of the business, otherwise the accounting reports may be misrepresented. The value of unsold stock affects the calculation of gross profit because the greater the value of stock, the greater the value of gross profit. SSAP 9 states that finished goods should be valued at prime cost plus factory overheads at normal production levels; at production cost is the most suitable.

The calculation of 'profit' in the manufacturing account

An assessment of profit may be determined in the manufacturing side of the business. This may be calculated if a *market value* of the goods manufactured can be given. In the previous exercise, 260 televisions were produced by ABC Company Limited at a production cost of £58,500. If the televisions could have been purchased from *other manufacturers* at, say, £280 each, it is possible to calculate whether it is worth ABC producing the televisions in the first place! For example:

260 @ £280 market value =	£72,800
ABC's production cost	£58,500
Profit on manufacturing side	£14,300

It seems it *is* worth it. ABC can make £14,300 by manufacturing the televisions themselves. The trading account showed a gross profit of £26,582:

Manufacturing profit = £14,300
Trading profit = £12,282

£26,582

If a manufacturer wanted to emphasise the profit made by the production side of the factory, the manufacturing account must include the market valuation of those goods manufactured: see the manufacturing account of ABC Company Limited, 31 December (extract), as shown in Table 27.5, and the trading account in Table 27.6.

TABLE 27.5   ABC's manufacturing account

	£
Cost of production	58,500
Manufacturing profit	14,300
Being market value 260 @ £280	72,800

TABLE 27.6   ABC's trading account

	£	£
Sales		79,695
Stocks of finished goods (1/1)	4,264	
Market value of production	72,800	
	77,064	
– Stock of finished goods (31/12)	9,651	67,413
Trading profit		12,282
Manufacturing profit		14,300
Gross Profit		26,582

From this method of presentation, the manufacturer has an assessment of:

the actual manufacturing profit	£14,300
the trading profit	£12,282
Gross Profit	£26,582

Thus, the profit figure is the same as before and the net profit is unaffected by this method of presentation

Mark-up and margins of profit

The 'mark-up' is usually expressed as a percentage and is *added* to the cost price of goods in order to arrive at to the selling price.

ABC company produced and sold 260 units earning a revenue of £79,695:

$$\text{Selling price per unit} \quad = \frac{£79,695}{260} = £306.5 \text{ per unit}$$

$$\text{Total cost price per unit} = \frac{£69,261}{260} = £266.38 \text{ per unit}$$

$$\textit{Profit} \text{ per unit} \qquad = \qquad\qquad £40.12 \text{ per unit}$$

Mark-up percentage

This is always based on the *cost price*

$$= \frac{\text{Profit} \times 100}{\text{Cost}}$$

$$= \frac{£40.12 \times 100}{£266.38} = 15\% \text{ mark-up}$$

The percentage mark-up on cost is the guideline to selling price. How much to mark up may be a problem. How much will the market be prepared to pay? What are the prices of the firm's competitors? What will be the cost of 'follow-up' services? ABC Co. has marked up its stock by 15% at present prices. Will competition in the market place become more intense and force the company to review its mark-up?

Margin percentage

This is always based on the *selling price*

$$= \frac{\text{Profit} \times 100}{\text{Selling Price}}$$

$$= \frac{£40.12 \times 100}{£306.50} = 13\% \text{ margin}$$

The margin percentage is a guideline to profit based on sales. In this case, every £100 sales will produce a profit of £13. Sales of £1,000 produce a profit of £130 and so forth. The margin percentage is a useful indicator of profit based on the value of sales and may be compared with previous trading performances and with other businesses in the same field in order to evaluate profitability.

Questions

1. From the following information, prepare Freddy Smith's manufacturing account, trading and profit and loss account for the year ended 31 December:

	£
Stocks (January 1)	
Raw materials	5,675
Work-in-progress	2,225
Finished goods	7,550
Purchases of raw materials	40,850
Sales	101,255
Returns (Dr.)	7,235
Factory	
Wages (Direct)	18,600
Power	2,675
Depreciation of plant	3,765
Rent and rates	3,720
Insurances	500
Office	
Light and heat	846
Insurances	245
General expenses	170
Wages	6,750
Rent and rates	975
Stocks (December 31)	
Raw materials	6,200
Work-in-progress	2,135
Finished goods	8,225

At 31 December

● Wages owing: £854 (office)
● Depreciation of office equipment £500
● Rent and rates pre-paid: 15% of both factory and office

2. From the following information, prepare Jack Jones's manufacturing account, trading account, and profit and loss account for the year ended 31 December:

	£
Sales	155,000
Stocks (January 1)	
Raw materials	5,856
Work-in-progress	1,500
Finished goods	10,575
Purchase of raw materials	85,424
Stocks (December 31)	
Raw materials	6,255
Work-in-progress	1,480
Finished goods	12,555
Factory	
Wages (direct)	22,575
Wages accrued (direct)	425
Factory and machinery maintenance	2,550
Depreciation on plant and machinery	4,500
Power	875
Salaries	6,500
Rent, rates, and insurance	2,142
Lighting and heating	532
Offices Expenses	
Rent, rates, and insurance	1,150
Lighting and heating	350
Administrative expenses	2,335

At 31 December

● Rates were pre-paid: £125 for factory and £60 for office
● £70 for factory salaries was owing
● A bill of £65 was due to the Gas Board for office heating

3. Harry is a manufacturer. From the following details relating to his business, prepare separate accounts to show for the year ended 31 December:

(a) the factory cost of goods;
(b) the manufacturing profit;
(c) the trading profit;
(d) the net profit.

	£
Stocks (1 January)	
Raw materials	6,757
Finished goods	10,560
Stocks (31 December)	
Raw materials	5,583
Finished goods	12,565
Wages: factory (Direct)	15,500
office	12,765
Rent, rates and insurance	4,580
(factory four-fifths; office one-fifth)	
Sales of finished goods	101,500
Purchases of raw materials	40,875
Manufacturing expenses	5,945
Selling expenses	12,855
Administrative expenses	7,400
Depreciation: machinery	2,150
office furniture	500
accounting machines (office)	150

Other Information

● (1/1) Stocks of work-in-progress (NIL)
  (31/12) Stocks of work-in-progress (NIL)
● The market valuation of the cost of production is £78,000

Required:

(a) Calculate, on the basis of 2,000 units produced in the year:
   (i)Direct labour cost per unit
   (ii)Direct material cost per unit
   (iii)Factory overheads per unit
   (iv)Production costs per unit
(b) Was manufacturing cost-effective?

Compare the market value per unit cost with production cost per unit.

4. ABC Co. Ltd is a manufacturer. From the following details relating to his business prepare separate accounts to show for the year ended 31 December:

(a) the factory cost of goods;
(b) the gross profit;
(c) the net profit.

	£
Stocks (1 January)	
Raw materials at cost	4,200
Finished goods at factory cost	7,525
Work-in-progress	5,450
Stocks (31 December)	
Raw materials at cost	4,875
Finished goods at factory cost	9,674
Wages: factory (direct)	27,855
office	15,640
Rent, rates and insurance	3,600
(factory four-fifths; office one-fifth)	
Sales of finished goods	121,565
Purchases of raw materials	45,750
Manufacturing expenses	4,380
Selling expenses	3,895
Administrative expenses	1,675
Depreciation: machinery	4,500
office furniture	1,500
office equipment	350
At 31 December	
Work-in-progress	5,980
Factory wages accrued	255

Based on 10,500 units produced by ABC Co. during the year, calculate:

(d) the prime cost per unit;
(e) the overhead factory cost per unit;
(f) production costs per unit;

(g) total costs per unit;

(h) assuming that 10,000 units were sold during the year, calculate both the mark-up % and margin % applied by the company.

5. Prepare the manufacturing, trading and profit and loss accounts of Fred's Co. Ltd for the year ended 31 December. Production output: 10,000 units in year.

	£
Stocks (1 January)	
Raw materials	4,250
Work-in-progress	—
Finished goods (2,050 Units)	10,250
Stocks (31 December)	
Raw materials	5,150
Finished goods: units in balance valued at production cost	
Work-in-progress	—
Purchases of raw materials	32,600
Sales (10,800 units)	86,500
Factory	
Direct wages	15,255
Power (direct)	1,650
Indirect salaries	4,780
Factory maintenance	1,585
Rates, insurance and general expenses	750
Indirect materials	1,480
Depreciation of plant	1,875
Office	
Rates, insurance and general expenses	455
Selling and distribution costs	2,875
Bad debts	450
Administration expenses	3,450
Discount (Dr.)	375
Depreciation of office equipment	500
Commission received	1,750
At 31 December.	

(a) Direct wages owing £250.
   Rates in advance (office) £50.

(b) A provision for bad debts to be created to equal 5% of debtors (Debtors £7,850).

(c) £150 was still due for factory power.

6. The following information is taken from the accounts of Peter Jackson, a businessman producing science equipment for colleges:

Trial balance of P. Jackson as on 30 June 19-5

	£	£
Stocks (1/7/19–4)		
Raw materials	6,885	
Finished goods	3,500	
Motor vehicle (cost)	8,750	
Premises (cost)	36,900	
Accumulated depreciation of vehicle (2 years)		1,750
Purchases (raw materials)	55,725	
Direct wages	45,780	
Sales		180,344
Discounts	855	1,044
Returns	548	
Salaries (assistants)	18,346	
Overheads (factory)	14,385	
Overheads (office)	7,044	
Creditors		6,755
Debtors	7,400	
Bank		2,045
Cash	400	
Drawings	10,420	
Capital		?

On 30 June, the following additional information was also available:

(a) Stocks in hand were valued:
    Raw materials £7,432
    Finished goods £4,200

(b) The motor vehicle is depreciated on straight line and is now 3 years old.

(c) Of the factory overheads, £240 is pre-paid and £600 is accrued.

Required:

Prepare the manufacturing account, trading and profit and loss account for the year ended 30 June 19–5 and a balance sheet as on that date.

7. XYZ Co. Ltd is a company which manufactures electrical components for the car industry. Production is planned for 50,000 units in the financial year ended 31 December.

The trial balance extracted from the ledgers on 31 December:

	£	£
Authorised and issued share capital:		
70,000 @ £1 ordinary shares		70,000
Share premium		7,000
Premises (cost)	86,000	
Plant (cost)	12,000	
Provision for depreciation of plant		6,000
Debtors	10,498	
Creditors		58,409
Stock (1 Jan.):		
Raw materials	5,892	
Finished goods (2,500 units)	8,500	
Provision for bad debts		200
Bad debts	528	
Bank/cash	2,910	
Direct wages	56,804	
Raw materials purchases of	156,820	
Sales (48,000 units)		204,000
General expenses ($\frac{1}{2}$ factory)	2,944	
Profit and loss balance (1 Jan.)		5,830
Rates and insurance ($\frac{1}{2}$ factory)	610	
Office wages	5,220	
Delivery charges	2,400	
Discount	313	
	351,439	351,439

Further information at 31 December

● Stocks: Raw materials unused £20,893.
            50,000 units of finished goods were produced.
            The unsold stock to be valued at production cost/
            unit.
● The provision for bad debts to be increased to £750.
● The plant is to be depreciated 10% on net value.
● A taxation provision of £750 is to be made.
● The directors have recommended a 5% dividend on the
  share capital.
  A general reserve is to be created by a transfer of £2,000
  in the appropriation account.

Required:

(a) Prepare the company's manufacturing, trading, profit and
    loss and appropriation accounts for the period ended
    31 December, and a balance sheet as at that date.
(b) Calculate on the basis of the number of units produced,
    the direct labour, direct materials and total overheads
    per unit.

8. *Trial Balance ABC Co. Ltd, year ended 31 December*

	£	£
Premises	20,000	
Plant and equipment at cost	75,000	
Motor vehicles at cost	4,000	
Provision for depreciation of plant and equipment		20,000
Provision for depreciation of motor vehicles		2,200
Stock of raw materials 1 January	8,000	
Stock of finished goods 1 Jan. 500 units	6,000	
Purchases of raw materials	75,600	
Direct wages	42,000	
Manufacturing expenses	28,500	
Selling and distribution costs	35,750	
Administrative expenses	13,825	
Discount		430
General expenses	6,600	
Debtors, creditors	2,570	16,650
Bank	3,805	
VAT	2,630	

Sales 11,250 units		225,000
Capital:		
60,000 @ £1 ordinary		60,000
	324,280	324,280

Additional information 31 December

● Stock of raw materials £10,600
  Stock of finished goods: unsold stock is to be valued at production cost. The firm's capacity of 12,000 units was produced in the year.
● Depreciation:
  Plant and equipment 10% of book value
  Motor vehicle (sales and distribution) 20% of cost
● Accruals:
  Direct wages £2,800
  Administrative expenses £250
● General expenses of £4,200 attributed to factory, the remainder to be allocated as administrative expenses
● Pre-payments:
  Sales and distribution cost £345
● It is proposed to provide a dividend of 5% to shareholders. A provision of £8,000 is to be made for taxation purposes and a general reserve of £6,000 is to be created.

Required:

(a) Prepare the firm's manufacturing account, trading and profit and loss and appropriation accounts for the period ended 31 December.
(b) Prepare the firm's balance sheet as at 31 December including in its presentation the working capital.
9. The following list of balances as at 31 December has been extracted from the books of Fairdeal Manufacturers Limited which commenced business on 1 January.

	£
Factory plant and machinery at cost 1 January	120,000
Motor delivery vehicles at cost 1 January	25,000
Purchases of raw materials	41,000
Factory labour: machine operatives	36,000
supervisory	7,000
Factory plat and machinery repairs	8,710
Heat, light and power	24,750
Rates and insurance	2,550
General administrative expenses	9,400
Administrative salaries	12,090
Trade debtors	12,000
Trade creditors	7,100
Bank overdraft	4,900
Sales	136,500
Ordinary shares of £1 each, fully paid	120,000
Share premium account	30,000

Additional information:
● Raw material stocks, at cost, at 31 December were valued at £3,000
● Work in progress at 31 December was valued at £24,000
● Depreciation is to be provided on fixed assets at the following rates on cost:

	% per annum
Factory plant and machinery	10
Motor delivery vehicles	25

● Rates and insurances pre-paid at 31 December amounted to £600; heat, light and power accrued due at 31 December was £2,300
● Rates and insurances and heat, light and power charges are to be apportioned three quarters to manufacturing and a quarter to the profit and loss account
● Manufactured goods are to be transferred from the manufacturing account to the trading account at wholesale prices; the wholesale price of goods manufactured during the year ended 31 December was £100,000*
● Finished goods stock at 31 December, at wholesale prices, was valued at £10,000*

Required:

(a) Prepare the manufacturing, trading and profit and loss account for the year ended 31 December for Fairdeal Manufacturers Limited.

(b) Prepare the balance sheet as at the same date for Fairdeal Manufacturers Limited.

* The finished goods at wholesale (market value) prices is 10% of the value of the wholesale price of manufactured goods $\left[\dfrac{10,000}{100,000}\right]$

It is assumed a provision for unrealised profit is made to equal 10% of the 'profit' on manufactured goods [£540 – check answer].

The double entry is:

  Debit: profit and loss account (provision for unrealised profit) £54
  Credit: Stock of Finished Goods £54

[Association of Accounting Technicians]

CHAPTER 28

Costing Principles and Classification of Costs

In our economic system, there is a wide diversity of businesses which require all kinds of information. In large organisations and particularly in factories making a whole range of products, it becomes even more important to feed management with the right type of information they will need in order to assist them in making the right decisions at the right time. In the manufacturing account, discussed in the last section, we needed to find out the different types of direct and indirect cost which made up the production cost. From these figures we could calculate the overall factory cost and the factory unit cost, which it is essential for management to know because it assists them to set the selling price. There is also a need to break down costs into fixed and variable categories in order to make further calculations which will affect both absorption and marginal costing, and this will be discussed in more detail as this part of the book progresses.

Costing

Management needs to have all kinds of information at its fingertips and costing is a basic essential in providing such information. For example:

- How much will it cost to produce 500 units of a certain product?
- Is it possible to reduce the selling price to match competitors?
- How many extra units must be produced to pay for an advertising campaign?
- How much will a new product cost in terms of labour, materials and overheads?

- What will happen if we close a section of the plant down?
- Can we afford to employ more labour?
- Can we sell a special order at 25% less than normal selling prices?
- How many units must be sold before it is possible to break even?

It is these types of question which need sound and correct answers. The guessing game doesn't come into it! Therefore, where management need information, costing helps to provide it. It is not surprising, then, that cost accounting is sometimes referred to as management accounting because of the information it supplies to help management make better, more informed decisions.

One of the most common costing questions which arises is simply 'How much does it cost to make?' This was seen in the manufacturing, trading and profit and loss accounts. Significantly, however, costing helps to decide what the future costs and prices will be, with the question posed: 'How much will it cost to make?' and therefore assists management in deciding whether a project goes ahead or not.

Costing principles

The type of information that requires an answer from costing such as 'How much will it cost to make?' involves both costing principles and the techniques used to get that information.

For example, if management wanted to know the full cost of making a specific unit, the technique of absorption costing will be used. If it wanted to know the break-even point of the product, then marginal costing would be used. If management wanted information concerning the future plans of the business in terms of what the costs are planned to be so as to be able to compare them with what actually happens, then this is the technique of what is called budgetary control. The types of cost we shall develop will concern the following concepts.

Absorption costing

A product or service absorbs all the costs in terms of labour, materials and a charge for overheads. Both fixed and variable costs are included in absorption. Note that fixed costs are insensitive to output changes, such as rent, rates and insurance costs. Variable costs are those that are sensitive to output change, best seen by direct materials and a proportion of direct labour and other variables such as power. The absorption cost is calculated on normal output levels in order to arrive at what is considered normal selling prices. Absorption costing methods may include job, batch, contract and process costing.

Marginal costing

This refers to variable costs and is really seeking to answer 'How much *extra* cost is included?' Whereas the absorption cost is looking to find the normal cost per unit, marginal costing is looking at cost and price in terms of output changes: whether there is an increase or decrease to levels of output and, if special orders occur which will increase output, to provide special prices for them. In Chapter 34 marginal costs are discussed in much greater detail, emphasising the importance of 'contribution'.

Budgeting

This is a management tool to help form future plans and to enable a comparison of a forecast of results with actual results when they occur. In this way, a yardstick is provided to see if things go according to plan and, if they don't, to find out why and then do something about it. This gives management what is called 'budgetary control'.

Standard costing

This assists management in providing pre-determined costs and is linked to budgeting. The standard cost for a product can be pre-determined for labour, materials and a charge for overheads. When the actual costs are measured, these can then be compared with the standard costs in order to monitor the progress of costs and incur control (see Table 28.1).

For management purposes, they will want to know why the variances (differences) occurred. Labour and overheads were more than planned, but materials were less. In this way, costs become more accountable and any corrective or other appropriate action can be taken.

Cost classification

The idea concerning the classification of costs boils down to finding out where money is being spent: not just how much money,

TABLE 28.1   Comparison of costs

	Standard cost per unit	Actual cost per unit	Variance per unit
Direct labour	2.80	2.95	+ 15
Direct materials	5.50	5.25	− 25
Overheads	8.95	9.55	+ 60

but in which areas. There is a need in cost accounting to know which areas of the business are spending money and thereby impose some element of control on the departments or cost centres who are spending it.

For example, if the motor vehicle expenses were £6,000, this could be written off in total as a charge against the profit and loss account. But who actually used the motor vehicles? Was it all used by the representatives of the sales office? Or do other departmental heads use cars on the business? For simplicity, if there were six cars, four of them used by the sales office, one by the factory manager and the other by the administrative head, the vehicle expenses would be divided:

Production overheads	£1,000
Sales and distribution	£4,000
Administration	£1,000

In other words, each department's share of the expense is shown so that the operating costs of a business can be identified and also controlled.

After viewing the presentation of the manufacturing account, it was seen that costs were broken down into different areas of the business:

Production Costs
    Prime cost
    Factory overheads

These were costs met by the factory, as distinct from those of the office.

Office Costs
    Sales and distribution expenses
    Administration

Rent, rates, insurances
Financial expenses
Salaries
Miscellaneous expenses

These are the general office expenses found in the profit and loss account. There are cases where a certain type of expense, such as rent, rates and insurance, ought to be divided into the *area of the business* where such an expense is used.

Total rent and rates	£20,000	
75% Factory proportion	£15,000	Factory overheads
20% Sales office	£4,000	Sales and distribution
5% Administration office	£1,000	Administrative expenses

Example

Using the cost classification sheet, break down the figures shown in Table 28.2 into their appropriate sections of costs.

The above costs relate to T. J. Freeze Ltd, which manufactures 2,000 units per annum. Further information for the financial year is given in Table 28.3.

Required:

(a) Using the information from the cost sheet and from above, prepare T. J. Freeze Ltd's manufacturing and trading and profit and loss accounts for the year ended 31 December.
(b) Calculate prime cost/unit, production cost/unit and total cost/unit, based on the production of 2,000 units in the year.

The answers are shown in Figure 28.1 and Tables 28.4 and 28.5.

TABLE 28.2 T.J. Freeze Ltd: costs

	£
Wages: 60% direct to production	
30% to sales staff.	70,000
10% to Administration	
Purchasing: 75% direct materials	
15% factory overheads	80,000
10% office stationery	
Rent, rates: (as below under Power)	20,000
Depreciation: 80% factory machines	5,000
20% office machines	
Power: 75% factory	
20% sales office	2,000
5% administration office	
Sales representatives' motor expenses	4,800
Telephone charges:	
25% factory	
50% sales office	1,500
25% administration office	
Financial expenses	420
Interest charges on overdraft	280

TABLE 28.3 Further information

	£
Stocks (1 January)	
Raw materials	8,755
Finished goods (100 units)	6,700
Work-in-progress	—
Stocks (31 December)	
Raw materials	6,215
Finished goods in stock	
valued at prime cost/unit	
Work-in-progress	—
Sales (1,800 units)	198,000

FIGURE 28.1 Cost classification sheet

	Wages, salaries (£)	Purchasing (£)	Rent, rates (£)	Telephone (£)	Motor expenses (£)	General expenses (£)	Stationery (£)	Power (£)	Interest charges (£)	Depreciation (£)	Transfer to: Manufacturing a/c
COSTS:											
Direct labour	42,000										42,000
Direct materials		60,000									60,000
Direct expenses											
Indirect labour											
Indirect materials		12,000									12,000
Indirect expenses			15,000	375				1,500		4,000	20,875
											Profit and Loss account
Distribution costs	21,000		4,000	750	4,800			400			30,950
Administration expenses	7,000		1,000	375		420	8,000	100	280	1,000	18,175
Total Cost	70,000	72,000	20,000	1,500	4,800	420	8,000	2,000	280	5,000	184,000

**TABLE 28.4 Manufacturing account
T. J. Freeze Ltd, year ended 31 December**

	£	£	£
DIRECT COSTS			
Stock of raw materials (1/1)	8,755		
Purchases of raw materials	60,000		
	68,755		
– Stock of raw materials (31/12)	6,215	62,540	
Direct wages		42,000	
Prime Cost			104,540
INDIRECT COSTS			
Indirect materials	12,000		
Indirect expenses	20,875		
Factory Overheads			32,875
Work-in-progress			137,415
Stocks			—
Cost of Production			137,415

Prime cost/unit $= \dfrac{\text{£}104{,}540}{2{,}000}$ = £52.27

No. of units in stock (31/12) = 300 (2,100 – 1,800 units)

Value of finished goods (31/12) = 300 × £52.27
= £15,681

TABLE 28.5 Trading and profit and loss account T. J. Freeze Ltd, year ended 31 December

	£	£	£
Sales			198,000
– Cost of sales:			
Stock of finished goods (1/1)	6,700		
+ Cost of production	137,415		
	144,115		
– Stock of finished goods			
(31/12)	15,681		128,434
Gross Profit			69,566
Less			
Distribution costs	30,950		
Administration expenses	18,175		49,125
Net Profit			20,441

Questions

1. The following information relates to ABC Co. Ltd for the year ended 31 December. The company makes television products, and its trading figures were:

	£
Sales (1,550 units)	215,000
Rent, rates, insurance	10,000
Power	12,000
Depreciation	18,000
Motor expenses	16,000
Telephone, postage	2,500
Stationery	4,200
Advertising	7,500
Wages, salaries	42,000
Purchases	68,000
Administration	5,700

● Wages: 50% direct, 20% indirect, sales office 15%, administration office 15%.

- Factory rent is 75%. The rest is divided equally between sales and administration offices.
- Purchases are 70% direct materials, 20% indirect materials, the rest being equally divided between sales and administration offices.
- The factory heating was £9,000 power. The rest is equally divided between sales and administration.
- Motoring expenses: 75% sales office, 25% administration.
- Telephone, postage; 80% used by the sales office, 15% by administration; 5% by the factory.
- Stationery: the finance section uses 60%, the factory uses 30% for its clock cards. The remainder is used by the sales office.
- Depreciation: £15,000 to factory plant and machinery. Of the rest, two-thirds is machines in administration, one-third in the sales office.

Other information relating to ABC Co. Ltd:
The company produces 1,500 units in the financial year. Unsold stock of finished goods are valued at production cost/unit.

Stocks (January 1)	
Raw materials	£ 4,200
Finished goods	
(200 units)	£14,950

Stocks (December 31)	
Raw materials	£ 5,100
Finished goods –	
Valued at production cost	

There were no significant stocks of work-in-progress.

Required:

(a) A cost sheet classifying the cost into their appropriate categories.
(b) A manufacturing, trading and profit and loss account of ABC Co. Ltd for the year ended 31 December.

2. The following information refers to the accounts of J. Jones, manufacturer, for the financial year ended 31 December. Production for the year was 5,000 units.

	£
Wages	
Direct factory	19,450
Indirect factory	12,145
Sales office	15,615
Administration	8,500
Purchases	
Raw materials	15,575
Indirect materials	1,450
Sales office stationery	850
Administration	1,955
Factory power (direct)	675
Factory maintenance	1,800
Factory rent, rates	2,560
Depreciation of plant	1,500
Office rent, rates ($\frac{1}{3}$ sales office)	957
Office light, heat ($\frac{1}{3}$ sales office)	366
Sales (4,800 units)	86,400
Administrative expenses	475
Discount (Dr.)	155
Depreciation of office Machinery and equipment ($\frac{1}{3}$ sales office)	900
Stocks (1 January)	
Raw materials	2,375
Work-in-progress	1,975
Finished goods (550 units)	4,750
Stocks (31 December)	
Raw materials	2,485
Work-in-progress	1,900
Finished goods: Unsold stock to be valued at production cost	

Other information on 31 December

- Accrued direct wages £850.
- An unpaid invoice for office light and heat £42.
- A provision for bad debts to equal 5% of debtors (debtors £5,500) to be charged to administration office.

Required:

- (a) Prepare a cost sheet to record the appropriate costs as above.
- (b) Prepare the firm's manufacturing account for the year ended 31 December, transferring sub-totals from the cost sheet.
- (c) Prepare the firm's trading and profit and loss account for the year ended 31 December, transferring sub-totals for distribution costs and administration expenses.

CHAPTER 29

Accounting for Materials

The purchase of stock is of great importance to many organisations, particularly in manufacturing or those businesses which need to buy and sell goods. The right amount of stock must be bought at the right price, at the right time. If a business over-spent on stock, it could tie up too much of its working capital on materials.

If too much stock was purchased, there could be problems of storage and some of it may become obsolete or damaged. If too little stock was bought, the business may run out of certain items which could cause hold-ups in production and the loss of valuable orders. The optimum level of stock should be held at all times, neither too much nor too little.

When stock is delivered, it should always be carefully checked to ensure that the correct quantity of items are received. The driver of the goods has a delivery note, to be signed once, the goods have been checked in. If there are two copies, one is retained by the store as a record of delivery, the other copy going with the driver. If the number of parcels or packages do not correspond with the delivery, the delivery note need not be signed by the person receiving the goods. A brief statement on the note as to the reason why it isn't signed could be written: for example, five packages received, not six. The signing of incoming goods is a serious business and only authorised persons should be given this responsibility.

Many businesses prepare a GRN, which enters details of the goods once they have been checked in. A copy of this would go to the buying office so that it can be checked against the purchase invoice. The storeman would retain a copy and enter the details of the goods on a stock bin card. Each stock item would have its own card to record the quantities of goods received and issued and the balance in stock.

Documentation procedure

The accountant may be involved in designing control systems to ensure that materials are:

(a) properly ordered;
(b) inspected and received;
(c) stored in appropriate places;
(d) issued to production or other departments on request.

In a manufacturing business, the cost of raw materials, work-in-progress and finished goods will call on a significant amount of investment in working capital; therefore it is of essential importance that the right level of stock is produced as efficiently as possible. If stock levels fail to be managed properly (for example, a shortfall holds up production), then the costs of idle time can diminish potential profits within a very short period.

The procedure for the ordering of materials into a typical manufacturing organisation may be illustrated as follows:

Purchase requisition	An internal request for stock items from anyone who may originate the request, the storekeeper or production manager, to those responsible for ordering materials.
Purchase order	The buyer will make out the order to send to the appropriate supplier, bearing in mind price, delivery dates and reliability of supplier.
Progress of deliveries	It is the responsibility of the buyer to ensure that materials are chased up and arrive on time, particularly urgent orders.
Delivery of materials	The document which accompanies the goods on arrival is the delivery note and is signed by the person receiving the goods, usually the storeman, as proof of delivery.
Goods received note	The document made out once the goods have been checked in, inspected and signed for. A copy is sent to buying office to check against incoming invoice. The goods are then stored.
Issues to store	Materials issued from stores to production as and when required; the stores issue voucher is an authorisation to release stocks and record of usage.

Stock bin card   Details of goods received and issued for each stock item. Kept with physical stock and helps to control stock movements.

The source documents

The main documents to consider are:

Purchase requisition

This is the internal request for materials to be purchased by the chief buyer or purchasing manager, and proper authorisation must be made before a requisition is signed and goods purchased. The storekeeper in respect of materials, would send requisitions when stock is approaching re-ordering levels. See Figure 29.1.

FIGURE 29.1 Purchase requisition

PURCHASE REQUISITION				
DATE 2/1		SERIAL NUMBER R 2953/9		
FROM H. Smith				
QUANTITY	DESCRIPTION	CODE NO.	JOB NO.	DEPARTMENT
275	25 mm bolts	17484 TW	0184/95	Stores 3
SIGNATURE *H Smith*		AUTHORISATION	*fg*	

Purchase order

The buying or purchasing department will be responsible for sending the purchase order to the suppliers. Price, delivery dates, reliability and quality are all significant elements the buyer must consider before placing orders. However, most orders will tend to be routine and sent to the usual suppliers. Copies of the order may also go to the section which made the requisition, the goods inward section to await the goods, and one for the file.

The goods received note

Once materials have been checked in by the storeman and the delivery note signed, the GRN is raised as evidence that the materials have arrived and been placed in stock. The GRN is an essential source document because a company must only pay for materials it actually receives. When the purchase invoice arrives from the supplier, the GRN will be checked against it. A copy of the GRN must go to the buying department, and the section which made the requisition will receive a copy in order to record the materials on the appropriate stock bin card in the receipts column. See Figure 29.2.

FIGURE 29.2 The GRN

GOODS RECEIVED NOTE				
DATE 8/1		SERIAL NUMBER G364		
SUPPLIER SPALDINGS (Lines)				
QUANTITY	DESCRIPTION	CODE NO.	JOB NO.	DEPARTMENT
275	25 mm bolts	17484/TW	0184/95	Stores
TRANSPORT BY British Geoffrey Diamond Ltd DELIVERY ADVICE/NOTE NO. 692/18				
RECEIVED BY H. Smith CHECKED BY PS				

The stores issue voucher

When materials are issued to production, a voucher is raised to authorise the transfer of materials to a specific job or contract. The appropriate stock bin card will record, in the issue column, the materials released from store (see Figure 29.3).

FIGURE 29.3   Stores issue voucher

STORES ISSUE VOUCHER				
DATE 10/1 SERIAL NUMBER S 295				
FROM J Davies				
QUANTITY	DESCRIPTION	CODE NO.	JOB NO.	DEPARTMENT
175	25 mm bolts	17484 TW	0184/95	Shop 3
RECEIVED BY L White AUTHORISED BY				

The stores returns voucher

This form reverses the procedure given with the stores issue voucher. If materials are returned to store, the voucher indicates what has been sent back, perhaps because of surplus or wrong stock, and the appropriate stock bin card will enter details in the receipts column.

Bin cards

The storeman needs to show movements of individual stock receipts and issues. The bin card (or stores card) is a simple record of stock movements and is kept with each category of stock. Physical checks can be made against the records maintained by the stores or cost office (the stock record card) and a system of control is provided.
    The bin card should be designed to give all the information we need concerning each item of stock. This includes, at the top of the card, its description, code number if applicable, unit of storage (such as boxes, packages or single units) and the level of stock required, including maximum, minimum and re-order levels (see Figure 29.4). Once the re-order level is reached, the storeman will inform the stock control clerk who will need to make out the purchase requisition to the purchasing department, along with other requests for stock.
    The bin card is used to record all inputs and outputs of stock as well as the stock balance. The card helps to control the stock of

FIGURE 29.4   The Bin card

BIN CARD						
ITEM Bolts (25 mm)			MAXIMUM STOCK 750			
CODE No. 17484 TW			MINIMUM STOCK 100			
			RE-ORDER LEVEL 250			
RECEIPTS			ISSUES			
Date	GRN No.	Quantity Received	REQ No.	Quantity Issued	Stock Balance	Notes
8/1	G364	275			275	New stock
10/1			5295	175	100	
21/1	G590	200			300	
28/1			5487	120	180	
1/2	G783	500			680	
27/2			5655	200	480	
4/3	SR24	25			505	Returns

each item and this will help management to identify stock movements, minimise unnecessary waste, or even stock theft. Under the heading 'Costing of direct materials' on the following pages below, the value of the stock held in the bin is also indicated on the stock record card, sometimes referred to as the stores ledger account.

Stock control levels

For the purpose of controlling stock movements, each bin card should indicate the following levels of control:

(a) the minimum stock level;
(b) the maximum stock level;
(c) the re-order level.

From time to time a business needs to estimate, for each stock item, the average usage and the anticipated delivery time (lead time), so that as stock levels fall to the re-order level, an order can then be placed to replenish the stock item. In theory, at least, by the time the stock order has come in, the stock item would be at the minimum level.

The difference between the minimum stock held and zero stock is referred to as 'buffer stock', which gives a vital few days to chase up any supplier whose order is delayed.

As the optimum level of stock should be carried for each item, it is important to calculate the re-order, minimum and maximum levels required for each stock item. The formulae for these are:

Re-order level	=	maximum usage × maximum lead time
Minimum stock level	=	re-order level less (average usage × average lead time)
Maximum stock level	=	re-order level + re-order quantity less (minimum usage × minimum lead time)

Example

A business uses the following data for an item of its stock:

Average usage	400 units per day
Maximum usage	500 units per day
Minimum usage	200 units per day
Minimum lead time	15 days
Maximum lead time	25 days
Economic re-order quantity	4,000 units

You are required to calculate the re-order, minimum and maximum levels of stock.

Re-order level	=	500 × 25	= 12,500 units
Minimum stock level	=	12,500 − (400 × 20)	= 4,500 units
Maximum stock level	=	12,500 + 4,000 − (200 × 15)	= 13,500 units

The economic re-order quantity refers to the optimum order level: that is, the best amount of stock to order at any time the stocks need replenishing to the levels wanted. The formula for the re-order quantity is:

$$Q = \sqrt{\frac{2AC}{H}}$$

Q = the economic re-order quantity
A = the annual demand of the stock item
C = the cost of ordering one consignment
H = the cost of holding 1 unit in stock

The economic re-order level in the above example was 4,000 units which was calculated from:

A = the annual demand: 400 units per day $\times$ 240 working days = 96,000 units

C = the cost of ordering one consignment from suppliers, estimated £12.50 on average

H = the cost of holding one unit in stock, estimated £0.15p. . . .

$$Q = \sqrt{\frac{2 \times 12.50 \times 96,000}{0.15}}$$

$$= \sqrt{\frac{2,400,000}{015}} = \sqrt{16,000,000}$$

$$= 4,000 \text{ units.}$$

The re-order quantity of 4,000 units should, then, be sufficient to bring stocks up to no greater than the maximum level once the stock arrives in store.

Continuous stocktaking

Stocktaking refers to the physical counting of stock at any given time, and these figures are checked against balances indicated on stock records. Continuous stocktaking is a system whereby a proportion of stock items are checked each day. A sufficient number of items are checked so that, in the course of a year, all items are checked at least once. Those items which have a high value per unit should be checked more frequently to obtain a tighter stock control of them.

Periodic stocktaking

This is in contrast to the above and is usually required on an annual basis, at the end of the accounting period, so that the stock end figure is used in the final accounts. The disadvantage of this is that, due to counting all stock items, disruptions can easily occur and production time may be lost. Discrepancies are also likely to be greater between the stock records and the physical count.

Perpetual inventory

This is a stock recording system whereby the balance is shown on the record for a stock item after every movement, either receipt or issue. With this system the balances on a stock record card (as shown on the following pages) represent the stock on hand and the balances would be used in preparing the periodic accounts. The recording and pricing of stock issues form the basis for the operation of the cost accounting system.

ABC inventory analysis

This system attempts to put the emphasis of stock control on the most significant items in stock: that is, in terms of relative annual cost. The annual cost of each item is established and all items are then ranked in order. In general, about 20% of the stock items often account for about 80% of stock purchasing (Pareto's Law). It therefore makes some sense to concentrate on checking the top 20% of stock items, due to 80% investment in them.

Stock wastage

It is inevitable that some proportion of stock will be wasted or lost due to several reasons. The wastage of stock must be kept at a minimum otherwise more money is required to keep stock at the right levels. Waste of materials in production can also lead to idle time on the assembly lines, causing costs to increase. Some of the causes of stock wastage are:

(a) If liquids are purchased, these may be vulnerable to changes in temperature and evaporation losses occur.
(b) Some units bought in bulk may be difficult to break up accurately, and only estimates are made when the stock is issued.
(c) Human error may occur, particularly where there may be a high labour turnover and where induction training is poor. Errors may result on different levels of assembly and more stock is scrapped because it fails to meet the appropriate quality.
(d) In production, plant and machinery can break down, causing more waste of material.
(e) Facilities for storage of stocks may be inadequate and this may cause premature deterioration and even scrap.
(f) Obsolescence may result in stock being replaced due to technological, fashion or other factors.

Example

A new trainee was placed on the assembly line collecting roof tiles. It was found that, in the first week, production was 10% less than normal on a specific batch, due to the tiles being broken or smashed when collected off the line. These had no residual value and had to be scrapped.

Normal cost of batch: 2,000 tiles @ 1.20 each	£2,400
Actual tiles produced: 1,800 tiles @ 1.20 each	£2,160
Loss due to 10% scrap	£ 240

The £240 scrap can be treated as a loss on factory overheads in the manufacturing account.

SSAP No. 9 [Stocks and Work-in-Progress]

This states that stock should be valued at its cost or, if lower than cost, at its net realisable value (its expected selling price). In other words, if some stock items are valued lower than their cost because of age or damage, etc., the expected selling price should be stated rather than cost, to give a more realistic assessment of stock value in the financial period under review.

If an organisation uses a computer, there are programs available to maintain stock records which have various functions like keeping up-to-date stock records, minimum and maximum stock levels, re-order levels and current balances of each stock type. Effective stock control should ensure that computer records are checked with actual physical records to avoid cases of fraud or pilfering of stock. Table 29.1 gives an example of stock valuation showing 'at cost or lower of net realisable value':

In the final accounts for the year ended 31 December 1988, the figure in the final column, £430, would be taken, along with other stock valuations, as the stock end value. This indicates that the items of stock valued at less than their cost should be assessed against the profit for the current period.

Costing direct materials

In manufacturing concerns the valuation of direct materials (materials used in producing a product) is usually straightforward in that the quantity used is valued at the supplier's price, for example:

TABLE 29.1   Lower of cost and net realisable value (Stock valuation at 31 December 1988)

Stock code	No. in stock	Cost price £	Value at cost £	Net realisable value (NRV) £	Lower of cost or NRV £
EO 145	10	5.00	50.00	40.00	40.00
EO 146	20	10.00	200.00	250.00	200.00
EO 147	5	12.00	60.00	60.00	60.00
EO 148	25	5.00	125.00	100.00	100.00
EO 149	10	2.50	25.00	10.00	10.00
EO 150	2	25.50	51.00	20.00	20.00
			511.00	480.00	430.00

500 units @ 50p each   =   £250
100 units @ 40p each   =   £ 40

Stocks of materials are normally held in stores and issued to production as and when required. Stock cards or computer records (on VDUs – visual display units) are used to show what has come in and gone out of stock and the balance on hand.

When costly parts (such as car engines or gear boxes) are valued, the cost price of each part is clearly known and used for stock valuation purposes. However, for items of stock having a *low value* and bought frequently in large quantities (such as nuts, bolts, brackets, screws, washers, etc.), it may not be possible or desirable to itemise the value of each item, particularly when costs may vary from time to time.

To cost these low-value items in production there are three distinct methods of valuation which basically consider the stock being issued in a particular order. The three methods are:

● FIFO   First-in, first-out
● LIFO   Last-in, first-out
● AVCO   Average cost of stock

In actual physical terms, the order of movement of stock does not matter. It does matter how the stock is valued.

● FIFO   assumes that stock in first is the first stock out
● LIFO   assumes that stock in last is the first stock out and
● AVCO   takes the weighted average of units in stock

and each method is valued accordingly.

Example

Stock received: 300 @ £1   = £300 January
200 @ £1.20 = £240 March
Stock issued: 400 between January to March

Using the three methods of stock valuation, what is the value of the stock still in hand for each method?

FIFO   100 × £1.20 =   £120
LIFO   100 × £1.00 =   £100
AVCO 100 × £1.08 =   £108   (£540/500 = £1.08)

So, for valuation purposes the FIFO method in this case values stock the highest (when prices rise) and LIFO and lowest. AVCO is in between the two.

Most organisations tend to use either the FIFO or AVCO methods. LIFO is rarely used because in times of rising prices it values stock the lowest and therefore has the effect of under-stating profit.

Remember an important concept in accounting from a previous section? The concept referred to is 'consistency'. Once a method has been chosen it should be consistently used and in this way stock valuation in one period can be accurately and fairly compared with another.

The following pages illustrate the stock record sheets or cards (see Figures 29.5–7) of the same item of stock (25 mm bolts) using the three distinct methods of valuation. Note that the stock end on 28 February shows:

- FIFO   values the balance in stock at £7,680
- LIFO   values the balance in stock at £7,120
- AVCO   values the balance in stock at £7,303

Clearly, the prices of the stock item rose because the FIFO valuation is the highest and LIFO the lowest, as one would expect.

Let us assume that, for simplicity purposes, the stock cards showing stock values at FIFO, LIFO and AVCO represented the total value for stock at the end of the period, 28 February. What effect would they have on the trading account?

By using FIFO, the gross profit would be greater than either LIFO or AVCO because it has a higher value of closing stock. LIFO clearly has the lower profit because its stock value is the lowest, particularly in times of rising prices. AVCO has a profit which falls between the other two.

FIGURE 29.5   Stock record card: FIFO

STOCK RECORD CARD									
UNIT: BOLTS (25 mm) QUANTITY LEVEL: Minimum: 100									
CODE: 17484 TW Maximum: 750									
SUPPLIERS: Spaldings (Lincs) Re-order level: 200									

	Received			Issued			BALANCE			
DATE	Qty	Unit Price £	Cost £	Qty	Unit Price £	Cost £	No in Stock	Unit Price £	Value £	
Jan 5	150	12-	1,800				150	12	1,800	
7	125	10-	1,250				125	10	1,250	
							275		3,050	
10				150	12	1800				
				25	10	250	100	10	1,000	
21	200	14-	2,800				200	14	2,800	
							300		3,800	
28				100	10	1,000				
				20	14	280	180	14	2,520	
Feb 1	500	16-	8,000				500	16	8,000	
							680		10,520	
27				180	14	2,520				
				20	16	320	480	16	7,680	Stock (end) 28/2

FIGURE 29.6   Stock record card: LIFO

STOCK RECORD CARD

UNIT: BOLTS (25mm)   QUANTITY LEVEL: Minimum: <u>100</u>
CODE: 17484 TW   Maximum: <u>750</u>
SUPPLIERS: Spaldings (Lincs)   Re-order
                                               level: <u>200</u>

DATE	Received			Issued			BALANCE			
	Qty	Unit Price £	Cost £	Qty	Unit Price £	Cost £	No in Stock	Unit Price £	Value £	
JAN 5	150	12-	1,800				150	12	1,800	
7	125	10-	1,250				<u>125</u>	10	<u>1,250</u>	
							275		3,050	
10				125	10	1,250				
				50	12	600	100	12	1,200	
21	200	14-	2,800				<u>200</u>	14	<u>2,800</u>	
							300		4,000	
28				120	14	1,680	100	12	1,200	
							<u>80</u>	14	<u>1,120</u>	
							180		2,320	
FEB 1	500	16-	8,000				<u>500</u>	16	<u>8,000</u>	
							680		10,320	
27				200	16	3,200	100	12	1,200	
							80	14	1,120	
							<u>300</u>	16	<u>4,800</u>	
							480		7,120	Stock end 28/2

FIGURE 29.7　Stock record card: AVCO

STOCK RECORD CARD

UNIT:　　　　BOLTS (25mm)　　QUANTITY LEVEL:　Minimum: 100
CODE:　　　　17484 TW　　　　　　　　　　　　　　　Maximum: 750
SUPPLIERS: Spaldings (Lincs)　　　　　　　　　　　Re-order
　　　　　　　　　　　　　　　　　　　　　　　　　level:　　　200

	Received			Issued			BALANCE			AVCO Notes
DATE	Qty	Unit Price £	Cost £	Qty	Unit Price £	Cost £	No in Stock	Unit Price £	Value £	
JAN 5	150	12-	1,800				150	12	1,800	
7	125	10-	1,250				125	10	1,250	
										3,050/ 275
							275	11.09	3,050	unit
10				175	11.09	1,941	100		1,109	price =
21	200	14-	2,800				300	13.03	3,909	value div. by stock.
										3,909/ 300
28				120	13.03	1,564	180		2,345	
FEB 1	500	16-	8,000				680	15.21	10,345	10,345/ 680
27				200	15.21	3,042	480	15.21	7,303	Stock end 28/2

Although the 1985 Companies Act does not outlaw the use of LIFO, SSAP No. 9, Stocks and Work-in-Progress, states that it should not be used because it does not provide an up-to-date valuation of stock, thereby distorting what should be the true profit. FIFO and AVCO methods are recommended with the overall proviso that stocks should never recognise profit in advance and should be valued at cost, or, if lower than cost, at their net realisable value.

However, it must also be recognised that a closing stock value in one period becomes the opening value of stock in the next. Thus FIFO's closing stock of £7,680 is the next period's opening stock value, which actually increases the cost of sales more than the other two methods. By virtue of this, the irregularities of differences in profit tend to cancel each other out. What is of vital importance is that, once a method has been adopted, it must be used consistently over and over again, to avoid any profit distortions.

Questions

1. Make a list of all the significant documents used in the acquisition of materials.
2. Why is it important to have a system of stock control in a large manufacturing organisation?
3. Why is it important to record the stock levels on a bin or stock record card?
4. The following data relates to an item of raw material:

cost of raw material	£10/unit
usage per day*	100 units
minimum lead time	20 days
maximum lead time	30 days
cost of ordering materials	£400 per order
carrying costs	10% of cost per unit of raw material

* Assume that the usage per day is the normal level and includes both maximum and minimum levels. You are also to assume that there is a 5-day, 48-week working year.

Required:

(a) the re-order level;
(b) the re-order quantity;
(c) the maximum level;
(d) the minimum level.

(Association of Accounting Technicians)

5. You are given the following information regarding material stock code Q242:

● The average demand for the material is 400 kilos per week, 50 weeks for the year
● The cost of ordering is £150 per order
● Q242 costs £6.00 per kilo and carrying costs (holding costs) are $33\frac{1}{3}\%$ of this figure for each kilo held
● The maximum usage in any one week is 600 kilos, the minimum 400 kilos

On average, the orders take between 1 and 3 weeks to be delivered. Note that these figures are based on weeks rather than days of use.

Required:

(a)   the optimum order quantity to be placed;
(b)   the re-order level;
(c)   the minimum stock level;
(d)   the maximum stock level.

(Association of Accounting Technicians)

6. (a) Write short notes which will clearly differentiate between:

● Continuous stocktaking
● Periodic stocktaking
● Perpetual inventory

(b) Calculate the normal stock control levels from the following information:

Economic order quantity	12,000 kilos
Lead time	10–14 working days
Average usage	600 kilos per day
Minimum usage	400 kilos per day
Maximum usage	800 kilos per day.

(ACCA)

7. The goods listed below were in stock at Jack's Store on 31 December.

Record the items on a stock card/sheet and calculate the value of stock at the end of the year, 31 December.

Code no.	Items	Quantity	Cost per unit £	NRV per unit £	Lower of cost or NRV £
427	Jeans	50	10.5	12.5	525.
428	Jeans	10	15.20	14.	
859/1	Sweaters	120	8.75	7.5	
859/2	Sweaters	60	12.50	15.95	
859/3	Sweaters	15	9.95	12.50	
870	Men's socks	50	1.15	1.50	
870/1	Men's socks	5	3.90	1.00	

8. The stock issues of a manufacturer for the months June to August inclusive were as follows:

Stock Issues – June, July, August

		Quantity (units)	Cost per unit £	Value of stock £
1/6	Balance	200	2.00	400.00
15/6	Purchases	100	1.95	
30/6	Purchases	200	2.10	
		500		
30/6	Issues	150		
1/7	Balance	350		
21/7	Purchases	200	2.15	
		550		

30/7	Issues	200	
1/8	Balance	350	
10/8	Purchases	150	2.20
21/8	Purchases	100	2.20
		600	
31/8	Issues	250	
1/9	Balance	350	

Required:

Write up a stock record card for the months June to August and calculate the value of stock on 1 September in terms of both FIFO and LIFO order issues.

9. Complete the stock record card by entering the 'balance in hand' figure on the right of the card. Calculate the value of stock end if purchases were £2.50 per ream up to 12/9 and £3.00 after 12/9 (use FIFO method).

STOCK RECORD CARD
MONTH: Sept

Item: Typewriting Paper – Size A4   Quantities
Suppliers: 1 ABC Co Ltd   MIN: 100 Ream
          3 XYZ Ltd 4   MAX: 200 Ream
                                   Re-order level:

DATE	ORDERED			RECEIVED			ISSUED		BALANCE
	Supp.	O/No.	Qty	Supp.	O/No.	Qty.	Dept.	Qty	130 Reams
Sept 1	1	347	150						
3	2	348	125						
6							P	36	
6							A	20	
9				1	347	150			
10							T	25	
12				2	348	100			
14							B	55	
14							M	60	
16	2	349	100						
18							A	25	
19				2	349	90			
20							P	79	

10. Use FIFO and LIFO methods to value the following stock:

```
Jan.  1    Balance                          50 units @ £3 unit
     10    Purchased 100 units @ £3
     16    Purchased 100 units @ £3.20
     24    Issued        80 units
Feb.  7    Purchased 200 units @ £3.50
     14    Issued       240 units
     20    Issued        80 units
     28    Purchased  50 units @ £3.40
```

Required:

(a) Prepare two stock cards to illustrate FIFO and LIFO methods of stock recording.
(b) What effect would these methods have in the trading account?

11.

(a) Complete the stock card below by showing the value in the end column. When the stock is sold, it is on the basis of FIFO. This means that for value purposes, the stock first in is assumed to be the first sold out.

```
Type of                          Stock level    150–200
goods      Unit 5                Re-order level    100
Code no.   11/13
Supplier   Arena, Metro
```

Date	Quantity received	Unit value £	Sales	Stock balance	Unit value £	Value £
June 1	Balance			200	4.00	800
5			80	120	4.00	480
12	Arena 200	4.25		200	4.25	850
				320		1330
15			140			
18			50			
20	Metro 120	4.00				
28			145			

Note: As a check, you should have 105 units in stock value on 28 June.

(b) The end of the firm's financial year is 30 June. The value of the unsold stock, Code No. 11/13, is entered on a stock sheet along with other stocks in order to calculate the value of unsold stock at the end of the accounting period.

The firm values its unsold stock at the 'lower of cost or net realisable value'. This basically means that if the expected selling price is less than the cost price, then the lower figure will be used to assess the stock value.

Complete the stock sheet as on 30 June:

Code no. and comments	Stock balance quantity	Unit value £	Value £	Net realisable value £		Lower of cost net realisable value
11/13	105			105	5.00	525
11/27 (old stock)	215	10.00	2150	215	7.00	1505	1505.00
11/33	150	6.50		150	7.50	
11/42 (damaged)	10	8.50		10	2.00	
11/50	85	12.75		85	15.50	
					total	

(c) Completion of Trading and Profit and Loss account.

Sales for the financial year were	£38,850
Purchases for the financial year were	£27,500
Stock (1/7) commencing	£ 2,650
Distribution Costs	£ 3,750
Administration Expenses	£ 1,225

Prepare the firm's trading and profit and loss account for the period ending 30 June. Use the stock valuation from the stock sheet above.

12. John Gaunt commenced trading on 1 January year 1 as a distributor of the Red Diamond Mark 1 Farm Tractor with an initial capital of £50,000 used to open a bank account.

Upon commencing trading, John Gaunt bought fixtures and fittings costing £10,000 which he installed in his rented premises.

Overhead expenses, including rent of premises but excluding depreciation, have been incurred as follows:

Year ended 31 December, Year 1	£24,000
Year ended 31 December, Year 2	£26,000
Year ended 31 December, Year 3	£31,000

Depreciation on fixtures and fittings is to be provided at the rate of 20% per annum using the reducing balance method.

Purchases and sales of the Red Diamond Mark 1 Farm Tractor up to 31 December Year 3 were as follows:

	Purchases	Sales
Year 1	6 at £25,000 each	4 at £30,000 each
Year 2	8 at £25,000 each	⎰3 at £30,000 each
		⎱4 at £32,000 each
Year 3		
February		1 at £34,000
March	4 at £28,000 each	
May		3 at £37,000 each
July	5 at £30,000 each	
September		4 at £38,000 each
October	2 at £32,000 each	
December		2 at £38,000 each

John Gaunt has accepted, with some reluctance, his accountant's advice to use the FIFO basis for stock valuation as from 1 January Year 3 instead of the LIFO basis which he claims to have used in earlier years.

All John Gaunt's business transactions are on a cash (non-credit) basis.

John Gaunt does not intend to take any drawings from the business until Year 4.

Required:

(a) Prepare, in as much detail as possible, John Gaunt's trading and profit and loss account for *each* of the years ended 31 December, using:
   the last in first out basis of stock valuation; and
   the first in first out basis of stock valuation.
(b) Prepare John Gaunt's capital account for the year ended 31 December Year 3.
(c) A concise report to John Gaunt in support of the accountant's advice concerning the stock valuation basis.

[Association of Accounting Technicians]

Accounting for Labour

Earlier in this text, Chapter 24 dealt with the payroll, so that if you wish to familiarise yourself with the calculations of gross and net pay, you can refer to that. This chapter is more concerned with the different remuneration systems available to an organisation and the treatment of labour costs in the costing system.

In the last chapter, it was noted that the main components of an absorption cost were direct materials, direct labour and overheads. This looks into labour costs in further detail.

Methods of remuneration

The design of a pay system is a most important and complex responsibility of management and it can exert a profound influence for good industrial relations if it is carried out fairly and properly. There are two basic structures of pay, one based on time and the other based on an incentive scheme which is related to performance:

(a) time rates;
(b) payment by results.

Time rates

This is the most common method of payment and was discussed in Chapter 24. It simply means that an employee will be paid a certain fixed amount of money for a specified unit of time. For example, an employee's basic pay might be £5.80 per hour for a 37.5 hour week. Overtime is rewarded at a rate of 1.25 hours for extra hours worked during Monday to Friday, and at a rate of 1.5 for Saturday work.

Most working people are paid by this method and there are a number of situations where it would be inappropriate to pay employees by any other method than time rates: for example, where it would be impossible or difficult to measure an individual's output (office workers). A major criticism of time rates is that it does not provide financial incentives to motivate an employee to better efforts.

Payment by results (PBR)

This payment scheme is, of course, related to performance and gives employees the vital ingredient of incentive to work more productively. Such schemes often operate in organisations where the work is standard and repetitive, typically found in so many of our factories. The major objective is to stimulate an employee's effort to produce more, which should then achieve a lower cost per unit. For management, there is greater production; for the employee, more pay.

The most common systems are associated with that of work study, where a task will be given a specific time allowance, and a bonus is paid on any time which might be saved in completing it. This is usually referred to as a 'premium bonus scheme'.

For example, the Halsey method is a bonus system whereby half the time saved is paid; there is also the Halsey–Weir method, where a bonus of one-third of the time saved is paid.

Measuring the time on PBR

If we were to measure the time taken for a specific job, say, cutting a metal pattern, 100 units is the job lot:

Time allowed to measure pattern:	
3 minutes per unit:	5.0 hours
Time Allowed to make pattern	
1.5 minutes per unit:	2.5 hours
Time allowed to cut out	
1.5 minutes per unit:	2.5 hours
Total time allowed:	10 hours

If the rate of payment was £5 per hour, with no incentive scheme available, an employee may or may not take up the time allowed, or may even take longer. Each hour would be paid at £5 per hour irrespective of the actual time taken.

If the Halsey bonus scheme operated, whereby half the time saved is paid at the going rate of £5 per hour, how much would an employee earn if it only took him 8 hours to do the job?

Time allowed to do job   10 hours
Time taken to do job   8 hours
Time saved   2 hours

Bonus for the job $\dfrac{2 \text{ hours} \times £5.00}{2} = £5.00$

Therefore, the total pay for that job would be:

$$
\begin{array}{r}
8 \text{ hours time taken} \\
+ \; \underline{1 \text{ hour}} \quad \text{time saved} \\
9 \text{ hours pay at £5 per hour} = £45 \text{ for the job (for} \\
8 \text{ hour's work).}
\end{array}
$$

Group bonus schemes

The above is an example of an individual bonus scheme. There are situations where an employee is part of a team and it may be difficult to measure individual performances. In such cases, it is possible to measure the group or team's performance and to pay each of them an equal share of the group bonus.

Measuring units on PBR

Another incentive for employees is what are called 'piece rates'. This is simply where an employee is paid an agreed rate per unit for the number of units produced: for example, if the rate is 0.50p per 100 units produced, then an employee who has an output of 24,000 units in a week will earn £120. The system of piece work is usually confined to what is called 'outworkers': that is, where assembly work is carried out, often on a part-time basis and sometimes in an employee's home. For example, a worker may produce circuit boards for a local industry and be paid at a rate of £12 per board. The more boards produced, the more pay is earned.

Example

The following amounts are paid per unit:

Units produced	Rate/unit
1–500	20p
501–600	24p
601 and above	30p

How much would an employee earn if her output was 620 units?

500 × 20p	£100.00	
100 × 24p	£ 24.00	
20 × 30p	£ 6.00	£130.00

Direct and indirect wages

In Chapter 27, on manufacturing accounts, we noted that labour could be either direct or indirect. As a reminder, a direct employee is a person who works directly on the job and whose pay is directly traceable to a job, such as an assembly worker or machinist. An indirect employee is not part of direct labour and the cost is, in effect, part of production overheads. Indirect employees may include storekeepers, production controllers, expeditors, cleaners, etc., who are necessary for the operation of the factory but not directly involved with making of the product.

Treatment of overtime premium

Many organisations ask their employees to work overtime in order to make maximum use of their resources. They are prepared to pay overtime rates (premiums) above their normal rates of pay: for example, at time and a quarter or time and a half, etc. In most cases the payment of overtime is treated as an *overhead cost* rather than as part of labour costs. For example, Jim works on job lot J225 for 4 hours on a Saturday at time and a half. Basic rate is £4 per hour. Jim's pay is £24 but, in the costing system, only £16 is charged to job lot J225; the other £8 is a charge to overheads.

However, in a case where a customer specifically wants a job done urgently, and pays the overtime premium, then the whole cost of direct wages, £24, is charged to the job.

Keeping records of pay

In the payroll section of Chapter 24, clock cards gave an employee's record of attendance at the place of work. In the costing system, it is also important to know what tasks/jobs an employee has been working on in order to make calculations concerning the cost of a job or the cost attributed to a particular area or cost centre. The usual records include:

the personnel record card
time sheets
job or route cards

Personnel record cards

The personnel office will maintain a file for each employee which will record his or her personal details, rates of pay and also employment history. Much of this information is confidential and restricted to the personnel office. The payroll and costing departments would have their own data to work on and be denied access to personal details.

Time sheets

Time sheets are normally required for direct employees, one for each, giving details of the jobs and the hours they have completed, normally on a weekly basis. Employees usually fill them out themselves and get a supervisor to agree and sign it. In this way, jobs and wage costs can, with reasonable accuracy, be charged to all the jobs being produced.

Job cards

Job or route cards are used for each specific job or batch. A number will be issued for the job and any materials from stores will be quoted on it and on the stores issue notes. All direct employees' hours worked on the job will also be recorded on the job card as well as on the time sheets. The job card will therefore be a record of the production process in labour hours and materials used on the job. In the following chapter we will note how a fair share for overheads is also attributed to a job in order to calculate the whole of its absorption cost: that is, its direct labour, direct materials and overheads:

Questions

1. Calculate gross pay using time rates on the following:

    (a) Freddie 36 hours @ £5.00 per hour
    +4 hours at time and a quarter
    (b) Jennie   38.5 hours @ £3.00 per hour
    +6 hours at time and a half
    (c) Jean   45 hours at £6.90 per hour
    +4 hours at time and a third

2. Calculate the cost of direct labour if the hourly rate was

£4.20 per hour for Jobs 1 and 3 and £3.60 per hour for Jobs 2 and 4:

    Job 1: time taken   20 minutes
    Job 2: time taken   30 minutes
    Job 3: time taken   10 minutes
    Job 4: time taken   45 minutes

3. See Harry Smith's time sheet and calculate how much labour cost will be charged to each of the job lot numbers and also Harry's gross pay. He is paid at £4.00 per hour.

Harry Smith's
TIME SHEET   WEEK COMMENCING Week 32

CUSTOMER/JOB NO.	MON	TUES	WED	THURS	FRI	SAT	SUN	TOTAL
227/15	3	4	4	3	4	2		
229/15	1.5	2	2	3	1	–		
224/15	2	1.5	3	1	2	2		
226/15	2			2				
Totals	8.5	7.5	9	9	7	4		

SIGNED _____

4. A piece work system is in operation whereby Sheila is paid a basic rate of attendance money of £2.25 per hour for a 38-hour week and piece rate of:

    from 200   to 1,000 units 10p   unit
          1,001 to 5,000 units 15p   unit
          over   5,000 units 17.5p unit

Calculate Sheila's earnings in a 4-week period in which she produces 5,080 units and completes a full 38 hours each week.

5. Calculate the gross pay of Annie Ross from the following information in which a bonus system operates whereby she is paid a daily bonus (at normal rates) of a one-third time saved:

	Time allowed (hours)	Time taken (hours)
Monday	10.5	9
Tuesday	11	8
Wednesday	12	9
Thursday	8	9
Friday	7.5	6

Sheila's basic hourly rate is £4.00 per hour for a 36-hour week. The overtime rate (premium) is 50% above the normal basic pay.

[Chartered Institute of Purchasing & Supply]

6. The following details relate to Jacobs Ltd, a factory:

Employee	Jack	Jill
Hours worked in week	44	40
Rate per hour	£3.50	£4.50
Units produced	480	390

The time allowed for each unit is 7 standard minutes. Each minute is valued at 0.05p (piece work).

Calculate earnings where the work is based on:

(a) piece work rates with earnings guaranteed at 80% of pay calculated on an hourly basis;
(b) premium bonus scheme in which the bonus is 75% of time saved, and this is added to pay calculated on an hourly basis;
(c) describe two situations in which the time basis of remuneration is likely to be more appropriate than piece work.

[Association of Accounting Technicians]

7. The following is a summary of the timesheets of a workshop in a manufacturing company:

Employee	Grade	Weekday hours at normal rates	Weekday hours at time plus a quarter	Weekend hours at time plus a half	Total hours taken
R. Blount	A	36	4	4	44
K. Short	B	36	2	4	42
M. Lewis	C	36	—	—	36
H. Bull	A	36	6	4	46
P. Kent	E	36	—	—	36

The basic hourly rates of pay are as follows:

    Grade A   £3.80
    Grade B   £4.40
    Grade C   £5.00
    Grade D   £5.50
    Grade E   £6.00

The company operates a payment by results scheme where they are paid a bonus of half the time saved at their basic hourly rate.

Required:

(a) Calculate the gross wage (excluding bonus) of each of the five employees.
(b) Calculate the bonus payable to each employee – the time allowed agreed for the week was as follows: R. Blount 50 hrs; K. Short 48 hrs; M. Lewis 42 hrs; H. Bull 54 hrs; and P. Kent 40 hrs; and then state the gross pay including bonus for each of the five employees.
(c) State two other methods of remunerating direct employees and briefly outline the benefits/disadvantages of each method.

                    [Chartered Institute of Purchasing & Supply]

CHAPTER 31

Accounting for Overheads; Cost Centres

When manufacturing or other organisations need to calculate the cost of a job, the cost of direct labour and direct materials is usually straightforward. But what of overheads? There is likely to be a considerable amount of expenditure by the organisation on light, heat, power, rent, insurance, rates, administration and other indirect costs, which is difficult to attribute to an individual cost unit. If a business produced a single product, apportioning overheads would be quite easy. The overhead costs in a specific period would be totalled and divided by the total number of units produced to arrive at the overhead cost per unit, for example:

$$\frac{\text{Overheads for the year}}{\text{Units produced}} \quad \frac{£192,000}{16,000} = £12.00 \text{ per unit}$$

However, if an organisation manufactured half a dozen products which went through various different stages of production, then apportioning overhead costs would be far more difficult to measure. This includes apportioning overhead costs fairly over those sections which benefit from them and then charging an appropriate rate in order to recover the overheads per job or unit. The rate to be charged would depend on the method used and the type of production in terms of labour and machinery used in the process of manufacture.

Absorption cost

The absorption cost includes all costs on a given capacity of production, both fixed and variable, broken down into:

● Direct labour
● Direct materials
● Overheads (both factory and office)

The overheads will mostly be made up of the indirect costs. For example, if an output of 16,000 units was manufactured:

Direct labour	@ £4.50p unit	£72,000
Direct materials	@ £14.80 unit	£236,800
Total overheads		£192,000
Total absorption cost =		£500,800

Absorption cost per unit: £500,800/16,000 = £31.30
Overhead cost per unit: £192,000/16,000 = £12.00

However, if we wanted to charge a proportion of overheads to those sections or departments which incurred the costs to give management better control, then a system of dividing overheads needs to be devised.

Apportioning overheads to cost centres

The use of cost centres provides management with information concerning the location of expenses. An organisation can be divided into distinct sections (for example, different production and service departments), which can be used to allocate and apportion costs and thereby identify the cost of activities or operations in them. The monitoring of these costs to those sections which incur them will help maintain a better control of expenses and assist management with budgeting programmes.

The Institute of Cost & Management Accountants has defined:

Cost Centre:
   A location, person or item of equipment of which costs may
   be ascertained and related to cost units
Production Cost Centre:
   A cost centre where production is carried out
Service Cost Centre:
   A cost centre for the provision of a service or services to
   other cost centres.

To find the total overheads charged to a product, the service cost overheads may be apportioned to the production centres. The indirect costs, both for factory and office overheads, which may benefit a number of cost centres, may not be so easily traceable to an individual centre, therefore a sound basis of apportioning these costs needs to be identified and adopted. For example, insurance for buildings and stock charged to the organisation as a whole may be £1,800. How will this be fairly apportioned to the cost centres as part of their charge for overheads?

Allocation of costs

The allocation of a cost implies that the costs incurred can be identified to a specific cost centre. Some costs should be a straightforward allotment of expenses because they can be more easily traced to an individual cost centre: for example, indirect wages or indirect materials may be allotted to specific cost centres because they can be traced directly to them.

Apportioning costs

Apportioning of cost applies when an expense is incurred for the benefit of two or more centres. Most of the overheads need apportioning over a number of cost centres, such as rent, rates and insurance.

Example: Insurance of buildings, £1,800, was charged to an organisation which operated three production centres and one service centre. It was decided to apportion the cost in relation to the floor areas (square metres) occupied by each centre:

Production Centres 1 1,400 sq. metres
        2 2,600 sq. metres
        3   800 sq. metres
Service Centre   4 3,200 sq. metres

Basis of apportionment:		Insurance of Buildings
Centre 1	1,400/8,000 metres = 17.5% of £1,800	£315
2	2,600/8,000 metres = 32.5% of £1,800	£585
3	1,000/8,000 metres = 12.5% of £1,800	£180
4	3,000/8,000 metres = 37.5% of £1,800	£720 £1,800

The bases of apportionment include the elements shown in Table 31.1, although this is not an exhaustive list.

TABLE 31.1   Bases of apportionment

Type of cost	Base
Rent, rates	Floor area
Insurance (buildings)	Floor area
Insurance (employees)	No. of employees
Insurance (stocks)	Value of stocks
Light, heat, power	Metered no. of units or floor area
Canteen expenses	No. of employees
Depreciation of assets	Net book value of assets
Distribution costs	Volume/value of sales
Wage office costs	No. of employees

Example

A company has two production departments, A and B, and one service department, C. Some of its overheads have already been allocated in Table 31.2. You are to apportion the remaining overheads on a fair basis given the criteria.

	A	B	C
Floor areas (sq. metres)	150	100	50
Value of plant, equipment	8,000	4,000	4,000
No. of employees	50	30	20
Metered units	3,000	2,000	1,000
Output (volume)	12,000	8,000	
Value of stock	15,000	7,500	

TABLE 31.2   Overhead cost analysis

	A	B	C	Total	Notes
Indirect materials	1,800	750	450	3,000	Allocated
Indirect labour	27,400	23,100	18,500	69,000	Allocated
Power				3,000	
Rent and rates				60,000	
Insurance (stock)				1,500	
Distribution costs				8,000	
Administration			10,000	10,000	Allocated
Canteen costs				4,500	
Interest charges			1,000	1,000	Allocated

So total value of overheads in the service centre is to be proportioned 70% to centre A and 30% to centre B, primarily as the basis of output capacity.

Required:
Complete the table by apportioning and totalling the overhead charges to their appropriate cost centres. (The answer is given in Table 13.3.)

TABLE 31.3 Apportionment of overhead charges

	A	B	C	Total	
Indirect materials	1,800	750	450	3,000	Allocated
Indirect labour	27,400	23,100	18,500	69,000	Allocated
Power	1,500	1,000	500	3,000	Floor area
Rent, rates	30,000	20,000	10,000	60,000	Floor area
Insurance (stock)	1,000	500		1,500	Stocks
Distribution costs	4,800	3,200		8,000	Sales
Administration			10,000	10,000	Allocated
Canteen costs	2,250	1,350	900	4,500	Employees
Interest charges			1,000	1,000	Allocated
	68,750	49,900	41,350	160,000	
Service Centre	28,945	12,405	(41,350)		
	97,695	62,305		160,000	

Calculation of overheads absorption rates

The main purpose of cost accounting is to lend support to management and assist in its decision making. Part of this is to explain, in some detail, how costs have been incurred and where: by job, by process or by product. Each product must be charged with its *fair share* of overheads. This can be done by using what is called an 'overhead absorption rate', also referred to as overhead recovery rate.

There are several different methods which can be used to calculate this rate. The choice will depend on the type of production capacity which operates at a specific stage of production. In most cases, this depends on the number of labouror machine hours used. If machines did most of the work, the overheads could be charged on the machine hour rate; if direct labour was dominant, rather than machine hours, then the direct labour hour rate could

be used. The formula for calculating these is simply the overheads for a specific centre, divided by the type of absorption rate used.
Methods used include:

- Direct labour hour rate: overheads/direct labour hours
- Machine hour rate: overheads/machine hours
- % Direct labour cost: overheads/cost of direct labour (%)
- % Direct material cost: overheads/cost of materials (%)
- Cost per unit rate: overheads/no. of units

In the above example of Production Centres A and B, let us assume that, in A, there were 19,200 direct labour hours worked, costing £130,260. Output was 12,000 units. In B, 10,800 machine hours were used to produce an output of 8,000 units. From these figures we can calculate the following overhead absorption rates:

Production Centre A

Direct labour (DL) hour rate: $\dfrac{\text{Overheads}}{\text{DL hours}}$ $\dfrac{97,695}{19,200}$ = £5.09 per DL hour

% Direct labour cost: $\dfrac{\text{Overheads}}{\text{DL cost}}$ $\dfrac{97,695}{130,260}$ = 75% of direct labour

Cost per unit: $\dfrac{\text{Overheads}}{\text{No. of units}}$ $\dfrac{97,695}{12,000}$ = 8.14 per unit

This would mean that, if it took 10 direct labour hours to do a job, the overhead charge would be £50.90 (10 × £5.09) based on using this method. If direct labour cost £80, the overhead charge would be £60 (75% of £80) based on the second method. If 10 units were produced, £81.40 (10 × £8.14) would be the overhead charge based on the third method.

Production Centre B

Machine hour rate: $\dfrac{\text{Overheads}}{\text{Machine hrs}}$ $\dfrac{62,305}{10,800}$ = £5.77 per machine hour

Cost per unit rate: $\dfrac{\text{Overheads}}{\text{No. of units}}$ $\dfrac{62,305}{8,000}$ = £7.79 per unit

The same method would apply in charging overheads depending on the number of machine hours it took or the number of units produced. If a job took 120 machine hours, the overhead charge for the job would be £692.40 (120 × £5.77).

If a blanket rate was used (that is, the total factory overheads divided by the total number of units produced or by the total labour or machine hours operated) the absorption rate would clearly not be as accurate because it would fail to take into account the individual circumstances involved in each process or stage of production.

Overhead absorption rates may be used in non-manufacturing organisations. Services like solicitors and accountants can also estimate charges for overheads to be added to the hourly cost charged to their clients. Their input of hours could therefore be regarded as direct labour. For example, it was estimated that a partnership of three solicitors each worked 35 contact hours a week for a period of 45 weeks a year, and total overheads were £36,855:

Overheads charged per hour: $\dfrac{£36,855}{4,725 \text{ [hours]}} = £7.80$ per hour

The overhead cost would then be added to the hourly fee charged by the solicitors, which would represent their income. For example, if they wanted to earn £30 an hour for their service, the charge to clients would need to rise to £37.80 per hour.

Under/Over-recovery

If pre-determined estimations differ from actual figures, either above or below, then overheads will either be under- or over-recovered. In our solicitor example, if each of them averaged 36 contact hours per week:

3 × 1 hr × 45 weeks × £7.80 = £1,053 is over-recovered in the year, thereby increasing profits by this figure.

On the other hand, if each of them only worked an average of 34 hours, the reverse would be true and £1,053 would be under-recovered, having the effect of reducing profits by the same margin.

Questions

1. As a cost accountant you have collected the following information relating to three production departments:

	B	D	T
Area (square feet)	20,000	15,000	15,000
No. of employees	400	400	600
Book value of plant	£600,000	£800,000	£600,000

Budget expenses for the year are:

	B £	D £	T £	Total £
Rent				75,000
Rate				50,000
Depreciation				50,000
Loan Interest	12,500	12,500	12,500	37,500
Lighting				12,500
Heating				50,000
Indirect	10,000	7,500	5,000	22,500
Canteen deficit				8,750
Personnel and welfare expenses				35,000
Wages office expenses				43,750
Power	25,000	30,000	30,000	85,000
Repairs and maintenance	5,000	8,750	6,250	20,000

Other budgeted information:

	B	D	T
Direct labour hours	33,500	20,000	65,000
" " rates per hour	£4	£3	£5

Required:

(a) You are required to calculate overhead recovery rates for each cost centre (direct labour hour method). Show the basis of apportion.
(b) A product takes 2 hours in Dept B, followed by 3 in Dept D and then 5 hours in Dept T; direct material costs £10 in B, £20 in D and £15 in T. Prepare a breakdown of the production cost (by element of cost) for that product.

[BTEC National]

2. You are accountant to a firm with four production departments in its factory. Currently one factory overhead recovery rate, which is a percentage of direct labour cost, is used. The current recovery rate is calculated on the basis of the following budget:

Department	Labour cost (£000s)	Direct labour hours (000s)	Machine hours (000s)	Factory overhead (£000s)
A	160	40	10	25
B	225	90	—	90
C	90	30	60	45
D	175	70	—	35 £195,000

Job number 42 has just been completed and is ready for final pricing. The details so far are:

Department	Direct material	Direct labour cost	Direct labour hours	Machine hours
A	£400	£1,520	400	50
B	£570	£1,200	500	—
C	£1,300	£370	100	220
D	£320	£1,740	600	—

After adding factory overhead to prime cost, 10% of the resulting total factory cost is added to cover administrative costs, and a further 50% of total cost is added as profit, to arrive at selling price.
Required:

(a) calculate the current overhead recovery rate;
(b) show the total selling price of Job 42, using the rate calculated in (a);
(c) calculate individual departmental overhead recovery rates, using the most appropriate bases and justifying your choice;
(d) show the total selling price of Job 42, using the rates calculated in (c).

[BTEC National]

3. *Factory Data:*

	Produc	tion		Service		
	A	B	C	X	Y	Totals £
Area (sq. metres)	54,000	45,000	36,000	27,000	18,000	180,000
No. of lights	640	700	560	350	750	3,000
Machine horse power (KW)	35,000	35,000	56,000	10,500	3,500	140,000

Budgeted Expenditure for next year

	A £	B £	C £	X £	Y £	Totals £
Rent	—	—	—	—	—	100,000
Rates	—	—	—	—	—	50,000
Light	—	—	—	—	—	30,000
Machine Power	—	—	—	—	—	60,000
Heat	—	—	—	—	—	470,000
Indirect wages	15,000	17,000	10,000	10,000	12,000	64,000
Supervisors' wages	33,300	27,100	32,700	9,850	18,050	121,000
Repairs and maintenance	14,800	38,900	51,700	9,900	19,700	135,000

It has been decided to allocate service departments X and Y in the following proportions:

	A	B	C	X	Y
Dept X	20%	50%	20%	—	10%
Dept Y	20%	30%	50%	—	—

Budgeted Direct Labour Hours:
A = 36,250 hrs, B = 53,125 hrs, C = 40,000 hrs
Direct wage rates for next year are budgeted as:
A £4 per hour, B £4.50 per hour and C £5.25 per hour.

Required:

(a) Apportion the overheads to each cost centre and then allocate the service cost centres to production centres.
(b) Calculate the overhead absorption rates for A, B, C, using direct labour hours.

(c) Calculate the cost of a new product which takes 4 direct labour hours in A, 6 hours in B and 4 hours in C. The direct material cost is £45 per unit.

[BTEC National]

4. PTS Limited is a manufacturing company which uses three production departments to make its product. It has the following factory costs which are expected to be incurred in the year to 31 December.

		£
Direct wages	Machining	234,980
	Assembly	345,900
	Finishing	134,525

		£
Indirect wages and salaries	Machining	120,354
	Assembly	238,970
	Finishing	89,700

	£
Factory rent	12,685,500
Business rates	3,450,900
Heat and lighting	985,350
Machinery power	2,890,600
Depreciation	600,000
Canteen subsidy	256,000

Other information is available as follows:

	Machining	Assembly	Finishing
Number of employees	50	60	18
Floor space occupied (m²)	1,800	1,400	800
Horse power of machinery	13,000	500	6,500
Value of machinery (£000)	250	30	120
Number of labour hours	100,000	140,000	35,000
Number of machine hours	200,000	36,000	90,000

Required:

(a) to prepare the company's *overhead* analysis sheet;
(b) to calculate appropriate overhead absorption rates (to two decimal places) for each department.

[Chartered Institute of Management Accountants]

5. A furniture making business manufactures quality furniture to customers' orders. It has three production departments and two service departments. Budgeted overhead costs for the coming year are as follows:

	Total £
Rent and rates	12,800
Machine insurance	6,000
Telephone charges*	3,200
Depreciation	18,000
Production supervisor's salaries	24,000
Heating and lighting	6,400
	70,400

*Use floor area.

The three production departments (A, B and C) and the two service departments (X and Y) are housed in the new premises, the details of which, together with other statistics and information is given below.

	DEPARTMENTS				
	A	B	C	X	Y
Floor area occupied (sq. metres)	3,000	1,800	600	600	400
Machine value (£000s)	24	10	8	4	2
Direct labour hrs budgeted	3,200	1,800	1,000		
Allocated Overheads: Specific to each department (£000s)	2.8	1.7	1.2	0.8	0.6
Service Department X's costs apportioned	50%	25%	25%		
Service Department Y's costs apportioned	20%	30%	50%		

Required:

Prepare a statement showing the overhead cost budgeted for each department, showing the basis of apportionment used. Calculate also suitable overhead absorption rates.

[Association of Accounting Technicians]

6. One of the directors of Company X has been looking at the budgets that have been recently prepared and shows concern at the production costs budget. The overhead absorption rate, based on a percentage on direct wages has increased from 200% to 300%.

Required:

(a) An explanation of how overhead absorption rates are calculated and used.
(b) An explanation of what factors may have caused the above increase.
(c) An explanation of the circumstances that could make this increase acceptable.
(d) Suggest possible apportionment methods for the following overhead cost items:

● Rent and rates
● Supervisors' salaries
● Canteen costs
● Machine depreciation

(e) Calculate under- or over-absorption of overhead from the following information.

	Machine Dept	Finishing Dept
Budgeted labour hrs	2,200	4,000
Budgeted overhead costs	£11,000	£16,000
Actual labour hrs	2,350	3,900
Actual overhead costs	£11,250	£16,720

[Association of Accounting Technicians]

CHAPTER 32

Job, Batch and Contract Costing

Absorption costing involves the total cost of a unit in terms of direct labour, direct materials and a charge for overheads. It includes both fixed and variable costs applied to the cost of a product or service. The overheads charge can be made by applying an overhead absorption rate as we discussed in the previous section. Absorption costing is part of what is called 'specific order costing', whereby the manufacture of products is individual rather than mass produced. There are three main methods of this type of absorption cost: job, batch and contract costing, which are developed further in this section.

Job, batch and contract costing methods involve costs which can be easily identified and allocated to customers according to their specific requirements.

Job costing

This system focuses its attention on the individual product. It is used where specific pieces of work are undertaken to satisfy customer needs. For example, if you wanted your house decorated or central heating installed, a painter and decorator or heating engineer would come round, measure up the job and give you a quotation for how much it would cost (see Figure 32.1).

In manufacturing, the customer requirement is also identified by having the order numbered on a job card; all stages of production costs in terms of labour, materials and overheads are assigned to the job card so that the costs are clearly identified for that particular job. The job cost card, therefore, indicates all relevant costs for a job and in effect, represents the business's work in progress to date.

FIGURE 32.1 Sample quotation

Quotation for Job No. 385/95
External Painting of House: 14 Hickory Dock Road, Docking

Labour:			
36 hours @ £6.75		£243.00	
Materials:			
24 litres of paint @ £4.20	£100.80		
7 litres of gloss @ £5.45	£ 38.15		
Other miscellaneous	£ 6.50	£145.45	
10% Overhead charge		£ 38.85	£427.30

Estimated Total Cost: £427.30

The preparation of job cards also allows the calculation of the selling price and profit margins for each job undertaken. The cost office also prepares cost sheets on which labour, materials and overhead costs are recorded for each job.

Example

You are working in the costing office of a firm of jobbing engineers. The details of Job No. B520 are as follows:

Direct Materials:
Requisition nos756 for 940 units @ £0.625 each
831 for 470 units @ £0.74 each
915 for 940 units @ £0.425 each

Direct Labour:

	Time allowed	Time taken	Rate (hr)
Operation 1	100 hours	92 hours	£3.50
2	80 hours	74 hours	£4.00
3	110 hours	102 hours	£5.00

A bonus system is in operation at the factory where the bonus is equal to half the time saved.

Add to the production cost factory overheads at 40% of the *prime cost*. Add to the factory cost: administration overheads at 15% of the *factory* cost. (The profit margin is 20% and goods are subject to VAT at 17.5%) Prepare a statement showing the amount to be invoiced to the customer for Job No. B520.

Solution

FIGURE 32.2 Job cost card

JOB B520	£	£
Direct materials		
756 940 × 0.625	587.50	
831 470 × 0.74	347.80	
915 940 × 0.425	399.50	1,334.80
Direct labour		
Op. 1 96 × 3.5	336.00	
2 77 × 4	308.00	
3 106 × 5	530.00	1,174.00
		2,508.80
Production overheads 40%		1,003.52
Factory cost		3,512.32
Administration overheads 15%		526.85
		4,039.17
Profit margin (25% mark up)		1,009.79
		5,048.96
VAT		883.57
Invoice total		5,932.53

Batch costing

A production order from a customer can be for an individual item or it can also be for a batch of identical items. To find the unit cost, the total batch cost is divided by the quantity of units produced. Job cards will be prepared in the same way as used in job costing. Problems could arise of how to apportion cost when a production batch is mixed with another batch for common activities, in order to save time and money. In this case, it may be prudent to charge the cost as an overhead item.

Sometimes a batch of components may be required within the factory to replace stocks of materials which are continually used

FIGURE 32.3 Example of batch cost

Internal Batch Order for Cost Centre A:
500 units Job No. 745/21: Costs per Unit

			£
DL	166.67 hours @ £7.20 hour		1,200.00
DM			
Code Numbers			
4481/33:	500 × 0.96	£ 480	
4481/44:	500 × 2.40	£ 1,200	
4481/56:	500 × 0.80	£ 400	2,080.00
Overheads			1,600.00
Batch cost			4,880.00

Overhead absorption rate: £9.60 per DL hour.
Costs allocated to Cost Centre A: 500 units × £9.76 per unit = £4,880

Note: Cost per unit of batch $\quad = \dfrac{£4,880}{500}$

$$= \quad £9.76$$

---

as parts to make other products. In this case an internal batch order is raised by the cost centre or department which requires to keep its stocks up to the required levels. (See Figure 32.3.)

Contract costing

There are also other jobs which may take a great deal of time and money. Contract costing is best applied to building and construction programmes where contractors may carry out a number of contracts within the financial period, or some may take a number of periods to complete, such as new office block in town, a group of houses on an estate, or a ship in dock. If work is not completed within strict time schedules, the contractor may be penalised for failing to meet deadline dates and incur additional costs. The contract price is estimated in advance and often there are in-built clauses in the contract, which allow the contractor to make additional charges on a cost-plus basis where conditions may be beyond his control.

Contract costing allows an organisation to identify and collect costs against each contractee (the persons who want the job done). At the end of the financial year, a company will balance off all its contract accounts and calculate any profit or loss to date on each of them and transfer the figures to the profit and loss account. The total work still in process (work in progress to be completed) is entered as stock in the current assets of the balance sheet in accordance with SSAP 9, Stocks and Work in Progress.

The amount of profit to take on an unfinished contract will take into account the Prudence Concept of SSAP 2, Disclosure of Accounting Policies, which, if you look back, tends to under-state rather than over-state profits. In this instance, the profit calculation to date is based on the following formula:

$$\text{Surplus to date} \times \frac{2}{3} \times \frac{\text{Cash received}}{\text{Certified value of work}}$$

In the above formula, the term 'certified value' is that value given by the architect to verify that any work completed is in accordance with the agreed specifications and conditions of the contract and that the appropriate stage payment can be made. It is also quite a common practice for the client (contractee) to retain a certain amount, usually 5–10% of any certified work, until 6–12 months after the final completion of the contract in the event that something is not quite up to standard. This is known as the 'retention money'. In line with prudence, in the event that a loss is made to date, the above formula is not used, because the whole loss would be written off against profits.

Example

A contracting company, AJAX Constructors Ltd. negotiated a contract to build a new silo system for a grain manufacturer. The contract price was agreed at £1,250,000 and, on 1 July, the contract work began. The details for the year ended 31 December were as shown in Table 32.1.

Required:

(a) Calculate the cost to date, as on 31 December, and the cost of the work certified.
(b) The estimated profit to date, at 31 December.

Solution

(a) The cost of the contract to date 31/12:

TABLE 32.1 AJAX contract costing

Expenditure	£	
Direct materials	340,000	
Direct labour	485,000	
Overheads	33,000	
Plant, equipment installed	24,000	
As on 31 December:		
Overheads outstanding	2,200	
Stock of materials	20,300	
Direct labour accrued		4,500
Plant, equipment depreciated by 30% per annum		
Work certified by architect valued		1,000,000
Work as yet uncertified valued		50,000
Cash received from clients,		885,000

Direct materials	£340,000	
– Unused	£20,300	£319,700
Direct labour	£485,000	
+ Accrued	£4,500	£489,500
Overheads	£33,000	
+ Accrued	£2,200	£35,200
Depreciation of plant, equipment (6 months)		£3,600
Cost of work to date		£848,000
Less Work uncertified on 31/12		£50,000
Cost of certified work 31/12		£798,000

Surplus to date= Certified work – Cost of certified work
£202,000   = £1,000,000   – £798,000

(b) Profit to date =Surplus to date $\times \dfrac{2}{3} \times \dfrac{\text{Cash received}}{\text{Certified value to date}}$

$$= \quad 202{,}000 \quad \times \frac{2}{3} \times \frac{885{,}000}{1{,}000{,}000}$$

$$= \quad £119{,}180$$

In the final accounts, the above figures would be entered in the contractor's trading account:

Cost of sales = Certified work to date + Profit to date
£917,180   = £798,000   + £119,180

Turnover   = Cost of sales + Profit to date
£1,036,360   = £917,180   + £119,180

Trading Account to 31 December
Turnover (Sales)   £1,036,360
Less
Cost of Sales   £917,180

Gross Profit   £119,180

Note that the cost of sales is a combination of cost of certified work to date and the attributable profit because of the element of work in progress which has been completed. It has not yet been certified by the architect, but a proportion of it should still be accounted for as part of the current year's cost of the contract.

Questions

1. You work in the costing department of a printing firm which carries out a number of 'jobbing contracts' per year. You are in the process of working out the amount to invoice a customer for a job (Job No. J420) which has just been completed. The basic cost data for the period is as follows:

Direct labour details:

Printing department	Hours worked	Time allowed
Job No. J405	130	150
Job No. J410	270	300
Job No. J420	60	70
Job No. J425	540	480
	1,000	1,000

Folding and binding dept	Hours worked	Time allowed
Job No. J400	200	230
Job No. J405	140	160

Job No. J420	20	26
Job No. J410	80	90
	440	506

In the Printing Department the basic hourly rate is £4 per hour and employees are paid a bonus equal to one half of time saved.

In the Folding and Binding Department the basic hourly rate is £3.50 per hour and employees are paid a bonus equal to one-half of time saved.

Direct material details:

All supplies used on Job Number 420 were bought specifically for the job. Invoice details were:
Invoice from Manchester Paper Mill Limited:

- 20 rolls of paper at £50 per roll
- Less 20% trade discount.

Invoice from Brighter Inks PLC:

- 5 litres of ink at £30 per litre
- Less 20% trade discount.

Production overheads

Printing Department – overheads are absorbed as a percentage of direct labour cost – the current rate being 120%.

Folding and Binding – overheads are absorbed on the direct labour hour method (actual time taken), the current rate being £8 per hour.

Administrative and distribution overheads

The current rate is 15% of total factory cost.

Profit

The standard profit margin applied is 20%.

VAT (sales tax) = 15%.

Required:

Prepare a detailed statement of the value to be charged to the customer for Job No. 420.

[Chartered Institute of Purchasing & Supply]

2. In the Albany Manufacturing Company Limited there are three Production Departments and two Service Departments. Budgeted overhead costs have been allotted to the departments as follows:

	Production departments			Service departments	
	A	B	C	M	N
	(£000)	(£000)	(£000)	(£000)	(£000)
Indirect labour	200	280	120	140	60
Other expenses	80	40	40	60	100
	280	320	160	200	160

The overheads of the Service Departments M and N are to be apportioned to Productions Departments A, B and C as follows:

Department M 30% to A   30% to B   20% to C   20% to N
     "   N 40% to A   50% to B   10% to C

The jobs are costed using an overhead absorption rate per direct labour hour.

The budgeted direct labour hours are A: 8,000; B: 16,000; C: 8,000.

Required:

(a) Apportion the Service Department overheads to the Production Departments.
(b) Calculate the Production Department overhead absorption rates.
(c) Calculate the production cost of a job which takes 4 hours in Department A, 6 hours in Department B and 3 hours in Department C and its prime cost is £750.
(d) What do you understand by the term 'total absorption costing'?

[Chartered Institute of Purchasing & Supply]

3. You work for a small firm of jobbing engineers who accept work on a cost-plus basis. One of the jobs, Job Number 153 for 80 finished units, is now complete and needs costing and pricing.

> *Information re: Job. No. 153*
> *Direct Material*

> 80 units of B @ 45p per unit
> 160 units of C @ 53p per unit
> 320 units of D @ 68p per unit

> *Direct Wages*

	Time allowed	Time taken	Basic hourly rate	m/c hours
Operation 1	160	144	£3	288
Operation 2	240	228	£2.90	60

A Halsey bonus system operates.

> *Production Overheads*

> Operation 1   £2 per machine hour taken
> Operation 2   £3 per Direct Labour hour taken

> *Administrative Overheads*
> 15% of total production cost.

> *Selling and Distribution Overheads*
> £2 per finished item.

> *Profit*
> There is a profit margin of 20%.

Required:

Prepare an analysed breakdown of the selling price for Job No. 153.

4. The following information relates to a small engineering company:

> *Budgeted data for next year.*

		£000
Overheads	Business rates and building insurance	800
	Repairs and maintenance of machines	200
	Depreciation of machinery	280
	Power consumption	180
	Production manager's salary and expenses	50
	Supervisors' salaries – Dept. A	30
	" B	30
	" C	25
	Heating and lighting	120

Basic hourly wage rates:	Dept. A	£5 per hour
	" B	£6 " "
	" C	£6 " "

Other information:

	Floor area in square metres	Machine value £000	Machine hours	Number of employees
Department A	10,000	1,500	6,000	100
B	14,000	2,000	6,000	75
C	16,000	500	8,000	75

The Production Manager's costs are to be apportioned in proportion to each department's machine hours.

Required:

(a) Prepare an overhead analysis sheet.
(b) Compute machine hourly overhead absorption rates for each department (round to the nearest whole pound).
(c) Prepare a price quotation for a job which requires 30 hours' machining in Department A, 20 hours' machining in Department B and 45 hours' machining in Department C. £2,000 of material will be required from stores. Administrative and distribution overheads are absorbed by adding 20% to total production costs. The company operates a standard profit margin of 25%.

[Chartered Institute of Purchasing & Supply]

5. A medium-sized building contracting organisation has its financial year end on 31 October 19–5. The expenditure charged against Contract No. 294/3 was as follows:

	£
Materials	372,000
Direct expenses	80,000
Wages	400,000
Sub-contractors costs	48,600
Allotment of Head Office overheads	36,000

The contract, which was for £2,900,000, had been started on 10 November 19–4. By 31 October 19–5 receipts from the client amounted to which represented 95% of the certified value. On 31 October 19–5 the value of materials unused was £24,000 and the cost of work completed but not yet certified was £30,000.

Required:

Prepare the account for Contract No. 294/3 for the year ending 31 October 19–5 – clearly showing the amount of profit transferred to Profit and Loss Account.

Note: The attributable profit formulae is:

$$\text{Surplus to date} \times \frac{2}{3} \times \frac{\text{cash received}}{\text{certified value}}$$

[Chartered Institute of Purchasing & Supply]

6. The accounts of a contractor disclosed that the following expenditure had been charged to contract number 19 during 19–5:

	£
Materials	248,000
Wages	320,000
Depreciation of plant	26,000
Head Office allotment of overheads	24,000
Payments to sub-contractors	32,400

The contract, which was for £1,500,000, had started in February 19–5. By 31 December receipts from the client amounted to £648,000, which represented 90% of the certified value. On 31 December the value of materials unused was £16,000 and the cost of work completed but not yet certified was £20,000.

Required:

Prepare the contract account for the year ending 31 December 19–5, clearly showing the amount of profit to take to the profit and loss account.

Note: You should use the following formule to determine profit:

$$\text{Surplus to date} \times \frac{2}{3} \times \frac{\text{cash received}}{\text{certified value}}$$

[Chartered Institute of Purchasing & Supply]

7. (a) A long-term contract is one that will usually extend for longer than one year.

● Give two examples of long-term contract work
● List three characteristics of a long-term contract other than its length

(b) In order to overcome the problem of profit recognition with a contract that extends over a number of years, attributable profit is allowed to be recognised before the contract is completed.

● Explain the problem of profit recognition that is associated with long-term contracts
● Outline what you understand by attributable profit and in what circumstances it should and should not be taken
● If it is thought that a loss might arise as a whole on a contract how should this be treated?

(c) A long-term contract to build a factory in Radley was started up in November 19–4 and is expected to be completed in February 19–6. The value of the contract is £1,400,000 and it is at the stage that profit can be attributed to it. When work has been certified, the company that issued the contract for the factory is sent an invoice for progress payments. You are given the following information relating to the year ended 31 October 19–5

	£
Materials issued to site from store	600,000
Materials returned to store	50,000
Materials remaining on site 31 October	20,000
Wages paid	250,000
Wages accrued	30,000
Sub-contractors' charges	25,000
Plant purchased at cost	100,000
Value of plant on site at 31 October	60,000
Overheads allocated to contract	25,000
Value of work certified at 31 October	1,200,000
Progress payments received at 31 October	1,000,000

All costs to date form cost of work certified.
Prepare the following for the year ended 31 October 19–5:

● The Radley contract account
● The contractee's account

[Association of Accounting Technicians]

CHAPTER 33

Process and Standard Costing

The previous chapter on job, batch and contract costing and this current chapter are all part of using an absorption costing system. The basic concept for each of these methods is the same: we are trying to calculate the cost of labour, materials and overheads in the cost of a job, batch, contract or process. With standard costing, we are trying to pre-determine what these costs are to improve the quality of budgetary control which is dealt with in Chapter 35. Process costing is part of what is termed 'operation costing', where the production of products or services is part of a continuous flow or process of operations, and where the cost of one stage is carried on and added to the next stage until all operations are completed. The cost per unit at any process of production is found by dividing the costs of that process by the number of units produced.

Process costing

In manufacturing there are many products which spring to mind that are simply not worth bothering about on an individual basis because the unit price could be so low: a bar of chocolate, a bottle of shampoo, a tin of paint, a packet of margarine, a bottle of milk and so on. These products are best dealth with in process costing rather than job or batch costing. Note that the finished output of one stage becomes the input for the next until all processes are complete and the units transferred to the stock of finished goods.

At the end of any cost period, there may be an element of work in progress still to be calculated, in which case a technique called 'equivalent units' is used.

> **Example**

A manufacturer produces 40,000 to 45,000 units a week of a product which has two distinct stages of process:

Stage 1:

Direct labour	£ 4,600	
Direct materials	£ 7,800	
Overheads	£10,000	£22,400

At the end of one week, 42,000 units were completed. Partly completed units (work in progress) included:

5,000 units with 50% direct labour and overheads,
8,000 units with 100% direct materials

To calculate the total cost for Stage 1 and the cost per unit for this process, we need to find out the cost for labour, materials and overheads, including the *equivalent units* produced:

Direct labour cost = £4,600 units + 5,000 units × 50%
                   = 2,500
extra equivalent units of direct labour; 44,500 units in total. To find the work in progress (WIP):

$$\text{DL cost per unit} = \frac{\text{DL cost}}{\text{Output + Equiv. units}} \quad \frac{4,600}{44,500} = 0.103\text{p}$$

WIP = 0.103p × 2,500 units = £258

Direct materials cost £7,800 plus 8,000 × 100% = 8,000 extra equivalent units of direct materials, a total of 50,000 units.

$$\text{DM cost per unit} = \frac{\text{DM cost}}{\text{Output + Equiv. units}} \quad \frac{7,800}{50,000} = 0.156\text{p}$$

WIP = 0.156p × 8,000 units = £1,248

Overheads cost £5,000 plus 5,000 units × 50% = 2,500 extra equivalent units, a total of 44,500 units.

$$\text{Overheads per unit} = \frac{\text{Overheads cost}}{\text{Output + Equiv. units}} \quad \frac{10,000}{44,500} = 0.225\text{p}$$

WIP = 0.225p × 2,500 units = £562

Total WIP:	DL	£ 258.00	
	DM	£1,248.00	
	Overheads	£ 562.00	£2,068

Process Cost: Stage 1

Direct labour	£4,600	
Direct materials	£7,800	
Overheads	£10,000	£22,400
Less WIP		£ 2,068
	Cost:	£20,332

Stage 1: Cost per unit £20,332/42,000 = 48.4p

Stage 2:
The cost of Stage 1 is then transferred to the next process of operations. In our example, this is the final stage.

Stage 2

Stage 1 Cost	£20,332	(42,000 units)
Direct materials	£ 2,520	
Direct labour	£ 2,988	
Overheads	£ 6,500	£32,340

At the end of this process, 41,800 units were finished goods, transferred to store. For work in progress, direct materials were 100% complete and both labour and overheads, 80%. 200 units were unfinished.

The work in progress for Stage 2:

Direct labour and overheads: 80% of 200 units = 160 *equivalent units*.
Direct materials were 100% complete = 200 units.
Stage 1 costs were 100% complete = 200 units.

Stage 1 cost $\dfrac{£20,332}{42,000}$ = 48.4p per unit

WIP   48.4p × 200 units   = £96.80

Direct materials $\dfrac{£2,520}{42,000}$ = 6p per unit

WIP   6p × 200 units   = £12.00

Direct labour $\dfrac{£2,988}{41,960*}$ = 7p per unit

WIP   7p × 160 units   = £11.20

Overheads $\dfrac{£6,500}{41,960}$ = £15.5p per unit

WIP   15.5p × 160 units   = £24.80

*41,960 units = 41,800 completed + 160 equivalent units.

Total WIP: Stage 1   £96.80
             DM   £12.00
             DL   £11.20
             Overheads £24.80   144.8

The factory cost is calculated by deducting the WIP from the total cost of Stage 2 process (see Table 33.1).

TABLE 33.1 Total factory cost

	£	£
Stage 1	20,332	
Stage 2		
DM	2,520	
DL	2,988	
Overheads	6,500	32,340
Less WIP (rounded up)		145
		32,195

Factory cost per unit: £32,195/41,800 units = 77p

Note that the work in progress sum of £145 at the end of the period is carried forward as the opening work in progress in the next sum:

Normal and abnormal losses due to wastage

In the course of this type of production, losses will occur through wastage because a percentage of products will fail to pass inspection and are therefore scrapped; or, where liquids are used, some measure may be lost due to evaporation or other reactions in the method of process, etc. The basic principle in costing which deals with waste is that the expected normal loss in the process is added to the cost per unit. If there are any abnormal gains or losses in process, these should be excluded from the normal output and posted separately to the profit and loss account at the end of the period.

In our example above, the factory cost per unit was 77p which was based on an output of 41,800 units. Suppose that normal wastage was about 5%. This would mean that, if no wastage had occurred, the output would have been 44,000 units. (Check: 44,000 less 5%.) The cost per unit would have been less:

$$\frac{\text{Factory Cost}}{\text{Output}} \quad \frac{£32,195}{44,000} = 73\text{p per unit}$$

However, because of normal expected wastage, the factory cost was divided by the output of 41,800 units, increasing the cost per unit by 4p. If output had only been 41,000 units, there would have occurred an *abnormal loss* of a further 800 units which would need to be treated differently, the loss being carried over to the profit and loss account. How do we deal with an abnormal loss? Follow the next example.

Example

A product passes through two processes in its production. During a cost period, the data was as shown in Table 33.2.

There was no work in progress at the end of either process. Calculate the unit cost of each process and the transfer of gain or loss to the profit and loss account.

TABLE 33.2 Cost period data

	Process 1 £	Process 2 £
Input: 8,000 units		
Direct materials	96,000	
Direct materials added in process		24,480
Conversion costs:		
Direct labour	109,300	130,320
Overheads	69,100	57,580
Outputs (units)	7,400	7,000
Normal loss (% of input)	10%	5%
Scrap value of each lost unit	£1	£4

Solution

Process 1

Normal loss 10% of 8,000 units = 800
Actual loss   = 600   200 units
                                                              (abnormal gain)

The formula to calculate the unit cost:

$$\frac{\text{(Total input costs – Normal scrap value)}}{\text{Expected normal output}}$$

Total Costs: £

Direct materials 96,000
Direct labour   109,300
Overheads   69,100   274,400

Normal scrap value 800 units × £1 = £800
Expected normal output   8,000 less 10% = 7,200 units

$$\text{Unit cost} = \frac{(£274,400 - 800)}{7,200} = £38 \text{ per unit}$$

Cost of Process 1 = 7,400 units × £38 = £281,200

Abnormal gain transferred to profit and loss account:

200 units saved × £38   = £7,600
less scrap lost 200 × £1   £ 200   £7,400

Process 2

Normal loss 5% of 7,400 units = 370
Actual loss   = 400 (30 units, abnormal
                                        loss)

Total Costs:

Process 1   £281,200
Direct materials £ 24,480
Direct labour   £130,320
Overheads   £ 57,580   £493,580

Normal scrap value 5% × 7,400 units = 370 × £4 = £1,480
Expected normal output 7,400 units less 5% = 7,030 units

$$\text{Total cost per unit} = \frac{(£493,580 - £1,480)}{7,030} = £70 \text{ per unit}$$

Abnormal loss transferred to profit and loss account:

30 units lost × £70   = £2,100
less additional scrap 30 × £4 = £ 120   £1,980

Factory cost: 7,000 units × 70 =   £490,000
Units transferred as stock of finished goods: 7,000

Profit and loss account (extract):

Other revenue:
  Wastage Gain   £7,400
  – Wastage Lost £1,980   £5,420

Standard costing

Standard costing is a management tool used to check the efficiency of production of an organisation, by comparing actual results with pre-determined calculations which management consider the standard to attain. It is management's way of budgetary control, particularly of high-cost units such as domestic appliances, televisions, motor cars, etc. One of the main purposes of cost accounting is to provide management with systems which will help them to achieve control of costs.

It includes the strict measurement of work rates, material costs, plant efficiency, etc., which go towards preparing the master budget. This is a forecast of pre-determined costs based on a given output, considered to be the normal capacity of production (for example, 1,200 units a month). A flexible budget can be prepared if the output varies from the master budget. If only 1,100 units were produced, then the expected standard cost for this number of units would be the flexible budget. It is the normal practice of management to check actual results with that of the flexible budget in order to get a better, more realistic appraisal of any differences in costs which may occur.

If management, for example, calculated the standard cost (in terms of materials, labour and overheads) of producing a motor vehicle for £7,500 and the actual cost came out at £8,000 each, then management will want to know why there is an unfavourable differences of £500. The difference (variance analysis) will help management find out why and where figures differed from their pre-determined forecast. The use of variances is one of the most significant aspects of standard costing where the outcome will either be a favourable or unfavourable (adverse) balance. Variance analysis provides the key to effective control of costs and attempts to discover why differences in costs may have arisen, and also provides management with ideas of what could be done about them.

In standard costing, an attainable standard is a standard which management believe can be attained if work is carried out efficiently and where allowances are made for what has been considered normal losses, waste and machine downtime. An ideal (potential) standard is a standard which can be achieved under the most favourable conditions with no allowances made for normal losses. Management must decide what the level of output is likely to be in the year ahead and provide a plan of costs, taking into account the organisation's previous experience in production and also the economic indicators, particularly that of inflation and levels of demand.

Variances

The variances which can be used in standard costing mostly concern production, with emphasis on direct materials, direct labour and production overheads. There are also variances for sales and non-manufacturing such as distribution and administration overheads. In examinations, questions concerning direct materials and direct labour variables are the most commonly used and the text will concentrate on these.

Production variances

> Direct materials price variance
> Direct materials usage variance
>
> Direct labour rate variance
> Direct labour efficiency variance
>
> Variable production expenditure variance
> Variable production efficiency variance
>
> Fixed production overhead expenditure variance
> Fixed production overhead volume variance

Sales

> Selling price variance
> Sales volume variance

Non-production

> Distribution (or marketing) variance
> Administration variance

Example

The following standard costs apply in a business that manufactures a single product:

Standard weight to produce 1 unit	12 kilograms
Standard cost per kilo	£9
Standard hours to produce 1 unit	10 hours
Standard rate per hour	£4 per unit

Actual output was 290 units and actual production costs in the accounting period were:

Materials used 3,770 kilograms   Materials cost £35,815
Hours worked 2,755 hours   Wages paid   £11,571

Budgeted sales 280 units at £90 each (cost £80)
Actual sales   285 units for £25,080.

Required:

(a) Calculate the relevant material, labour and revenue variances;
(b) explain why the variances may have occurred.

Solution

Direct material variances

This is where the actual costs differ from the standard due to the purchase price of components which might be more or less than the standard (material price variance), or where more or fewer components are used than the specified standard (material usage variance).

Material price variance:
  (Actual quantity × Standard price) – Actual cost
     (3,770 kilos × £9)   – £35,815
  = (1,885) *adverse* balance

Material usage variance:
  (Standard quantity – Actual quantity) × Standard price
     (3,480 kilos – 3,770 kilos)   × £9
  = (2,610) *adverse* balance

The total material cost variance is £4,495 (adverse) due to more materials used than standard through wastage, inefficiency, machine breakdowns, etc., and purchase prices being more than expected.

Direct labour variances

These follow the same pattern as the material variances to find out whether the hourly rate paid is more or less than the standard rate (labour rate variance) and whether more or less time is taken than the specified standard time (labour efficiency variance).

Labour rate variance:
(Actual hours × Standard rate) – Actual cost
(2,755 hours   × £4)   – £11,571
= (£551) *adverse* balance

Labour efficiency variance:
(Standard hours – Actual hours) × Standard rate
    (2,900 hours – 2,755 hours)   × £4
= £580 *favourable* balance

The total labour variance works out as £29 favourable, due to greater efficiency of hours used although the labour rate was higher than the standard.

Sales variances

The same principles apply for sales price and sales volume variances, where the product is sold for more or less than the budgeted (standard) price (sales price variance), and where the quantity sold is higher or lower than the budgeted quantity (sales volume variance).

Sales price variance:
(Actual quantity × Standard price) – Actual sales
    (285 units × £90)   – £25,080
= £570 *adverse* balance

Sales Volume Variance:
(Standard quantity – Actual quantity) × Sales margin
    (280 units – 285)   × £10
= £50 *favourable* balance

The total sales variance is £520 adverse due to the greater difference in sales prices, although slightly offset by a more favourable volume variance.

Looking at the overall picture, the worst situation was that of materials where almost £4,500 was adverse, and this would lead management in deciding what to do about it. Perhaps a new buyer may be needed or a more efficient method of production is required. Labour was close to the pre-determined standards and sales prices may have had to be reduced to stimulate greater demand for the product.

Overhead variances

For these variances the same principle applies again. The variance is the difference between the standard overhead charges and actual overheads charged. The overhead absorption rate is used for the calculation of overheads charged, in our example, direct labour hours (£11,000/2,200 hours = £5 per DL hour).

Example

The following figures relate to a cost centre where:

Budgeted labour hours	2,200 hours
Budgeted overheads:	£11,000
Actual labour hours:	£2,350
Actual overheads:	11,250 hours

Calculate the fixed overhead expenditure and overhead volume variance.

Fixed overheads
expenditure variance: Budgeted overheads – Actual overheads
    £11,000 – £11,250
    = £250 *adverse* balance

Fixed overheads
volume variance: (Actual hours × Standard rate) – Actual overheads
    (2,350 hours × £5) – £11,250
    = £500 *favourable* balance

The total overhead variance is £250 favourable due to more actual hours recovering £5 per labour hour than the standard, even though the actual overheads were more than the budget figure.

Questions
---

1. The process costs for a new product was as follows:

        Material Code 223 2.50 per kilo
                Code 224 0.80 per kilo
        Labour 2,200 hours at £3 per hour
        Overhead absorption is 100% of labour cost

During the first period of production, 3,000 units were finished and 400 partly finished. The work in progress was considered 100% for materials and 75% for labour and overheads.

Required:

Prepare the process cost of the work completed, including work in progress and the value of finished goods to store.

2. A new process has been started by a company and its costs for the first month were:

> Material   A   200 units at £10 per unit
> B   1,500 units at £3.20 per unit
> Conversion costs (labour and overheads) £26,400.

During the first month, 1,500 units were finished and taken into stock. The work in progress had 200 units considered 75% complete for conversion costs and 100% for materials.

Required:

Prepare the process cost of the work completed, the value of work in progress and the value of finished goods to store.

3. A product passes through two stages of process, A and B. The cost of Process A was 5,000 units at 8.5p per unit. In Process B the following costs were incurred:

> Direct materials   £7,180
> Direct labour   £8,500
> Overheads   90% of labour
> Output (units)   4,700 units

Rejection rate at end of process of manufacturing is normally 5%
The scrap value of each unit lost is £1.50 each.
There was no work in progress at the end of the process.

Required:

Calculate the total unit cost of manufacture and transfer any gain or loss to the profit and loss account.

4. A compound is manufactured as a result of two distinct processes. Details of Process 2 for the month of July were:

Work in progress opening stock	Nil
Direct materials from Process 1	10,000 kilos. valued at £40,500
Direct labour	1,000 hours at £5.616 per hour
Overheads	50% of direct labour
Output of finished goods	8,000 kilos
Closing stock of work in progress	900 kilos

Quality control at the end of the process normally leads to a rejection rate of 10%. Closing work in progress is 100% for direct materials and 75% for labour and overheads.

Required:

Prepare the process cost of the work completed, the value of WIP and the amount of abnormal loss transferred to the profit and loss account.

(Association of Accounting Technicians)

Note: To assist you in this question, when calculating the WIP you need to add the abnormal loss of units to the output of finished goods (f.g.) and the equivalent units. Abnormal loss is 100 units (9,000 − 900 actual).
Direct materials: 8,000 (f.g.) + 900 WIP + 100 loss = 9,000 equiv. units
Direct labour: 8,000 (f.g.) + 675 WIP + 100 loss = 8,775 equiv. units.
The loss of 100 units at unit cost is transferred to profit and loss.

5. Your work as a management accountant and have to give a talk to your colleagues in the Production Department about the introduction of a standard costing system.

Required:

(a) Define standard costing.
(b) What is the purpose of standard costing?
(c) What are the benefits of standard costing?
(d) What are the problem associated with introducing and maintaining a standard costing system?

[Chartered Institute of Purchasing & Supply]

6. Your financial director is shortly to go on a one-day conference on standard costing and its benefits for manufacturing industry. He has asked you to draft a short report on standard costing before he goes to the conference.

   You decide to include a table of variances in the report and have, therefore, made up the following data in respect of a product:

   Standard Cost of *One Unit* of Output:

	£
Direct material 20 kilos at £2.00 per kilo	40
Direct wages 10 kilos at £4.00 per hour	40
	80

   Actual Cost of *100 Units* of Output:
   Direct material £4081   (2,182 kilos)
   Direct wages   £4312   (980 hours)

   Required:

   (a) Draft the brief notes which will form the basic contents of the report. You should discuss the purpose of standard costing and discuss any possible problems.
   (b) Using the above data calculate the following variances:

   ● Direct material price variance
   ● Direct material usage variance
   ● Total direct material cost variance
   ● Direct labour rate variance
   ● Direct labour efficiency variance
   ● Total direct labour cost variance

   (c) Suggest possible explanations for the variances.

   [Chartered Institute of Purchasing & Supply]

7. A manufacturer produce a single product, IRIS, which has the following standard data:

	Per unit of IRIS £
Direct material 2 kilos at £10 per unit	20
Direct labour 5 hours at £10 per hour	50
Selling price	100

1,000 units of IRIS are budgeted to be produced and sold for each of the 13 reporting periods in the year. Administrative fixed costs of £4,000 per period are also budgeted.

In the second reporting period the actual data was as follows:

Units of IRIS produced	1,000	units
Sales of IRIS	900	units
Total revenue from sales	£99,000	
Kilos of material purchased	2,400	kilos
Total cost of purchases	£21,600	
Direct labour- hours	4,000	hours
- total cost	£36,000	
Administrative fixed costs	£6,000	

There are no opening or closing stocks of materials and no opening stock of finished goods.

Finished goods in stock at end of period 2 are to be valued at standard cost (£70 per unit).

Required:

(a) Prepare a statement showing the budgeted profit for period 2.
(b) Prepare a statement showing the actual profit for period 2.
(c) Calculate the relevant material and labour cost variances for period 2.
(d) Briefly explain the major purposes of standard costing.

[Chartered Institute of Purchasing & Supply]

8. A manufacturer produce a single product, the standard cost data for which is as follows:

Standard weight of material to produce one unit	18 kilos
Standard price per kilo	£8
Standard labour hours to produce one unit	9 hours
Standard wage rate per hour	£5

The actual production and costs for April were:

Material used	5,810 kilos
Material cost	£44,100

Hours worked   2,610 hours
Wages paid   £15,620

The actual output was 300 units.

Required:

(a) Compute the relevant material and labour cost variances and present them in a suitable tabular form.
(b) Suggest possible explanations for the cost variances.
(c) How might the Purchasing Department help in the setting of material price standards?

[Chartered Institute of Purchasing & Supply]

Chapter 34

Marginal Costing

In the previous sections, we discussed absorption costing in all its various guises: job, batch, process costing, etc. Absorption costs absorb a product in terms of its materials, labour and overhead costs. These are the three essential components in costing and that is why there were three separate sections which dealt with them.

In contrast, marginal costing is related to those costs which can be directly traceable to a specific unit. These costs are sensitive to the level of output. For example, if only one unit was produced, then the costs which can be directly traced to producing that unit represent a marginal cost. If production increased to two, then the marginal cost would also increase to two.

For marginal costing to be calculated, it is necessary to divide costs into two categories: variable and fixed costs. Variable costs are those direct costs traceable to a unit like direct materials and are sensitive to output change. Fixed costs are far less sensitive to change and are the indirect costs, such as rent and rates. Therefore, if output were to change, either increasing or decreasing, it would hardly affect the cost of rent or rates but it would affect direct materials or direct labour costs. The terms marginal and variable costs are interchangeable, so that £10 per unit variable cost may be described as £10 per unit marginal cost.

It is important to make this distinction because the level of activity will have a direct bearing on the amount of profit or loss on a given output of production. In general, the more units produced, the more the fixed cost per unit will decrease, thereby increasing potential profits. On the other hand, if output levels fall, then the fixed costs per unit will increase, reducing the profit. The variable cost per unit should be the same and will rise in relation to the volume produced.

> Output level: 500 units
> Variable cost: £10.00 per unit

Fixed costs: £25,000
Cost per unit: 500 × £10 = £ 5,000
    Fixed Costs   + £25,000   £30,000
                        ─────────   ─────── = £60.0 per unit
                                       500

Output level: 600 units
Cost per unit: 600 × £10 = £ 6,000
Fixed costs   + £25,000   £31,000
                           ─────────   ─────── = £51.67 per unit
                                          600

Therefore, by increasing the level of output, fixed costs are 'diluted', making the cost per unit cheaper, with potentially more profit. If output was to decrease, the cost per unit would be greater.

Table 34.1 concerns ABC Company, which has a normal output capacity of 260 televisions per month. It has the facilities to increase this by at least 20%. Study the figures and take particular note of 'contribution', which plays an essential part of marginal cost calculations.

Production capacity: 260 televisions

$$\text{Absorption cost } \frac{69{,}261}{260} = \text{£266.39 per television}$$

The absorption cost is the total of fixed and variable costs.

Once the absorption cost is known, a firm can then estimate a mark-up on cost price which will represent its profit. For example:

Absorption cost based on
    260 televisions   £266.39
+ Mark-up 20%   £ 53.28
                               ───────
Possible selling price   £319.67   per television

If the public chose to buy something more competitive elsewhere, then the 20% mark-up will have to be reconsidered, or the costs reduced.

Marginal (variable) costs

This refers to the *extra* costs involved in producing one or more units over and above the projected forecast of production (or one or more units fewer).

TABLE 34.1   ABC data

	£	£
1. Direct labour		23,463
2. Direct materials		22,473
3. Overheads:		
Factory	12,564	
Office	10,761	23,325
		69,261

TABLE 34.2   ABC's marginal costs

Marginal cost per TV	£	£
(a) Direct materials $= \dfrac{22,473}{260} =$		86.43
(b) Direct labour: (bonus)		2.50
(c) Extra overheads		
Power		0.30
Other		0.20
		89.43
Total marginal cost to produce 15 extra sets		× 15 £1,342

Marginal cost may be required in order to find out the effect on expenses when producing more or fewer items.

If ABC Company had produced 275 televisions within its production capacity, how much *extra* did the 15 televisions cost?

Consider:

(a) All direct materials are extra.
(b) Direct labour earns £2.50 bonus for each set produced.
(c) Power to produce one television costs 30p.
(d) Other overheads are an extra 20p per set.

How much is the marginal cost per television? See Table 34.2.

Variable costs are costs as in Table 34.2, which are sensitive to changes in production levels. The more units produced, the greater the variable (or marginal) cost.

Fixed costs

Those costs which are deemed not so sensitive and which must be paid regardless of production levels are known as *fixed costs*.

Fixed costs do not change even if one extra or one less is produced. Factory overheads and office overheads tend to remain relatively fixed.

These cost types may now be broken down into their fixed and variable categories (see Table 34.3). Figures are based on a 260-unit capacity of production.

TABLE 34.3 Cost types

Capacity: 260 TVs	Total cost	Fixed cost	Variable cost	Notes
	£	£	£	
Direct labour	23,463	22,813	650	(£2.50 bonus)
Direct materials	22,473	—	22,473	100% variable
Overheads	23,325	23,195	130	(50p per TV)
	69,261	46,008	23,253	

(a) Total absorption cost: $\dfrac{£69,261}{260}$ = £266.39

(b) marginal cost: $\dfrac{£23,253}{260}$ = £89.43

To produce *extra* televisions, therefore, will *not* incur the full absorption cost because some costs are relatively fixed for a certain capacity of production.

The above example shows that extra sets produced will incur 100% of the costs of the materials directly, but other extra costs involved are relatively low. It is very useful for management to *know* the marginal costs because it is these that directly affect 'contribution' towards profit, before fixed costs are deducted.

The importance of contribution

If an order for an extra 50 televisions was received, asking for a special mark-down price of, say, £140 per set, management could accept the order knowing that marginal costs were around £90. That is, of course, if the 50 extra could be produced within the normal production capacity. If more labour was to be hired, then direct labour costs would have to be added to marginal costs.

Calculate:

(a) The estimated profit if 260 units were produced and sold at £320 per unit.
(b) The *extra* profit if 275 units were produced and sold.

Profit calculation using marginal costing

(a) see Table 34.4

TABLE 34.4   Estimated profit on 260 units

	£
Revenue	
260 units @ £320	83,200
Deduct	
Variable costs:	
260 unit @ £89.43	23,252
CONTRIBUTION*	59,948
Deduct	
Fixed costs:	46,008
Profit	13,940

* Contribution = Revenue – Variable Costs

The more contribution, the more profit is available before fixed costs are deducted.

When production levels change, contribution will move proportionately so that any extra contribution, as a result of higher production levels, produces more profit. Conversely, if production levels are less than those forecasted less contribution results in less profit.

Contribution plays a very significant part in marginal costing.

TABLE 34.5   Estimated profit on 275 units

	£
Revenue:	
275 units @ £320	88,000
Deduct	
Variable costs:	
275 @ £89.43	24,594
Contribution	63,406
Deduct	
Fixed costs	46,008
Profit	17,398

(b) See Table 34.5.

The *extra profit* on 15 more units?	(£17,398 – £13,940)	= £3,458
The *extra contribution*?	(£63,406 – £59,948)	= £3,458

Check on profit

Revenue earned:

£320 × 15 = £4,800

To produce an extra 15 units, the variable or marginal cost was

£89.43 × 15 = £1,342

Extra profit: =   £3,458 (*Note*: No change in fixed costs.)

The use of 'contribution per unit'

The contribution per unit can be used to make quick calculations in marginal costing:

Revenue:	£320.00
– Variable cost	£ 89.43
Contribution per unit	230.57

Extra profit on an extra 15 units?

Contribution per unit × 15
£230.57   × 15
                       = £3,458 extra profit

Total profit on 275 units?

= [Output × contribution/unit] – fixed costs
= [275 ×   230.57   ] – £46,008
= £17,398 profit

If only 250 units were produced, what effect would it have on profit?

= [output x contribution/unit] – fixed costs
= [250   x   230.57]   – £46,008
= £11,634 profit

Breakeven

Management need to know at what point in production the firm has 'brokeneven'. This refers to the point at which the business has earned sufficient revenue to cover all costs. Any further revenue earned after this point will be a contribution towards profit.

Revenue less than the break-even point means losses. This is an important calculation for management because it needs to know at what point its costs are covered in terms of production units and revenue earned, and when this has been achieved.

The Independent newspaper needed something like a daily circulation of 330,000 newspapers to breakeven. Some of the major airlines need to have 60% of their seats sold to breakeven. A number of manufacturers need to produce to at least 70% of their capacity to breakeven, while others can manage on about half capacity.

The calculation of breakeven in production units:

Breakeven (in units) $= \dfrac{\text{Fixed costs}}{\text{Contribution/Unit}}$

$= \dfrac{£46,008}{£230.57}$

= 199.54 units (200 rounded up) television sets

Check:
Contribution/unit × 200

	= £46,114	(Contribution)
less Fixed cost	£46,008	
(profit)	+ £106	(because of rounding up to 200)

Profit on 201 produced?
Contribution/unit × 1

=	£230.57
	+£106.00
	£336.57 profit

Check:
Contribution/Unit × 201

=	£46,344.57
less Fixed Cost	£46,008
	£336.57 profit

The contribution to sales ratio [or profit/volume (PV) ratio]

To find the break-even revenue is simply a matter of multiplying the number of units produced by the revenue per unit:

No. of units to breakeven	=	200
Selling price per unit	=	£ 320
Break even revenue	=	£64,000

If the contribution to sales ratio is used, break-even revenue may be calculated more directly.

$$\text{Contribution to sales ratio} = \frac{\text{Contribution/Unit}}{\text{Sales/Unit}}$$

$$= \frac{£230.57}{£320.00}$$

$$= 0.721 \quad (0.7205)$$

$$\text{Calculation of break-even revenue} = \frac{\text{Fixed costs}}{\text{Contribution/sales}}$$

$$\frac{£46,008}{0.721}$$

= £63,811 Revenue needed to breakeven

The contribution to sales ratio may also be used to estimate profit on the sales revenue. If, in the financial year, £76,800 had been earned to date, what profit is estimated on this revenue?

Revenue × Contribution/Sales ratio (C/S ratio)

£76,800 × 0.7205	=	£55,334
less Fixed costs		£46,008
		9,326 (profit)

Check:

No. of units to earn £76,800 revenue?

$$= \frac{\text{Sales}}{\text{Unit price}} = \frac{£76,800}{£320}$$

$$= \quad 240 \text{ units sold}$$

Can you take it from there?

240 units sold × contribution/unit (£230.57 = £55,336 (Contribution)
Less Fixed costs: £46,008
                                                        £9,328 (profit)

Calculate estimated profit on £89,600 sales revenue ... £18,548 profit
Calculate estimated profit/loss on £62,400 revenue ... [£1,048] loss

The break-even chart

The break-even chart is a graphic illustration showing the point at which revenue covers total costs – that is, the break-even point. In business it is rarely used because prices constantly change, making it difficult to use the chart effectively. However, the chart is useful because it does show the estimated point at which break-even takes place, both in units and revenue. In practice, it can be a guide to show a band of break-even rather than a point; for example, instead of 200 units representing break-even, it may be a band between 190 and 210 units. The construction of the chart is shown below.

Fixed costs for the financial period:	£2,000
Variable costs per unit:	£6.00
Sales price per unit:	£10.00
Contribution:	£4.00 per unit (£10 – £6)

Break-even point:
$$\frac{\text{Fixed costs}}{\text{Contribution/Unit}}$$

$$\frac{£2,000}{£4} \quad = \quad 500 \quad \text{units}$$

Break-even revenue: 500 × £10 unit

$$= \quad £5,000$$

The Cost Chart (Fig. 34.1)

Total costs = Fixed + Variable costs

Figure 34.1   Chart showing costs only

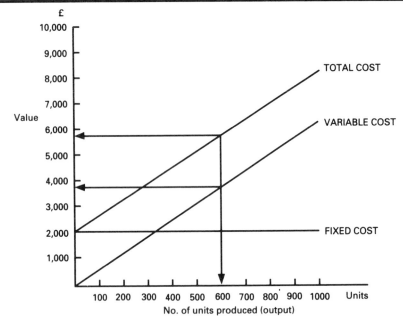

Variable cost: 600 units = £3,600
Total cost: 600 units = £5,600

and these *start at £2,000* because, irrespective of production levels, fixed costs of £2,000 are incurred.
From the chart:

What is the variable cost on 600 units?
What is the total cost on 600 units?

The break-even chart (Fig. 34.2)

Figure 34.2   Chart showing break-even point

The break-even chart shows the additional line of revenue. Revenue commences at zero because it is dependent on the number of units sold and produced.

From the chart:

What sum of revenue is earned on 600 units?

600 × £10 = £6,000

The break-even point is the point where the revenue line crosses the total cost line – that is, at 500 units. Revenue at this point is £5,000. Any point beyond 500 units means profit. Any point below 500 units means loss.

From the chart: Approx. figures

What is the loss on 450 units?   Check: £200 loss
What is the profit on 610 units?   Check: £440 profit

If revenue was £6,250, what profit?   Check: £500 profit
If revenue fell to £4,200, what loss?   Check: £320 loss

If the output was 750 units, what is the estimated profit?
  Check: £1,000 [750 × 4] – 2,000

Use both the chart and costing figures for your answer.

Variations in price

If the sales price increased by 25% and fixed costs increased to £3,900, calculate the new break-even point. The variable costs remain the same.

What profit is made if the budgeted capacity remains on 750 units?

$$\text{Break-even point:} \quad = \frac{\text{Fixed Costs}}{\text{Contribution/unit } (12.5 - 6.00)}$$

$$= \frac{£3,900}{£6.5}$$

$$= 600 \text{ units to breakeven}$$

$$\text{Profit on 750 units} = [750 \text{ units} \times £6.5] - £3,900$$

$$= £975 \text{ profit}$$

Which is the more profitable? The variation in price with increased fixed costs, or the budgeted capacity as before? Answer: as before, £1,000 profit.

Management may use variations in price, change its costs and regulate output in order to meet the needs of the market. Market research assesses the level and nature of demand in the market and if there is likely to be changes in consumer buying; management needs to change its strategy (or planning) in order to maintain its share of the market, or indeed increase its share.

Which is the best plan?

Using the figures based on an output of 750 units as before and the data below,

Variable cost/unit	£6
Fixed costs	£2,000
Sales price	£12 per unit

determine which of (a), (b), (c) or (d) below is the best course of action.

(a) Base the estimated profit on the above budgeted plan.
(b) Reduce the price by £1.00 per unit, research having indicated a 20% sales increase.

(c) Launch an advertising campaign costing £400, which produces a sales increase of 10%.
(d) Reduce the sales price by 15%, giving a market increase of 30%.

To give you a start:

(a) Estimated profit on 750 units:
   Contribution/unit   =   £6.00 × 750 units
   Contribution   =   £4,500
   less Fixed costs   =   £2,000
   _____
   Profit   £2,500

Can the proposals in (b), (c) and (d) better £2,500 profit?

(b) Reduce the price £1
   Sales increases 20%
   Contribution/unit   =   £5.00 x 900 units
   Contribution   =   £4,500
   less Fixed costs   =   £2,000
   _____
   Profit   £2,500

No change!

Try (c) and (d):   (c) = £2,550 profit, (d) = £2,095 profit.

A summary of marginal cost formula

Contribution:	Selling price – Variable cost
Profit or Loss:	(Output × Contribution/unit) – Fixed costs
Break-Even Point:	$\dfrac{\text{Fixed costs}}{\text{Contribution per unit}}$
% Margin of Safety:	$\dfrac{(\text{Planned output} - \text{Break-even point})}{\text{Planned output}}$
Contribution/Sales Ratio: (C/S)	$\dfrac{\text{Contribution per unit}}{\text{Sales per unit}}$
Break-Even Revenue:	$\dfrac{\text{Fixed costs}}{\text{Contribution/Sales Ratio}}$
Estimated Profit from Sales Value:	(Sales × Contribution/Sales Ratio) – Fixed costs

---

Example

As a costing assistant for a manufacturing company, you are asked to make a number of calculations. The company has a plant capacity of 10,000 units per annum, but at present is working only to about 90% capacity. The pricing policy of the enterprise is to add a 20% mark-up to cost.

The information you are given is listed in Table 34.6.

TABLE 34.6   Costs based on a budget of 10,000 units per annum

	£	
Direct labour	100,000	100% variable
Direct materials	200,000	100% variable
Factory overheads	80,000	£2 per unit variable
Administrative overheads	120,000	
Total estimated costs:	500,000	

Required:

(a) Prepare a table to show total, fixed and variable costs based on a planned output of 10,000 units per annum.
(b) Calculate the contribution per unit.
(c) What is the estimated profit on the planned output? If sales were only 9,000 units, calculate the estimated profit or loss.
(d) Calculate the break-even point.
    What is the loss on 10 units below break-even?
    What is the profit on 10 units above break-even?
(e) Calculate the contribution/sales ratio (profit/volume ratio).
    Calculate the profit or loss on sales of £425,000.
(f) If the selling price was reduced by 10% and advertising costs were £20,000, to gain an estimated extra 1,500 units sold, would it be worth going ahead with the project?
(g) An improved model is to be launched. Variable costs will increase by £8 per unit. Fixed costs will increase by an estimated £50,000. The selling price to launch the new model is £65.
    What extra sales are required to cover these costs?

TABLE 34.7 Table of costs

	Output: 10,000 units		
	Total £	Fixed £	Variable £
Direct labour	100,000	—	100,000
Direct materials	200,000	—	200,000
Factory overheads	80,000	60,000	20,000
Administrative overheads	120,000	120,000	—
	500,000	180,000	320,000

(a) See Table 34.7.

(b) Contribution per unit:

Selling price £60 – Variable cost/unit £32
Contribution: £28

(c) Estimated profit on planned output:

10,000 × £28 per unit		£280,000
Estimated profit	=	£100.000

Profit on 9,000 units:

1,000 units × Contribution/unit		1,000 × £28
	=	£28,000 *less* profit
Estimated profit	=	£72,000

(d) Break-even point:

Fixed Costs		£180,000
Contribution/Unit	=	28
	=	6,429 units (rounded up)

Check:

Revenue:	6,429 × £60	=	385,740
– Variable costs	6,429 × £32	=	205,728
Contribution:			180,012
– Fixed costs			180,000
			12

Loss on 10 units below:

10 × Contribution/unit	=	10 × £28
	=	£280 (loss £268)

Profit on 10 units above:

10 × Contribution/unit	=	10 × £28
	=	£280 (profit £292)

(e) Contribution: Sales ratio:

$$\frac{\text{Contribution/unit}}{\text{Sales/unit}} \qquad \frac{£28}{£60}$$

	=	0.46667

Profit/loss on sales of £425,000:

Sales × Contribution: sales ratio	=	£425,000 × 0.46667
Contribution	=	£198,335
– Fixed cost	=	£180,000
Estimated profit		£ 18,335

(f) Is the project worth going ahead? YES

New selling price: £60 – 10% = £54
New contribution/unit: £22 × 1,500 extra units sold:

	=	£33,000
less costs for advertising		£20,000
Estimated profit		£13,000

(g) Extra sales required:

Selling price £65 – Variable costs £40
New contribution/unit = £25
To cover an extra £50,000 fixed costs:

$$\frac{\text{Fixed costs}}{\text{Contribution/unit}} = \frac{£50,000}{£25}$$

Extra sales required = 2,000 units

The limiting factor

The amount of contribution per unit a business makes is essential to profit. The greater the contribution, the greater potential to make profits. If a company made two or more products, it may have to decide, in some cases, in what quantities to produce them which would make the most benefit to contribution.

If there was a restriction or constraint in any way, in the production or demand for products, a choice may have to be made on the products which will achieve the greater contribution. The constraint is referred to as the 'limiting factor'.

Example

A business makes two major products, refrigerators and washing machines (see Table 34.8).

TABLE 34.8 Product data

	Refrigerators £	£	Washing machines £	£
Sales per unit		120		250
Variable costs:				
direct materials	40		100	
direct labour	24		50	
overheads (variable)	10	74	20	170
Contribution/unit		46		80

In terms of contribution per unit, the washing machines are better although we do not know the quantities produced of each product. If an output of 200 refrigerators and 150 washing machines were produced:

total contribution refrigerators   200 × 46 = £9,200
total contribution washing machines 150 × 80 = £12,000

Again, the washing machines come out on top.

If direct materials were in short supply in a given month, which of the two products makes the better contribution in terms of materials?

$$\frac{\text{Contribution}}{\text{Direct materials}} = \text{contribution to £1 direct materials used}$$

Refrigerators: $\frac{46}{40}$ = £1.15 contribution/direct materials

Washing machines: $\frac{80}{100}$ = £0.80 contribution/direct materials

In this case, the refrigerators are the better prospect and perhaps should be given the first priority in production.

If only 80% direct materials were available, each product requiring the same type of materials but in different quantities:

Cost of materials:

Refrigerator: 200 units × £40 per unit = £8,000
Washing machine: 150 units × £100 per unit= £15,000 £23,000

If only 80% of materials could be purchased: £23,000 × 80% = £18,400

Produce refrigerators first, having the higher material contribution per unit:

200 × £40 per unit = 8,000 materials to make 200 units

which leaves £10,400 for washing machines:

$$\frac{£10,400}{100} = 104 \text{ units to make}$$

Total contribution: Refrigerators   200 × 46 = £9,200
                     Washing machines 104 x 80 = £8,320 £17,520

The contribution: sales ratio

If the sales potential of either product was the same, the C/S ratio could be used to rank the two products:

Refrigerators: $\dfrac{C}{S} = \dfrac{46}{120} = 38.33\%$

Washing machines $\dfrac{C}{S} = \dfrac{80}{250} = 32\%$

If sales for either product had a potential of £12,000 per week then refrigerators have the greater profit by £760:

Refrigerators	£12,000 × 38.33%	= £4,600
Washing machines	£12,000 × 32%	= £3,840.

   In practice, it is never quite as straightforward as it appears. Many other factors come into play, not least the customers, the investment in plant and machinery and the workforce. It is not just a case of figure-crunching: the effect on reliable customers, the morale of workers and the cost of expensive equipment are all influential in deciding what the best course of action might be.

To make or buy?

Another important point in marginal costing is to decide whether to make products or buy them from elsewhere if they look cheaper to purchase. This time we must look at the fixed costs because they play an influential part in making the decision.
   If, in producing the refrigerators, the business also made the motors of the these units, costing £22 each:

Variable cost of motor/unit	£10	
Fixed overheads charged	£12	£22
Purchase from external supplier		£18

A cost of £4 per unit cheaper.
   Is it a case of down tools, shut the motor shop and buy from outside? Buying 200 motors a week would save the business £800; or would it?
   Do the fixed costs conveniently disappear once the making of a product is closed down? No. When the existing facilities for production are available for use, the fixed costs still remain and burden the other products with a greater proportion of fixed costs per unit:

Refrigerators:

	+ Motor	Total
Variable costs	£64	£10	£74
Fixed Overheads	£24	£12	£36
	£88	£22	£110

If the motor was purchased externally, the fixed cost of £12 still remains as part of the product cost. A refrigerator will incur £36 fixed costs and a total absorption cost of £100 per unit (not £88 per unit).

Therefore, when deciding whether to make or buy, all the costs must be considered, particularly fixed costs that do not go away if a section or a product is closed down.

The use of marginal costing assists management by providing further information with which to improve decisions making, in particular when output levels differ from those planned, or special prices for special orders need to be calculated. In the real world, however, you must remember solutions are not always based on figures alone. The limiting factor, used to find out which would be the best combination of units to produce, is fine in theory; but in practice, it's the regular and reliable customers who need to be satisfied first, irrespective of the order of contribution made to profits. Every business needs good orders and good customers to survive. In a similar way, it may be more prudent to close down an activity because it is cheaper to buy externally; but, apart from the difficulty of reducing fixed costs anyway, there is the painful problem of making your labour unemployed and paying for redundancies. It may also lower the morale of existing employees which may have a knock-on effect on their productivity. The closure would also mean the disposal of plant, equipment and other assets which may produce very little capital as scrap or disposal value.

Questions

1. The following costs relate to an output of 2,000 units:

	£	£
Direct labour	25,000	
Direct materials	40,000	
Overheads	35,000	100,000

Variable Costs

Direct materials	100%
Direct labour	£1.50 per unit.
Power (part of overheads)	0.50 per unit.

Revenue

Sales per unit   20% above cost price.

Required:

(a) A table to show total, fixed and variable costs based on an output of 2,000 units.
(b) The contribution per unit.
(c) The estimated profit based on 2,000 units.
(d) The estimated profit on 2,100 units
    and on 1,950 units.
(e) The break-even point.
    The profit on 1 above break-even.
    The loss on 1 below break-even.
(f) *Variation*. If sales price per unit were to decrease by 10% and output was to increase by 10%, what is the estimated profit (or loss)?

2. Mr Baldwin's small factory produces jeans. Output per month is 500 units.

Monthly costs	£	Variable Cost:
Direct labour	2,000	£0.50/Unit
Direct materials	2,000	100%
Overheads (fixed)	1,000	—
Costs per month	5,000	
Selling price:	Mark-up of 25% on cost	

Required:

(a) The contribution per unit.
(b) The estimated profit per month based on 500 units.
(c) The break-even point per month.
   The break-even revenue per month based on C:S ratio (contribution: sales ratio).
(d) If during the first 6 months revenue reached £42,500, what is the estimated profit?
(e) If sales in a month were £5,950, what is the estimated profit/loss in the month?
(f) Variations due to market changes:
   Propose to reduce the sales price by £1.00 and sales estimated to rise by 20% per month, or increase advertising cost by £2.50 per month and improve the jeans with stronger zip costing £0.30 per unit, with sales estimated to rise by 15% per month.
   Which is the better of the two proposals?
(g) If advertising costs increase by £765 during the first year, how many extra units need to be sold to cover this cost?

Note: Treat as a fixed cost and divide by contribution per unit.

3. Lillee and Thompson produce sports gear under the trade name 'Down Under'. The present year expects costs to be:

	£
Direct labour	48,000
Direct materials	55,000
Production overheads	22,500
Distribution costs	15,000
Administration costs	13,500
Financial and general costs	4,000

Sales revenue: £4 per unit

Variable costs

Direct labour	75%
Direct materials	100%
Production overheads	10%
Distribution costs	10%

Expected production capacity: 50,000 units.

Required:

(a) A table to show the division of fixed and variable costs based on a capacity of 50,000 units.
(b) Calculate the unit contribution.
(c) If an order for 1,000 units was received, what would the extra cost be, based on marginal costing?
(d) Could the firm accept the above order at £2.80 per unit?
(e) Calculate the break-even point.
   Calculate the break-even revenue based on the cost: sales ratio.
(f) Calculate the loss on 50 units below break-even.
(g) What is the estimated profit on 50,000 units?
(h) What is the profit/loss on a production of 39,500 units?

4. The following costs relate to a budgeted sales forecast of 30,000 units per year:

Costs	Budgeted £	Fixed £	Variable £
Production cost	287,500	25,000	262,500
Administration	35,000	30,000	5,000
Distribution	95,000	62,500	32,500
	417,500	117,500	300,000
Revenue per unit:	£15.00		

Required:

(a) The number of units needed to sell to cover costs.
(b) If sales decline to 20,000 units, what is the estimated profit or loss?
(c) If £80,000 is spent on advertising, how many extra units need to be sold to cover cost?
(d) On sales of £345,750 after 10 months, what is the estimated profit/loss at this point?
(e) The following proposals have been made:

● Spend £2.00 per unit improving the product, expecting sales to rise to 40,000 units
● Pay £1.00 per unit sales commission, expecting sales to rise to 38,500 units

● An additional order of 8,000 units at £12.50 per unit for export (export costs £10,000)

Which of these three proposals do you consider the best?

5. Smith Engineering Ltd has prepared the quarterly budget figures for three months ending 31 March 1986 as follows:

	Budget forecast total £	Fixed costs £	Variable costs £
Cost of production	115,000	10,000	105,000
Cost of distribution and sales	38,000	25,000	13,000
Administration expenses	14,000	12,000	2,000
	167,000	47,000	120,000

Sales forecast:
12,000 units @ £15 each.

As an assistant to the cost accountant you have been asked to calculate the following:

Required:

(a) What is the minimum number of sales units required to cover costs?
(b) If demand was to fall to 8,000 units, what is the effect on the forecast profit?
(c) If an additional £16,000 was spent on advertising the product, how many *more* units need to be sold to cover costs?
(d) Alternative proposals were to be considered:

● Redesign and improve packaging costing £1.50/unit (test marketing indicates that sales would increase by 25%)
● Reduce the selling price by £1 (research indicates that sales would increase by a third)

Should the company consider one of the above proposals or leave things as they were in the budgeted forecast?

6. As a costing assistant you need to prepare budget estimates for the next financial year. At current production levels,
   the company produces 6,000 units per year and has the
   capacity to increase this by another 1,000 units. The firm's
   pricing policy is to mark up by 25% on cost.
      The estimated costs for the next financial period based
   on an output of 6,000 units are:

	£
Direct labour	78,000
Direct materials	114,000
Factory overheads:	
Indirect labour	12,000
Indirect expenses	33,000
Office overheads	123,000
	360,000

Your research reveals that direct labour and direct materials
   are 100% variable.
Indirect labour is 10% variable as a result of sharing a bonus
   payment scheme.
Power (indirect expenses) is estimated at £1.80 per unit
   variable.
All other costs are to be considered fixed.

   Required:

(a) Prepare a suitable table to show fixed and variable costs
    based on an output of 6,000 units.
(b) Calculate:
      The contribution per unit.
      The break-even point.
(c) Prepare a chart based on an output of 6,000 units to
    illustrate:
    The company's break-even point.
    The profit/loss based on a production of 6,500 units.
    The profit/loss based on a production of 3,500 units.

7. As an assistant to the cost accountant of a manufacturing
   company, you have been asked to prepare some costing
   information relating to the launch of the company's new
   product.

Expected output:	10,000 units
Cost per unit	£
Direct materials	30
Direct labour	70
Variable overheads	40

Total fixed costs attributed to the product is £240,000.
Selling price per unit: £200.

Required:

Calculate:

(a) The contribution per unit.
(b) The break-even point.
(c) The margin of safety, expressed as a percentage.[*]
(d) The maximum profit on the expected output of 10,000 units and the estimated profit if production fell to 8,500 units.
(e) The following proposals have been put forward:

● By reducing the price to £190 per unit, 12,000 units are estimated to be sold
● By increasing the price to £210 per unit, 9,500 units are estimated to be sold
● By retaining the existing price at £200 and an extra £60,000 is spent on advertising, sales being estimated at 11,800 units

Which of these proposals do you consider is the best? Explain briefly why.

[*]margin of safety	=	Output - break-even point
as a %	=	Margin of safety × 100
		Output

8. A firm makes two products, A and B. Their cost data per unit is:

		A		B
Output per week:		50 units		80 units
Sales/unit		100		60
variables:				
materials	40		15	
labour	12	52	20	35
Contribution		48		25
Fixed costs		30		20

Required:

(a) What different methods can be used to decide the best contribution available on different products?
(b) If there is a shortfall of materials and only 80% is available, what would management be advised to do?
(c) What factors should management consider before deciding either to keep production going or simply to buy from outside a product which appears cheaper to purchase? (For example, if product B could be purchased for £50 per unit.)

9. You work in the Management Accounts Department of a Manufacturing company which makes three products from one basic raw material. Due to a serious accident at the supplier's factory there will be a shortage of the basic raw material next year. Next year's budgeted data is as follows:

Maximum amount of raw materials available – £2,094,000

Product	X	Y	Z
Maximum possible sales (units)	24,000	32,000	25,000
Variable costs per unit:			
Direct material	£24	£32	£38
Direct labour	£32	£21	£23
Overheads	£12	£10	£12
Selling price	£80	£88	£94

Total annual fixed costs are £585,000.

Required:

(a) Calculate the maximum profit that the company can make in the next year.
(b) If there was no shortage of the basic raw material, should the company consider accepting a 'special order' for 5,000 units of Product Y at a price of £74 (the additional costs of handling this order are estimated at £7,500)? In your answer clearly state the extra profit/loss if the order is accepted.

[Chartered Institute of Purchasing & Supply]

CHAPTER 35

Budgeting and Planning

In a well-structured organisation the budget is at the centre of the financial control system. When budgets are being prepared the responsibility for each main section is normally allotted to the functional heads of each department, such as the sales manager, production manager, finance manager, and so forth.

The basic purpose of a budget is to control the organisation's expenditure and to plan ahead for the future. After budgets have been prepared by heads of departments, they should be communicated to all personnel who need to know in order to involve them in the forward planning of the organisation. Budgets assist those in management by motivating them towards the major objectives of the organisation. Expenditure for the year ahead can be planned, profits estimated and targets set. Actual results can then be measured against the budgeted plans, and differences (variances) may be analysed, debated and acted upon where appropriate.

Budgets are prepared by management in order to attempt to achieve company policy; their preparation is usually a time-consuming exercise. The main steps may be summarised as follows:

(a) the objectives of the organisation should be clearly stated;
(b) an initial forecast of expenditures and revenues is prepared;
(c) the necessary computations are made in terms of manpower, materials, equipment, overheads, etc.;
(d) the initial budget is reviewed and amended where appropriate until it is accepted.

In order to set realistic objectives, management must obtain as much information as it can in terms of both internal and external factors. Externally, the organisation must consider the economic and political climate and obtain as much information as possible about competitors. Internally, it must assess the strengths and weaknesses of its own structure and consider the alternative plans available in order to compete effectively and gain its optimum share of the market.

The main types of budget are:

- Sales budget
- Production budget
- Personnel budget (or manpower)
- Capital expenditure budget
- Administration budget
- Cash budget
- Operating budget

The initial forecast must start with the expected level of sales. Selling is the life-line of an organisation and its cornerstone. Without sales, there is no organisation and therefore it is essential to make an accurate estimation of what sales (for every product) are likely to be. From the sales budget, other budgets should then fall into place.

The production budget must ensure that it can meet the demands set by the sales budget. It must take into account the stocks it already holds and be sure it has the necessary materials, labour, machinery and so forth to meet the appropriate sales demand. It is of little use to budget for a 30% sales increase if production cannot cope with even a 10% increase. If management wants a 30% increase, it must prepare, plan and be ready to finance it.

The personnel budget must ensure that the organisation has the right manpower at the right time, with the appropriate financial support to meet manpower and training needs.

The capital expenditure budget takes into account capital costs and involves the purchase of fixed assets like plant, machinery, equipment, new premises and other items expected to be used in the organisation over the long term. Fixed assets need replacement because they are likely to be worn out eventually or become obsolete. The budget needs to forecast what resources need to be put aside either for replacement or expansion purposes.

The administration budget usually takes into account all the overheads of the organisation from the administrative point of view and involves, largely, the fixed costs like rent, rates, stationery, heating, telephone, etc.

The cash budget (or cash flow) is often regarded as the most crucial. It involves all the other budgets in its forecast because it must include all sources of expected revenues in the months ahead (normally 1 year) against all sources of expected expenditure. In other words, it shows the forecast of the flow of cash into and out of the organisation and, in so doing, affects the bank balance. An organisation must have sufficient liquidity (or cash) to meet its day-to-day needs, otherwise it will run into financial difficulties and may have a cash crisis. If it runs out of money because of poor forward planning, how can it pay for wages, materials and a long list of overhead costs? On the other hand, if it can be foreseen that there may be a cash shortage ahead, management can negotiate, ahead of time, the necessary liquidity it needs and, in so doing, it emphasises the financial soundness of the organisation.

The operating budget represents a forecast of the final accounts. What will the estimated profit (or loss) be in 6 or 12 month's time? The business will plan its objectives and aim to make a satisfactory return on capital employed. All other budgets will contribute in preparing the operating budget and the forecast of profit or loss can then be compared against actual results, usually on a monthly basis, to see if activities go according to plan. This will assist management in making decision.

The cash budget

A new company has gathered the following information for the six months from 1 January 1988 to 30 June 1988.

(a) Sales (in units) £40 per unit:

Jan.	Feb.	Mar.	Apr.	May	June	
200	300	200	400	300	400	units

(b) Production is 300 units per month for the whole 6 months.
(c) Fixed overhead costs will be £3,000 per month, payable in the month after production.
(d) Variable overhead costs will be £15 per unit payable in the month of production.
(e) Direct wages will be £5 per unit payable in the month of production.
(f) Equipment costing £10,000 will be purchased in February and paid for in March. Once installed, it will allow production to increase to 500 units per month.
(g) Materials will cost £8 per unit and suppliers will be paid in the month following purchases.
(h) All sales of units are on credit. Debtors are expected to pay in the month following their purchase.
(i) Cash at bank on 1 January = £10,000.

Required:

A schedule of payments and a cash budget (see Tables 35.1 and 35.2).

TABLE 35.1   Schedule of payments

	Jan. £	Feb. £	Mar. £	Apr. £	May £	June £
Fixed overheads		3,000	3,000	3,000	3,000	3,000
Variable overheads						
(300 x £15)	4,500	4,500	4,500	4,500	4,500	4,500
Direct wages						
(300 x £5)	1,500	1,500	1,500	1,500	1,500	1,500
Equipment			10,000			
Materials						
(300 x £8)		2,400	2,400	2,400	2,400	2,400
	6,000	11,400	21,400	11,400	11,400	11,400

TABLE 35.2   Cash budget

	Jan. £	Feb. £	Mar. £	Apr. £	May £	June £
Bank balance b/f	10,000	4,000	600	(8,800)	(12,200)	(7,600)
+ Receipts*	—	8,000	12,000	8,000	16,000	12,000
	10,000	12,000	12,600	(800)	3,800	4,400
– Payments	6,000	11,400	21,400	11,400	11,400	11,400
Bank balance c/f	4,000	600	(8,800)	(12,200)	(7,600)	(7,000)

* Receipts calculated (*a*) £40 unit sales, allowing for one month credit.

Analysis of the cash budget

The cash budget clearly highlights that the company does not have sufficient capital to finance the above plan. However, if it could lease the new equipment rather than buy it, or obtain more capital by March, the problem would be solved. If the company had not prepared a cash-flow budget it would have had a deficit from March to June of a proportion it may not have planned. By preparing a cash flow, the organisation can demonstrate it has some control in its financial affairs and is therefore more likely to accommodate the deficit period by negotiation with its creditors. The cash flow emphasises the common business problem that, in order to finance an increasing level of sales, stocks have to be increased, equipment purchased, etc. Extra expenditure is incurred before the revenue from extra sales comes in.

In conclusion, budgets are both a planning and control tool because they help management to evaluate the financial implications of various courses of action ahead of time and to monitor those plans by comparing actual results of budget plans.

Budgets are an example of management by objectives because variations between actual and budgeted results can be highlighted, analysed and discussed in order to gain the optimum levels of profits for the organisation.

Example: cash budget through to budgeted final accounts

This is a testing question and needs to be followed carefully.

You have been asked by a business colleague of yours to 'cost out' his plans to set up a limited company to import and sell mountain bikes, which are apparently the very latest in the UK.

Information

1. The company will be called Bikers (Import) UK Ltd and will issue 90,000 x £1 ordinary shares at par on the following terms:

   1 Jan. on application 20%
   7 Jan. on allotment 30%
   4 Apr. First and final call 50%

2. The following is the pattern of fixed asset acquisitions:

   January £60,000 by cheque
   and October £20,000 by cheque.

3. Provide depreciation at the rate of 15% on the total fixed asset value on 31 December.

4. Sales are expected to be: Jan. £12,000; Feb. £16,000; Mar.–June inc. £20,000 monthly; July–Dec. inc. £25,000 monthly.
5. An initial stock will be purchased on 1 Jan. £20,000 (selling value) and subsequent purchases are to be arranged so that the stock *at the end of each month* will still be at this same figure. The sales margin is to be 30%. Therefore a stock of £14,000 is required in balance each month ending.
6. Estimated wages will be £2,500 each month, payable in that month.
7. Estimated rent and rates will be £1,000 each month, payable in that month.
8. Estimated operating expenses will be £1,500 each month, payable one month in arrears.
9. Trade creditors will be paid in the month *after goods are received* and debtors *will settle their accounts two months* after the sale.
10. Assume that the Directors will propose an Ordinary Dividend of 2 pence per share.
11. Assume that the Directors will provide for Corporation Tax at the rate of 30% of net profit.

Required:

(a) Prepare a 'schedule of payments' for the period January–December inclusive.
(b) Prepare a cash budget for the period January–December inclusive.
(c) Prepare a forecast trading, profit and loss and appropriation account for the year.
(d) Prepare a forecast balance sheet as at 31 December.

Solution

The main problem is to calculate the value of budgeted purchases – notes 4 and 5 above give us the details. First, convert sales figures to cost – i.e., 70% of sales value (see Table 35.3).

Note 5 tells us that the budgeted stock at the end of each month is to be £14,000 (70% of £20,000). The budgeted purchases will be as shown in Table 34.4.

TABLE 35.3 Conversion of sales figures to cost

	Jan.	Feb.	Mar.	Apr.	May	June
Sales £	12,000	16,000	20,000	20,000	20,000	20,000
70% of sales = cost of sale	8,400	11,200	14,000	14,000	14,000	14,000

	July £	Aug. £	Sept. £	Oct. £	Nov. £	Dec. £
Sales £	25,000	25,000	25,000	25,000	25,000	25,000
70% of sales = cost of sales	17,500	17,500	17,500	17,500	17,500	17,500

TABLE 34.4 Budgeted purchases

Jan. £	Feb. £	Mar. £	Apr. £	May £	June £	July £	Aug. £	Sept. £	Oct. £	Nov. £	Dec. £
8,400 *14,000											
22,400	11,200	14,000	14,000	14,000	14,000	17,500	17,500	17,500	17,500	17,500	17,500

i.e., in January we purchase our 'base stock' of £14,000* and what we plan to sell in January, then in each month following we plan to purchase what we intend to sell – leaving us with a constant stock at cost of £14,000 at beginning and end of each month.

Note: Many questions actually tell you what the purchases figure is. All you have to do is take note of any credit period given for the cash budget – in this example Bikers expect *one month's credit* from suppliers, e.g., January purchases will be paid for in February.

(a) Prepare the *schedule of payments*, i.e., list what amounts are going to be *paid* in each month (see Table 35.5).
(b) Prepare the *cash budget* (see Table 35.6): in this example there are two sources of revenue:

● The receipts from the initial share issue, i.e., £45,000 duringJanuary and £45,000 during April

TABLE 35.5 Schedule of payments

	Jan. £	Feb. £	Mar. £	Apr. £	May £	June £
Purchase of fixed assets	60,000	—	—	—	—	—
Payments to suppliers	—	22,400	11,200	14,000	14,000	14,000
Wages	2,500	2,500	2,500	2,500	2,500	2,500
Rent and rates	1,000	1,000	1,000	1,000	1,000	1,000
Operating expenses	—	1,500	1,500	1,500	1,500	1,500
	63,500	27,400	16,200	19,000	19,000	19,000

	July £	Aug. £	Sept. £	Oct. £	Nov. £	Dec. £
Purchase of fixed assets	—	—	—	20,000	—	—
Payments to suppliers	14,000	17,500	17,500	17,500	17,500	17,500*
Wages	2,500	2,500	2,500	2,500	2,500	2,500
Rent and rates	1,000	1,000	1,000	1,000	1,000	1,000
Operating expenses	1,500	1,500	1,500	1,500	1,500	1,500*
	19,000	22,500	22,500	42,500	22,500	22,500

* At the end of December £17,500 will be owing in respect of December purchases and £1,500 owing in respect of expenses incurred in December. Thereafter, these amounts will appear under current liabilities on the budgeted balance sheet at 31 December.

● Receipts from customers: note 9 informs us that Bikers Ltd intend to *give 2 months credit*. Therefore, January sales will be received in March and so on.

(c) Prepare the budgeted trading and profit and loss account for the year (see Table 35.7).

(d) Prepare the budgeted balance sheet (see Table 35.8).

TABLE 35.6 The cash budget

	Jan.	Feb.	Mar.	April	May	June
Balance b/f	Nil	(18,500)	(45,900)	(50,100)	(8,100)	(7,100)
Receipts	45,000	—	12,000	61,000*	20,000	20,000
	45,000	18,500	33,900	10,900	11,700	12,700
Payments	63,500	27,400	16,200	19,000	19,000	19,000
Balance c/f	(18,500)	(45,900)	(50,100)	(8,100)	(7,100)	(6,100)

	July	Aug.	Sept.	Oct.	Nov.	Dec.
Balance b/f	(6,100)	(5,100)	(7,600)	(5,100)	(22,600)	(20,100)
Receipts	20,000	20,000	25,000	25,000	25,000	25,000
	13,700	14,700	17,200	19,700	2,200	4,700
Payments	19,000	22,500	22,500	42,500	22,500	22,500
Balance c/f	(5,100)	(7,600)	(5,100)	(22,600)	(20,100)	(17,600)

* i.e., February sales £16,000 + £45,000 balance of share issue.

TABLE 35.7 Bikers (Import) UK Ltd budgeted trading and profit and loss account for year ending 31 December

	£	£
Sales		258,000
Cost of Sales		
Opening stock	0	
Purchases	194,600	
	194,600	
Closing stock	14,000	180,600
Gross Profit		77,400
Wages (12 x £2,500)	30,000	
Rent and rates (12 x £1,000)	12,000	
Operating expenses (12 x £1,500)	18,000	
Depreciation of fixed assets (£80,000 x 15%)	12,000	72,000
Net Profit (b/t)		5,400
Proposed corporation tax (30% of £5,400)		1,620
Net Profit (a/t)		3,780
Proposed ordinary dividend (90,000 x 2p.)		1,800
Profit and Loss		1,980

TABLE 35.8 Bikers (Import) UK Ltd budgeted balance sheet as at 31 December

	£ Cost	£ Depreciation	£ Net
Fixed Assets			
Various	80,000	12,000	68,000
Current Assets			
Stock	14,000		
Debtors	50,000	64,000	
Current Liabilities			
Creditors	17,500		
Accruals	1,500		
Overdraft	17,600		
Taxation owing	1,620		
Dividends owing	1,800	40,020	23,980
			£91,980
Capital and Reserves			
£1 ordinary shares			90,000
Profit and loss account balance			1,980
			£91,980

Questions

1. The following is the budget data for J. Robertson and David for the months April to December (in £000s).

	Apr	May	June	July	Aug.	Sep.	Oct.	Nov.	Dec.
Credit Sales	20	30	35	34	36	25	26	27	28
Credit purchases	20	22	22	23	17	18	19	20	30

Rent and rates are paid quarterly in advance: first payment due on 1 April (£12,000 per year).
Salaries paid in the month: £2,000 per month.
Wages paid in the month: £1,000 per month + 10% increase from 1 September.
General expenses paid in the month: £500 per month.
Opening bank balance: £10,000 overdraft on 1 July.

Note: Debtors pay at the end of the month following the sale.
   Creditors must be paid at the end of the month in which the purchase was made.
   A tax payment of £15,000 is to be made in July.

Required:
Prepare a cash budget for July to December inclusive.
2. The following information refers to Jones Ltd and shows the forecast from June 19–4 to March 19–5.
Sales are £48 per unit: unit sales forecast:

	June	July	Aug.	Sept.	Oct.	Nov.	Dec.	Jan.	Feb.	Mar.
Units	940	980	1,020	1,040	1,080	1,180	1,240	1,280	1,360	1,380

Debtors expected to pay 2 months after invoice.
Production in units:

	June	July	Aug.	Sept.	Oct.	Nov.	Dec.	Jan.	Feb.	Mar.
Units	1,000	1,040	1,040	1,100	1,200	1,240	1,300	1,360	1,400	1,400

Materials cost £20 per unit payable in the month of production.
Labour cost £12 per unit payable in the month of production.
Fixed expenses cost £3,000 per month payable in month of production.
Variable expenses cost £8 per unit payable in month following production.
Capital expenditure on equipment £15,000 is anticipated in December.
Bank account balance estimated in September is £4,000 overdraft (agreed bank limit £20,000).

Required:

Prepare a cash budget for the period September 19–4 to February 19–5 inclusive, showing the cash balance at the end of each month. Comment briefly on the forecast of cash flow.
3. You work for a firm of accountants who have just taken on a client, R. Snall & Co. In addition to the year end accounts, the client requires a 'cash forecast' and has supplied various data.

Information

● Opening cash (including bank) balance £2,000
● Production in units:

April	May	June	July	Aug.	Sept.	Oct.	Nov.	Dec.	Jan.	Feb.
480	540	600	640	700	740	760	680	620	520	500

- Raw materials used in production cost £10 per unit, which is payable in the month of production
- Direct labour costs of £17 per unit are payable in the month of production
- Variable expenses are £3 per unit, payable $\frac{2}{3}$ in month of production and $\frac{1}{3}$ in the month following production
- Sales at £40 per unit:

Mar.	April	May	June	July	Aug.	Sept.	Oct.	Nov.	Dec.
520	400	640	580	800	600	700	800	780	800

Debtors to pay their accounts in the month following the sale
- Fixed expenses of £1,200 per month payable each month
- Machinery costing £21,000 to be paid for in August
- Receipt of an investment grant of £7,000 is due in November
- Drawings to be £800 per month

Required:

(a) Prepare a schedule of payments for the six months July–December.
(b) Prepare a cash budget for the six months July–December.
(c) Prepare a draft memorandum to the client, commenting on the results of your cash budget.

4. Mr Ben is to open a retail shop on 1 July. He will put in £70,000 cash as capital. His plans are as follows:

Information

- On 1 July to buy and pay for premises £50,000, shop fixtures £7,000 and a motor van £4,000.
- To employ two sales assistants, each to get a salary of £350 per month, payable at the end of each month (ignore tax and NI).
- To buy the following goods:

	July	Aug.	Sept.	Oct.	Nov.	Dec.
(units)	500	540	660	800	900	760

● To sell the following goods:

	July	Aug.	Sept.	Oct.	Nov.	Dec.
(units)	345	465	585	705	885	945

● Units will be sold for £25 each. One-third of the sales are for cash, the other two-thirds being on credit. Customers are expected to pay their accounts in the month following that in which they buy the goods.
● Units will cost £16 for July to September inclusive and £18 thereafter. Suppliers are to be paid in the month of supply.
● Mr Ben will withdraw £700 per month as drawings.
● His other expenses are estimated at £400 per month payable in the month following.
● Stock at 31 December is to be valued £18 per unit.
● Provide for depreciation on shop fixtures at 10% p.a. and 25% p.a. on the motor van.

Required:

(a) Prepare a schedule of payments for July to December inclusive.
(b) Prepare a cash-flow budget for the period July to December inclusive, showing the balance at the end of each month.
(c) Prepare a budgeted profit statement for the 6 months ending 31 December.
(d) Prepare a budgeted balance sheet as at 31 December.
(e) Comment on the expected results of the business, making use of any financial indicators you may wish to illustrate your comments.

5. Smith & Jones wish to form a new private limited company in the name of S & J Co. Ltd. The new company is to commence its operations with effect from 1 July. The data estimated for the period from 1 July to 31 December is as follows:

● Smith is to put £50,000 into the business bank account on 1 July, and will be issued with 50,000 £1 ordinary shares. Jones will put £100,000 into the business bank account

on the same date and will be issued with 50,000 £1 ordinary shares and £50,000 of debenture stock at 12% interest.
● The sales will be on a credit basis and are estimated to be:

July	£25,000	Oct.	£50,000
Aug.	£45,000	Nov.	£45,000
Sep.	£65,000	Dec.	£60,000

All debtors are expected to settle their accounts two months after the month in which the goods are bought.

● Purchases, all on credit, are estimated to be:

July	£65,000	Oct.	£45,000
Aug.	£35,000	Nov.	£30,000
Sep.	£50,000	Dec.	£45,000

Creditors' payments are arranged to be paid in the month following the purchase.

● Wages and salaries are estimated to be £1,750 per month payable on the last weekday of each month.
● Smith and Jones will each draw director's fees of £1,000 per month payable on the last weekday of each month.
● Debenture interest is to be paid $\frac{1}{2}$ yearly, the first payment is due in December.
● Premises are to be purchased for £85,000 and paid for in August.
● Fixed costs are estimated to be £1,500 per month for the first four months of business and then increase by 20% thereafter. These costs are payable one month in arrears.
● Equipment is to be purchased on 1 July for £30,000, half of which is to be paid in July and the other in October.
   It is also to be depreciated by 20% per annum on the straight-line basis.
● Stock is estimated to be valued at £40,000 on 31 December.

Required:

(a) Prepare a cash-flow budget for the period July to December (inclusive).
(b) Prepare a budgeted profit and loss account and a balance sheet for the half year to 31 December.
(c) Prepare a draft report to Smith and Jones concerning the

importance of budgetary control. Include aspects such as purpose, functions and problems involving the preparation of budgets.

[BTEC National]

6. You work for a small manufacturing company which is developing a system of budgetary control and the following data is available:

Balance Sheet as at 31 May

	£	£	£
Fixed Assets			
Premises			50,000
Plant (orig. cost £10,000)			6,400
			56,400
Current Assets			
Stock	18,800		
Debtors	11,200		
Bank	600	30,600	
Current Liabilities			
Creditors	18,600		
Proposed dividend	2,000	20,600	10,000
			£66,400
Capital and Reserves			
£1 Ordinary Shares			50,000
Profit and loss account balance			16,400
			£66,400

Month	Credit sales	Cash sales	Credit purchases
May (actual)	£11,200	£5,600	£18,600
June (budgeted)	13,400	8,000	19,000
July (budgeted)	16,400	9,000	20,000
Aug. (budgeted)	16,000	9,000	10,400

● All trade creditors will be paid in the month following receipt of the goods and all trade debtors will take one month's credit

- On 1 June plant costing £5,000 is to be purchased (depreciation is charged on the straight-line basis of 10% p.a. on cost)
- The following monthly expenses, to be paid monthly, are estimated as: wages £1,800; general expenses £700
- Rent is £3,600 per year, payable in full in June, for the year to 30 June the following year
- The proposed dividend will be paid in July
- The sales margin is estimated at 20%

Required:

(a) Prepare a schedule of payments for June–August inclusive.
(b) Prepare a schedule of receipts for June–August inclusive.
(c) Prepare a cash-flow budget for June–August inclusive clearly showing the balance at the end of each month.
(d) Prepare a budgeted trading and profit and loss account for the three months, and a balance sheet as at 31 August.
(e) Comment upon the resulting profitability and liquidity position.

[BTEC National]

7. The following information relates to a businessman, D. Balfour, who will be starting his enterprise on 1 July, with £5,000. He has made a forecast for the next six months concerning his cash flow:

- Production will concern the making of an electrical component for the computer industry. His plan is to produce 500 units per month in the first six months.
- Sales: each unit has a selling price of £12.50. The sales estimate for 6 months to 31 December is:

July	Aug.	Sept.	Oct.	Nov.	Dec.
400	480	480	560	640	400 (units)

- Variable overheads (based on output) will be £1.50 per unit, payable in the month of production.
- Fixed costs will be £1,000 per month payable *after* the month of production.
- Production wages (direct) will be £3 per unit payable in the month of production.

- Salaries will be £500 per month until October but expected to rise by 10% in the months following.
- Equipment, to cost £8,000, will be purchased in September. 25% deposit will be paid in September with the balance to be paid equally in October and November.
- Materials will cost £2 per unit and suppliers will be paid in the month *after* the purchase.

All unit sales are on credit. Debtors are expected to pay in the month *following* their purchase, £5,000 was deposited in the business bank account on 1 July.

As Mr Balfour's financial assistant, you have been asked to prepare:

Required:

(a) A schedule of payments for the 6 months ending 31 December and a cash budget to cover the same period.
(b) An operating budget which will show the trading and profit and loss forecast for the 6 months ending 31 December and a forecast balance sheet as on 31 December (*Note*: closing stock to be valued at £6.50 per unit.)

[BTEC National]

8. You work as an assistant to a firm of accountants who deal with a variety of financial and management accounts. One of their new clients is a partnership called Johnston & Buckley who have submitted their proposed budget figures to you.

The new partnership takes effect from 1 July and its business is an estate agency. The data below is estimated for a six-month period, ending 31 December.

- Johnston and Buckley are to put £50,000 each into the business bank account on 1 July.
- The goodwill of the new business is estimated to cost a total of £24,000, payable in two instalments, 1 July and 1 October. Initially, this is to be treated as an intangible asset before eventually being written off.
- The forecast of sales commission is estimated to be as follows:

	£		£
July	12,500	Oct.	9,000
Aug.	13,000	Nov.	4,000
Sep.	12,000	Dec.	2,500

All clients are expected to settle their accounts one month after the sales go through.

● Johnson & Buckley will each draw £1,800 per month, but this will commence from August.
● Staff salaries are estimated to cost £1,650 per month, payable in the month.
● Light and heat is estimated to cost £140 quarterly, paid by standing order, the first quarter being due on 10 October.
● Premises are to be purchased for £75,000 and motor vehicles for £10,000, both to be paid for in August.
● Motor expenses are expected to be £200 per month, payable in the month.
● General expenses are estimated to be £350 per month, payable one month in arrears.
● Rates, water, insurance and other various costs are estimated to be £1,500 per month for the first 4 months of business, rising by 20% thereafter. These costs are payable one month in arrears.
● Equipment is to be purchased on 1 July for £30,000, half of which is to be paid immediately and the balance in October. It is to be depreciated by 20% per annum on the straight-line method. The motor vehicles are to be depreciated by 25% per annum on the reducing balance method.
● Advertising is to cost £1,000, the first half is due for payment on 1 September, the other on 1 December.
● Accounting fees are £390 to be paid for in August.
● It is estimated that the interest on bank overdraft and bank charges will accrue by £2,000 on 31 December.

The partnership agreement indicates that 10% interest p.a. is to be paid on capital and that profits are to be shared on a ratio of 60:40 in favour of Johnston.

Required:

(a) Prepare a cash budget for the six-monthly period July to December, inclusive.

(b) Prepare a budgeted profit and loss account* and a balance sheet for the half year to 31 December.

* There is no need for a trading account because this is an estate agency. Sales less expenses to arrive at net profit will be acceptable.

[BTEC National]

CHAPTER 36

Capital Investment Appraisal

In most organisations, management has certain criteria on which its investment decisions are taken, and there are usually more investment proposals than there is finance to back them.

Capital appraisal is a way whereby an organisation can decide which is the best way to invest its money when it comes to capital expenditure. Decisions are made on the basis of:

(a) the sum invested in a capital project;
(b) the estimated returns from the project; and
(c) the length of time the project is expected to last.

Three methods of capital appraisal will be discussed. These are:

● The 'pay-back' method
● The return on investment method (ROI)
● The discounted cash flow method (DCF)

The pay-back method

This method approaches capital appraisal from the point of view of how long it takes the project to pay back the original sum invested. If an organisation has £10,000 to invest, what could it do with the money? What would be the wisest choice? Note that capital appraisal calculations are only estimations, and what may look and seem a good investment on paper may turn out to be a disaster in practice!

An organisation could consider investing its money in new motor vehicles, or in stocks and shares, or in extending its premises or buying another business, and so on. Which choice would provide the best return in terms of value for money? How long is it intended that the investment last? A bit of a gamble certainly but, with large sums to be invested, investigation into how much the returns will yield is essential in order that management makes the best choice available at the time.

Consider two plans.

Plan A £10,000 invested in a vehicle appropriate to give driving lessons for a man wanting to be a driving instructor

Plan B £8,000 invested in a portfolio of securities estimated to produce about 20% (compound) return on investment

Which of the two plans will pay back the original investment in the quicker time? See Table 36.1.

TABLE 36.1 Comparison of Plans A and B

Year	Plan A Driving school vehicle £		Plan B Portfolio of securities £	£
	Initial Investment	10,000	8,000	
1	Estimated return		Estimated	
	(Revenue – expenses)	3,000	Return 20%	1,600	9,600
2	(Revenue – expenses)	3,200	"	1,920	11,520
3	(Revenue – expenses)	3,500	"	2,304	13,824
4	(Revenue – expenses)		$(9\frac{1}{2}$ months)	2,199	16,023
	(1 month)	300		8,023	
		10,000			

Analysis

Plan A is estimated to be the better of the two plans in monetary terms, taking 3 years and 1 month to recover the original investment of £10,000, whereas Plan B is estimated to take about $8\frac{1}{2}$ months longer to recover the initial sum.

Nothing is absolutely certain. These figures can only be estimations. How can it really be possible to calculate with 100% certainty what returns will be x number of years ahead? It may well be that the investor prefers Plan A because it gives him a job as well as income. On the other hand, he may prefer his capital doing the earning on its own.

TABLE 36.2   Capital project's profits

	£	£
Year 1	8,000	
2	12,000	
3	24,000	
4	20,000	
5	16,000	80,000
		5 years
	=	16,000 average

$$\text{ROI} \quad = \quad 16\%$$
$$\frac{(16{,}000 \times 100)}{100{,}000}$$

Return on investment method (ROI)

The ROI is the average profit for the project expressed as a percentage of the capital outlay. For example, a capital project investing £100,000 is estimated to have profits as shown in Table 36.2.

ROI is a fairly straightforward method, as is the pay-back method, but both these tend to ignore the fact that any money received in the future will be worth less than it is today. This brings in the third method, discounted cash flow.

Discounted cash flow (DCF)

When considering different investments with returns which are not the same, it should be noted that only by discounting the earnings to present values can any valid comparisons be made. For example, £100 due in one year is only worth £90.91 now if interest rates were 10% per annum:

Current value	£90.91
+ 10% interest	£9.09
	£100.00

£100 due in 2 years time is only worth £82.64 in today's money assuming interest rates of 10%:

Current value*	£82.64	
+ 10% interest	£8.26	Year 1
	£90.90	
+ 10% interest	£9.10	Year 2
	£100.00	

* Known as 'Net Present Value' (NPV).

The discounting of future earnings is really the opposite of compounding interest rates. For example, what will a sum of £100 amount to in 3 years' time if the interest rate is 8% per annum?

Compound Interest (CI) = $P(1 + R)^N$

P = principal invested
R = rate of interest
n = number of years invested

$$CI = 100(1.08)^3$$
$$= £125.97$$

Therefore, we could also say that a sum of £125.97 earned in a period of 3 years' time is worth only £100 in today's monetary value, given that the current rate of interest is 8%.

We can now look at the problem of future earnings at the going rate of interest and see what they are worth in today's value: that is, the present value of any future investment(s).

The formula to get the future earnings in today's money is:

$$NPV = \frac{FV}{(1 + R)^n} = \frac{125.97}{(1.08)^3} = £100$$

FV = future value

DCF is a most useful method when trying to evaluate alternative investment plans on capital expenditure projects. A business which is considering a number of different investment ideas will want to try to estimate the profit/returns on these projects. Therefore, in order to estimate the net benefits of these to the business, a useful way is to calculate their NPVs by using DCF at the current rates of interest.

Example

We have £5,000 to invest at current rates of interest of 8%. If this was deposited in a bank or building society over, say, 3 years it would earn £1,298 in interest (using the formula: $CI = P(1.08)^3$.

If we invested in Project A, it is estimated to earn £2,500 in 3 years or, in Project B, £3,000 in 4 years. Which would be the better of the two investment plans?

Both projects are obviously better than investing money in the bank at 8% but, in NPV terms, which is the better of the two?

Project A $\dfrac{2,500}{(1.08)^3}$ = £1,984

Project B $\dfrac{3,000}{(1.08)^4}$ = £2,205

Project B would therefore be the better of the two investments, as it has a higher NPV. However, it may be decided
that the return is good enough after 3 years and project A
chosen instead.

Although there are always going to be uncertainties in this
area of capital investments, who knows how quickly interest
rates change, or how estimates of profit can go disastrously
wrong? The DCF method at least attempts to calculate those
future returns in the light of today's monetary values.

Consider the following alternative proposals which have a different initial cost of investment. The business plans to borrow the
money at 12%, therefore this will be the discount factor. Project X
requires an investment of £60,000; project Y an investment of £80,000.
Using the formula method for each year's returns the results were
as shown in Table 36.2.

In project A, the gross returns of profit were £65,500, at NPV
worth £46,040. If the initial capital borrowed is deducted, this gives
a negative cash return of £13,960.

TABLE 36.2   Estimated annual returns*

Project	X £	NPV £	Y £	NPV £
Investment	60,000		80,000	
Estimated returns:				
Year 1	10,000	8,928	13,000	11,607
Year 2	12,000	9,566	15,000	11,958
Year 3	13,000	9,253	16,000	11,388
Year 4	14,500	9,215	18,000	11,439
Year 5	16,000	9,078	20,000	11,348
	65,500	46,040	82,000	57,740
Less initial capital		(60,000)		(80,000)
		(13,960)		(22,260)

* 12% interest rate.

In project B, the return at NPV was estimated at £57,740; again, a negative cash return of £22,260, even worse than project A. Obviously, it isn't worth going ahead with either of these projects if the returns are less than the initial capital borrowed.

However, we do not know what the borrowing was used for. If the investment was in plant, machinery and equipment, there could be some residual value to be considered. If the sale value of project A was, say, £20,000, then clearly there is an overall surplus of £6,040. If the residual value of project B was £30,000, the surplus would be £7,340.

If the investment had been on the purchase of two flats, there would still be the value of the properties to sell, and this would have to be taken into account when deciding which investment would be the best choice.

Using DCF tables (see Table 36.5)

Rather than use the formula for each of the year's returns, tables are available for ease of calculations. In our example:

Project A @ 12% (final column of table):

Year 1 10,000 × 0.893 discount factor = £8,930
Year 2 12,000 × 0.797 discount factor = £9,564
Year 3 13,000 × 0.712 discount factor = £9,256

The total NPV for project A = £46,044 and for project B = £57,744; both very close to the calculations by formula. Check the figures yourself.

Finally, if we look at these two projects with the pay-back and ROI methods:

(a) it takes approximately 5 years to pay back each investment so there is no distinct advantage;
(b) the average return on the investments also appears very similar, so again no distinct advantage;

$$\text{Project X} \quad \frac{\text{Total returns £65,500}}{\text{No. of years} \quad 5}$$

$$= \frac{£13,100}{£60,000} \times 100 = 21.83\%$$

$$\text{Project Y} \quad \frac{\text{Total returns £82,000}}{\text{No. of years} \quad 5}$$

$$= \frac{£16,400}{£80,000} \times 100 = 20.5\%$$

To conclude, there isn't an awful lot to choose between the two projects with either the pay-back or ROI methods. With DCF, project X is the better figure because its NPV after the initial capital is deducted has a more favourable negative balance.

However, it would be an advantage to know what the two investments were. If, for example, it was to purchase either one of two flats, other factors need to be considered, such as their location, their physical condition and the market which will prevail at the time of their disposal.

Example

Table 36.3 shows the net surplus returns for two projects which have an initial capital investment of £300,000.

TABLE 36.3   Net surplus returns for Projects A and B

	Project A £	Project B £
Earnings Year	100,000	80,000
2	120,000	100,000
3	100,000	100,000
4	60,000	100,000
5	40,000	40,000
Total return	420,000	420,000

Pay-back method

Project A pays back during the third year whereas Project B pays back during the fourth, and therefore on this basis it appears that Project A is the better of the two.

Return on investment

As the total return is the same (average return per year £84,000), both project A and B will give identical returns over the 5 years and therefore there is no basis for comparison here.

$$\text{ROI} \quad \frac{£84,000 \times 100}{£300,000} = 28\%$$

Discounted cash flow (assuming interest rates at 10%)

TABLE 36.4   DCF for Projects A and B

Year	Project A Earnings £	Project A NPV* £	Discount factor	Project B Earnings £	Project B NPV* £
0		300,000			300,000
1	100,000	90,900	0.909	80,000	72,720
2	120,000	99,120	0.826	100,000	82,600
3	100,000	75,100	0.751	100,000	75,100
4	60,000	40,980	0.683	100,000	68,300
5	40,000	24,840	0.621	40,000	24,840
		330,940			323,560

* The earnings are multiplied by the relevant discount factor.

DCF tables are available which relate to variable rates of interest over a period of time in years.

Project A has a superior earnings on a NPV basis compared with Project B, a difference of £7,380 in current terms, represented over the 5-year spell (£330,940 or £323,560).

The choice of appraisal method is left to management to decide, but many organisations will use more than one method. Generally, the larger the organisation the more sophisticated the range of methods used. The market standing of the organisation may well influence the choice. For example, a newly formed company may well look for the project with the fastest pay-back while an older company may seek a longer-term view with a steadier return. Note that if the NPV comes out less than the original investment, it is hardly worth considering the project at all. Table 36.5 gives a handy DCF reckoner.

TABLE 36.5 DCF tables from 1% to 12% over a period of 15 years

Future years	% Rate of discount 1	2	3	4	5	6	7	8	9	10	11	12
1	0.990	0.980	0.971	0.962	0.952	0.943	0.935	0.926	0.917	0.909	0.901	0.893
2	0.980	0.961	0.943	0.925	0.907	0.890	0.873	0.857	0.842	0.826	0.812	0.797
3	0.971	0.942	0.915	0.889	0.864	0.840	0.816	0.794	0.772	0.751	0.731	0.712
4	0.961	0.924	0.888	0.855	0.823	0.792	0.763	0.735	0.708	0.683	0.659	0.636
5	0.951	0.906	0.863	0.822	0.784	0.747	0.713	0.681	0.650	0.621	0.593	0.567
6	0.942	0.888	0.837	0.790	0.746	0.705	0.666	0.630	0.596	0.564	0.535	0.507
7	0.933	0.871	0.813	0.760	0.711	0.665	0.623	0.583	0.547	0.513	0.482	0.452
8	0.923	0.853	0.789	0.731	0.677	0.627	0.582	0.540	0.502	0.467	0.434	0.404
9	0.914	0.837	0.766	0.703	0.645	0.592	0.544	0.500	0.460	0.424	0.391	0.361
10	0.905	0.820	0.744	0.676	0.614	0.558	0.508	0.463	0.422	0.386	0.352	0.322
11	0.896	0.804	0.722	0.650	0.585	0.527	0.475	0.429	0.388	0.350	0.317	0.287
12	0.887	0.788	0.701	0.625	0.557	0.497	0.444	0.397	0.356	0.319	0.286	0.257
13	0.879	0.773	0.681	0.601	0.530	0.469	0.415	0.368	0.326	0.290	0.258	0.229
14	0.870	0.758	0.661	0.577	0.505	0.442	0.388	0.340	0.299	0.263	0.232	0.205
15	0.861	0.743	0.642	0.555	0.481	0.417	0.362	0.315	0.275	0.239	0.209	0.183

Questions

1. The following represents the net returns for two projects which have an initial capital investment of £200,000:

Project earnings	Year	X £	Y £
	1	40,000	80,000
	2	80,000	120,000
	3	120,000	100,000
	4	80,000	40,000
	5	60,000	20,000

Required:

(a) State which of the two projects pays back the quickest.
(b) Which of the two gives the better ROI?

2. Find out the NPVs of the following:

Capital return £	Time (years)	Interest rates at time %
(a) 5,000	4	10
(b) 30,000	6	12
(c) 100,000	5	8

3. The following are the net surplus figures for three projects which have an initial investment of £400,000:

Project earnings Year	A £	B £	C £
1	80,000	160,000	100,000
2	160,000	240,000	150,000
3	240,000	200,000	250,000
4	160,000	80,000	120,000
5	100,000	20,000	100,000

Required:

State which project you would recommend and why. (The organisation has a target return on capital of 10%.)

4. The following are the net surplus figures for two projects which have an initial capital investment of £500,000:

Project earnings Year	L £	M £
1	80,000	60,000
2	120,000	180,000
3	280,000	320,000
4	200,000	200,000

State which project you consider the better and why. (Company target return is 12%.)

5. Calculate the NPV of a pension plan which will earn £20,000 per annum in ten years' time at interest rates expected to average 12%.

6. A house is purchased in 1985 for £62,000 and sold in 1990 for £120,000. If interest rates average 11% per annum, in the 5 years, what is the real increase in value of the property taking NPV into consideration?

7. An investment of £30,000 is expected to earn a sum of £33,460 in Special Bonds over a period of 4 years. This is to be compared with an alternative investment in Unit Trusts, earning £42,580 over a period of 6 years. If interest rates are estimated to be 12% per annum, which of the two investments will give the best return at NPV?

PART VII

FURTHER ACCOUNTING ISSUES

Control Accounts

When an enterprise grows, inevitably the paper work grows with it. The accounting system needs to expand, and the work has to be sub-divided. Instead of having a single ledger, there may become a need for several ledgers (nominal, sales and bought ledgers).

This is particularly the case where a firm may have numerous debtors and numerous creditors. These will be removed from the mainstream of the general ledger and *personal* ledgers will be used to accommodate debtors and creditors. Some large firms will have several hundred of these personal accounts and therefore a need arises for such individual accounts to be cross-checked with a 'master' control balance. The control accounts are held in the general ledger and represent the *totals* of debtors and creditors. Whatever happens to an individual personal account, the total effect will be reflected in the control accounts. The control accounts not only cross-check the individual accounts; they are also used for management purposes. For example, if the total liability for creditors is required, the control account should give the answer without the necessity of adding each of the creditors' balances.

Control accounts are only a cross-check with individual balances for debtors and creditors. [See Chapters 7 and 8.]

If the individual debtors, for example, do not balance with debtors control, detailed checking is required to find the errors. Thus the trial balance should be easier to balance because the control accounts have 'controlled' individual personal accounts. They are arithmetical proofs of individual ledgers for debtors and creditors.

| **Examples** |
---

1. *Sales Ledger Control* (Debtors control a/c)
The following are balances from the ledgers of ABC Company, and Table 37.1 shows a debtors control account.

	£
Sales ledger Dr. balances at 1 June	7,300
Credit sales (June)	12,500
Cash/cheques received from debtors	11,500
Returns from customers	400
Discounts allowed to customers	280
Debtors' cheques returned from bank marked 'R/D'	
– cheques dishonoured	330
Sales ledger Dr. balance at 30 June	7,950

TABLE 37.1   Debtors control account

		Dr.	Cr.	Balance
June	1 Balance			7,300 Dr.
	30 Sales	12,500		19,800
	Bank/cash		11,500	8,300
	Discounts		280	8,020
	Returns inward		400	7,620
	Cheques dishonoured	330		7,950
	Balance (Sales Ledger)			7,950

Note: The 30 June balance from the sales ledger is verified with the control balance above. FINE!

2. *Purchases Ledger Control* (Creditors Control account)
This is shown in Table 37.2.

		£
Purchases ledger Cr. balances at 1 June		12,500
Credit purchases for June		19,750
Cheques paid to supplies		18,200
Discounts received		478
Returns to suppliers		545
Debit note from suppliers, resulting from under-charge		50
Credit balances from purchases ledger at 30 June		13,427

TABLE 37.2 Creditors control account

		Dr.	Cr.	Balance
June 1	Balance			12,500
30	Purchases		19,750	32,250
	Bank	18,200		14,050
	Discounts received	478		13,572
	Returns outward	545		13,027
	Under-charge		50	13,077
	Balance (B/L)			13,427

Note: There is a discrepancy of £350 between the purchases ledger (£13,427) and the control a/c (£13,077). Somewhere an error has been made and records must be checked until it is found.

Any transaction which affects either a debtor (in the sales ledger), or a creditor (in the bought ledger) must be reflected in the appropriate control account. The control accounts are totals of respective debtors and creditors.

Sometimes it happens that a debtor overpays his account or, conversely, a creditor is overpaid, and this temporarily gives rise to

a debtor's account with a credit balance, or
a creditor's account with a debit balance

This will be reflected in the control accounts and these may have both debit and credit balances at the beginning and end of the account (see Table 37.3).

	Dr. £	Cr. £
1 March		
Sales ledger control balances	5,275	130
Bought ledger control balances	210	2,500
31 March		
Sales ledger control balances	5,725	85
Bought ledger control balances	140	1,900
Credit sales		14,250
Credit purchases	9,600	
Cheques, cash from customers	13,140	
Returns inward	175	
Returns outward		830
Bad debts	380	
Cheques, cash to suppliers		9,240

Note: Contra entries between debtors and creditors £60. These refer to accounts 'set off' against each other: for example, where a debtor is also a supplier of goods. One sum may be set off against another by debiting the creditor and crediting the debtor.

TABLE 37.3   Sales ledger control a/c

Dr.					Cr.
1 Mar.	Balance b/d	5,275	1 Mar.	Balance b/d	130
31	Sales	14,250	31	Bank/cash	13,140
	Balance c/d	85		Returns In	175
				Bad debts	380
				Transfer (contra)	60
				Balance c/d	5,725
		19,610			19,610
1 Apr.	Balance b/d	5,725	1 Apr.	Balance b/d	85

Note: The credit balance of £85 b/d has its balance c/d on the debit side. The net figure owing by debtors = £5,640.

TABLE 37.4   **Sales ledger control account**

		Dr. £	Cr. £	Balance £
1 Mar.	Balances	5,275	130	5,145 Dr.
31	Sales	14,250		19,395
	Bank/cash		13,140	6,255
	Returns inward		175	6,080
	Bad debts		380	5,700
	Contra		60	5,640*
1 Apr.	Balances (sales ledger)	5,725	85	5,640 Dr.

* Net result of Dr. and Cr. balances.

TABLE 37.5 **Purchase ledger control account**

Dr.					Cr.
1 Mar.	Balance b/d	210	1 Mar.	Balance b/d	2,500
31	Bank/cash	9,240	31	Purchases	9,600
	Returns outward	830		Balance c/d	140
	Contra	60			
	Balance c/d	1,900			
		12,340			12,340
1 Apr.	Balance b/d	140	1 Apr.	Balance b/d	1,900

Note: The debit balance of £140 has its corresponding c/d balance on the debit side. The net figure owing to creditors = £1,760.

If the control account was recorded in the running balance method the sales ledger control account would appear as in Table 37.4 and the purchase ledger control account would appear as in Table 37.6.

TABLE 37.6   Purchase ledger control account

		Dr. £	Cr. £	Balance £
1 Mar.	Balances	210	2,500	2,290 Cr.
31	Purchases		9,600	11,890
	Bank/cash	9,240		2,650
	Returns outward	830		1,820
	Contra	60		1,760*
1 Apr.	Balances (B/L)	140	1,900	1,760 Cr.

* Net result of Dr. and Cr. balances.

Questions

1. From the following details for the month of January, pre-pare Freddy Smith's sales ledger control account and purchases ledger control account.

   The opening balances in the purchases ledger and sales ledger were £4,420 credit and £2,420 debit respectively.

	£
Credit purchases from suppliers	36,480
Credit sales to customers	30,500
Cash paid to creditors	36,840
Receipts from trade debtors	26,175
Discounts received	825
Discounts allowed	720
Purchase returns	815
Debit note to debtor	119
Bad debt written off	730
Credit balances in purchases ledger transferred to sales ledger	180
Returns inward	414

On 31 January, the purchases ledger had a balance of £2,240 and the sales ledger £5,080. Check these figures with your control accounts.

2. The following information has been taken from the books of Harry Jones relating to the year ended 31 December.

	£
Sales ledger balance 1 January	2,246
Bought ledger balance 1 January	1,608
Credit sales	38,127
Cash sales	9,750
Purchases on credit	27,121
Receipts from customers	27,560
Payments to suppliers	19,422
Discount allowed	810
Dishonoured cheques from customers	925
Returns outward	316
Returns inward	1,427

Required:

Prepare the sales and bought ledger control accounts for the year ended 31 December.

3. The following figures for the month of May relate to the sales ledger of George Harrison:

Balances brought forward from:	£
1 May	13,740
31 May	16,996
Sales	12,450
Returns inward	150
Cash from customers	9,208
Discounts allowed	245
Bad debts	222
Cheques returned from bank marked insufficient funds	442
Cash sales	4,173
Debit notes to customers	154
Interest charged to customers (on overdue accounts)	58
Debit balances in sales ledger transferred to purchases ledger	42

Required:

(a) Prepare the debtors control account for the month of May.
(b) From the figures you have prepared, what conclusions do you arrive at?

4. You work as an accounts clerk for a manufacturing company, Rock Ltd, and have to write up the control accounts for the month of February. Details of transactions are as follows:

	£
Feb. 1 Purchase ledger (credit balance)	26,100
Purchase ledger (debit balance)	460
Sales ledger (debit balance)	51,400
Sales ledger (credit balance)	630
Total transactions in the month:	
Bad debts written off	420
Credit purchases	37,590
Cash purchases	5,200
Returns outwards	510
Returns inwards	1,480
Cheques paid to creditors	24,270
Cheques received from debtors	47,360
Contras	800
Dishonoured cheques (i.e., from debtors)	140
Credit sales	74,900
Cash sales	9,250
Discount allowed	1,840
Discount received	960
Cheque received from a supplier	460

Required:

(a) Prepare the sales ledger control account for February.
   [The sales ledger schedule total was £73,910.]
(b) Prepare the purchase ledger control account for February.
   [The purchase ledger schedule total was £37,200.]
(c) Describe one other system of internal check which can be used to ensure accuracy of posting.
   Which of the two control accounts agreed?

How much was the discrepancy in the control account which failed to balance?

[Institute of Bankers]

5. You work as an accounts clerk for a wholesale company, Zarak Ltd, and have to write up the control accounts for the month of August. Details of transactions are as follows:

	£
Aug. 1 Sales ledger (debit balance)	48,000
Sales ledger (credit balance)	520
Purchase ledger (credit balance)	24,200
Purchase ledger (debit balance)	350
Total transactions in the month:	
Credit sales	61,740
Cash sales	5,210
Credit purchases	34,720
Cash purchases	3,905
Discount allowed	760
Discount received	980
Returns inwards	1,750
Returns outwards	430
Cheques received from debtors	51,720
Cheques paid to creditors	23,890
Dishonoured cheques (i.e., from debtors)	880
Contras	750

Required:

(a) Prepare the sales ledger control account for August. [Sales ledger schedule total was £54,300.]
(b) Prepare the purchase ledger control account for August. [Purchase ledger schedule total was £32,520.]
(c) Briefly explain why control accounts are used. Which of the two control accounts did not balance with the schedule?

6. You are an assistant in the accounts office responsible for nominal ledger entries in a firm of Wholesalers, Smith & Jones. The following information is available to you from

which it is proposed to prepare Control accounts for both sales and bought ledgers for the month ended 31 March.

Balances at 1 March: £

Bought ledger balances	(Cr.)	149,940
Bought ledger balances	(Dr.)	320
Sales ledger balances	(Dr.)	311,100
Sales ledger balances	(Cr.)	425
Sales		130,155
Purchases		65,250
Bad debts written off		225
Dishonoured cheques		485
Discount to customers		310
Discount from suppliers		395
Cash repayments to customers		120
Contra entries between debtors and creditors		765
Returns inward		2,155
Returns outward		580
Cheques, cash from customers		127,255
Bills payable (Dr. P/L control)		150
Cash sales		1,575
Cheques, cash to creditors		62,350
Cheques received from suppliers		125
An increase in the provision for bad debts		277

At 31 March, the following balances were taken from the personal ledgers:

Sales ledger balances	(Dr.)	309,545
	(Cr.)	140
Bought ledger balances	(Cr.)	152,655
	(Dr.)	150

Required:

(a) Prepare the sales ledger control account and the purchases ledger control account for the month of March.
(b) Comment on any discrepancy that may appear in your figures.

[BTEC National]

7. As a member of the accounting team of ABC Co. Ltd you are asked to prepare the control accounts of both the sales ledger and bought ledger for the month ended 31 March.

The following were balances taken from the books of ABC Co. Ltd for the month of March:

	£
1 March	
Bought ledger Cr. balance	12,860
Bought ledger Dr. balance	225
Sales ledger Dr. balance	34,755
Sales ledger Cr. balance	372
31 March	
Purchases journal	23,805
Sales journal	37,215
Discount received	621
Discount allowed	558
Cheques received from customers	29,950
Cash/cheques to suppliers	22,140
Contra entries between debtors and creditors	420
Cash purchases	1,285
Bad debts written off	470
Returns outward journal	950
Dishonoured cheques from customers	155
Interest charged to customers on overdue accounts	85
Returns inward journal	1,472
Received from creditor in respect of overpayment	25
Bills receivable (Cr. S/L control)	1,150
Cash refund to customer	50
Provision for bad debts	750

The balances extracted from the personal ledgers of ABC Co. Ltd on 31 March were:

		£
Bought ledger	Cr. balance	12,484
Bought ledger	Dr. balance	150
Sales ledger	Dr. balance	38,124
Sales ledger	Cr. balance	456

Required:

(a) Prepare the bought ledger control account and the sales ledger control account for the month ended 31 March.
(b) From the figures you have prepared for (a), what conclusions can you draw?
(c) Briefly explain by means of memorandum to the junior accounts clerk, why in some business enterprises there is a need to keep control accounts.

[BTEC National]

8. The trial balance as at 1 January of Highground Dealers Limited included the following items:

	Debit £	Credit £
Purchases ledger control account	245	152,498

The following relevant information has been provided by the company for the first three months:

	Purchases at list prices £	Purchases returns at list prices £	Cash paid £	Discounts received £	Purchases ledger debit balances at month end £
January	142,000	4,200	157,760	2,510	180
February	98,000	5,700	126,150	1,870	276
March	112,000	6,500	85,700	1,430	355

The company's stock in trade increased from £30,000 on 1 January to £38,000 at 31 March.

Highground Dealers Limited normally obtains a gross profit of 40% on the cost of all goods sold; however, in February the company sold, at half the normal sales price, a quantity of goods which it had bought for £10,000.

The company obtains its purchases at list prices less 10%.

On 28 February the following account in the sales ledger was closed by the transfer of the balance to K. Marden's account in the purchases ledger:

K. Marden   £3,000 debit

Required:

(a) Prepare the purchases ledger control account of Highground Dealers Limited for each of the three months to 31 March.
(b) Prepare a computation of the gross profit for the three months ended 31 March of Highground Dealers Limited.

[Association of Accounting Technicians]

CHAPTER 38

The Trial Balance, Journal and Suspense Accounts

The trial balance is used to check the arithmetical accuracy of the double-entry system. At frequent intervals, ledger account balances are listed to see if total debits equal total credits. If the trial balance fails to balance, the ledger accounts need to be checked to locate the errors and to correct them.

The trial balance is not a fool-proof system because some types of error will not be disclosed:

- Errors of compensation
- Errors of principle
- Errors of omission
- Errors of commission
- Errors of original entry

The following are examples of errors made in the ledgers where the use of a trial balance has failed to disclose them.

An error of compensation

This refers to an error where the *same* mistake has been made to both sides of a transaction.

8/6: A cheque of £451 was received from a debtor, T. Smith, but was entered incorrectly as £415 in the records:

Entry: Dr. Cash Book £415
            Cr. Smith a/c (Sales Ledger) £415

Both debit and credit entries have recorded the same error and the trial balance would fail to disclose it and therefore would still balance.

Correction of error

> Dr.   Cash Book   £36
>   Cr.   Smith a/c   £36
> (making up the under-stated £415 to the correct £451)

An error of principle

This refers to an error where a transaction has been posted to the wrong group of accounts. An asset account incorrectly posted as an expense is a good example.

10/6: Office equipment bought on credit from ABC Suppliers Ltd, at £2,500, was incorrectly posted to the purchases account instead of office equipment:

> Entry: Dr.   Purchases a/c   £2,500
>   Cr.   ABC Suppliers Ltd   £2,500

Correction of error

> Dr.   Office Equipment a/c   £2,500
>   Cr.   Purchases a/c   £2,500
> (this will clear the over-stated purchases of £2,500 and correctly increase the asset by £2,500)

An error of omission

This refers to an error where a transaction has been omitted altogether – a sales or purchase invoice mislaid, a gas or electricity bill neglected or missing. No transaction would be entered in the books and the trial balance would fail to disclose the omission and still balance, of course.

14/6: A sales invoice to J. Jackson had been misplaced and no entries were made in the books:

> Entry: Dr.   J. Jackson a/c (Sales Ledger)   £200
>   Cr.   Sales a/c   £200

Correction of error

When the invoice has been found, the above entry is required in the sales and nominal ledgers.

An error of commission

This refers to an error where a transaction has been posted to the wrong account, but to the same group of accounts – a nominal account like a gas bill incorrectly posted to another nominal account like office expenses. The trial balance would still balance because both are debit entries to the expense account.

26/6: A gas bill of £185 had been incorrectly entered in office expenses instead of light and heat account:

Entry: Dr. Office Expenses a/c £185
          Cr. Cash Book £185

Correction of error

Dr. Light and Heat a/c £185
  Cr. Office Expenses a/c £185
(this clears the over-stated office expenses by £185 and correctly increases the light and heat account by £185)

An error of original entry

This refers to an error which has been made on an original document, such as an invoice or credit note which may have omitted or miscalculated something. The trial balance would still balance because the wrong figures would be used for both debit and credit entries.

30/6 An invoice for £380 + VAT sent to F. Jones, a customer, where VAT had been calculated at 15% instead of 17.5%:

Entry: Dr. F. Jones £380 + £57 VAT = £437.000
          Cr. Sales   £380
               VAT   £ 57

Correction of error

When the error was located, the VAT had to be increased by £9.50 (17.5% of £380 = £66.50)

Dr. F. Jones £9.50
  Cr. VAT   £9.50

The location of errors

All these types of error will not be disclosed by the trial balance because both debit and credit entries are equal and therefore the total columns will also be equal. The trial balance is still an essential part of the double-entry system because, even though it has its limitations, a cross-check with the ledger balances is needed to ensure their arithmetical accuracy. What has to be borne in mind is that not all trial balances are correct, even though the totals may match up.

If the trial balance fails to balance, then the error or errors must be located and correcting entries made. It may be necessary to comb through the ledgers carefully to check for any arithmetical inaccuracies or any obvious double-entry error (for example, posting two debits or two credits for the same transaction). It may be necessary to check back to the subsidiary books such as the day books, Cash Book or Petty Cash Book, to ensure that the correct figures were posted to the relevant ledger accounts because there may have been an incorrect addition to a column of figures.

The journal

The journal is used for those transactions which are normally outside the scope of the other subsidiary books.

When the book-keeping system was in its early stages of development, the journal acted as the only subsidiary book in use. All transactions were entered in the journal prior to ledger posting. Later on, as the book-keeping system developed, it was found that the use of the journal as the only book of original entry was inadequate. There were so many repetitious entries to be made that separate subsidiary books were soon in use. The day books gave the answer for sales, purchases and returns, and the Cash Book for those transactions of a cash/cheque nature.

The journal has now a lesser role than when it was first in use. It is left with the function of *providing some original entry for those miscellaneous types of transaction* that do not quite 'fit in' to the other subsidiary books.

For example, purchasing plant and machinery on credit. This cannot be entered in the purchases day book because the asset, plant and machinery is not for resale; neither can it be entered in the Cash Book because the transaction is not in cash. The answer: use the journal.

The journal is commonly used in the following circumstances:

(a) the correction of errors;
(b) the opening entries in a new accounting period;
(c) the transfer of balances between accounts including revenue and expenses to trading and profit and loss;
(d) the writing-off of bad debts;
(e) the purchase or sale of fixed assets;
(f) providing adjustments to the final accounts such as de-preciation, accruals, pre-payments, provision for bad debts, discounts, etc.;
(g) making any other adjustments to accounts which are outside the scope of other subsidiary books.

Presentation of the journal

The journal has a debit and credit column to facilitate posting to the ledgers. The debit entry is always entered first and the credit entry, by tradition, is slightly indented. There is also a narrative (comment) after the entry, giving a brief explanation of what the entry was for. Study the two examples of year-end adjustments given below:

(a) The motor van is to be depreciated by 20% by reducing balance method. As on 30/6, cost £2,500, Provision for depreciation £500.
(b) The provision for bad debts is to be adjusted to equal 5% of debtors. As on 30/6, debtors £12,420, Provision for bad debts £300.

Journal: Examples of year-end adjustments

Date	Account details	Folio	Dr.	Cr.
30/6	Profit and Loss a/c, depreciation of motor van	NL 80	400	
	Provision for depreciation of motor van	NL 30		400
	Depreciation @ 20% reducing balance at year end			
30/6	Profit and loss a/c, provision for bad debts	NL 80	321	
	Provision for bad debts	NL 45		321
	Provision adjusted to equal 5% of debtors			

Figure 38.1 represents the Journal, showing the corrected errors of G. Harrison (that is, the five errors which the trial balance failed to disclose). Ledger entries are shown in Tables 38.1 and 38.2.

Figure 38.2 gives further examples of the journal entries recorded for:

(a) the commencement of a new accounting period, 1 January;
(b) the transfer of revenue and expense accounts and stock account to trading and profit and loss account, 31 December;
(c) the purchase of a motor van on credit on 31 December

The suspense account and the correction of errors

The purpose of using a suspense account is to balance the trial balance temporarily. When errors are made which produce an incorrect trial balance because the totals disagree, a suspense account may be entered in the trial balance by inserting the difference between the trial balance totals. A suspense account is opened in the nominal ledger and is written off when the error or errors are located. The journal is used to make the appropriate corrections. An example is given in Figure 38.3.

Errors must eventually be found and corrected. When they are found, journal entries are necessary to correct them and the appropriate accounts adjusted to their correct value. The following errors were located in the books of G. Harrison:

(a) sales were under-valued by £100 in cash sales when posted to sales account;
(b) general expenses of £40 had been omitted from Cash Book posting to the nominal account, 'general expenses';
(c) the purchase of furniture of £300 was wrongly debited to the purchases account;
(d) discount received of £100 had not been posted to the discount account in the nominal ledger.

Required:

(a) Open a suspense account in the nominal ledger on 30 June with an opening balance of £160 Cr.
(b) Make the appropriate journal entries to correct the errors (see Figure 38.3).
(c) Adjust the accounts in Harrison's nominal ledger (see Table 38.4).

FIGURE 38.1 Correction of Errors

THE JOURNAL: G. Harrison

	Folio	Dr.	No. 2	Cr.	
		£		£	
June					
8 Cash Book (Bank)		36			
T. Smith Sales Ledger				36	
Error of compensation.					
£451 cheque entered as £415.					
10 Office Equipment		2,500			
Purchases				2,500	
Error of principle:					
An asset incorrectly entered					
as an expense					
14 J. Jackson (Sales Ledger)		200			
Sales				200	
Error of omission:					
Sales invoice No. 2176 omitted					
no entries in the books.					
26 Light & Heat		185			
Office Expenses				185	
Error of commission:					
Gas bill incorrectly entered					
as office expense.					
30 F. Jones		9	50		
VAT				9	50
Error of original entry					
VAT charge at 15% instead of 17.5%					

TABLE 38.1 Error correction: sales ledger

		Folio	Dr. £	Cr. £	Balance £
T. Smith a/c					
June 1	Balance				451 Dr.
2	Bank	CB 5		415	36
8	Bank	J 2		36	—
J. Jackson a/c					
June 1	Balance				50 Dr.
14	Sales	J 2	200		250
F. Jones a/c					
June 1	Balance				120 Dr.
15	Sales VAT		437		557
30	VAT	J 2	9.5		566.50

TABLE 38.2 Error correction: nominal ledger

		Folio	Dr. £	Cr. £	Balance £
Office Equipment a/c					
June 1	Balance				1,000 Dr.
10	Purchases	J 2	2,500		3,500
Light & Heat a/c					
June 1	Balance				350 Dr.
26	Office exps.	J 2	185		535
Office Expenses a/c					
June 1	Balance				595 Dr.
26	Light & Heat	J 2		185	410
VAT a/c					
June 1	Balance				40 Cr.
15	Sales			57	97
30	Sales	J 2		9.5	106.50
Sales a/c					
June 1	Balance				590 Cr.
14	Jackson	J 2		200	790
15	Jones	J 2		380	1,170

FIGURE 38.2   G. Harrison's Journal

			Dr.		Cr.	
			No. 3			
			£		£	
(a)	Jan. 1	Premises	12,000			
		Fixtures & Fittings	1,500			
		Equipment	2,480			
		Motor Van	1,000			
		Stock	1,500			
		Debtors	765			
		Bank	400			
		Prepaid Expenses	120			
		Creditors			950	
		Accrued Expenses			88	
		Mortgage on Premises			8,000	
		Bank Loan			1,000	
		Capital: G. Harrison			9,727	
			19,765		19,765	
		Assets, Liabilities & Capital				
		of G. Harrison on 1 January ...				
(b)	Dec. 31	Sales	11,000			
		Trading a/c			11,000	
		Trading a/c	5,000			
		Purchases			5,000	
		Transfer of sales and purchases				
		to trading				
		Trading a/c	1,000			
		Stock (1/1)			1,000	
		Stock (31/12)	1,500			
		Trading a/c			1,500	
		Transfer of stock (beg.) and				
		stock (end) to trading				
		Profit & Loss a/c	884			
		Salaries			884	
		Transfer of expense to				
		profit & loss				
(c)	Dec. 31	Motor Van	7,500			
		Jake's Garage			7,500	
		Purchased on credit				
		over 3 years				

TABLE 38.3   **Extract of trial balance taken from the books of G. Harrison 30 June**

Account	Dr. £	Cr. £
Sales		18,600
Purchases and	12,500	
Furniture and fittings	4,200	
General expenses	150	
Discount		35
	36,660	36,500
Suspense		160
	36,600	36,600

(d) If Harrison had a net profit on 30 June of £8,500, how would the above errors affect the profit?

(e) one of Harrison's debtors, J. Smith, had been written off as bad. He owed £250. Show how this would be entered in the journal.

How profit is affected

If the trading and profit and loss account had already been prepared before the errors were located, the correction of the above would have changed the value of net profit:

Net profit (before errors)			£8,500	
Add	Sales (undercast)	£100		
	Discount received	£100		
	Purchases	£300	500	£9,000
Less	General expenses	£40		40
Net profit (after errors)				£8,960

FIGURE 38.3   G. Harrison's Journal Entries

JOURNAL: *G. Harrison*

			Dr.		No. 4 Cr.	
			£		£	
June						
30	Suspense a/c		100			
	Sales				100	
	Sales a/c under-valued					
30	General Expenses		40			
	Suspense a/c				40	
	Failed to complete double-entry					
	from Cash Book					
30	Furniture & Fittings		300			
	Purchases				300	
	Error of Principle, Furniture					
	incorrectly posted to purchases.					
30	Suspense a/c		100			
	Discount Received				100	
	Failed to complete double-entry					
	from Cash Book					
30	Bad Debts		250			
	J. Smith				250	
	Debtor written off as bad					

TABLE 38.4   G. Harrison's nominal ledger

	Folio	Dr. £	Cr. £	Balance £
Suspense a/c				
June 30 Trial balance			160	160 Cr.
Sales	J 4	100		60 Cr.
General expenses	J 4		40	100 Cr.
Discount	J 4	100		—
Sales a/c				
June 30 Balance				18,600 Cr.
Suspense	J 4		100	18,700
General Expenses a/c				
June 30 Balance				150 Dr.
Suspense	J 4	40		190
Furniture & Fittings a/c				
June 30 Balance				4,200 Dr.
Purchases	J 4	300		4,500
Purchases a/c				
June 30 Balance				12,500 Dr.
Furniture and fittings	J 4		300	12,200
Discount Received a/c				
June 30 Balance				35 Cr.
Suspense	J 4		100	135 Cr.

Questions

1. Make the appropriate journal entries to correct the following errors:

   (a) an amount of £300 had been included in the salaries account for a job which involved repairing the proprietor's garage (J. Jones);
   (b) a cheque of £350 from P. Smith had been credited to R. Smith in error;
   (c) the purchase of calculators for the office staff, costing £125, had been posted to the purchases account;
   (d) an invoice for rates owing to Wimborne DC for £178 had been mislaid.

2. On 1 January, Tom Jones had the following assets and liabilities:

	£
Premises	20,000
Vehicle	500
Equipment	2,100
Stock	1,860
Debtors	675
Mortgage on premises	15,000
Bank (overdrawn)	450
Creditors	1,155

Prepare an opening journal entry of 1 January showing Tom Jones's assets, liabilities and capital as at this date.

3. Make the necessary journal entries for the following:

(a) a debtor, Harry Smith, failed to pay his account of £256 and it was decided to write the debt off;
(b) a machine valued £500 was purchased on credit terms from Equipment Supplies Co. Ltd;
(c) the motor vehicle (cost £2,800) was to be depreciated by 25% of cost;
(d) sales £14,500 and purchases £9,850 are to be transferred to the trading account for gross profit calculation;
(e) a gas bill of £85 had been wrongly posted to the rates account.

4. An extract of Harry's trial balance:

	Dr. £	Cr. £
Suspense a/c		247
	20,534	20,534

Subsequently the following errors were found:

● Goods £285 to R. Smith had been posted to J. Smith in error
● Accounting equipment sold for £600 credited to sales account

- Cash discount of £8 allowed to J. Jones and credited to him, but no entry was made to the discount account
- The addition of the sales day book was under-cast by £200
- Salaries accrued £55 at the end of the previous year had not been brought forward to the new accounting period
- A sales invoice of £275 had been misplaced. No entries had been made

Required:

(a) Journal entries necessary to correct the books.
(b) The suspense account entries.

5. The accounts of a business were extracted on 30 June as follows:

	£	£
Bank account	1,245	
Capital account		34,900
Stock	3,400	
Premises	20,000	
Furniture and fittings	900	
Wages and salaries	15,400	
Office expenses	1,060	
Purchases	13,900	
Sales		21,900
Drawings	3,800	
Debtors	2,600	
Creditors		3,230
	62,305	60,030

It was subsequently discovered that the following errors had been made in the listing of the balances:

- The bank account was overdrawn £1,245
- A sum of £200 drawn out by the owner for his personal use had been included under 'office expenses'
- Purchases on credit totalling £1,000 had not passed through the books
- The balance of the discount allowed account, £160, had been omitted

- £2,400 included under wages and salaries and £600 included under purchases represented extensions to premises
- Office cash of £55 had been omitted from the list of balances

Required:

(a) A suspense account in the ledger.
(b) A corrected trial balance for the month ending 30 June.

6. You work as a senior accounts clerk for R. Underwood, and have been assisting in the preparation of the final accounts. The trial balance as at 30 April did not agree, and a suspense account was opened for the difference. The following errors have now been traced:

- The total of the returns outward book, £248, had not been posted to the ledger
- An invoice received from a supplier, A. Biggs, for £200 had been mislaid, so entries for this transaction had not been made
- A payment for repairs to vehicles, £72, had been entered in the vehicle repairs account as £70
- When balancing the account of G. Bradford in the ledger, the debit balance had been brought down in error as £28, instead of £82
- £100 received from the sale of office equipment had been entered in the sales account
- A private purchase of £230 by R. Underwood had been included in the business purchases
- The purchase day book was undercast by £92

Required:

(a) Show the requisite journal entries to correct the errors.
(b) Write up the suspense account showing the correction of the errors.
(c) If the originally calculated profit was £10,500, show your calculation of the correct figure.
(d) State four types of errors which do not affect the agreement of the trial balance, giving an example of each.

7. Hawkers & Pedlar have produced a trial balance for the year ended 31 March, which does not balance. A suspense account of £507 cr. was opened for the difference. An examination of the firm's books disclosed the following errors:

- An invoice from R. Pitman, amounting to £300 for goods purchased, has been omitted from the purchase day book and posted direct to the purchases account in the nominal ledger but not entered in the purchase ledger
- The sales day book has been under-cast by £450
- Discount allowed for the month of March, amounting to £242, has not been posted to the nominal ledger
- A cheque, amounting to £540, for the purchase of furniture and fittings had been correctly entered in the Cash Book but entered in the nominal ledger account as £450
- A sales invoice, amounting to £730, sent to J. Knight, has been omitted from the books completely
- A payment, amounting of £233, for heating and lighting had been correctly entered in the Cash Book but posted, in error, to the motor expenses account at £322
- An invoice regarding the purchase of a new printer included £180 in respect of computer stationery; the total invoice value had been posted to the equipment account in the nominal ledger

Required:

(a) Write up the journal entries, where necessary, to correct the errors. (Narratives not required.)
(b) Draw up the suspense account.
(c) If the net profit for the year excluding the seven errors was £22,031, produce a statement showing the corrected profit figure.

8. The draft trial balance of James McLippie and Son as at 30 April did not agree and the difference was posted to a suspense account. Subsequent investigation of the accounts revealed the following errors of £1,352 debit.

- The discount received column in the cash book had been over-cast by £100
- J. Stanley, a customer, had not been credited with £8

discount although this had been correctly entered in the Cash Book
- The sales book had been over-cast by £900
- An invoice made out (correctly) for £45 in respect of sales made to H. Purcell had been recorded in the sales book as £54 (this is quite apart from the error in the sales book referred to above)
- The purchases book had been under-cast by £360
- Goods returned from J. Blow, a customer, had been recorded in the returns inward book as £108; in fact, the value of the goods returned had been subsequently agreed with the customer at £88 but no adjustment had been made in the accounting records
- VAT (at 15%) amounting to £15 collected on cash sales of £100 had not been entered in the VAT column in the Cash Book; instead the sales had been recorded in the cash column as £115

Required:

(a) Prepare journal entries to show how the above errors would be corrected.
(b) The suspense account entries.
(c) If the profit had been calculated at £13,564 before the errors were disclosed, what is the profit for the year after correcting the above errors?

[Association of Accounting Technicians]

9. The trial balance of J. Sharp, a retailer, does not balance. You are asked to look through his accounts and subsequently you do find the errors below. The trial balance of the proprietor on 30 June was as follows:

	Dr. £	Cr. £
Premises	20,000	
Motor van	500	
Equipment	2,100	
Stock	1,860	
Debtors	675	
Creditors		1,155

Capital, J. Sharp		12,500
Bank		455
Sales		35,750
Purchases	20,195	
General expenses	1,250	
Wages	3,970	
Suspense		690
	50,550	50,550

Errors found:

- A piece of equipment worth £500 had wrongly been posted to purchases account
- A gas bill of £85 had been paid but had not gone through any of the books
- Discount allowed, £68, had not been posted to the ledger
- Sales were under-cast by £800
- A cheque from a debtor (R. Smith), £150, had been recorded as £105 in his account but correctly in the corresponding account
- The total from the returns inward account, £87, had not been posted to the ledger

Required:

(a) Prepare suitable journal entries to correct the above errors and write up the suspense account.
(b) Prepare the corrected trial balance of J. Sharp as on 30 June.
(c) State which of the above errors would not be found by the trial balance.

[Associated Examining Board]

10. The trial balance as at 31 March of Allsquare Engineers Limited did not balance and therefore a suspense account was opened showing a credit balance of £549. Unfortunately, the errors in the accounts were only traced after the completion of the draft final accounts for the year ended 31 March which showed the following results:

	£
Profit on manufacturing*	12,760
Gross profit	23,410
Net profit	9,746

* Manufactured goods are transferred to the trading account at whole sale prices.

The following errors were discovered:

2 January	Credit sales to T. Sparkes of £1,200 not recorded in the sales day book.
15 January	A receipt of £500 from K. Dodds, debtor, was recorded in the Cash Book only.
February	Discounts received of £376 have been recorded correctly in the purchases ledger control account and then debited in the discounts allowed account.
	Discounts allowed of £224 have been recorded correctly in the sales ledger control account and then credited in the discounts received account.
31 March	Payments to suppliers totalling £21,257 have been debited in the purchases ledger control account as £21,752.
	Depreciation for the year ended 31 March on manufacturing equipment was correctly recorded in the provision depreciation account but not posted to the manufacturing account. The correction of this error cleared the suspense account.

Required:

(a) Write up the journal entries to correct the above errors.
(b) The suspense account as it would appear after the correction of all the accounting errors.

[Association of Accounting Technicians]

CHAPTER 39

Incomplete Records

Many small business organisations do not keep a full set of adequate accounting records because they have neither the time nor the necessary accounting experience to do so.

Sole traders, in particular, keep only partial or 'incomplete records' and rely on the services of an accountant to write up their accounts at the end of the financial year. This is required for the purpose of calculating the taxation due to the Inland Revenue and also to have some idea of how the business has performed.

Some financial data are available, of course, because all businesses need to have essential information such as:

- How much they owe suppliers
- How much customers owe them
- How much cash is available
- How much VAT is payable to Customs & Excise

and so forth. Because of these reasons the accountant is able to use the financial information which may be available, like invoices, credit notes, till rolls, bank statements, cheque stubs, receipts for cash, etc., to prepare a set of accounts (that is, the trading and profit and loss account and balance sheet).

From incomplete financial data, therefore, it is still possible to reconstruct accounts by relating and piecing them together in order to prepare the final accounts.

Procedure

The procedure for reconstructing accounts is varied. Many accountants like to use a work sheet which shows a logical sequence of workings extending to a trial balance. Any adjustments such as accruals and pre-payments may also be included, and the final accounts can then be prepared. The following method is a basically simple procedure which pieces the accounts together without necessarily resorting to a work sheet.

1. Establish the owner's capital (net worth) at the beginning of the financial year by listing his assets against his liabilities.
2. Prepare a bank/cash summary in the form of a simplified Cash Book which will identify receipts and payments of money into and out of the business. The accountant would do this from records such as bank statements, till rolls, cheque stubs, etc.
3. Establish the sales and purchases for the year from the reconstruction of debtors' and creditors' accounts. Financial data available to the accountant could come from invoices, credit notes, cheque stubs, statements, cash receipts, etc.
4. Prepare the trading and profit and loss accounts including items for adjustments, and the balance sheet for the year under review.

The role of the accountant in this capacity is to prepare the final accounts of the business as accurately as possible from the given financial data available. He does not audit the accounts. The accounts may be checked by other accountants expressing, in their view, the trueness and fairness of them.

Example 1
---

1. *Establishing the owner's capital*
   E. T. Gibbs is a sole trader in business as an electrician. He uses his garage as a small workshop but most of his business is on contract with clients which takes him to various parts of the locality where he works.
   On 1 January, his statement of affairs at the beginning of the financial year was as shown in Table 39.1.
2. *Preparing a bank/cash summary*
   From bank statements, till rolls, cheque book records and other sources, it is possible to draw up a bank summary to establish where money has come from and where it has gone, as well as calculating the bank/cash balance at the end of the financial year. E. T. Gibbs's records provided the bank summary shown in Table 39.2 on 31 December.
   The figures from the bank summary are used to help reconstruct the final reports. At the end of the financial year, E. T. Gibbs had £3,055 in the bank, an increase of £1,085 from the beginning of the year.

TABLE 39.1 E. T. Gibbs: Statement of affairs, 1 January

	£	£
Tools and equipment	250	
Motor vehicle	950	
Debtors	2,150	
Bank balance	1,970	
Stock	3,180	8,500
Creditors		2,800
Capital 1 January		5,700

TABLE 39.2 E. T. Gibbs: Bank summary

Receipts	£	Payments	£
Bank balance (1 Jan.)	1,970	Payments to suppliers	30,125
Receipts from customers	39,750	Personal drawings	3,880
Cash sales	2,185	Wages (assistant's)	4,375
		General expenses	560
		Motoring expenses	835
		Insurance	160
		Telephone and rates	395
		Light and heat	170
		Advertising	350
		Bank balance (31 Dec.)	3,055
	43,905		43,905

3. *Establishing sales and purchases for the year*
As receipts from debtors and payments to suppliers do not necessarily correspond with the sales and purchases totals, it is therefore necessary to construct the debtors' and creditors' accounts in order to arrive at the sales and purchases totals (see Tables 39.3 and 39.4). The accountant may get this information from invoices sent to customers and invoices received from suppliers plus credit notes, bank statements, cheque stubs, and so forth. Many sole traders actually write on invoices and statements the dates when settlement of accounts occurred, including any cash discounts paid or received.
E. T. Gibbs had for the year ended 31 December:

TABLES 39.3 Sales for the year

S/L Control a/c Dr.		£	Cr.	£
Jan. 1	Balance	2,150	Bank/cash	39,750
			Discount allowed	650
Dec. 31	Sales*	41,125	Returns inward	200
			Dec. 31 Balance	2,675
		43,275		43,275

* To reconstruct debtors in order to find the sale, the opening Dr. balance of debtors (£2,150) is substracted from the total of the Cr. column (£43,275) = £41,125.

TABLE 39.4 Purchases for the year

P/L Control a/c Dr.	£	Cr.		£
Bank/cash	30,125	Jan. 1	Balance	2,800
Discount received	875			
Returns outward	1,350	Dec. 31	Purchases*	32,720
Dec. 31 Balance	3,170			
	35,520			35,520

* To reconstruct creditors in order to find the purchases, the opening Cr. balance of creditors (£2,800) is subtracted from the total of the Dr. column (£35,520) = £32,720.

Once the sales and purchases have been reconstructed from debtors and creditors, they can be transferred to the trading account.

● Discount allowed   £ 650
● Discount received   £ 875
● Returns inward   £ 200
● Returns outward   £1,350
● Closing debtors   £2,675
● Closing creditors   £3,170

4. *Preparing the final accounts: trading, profit and loss account and balance sheet*
The only further information required before preparing the final accounts is to check on any adjustments such as accruals, pre-payments and depreciation. The stock position at the end of the financial year must also be calculated by the owner.
Table 39.5 shows information that was available relating to E. T. Gibbs on 31 December.

TABLE 39.5 E. T. Gibbs data

	£
Stock	3,246
Electricity owing	35
Depreciation	
tools and equipment and	20
Motor vehicle	100
Debtors' balances	2,675
Creditor's balances	3,170

Table 39.6 gives the trading and profit and loss accounts and Table 39.7 the balance sheet of E.T Gibbs.

TABLE 39.6 Trading and profit and loss account, E. T. Gibbs, for year ended 31 December

	£	£
Sales (credit)	41,125	
Cash sales	2,185	
- Returns inward	(200)	43,110
Cost of Sales		
Stock (1 Jan.)	3,180	
+ Purchases	32,720	
- Returns outward	(1,350)	
	34,550	
- Stock (31 Dec.)	3,246	31,304
Gross profit		11,806
Expenses		
Wages (assistant)	4,375	
General expenses	560	
Motor expenses	835	
Telephone and rates	395	
Light and heat (+ £35 accrued)	205	
Advertising	350	
Discount allowed	650	
Depreciation (tools, motor)	120	
Insurance	160	7,650
		4,156
+ Discount received		875
Net Profit		5,031

TABLE 39.7 Balance sheet: E. T. Gibbs: as at 31 December

	£	£	£
Fixed Assets			
Tools and equipment	250		
– Depreciation	20		230
Motor vehicle	950		
– Depreciation	100		850
			1,080
Current Assets			
Stock	3,246		
Debtors	2,675		
Bank	3,055	8,976	
Less			
Current Liabilities			
Creditors	3,170		
Accrued expenses	35	3,205	
Working capital			5,771
			6,851
Financed by			
Capital			
E. T. Gibbs (Jan. 1)	5,700		
+ Net Profit	5,031		
	10,731		
– Drawings	3,880		6,851

Note: Mr Gibbs made £5,031 profit calculated from the figures he forwarded to his accountant. For personal use, he withdrew £3,880 during the financial year, thereby increasing his net worth in the business to £6,851, an increase of £1,151.

The profit of £5,031 will be the basis of his tax liability to the Inland Revenue, less the appropriate taxable allowances as per his tax coding. His tax liability is therefore

Profit	£ 5,031	
– Allowances	£ 4,200	
Taxable income	£ 831	@ 25%tax
Tax payable		= £207.75

Example 2

You have just completed a business studies course and have been asked by an old school friend, J. Starky, to have a look at his books. J. Starky has been running a retailing business for the past year and needs to know what his 'state of affairs' is for taxation purposes.

J. Starky's Summary Cash Book for the year ended 31 March 19–5 is as shown in Table 39.8.

His assets and liabilities were as shown in Table 39.9.

TABLE 39.8 J. Starky's Summary Cash Book

	£		£
1/4/19–4 Balance b/f	10,000	Payments to	
Cash sales	50,000	suppliers	157,340
Cash received from		Cash purchases	7,880
debtors	219,500	Rent	22,500
		Rates	900
		Salaries	13,080
		Wages	30,500
		General Expenses	22,000
		Drawings	15,000
		31/3 Balance c/f	10,300
	£279,500		£279,500

TABLE 39.9 Assets and liabilities

	£ 1 April 19–4	£ 31 March 19–5
Creditors for goods	28,400	30,010
Rent owing	1,000	500
Stock	54,000	53,000
Debtors	46,600	55,700
Pre-paid rates	170	295
Fixtures and fittings	10,000	10,000
Vehicle	7,500	7,500

In preparing the accounts you decide:

● To depreciate the vehicle by $33\frac{1}{3}$%
● To depreciate the fixtures and fittings by 10%
● To make a provision for bad debts of 5%
● To assume (based on J. Starky's estimate) that J. Starky has taken *£1,000 worth of goods* from the business for his own use.

Solution

Calculation of sales and purchases: as per the requirements of the matching (accruals) concept we should include the cost of purchases made in the year and the value of sales generated in the final accounts – which is not the same as payments made and cash and bank receipts.

S/L Control a/c

1/4 Balance b/f	46,600	Cash from debtors	219,500
\ credit sales =	228,600*	31/3 balance c/f	55,700
	275,200		275,200

Total sales = £228,600 + £50,000 (cash sales) = £278,600

* i.e., the balancing figure.

Control account to find value of purchases:

P/L Control a/c

Payments to suppliers	157,340	1/4 Balance b/f	28,400
31/3 Balance c/f	30,010	∴ Credit purchases	158,950*
	187,350		187,350

Total purchases = £158,950 + £7,880 (cash purchases) = £166,830.

Table 39.10 shows Starky's trading and profit and loss account, and Table 39.11 shows his balance sheet.

TABLE 39.10   J. Starky: trading and profit and loss account for year ending 31 March, 19–5

	£	£	£
Sales			278,600
Less cost of sales:			
Opening stock		54,000	
Purchases	166,830		
Less goods for own use	(1,000)	165,830	
		219,830	
Closing stock		53,000	166,830
Gross Profit			111,770
Rent (22,500 − 1,000 + 500)*		22,000	
Rates (900 + 170 − 295)*		775	
Salaries		13,080	
Wages		30,500	
General expenses		22,000	
Depreciation: Vehicle		2,500	
Depreciation: Fixtures and fittings		1,000	
Provision for bad debts (5%)		2,785	94,640
Net Profit			£17,130

* Both rent and rates figures have to be adjusted in respect of opening and closing accruals and prepayments.

TABLE 39.11 J. Starky: balance sheet as at 31 March, 19–5

	£ Cost	£ Depn.	£ Net
Fixed Assets			
Fixtures and fittings	10,000	1,000	9,000
Vehicle	7,500	2,500	5,000
	17,500	3,500	14,000
Current Assets			
Stock	53,000		
Debtors (55,700 - 2,785)	52,915		
Pre-payments	295		
Bank	10,300	116,510	

TABLE 39.11 *continued*

	£	£	£
Current Liabilities			
Creditors	30,010		
Accrued rent	500	30,510	
			86,000
Working Capital			£100,000
Financed by			
Capital			98,870
Add profit			17,130
Less drawings			16,000
			£100,000

Questions

1. The balance sheet of Harry Jones, a trader, was as follows on 1 January.

	£		£
Capital	7,000	Equipment	2,900
Creditors	560	Stock	3,100
		Debtors	950
		Balance at Bank	610
	7,560		7,560

The information given below relates to Harry's business transactions for the year to 31 December.

	£
Payments to suppliers	39,950
Payments received from customers	49,645
Bank drawings for private use	2,310
Salaries and wages	4,165
Expenses	2,242
Discounts allowed	150
Discounts received	585

At 31 December the stock in trade was valued at £4,850. Expenses paid in advance amounted to £200, trade debtors to £4,845 and trade creditors to £3,550. Depreciation of equipment is at 15% per annum.

Required:

(a) The total account for debtors and the total account for creditors for the year, thus ascertaining the sales and purchases for the year.
(b) A summarised bank account for the year.
(c) The trading and profit and loss account for the year ended 31 December.
(d) The balance sheet at 31 December.

2. The following information relates to Freddy Smith at the commencement of the accounting period 1 January.

	£	
Stock	3,200	debit balance
Debtors	3,850	debit balance
Creditors	2,460	credit balance
Rates in advance	70	debit balance
Capital	6,500	credit balance

Smith did not keep proper books of account but from his cheque stubs it was possible to draw up a summary of his bank details for the year:

	£		£
(1/1) Balance (beg.)	1,840	Rent, rates	1,050
Cash received	68,375	Suppliers for	
from customers		materials, etc.	43,955
Interest from		Light and heating	545
bank	150	Wages, salaries	8,825
		Insurances	490
		Misc. expenses	2,240
		Motoring expenses	1,985
		Advertising	650
		(31/12)	
		balance	10,625
	70,365		70,365

At the end of the year the following balances were extracted:

31 December	£
Stock	4,750
Debtors	8,242
Creditors	5,465
Rates in Advance	55

Freddy also took £5,000 from the bank for his own Christmas present at the end of the year!

Required:

Prepare a trading and profit and loss account for the year ending 31 December and a balance sheet as at that date.

3. The following information was extracted from the books of Jack Rogue at 31 December.

	£		£
(1/1) Opening balance	1,120	Cash paid to suppliers	40,800
Cash received		Rent and rates	2,155
from credit		Lighting and heating	325
customers	58,750	Salaries	6,450
		Insurances	120
		General expenses	1,145
		Drawings	6,525
		Motor vehicle expenses	875
		Closing balance (31/12)	1,475
	59,870		59,870

Balances	1 January £	31 December £
Stock	3,955	4,555
Debtors	3,525	4,625
Creditors	3,410	4,150
Motor vehicle	2,750	2,500
Insurance paid in advance	60	75

Required:

Jack's trading and profit and loss account for the year, and balance sheet as at 31 December.

4. The following balances represent the accounts of F. Smith, a sole trader who does not keep a full set of accounts:

	1 January £	31 December £
Premises	25,000	25,000
Tools and equipment	2,150	
Motor vehicle	2,500	1,950
Debtors	1,750	2,780
Stock	2,565	3,425
Bank	—	
Mortgage on premises	15,250	13,295
Creditors	3,150	4,825
Overdraft	1,765	—

Smith's receipts and payments for the year were as follows:

Receipts	£	Payments	£
From credit customers	42,720	Light and heat	350
Cash sales	5,400	Wages to assistant	3,240
		Rates	390
		Insurance	270
		Telephone	120
		Drawings	5,160
		Payments to suppliers	33,470
		New equipment	2,000
		Motor expenses	450
		Miscellaneous expenses	375

Further information

● Discount to customers £545; discount received from suppliers £425
● Tools and equipment to be depreciated 10%, including new purchases
● Debtors are to be provided against going bad by 5% (from 31 December balance)

- Wages to assistant owing £55
- The owner took stock for personal use valued at £750
- The mortgage repayment (£1,955) has not been included under payments for the year

Required:

(a) A summarised bank account for the year ended 31 December. (Assume all cash is paid direct into the bank and all payments are by cheque.)
(b) A trading and profit and loss account for the year ended 31 December, and a balance sheet as at that date.

5. The following information relates to the books of J. Archer, who has been running a retailing business for the past year and who needs to know what his state of affairs is for taxation purposes.

   The summary of his receipts and payments for the year ended 31 March 19–5 was:

	£		£
Bank balance (1/4/19–4)	10,000	Payments to suppliers	157,340
Cash sales	50,000	Cash purchases	7,880
Receipts from debtors	219,500	Rent and rates	22,900
		Salaries	13,580
		Wages	30,500
		General expenses	20,500
		Light and heat	1,500
		Telephone	850
		Motor expenses	2,150
		Drawings	12,000
		Bank balance (31/3/19–5)	10,300
	279,500		279,500

J. Archer's assets and liabilities were:

	1 April 19–4 £	31 March 19–5 £
Creditors	28,400	30,010
Rent owing		500
Stock	54,000	53,000
Debtors	46,600	55,700
Pre-paid rates		295
Fixtures and fittings	10,000	9,000
Motor vehicle	7,500	6,450

In preparing the accounts it is decided to:

● Depreciate the fixtures by a further 10% *of the 31/3/ 19–5 value*
● Make a provision against bad debts of 5%

Required:

(a) Prepare a trading and profit and loss account for the year ended 31 March 19–5 and a balance sheet as at that date.
(b) Make a brief assessment of Archer's trading performance using any accounting ratios you think are necessary.

6. Jack Jones is a retailer who does not keep a proper set of accounts. He keeps a record of receipts and payments through the bank, and documents (such as invoices and bills) relating to the business.
   On 1 January, his statement of affairs showed the following balances (other than his bank account):

	£
Premises	15,000
Fixtures and fittings	2,500
Motor van	1,350
Debtors	2,750
Stock	3,000
Creditors	2,600
Bank loan (5 years)	4,000

His summarised bank account for the financial year:

Receipts	£	Payments	£
Bank balance (Jan. 1)	2,000	Wages (casual)	1,550
Shop takings + receipts		Light and heat	295
from debtors	47,250	Advertising	300
Commission	500	Rates and water	250
		Personal drawings	2,875
		Payments to suppliers	38,550
		Motor van expenses	750
		Shop equipment	1,300
		Telephone	290
		Bank + interest charges	215
		General expenses	500
		Repairs to property	700
		Bank balance (Dec. 31)	2,175
	49,750		49,750

Note: Discount allowed to customers £225.
Discount received from suppliers £550.

Further information

● Balances at the end of the financial year, 31 December, other than bank account:

Debtors	£1,800
Creditors	£2,465
Stock	£3,815

● The owner took £800 goods for his own use during the year
● Depreciation: the motor van is revalued to £1,000.
    fixtures are to be reduced by 20%
    premises remain at cost
● Rates in advance £40; advertising pre-paid £50; casual wages due to be paid £75
● A provision for bad debts to equal 5% of current debtors is to be made

Required:

(a) Prepare a statement of affairs on 1 January to show Jack Jones's financial position.
(b) Reconstruct debtors' and creditors' accounts in order to calculate sales and purchases for the financial year.
(c) Prepare the trading and profit and loss account for the year ended 31 December; also a balance sheet as at this date.
(d) Write a short report to Jack outlining the financial results for the year. Use any accounting ratios you feel appropriate.

[BTEC National]

7. You work as a self-employed accountant and are about to draw up the final accounts for a client, D. White. D. White does not keep a full set of accounts but has kept a receipts and payments book for the year.

Data extracted on 31 December

Summary of Receipts and Payments Book

	£		£
Balance b/f (1/1)	1,488	Cheques to	
Cheques from		Suppliers	148,992
Debtors	208,500	Salaries and wages	27,800
		Rent and rates	6,700
		Lighting and heating	1,420
		Misc. expenses	5,255
		Drawings	14,900
		Purchase of	4,000
		equipment	
		Balance c/f	921
	209,998		209,988

	January £	December £
Stock	11,900	12,850
Debtors	15,210	16,930
Creditors (for purchases)	11,840	13,120
Accruals for salaries and wages	490	560
Pre-payment of rates	810	900
Fixed assets	56,000	?

Note: Fixed assets are to be depreciated by 15%.

Required:

(a) Prepare the trading and profit and loss Account of D. White for year ending 31 December.
(b) Prepare the balance sheet of D. White as on 31 December.

[Institute of Commercial Management]

8. Justin Harris carries on a retail business and does not keep his books on a double entry basis. The following particulars have been extracted from his books.

	1 July 19–4 £	30 June 19–5 £
Fixtures and fittings	48,000	?
Stock in trade	32,000	36,000
Trade debtors	4,000	6,400
Trade creditors	14,000	12,000
Cash in hand	720	1,440
Balance at bank	9,800	8,800

At 1 July 19–4, the only outstanding expense items were lighting accrued, £160, and rates in advance, £400.

At 30 June 19–5, there was £1,000 owing for rent, rates had been paid in advance by £480, wages accrued amounted to £360, and there was a stock of heating fuel valued at £600.

The following cash and bank transactions took place during the year ending 30 June, 19–5

	£
Carriage inward	3,360
Wages	18,360
Sundry expenses	1,000
Printing, stationery and advertising	2,240
Rent and rates	5,000
Heating and lighting	2,760
Cash received from customers	205,000
Cash paid for purchases	160,400
Cash withdrawn from business for own use	12,160

During the year Harris had taken goods from his business for his own consumption amounting to £30 per week, and had not paid any money into the business for them.

Depreciation of fixtures and fittings to be charged at 10%. There have been no sales or purchases of fixtures and fittings during the year.

Required:

Prepare a trading and profit and loss account for the year ended 30 June 19–5, and a balance sheet at that date.

[Institute of Commercial Management]

9. You work for a firm of accountants which prepares the accounts for Murry Limited. During the night of 2nd June, Murry Limited suffered a fire which destroyed all the company's stock records and a quantity of stock. The stock was covered by insurance against loss by fire. You have been asked by your firm to assist with preparing the insurance claim for Murry Limited.

You have ascertained the following information:

	On 1 January £000s	On 2 June £000s
Stock at cost	264	?
Trade debtors	78	94
Trade creditors	90	106

The following transactions took place between 1 January and 2 June.

	£000s
Cash purchases	34
Payments to creditors	548
Cash received from debtors	628
Cash sales	160
Discount received	20
Discount allowed	16

The physical stock-take, carried out first thing in the morning on 3 June, showed the remaining stock (undamaged) to have a cost value of £182,000. Murry Limited operate a standard margin of 30%, i.e., a gross profit of 30% on selling price.

Required:

(a) Calculate the total value of purchases for the period.
(b) Calculate the total value of sales for the period.
(c) Use the information in tasks (a) and (b) to calculate the cost of the damaged stock.

10. The assets and liabilities as at the close of business on 31 October 19–4 of J. Patel, retailer, are summarised as follows:

	£	£
Motor vehicles:		
At cost	9,000	
Provision for depreciation	1,800	
		7,200
Fixtures and fittings:		
At cost	10,000	
Provision for depreciation	6,000	
		4,000
Stock		16,100
Trade debtors		19,630
Cash		160
		£47,090
Capital — J. Patel		30,910
Bank overdraft		6,740
Trade creditors		9,440
		£47,090

All receipts from credit customers are paid intact into the business bank account, whilst cash sales receipts are banked after deduction of cash drawings and providing for the shop till cash float. The cash float was increased from £160 to £200 in September 19–5.

The following is a summary of the transactions in the business bank account for the year ended 31 October 19–5.

Receipts	£	Payments	£
Credit sales	181,370	Drawings	8,500
Cash sales	61,190	Motor van (bought	
		1 May 19–5)	11,200
		Purchases	163,100
Proceeds of sale		Establishment and	
of land owned		administrative expenses	33,300
privately		Sales and distribution	
by J. Patel	16,000	expenses	29,100

Additional information for the year ended 31 October 19–5:

● A gross profit of $33\frac{1}{3}\%$ has been achieved on all sales
● Bad debts of £530 have been written off during the year
● Trade debtors at 31 October 19–5 were reduced by £8,130 as compared with a year earlier
● Trade creditors at 31 October 19–5 amounted to £12,700
● Depreciation is to be provided at the following annual rates on cost:

Motor vehicles	20%
Fixtures and fittings	10%

● Stock at 31 October 19–5 has been valued at £23,700

Required:

A trading and profit and loss account for the year ended 31 October 19–5 and a balance sheet as at that date for J. Patel.

[Association of Accounting Technicians]

CHAPTER 40

The Extended Trial Balance

The trial balance is an indication or test of arithmetical accuracy of the double-entry system as we saw Chapter 37.

At the end of a financial period, the trial balance is extracted from the accounts of the general ledger in readiness for the preparation of the final accounts. All adjustments relating to the end of the period must also be taken into account to ensure the correct matching of revenue with expenses and to correspond with SSAP 2, Disclosure of Accounting Policies (accounting concepts).

The extended trial balance (ETB) is a form of a worksheet where extra columns are provided alongside the trial balance figures in order to accommodate any adjustments or changes which may be required for the preparation of the final accounts. Indeed, the final two columns of the ETB are the profit and loss account and the balance sheet. The worksheet is then used to type up the formal financial statements for the client or the party requesting them.

An abbreviated example of the layout of the ETB is shown in Table 40.1.

The relevant empty columns of the ETB will be used for:

(a) Adjustments column: making any adjustment to the trial balance figures. This would include the correction of errors disclosed, writing off bad debts, making provisions for depreciation, bad debts or discounts and for adjusting figures for VAT, etc.

(b) Creditor/accruals column: the inclusion of any outstanding expenses which will increase expenses for the period or any figures which will affect an increase/decrease in creditors.

(c) Debtors/pre-payments column: any expenses paid in advance,

TABLE 40.1 ETB layout

Folio description	Trial balance		Adjustments	
	Dr.	Cr.	Dr.	Cr.
Premises	57,500			
Equipment	23,000			
Provision for depn		6,000		
Motor vehicle	8,000			
Provision for depn,		2,000		
and continues across the page:				

Creditors/ accruals	Debtors/ pre-payments	Profit and loss account		Balance sheet	
		Dr.	Cr.	Dr.	Cr.

reducing the expense for the period, and any figure which will affect an increase/decrease to debtors.

(d) Profit and loss column: entering all revenue and expenses, including the opening and closing figures for stock.

(e) The balance sheet column: entering all asset, liability and capital accounts, including all adjustments affecting them.

In practice, the ETB uses extra columns for cash and banking transactions.

Example

This is taken from question 7 (Arthur Jones) in Part III. Chapter 15 of the text, and will indicate how the ETB is prepared. This example is used because it has the type of adjustments which we can readily identify and use, and also you can check the answer with that given in the text and with the answer provided from the ETB. See Figure 40.1.

The continuation of Arthur Jones's extended trial balance with further adjustments/errors

Let us assume that, when the trial balance was prepared, fixtures and fittings valued at £3,750 had to be included. This would mean that the trial balance would fail to balance by

684

FIGURE 40.1 Arthur Jones: data

Folio	Description	Trial balance Dr.	Trial balance Cr.	Adjustments Dr.	Adjustments Cr	Creditors/ Accruals	Debtors/ pre-payments	Profit and loss account Dr.	Profit and loss account Cr.	Balance sheet Dr.	Balance sheet Cr.
	Premises	57,500								57,500	
	Equipment	23,000								23,000	
	Prov. for depn		6,000		3,400						9,400
	Motor van	8,000								8,000	
	Prov. for depn		2,000		1,500						3,500
	Stock (1/1)	8,300						8,300			
	Purchases	30,800			800			30,000			
	Sales		66,600						66,600		
	Returns inward	700						700			
	Returns outward		900						900		
	Wages	16,500				550		17,050			
	Carriage inwards	500						500			
	Carriage outwards	400						400			
	Commission received		500						500		
	Bank interest	350						350			
	Lighting, heating	1,650						1,650			
	Postage, stationery	600					95	505			
	Insurance	1,200						1,200			
	Telephone	500						500			
	Rent received		750			180			930		
	Debtors	7,000								7,000	
	Provision for bad debts				700						700
	Creditors		11,750								11,750
	Bank	1,950								1,950	
	Discount allowed	100						100			
	Bad debts	450						450			
	Capital account		71,000	800							70,200
	Depreciation – eqpt			3,400				3,400			
	Depreciation – van			1,500				1,500			
	Bad and doubtful debts			700				700			
	Stock (31/12)								9,500	9,500	
	Profit and loss a/c							11,125			11,125
		159,500	159,500	6,400	6,400	730	95	78,430	78,430	107,225	107,225
								11,125		11,125	

Notes: 1. The adjustments column imposes the double-entry principle; for example, depreciation is debited to profit and loss as an expense and the provision for depreciation is credited in the balance sheet. The totals must agree.
2. The accruals and pre-payments columns simply list those items to be adjusted and are totalled. Totals need not agree.
3. The profit and loss account indicates debits for expenses and credits for revenue. The difference between these equals the net profit (£11,125). Totals must agree.
4. The balance sheet has assets as debits and liabilities, capital and profit as credits. Totals must agree.

this sum and a suspense account must be opened with a balance of £3,750 credit.

Subsequently, the errors have been located and the following information is revealed:

● Discount received, £80, had not been posted to the ledger account
● A debtor, Harry Smith, had to be written off as bad (£150); the 10% provision still remains but needs adjustment
● The bank account of £1,950, in effect, was a credit balance
● Purchases in the day book had been under-cast by £650
● The VAT account in credit of £420 had been omitted from the list of balances
● A stationery invoice had £9 inclusive of VAT which had not been posted to the VAT account

Required:

(a) Enter the furniture and fittings £3,750 and suspense account £3,750 in the ETB. £3,750 also needs to be recorded as a *debit* in the adjustments columns to counter the corrections to be made (see Figure 40.2).
(b) Prepare the appropriate journal entries for the above transactions, and write up the suspense account (see Table 40.2 and 40.3).
(c) Show the effect of these transactions on the net profit (see Table 40.4).
(d) Prepare the appropriate entries in the ETB (see Figure 40.2).

Try to follow the adjustments and corrections line by line in the ETB. Finally, if we were to prepare a draft copy of the financial statements (that is, the profit and loss account and balance sheet) from the ETB, it should be relatively straightforward. See if you can prepare it yourself, then check it with the Tables 40.5 and 40.6.

The ETB is used widely in accounting practice, particularly for clients' accounts. As a worksheet, it summarises all the relevant figures which have been calculated, either from ledger accounts or, more likely, from the various business documents provided by the client for the financial year. Although it looks a little complicated by its multi-columns, once it has been used a number of times it provides an appropriate record of

FIGURE 40.2 Arthur Jones's ETB: solutions

Folio	Description	Trial balance Dr.	Trial balance Cr.	Adjustments Dr.	Adjustments Cr.	Creditors/ accruals	Debtors/ pre-payments	Profit and loss account Dr.	Profit and loss account Cr.	Balance sheet Dr.	Balance sheet Cr.
	Furniture and fittings	3,750								3,750	
	Premises	57,500								57,500	
	Equipment	23,000								23,000	
	Prov. for depn		6,000		3,400						9,400
	Motor van	8,000								8,000	
	Prov. for depn		2,000		1,500						3,500
	Stock (1/1)	8,300						8,300			
	Purchases	30,800		650	800			30,650			
	Sales		66,600						66,600		
	Returns inward	700						700			
	Returns outward		900						900		
	Wages	16,500				550		17,050			
	Carriage inwards	500						500			
	Carriage outwards	400						400			
	Commission received		500						500		
	Bank interest	350						350			
	Lighting, heating	1,650						1,650			
	Postage, stationery	600			9			591			
	Insurance	1,200					95	1,105		95	
	Telephone	500						500			
	Rent received		750			180			930	180	
	Debtors	7,000			150					6,850	
	Provision for bad debts			15	700						685
	Creditors		11,750								11,750
	Bank	1,950			3,900						1,950
	Discount allowed	100						100			
	Bad debts	450		150				600			
	Capital account		71,000	800							70,200
	Depreciation – eqpt			3,400				3,400			
	Depreciation – van			1,500				1,500			
	Bad and doubtful debts			700	15			685			
	Stock (31/12)								9,500	9,500	
	Suspense		3,750	3,750							
	Discount received				80				80		
	VAT			9	420						411
	Profit and loss a/c							10,429			10,429
		163,250	163,250	10,974	10,974	730	95	78,510	78,510	108,875	108,875

TABLE 40.2 Journal entries: Arthur Jones

	Dr.	Cr.
Suspense	80	
Discount received		80
Bad debts	150	
debtors		150
Prov. for bad and doubtful debts	15	
bad and doubtful debts		15
Suspense	3,900	
bank		3,900
Purchases	650	
Suspense		650
Suspense	420	
VAT		420
VAT	9	
Stationery		9

TABLE 40.3 Suspense account

	Dr.	Cr.	Balance
Trial balance		3,750	3,750 Cr.
Discount received	80		3,670 Cr.
Bank	3,900		230 Dr.
Purchases		650	420 Cr.
VAT	420		0

TABLE 40.4 Effect on profit

	£
Net profit	11,125
Add	
discount	80
stationery	9
Deduct	
bad debts	(£135)
purchases	(£650)
Net profit (adjusted)	10,429

TABLE 40.5 Arthur Jones: profit and loss account, year ended 31 December

	£	£
Sales		65,900
Cost of sales:		
Stock (1/1)	8,300	
Purchases	30,650	
Carriage inwards	500	
Returns out	(900)	
Stock (31/12)	(9,500)	29,050
Gross Profit		36,850
Expenses:		
Wages	17,050	
Carriage out	400	
Bank interest	350	
Light and heat	1,650	
Printing and stationery	496	
Insurance	1,200	
Telephone	500	
Discount	100	
Bad debts	600	
Depreciation	4,900	
Bad and doubtful debts	685	27,931
		8,919
Other Revenue:		
Discount received	80	
Rent received	930	
Commission received	500	1,510
Net Profit		10,429

TABLE 40.6 Arthur Jones; balance sheet as on 31 December

	£	£	£
Fixed Assets			
Premises	57,500		57,500
Furniture and fittings	3,750		3,750
Equipment	23,000	9,400	13,600
Motor van	8,000	3,500	4,500
	92,250	12,900	79,350

Current Assets		
Stock	9,500	
Debtors	6,165	
Pre-payments	95	
Accrued revenue	180	15,940
Current Liabilities		
Overdraft	1,950	
Creditors	11,750	
Accruals	550	
VAT	411	14,661
Net Current Assets		1,279
Capital Employed		80,629
Capital	70,200	
profit	10,429	80,629

calculations in readiness for the preparation of the year-end accounts.

Questions

1. The Trial Balance figures as on 31 March for R. Westlake Ltd.

	£	£
Premises	130,000	
Equipment and machines	28,120	
Motor vehicle	8,600	
Stocks	4,800	
Bank overdraft		8,390
Petty cash	980	
Debtors and creditors	7,420	5,160
Mortgage and premises		84,000
Loan (8 years)		7,300
Sales		51,000
Purchases	17,400	
VAT		2,740
Wages	16,300	
Lighting and heating	2,280	
Telephone	1,870	
General expenses	370	

	£	£
Interest	2,300	
Business rates	2,070	
Director's fees	4,600	
Insurance	1,480	
Capital		70,000
	228,590	228,590

Notes:

● Stocks are valued at £5,350 as at 31 March
● Wages - a bonus of £750 is outstanding on 31 March
● Insurance premium is pre-paid to June (£290)
● The equipment and motor vehicle are both to be depreciated by 10%

Required:

(a) Prepare an extended trial balance for R. Westlake Ltd on 31 March.
(b) Prepare the trading and profit and loss account of the firm for the month ended 31 March.
(c) Prepare the balance sheet as at that date.

2. The following figures have been extracted from the ledgers of Frances Mitchell:

Trial balance as at 30 June:

	Dr £	Cr £
Sales		276,156
Purchases	164,700	
Carriage inwards	4,422	
Carriage outwards	5,866	
Drawings	15,600	
Rent and rates	9,933	
Insurance	3,311	
Postage and stationery	3,001	
Advertising	5,661	
Salaries and wages	52,840	
Bad debts	1,754	
Debtors	24,240	

Creditors		25,600
Returns outwards		131
Cash	354	
Bank	2,004	
Stock	23,854	
Equipment (cost)	116,000	
Capital E. Mitchell		131,653
	433,540	433,540

The following information was available on 30 June:

● Wages are accrued by £420
● Rates have been pre-paid by £1,400
● Stock of unused stationery valued £250
● A provision for bad debts is to be created to equal 5% of debtors
● Unsold stock at the close of business valued at £27,304
● Depreciate equipment 10% of cost

Required:

(a) Prepare an extended trial balance for F. Mitchell as on 30 June.
(b) Prepare the trading and profit and loss account for the year ended 30 June and a balance sheet as at that date.
(c) Advise F. Mitchell on the position of the working capital of the business.

(Institute of Bankers)

3. The following trial balance has been extracted from the ledger of M. Yousef, a sole trader:

Trial balance as at 31 May:

	Dr £	Cr £
Sales		138,078
Purchases	82,350	
Carriage	5,144	
Drawings	7,800	
Rent and rates and insurance	6,622	
Postage and stationery	3,001	
Advertising	1,330	

	Dr £	Cr £
Salaries and wages	26,420	
Bad debts	877	
Provision for bad debts		130
Debtors	12,120	
Creditors		6,471
Cash on hand	177	
Cash at bank	1,002	
Stock (opening)	11,927	
Equipment		
at cost	58,000	
accumulated depreciation		19,000
Capital		53,091
	216,770	216,770

The following additional information as at 31 May is available:

● Rent is accrued by £210
● Rates have been pre-paid by £880
● £2,211 of carriage represents carriage inwards on purchases
● Equipment is to be depreciated at 15% per annum using the straight-line method
● The provision for bad debts to be increased by £40
● Stock at the close of business has been valued at £13,551

Required:

(a) Prepare an extended trial balance for M. Yousef as at 31 May.
(b) Prepare the trading and profit and loss account for the year ended 31 May and a balance sheet as at that date.

[Association of Accounting Technicians]

4. The following information is taken from the accounts of Mary Walker, a businesswoman selling science equipment to colleges:

Trial balance of M. Walker as on 30 June:

	£	£
Stock [opening]	6,855	
Motor vehicle (cost)	8,750	
Premises (cost)	36,900	
Accumulated depreciation of vehicle		1,750
Purchases	55,725	
Sales		120,344
Discounts	855	1,044
Returns	548	738
Salaries (assistants)	18,346	
Overheads	14,385	
Creditors		6,755
Debtors	7,400	
Bank		2,045
Cash	400	
Drawings	10,420	
Capital		27,908
	160,584	160,584

On 30 June, the following additional information was also available:

● Stock in hand valued at £7,455
● The motor vehicle is depreciated on the straight-line principle and is now three years old
● Of the overheads, £240 is pre-paid and £600 is accrued

Required:

(a) Prepare an extended trial balance for M. Walker as at 30 June.
(b) Prepare M. Walker's trading and profit and loss account for the year ended 30 June and a balance sheet as on that date.

[BTEC National]

5. The following trial balance was extracted from the accounts of Freddy Smith on 30 June

	Dr £	Cr £
Sales		27,615
Purchases	16,470	
Returns	205	315
Stock [opening]	2,355	
Carriage inwards	442	
Carriage outwards	580	
Drawings	2,560	
Maintenance and rates	1,998	
Insurance, telephone	334	
Light, heat	546	
Postage, stationery	350	
Bad debts	175	
Motor expenses	560	
Wages	5,285	
Provision for bad debts		65
Cash	200	
Bank overdraft		2,005
Equipment [cost]	11,600	
Prov. for depreciation of equipment		1,160
Motor van [cost]	2,500	
Prov. for depreciation of van		1,500
Debtors, creditors	2,420	2,560
Bank loan [deferred]		4,500
Capital: F. Smith		8,860
	48,580	48,580

The following additional information was available on 30 June:

● Unsold stock was valued at £2,895
● Accrued expenses: wages, £185; electricity bill, £90
● Pre-payments: stock of unused stationery, £110; insurance, £80
● The bad debts provision is to be adjusted to equal 5% of debtors
● Depreciation: the van at 25% on the reducing balance method; equipment at 10% of cost.

Required:

(a) Prepare an extended trial balance for F. Smith as an 30 June.
(b) Prepare the trading and profit and loss account of F. Smith for the period ended 30 June
(c) Prepare the balance sheet of F. Smith as on 30 June, showing net current assets. Calculate the current ratio.

[BTEC National]

6. You work for a firm of accountants, Carter & Cutler, and are asked to prepare a draft of the end of year accounts for a client, P. Jackson.
The following trial balance was extracted from the accounts of P. Jackson on 30 June.

	Dr. £	Cr. £
Suspense account		549
Bank		6,500
Purchases/sales	46,000	75,250
Motor vehicle	12,500	
Provision for depreciation (Motor vehicles)		5,000
Rent and rates	1,400	
Light and heat	700	
Carriage inwards	500	
Discounts [balance]	400	
Opening stock	6,300	
Commissions received		1,500
Drawings	9,611	
Returns	1,800	1,500
Office salaries	16,000	
Debtors/creditors	24,000	16,000
Provisions for bad debts		2,000
Fixtures and fittings	8,000	
Provision for depreciations (Fixtures and fittings)		2,400
Land and buildings	65,000	
Bank loan (repayable long-term)		10,000
Interest on loan ($12\frac{1}{2}$% pa)	938	
Capital		72,450
	193,149	193,149

Notes: as on 30 June

- Closing stock £5,300
- During the financial year P. Jackson took goods for own use from the business which cost £2,000
- Revenue accrued: £426 still to be received on commission
- Rates had been paid £200 in advance
- £312 is owed for interest on the bank loan and £540 is due on salaries
- Provision for bad debts is to be increased to 10% of the debtors
- Provision for depreciation of 10% p.a. on cost is to be made on fixtures and fittings
- The motor vehicles are to be revalued to £6,000

The trial balance as on 30 June, did not balance, so a suspense account had to be opened with a credit balance of £549.

However, the following errors were revealed shortly after the accounts had been further scrutinised:

- Credit sales of £1,200 had been omitted from the books (a sales invoice had been found relating to June)
- A receipt of £500 from a debtor had been recorded in the Cash Book only, the posting being omitted
- Discounts received (£376) had been recorded correctly in the purchase ledger, but had in error been posted to the debit side of the discounts account
- Discounts allowed (£224) had also been recorded correctly in the sales ledger, but had in error been posted to the credit side of the discounts account
- Payments made to the firm's supplier totalling £21,257 had been debited as £21,752 in the purchase ledger control account
- Finally, the accountant's bill of £750 had been paid and recorded in the Cash Book but no further entry had been made

Required:

(a) Prepare the necessary journal entries to record the above errors and show the suspense account as it would appear after the correction of all the accounting errors.

(b) Adjust the relevant accounts in the trial balance affected by the errors.

(c) Prepare an extended trial balance for P. Jackson as at 30 June.

(d) Prepare the trading and profit and loss account of P. Jackson for the year ended 30 June.

(e) Prepare the balance sheet of P. Jackson as on 30 June, showing net current assets and the current ratio (in brackets).

CHAPTER 41

Examination Success

Many candidates go into examinations inadequately prepared. They have little idea what the questions are likely to be about and they may not have studied all of the syllabus.

Every candidate must know the full extent of the subject they are undertaking and they should have experienced a number of typical past examination questions in order to know what to expect, both in the coverage of the questions and the depth of knowledge required.

All major aspects of the syllabus should have been studied. It is always too much of a risk to think that a section of work won't be needed because there were questions on it in the previous year.

Exam revision

You should make a list of topics which covers all major areas of an examination. Revise each topic carefully and ensure you understand its basic underlying principles. For example, if you were revising financial statements:

- What are they used for?
- How are they prepared?
- How are adjustments such as accruals, pre-payments and depreciation treated?
- What accounting ratios could be used with the profit and loss account and the balance sheet?

Once a check list has been completed, questions concerning the topic, preferably from previous exam papers, should be attempted and mastered.

You will need to organise and manage your time carefully, to ensure you are fully prepared for the exams you wish to take. If you are attempting a number of exam papers, try to organise certain days of the week so that you spend adequate time on each subject: for example, Monday evenings, Accounting; Wednesday evenings, Economics: etc. Ensure you have sufficient exam questions to practise on and always try to obtain the recommended answers so that you can check your progress.

Wherever possible, nearer the exam time, try to set up your own 'mock exam' at a week-end and attempt to do four or five different questions within the time limits. Many examinations are of a 3-hour duration, so set yourself the requisite number of questions and a time to complete them. It is of essential importance to know how long you have to complete a question.

The examination

Always get to the examination room in plenty of time. Choose a desk where you think you will be comfortable (for example, at the back, front, or side) and make sure you have a watch or can easily see the clock in the room. Relax, breath deeply, concentrate. The papers may already be face down on the desks. When you are allowed to turn the papers over:

(a) Read the paper briefly but carefully to get the general idea of it.

(b) Check how many questions you need to do and whether you need to attempt some questions which are compulsory and others where you are given a choice. You may be asked to do questions from different parts of the paper (for example, two from Section A and two from Section B).

(c) If you have to do *five questions* from a paper in 3 *hours*, this means that you should not spend more than about 35 minutes per question.

(d) Whilst you go through the paper, try to make a choice of the questions you would like to attempt. This stops you re-reading the exam paper over and over again.

(e) Attempt what you consider to be the easiest question first to give you some early confidence and help you get on your way.

(f) Although you will need to write rather quickly, try not to sacrifice presentation altogether. You still need to present your accounts legibly and allow yourself plenty of space for each question. The examiner is not impressed with small print crammed into limited space.

(g) Try to remember to use a fresh page for each question. If you need to alter some figures or add more material to a question, it can be done more easily if each question is on a separate paper.

(h) Use a ruler to draw lines rather than doing it free-hand. Major totals should always be underscored. It improves presentation and makes your work look more organised.

(i) Try to finish the number of questions you are set. *Do not spend all your time completing just half of the questions.* The chances of you succeeding would be minimal, particularly if the pass mark was 50%.

(j) If you do have any time left at the end, always go over the questions again, checking to see if there are any obvious errors. If you do alter anything, strike out the error in pencil and insert the correction. Do so as neatly as possible.

(k) Ensure that you have your name and candidate number on the examination booklet and also on any extra pages that you may have used.

Finally, make sure that you prepare for your exams thoroughly, leaving adequate time for good revision. Whether you want to revise up to the very last minute or would rather have a pleasant evening off before the day of an exam is simply a matter of choice; but you need to work hard!

Best wishes with all your examinations.

Preparation of Balance Sheets and Calculation of Current Ratios

Situation

You have been given a summary of the balance sheet of your organisation for the last four years from your supervisor, the Finance Manager. He wants you to produce separate balance sheets for the purpose of calculating working capital and current ratios.

Information

Use the data from the table below relating to the last for years' balance sheets.

Balance sheet figures over the last 4 years

	£000s			
	Year 1	Year 2	Year 3	Year 4
	£	£	£	£
Premises	100	100	100	110
Plant, machinery and equipment	60	80	85	90
FIXED ASSETS	160	180	185	200
Stocks	70	80	100	115
Debtors	30	42	75	75
Bank/cash	65	38	—	10
CURRENT ASSETS	165	160	175	200

| | £000s | | | |
	Year 1	Year 2	Year 3	Year 4
	£	£	£	£
Creditors	85	95	100	120
Bank overdraft			35	
CURRENT LIABILITIES	85	95	135	120
Loans more than 12 months:	50	65	50	85
NET ASSETS	190	180	175	195

Required:

(a) Prepare separate balance sheets for each of the 4 years and clearly indicate the working capital in your presentation.

(b) Calculate the working capital ratio (current ratio) for each of the four years and prepare brief notes to your superior to indicate your findings.

(c) If the above organisation is a public limited company, outline how the company could be financed.

Planning Your Own Business

Situation

A number of years after leaving college you and a small group of friends
want to start your own business enterprise.

You will need to research thoroughly the kind of business venture you
want to undertake and ensure there is sufficient demand for your product or service. You will need answers to the following questions:

- Is there an adequate market for your product or service?
- What is the competition like?
- Who are the potential customers?
- What prices are you likely to charge?

You must also decide what type of business organisation you want to set
up and whether you need to acquire business premises. You will need to
take into consideration:

(a) the relevant Acts;
(b) legal implications such as Health and Safety, contracts of employ-
    ment, dismissal procedure;
(c) the tax authorities to be notified.

You will need to know what kind of stock you require if you decide to
produce or trade in products, and also what quantities to buy, where to
buy and what prices to pay.

If further capital sums are required you will need to know where extra
funding may be found.

Required:

Prepare your own detailed business plan which will outline clearly how
you propose to establish, organise and control your new business ven-

ture. When drawing up your plan, the finance should be within the range of £5,000–£25,000 and it is assumed that you can raise up to 50% from your own personal sources.

Your business plan is not likely to include any great detail with regard to the day-to-day running of the business, so you are required to supplement the plan with the following detailed appendices:

(a) *Image*:		Design a logo and letterhead which you think will give a positive image. Draft a mission statement.
(b) *Management*:		Detail the management policies to be used to ensure quality of the product/service; motivation of staff; communications. (Refer to various theories and apply these to your business.)
(c) *Policies*:		Draw up policy documents to demonstrate: equality of opportunity; recruitment and selection process; appraisal.
(d) *Administration Systems*:		By use of flow charts and accompanying narrative, show *two* processes relevant to your business, detailing points of effective control.
(e) *Layout*:		Having due regard to legislation: draw up an accurate floor plan showing all relevant contents and give details of colour schemes, etc. Prepare a brief paper which sets out these considerations in designing the layout.

The above information will depend on the nature of your business and its requirements. Present your answer in a suitable format as a supplement to your business plan.

The law requires that you keep accurate financial records and it is necessary for any successful venture to have adequate finance and to be able to forecast figures ahead of time.

You will need to prepare budgets to indicate your financial plans, so you are required to forecast the first year's trading

You will need to forecast:

(a) cash budget;
(b) trading and profit and loss;
(c) balance sheet.

You should also take into consideration:

● The volume of sales (from market research)
● For manufacturing concerns, figures indicating the factory cost

- The provision for depreciation of any fixed assets
- The calculation of stock figures
- The break-even point in either output or sales value

(d) From the findings of the information above, you are asked to prepare a report which will indicate a forecast of the financial performance of your new business.

(e) Whether or not your business needs to be registered for VAT, prepare a brief report which explains how your accounts would be affected.

An Investigation into Different Forms of Business Organisation in Your Area

Situation

You are to assume you are currently employed by a market research agency. The agency has been approached by one of the major US banks in this country, who wish to expand their financial services to a wide range of UK business enterprises. The bank has just established its new head offices in your area and requires the agency to undertake a number of surveys about business in this area as a pilot project. The assignment is based on the collection of data on four organisations found in the area, namely:

(a) A *Public* Limited or a *Private* Limited Company;
(b) A *Partnership* and a *Sole Trader*;
(c) A *Public Sector* organisation.

Required:

(a) Collect information individually or in groups about the organisations you have selected by using a variety of sources including:

● public reference library
● college library
● Careers Office
● PRESTEL
● employees of organisations known to you

706

When you have completed the initial research you should arrange for speakers from selected organisations to address the class and answer questions.

Under the guidance of your lecturers you should, as a class:

- Decide upon the different types of business you will use for this task and which speakers or companies will be approached
- Draft a letter of invitation
- Complete any other necessary correspondence
- Make arrangements for rooms, times, etc
- One member of class should welcome and introduce the speaker and another propose the vote of thanks
- You should *all* prepare written questions to be asked after the talk, which will be submitted to the lecturer for assessment

(b) Using the information collected in (a) each student should write a report to the Marketing Manager to describe, compare and contrast the different types of organisations in terms of

- How the organisation was legally established
- Where it obtained (and in what form) finance for its establishment
- The ownership of the organisation
- Its management and operation
- Control exercised over the organisation
- Its organisational structure

(c) Individually, you should give a brief oral presentation on any one of the organisations studied and be prepared to answer questions from the class.

(d) To ensure the prospective clients are viable, long-term customers worthy of support and help, the bank requires detailed financial information about the organisations. Your market research agency is required to:

- Prepare balance sheets for each of the organisations chosen or, in the case of the public sector organisation, a similar document indicating sources of finance and a programme of expenditure for the current financial year (present the figures in vertical form)
- From the figures you have prepared, calculate accounting ratios to evaluate the liquidity, where relevant, of each of the organisations and briefly comment on the organistion's ability to cover its debts, as an appendix to the balance sheet.

Manufacturing Accounts and Costing

Information

The trial balance of the company as on 31 December was as follows:

	£	£
Ordinary share capital:		
70,000 (*a*) £1 shares issued and paid		70,000
Share premium account		7,000
Profit and loss (1 January)		5,820
Premises (cost)	86,000	
Plant, equipment, machinery (cost)	12,000	
Provision for depreciation:		
Plant, equipment, machinery		6,000
Debtors	10,498	
Creditors		58,409
Stock: raw materials (1 January,)	5,892	
finished goods (1 January)		
2,500 units	8,500	
Provision for bad and doubtful debts		210
Bad debts written off	528	
Bank/cash	2,910	
Direct wages	56,804	
Purchases of raw materials	156,820	
Sales: 48,000 units in year		204,000
General overheads ($\frac{1}{2}$ factory)	2,944	
Rates and insurance ($\frac{1}{2}$ factory)	610	
Office salaries	5,220	
Carriage outwards	2,713	
	351,439	351,439

Further information on 31 December

- The value of unsold stock of raw materials was £20,893
- In the year, 50,000 units were produced (the unsold stock in the warehouse is to be valued at production cost)
- Depreciation of plant, equipment and machinery is to be at 10% of net value
- The provision for doubtful debts is to be increased to £750
- The Directors have recommended a 5% ordinary dividend and a general reserve is to be created by the transfer of £4,000

Required:

(a) You are to prepare the company's manufacturing account, trading and profit and loss account and appropriation account for the year ended 31 December.
(b) Prepare the company's balance sheet as at 31 December, showing clearly the net current assets of the company as well as the capital employed.
(c) Based on the number of units produced in the year, make calculations to show:

- The direct labour cost per unit
- The direct material cost per unit
- The *total* overheads per unit (factory and office)
- Using the trial balance figures for the selling price per unit, calculate the mark-up on cost per unit

Costing forecast

The budget figures for the following year are estimated as follows:

Production Output:	60,000 units	
Direct Labour:		£ 63,500
Direct Materials:		£147,000
Factory Overheads:		£ 15,000
Service (office) Overheads:		£ 14,500

Variables:

Direct materials:	100% variable
Direct labour:	30p per unit as a productivity bonus
Factory overheads:	2p per unit for power
All other costs:	Fixed

(d) Prepare a suitable table to show fixed, variable and total costs based on the figures above. Calculate the contribution per unit.

(e) Calculate the break-even point. Prepare a break-even chart to illustrate the break-even point. On your chart show:

Profit/loss   on   42,000 units produced
                  on   30,000 units produced

Allied Components Plc: Diversification

Situation

Allied Components makes electrical components used in the production of electrical appliances. Because of intense competition, especially from the Far East, the Board has taken a decision to diversify Allied's business interest.

Two plans are put forward:

1. To produce other products using existing plant and equipment. This plan is favoured by the Production Director because his research and development team has devised new plans for other products.
2. To purchase another manufacturing organisation in order to give Allied a wider product range and diversify its markets. This plan is favoured by the Finance and Sales Directors who would like to use the company's funds to acquire subsidiaries. Particular interest has been shown in purchasing one of two private companies which specialise in producing circuit boards used in a wide variety of products. Both companies appear to be sound financial investments.

   The companies are:

   Arrowsmith Ltd   An older, well-established company having a stable record of production and profits over a number of years; good labour relations record.

   Hardcastle Ltd   A relatively new company which has rapidly become established. Only a few years' trading figures available but early trend shows rising profits. Young and more aggressive management but more strained labour relations.

The Financial Director has been able to secure the most recent figures of both these organisations and you have been asked as one of his assistants to prepare a draft of the final accounts of the two companies and to give a reasoned assessment of them. You have also acquired accounting ratios from 'Inter-Firm Comparison Ltd' provided by the British Institute of Management.

Accounting date to year ended 31 December 19–5

	Arrowsmith Ltd £	Hardcastle Ltd £
Turnover	356,000	327,000
Stock (1/1)	62,000	58,750
Cost of production	256,500	201,500
Stock (31/12)	84,000	68,750
Sales and Distribution costs	28,100	44,800
Administration expenses	44,400	38,700
Interest payable	4,000	5,500
Taxation provision	15,500	14,500
Transfer to reserves	20,000	25,000
Dividends Proposed	9,000	2,500
Fixed assets (net values)	156,500	135,100
Debtors	84,200	76,750
Bank/cash	4,800	(10,800) O/D
Pre-payments	—	500
Accruals	500	4,900
Creditors	86,500	89,400
Loans (long-term)	40,000	52,000
Issued and paid-up capital		
Ordinary (a) £1 shares	100,000	50,000
Reserves (1/1)	57,500	27,500

Accounting ratios are provided by the British Institute of Management on electronic industries. The figures have been supplied for guidance as to financial performance.

Accounting Ratios:

	%
Gross margin	40.
Net profit (b/t)/sales	14.5
Net profit (a/t)/capital employed	20.75
Net profit (a/t)/net worth	29.55
Production cost/sales	60.5
Sales and Dist. cost/sales	9.5
Administration exp./sales	11.0
Current ratio	1.85:1
Acid test	0.95:1

Capital gearing	80%
Current assets/sales £1,000	£450
Fixed assets/sales £1,000	£421
Investment Ratios	
Earnings per share	£0.55
Cover	8 times
Dividend per share	£0.05
Yield	4.5%
P/E ratio	12 times

The current market value per share for Arrowsmith is 174p and for Hardcastle 256p.

Required:

(a) Prepare a draft copy of the trading and profit and loss accounts of the two companies for the year ended 31 December 19–5. Prepare the balance sheets as at that date.
(b) Using the inter-firm comparison ratios as a guide, prepare the accounting ratios of both companies on which to form your assessment. Include investment ratios for both companies, as listed.
(c) Evaluate the case for and against the company which appears to be the better of the two investments. Draw attention to the limitations accounting ratios tend to impose on the assessment of financial performance.

Incomplete Records and the Extended Trial Balance

You are employed in the accounts office of Johnson & Palmer, Chartered Accountants and have been given the task of completing the year-end accounts of a client, Jack Jones, for the period ending 30 June 1995. The figures taken from the previous accounts on 30 June 1995 were as follows:

	£	£
Premises	50,000	
Fixtures, fittings and equipment	12,500	
Provision for depreciation of fixtures, fittings, etc.		1,250
Motor vehicle	4,500	
Provision for depreciation of motor vehicle		1,970
Debtors	4,800	
Creditors		6,530
Stock	12,750	
Stationery pre-paid	155	
Light and heat accrued		150
VAT	385	
Mortgages on premises		25,500
Bank (overdrawn)		4,680
Capital account		?

Required:

(a) Prepare the necessary journal entry to bring the account balances forward to the new accounting period, commencing 1 June 1995.

714

Summarised bank statement to 30 June 1995

	Bank £		Bank £
		Balance on 1/7/94	4,680
Takings (inc. debtors' receipts)	48,998	Payments to suppliers	36,558
New capital by Jones	2,500	Light, heat	553
VAT	580	British Telecom	185*
		Motor expenses	1,344*
		New equipment (1/1)	2,100
		Wages	8,960
		Maintenance and repairs	958*
		General costs	340
		Stationery	428*
		Petty cash	100
		Mortgage repayments	2,160
		Bank charges/interest	255

* VAT @ 17.5% is inclusive in these figures.
Note: Discount allowed to date £296.53.
    Discounts received to date £630.50.

> When checking the bank's statements, it was found that further charges of £24.82 had been incurred and also that a cheque of £185 from Kings, a customer, had been returned to the drawer as having insufficient funds.
>
> (b) Balance the bank summary as on 30 June 1995.

Further information provided as on 30 June 1995:

● Stock: the value at cost was £14,200
● The trade debtors were £3,950
● Trade creditors were £7,280
● The owner, Jack Jones, has taken £400 cash from the till for his own use and this has not been recorded in any of the books.
● VAT: the business is zero-rated for VAT but approximately 30% of purchases are inclusive of VAT
● Depreciation of fixed assets:
   The vehicle is depreciated by 25% reducing balance
   Fixtures, fittings, equipment by 10% reducing balance with any new acquisitions charged on a monthly basis
● Gas and electricity bills in arrears amounted to £185; overtime accrued on wages was £150; stationery unused was valued at £200 (exc. VAT)
● A customer's account for £370 is to be written off as a bad debt
● On mortgage repayments, £1,650 was interest charged

(c) You are to prepare ledger accounts for sales and purchase ledger control accounts, the VAT account and the mortage account. (This will help you in preparing the extended trial balance.)

(d) Enter all the above information in the extended trial balance as on 30 June 1995 and complete all appropriate entries (that is, adjustments, accruals, pre-payments, etc.) concluding with the profit and loss and balance sheet columns.

(e) Prepare the trading and profit and loss account for Jack Jones for the period ending 30 June 1995, and a balance sheet as at that date.

[Association of Accounting Technicians]

Glossary of Terms

ACCOUNT	A formal record of one or more business transactions expressed in money and kept in a ledger/journal.
ACCRUAL	The accounting treatment of expense incurred in one financial year but paid in the next financial year.
ADVICE NOTE	Note accompanying the delivery of goods.
ASSET	Any resource owned by a business, tangible or intangible.
AUDIT	An examination of the accounts and supporting records by an independent accountant.
AUDITOR	The person who carries out the audit.
BAD DEBT	An amount receivable but deemed to be uncollectable.
BALANCE	The difference between the debit and the credit entries in an account.
BALANCE SHEET	A statement of assets held in a business at a particular time – the Position Statement.
BANK RECONCILIATION	A statement explaining the difference between the Cash Book and the statement issued from the bank.
BOOK VALUE	The original cost of an asset less the cumulative depreciation.
BOOK-KEEPING	The process of recording financial transactions in the ledger/journal.
BOOKS OF PRIME ENTRY	Books into which transactions are first recorded before transfer to the ledger.
BUDGET	The expression of a business plan in money terms.
CAPITAL	Usually refers to the owner's net worth: that is, the total capital employed minus long-term liabilities.
CASH BOOK	A book in which all the cash/bank receipts and payment are recorded.

717

CASH DISCOUNT	An amount allowed for prompt settlement of an invoice.
CASH FLOW STATEMENT	A statement prepared for limited companies which identified the inflow and outflow of funds, replacing the funds flow statement.
CONTRA	The setting-off of matching debit with credit against each other.
CREDIT NOTE	The document which shows the amount and other particulars regarding the reduction or cancellation of the amount originally invoiced.
CREDITOR	One to whom money is owed.
CURRENT ASSET	An asset held for less than one year which can be converted to cash, such as stock, work in progress or debtors.
CURRENT LIABILITY	A short-term debt which must be repaid before the anniversary of the next balance sheet.
DEBTOR	One who owes money to the business.
DEPRECIATION	The estimated loss in value of a fixed asset as a result of wear and tear or obsolescence.
FINAL ACCOUNTS	The profit and loss account and balance sheet drawn up at the end of the financial year.
FIXED ASSET	An asset held for more than one year, such as land, building, plant and machinery, office equipment.
GOODWILL	The excess paid for a business over the book value of assets minus liabilities being acquired on purchase.
INTANGIBLE ASSET	An asset which has no physical substance but possesses a value, such as goodwill or development costs.
IMPRESS SYSTEM	Most usually associated with petty cash, whereby a fixed amount of money is advanced to the Petty Cashier who is reimbursed on a regular basis for the amounts paid out on petty cash vouchers.
INVOICE	The document which shows the quantity, price, terms and other particulars regarding goods or services provided.
LEDGER	The main book of account in which entries are recorded and divided into the purchases, sales and nominal ledgers.
LIABILITY	Amount owing to third party.
MARGIN	Profit expressed as a percentage of selling value.
MARK-UP	Profit expressed as a percentage of cost value.
PAR	The nominal or face value of a security.
PETTY CASH BOOK	A book kept by the Petty Cashier in which small cash disbursements are recorded. It's a subsidiary of the Cash Book.

PETTY CASH VOUCHER	Document supporting an entry in the Petty Cash Book
POSTING	The act of transferring entries from the books of prime entry to their separate accounts in the ledger or cash book.
PRE-PAYMENT	The accounting treatment of expenses incurred in the current financial year which relates to the next financial year.
PROFIT AND LOSS ACCOUNT	A summary account which nets off all revenue expenditure against income showing as its balance the net profit for the accounting period.
PROVISION	Amount written off or retained out of profits to provide for depreciation or known liability.
RECEIPT	A written acknowledgement of payment for goods or services received.
STATEMENT OF ACCOUNT	A statement prepared to show the amount due. Usually a statement will show only the amounts and dates of transactions between the two parties since the preparation of the previous statement.
STATEMENT OF AFFAIRS	A report, usually prepared from incomplete records, that shows the assets, liabilities and net worth of a business.
STOCK IN TRADE	Goods held for subsequent sale in the ordinary course of business.
TANGIBLE ASSET	*See* FIXED ASSET.
TAXABLE INCOME	Earnings that are subject to tax.
TRADE DISCOUNT	A reduction that is allowed to certain customers on a list price. Usually the greater the quantity of items purchased the higher the discount.
TRIAL BALANCE	A list of all the balances in the ledgers of a business to prove the arithmetical accuracy of the debit and credit balances before preparing final accounts.
TURNOVER	Net sales – that is, sales less returns inwards.
VALUED ADDED TAX (VAT)	Tax levied by HM Customs & Excise on the supply of some goods and services.
WRITTEN DOWN VALUE	*See* BOOK VALUE.

Abbreviated Answers to Text Questions

Part I

Chapter 1   Financial Resources

Q1   Book-keeping's main function is the recording of financial information on a day-to-day basis and to classify and group this information into sets of accounts.

Accounting needs book-keeping records for the purpose of preparing financial statements (such as profit and loss a/c, balance sheet) to provide the interested parties with essential information about the financial aspects of the organisation.

Q2   The size of capital relates to the size of an organisation because the potential to raise capital depends on either one or more persons subscribing the initial finance. A sole trader has only his own resources while a plc can raise vast sums because it can invite the public, through its prospectus, to buy shares.

Other factors: the size of market available, the nature of the goods or services provided, the personal wealth of the entrepreneur.

Q3   (a) Personal wealth, resources available, such as bank loan.
(b) Share capital, debentures, retained profits and loans.

Q4   The private sector refers to economic activity in the hands of private individuals, providing goods and services in order to gain individual benefit.

The public sector refers to economic activity in the hands of the state, providing goods and services for the benefit of the nation.

Q5   The Council Tax and borrowing from various sources, but mainly from the Government's Works Loan Fund.

Q6   By imposing taxes and by borrowing money if there is a budget deficit.

PSBR – Public Sector Borrowing Requirement.
PSDR – Public Sector Debt Repayment.

Q7 Government revenue: direct and indirect taxation.
Government expenditure: Social Security, Health, Education, Defence and other government departments, such as Environment.

Q8 To regulate the economy, mainly by using taxation as a means of influencing *demand* for goods and services; to keep inflation under control; to invigorate the economy by providing subsidies and incentives for growth and investment; to stimulate employment through training programmes or financial initiatives; to direct the economy which will respond to the needs of the market.
Direct tax – taxes on income, such as income tax, corporation tax.
Indirect tax – taxes on goods and services, such as VAT, Customs & Excise tax.

Q9 By earning revenue through the sale of goods or services; by retaining profits for growth; from Government subsidies, grants and loans.
The more finance central government gives, the more influence it will exert.

Q10 Ordinary shares: true shares, voting rights, no fixed dividends. Preference shares: priority of dividends at fixed rates, no voting rights. Less risky than ordinary.

Q11 It may have insufficient capital to fund its own fixed assets or may wish to use funds for alternative purposes.

Q12 To free the economy from the public sector and to raise large sums, some to repay the PSBR.

Chapter 2   Business Planning

Q1 Any of the major banks or the local Business Enterprise scheme.

Q2 To see if the business is viable; to provide sound factual evidence and forecast figures for interested parties like banks.

Q3 Marketing and finance. Product must sell and cash flow essential.

Q4 Product, price, place and promotion. The mix must be right for success of business.

Q5 Its cost and the competitors pricing are major factors.

Q6 Local advertising and introductory offers.

Q7 To identify key staff, their responsibilities, strengths and weaknesses.

Q8 Without financial information, the business may lack direction and control.

Q9 It forecasts receipts and payments to identify cash movements and bank balances over a 12-month period.

Q10 The profit and loss account shows how profits are determined, matching revenue with expenses. The balance sheet indicates the financial position in terms of assets, liabilities and capital of a business.

Q11 Generally, VAT figures are excluded and shown as net. The balance due to Customs shown in the balance sheet.

Q12 A franchise is a monopoly right to trade by a contractual agreement between the supplier of the franchise and the trader.

Q13 The needs to be aware of legalities affecting trading activities; Sale of Goods Act indicates that goods must be fit for the purpose thereof.

Q14 Facts to be clear and concise, including finances. Determination, good communication, self-belief and confidence.

Chapter 3   The Role of the Accountant

Q1 A wide variety of work which is stimulating, challenging, absorbing and even exciting.

Q2 Auditors examine the accounting books to see that recording is as it should be and whether, in their opinion, the figures represent a true and fair view as to the state of a business's affairs at the end of the financial year.

Q3 Private practice can open up a wide range of financial services for different clients, whereas an accounts office will have more specialised work concerning its own affairs.

Q4 The day-to-day recording of financial information.

Q5 The same type of information such as sales, purchases, stock, wages, etc., can be fed into a program and be automatically up-dated and printed out at the touch of a button.

Chapter 4   Introducing the balance sheet

Q1 *J. Smith*
Assets: fixed £10,400, current £1,550, total £11,950.
Liabilities: deferred £7,500, current £115, total £7,615.
Capital £4,335. (a)   C   =   A   –   L   (b) Mortgage £7,000.
                            £4,335 = £11,950 – £7,615
(c) Bank £5 Creditors NIL. (d) On credit: stock £125, creditors £125.
(e)   C   =   A   –   L
    £4,335 = £11,960 – £7,625

Q2 *John Jones*
(b) Bank £1,760. (c) Assets: fixed £3,340, current £3,260, total £6,600.
Liabilities: deferred £1,000, current £1,800, total £2,800.
Capital £3,800. (d) Working capital (WC) £1,460. WC ratio 1.8 – adequate.

Q3 *M. Crooks*
(a) Assets: fixed £53,200, current £16,375, total £69,575.
    Liabilities: deferred £33,500, current £16,075, total £49,575.
    Capital £20,000.
(c)   C   =   A   –   L   (d) Just; working capital £300.
    £20,000 = £69,575 – £49,575 (e) Sell stock.

Q4 *R. David*
(a) Fixed assets £16,000. Working capital £7,485. Total £23,485.
    Deferred liabilities £11,500. Net assets £11,985.
    Capital £13,985 *less* Drawings £2,000 = £11,985.
(b) Need sufficient 'liquid' funds to pay current debts.

Q5 *H. Smith*

Balance Sheet: Assets: fixed £34,050, current £7,370 (working capital £950)

Liabilities: current £6,420. Deferred £24,000

Net assets £11,000. Capital £12,000 *less* drawings £1,000 = £11,000.

(a) Liabilities of £30,420 against £11,000 of capital. A strain to repay debts within 5 years.

(b) No. Only £100 cash available.

(c) Most of resources tied up in fixed assets.

(d)   C   =   A   −   L
       £11,000 = £41,420 − £30,420

Q6 *R. James*

(a) Fixed assets £44,000, working capital £5,750 = £49,750.
Less deferred liabilities £26,000 = £23,750.
Capital £20,000 − Drawings £4,500 + Profit £8,250 = £23,750.

(b) Good working capital: WC ratio 1.9.

(c) Yes − a very good return of 41.25%.

(d) Independence, challenge, self-motivation, etc.

Q7 (a) Capital (1/1) £24,500. Fixed assets £18,100, Working Capital £20,393 = £38,493 − Deferred Liabilities £20,753 = £17,740. Capital £17,740.

(c) A poor trading year. Capital reduced due to net loss and drawings.

Q8

	Year 1	Year 2	Year 3
(a) Working capital	£700	£920	£1,720
(b) Working capital ratio	1.5	1.8	1.9

(c) Year 2 probably best [Year 3 carries too much stock and has bank o/d].

Part II

Chapter 5   The Ledger System

Q1 Balances: credit, creditors, mortgage, overdraft and capital. All others debit.

Q2 Green a/c Nil balance, Bank a/c £135 Dr. Goods a/c £1,600 Dr.

Q3 R. David: Bank £3,950, Stock £1,800, Equipment £300, Briggs £350 all Dr. Capital £2,600, XYZ £1,300, Loan £2,500 all Cr. MV a/c Nil

Q4 J. Bird: Bank £35,000, Premises £26,000, Fixtures £1,250, MV £5,000 all Dr. Capital £60,000, Jackson £5,000, Loan £4,000 all Cr.

Chapter 5   (after revenue and expenses)

Q1 Trial balance totals = £19,965.

Q2 Trial balance totals = £13,800.

Q3 Trial balance totals = £7,318: Bank £64, J. Jones £148, H. Belafonte

£1,175, Purchases £632, Stock £2,150, MV £2,750, Equipment £399 all Dr. Diamond £100, Jake's £2,475, Manilow £584, Capital £4,159 all Cr.

Q4   Trial balance totals = £1,260: Smith £415, Lillee £201, Thomson £156, Purchases £345, Bank £143 all Dr. Capital £18, May £195, Cowdrey £152, Sales £895 all Cr.

Q5   Trial balance totals £25,950. Premises £15,000, Stock £2,150. Purchases £2,325, Equipment £2,275, MV £2,400, Bank £200, Gordon £500, Jones £287, White £813 all Dr. Loan £10,000, ABC £1,000, Jake's £1,500, Jackson £953, Brown £1,297, capital £11,200 all Cr.

Q6   Trial balance totals £7,000. Van £1,500, Bank £1,080, Cash £200, Equipment £1,800, Rent £250, Purchases £1,600, Stationery £40, motor exps £30, General exps £80, W'barrow £297, Smith £90, Returns in £33, all debits. Capital £3,000, HP £900, Sales £1,220, Steele £250, Daley £400, Land £1,080, Returns out £150 all credits.

Chapter 6   An Alternative Method of Recording

Error in example: J. Randle a/c £350 not £450.
Trial balance totals £6,597.

Q1   (a) *D. Robert*. Trial balance total: £40,840.
        (b) The personal a/cs Dr. – sales ledger: Smith & Hunt.
             The personal a/cs Cr. – bought ledger: Jones & Fox.
             All other a/cs in the nominal ledger.
        (c) Purchases, sales, wages and general expenses.

Q2   *R. Lee*: Trial balance total: £3,852.
        Purchases £2,585, Jackson £250, Fanshawe £300, Bank £717 all Dr. Capital £221, Sales £3,198, Newman £433 all Cr.

Q3   *F. Smith*: Trial balance totals: £29,051, Premises £20,000, MV £1,875, Stock £1,900, Bank £1,277, Rollin £500, Vines £450, Purchases £2,850, General expenses £115, Insurance £84, all Dr. Capital £6,263, Mortgage £16,750, Boston £2,950, Turner £600, Sales £2,488 all Cr.

Q4   *J. Briggs*: Trial balance totals: £26,380, Bank £265, Premises £17,000, Fixtures £1,000, Cash £595, Collins £2,850, Smith £720, Purchases £1,870, Salaries £600, Repairs £260, Stock £1,200, Drawings £20 all Dr. Capital £20,000, Jones £1,055, Sales £5,325 all Cr.

Q5   *G. Harrison*: Trial balance totals: £3,605. Cash/Bank £1,226, Lloyd £250, Jones £268, Purchases £1,195, General Expenses £57, Salaries £165, Insurance £54, MV £350, Drawings £40, all Dr. Capital £1,860, Bloggs £250, Sales £915, T. Jones £580 all Cr.

Q6   *L. Dawson*: Trial balance totals £44,980.
        Debits: Bank £14,258, Cash £2,658, Purchases £9,500, F + F £6,200, Advertising £56, Rent £6,000. Wages £170, Insurance £400, P + S £38, Drawings £500, Redhill £3,100, Shaw £2,100.
        Credits: Capital £30,000, Sales £11,480, Green £3,500.

Q7   Trial balance totals £6,060. Van £1,800, Equipment £1,750, Furn. £150, Purchases £1,595, Returns in £40, Bright £125, Taylor £150, O'heads

£250, Drawings £200, all debits. Capital £2,200, Bank o/d £50, XYZ £1,150, Good £235, Rawlings £960, Sales £1,405, Returns out £60, all credits.

Chapter 7   The Sales Day Book

Q1 (a) R. Carlton: SDB totals: sales £1,690, VAT £253.5, total £1,943.5.
  (b) Sales ledger, Dr. (c) Nominal ledger; sales and VAT Cr.
  Debtors total Dr. (d) To cross-check accuracy of sales ledger.
  Double-entry already completed.
Q2 (a) Sales £890. (b) Arthur £450, Brian £160, Colin £280 all Dr.
  Sales a/c £2,130 Cr.
Q3 (a) Sales £890, VAT £133.5, total £1,023.5.
  (b) Arthur £517.5, Brian £184, Colin £322, all Dr.
  (c) Sales a/c £2,130 Cr. VAT £8.5 Cr, Sales ledger control £1,023.5 Dr.
Q4 (a) Sales £2,460, VAT £369, total £2,829.
  (b) Debtors: Bremner £1,667.5, Gray £422, Lorimer £1,175, Jones £629.5, Giles £115 all Dr. in Sales Ledger.
  (c) Sales ledger control £4,009 Dr.
Q5 Totals: Total £1,109.55, bats £755, balls £111.75, pads £242.8.
  Debtors: Brearly £420.46. Botham £99.75, Boycott £415.85, Bailey £188.38, Benaud £335.5 all Dr.
  Debtors control: £1,459.94 Dr.
Q6 Totals: Sales £5,930, VAT £1,037.75, Total Debtors £6,967.75. Jackson £657, Thomson £1,520, Illingworth £901, Rocastle £2,803, James £1,710 all debits, total = £7,591, equals S/L control a/c.
Q7 (a) Totals: S161 = £840, S162 = £200, S163 = £560, VAT £280 = £1,880.
  (b) Davies £575.50, Smith £352.50, Forbes £508, S/L Control £1,436.
  (c) VAT a/c and each sales a/c would be credited.

Chapter 8   The Purchases Day Book

Q1 (a) Purchases day book. R. Jones.
  (b) Net purchases £157.87. VAT £26.94. Total £184.81.
  (c) Purchases and VAT Dr. Harrison a/c Cr. £184.81.
Q2 *Purchases day book – G. Harrison.*
  (a) Purchases £1,007.10, VAT £149.79, total £1,156.89.
  (b) Bought ledger (or purchases ledger). Credit. Because they represent liabilities to Harrison.
  (c) Nominal ledger: Purchases and VAT Dr., total creditors Cr.
  (d) Cross-check the bought ledger.
  (e) ROCCO.
Q3 Purchases day book: Purchases £880.
  Bought ledger Dick £500, Eric £380, Fred £160 all Cr.
  Purchases a/c £1,980 Dr.
Q4 Purchases day book: Purchases £880, VAT £132, total £1,012.

Bought ledger Dick £560, Eric £437, Fred £175 all Cr.
Nominal ledger: VAT £257 Dr. Purchases £880, Bought Ledger control £1,172 Cr.

Q5 (a) Purchases day book £4,497.5, sales day book £2,420.
(b) Bought ledger: ABC £3,937.5 XYZ £560 Cr.
Sales ledger: Green £1,575, Jones £495, Smith £350 Dr.
Sales a/c £2,420 Cr. Purchases a/c £4,497.5 Dr.

Q6 Purchases day book. Purchases £1,605, VAT 280.88, total £1,885.
Bought ledger: Mellows £646.25, Hudson £652.13, Paterson £470.
Moorcroft £117.50 all Cr. Bought ledger control a/c £1,885.88.

Q7 Total VAT £732.56, Footwear £1,862, Leisure £1,094, Sports £1,230 = Total £4,918.56. Debit each purchase a/c and VAT a/c. P/L control a/c £4,918.56 Credit.

Chapter 9   The Returns Day Books

Q1 Returns inward day book. Returns inward £130, VAT £19.5, total £149.5.
Sales ledger: Arthur £77, Brian £51, Colin £92.5 all Dr.
Nominal ledger: Returns Inward a/c £387 Dr. VAT a/c £144.5 Dr.
Sales ledger control a/c £220.5 Dr.

Q2 Returns outward day book. Returns outward £188, VAT £28.2, total £216.20.
Bought ledger: Dick £188, Eric £44.8, Fred £51 all Cr.
Nominal ledger: Returns outward a/c £540 Cr. VAT £96.8 Dr.
Bought ledger control a/c £283.80 Cr.

Q3 Purchases day book: Total £9,605. 92.
Returns outward day book: Total £991.41.
Dunlop's a/c £3,087.9, Metre a/c £3,395.75 Cr.
Sondico's a/c £2,130.86 Cr.

Q4 Purchases day book: Purchases £2,580, VAT £393.75, total £2,973.75.
Returns outward day book: Returns out £96.30, VAT £16.85, total £113.15.
Purchase ledger: Trueman £1,771.50, Statham £580, Tyson £1,292.25, Snow £951, Illingworth £659.35, Old £861.50. All credit balances.
P/L control a/c = £5,935.60.

Q5 Sales day book: Sales £510, VAT £76.5, total £586.5.
Purchases day book: Purchases £730, VAT £109.5, total £839.5.
Returns outward day book: Returns out £200, VAT £30, total £230.
Sales ledger: Hunt £149.5, Speedie £247, Milton £230. All debits.
Purchase ledger: Ball £287.5, Carlson £184, Smith £138. All credits.
S/L control a/c £626.5.
P/L control a/c £609.5.

Q6 Sales ledger: Appleby £230, Shuttleworth £320, Vincent £651 debits.
Purchase ledger: Morton £460, Pierce £180 credits.

Chapter 10   The Cash Book

Q1 Cash a/c £50, Bank £730 Dr. Dis. All. £17 Dis. Rec. £1.
Q2 Cash a/c £661, Bank £1,597 Dr. Dis. All. £6, Dis. Rec. £40.
Q3 Cash a/c £369.31, Bank £932 Dr. Dis. All. £50.65, Dis. Rec. £28.
Q4 Cash a/c £388, Bank £336.80 Dr. Dis. All. £15.20, Dis. Rec. £7.
Personal a/cs all Nil balances.
Q5 Bank a/c £62, Bank £101 Dr. Dis. All. £13, Dis. Rec. £9.
Q6 Bank a/c £62.85 Dr. Dis. All. £22.5 Debtors £502.5, Record Sales £225.36.
Other sales £901.44. Dis. Rec. £15, Creditors £1,435, Wages £280, Other
£427, Drawings £275.
Q7 *R. Lees*: Wine £830, Beer £1,030, Spirits £290, Other £134.
Total sales £2,284. VAT £342.6. Total Cash £2,626.6.
Both sales and VAT totals are posted on the credit side of their
ledger accounts.
(c) To be aware of which lines are selling. Better control of buying
and marketing.
Q8 Cash a/c £379, Bank £620, VAT £126, Telephone £180, all debits.

Chapter 11   The Bank Reconciliation Statement (BRS)

Q1 Bank a/c £253 Dr. BRS: £420 + £90 − £257 = £253.
Q2 Bank a/c £699 Dr. BRS: £864 + £205 − £370 = £699.
Q3 Bank a/c £2,791 Dr. BRS £3,084 + £404 − £697 = £2,791.
Q4 Bank a/c £377.5 Cr. BRS £379.4 − £24 + £22.10 = £377.5 O/D.
Q5 Bank a/c £206.35 Dr. BRS £625.15 + £156.20 − £575 = £206.35.
Q6 Bank £630 Cr. (Overdrawn) BRS £893 (Overdrawn) - Deposits Cr.
£1,215. = £322 Cr. − Unpresented cheques £952 = £630 (overdrawn).
Cash Book errors: Debit £426, £500.
Credit £840, £19, £23, £215, £99, £1,700.
Q7 Cash Book: Debits: £600, £420, £12?. Credits: £79, £1,353, £90, £200,
£70. Balance £2,200.
BRS £1,935 + £1,800 − £1,535 = £2,200.
Q8 Bank b/d £285 o/d, BRS £479 + £46 − £810 = £285 (Bank o/d).

Chapter 12   The Petty Cash Book

Q1 Petty Cash balance £0.61, VAT £17.70, Postages £29.84, Stationery
£36.66, Travel £81.18, Cleaning £20, Sundries £14.01, Reimbursement
£199.39, Cash float £200.
Q2 Petty Cash balance £23.15, Cleaning £27.59, Stationery £31.31, Postages
£8.35, Sundries £9.60, No VAT, Reimbursement £76.85, Cash float
£100.
Q3 Petty Cash balance £13.93, VAT £4.80, Cleaning £24.32, Stationery
£37.65, Postages £17.80, Sundries £19.50, Packing Materials £32, Reimbursement £136.07, Cash float £150.
Q4 Petty Cash balance £39.26, VAT £4.30, Travel £8.35, Cleaning £16.30,

Postages £13.28, Stationery £12.40, Refreshments £3.76, Sundries £2.35, Reimbursement £60.74, Cash float £100.

Q5   Petty Cash balance £9.80, VAT £4.19, Travel £13.27, Stationery £10.53, Cleaning £4.36, Refreshment £4.85, Postage £3, Reimbursement £40.20, Cash float £50.

Q6   Petty Cash balance £22.16, VAT £8.20, Post £29.61, Travel £32.80, Cleaning £31.50, Refresh. £23.49, Stationery £18.04, Sundries £34.20 = £177.84.

Chapter 13   Computed-based accounts

Q1   Printouts of accounts, including statements. Analysis of accounts, e.g. aged debtors and creditors. Automatic double-entry. Instant up-dating and review on screen. Integration with other aspects such as invoicing and stock control.

Q2   Example: Sales Ledger menu: Ledger Processing. Gives access to any customer a/c. Functions include up-dating files and the input of day-to-day information such as invoices and receipts.

Q3   Ledger Processing. Function No. 2 Ledger Posting – for entering day-to-day details relating to any account.

Q4   Invoices and Credit Notes. The Sales and Purchases Day Books provide the same information.
Customer and supplier accounts give more details such as address, turnover to date, invoice and cheque numbers, ageing of debts, etc.

Q5   Have you tried a computer yet hands-on?
If not, why not?

Part III

Chapter 14   Final accounts: calculating profits

Q1   *Wright*: Gross Profit £8,350, Net Profit £5,975. Fixed Assets £25,325, Working Capital £3,900. Capital employed £29,225.
Capital £25,000 – Drawings £1,750 + Net Profit £5,975 = £29,225.

Q2   *Armstrong*: Gross Profit £31,950, Net Profit £9,100. Fixed Assets £34,300, Working Capital £1,800. Capital employed £36,100 – Deferred liabilities £20,000 = £16,100. Capital £7,000 + Net Profit £9,100 = £16,100.

Q3   *Smith, F.*: Gross Profit £3,280, Net Profit £2,000. Fixed Assets £2,700 + Working Capital £1,300. Capital employed £4,000. Capital £2,000 + Net Profit £2,000 = £4,000.

Q4   *White*: Gross Profit £6,057, Net Profit £3,128. Fixed Assets £14,410, Working Capital £248. Capital employed £14,658.
Capital £12,730 - Drawings £1,200 + Net Profit £3,128 = £14,658.

Q5   *Robert*: Gross Profit £15,820, Net Profit £6,780. Fixed Assets £18,100, Working Capital £3,880. Capital employed £21,980. Capital £18,000 - Drawings £2,800 + Net Profit £6,780 = £21,980.

Q6   *Chappell, G.*: Gross Profit £904.88, Net Loss £240.29.

Fixed Assets £1,225, Working Capital £2,387.48 - £402.77 = £3,209.71.
Capital £4,050 - Net Loss £240.29 – Drawings £600 = £3,209.71.

Chapter 15 Final accounts: adjustments

Q1 *Wright*: Gross Profit £7,770, Net Profit £1,373. Fixed Assets £15,010.
Working Capital (–£1,837) insolvent. Capital employed £13,173. Capital
£16,000 – Drawings £4,200 + Net Profit £1,373 = £13,173.

Q2 *Hunt*: Gross Profit £4,950. Net Profit £403. Fixed Assets £1,900.
Working Capital £4,003. Capital employed £5,903. Capital £8,000 –
Drawings £2,500 + Net Profit £403 = £5,903.

Q3 *Waugh*: Gross Profit £150,100, Net Profit £57,400. Fixed Assets £89,000,
Current Assets £52,740, Current Liabilities £14,340, Working Capital
£38,400, Capital Empld £127,400, LTL £25,000 = £102,400.

Q4 P & L a/c Rent £2,400, accrued £600. Insurance £1,550, pre-paid £550.

Q5 P & L a/c Insurance £2,467, pre-paid £533.

Q6 *Farney*: Gross Profit £57,600, Net Profit £28,834. Fixed Assets £66,500,
Current Assets £47,124 (debtors £20,974), Current Liabilities £7,550,
Working Capital £39,574, Capital Emplyd £106,074, LTL £10,000 =
£96,074.

Q7 *Charcoal*: Bad debts £6,370, Provision for bad debts £8,418 (75% =
£2,558, 50% = £3,780, 10% = £2,080). P & L a/c: Bad debts provision
£8,388. Balance Sheet: debtors £88,210 – £8,418 = £79,792.

Q8 *Bradshaw*: (a) Prov. in 19–4 = £5,850, in 19-5 = £5,150. (b) In 19–4, P
& L cr. £950, balance = £5,850; in 19–5 P & L dr. £700, balance =
£5,150. (c) Provision increased by 16% in first year, reduced by 12%
second year. We do not know bad debts written off over 2 years.
(d) Debtors = £171,353 in balance sheet.

Q9 *Tip Top*: (a) Prov. balance = £242 (2% of £12,100); (b) Debtors: £12,360
– £260 bad debts – £242 prov. = £11,858 – £716 cr. = £11,142.
Creditors: £7,348 – £654 dr. = £6,694. P & L a/c £168 cr.

Q10 Rent: P & L a/c £5,300, pre-paid £500, Rates: P & L a/c £4,160,
accrued £760.

Chapter 16 Capital transactions

Q1 (a) capital; (b) revenue; (c) revenue; (d) capital; (e) revenue; (f) rev-
enue; (g) revenue; (h) capital; (i) revenue; (j) revenue; (k) rev-
enue; (l) revenue.

Q2 (a) capital; (b) capital; (c) capital; (d) capital; (e) capital or revenue;
(f) revenue; (g) revenue; (h) capital; (i) capital; (j) revenue; (k)
capital; (l) revenue.

Q3 (a) So that profits are not distorted and fixed assets are correctly
valued.
(b) Profit and fixed assets are under-stated by £2,320.

Q4 (a) (i) Ford £7,290, Toyota £6,480.
(ii) Journal: Dr Motor Vehicle £1,550, Cr Disposal £6,000, Bank
£9,500. Dr P + L £2,198, Cr Prov. for Depn £2,198.

Ledger balances: Motor Vehicle £23,500 Dr, Prov. for Depn of Vehicle £3,718 Cr, Disposal of Vehicle 0 (£10,000 Dr, Depn. £2,710, Trade-In £6,000, P + L £1,290 Cr). P + L account: Depn £2,198, Loss on sale £1,290. Fixed Assets: £23,500 – £3,718 = £19,782.

(iii) Ledger balances: Prov. for Depn of Vehicle £3,201 Cr, Disposal of Vehicle 0 (£10,000 Dr, Depn £2,953, Trade–In £6,000, P + L £1,047), P + L account: Depn Ford £243, Toyota £648, Mercedes £1,033 = £1,924, Loss on sale £1,047. Fixed Assets: £23,500 – £3,201 = £20,299.

(b) The statement is untrue because depreciation does not set cash aside for replacement, although profits are reduced due to the expense of it.

Q5 *Dooley*: Trial balance totals £28,393. Gross Profit £7,437. Net Profit £2,039. Fixed Assets £3,456, Working Capital £7,631. Capital employed £11,087. Capital £9,048 + Net Profit £2,039 = £11,087.

Q6 *Jones*: Gross Profit £37,500, Net Profit £11,125. Fixed Assets £75,600. Working Capital £5,725. Capital employed £81,325. Capital £71,000 – Drawings £800 + Net Profit £11,125 = £81,325. Note: Carriage Inwards in Trading a/c.

Q7 *ABC Co.*: Gross Profit £9,700, Net Profit £4,022. Fixed Assets £31,350. Working Capital £4,072. Capital employed £35,422 Deferred Liabilities £15,500 = £19,922. Capital £18,000 - Drawings £2,100 + Net Profit £4,022 = £19,922.

Q8 *Jones*: Gross Profit £3,440, Net Profit £2,005. Fixed Assets £15,580. Working Capital £5,249. Capital employed £20,829 – Deferred Liabilities £12,100 = £8,729. Capital £7,574 – £850 + Net Profit £2,005 = £8,729.

Q9 (a) Depreciation by time, wear/tear depletion and obsolescence.

(b) Obsolescence, wear/tear, depletion, N/A, time.

(c) The measure of wearing-out through time, use, obsolescence; allocated to charge a fair proportion of cost over-time of use.

(d) To keep control of investment capital on fixed assets as to its cost, depreciation, location, disposal or other factors

(e) It is the first or prime point of entry outside the scope of other journals, used for recording errors, adjustments and the purchase/sale of fixed assets.

Q10 Premises a/c £1,500,000 Debit. Plant & Machinery a/c £900,000 Debit. Provision for depreciation a/c £423,500 Credit.

Asset Disposal a/c Debit £10,000 to P & L a/c (as surplus on sale).

Balance Sheet: Fixed Assets: Cost £2,400,000, Depreciation £423,500. Net Book Value £1,976,500.

Revaluation Reserve a/c not used for distribution (of dividends).

Details of the revaluation: name of valuers, basis, date, etc.

Q11 Gross Profit £13,153, Net Profit £247. Fixed Assets £18,880, Current Assets £16,207 (debtors £11,622), Current Liabilities £15,840, Working Capital £367, LTL £3,500 = £15,747. Capital £18,860 + Profit £247 – Drawings £3,360 = £15,747.

Chapter 17 Partnership accounts

Q1 *A & B*: Appropriation a/c: Net Profit £14,680 – Salaries £6,000 – Interest on Capital £1,200 + Interest on Drawings £460 = £7,940. Profit Share £3,970 each partner.
Balance Sheet: Capital a/cs £24,000. Current a/cs A £3,470, B £2,245, both Cr.
Balance Sheet: Capital a/c A £15,000, B £15,000, C £10,000,
Total £40,000.
Profit Sharing Ratio 3:3:2.

Q2 *Smith & Jones*: Gross Profit £10,012, Net Profit £5,691. Appropriation a/c: Net Profit £5,691 – Salary £1,000 + Interest on Drawings £369 = £5,060. Profit Share 3:2. Smith £3,036, Jones £2,024. Current a/c balances: Smith £101. Dr. Jones £824. Cr.
Balance Sheet. Fixed Assets £27,500. Working Capital £3,223 Capital employed £30,723, Capital Accounts £30,000. Current Accounts £723 = £30,723.

Q3 *Lee and Crooks*: Gross Profit £14,565, Net Profit £5,097. Apprioriation a/c: Net Profit £5,097 – Salaries £2,500 + Interest on Drawings 549 = £3,146. Profit Share £1,573 each partner. Current Accounts Lee £626 Dr. Crooks £955 Dr. Balance Sheet: Fixed Assets £20,680, Working Capital £5,738. Capital employed £26,418. Capital a/cs £28,000. Current a/cs £1,582 Dr. = £26,418.

Q4 *May and Cowdrey*: Gross Profit £6,299. Net Profit £3,495. Appropriation a/c: Net Profit £3,495 – Salary £1,046 – Interest on Capital £700 = £1,749. Share of Profit: May £1,311.75, Cowdrey £437.25. Current a/cs: May £561.75 Cr. Cowdrey £733.25 Cr. Balance Sheet: Fixed Assets £9,164, Working Capital £6,131. Capital employed £15,295. Capital Accounts £14,000, Current a/cs £1,295 = £15,295.

Q5 (a) *Jones, Smith & Brown*: Gross Profit £60,970. S & D costs £6,767. Admin. costs £17,202. Net Profit £37,001. Appropriation a/c: Net Profit £37,001 – Salary £2,750 – Interest on capital £3,000 + Interest on Drawings £550 = £31,801. Share of Profit 5:4:1. James £15,900.5, Smith £12,720.4, Brown £3,180.1 Total £31,801.
(b) Current a/cs Jones £12,342.5, Smith £14,085.4, Brown £2,393.1 all Cr.
(c) Balance Sheet: Fixed Assets £72,800, Working Capital £33,021. Capital employed £105,821 – Deferred liabilities £27,000 = £78,821 (net assets). Capital a/cs £50,000. Current a/cs £28,821 = £78,821.

Q6 *Smith, Jones & Rogers*: Appropriation a/c: Net Profit £7,300 – Salary £900, – interest on capital £510, £480, £450, + interest on drawings £165 = £5,125. Profit share: Smith £2,050, Jones £2,050, Rogers £1,025. Current a/cs: Smith £1,095 Cr. Jones £1,075 Cr. Rogers (£370) Dr. Fixed Assets £30,700, Working capital £50, Capital employed £30,750 – Loan £4,950 = £25,800. Capital £24,000 + Current a/cs £1,800 = £25,800.

Q7 *French & Saunders*: (a) Appropriation a/c: Net Profit £19,800 – inter-

est on capital £3,600 + interest on drawings £800 = £17,000. Profit share £8,500 each partner. Current a/cs: French £2,100 Cr. Saunder (£7,160) Dr.
(b) Fixed Assets £61,000, Working Capital (£1,060), Capital employed £59,940 − Loan £20,000 = £39,940. Capital £45,000 + Current a/cs (£5,060) = £39,940. WC ratio 0.87 (insolvent), (c) Reduce the Drawings of £27,000. (d) Dr P + L a/c Cr French's current a/c.

Q8 *Wooldridge & James*: Approriation a/c: Net Profit £38,650 − salary £21,000 − interest on capital £8,300 + interest on drawings £1,550 (W £650, J £900), = £10,900. Profit share: Wooldridge £6,540, James £4,360.
Current a/cs: Wooldridge £7,990, James £2,660, both Cr.
Fixed Assets £114,000, Working Capital £5,650, Capital employed £119,650, − Deferred Liab. £29,000 = £90,650.
Capital £80,000 + Current a/cs £10,650 = £90,650.

Q9 *Bell, Ring & Gong*: Appropriation a/c: Net Profit £44,000 + £300 depn on motor vehicle acquired by Ring, £144,300 − £100 loss on sale of vehicle = £44,200. Salaries £23,000, Interest £7,400, Profit share: Bell £6,900, Ring £4,140, Gong £2,760.
Fixed Assets £74,850, Working Capital £8,350, Capital Empld = £83,200.
Capital a/cs: Bell £30,000, Ring £21,200, Gong £22,800 = £74,000. Current a/cs: Bell (£3,100), Ring £3,260, Gong £9,040 = £9,200.
Total partners = £83,200.

Chapter 18   Company accounts

Q1 *XYZ Co. Ltd*: (a) Net Profit (before tax) £15,500 − Provision for tax £3,760 = £11,740, Net Profit (after tax). + P & L balance £5,000 = £16,740 − provision for dividends £11,750 and Reserve £2,000 = P & L balance (31/12) £2,990.
(b) Balance Sheet. Fixed Assets £144,000. Current Assets £13,000 − current liabilities £22,010. Working capital (insolvent) £9,010 Capital employed £134,990. Capital £130,000. Reserve £2,000, P & L a/c £2,990 = £134,990.

Q2 *ABC Ltd*: Net Profit (before tax) £18,750 − Provision for tax £1,500 = £17,250, Net Profit (after tax) + P & L balance £5,460 = £22,710 − Provision for dividends £9,000 and reserves £10,000 = P & L balance (31/12) £3,710.
Balance Sheet: Fixed Assets £94,250, current assets £27,670 − current liabilities £18,210 = working capital £9,460. Capital employed £103,710. Capital £60,000, Reserve £40,000, P & L a/c £3,710 + £103,710.

Q3 *Bournemouth T Co. Ltd*: Gross Profit £31,310, Net Profit (before tax) £9,505 − Provision for tax £500 = £9,005 net profit (after tax), + P & L balance £1,300 = £10,305 − Provision for dividend £9,000 − Reserve £600 = £705 P & L balance (31/12). Balance Sheet: Fixed Assets £53,900, current assets £33,931 − current liabilities £15,526 = working capital £18,405, capital employed £72,305 − Deferred liabilities

£5,000 = £67,305. Capital £60,000, Premium a/c £6,000, Reserve £600, P & L a/c £705 = £67,305.

Q4 *Robertson & David Co. Ltd*: Gross Profit £151,800, Net Profit (before tax) £43,033, Provision for tax £19,200. Net Profit (after tax) £23,833 + P & L balance £7,780 = £31,613 – Dividends £22,400 – Reserve £4,000. P & L balance (31/12) £5,213. Balance Sheet: Fixed Assets £322,330. Current assets £102,169 – current liabilities £110,286. Working capital (insolvent) – £8,117. Capital employed £314,213 – deferred liabilities £40,000 = £274,213 (net assets). Capital £240,000. Reserve £29,000, P & L a/c £5,213 = £274,213.

Q5 *G. Chappell & Sons Ltd*: Gross Profit £19,324. Net Profit (before tax) £6,305. Provision for tax £1,250. Net Profit (after tax) £5,055 + P & L balance £1,170 = £6,225, – dividends £4,125 – Reserve £2,000 = P & L balance £100. Balance Sheet: Fixed assets £113,000, current assets £28,567 – current liabilities £9,967. Working Capital £18,600. Capital employed £131,600. Capital £125,000, Premium a/c £2,500, Reserve £4,000, P & L a/c £100 = £131,600.

Q6 *Harrison Ltd*: Gross Profit £94,225, Distribution cost £40,414, Admin. expenses £40,595. Interest payable £5,000, total expenses £86,009. Net Profit (before tax) £8,216. Provision for tax £3,750. Net Profit (after tax) £4,466 – Provision for dividends £3,750 + P & L balance (31/12) £716. Balance Sheet: Fixed assets £101,300, current assets £52,160, Current liabilities £60,744. Working capital (insolvent) – £8,584. Capital employed £92,716. – Deferred liabilities £40,000 = £52,716 (net assets). Capital £50,000, Reserve £2,000, P & L a/c £716 = £52,716.

Q7 *Jason Ltd*: Appropriation a/c: Net Profit £40,600 – tax £8,400 + P & L bal. £19,200 – Dividends £2,400, £9,000 = Reserves £40,000. Fixed Assets £160,000, Current assets £45,000, Current liabilities £30,000.
Working Capital £15,000, Capital employed £175,000.
Share capital £130,000 + Reserves £45,000 = £175,000.

Q8 *Compton Ltd*: Appropriation a/c: Net Profit £108,000 – tax £30,000 + P & L bal. £22,000, – Dividends £16,000, £48,000 – Reserves £20,000 = P & L bal. 31/3, £16,000. Fixed Assets £554,000, Working Capital £16,000, Capital employed £570,000. Share Capital £500,000, Reserves £54,000, P & L a/c £16,000 = £570,000.

Q9 *J. P. Davies, plc*: Appropriation a/c, Net Profit (after interest) £67,500 – tax £20,000, + P & L bal. £40,000 – Dividends £15,000, £40,000 – Reserves £25,000 = P & L bal. 30/6, £7,500.
Fixed Assets £355,000, current assets £419,000, current liabilities £296,500, Working Capital £122,500, Capital employed £477,500 – Deferred Liab. £100,000 = £377,500. Share Capital £300,000 + Reserves £70,000, P & L a/c £7,500 = £377,500.

Chapter 19   Cash flow statements

Q1   *ABC Co.*: 1 Profit £44,150 + depn £8,000 + WC changes £5,125 = £57,275; 2 Dividends (£8,000); 3 Tax (£2,500); 4, FA (£63,000) = (£26,225); 5 Financing £25,000 = (£1,225), Bank = (1,225).

Q2   *Bishop*: 1 Profit £147,450 + depn £24,000 + WC changes £15,375 = £186,825; 2 Dividends & Interest (£39,000); 3 Tax (37,500); 4, FA (£189,000) = (£78,675); 5, Financing £75,000 = (£3,675), Bank = (£3,675).

Q3   *Jackson*: 1 Profit £12,750 + depn £3,500 – WC changes (£7,070) = £9,180; 2 nil; 3 Tax (£5,100); 4, FA (£16,000) + sale £1,500 = (£14,500) = (£10,420); 5, Financing £10,000 = (£420), Bank = (£420).

Q4   *Jones*: 1 Profit £30,000 + depn £20,000 – WC changes (£26,000) = £24,000; 2 Dividends (£12,000); 3, Tax (£16,000); 4, FA (£30,000) + sale £9,000 = (£71,000) = (£75,000); 5, Financing £83,000 = £8,000, Bank = £8,000.

Q5   *Fox*: Year 1 FA £28,904, WC £2,000, LTL £5,000 = £25,904. Year 2 FA £38,244, WC (£1,500) LTL £2,500 = £34,244.
1 Profit £21,590 + depn £4,500 – WC changes (£5,276) = £20,814; 2 Dividends (£6,500); 3 Tax (£5,100); 4, FA (£13,840) = (£4,626); 5, Financing £2,500 = (£2,126), Bank = (£2,126).

Q6   *XYZ*: 1 Profit £7,500 + depn £3,800 – WC changes (£800) = £10,500; 2 Dividends nil; 3, Tax (£6,000); 4, FA (£9,000) + sale £3,500 = (£5,500) = (£1,000); 5, Financing nil, = (£1,000), Bank = (£1,000).

Q7   *Aspen*: 1 Profit £48,160 + depn £20,300 – WC changes (£4,140) = £64,320; 2 Dividends (£10,000); 3 Tax (£17,120); 4, FA (£70,400) = (£33,200); 5 Financing £20,000, = (£13,200), Bank = (£13,200).

Chapter 20   Accounts of clubs and societies

Q1   Profit from Bar £2,475. Revenue £9,330, Expenditure £8,675, Surplus £655. Fixed assets £26,950, current assets £4,855, Current liabilities £550, Working capital £4,305. Capital employed £31,255. Accumulated funds £30,600 + Surplus £665 = £31,255.

Q2   Revenue £15,175, Expenditure £7,878, Surplus £7,297. Fixed assets £13,500, Working capital £5,397. Capital employed £18,897. Accumulated funds £11,600 + Surplus £7,297 = £18,897.

Q3   Bank Account (31/3) £4,115. Revenue £7,827, Expenditure £3,842 = Surplus £3,985. Fixed assets £8,550. Working capital £3,735. Capital employed £12,285. Deferred liabilities £5,000 = £7,285. Accumulated funds £3,300 + Surplus £3,985 = £7,285.

Q4   (a) Refreshment surplus £1,640.
(b) Revenue £4,715, Expenditure £3,496 = surplus £1,219. Fixed Assets £19,299. Working Capital (£1,625), Capital employed £17,674, – Loan £5,955 = £11,719.
Accumulated funds £10,500 + surplus £1,219 = £11,719.

Q5   Bank a/c £2,825. Refreshment surplus £515. Revenue £3,980. Expenditure £1,953 = surplus £2,027. Fixed Assets £17,750, Working Capital

£2,827, Capital employed £20,577 – Loan £2,000 = £18,577.
Accumulated funds £16,550 + surplus £2,027 = £18,577.

Q6 Bank balance = £65. Surplus £43 (subs £160, depn £11, loss on sale £7). Fixed Assets £1,099, Working Capital £58 = £1,157. Acc. Fund £1,114 + surplus £43 = £1,157.

Q7 Bar a/c surplus = £318. Surplus on I & E = £5,577 (subs £17,670). Fixed Assets £106,200, Current Assets £19,465, Current Liabilities £2,088, Working Capital £17,377 = £123,577. Acc. Fund £118,000 + surplus £5,577 = £123,577.

Q8 Surplus £13,091 (subs £11,900, profit on tools £2,900, loss on exhib. £35), Fixed Assets £8,000, Current assets £8,880, Current Liabilities £545, Working Capital £8,335 = £16,335. Acc. Fund £3,244 + Surplus £13,091 = £16,335.

Part IV

Chapter 21 Accounting ratios and preparing reports

Q1 Gross Profits £10,000, £12,000, £13,050. Net Profits £3,850, £5,050, £4,675.
Gross Profit %'s £33.33%, 33.33%, 29%. Net Profit %'s 12.8% 14% 10.4%. Expense %: Distribution 10%, 8.9%, 9.1%.
Administration 10.5%, 10.4%, 9.5%.
Stock turnover = 10, 9.6 and 8 times per annum.
Credit days taken 73 in Yr 1 and Yr 2; 89 days Yr 3.
Return on capital 14.5%, 16.8%, 14.7%.

Q2

	Co. A	Co. B		Co. A	Co. B
Gross Profits	£4,000	£13,500	Fixed Assets	£7,000	£10,000
Net Profits	£2,450	£6,000	Working Capital	£2,275	£ 3,250
				£9,275	£13,250
Gross Profit %	44.4%	56.25%			
Net Profit %	27.2%	25%			
Return on capital	26.4%	45.3%			
Working capital ratio	2.14	1.9			

Q3

Harry Smith	Yr. 1	Yr. 2	Yr. 3
Working capital	£8,100	£6,280	£5,470
Working capital ratio	2.25	1.64	1.39
Acid test ratio	1.54	1.01	0.67

Year 1 obviously the most liquid year.

Q4

	Yr. 1	Yr. 2	Yr. 3
Gross Profit %	40%	33.33%	40%
Net Profit %	22%	13.33%	17.5%
Return on Capital Inv.	35.5%	19.0%	29.5%
Return on Capital Empld	22.9%	15.6%	27.3%
Current ratio	2.1	1.3	1.25
Net worth/total assets	72.5%	68%	65.3%

Year 2 inferior in all respects.
Big improvement in Year 3.

Q5

	Ball Bearings Ltd	Rocco Bank Ltd
Net Profit (after tax)	£1,500,000	£1,600,000
Earnings/Share	15p	80p
Dividend/Share	7p	20p
Cover	2.1	4
Current ratio	0.98	0.95
Acid test	0.5	0.95
Capital gearing	300% (high)	6.67% (low)
Net worth/total assets	11%	7.5%

Q6

	Sales	Cost of sales	Gross profit		Expenses	Net profit	NP%
Yr 1	£ 36,000	£27,000	£ 9,000	25%	£ 8,400	£ 600	1.67%
Yr 2	£ 54,000	£40,500	£13,500	25%	£ 9,500	£4,000	7.4%
Yr 3	£ 78,000	£58,500	£19,500	25%	£11,500	£8,000	10.3%
Yr 4	£120,000	£96,000	£24,000	20%	£19,000	£5,000	4.2%

Q7

	Yr. 1	Yr. 2	Yr. 3
Gross Profits	£36,000	£50,000	£70,000
Net Profits	£1,600	£7,000	£16,000
Profit Returns			
Gross Profit %	30%	$33\frac{1}{3}$%	35%
Net Profit %	1.33%	4.67%	8%
ROCE	2.67%	6.67%	10%
Stock Turnover	10.5	11.8	13

Steady improvement over the 3-year period. Sales and turnover of stock has increased each year to give a ROCE of 10% [still moderate]. Reduction of fixed costs and cost of sales for further improvement in Yr 4.

Q8	A	B	C
Net Profit (after interest)	£695,000	£695,000	£645,000
Net Profit (after tax)	£451,750	£451,750	£419,250
Retained Profit (after dividends)	£ 41,750	£ 31,750	£ 59,250
Eps	13.4p	12.9p	13.9p
Capital gearing	16.6%	0%	16.6%

Scheme C may be worth pursuit, having greater retained profits and marginally the highest eps.

Q9 (a)	Yr. 1	Yr. 2	Yr.3
Gross %	33.3	25.	20.0
Net %	10.0	4.4	2.6
ROCE %	15.0	8.0	5.8
WC ratio	3.5	2.14	1.73
Acid test	2.3	1.43	1.0
Sales/cap. empld	1.5	1.8	2.25
Debt collection	79 days	81 days	74 days
Owner's stake (%)	80.0	74.1	68.6
Eps	24p	12.9p	9.3p

(b) Turnover has been achieved but at declining profit and liquidity levels. Difficult to justify increased investment. Problem is the high COS, but variable overheads improved along with asset usage.

Q10	Co. A	Co. B
Gross %	25.0	25.0
Net %	5.63	7.5
Net % (−int)	7.5	7.71
ROCE %	8.2	7.5
ROCE % (−int)	10.9	7.7
WC ratio	4.0	4.0
Acid test	1.0	1.5
Gearing %	37.5	2.1
Interest cover	4 times	37 times
Stock turnover	6 times	3 times
Sales/cap. emplyd	1.45	1.0
Eps	15p	11.25p

(b) Profits & liquidity similar although A better ROCE & eps. Long-term solvency shows B stronger. A has better use of resources. Invest in B, larger company, stronger solvency, 40% a large slice.

Chapter 22   VAT and VAT returns

Q1 VAT outputs £58,590, VAT inputs £41,860, VAT balance = £16,730.
Q2 VAT a/c £127 Cr, Sales £11,600 Cr, Purchases £8,960 Dr, Eqpt, £840 Dr, Motor Vehicle £8,850 Dr, Operating Exps £720 Dr.
Q3 (a) monthly, annually; (b) invoice date; (c) on form VAT 100 as inputs; (d) after 12 months and written off; (e) no, only those for business purposes allowed by VAT Office; (f) as part of the expense, VAT is not separated; (g) VAT recorded in VAT a/c as an input.

Chapter 23   SSAPs and FRSs

Q1 *Chairman's Report*: (a) Accruals (1st line), consistency (depreciation) prudence (stock, lower of cost), going concern (whole report).
(b) Other: cost & materiality.
Q2 Peter Drucker suggests: market standing, product leadership, staff development and public responsibility.
Profit motivation still the most significant aspect.
Q3 See pages relating to 4 concepts.
Q4 (a) cost concept, realisation (turnover), consistency (depreciation) prudence (stock), going concern (whole accounting policy).
(b) check manufacturing accounts and the importance of stock value.

Part V

Chapter 24   Personal income

Q1 *Smith*: Gross Pay £162; Deductions £54.34; Tax £35.16; Net pay £107.66.
Q2 Gross Pay: Jack £134.40; Fred £123.90; Harry £151.90.
Q3 Piece-rates on 1,650 units £28.75; Basic pay £50; Total pay £78.75.
Q4 *Robbins*: Time allowed 54 hours. Time taken 39 hours. Time saved 15 hours. Bonus hours 50% of 15 hours = 7.5 hours. Gross pay 46.5 × £3 = £139.50.
Q5 Clock Card 44½hours. Overtime = 6½hours. Basic pay £91.20. Overtime pay £23.40. Total Gross pay £114.60.
Q6 Week 1 £215.25; Week 2 £238.35.
Q7 Tax £22.80 (20% = £11.53 on £57.69, 25% = £11.27 on £45.11).
Net pay: £226.80 − £54.24 = £172.56.
Q8 (a) £1.53 tax (lower rate 20%).
(b) £38.65 tax (lower rate £11.53, basic rate £27.12).
Q9 Gross pay per week = £707.69 less tax free £152.44 = £555.25 taxable pay. Tax: Lower rate, £57.69 = £11.53, Basic rate, £398.07 (£20,700 p.a.) = £99.51, Higher rate on rest, £99.49 = £39.79.
Total tax = £150.83.
Q10 (a) NIC 23.52; (b) 8.20.
Q11 Statutory deductions refer to income tax and NIC which must be deducted from pay by law. Voluntary deductions are a choice made by the employee.

Q12 (a) Tax Tables A & B; (b) NIC Tables 1 and 1A.

Q13 Not contracted out is part of the State pension scheme (SERPS), using Tables 1. Persons with their own pension plans use Tables 1A (contracted out).

Q14 NIC is used to pay for benefits such as pensions, unemployment and sick pay.

Chapter 25   Saving and borrowing

Q1 External investigation of high street banks and societies.

Q2 (a) Gross is without tax paid at 25% basic rate.
(b) 7% = 5.25% net, 7.15% = 5.3625% net, 6% = 4.5% net.
(c) £39.37, £40.22, £33.75.

Q3 Endowment: Premium paid to insurance co. with interest to lender, cash surplus at end of term.
Repayment: interest and loan repaid together, no surplus fund.

Q4 High interest rates charged each month. With HP goods are not legally owned until last payment.

Chapter 26

Q1 June £240, July £340, August £430 – monthly balances. Savings suggested: June £200; £100 July; £80 August.

Q2 January £340, February £440, March £330 – monthly balances. Savings: January £140; February £240; March £130.

Q3 April £625, May £350, June £85 – monthly balances. Open-ended suggestions for part (b).

Q4 (a) Gross salary £153.85
Net salary £103.86 (£104 for budget).
(b) Bank c/f Jan £176, Feb. £322, March £572.
(c) Saving £572 over 3 months, he could spend an average £190 per month.
(d) £90 month; £65 month.
(e) Finance from bank, HP co. or even credit card. Bank, a specific loan over 3 years probably the best.

Part VI

Chapter 27   Manufacturing accounts

Q1 *F. Smith*: Prime Cost £58,925, Factory overheads £10,102, Factory Cost £69,117. Gross profit £25,578, Net profit £15,384.25.

Q2 *J. Jones*: Prime Cost £108,025, Factory overheads £17,044, Factory Cost £125,089. Gross Profit £31,891, Net profit £28,051.

Q3 *Harry*: Prime Cost £57,549, Factory overheads £11,759, Factory Cost £69,308, Factory Profit £8,692, Gross Trading Profit £25,505. Net Loss £389, DL/Unit £7.75, DM/Unit £21.02, Factory overheads/Unit £5.88,

Prod. Cost/Unit £34.65. Yes – manufacturing was cost-effective, by £4.35/Unit. *Note*: Total Gross Profit £34,197.

Q4 *ABC Co. Ltd*: Prime Cost £73,185, Factory overheads £11,760, Factory Cost £84,415. Gross Profit £39,299, Net Profit £15,519. Prime Cost/Unit £6.97, Factory overheads/Unit £1.12, prod. Cost/Unit £8.04, Total cost/unit £10.30. Mark-up % 18.1, Margin % 15.3.

Q5 *Fred's Co. Ltd*: Prime Cost £49,005, Factory overheads £10,470, Factory Cost £59,475. Factory Cost/Unit £5.95. Gross Profit £24,212.5, Net Profit £17,515.

Q6 *P. Jackson*: Prime Cost £100,958, Factory overheads £14,745, Factory Cost £115,703. Gross Profit £64,793, Net Profit £38,717.
Fixed Assets £43,025, Working Capital £10,272, Capital employed £53,297.
Capital £25,000 + Net Profit £38,717 – Drawings £10,420 = £53,297.

Q7 *XYZ Co. Ltd*: Prime Cost £198,623, Factory Cost £201,000, Cost/Unit £4.02. Finished goods stock 31/12 £18,090. Gross Profit £12,590, Net Profit £1,802. P & L c/f £1,382, Fixed Assets £91,400. Working capital – £11,018 (insolvent). Capital employed £80,382. Shareholders' funds: £80,382.

Q8 *ABC Co*: Prime Cost £117,800, Factory overheads £38,200. Factory Cost £156,000. Factory Cost/unit = £13, Stock, FG £16,250, Gross Profit £79,250, Net Profit £27,000. Fixed Assets £70,500, Working Capital £5,500, Capital Emplyd £76,000, Capital & Reserves £76,000.

Q9 *Fairdeal*: Prime Cost £74,000, Factory overheads £49,460, Factory Cost £99,460, Manufacturing Profit £540. Trading Profit £46,500 + MF Profit £540 = £47,040, Expenses £35,044 (prov. for unrealised profit £54), Net Profit £11,996. Fixed Assets £126,750, Current Assets £49,546, Current Liabilities £14,300, Working Capital £35,246, Capital Emplyd = £161,996. Capital £120,000 + Premium £30,000 + Retained Profits £11,996 = £161,996.

Chapter 28   Costing principles and classification of costs

Q1 *ABC Co. Ltd*: Cost Sheet DL £21,000, DM £47,600 Factory overheads £54,885, Dist. overheads £35,370, Admin. overheads £27,045. Factory Cost/Unit £81.72. Prime Cost £67,700, Factory overheads £54,885, Factory Cost £122,585. Gross Profit £89,723. Net Profit £27,308.

Q2 *J. Jones*: Cost sheet: DL £20,300, DM £15,575, DE £675, Factory overheads £19,455, Dist. overheads £17,220, Admin. overheads £12,870. Factory Cost/Unit £11.194.
Prime Cost £36,440, Factory overheads £19,455. Factory Cost £55,970. Gross Profit £34,076. Net Profit £3,986.

Chapter 29   Accounting for materials

Q1 As per text: purchase requisition, purchase order, delivery note, GRN, stock requisition voucher, store issue voucher, stock card.

Q2 To ensure control of stock movements and buying optimum levels of stock.

Q3 To check quantities on any given item and to ensure re-orders are made on time.

Q4 (a) 3,000; (b) 4,382; (c) 5,382; (d) 500.

Q5 (a) 1,732; (b) 1,800 (600 × 3 weeks); (c) 1,000; (d) 3,132.

Q6 (a) as per text; (b) 11,200 re-order, 4,000 minimum level, 19,200 maximum level.

Q7 *Jack's store*: Lower of cost or NRV £525, £140, £900, £750, £149.25, £57.50 and £5. Total stock value = £2,526.75.

Q8 *Using FIFO*: value of stock 1/7 £715 1/8 £745 1/9 £765 = 100 units × £2.15 = £215.250 units × £2.20 = £550. Total value = £765.

Using LIFO: value of stock 1/7 £700 1/8 £700 1/9 £700 = 200 units × £2 = £400. 100 units × £1.95 = £195, 50 units × £2.10 = £105. Total value £700.

Q9 *Stock Card*: 12/9 299 reams × £2.5 = £747.5 20/9 Balance 170 reams: FIFO 80 × £2.5 = £200, 90 × £3 = £270. Total value £470.

Q10 *FIFO*: 24/1 Balance 100 units × £3.2, 70 units × £3, total 170 units value £530. 28/2 Balance 50 units × £3.40, 50 units £3.50, total 100 units value £345.

LIFO: 24/1 Balance 150 units × £3, 20 units × £3.20, total 170 units value £514. 28/2 Balance 50 units × £3, 50 units × £3.40, total 100 units value £320.

LIFO's stock value is £25 *less* than FIFO. Therefore gross profit would be £25 less if LIFO stock value used.

Q11 (a) Stock Card: 28/6 105 units @ £4 unit = £420 stock value.

(b) Stock Sheet: Total £4,003.75 (rounded up to £4,004).

(c) Gross Profit £12,704.

Net Profit £7,729.

Q12 (a)

		1986	1987	1988
Gross Profit	LIFO	20,000	43,000	80,000
	FIFO	20,000	43,000	96,000
Net Profit (Loss)	LIFO	(6,000)	15,400	47,720
	FIFO	(6,000)	15,400	63,720

(b) capital a/c 1986 = £44,000, 1987 = £59,400, 1988 = £123,120.

(c) FIFO identifies more closely with actual stock movement values and stock-end will reflect current value of stock. SSAP 9 recommends its use.

Chapter 30 Accounting for labour

Q1 (a) Freddie £205; (b) Jennie £142.50; (c) Jean £347.3.

Q2 £6.60.

Q3 227/15 = £80, 229/15 = £38, 224/15 = £46, 226/15 = £16.
Total gross pay = £180.

Q4   Attendance: £342; piece rates: £80 + £600 + £14 = £694.
Total pay = £1,036.

Q5   Basic pay £144, bonus pay £42, total pay = £186.

Q6   (a) Jack: £168 (more than 80% hourly = £154). Jill: £144 (£136.50
piece rate is less than 80% hourly rate of £180 = £144).

   (b) Jack: £185.50; Jill: £198.56.

   (c) When it is difficult to calculate (office workers) or when trainees
are on the job.

Q7   (a) Blount £178.50; Short £195.80; Lewis £180; Bull £188.10; Kent £216
(*note*: Bull is grade A pay).

   (b) Bonus: Blount £11.40; Short £13.20; Lewis £15; Bull £15.20; Kent
£12. Blount £190; Short £209; Lewis £195; Bull £203.30; Kent £228.

   (c) Piece work: good incentives, easy to understand, agreed unit
rates. Time rates: easy to understand, used where output difficult to measure or where quality more important than quantity.
Lack of incentives.

Chapter 31   Accounting for overheads and cost centres

Q1   (a) Overheads: B £167,500; D £160,000; T £162,500; DL Hour rate: B
£5.00; D £8.00; T £2.50.

   (b) Cost: DM £45.00; DL £42.00; overheads £46.50; total = £133.50.

Q2   (a) Overheads recovery 30% of DL cost.

   (b) Job 42: DM £2,590, DL £4,830, Overheads £1,449, Admin. £887 =
£9,756 + 50% profit £4,878 = £14,634.

   (c) Overheads recovery: A £0.625 DL Hour, B £1.00 DL Hour, C
£0.75 Machine Hour, D £0.50 DL Hour

   (d) Job 42: DM £2,590, DL £4,830, Overheads £1,215; total = £8,635.

Q3   (a) Overheads sub-totals: A £250,000, B £260,000, C £330,000, X
£100,000, Y £90,000. Totals: A £290,000, B £340,000, C £400,000.

   (b) Overheads recovery: A £8.00, B £6.40, C £10.00 per DL Hour.

   (c) Cost of pump: DL £64, DM £45, Overheads £110.40; total = £219.40.

Q4   (a) PTS Overheads: Machining £10,179,032, Assembly £6,468,847,
Finishing £4,669,495.

   (b) Overheads recovery: Machining £50.90 per Machine Hour, Assembly £46.21 DL Hour, Finishing £51.88 per Machine Hour.

Q5   (a) Overheads: Dept A £41,150, B £22,325, C £14,025.

   (b) Overheads recovery: A £12.86, B £12.40, C £14.02 DL Hours.

Q6   (a) Links the overheads with type of activity, e.g. DL Hours.

   (b) Increase in overheads or decrease in labour costs (more efficient).

   (c) More capital intensive, relying more on machines than labour.

   (d) Floor area; labour hours; no. of employees', plant value.

   (e) Machine: £500 over (150 hrs × £5.00 per hour = £750 excess −
£250 actual overheads cost increase. Finishing: £1,120 under (100
× £4.00 per hour not recovered = £400; add overheads cost increase of £720.

Chapter 32   Job, batch and contract costing

Q1 Job 420. Labour: Printing £260, Binding £80.50 = £340.50; Materials £920; Prod. overheads £472 = £1,732.50 + £259.88 = £1,992.38 + profit £498.10 + VAT £373.57 = total £2,864.05.

Q2 (a) Overheads: A £420, B £480, C £220.
  (b) Absorption rates: A £52.50, B £30.00, C £27.50 per DL hour.
  (c) job cost £1,222.50. (d) All overheads recovered in unit cost.

Q3 Job 153. Materials £338.40, Labour £1,134.60, Prod. overheads £1,260.00 = £2,733.00 + Admin. overheads £409.95, Sales overheads £160.00 = total cost £3,302.95 + profit £825.74 = SP £4,128.69.

Q4 (a) A £509; B £661; C £545; total £1,715.
  (b) A £85, B £110, C £68 per DL hour.
  (c) prime cost £2,540, Prod. overheads £7,810 = £10,350 + £2,070 = £12,420 + profit £4,140 = £16,560.

Q5 Cost of Certified Work = £882,600, surplus £197,400, Cert. Value £1,080,000, profit taken to P&L account £125,020.

Q6 Cost of Certified Work = £614,400, surplus £105,600, Cert. Value £720,000, profit taken to P&L account £70,400.

Q7 (a) Construction of buildings, roads, homes, etc. Long-term contract: unique product, high cost, contracts away from premises.
  (b) Need to be prudent and amount to realise; that part of surplus seen prudent to report in P&L, not taken in early stages. Losses taken as whole figure.
  (c) Cost of Work Certified £900,000, profit taken £166,667, closing contractee balance = £200,000.

Chapter 33   Process and standard costing

Q1 Total costs £16,600, WIP: DM £400, DL £600, overheads £600 = £1,600. Cost of processing = £15,000. Unit cost = £5.00, FG to store = £15,000.

Q2 Total costs £33,200, WIP: £3,200. Cost of processing = £30,000. Unit cost = £20.00, FG to store £30,000.

Q3 Total costs £65,830, abnormal loss 50 units. Cost per unit £13.78. Output value 4,700 × £13.78 = £64,766. To P&L a/c loss £614, (£689 − £75).

Q4 Total cost £48,924. WIP £4,698: DM £4,050, DL £432, overheads £216. Process cost: £48,924 − WIP £4,698 − Abnorm. loss £546 = £43,680. Cost per unit = £5.46. To P&L 100 × £5.46 = £546 (loss).

Q5 (a) predetermined measured quantities to be attained;
  (b) management tool to check production efficiency;
  (c) budgetary control of performance;
  (d) standards to be ideal or attainable , problems of inflation.

Q6 (a) assists in the process of planning and control of costs, the key being variance analysis.
  (b) DM price V, £283 fav.; DM usage V, £364 adv.; total = £81 adv.

DL rate V, £392 adv.; DL effic. V £80 fav.; total = £312 adv.
Total V = £393 adverse.

(c) Lower quality material but more scrap. Use of higher labour standard, more cost, but better efficiency.

Q7 (a) Budgeted contribution £30,000, profit = £26,000.

(b) Actual contribution £48,400, profit = £42,400.

(c) DM price V, £2,400 fav.; DM usage V, £4,000 adv.; DL rate V £4,000 fav.; DL effic. V £10,000 fav.; Total V = £12,400 fav.

(d) Management tool to check efficiency, etc.

Q8 (a) DM price V, £2,380 fav.; DM usage V, £3,280 adv.; DL rate V, £2,570 adv.; DL effic. V £450 fav.; Total V = 3,020 adv.

(b) Higher discounts, decrease in market prices but inferior quality. Higher grade of labour means more cost, but more efficient.

(c) Assist in assessment of market trends and better quantity discounts based on usage estimates.

Chapter 34   Marginal costing

Q1 (a) Table: Fixed costs £56,000, Variable costs £44,000. (b) Contrib./Unit £38 (£60 − £22). (c) Profit on 2000 units, £20,000. (d) 2,100 units, £23,800; on 1,950 £18,100. (e) Break-even 1,474 units. Profit (1 above) £38. Loss (1 below) £38. (f) Variation: £14,400 profit.

Q2 *Baldwin* (a) C/Unit £8; (b) Profit £1,250; (c) B/E 344 units, £4,300 revenue; (d) Profit £10,700; (e) £1,058; (f) £1,450 profit first, £1,427.5 profit second, first best; (g) 96 extra units.

Q3 *Lillee, Thompson*: (a) Table; Fixed costs £63,250, Variable cost £94,750; (b) C/Unit £2.105; (c) £1,895 extra cost; (d) Yes; (e) B/E 30,048 Units, £120,192 revenue; (f) Loss £104.2; (g) £42,000; (h) £19,897.50 profit.

Q4 (a) B/E 23,500 units; (b) £17,500 loss; (c) 16,000 units extra; (d) £2,250 loss; (e) £2,500 profit; £36,500 profit; £10,000 extra profit – total profit £42,500. Third is best proposal.

Q5 (a) 9,400 units; (b) £7,000 loss; (c) 3,200 units; (d) Profit £5,500; Profit £17,000; second is best proposal, current profit only £13,000.

Q6 (a) Fixed costs £156,000, Variable costs £204,000; (b) C/Unit £41, B/E 3,805 units; (c) 6,500 units = £110,500 profit, 3,500 units £12,500 loss.

Q7 (a) Contribution £60. (b) Break-even 4,000 units.

(c) Margin of safety 6,000 units, 60%.

(d) Estimated profits £360,000 and £270,000.

(e) Proposals: £360,000 profit; £425,000 profit; £408,000 profit. Therefore, second has best profit potential

Q8 (a) Contribution per unit, total contribution, contribution/materials or other cost, c/s ratio are some examples.

(b) Contribution/materials A = £1.20, B = £1.67. Make 34 of A, 80 of B. Total contribution, A = £1,632, B = £2,000.

(c) The effect of fixed costs, also morale of workforce, cost of equipment, etc.

Q9 (a) Contrib/DM: X = 0.5, Y = 0.78, Z = 0.55. DM allocated:
 Y = £1,024,000, Z = £950,000, X = £120,000; total £2,094,000. Profit
 X = £60,000, Y £800,000, Z £525,000 – Fixed Costs £585,000 =
 £800,000.
 (b) Extra contribution £55,000 – £7,500 = £47,500; order accepted.

Chapters 35   Budgeting and planning

Q1 Cash Budget (£)

	July	Aug.	Sept.	Oct.	Nov.	Dec.
Bal. b/f	(10,000)	(19,500)	(6,000)	8,400	7,800	10,200
Receipts	35,000	34,000	36,000	25,000	26,000	27,000
Payments	44,500	20,500	21,600	25,600	23,600	33,600
Bal. c/f	(19,500)	(6,000)	8,400	7,800	10,200	3,600

Q2 Cash Budget (£)

	Sept.	Oct.	Nov.	Dec.	Jan.	Feb.
Bal. b/f	(4,000)	(3,480)	(4,720)	(7,080)	(24,760)	(25,040)
Receipts	47,040	48,960	49,920	51,840	56,640	59,520
Payments	46,520	50,200	52,280	69,520	56,920	58,680
Bal. c/f	(3,480)	(4,720)	(7,080)	(24,760)	(25,040)	(24,200)

Obviously with an o/d limit of only £20,000, the final 3 months all
exceed this figure and the ceiling will need re-negotiation with the
bank.

Q3 Cash Budget (£)

	July	Aug.	Sept.	Oct.	Nov.	Dec.
Bal. b/f	2,000	4,040	(7,900)	(8,060)	(4,840)	11,680
Receipts	23,200	32,000	24,000	28,000	39,000	31,200
Payments	21,160	43,940	24,160	24,780	22,480	20,660
Bal. c/f	4,040	(7,900)	(8,060)	(4,840)	11,680	22,220

Q4 Cash Budget (£)

	July	Aug.	Sept.	Oct.	Nov.	Dec.
Bal. b/f	70,000	2,475	1,660	1,925	1,350	2,475
Receipts	2,875	9,625	12,625	15,625	19,125	22,625
Payments	70,400	10,440	12,360	16,200	18,000	15,480
Bal. c/f	2,475	1,660	1,925	1,350	2,475	9,620

Gross Profit £30,910. Net Profit £23,460. Proprietor's capital 31/12
£89,260.

Q5 Cash Budget (£)   July   Aug.   Sep.   Oct.   Nov.   Dec.

Balances c/f £131,250 (24,000) (39,250) (64,500) (49,750) (38,300)

Gross Profit £60,000, Net Profit £21,900.
Fixed Assets £112,000, Working Capital £59,900,
Capital employed £171,900 – Debentures £50,000 = £121,900.
Capital £100,000 + Profit £21,900 = £121,900.

Q6 Cash Budget (£)   June   July   August

Balance c/f   (9,900)   (11,000)   (8,100)

Sales £71,800 – COS £57,440 = Gross Profit £14,360.
Stock value £10,760. Net Profit £5,585.
(*Note*: Depreciation £375, Rent £900).
Fixed Assets £61,025, Working Capital £10,960, Capital employed £71,985.
Capital £50,000 + P & L a/c £21,985 = £71,985.

Q7 (a) Bank balance December £2,400.
(b) Gross Profit £17,760, Net Profit £7,860.
Fixed Assets £7,200, Current Assets £7,660, Current Liabilities £2,000,
Working Capital £5,660 = Capital Employed £12,860.

Chapter 36   Capital investment appraisal

Q1 (a) Y; (b) X = 38%; Y = 36%.
Q2 NPV: (a) £5,000 = £3,415; (b) £30,000 = £15,210; (c) £100,000 = £68.100.
Q3 Payback method: B is fastest.
Returns on investment: A 37%, B 35%, C 36% so A is best.
NPV: Earnings: A £556,500, B £560,940, C £546,610 so B is best.
Project B.
Q4 Payback method M is fastest.
Return on investment: L 34%, M 38%.
NPV: Eearnings L (£493,640), M £552,080.
Clearly project M is best.
Q5 NPV formulae £20,000/$(1.12)^{10}$ = £20,000 × 3.1058 = £6,440.
   tables   £20,000 × 0.322   = £6,440.
Q6 NPV formulae £58,000/$(1.11)^5$ = £58,000 × 1.6851 = £34,419.
   tables   £58,000 × 0.593   = £34,394.
Q7 NPV formulae £33,460 $(1.12)^4$ = £33,460 × 1.5735 = £21,265.
(Bonds) tables £33,460 × 0.636   = £21,280.
NPV formulae £42,580 $(1.12)^6$ = £42,580 × 1.9738 = £21,572.
(Trusts) tables £42,580 × 0.507   = £21,588.

Unit trusts marginally more profitable, £308 (tables).

Part VII

Chapter 37   Control accounts

Q1 *F. Smith*: Sales ledger control £4,820 Dr. A discrepancy of £260 with sales ledger.
Bought ledger control £2,240 Cr. Agrees with bought ledger balance.

Q2 *H. Jones*: Sales ledger control £11,501 Dr. Bought ledger control £8,991 Cr.

Q3 *G. Harrison*: Sales Ledger Control £16,977 Dr. A discrepancy of £19 with sales ledger.

Q4 *Rock Ltd*: Sales Ledger Control: Balance £73,910. (Debits £126,440, Credits £52,530.) Purchase Ledger Control: Balance £37,150. (Debits £27,000, Credits £64,150.) S/L control agrees. P/L control, £50 discrepancy. The trial balance and bank reconciliation are two other methods of cross-check and control.

Q5 *Zarak Ltd*: Sales Ledger Control: Balance £55,120. (Debits £109,820, Credits (£55,500.) Purchase Ledger Control: Balance £32,520. (Debits £26,400, Credits £58,920.) P/L control agrees. S/L Control £820 discrepancy.

Q6 *Smith & Jones*: Sales Ledger Control: £310,865; £1,320 discrepancy with Sales Ledger. Purchase Ledger Control: £150,905; £1,750 discrepancy with Purchase Ledger.

Q7 ABC Co.: Sales ledger control £38,324 Dr. £456 Cr. A discrepancy of £200 with sales ledger. Bought ledger control £12,484 Cr. (same as Bought Ledger) £150 Dr.

Q8 (a) Jan. bal.b/d £116,183, Feb. bal.c/d £68,329, Mar. bal.b/d £76,228.
(b) Gross Profit: COS = £294,040 − £10,000 = £284,040 × 40% = £113,616 less loss of £3,000 on sale = £110,616 gross profit.

Chapter 38   The trial balance, journal and suspense accounts

Q1 Journal entries: (a) Drawings Dr., Salaries Cr. (b) R. Smith Dr., P. Smith Cr. (c) Office Equipment Dr., Purchases Cr. (d) Rates Dr., Accrued expenses Cr.

Q2 Journal entries: Premises £20,000, Vehicle £500, equipment £2,100, Stock £1,860, debtors £675, all debit entries. Mortgage £15,000, Bank O/D £450, Creditors £1,155 and capital − T. Jones £8,530 all credit entries.

Q3 Journal entries (a) Bad debts £256 Dr., H. Smith £256 Cr. (b) Equipment £500 Dr., Equipment Supplies Co. £500 Cr. (c) P & L £700 Dr., Provision for depreciation of MV £700 Cr. (d) Sales £14,500 Dr., Trading a/c £14,500 Cr., Trading a/c £9,850 Dr., Purchases £9,850 Cr. (e) Light and Heat £85 Dr., Rates £85 Cr.

Q4 Journal entries (a) R. Smith Dr., J. Smith Cr.; Sales £600 Dr., equipment £600 Cr.; Discount allowed £8 Dr., Suspense a/c £8 Cr.; Sus-

pense a/c £200 Dr., Sales £200 Cr.; Suspense a/c £55 Dr., Salaries
£55 Cr.; Debtors a/c £275 Dr., Sales £275 Cr.

(b) Suspense a/c   Dr. Sales   £200   T. Balance   £247 Cr.
                       Salaries   £ 55   Disc. All.   £ 8
                                  £255   £255

Q5 (a) Suspense a/c Dr. Bank £2,490, Cr.   T. Balance £2,275
       Discount £160, Cash £55.
       (b) Corrected Trial Balance: Bank £1,245, Capital £34,900, Sales £21,900
       and Creditors £4,230, all Credit balances. Stock £3,400, Premises
       £23,000, Furniture £900, Wages and Salaries £13,000, Office Expenses
       £860, Purchases £14,300, Drawings £4,000, Debtors £2,600, Discount
       All. £160, Office cash £55, all Debit balances. Totals: Trial Balance
       £62,275.

Q6 *R. Underwood*: (a) Suspense a/c £248 Dr., Returns Out. £248 Cr.; Pur-
       chases £200 Dr., Biggs £200 Cr.; Vehicle Repairs £2 Dr., Suspense £2
       Cr.; Bradford £54 Dr., Suspense £54 Cr.; Sales £100 Dr., Office equip.
       £100 Cr.; Drawings £230 Dr., Purchases £230 Cr.; Purchases £92 Dr.,
       Suspense £92 Cr.
       (b) Suspense a/c £248 Dr. Credits: £100, £2, £54 and £92.
       (c) £10,584.

Q7 *Hawkins*: (a) Suspense a/c £300 Dr., Pitman £300 Cr.; Suspense £450
       Dr., Sales £450 Cr.; Discount Allowed £242 Dr., Suspense £242 Cr.;
       F & F £90 Dr., Suspense £90 Cr.; Knight £730 Dr., Sales £730 Cr.;
       Heat and Light £233 Dr., Suspense £89 Dr., Motor Expenses £322
       Cr.; Stationery £180 Dr., Equipment £180 Cr.
       (b) Suspense a/c Dr. £300, £450, £89. Credits: £507, £242, £90.
       (c) £22,878.

Q8 Suspense £1,352 Dr., Debits: Stanley £8, Credits: disc. £100, sales
       £900, purchases £360.
       Profit £13,564 less: £100, £900, £9, £360, £15; add £20 = adjusted
       profit £12,200.

Q9 Suspense £690 Cr., Debits: sales £800, Smith £45, Credits: disc. £68,
       returns in £87. Corrected totals of trial balance = 50,745. The first
       two errors listed would not be found.

Q10 (a) Debtor £1,200 Dr. sales £1,200 Cr.; suspense £500 Dr., Dodds
        £500 Cr.; suspense £752 Dr., disc. alld £376, disc. recd £376 Cr.; disc.
        alld. £224, disc. recd. £224 Dr., suspense £448 Cr.; suspense £495
        Dr., p/l control £495 Cr.; depn £750 Dr., suspense £750 Cr.
        (b) Suspense £549 Cr. Debits: Dodds £500, discounts £752, p/l con-
        trol £495, Credits: discounts £448, depn £750.

Chapter 39   Incomplete records

Q1 *H. Jones*: Debtors – to reconstruct sales £53,690. Creditors to recon-
       struct purchases £43,525. Bank a/c £1,588. Gross Profit £11,915. Net
       profit £5,708.

Balance Sheet: Fixed assets £2,465, Working capital £7,933. Capital employed £10,398. Capital £7,000 – Drawings £2,310 + Net Profit £5,708 = £10,398.

Q2 *F. Smith*: Bank a/c £10,625 – Cash Drawings £5,000 = £5,625. Sales a/c £72,767. Purchases a/c £46,960. Gross Profit £27,357. Net Profit £11,707. Balance Sheet: Fixed assets Nil. Current assets £18,672, current liabililties £5,465, working capital £13,207. Capital £6,500 – Drawings £5,000 + Net Profit £11,707 = £13,207. *Note*: Rates £1,065 in P & L a/c.

Q3 *Jack*: Capital = £8,000 (Assets £11,410 – Liabilities £3,410). Sales a/c £59,850, Purchases a/c £41,540. Gross Profit £18,910. Net Profit £7,605. Balance Sheet: Fixed assets £2,500. Working capital £6,580. Capital employed £9,080. Capital £8,000 – Drawings £6.525 + net Profit £7,605 = £9,080. *Note*: insurance £105 in P & L a/c.

Q4 *F. Smith*: Bank a/c commence payments with O/D £1,765 and include £1,955 mortgage repayment. Balance on 31/12 = £1,425 overdrawn. Sales a/c £49,695, Purchases £35,570. Gross Profit £15,735, Net Profit £9,261.
Balance Sheet: Fixed assets £30,685, Current assets £6,066, current liabilities £6,305, working capital (insolvent) – £239, capital employed £30,446. Deferred liabilities £13,295. Net assets £17,151. Capital £13,800 – drawings £5,910 + Net Profit £9,261 = £17,151.

Q5 *J. Archer*: Capital £99,700. Sales a/c £228,600. Purchases £158,950. Gross Profit £110,770, Net Profit £12,850. Fixed assets £14,550. Working Capital £86,000. Capital employed £100,550. Capital £99,700 – Drawings £12,000 + Net Profit £12,850 = £100,550. *Note*: Depreciation of fixtures £1,900.

Q6 *J. Jones*: Capital £20,000. Sales £46,525, Purchases £38,965. Gross Profit £9,175, Net Profit £4,225.
Fixed Assets £19,300, Working Capital £5,250, Capital employed £24,550 – Loan £4,000 – £20,550. Capital £20,000 + Net Profit £4,225 – Drawings £3,675 = £20,550.

Q7 *D. White*: Gross Profit £60,898, Net Profit £10,742. Fixed Assets £51,000, Current assets £31,600, Current Liabilities £13,680, Working Capital £17,920, Capital employed £68,920.
Capital £73,078 + Net Profit £10,742 – Drawings £14,900 = £68,920.

Q8 *Justin Harris*: Gross Profit £51,200, Net Profit £16,520.
Fixed Assets £43,200, Current assets £53,720, Current Liabilities £13,360, Working Capital £40,360, Capital employed £83,560.
Capital £80,760 + Net Profit £16,520 – Drawings £12,160, £1,560, = £83,560.

Q9 *Murray Ltd*: Credit purchases £584,000. Credit Sales £660,000. Sales £820,000 – COS £574,000 = Gross Profit £246,000. Closing stock £308,000 (£882,000 – £574,000).
Stock Loss £126,000. (£308,000 – £182,000).

Q10 Credit sales £173,770, cash sales £61,190 = £234,960. Credit purchases £166,360. Sales £238,140 (+ 50% on COS £158,760). Gross Profit £79,380. Net Profit £12,530. Fixed Assets £18,480, Current Assets £42,020,

Current Liabilities £12,700, Working Capital £29,320 = £47,800. Capital £30,910 + £16,000 + Profit £12,530 − Drawings £8,500, £3,140 = £47,800.

Chapter 40   The extended trial balance

Q1   Gross Profit £34,150, Net Loss (£1,252). Fixed Assets £163,048, Current Assets £14,040, Current Liabilities £17,040, NCL (£3,000), Capital Emplyd £160,048, LTL £91,300 = £68,748. Capital £70,000, loss (£1,252) = £68,748.

Q2   Gross Profit £110,615, Net Profit £16,667. Fixed Assets £104,400, Current Assets £54,340, Current Liabilities £26,020, Working Capital £28,320, = Capital Emplyd £132,720. Capital £131,653 + Profit £16,667 − Drawings (£15,600) = £132,720.

Q3   Gross Profit £55,141, Net Profit £5,888. Fixed Assets £30,300, Current Assets £27,560, Current Liabilities £6,681, Working Capital £20,879, = Capital Emplyd £51,179. Capital £53,091 + Profit £5,888 − Drawings (£7,800) = £51,179.

Q4   Gross Profit £65,409, Net Profit £31,632, (depn £875). Fixed Assets £43,025, Current Assets £15,495, Current Liabilities £9,400, Working Capital £6,095 = Capital Emplyd £49,120. Capital £27,908 + Profit £31,632 − Drawings (£10,420) = £49,120.

Q5   Gross Profit £11,353, Net Loss (£26). Fixed Assets £10,030, Current Assets £5,584, Current Liabilities £4,840, Working Capital £744, Capital Emplyd £10,774, LTL £4,500 = £6,274. Capital £8,860 − Drawings (£2,560) − Loss (£26) = £6,274.

Q6   (a) Suspense a/c Dr. Debtor £500, Discount received £752, creditors £495. Cr. Balance £549, Discount allowed £448, Accounts fees £750.

(b), (c) Sales £76,450, Debtors £24,700, Discount £96 Cr. Creditors £16,495, Accounts fees £750.

(d) Gross Profit £30,650, Net Profit £9,270.
Fixed Assets £75,800, Current Assets £28,156, Current Liabilities £23,847, Working Capital £4,309 = Capital Employed £80,109 less Long Term Liabilities £10,000 = £70,109. Capital £72,450 + Profit £9,270 − Drawings £11,611 = £70,109.

Index

absorption cost   483, 525
accountant   41
accounting   3
  cost   4
  equation   48
  financial   4
  management   5
  system   106
accounting concepts   408
accounting ratios   365
  limitations   382, 385
accounts   3, 67
  computer-based   44, 199
accounts office   43
accruals   234
accumulated funds   348
acid test ratio   370
adjustments to accounts   273
aged debtors   241
appropriation accounts
  companies   311, 316
  partnerships   288
Articles of Association   37, 310
Memorandum   37, 310
assets   30, 46
  current   49
  fixed   49
  intangible   49
  investment   49
  net   51
  net current assets   276
audit   42
auditing   42
auditor's report   42

bad debts   238, 399

recovery of   243
balance sheet   36, 46
balancing   70
bank reconciliation   168
bank statement   168
bar trading account   350
batch costing   540
book-keeping   4, 68
books of prime entry   105
bought (purchase) ledger   93, 121
break-even   575
  break-even chart   577
  break-even point   577
Budget   18
budgets   597
  business   597
  cash flow (budget)   34, 599
  personal   452
business plan   23
buying on credit   446

capital   7
  appraisal   616
  authorised   8, 317
  employed   225, 368
  expenditure   256
  gearing   377
  issued and paid up   8, 317
  nominal   316
  working   36, 55, 370
cash book   105, 149
  analysed   149
  modified   154
cash budget   599
cash discounts   150
  allowed, received   150

cash flow statement   332
Central Government   14
   Local Government   14
clock cards   428
clubs and societies   347
columnar (analysed) accounts
      113, 130
Community charge   14
Companies Act   43, 309
   1985 Act   311
   1989 Act   312
company accounts   309
computer-based accounts   44, 199
contra entry   160
contract costing   541
contribution   573
control accounts   629
   purchase control   127, 633
   sales control   111, 633
cost classification   484
costing   5
   absorption   483, 525
   batch   540
   contract   541
   job   538
   marginal   484, 569
   principles of   483
   process   552
   standard   484, 559
cost of sales   35, 220
Council Tax   15
credit control   240
   note   136
   rating   242
current accounts   288
current ratio   370

day books   105
debentures   10, 311
debt collection   240
deeds of partnership   287
depreciation of fixed assets   259
   disposal of   262
   fixed instalment   259
   reducing balance   261
direct costs   461
director's report   312
discounted cash flow   616
disposal of fixed assets   262
dividends   6, 311
double-entry   67
drawings   55, 288

efficiency ratios   371
errors   542
   correction of   643
evaluation (of results)   33, 383
expenses   75, 219, 221
extended trial balance   682

factor finance   12
factory cost   461
   overheads   463
final accounts   219
financial resources   3
finished goods   464
financial statements   219
fixed asset register   270
fixed costs   569
financial Reporting Statement
      318, 407
Financial Times Index   379
forecast   598
   cash flow   34
franchising   37

gearing   377
goodwill   49, 293, 416
   written off   295
gross profit   220

imprest system   185
income and expenditure
      account   348
income tax   428
incomplete records   661
indirect costs   462
insolvent   7, 370
interest on capital   287
   on drawings   287
investing money   443
investment ratios   378
Investors in industry   12
invoices   107, 121, 403

journal   106, 263, 645

legal requirements   37
liabilities   36, 49
   current   49
   long-term   49
limited company   6, 309
liability   6, 309
limiting factor   585
liquidity ratios   370

loan capital   9
local authorities   14
lower of cost and net realisable
     value   504

manufacturing account   461
margins of profit
     mark up   470
     margin   470
marginal cost   569
     formula   581
Memorandum of Association   37,
     310
mortgages   449

National Income Contribution   431
nationalised industry   18
net present value   618
net profit   221
net book value   260
nominal ledger   93, 222

ordinary shares   8, 311
     preference   9, 311
overheads   525
     absorption rates   529
     allocation of   527
     apportion of   527

partnership accounts   287
PAYE   429
petty cash book   185
     vouchers   186
Poll Tax   14
preference shares   9, 311
prepayments   235
prime cost   462
private sector   5
privatisation   19
process costing   552
production cost   463
productivity   376, 467
profit and loss account   219
profitability ratios   368
profits   219
provision for bad debts   238
     depreciation   259
     discounts   244
     dividends   311
     taxation   311
PSBR   16
PSDR   17

public finance   14
     sector   14
purchases day book   121
     ledger   93, 125
     returns   136

quick asset ratio   370

rate support grant   14
ratios   365
raw materials   461
real accounts   93
receipts and payments account   348
remuneration (pay)   425, 517
reserves   311, 317
residual value   259
return on capital   368
returns inward   136
     outward   137
revenue   75, 219, 258
revenue expenditure   256
running balance   91

sales day book   105
     ledger   93, 108
     return   136
share capital   6, 311
shareholders funds   378
share premium account   317
sources of finance   7
     owner's capital   8
     loan capital   9
     debentures   10
     profits   11
     leasing/hiring   11
     factor finance   12
     creditors   12
     government   12
SSAPs   266, 407, 503
     FRSs   318, 407
standard costing   559
stock control   499
Stock Exchange   8, 16, 379
stocktaking   501
stock turnover   373
stock valuation   468, 504
     AVCO   504
     LIFO   504
     FIFO   504
     lower of cost, net realisable value
          412, 504
structure ratios   376
suspense accounts   647

tax tables   431
taxation   4
  corporation tax   311
  income tax   428
trade discount   110
trial balance   81, 642

variable cost   569

VAT   16, 33, 187, 396, 411

wages   425
work-in-progress   462
working capital   36, 55, 369
working capital (current) ratio   64,
  370